Love and Capital

Also by Mary Gabriel

Notorious Victoria: The Life of Victoria Woodhull, Uncensored
The Art of Acquiring: A Portrait of Etta and Claribel Cone

Love and Capital

Karl and Jenny Marx and the Birth of a Revolution

MARY GABRIEL

LITTLE, BROWN AND COMPANY

New York Boston London

Little, Brown and Company
Hachette Book Group
237 Park Avenue, New York, NY 10017
www.hachettebookgroup.com

First Edition: September 2011

Little, Brown and Company is a division of Hachette Book Group, Inc.
The Little, Brown name and logo are trademarks of Hachette Book Group, Inc.

The publisher is not responsible for websites (or their content)
that are not owned by the publisher.

Copyright acknowledgments appear on pages 601–602.

Library of Congress Cataloging-in-Publication Data

Gabriel, Mary
    Love and capital : Karl and Jenny Marx and the birth
of a revolution / Mary Gabriel. — 1st ed.
        p. cm.
    Includes bibliographical references and index.
    ISBN 978-0-316-06611-2
    1. Marx, Karl, 1818–1883. 2. Marx, Karl, 1818–1883 — Family. 3. Marx, Karl,
1818–1883 — Friends and associates. 4. Marx family. I. Title.
    HX39.5.G334 2011
    355.40922 — dc22   2010044021

10   9   8   7   6   5   4   3   2   1

RRD–C

Printed in the United States of America

For John

and

In loving memory of my grandfather

Contents

CONTENTS

Part III
Exile in Victoria's England

Part IV
The End of *La Vie Bohème*

Part V
From *Capital* to the Commune

Part VI
The Red Terrorist Doctor

Part VII
After Marx

MAP OF
EUROPE
·1848·

MONARCHIES:

Absolute

Constitutional

Estates

Absolute & Constitutional

Grand Duchy

Papal States

★ **Free City**

✸ **Rebellion**

— **German Confederation**

0   150   300 *Miles*

0   150   300 *Kilometers*

IRELAND

Dublin

UNITED KINGDOM

Manchester

GREAT BRITAIN

London

Paris

FRANC

Bordeaux

San Sebastián

Bagnères-de-Luchon

Marsei

Lisbon

PORTUGAL

Madrid

SPAIN

Barcelona

Seville

Atlantic Ocean

M e d i t e

The boundaries of 1848 Europe were largely those imposed by the 1815 Congress of Vienna after the defeat of Napoleon, and despite calls for democratic freedoms, the territories within those boundaries were administered by monarchs. In 1848 rebellions swept Europe, marking the first and still the only such continent-wide revolt.

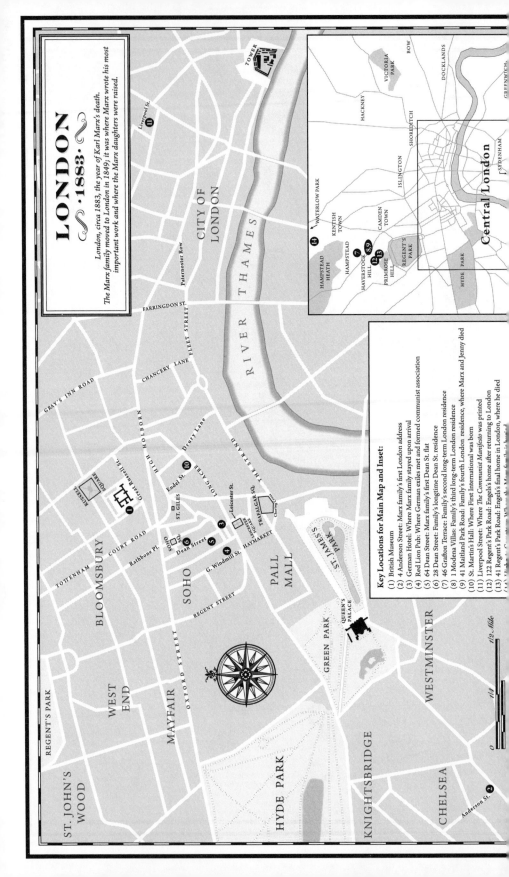

LONDON
·1883·

London, circa 1883, the year of Karl Marx's death. The Marx family moved to London in 1849; it was where Marx wrote his most important work and where the Marx daughters were raised.

Key Locations for Main Map and Inset:

(1) British Museum
(2) 4 Anderson Street: Marx family's first London address
(3) German Hotel: Where Marx family stayed upon arrival
(4) Red Lion Pub: Where German exiles met and formed communist association
(5) 64 Dean Street: Marx family's first Dean St. flat
(6) 28 Dean Street: Family's longtime Dean St. residence
(7) 46 Grafton Terrace: Family's second long-term London residence
(8) 1 Modena Villas: Family's third long-term London residence
(9) 41 Maitland Park Road: Family's fourth London residence, where Marx and Jenny died
(10) St. Martin's Hall: Where First International was born
(11) Liverpool Street: Where *The Communist Manifesto* was printed
(12) 122 Regent's Park Road: Engels's home after returning to London
(13) 41 Regent's Park Road: Engels's final home in London, where he died
(14) Hisbes's Convitors: Where the Manuel family is height

REGENT'S PARK

ST. JOHN'S WOOD

WEST END

MAYFAIR

OXFORD STREET

BLOOMSBURY

TOTTENHAM
COURT ROAD

RUSSELL SQUARE

GRAY'S INN ROAD

HIGH HOLBORN

CHANCERY LANE

FLEET STREET

FARRINGDON ST.

Paternoster Row

CITY OF LONDON

Liverpool St.

TOWER

GREAT RUSSELL ST.
ST. GILES
Endell St.
LONG ACRE
Drury Lane
SOHO SQ.
Rathbone Pl.
Dean Street
Leicester St.
TRAFALGAR SQ.
THE STRAND
Charing
HAYMARKET
G. Windmill St.

SOHO

REGENT STREET

PALL MALL

GREEN PARK

QUEEN'S PALACE

ST. JAMES'S PARK

WESTMINSTER

HYDE PARK

KNIGHTSBRIDGE

CHELSEA

Anderson St.

RIVER THAMES

Central London

HAMPSTEAD HEATH
WATERLOW PARK
KENTISH TOWN
HAMPSTEAD
HAVERSTOCK HILL
PRIMROSE HILL
CAMDEN TOWN
REGENT'S PARK
ISLINGTON
HYDE PARK
SHOREDITCH
HACKNEY
VICTORIA PARK
BOW
DOCKLANDS
GREENWICH
SYDENHAM

0   1/4   1/2 Mile

Character List

Adams, Charles Francis — lawyer, U.S. ambassador to Great Britain during Abraham Lincoln's administration, son of the sixth U.S. president, John Quincy Adams.

Adler, Victor — Austrian journalist, leader of the Austrian Social Democrats, and a close associate of Engels.

Albert (né Albert Francis Charles Augustus Emmanuel of Saxe-Coburg-Gotha) — married Queen Victoria in 1840 and became Prince Albert. He was instrumental in developing cultural and scientific institutions in England.

Alexander II (né Aleksandr Nikolayevich) — czar of Russia from 1855 to 1881. He ended serfdom in 1861 and allowed some modernization of Russia's economy and political life, but his government was repressive and accused of neglecting the vast majority of its citizens. He was assassinated in 1881.

Earl of Angus — descendant of one of the oldest family lines in Scotland dating to the tenth century, the first Earl of Angus was titled in 1389. He died in prison after being captured by the English.

Anneke, Fritze — ex-Prussian military officer, journalist, and an early communist agitator in Cologne, later a democrat. He was jailed for six months in 1848 for organizing workers, fought in the 1849 uprising in Baden, and emigrated to the United States, where he joined the Union army during the Civil War.

Annenkov, Pavel — wealthy Russian liberal journalist and friend of Marx.

Appian — historian born in Alexandria, capital of Roman Egypt, c. AD 95. He wrote *Roman History* sometime before 165.

Earl of Argyll — descendant of one of Scotland's most powerful and controversial families, Archibald Campbell, 7th Earl of Argyll, was executed in Edinburgh in 1661 for opposing Britain's Charles II.

Aveling, Edward—British doctor of zoology, journalist, secularist, theater critic, playwright, socialist, labor agitator, and common-law husband of Marx's youngest daughter, Eleanor. His pen name was Alec Nelson.

Aveling, Isabel (née Frank)—first wife of Edward Aveling, daughter of a wealthy poulterer in London's Leadenhall Market. Known as Bell.

Bakunin, Antonia (née Kwiatkowski)—daughter of a Polish merchant, wife of Mikhail Bakunin.

Bakunin, Mikhail—nineteenth-century Russian aristocrat turned anarchist and author, he had a loyal following in Italy, France, Poland, Spain, Switzerland, and Russia, and was Marx's lifelong political rival.

Balzac, Honoré de—French novelist who combined Romanticism with realism to produce a detailed and intimate picture of social, political, and economic life during the early nineteenth century in France.

Bangya, Janos—Hungarian journalist and police spy for Prussia who successfully infiltrated Marx's inner circle in London. He later worked for the secret police in Paris under Napoleon III.

Barbes, Armand—veteran French revolutionary and member of the early Society of the Seasons, which led a failed revolt in 1839. Imprisoned by Louis-Philippe and freed after the 1848 revolt, he briefly became a member of the National Assembly.

Barrett, Michael—Irishman hanged in 1868 outside London's Newgate Prison for his participation in a bombing at the Clerkenwell jail that killed twelve people. Barrett was the last man publicly hanged in England.

Barthélemy, Emmanuel—French follower of Auguste Blanqui and fighter in the 1848 June Days in Paris, he appeared in London at about the time Marx arrived in 1849 and frequented some of the same political associations. He believed Marx too conservative and plotted to kill him. Barthélemy was later executed in London for two murders.

Baudelaire, Charles—one of France's most influential poets, he examined mystical darkness as well as man's cruelty to man, which he described as evident in the nineteenth-century society around him. He was a friend of Marx's future son-in-law Charles Longuet in Paris in the 1860s.

Bauer, Bruno—Young Hegelian, radical German theologian and philosopher, and an early Marx colleague in Berlin.

Bauer, Edgar—German philosopher, writer, and Young Hegelian, he was attacked by Marx and Engels in *The Holy Family* along with his brother Bruno but remained friends with Marx in London.

Bauer, Heinrich—German shoemaker and a founder of the League of the Just in London, he later became a member of the Communist League, traveling from London to Germany to propagandize. He eventually emigrated to Australia.

Bauer, Ludwig—German doctor in London who attended the Marx family upon their arrival in London and pursued Marx for unpaid bills.

Bax, Ernest Belfort—British journalist and author of the first independent English review praising Marx's *Capital, Volume I.* Later active in the burgeoning British socialist movement along with Eleanor Marx, he was a future leader of the British Socialist Party.

Bazalgette, Joseph—nineteenth-century civil engineer charged with building a sewage system for London that would protect its citizens from outbreaks of cholera that killed thousands.

Bebel, August—a leading figure in the nineteenth- and early-twentieth-century German workers' political movement and the International, cofounder of the Social-Democratic Workers' Party, and member of the Reichstag, he would be a critical figure in the movement after Marx's and Engels's deaths.

Becker, Hermann—German lawyer and journalist who had begun publishing a series of Marx's collected works before being arrested in the spring of 1851 as a defendant in the Cologne Communist Trial. He was sentenced to five years in prison for attempted high treason. In later years he was mayor of Dortmund and Cologne, and a member of the Reichstag.

Becker, Johann—veteran German revolutionary resident in Switzerland, participant in the 1848 uprisings and the First International, and active in the Swiss working-class movement. He was a lifelong friend of Marx, Engels, and Jenny.

Berlin, Isaiah—twentieth-century Russian-born British liberal philosopher, historian of ideas, known first for his work on political freedom, *Two Concepts of Liberty.*

Bernays, Karl Ludwig (né Lazarus Ferdinand Coelestin)—Bavarian newspaper editor expelled for his liberal views, he worked with Marx on two newspapers in Paris and was jailed under pressure from Prussia for an antimonarchy article. He eventually emigrated to the United States. Known as F. C. Bernays.

Bernstein, Eduard—Swiss-based German newspaper editor and German Social Democrat viewed by Marx and Engels as among the most capable new-generation party men. Accused of revisionism after Engels's death, he was a close friend of Eleanor Marx after he moved to England. Known as Ede.

Besant, Annie (née Wood)—British secularist and writer. An early advocate of birth control, she was charged with obscene libel for promoting it. A former lover of Edward Aveling, she became one of his most vocal critics after he began his relationship with Eleanor Marx. In later years she became a theosophist and agitated for Indian independence.

Biskamp, Elard—fought in the 1848–1849 uprisings in Germany, founder of the London-based German émigré newspaper *Das Volk*. He worked with Marx on the publication in 1859.

Bismarck, Otto Eduard Leopold von—served in Prussia as ambassador to Russia and France and as prime minister, and became chancellor in the new German Reich created in 1871. He was perhaps the most important figure in uniting the German Confederation under a German Empire, and wielded enormous power domestically and throughout Europe. He instituted antisocialist laws and crackdowns on workers.

Black, Clementina—British author and portraitist, working-class activist, president of the Women's Industrial Council, and a friend of Eleanor Marx.

Blanc, Jean Joseph Louis—French socialist writer and activist, minister in France's 1848 provisional government, he oversaw a controversial jobs program whose dissolution triggered the June Days revolt. Known as Louis.

Blank, Marie (née Engels)—Friedrich Engels's closest sibling, married socialist Emil Blank.

Blanqui, Louis Auguste—veteran French revolutionary, anarchist, communist, propagandist, and participant in every major nineteenth-century revolt in France—1830, 1848, and 1871. Known as Auguste.

Blind, Karl—German writer who worked with Marx in London on refugee matters and socialized with the Marx family during the early 1850s in London.

Blos, Wilhelm—journalist, member of the Social-Democratic Workers' Party, future Reichstag deputy, and minister-president of Germany's Württemberg Government from 1918 to 1920.

Bonaparte, Pierre Napoleon—cousin of Napoleon III and member of France's Constituent and Legislative assemblies.

Born, Stephan (né Simon Buttermilch)—German typesetter and Communist League member introduced to Marx's inner circle in Brussels through Engels, later a leader of the German working-class movement in Berlin.

Bornstedt, Adalbert von—German journalist who worked as an Austrian spy and agent provocateur, he was the editorial assistant on the Paris newspaper *Vowarts!* and editor of the *Deutsche-Brüsseler-Zeitung* in Brussels.

Börnstein, Heinrich—German journalist and businessman who founded the Paris newspaper *Vowarts!*, he later emigrated to the United States and edited a newspaper in St. Louis.

Brandenburg, Friedrich Wilhelm von—illegitimate son of Prussian king Friedrich Wilhelm II, military commander, prime minister of the counterrevolutionary Prussian government formed in November 1849, he remained in that post until his death in November 1850.

Bühring, Karl Johann—German cabinetmaker and member of the Communist League. Marx used his passport to travel to Holland and Berlin in 1861.

Bürgers, Heinrich—radical German journalist and future Reichstag member who worked with Marx in Paris, Brussels, and Cologne. He spent six years in prison after being convicted in the Cologne trial of Communist League members.

Burns, John—British working-class leader and union organizer, member of the Social Democratic Federation, organizer of the London Dock Strike, member of the British Parliament, and cabinet minister in Liberal Party governments.

Burns, Lydia—Irish factory worker and younger sister of Mary Burns, she lived as Engels's common-law wife after the death of her sister in 1863. Known as Lizzy.

Burns, Mary—Irish factory worker in Manchester who lived as Engels's common-law wife until her death in 1863.

Burns, Mary Ellen—niece of Mary and Lizzy Burns, raised by Lizzy and Engels as their daughter. Known as Pumps.

Camphausen, Ludolf—Prussian banker, railway baron, and future prime minister of Prussia, he was a financial backer of the *Rheinische Zeitung* newspaper that Marx edited in Cologne.

Cavaignac, Louis Eugène—French general and minister of war under the 1848 government, he was given executive power to run France by the National Assembly during the June Days uprising in Paris and until presidential elections in December 1848.

Cervantes, Miguel de—Spanish novelist who lived a life of adventure before succumbing to a life of relative poverty, until age fifty-eight and the success of his novel *Don Quixote,* one of the Marx family's favorite books.

Champion, Henry Hyde—English socialist, journalist, and retired army artillery officer who helped organize the great London Dock Strike, he was an early supporter of an Independent Labour Party in Britain and helped write its rules.

Charles X (né Charles-Philippe de France)—French Bourbon monarch ousted in 1830 July uprising over his attempts to undo reforms, such as a limited constitution, enacted by his predecessor.

Chernysevsky, Nikolai—Russian journalist and leader of the radical intelligentsia in Russia in the 1850s and 1860s, he was banished to Siberia for nineteen years for his writings, which were interpreted as promoting revolutionary populism.

Clemenceau, Georges Eugène Benjamin—French republican, journalist, member of the National Assembly, interior minister, and twice France's prime minister (1906–1909 and 1917–1920). One of Charles Longuet's closest associates in Paris, he was instrumental in Longuet's return to France from exile in London.

Cluss, Adolf—German engineer, writer, Communist League member, and important Marx colleague in Washington, D.C., where he propagandized for Marxian socialism.

Cohen, Ferdinand—stepson of Karl Blind, he committed suicide in jail after an unsuccessful attempt to assassinate Bismarck in Berlin in 1866.

Collison, William—son of a London policeman, early agitator for the eight-hour workday, and founder of the Free Labour Association, which supplied nonunion labor to break up strikes, among other things.

Cooper, James Fenimore—nineteenth-century American author whose tales, set in untouched frontiers and forests, formed an exciting picture of the continent for European audiences.

Crosse, Arthur Wilson—London lawyer. He handled probate of Engels's will, and wrote wills for Eleanor Marx Aveling and Edward Aveling.

Culine, Hippolyte—French Workers' Party leader in the Lille region during the 1891 Fourmies May Day melee.

Cuno, Theodor—German socialist and International member, he worked on behalf of the International Working Men's Association in Italy and later emigrated to the United States, where he continued working-class and socialist agitation.

D'Agoult, Countess (née Marie-Catherine-Sophie de Flavigny)—former lover of Franz Liszt, with whom she had three children, and Georg Herwegh's lover when Karl and Jenny Marx were in Paris, she presided over a salon of radical thinkers. Pseudonym Daniel Stern.

Dale, George Edgar—Sydenham pharmacist who sent Eleanor Marx prussic acid.

Dana, Charles—American journalist and editor of the *New York Daily Tribune* from 1849 to 1862, he employed Marx as a foreign correspondent.

Daniels, Amalie—wife of Roland Daniels.

Daniels, Roland—Cologne doctor, close Marx associate, and member of the Communist League. He was tried and acquitted in the Cologne

Communist Trial but died shortly afterward from illnesses connected to his long pretrial incarceration.

Danielson, Nikolai—Russian confidant of Marx and Engels, writer, and economist. With Hermann Lopatin and Nikolai Lyubavin, he translated *Capital, Volume I* into Russian.

Dante Alighieri—Italian poet born in the thirteenth century, best known for *The Divine Comedy,* he is considered one of the world's greatest poets.

Darwin, Charles—nineteenth-century British naturalist whose 1859 book, *On the Origin of Species by Means of Natural Selection,* sparked popular debate on evolution and made him instantly famous as a founding scientist of the controversial theory.

Deasy, Captain Michael—U.S. Civil War veteran arrested in Manchester in 1867 as a Fenian leader, in a case that became legend in the Irish independence movement when three Irishmen were hanged for helping him escape.

Defoe, Daniel (né Daniel Foe)—English novelist and journalist, author of *Robinson Crusoe* and *Moll Flanders,* among other books, he was known for his realistic depiction of English society in the late seventeenth and early eighteenth centuries.

Demuth, Helene—domestic in the Westphalen household in Trier, who from age twenty-five lived with Karl and Jenny Marx as a member of the family. Known as Lenchen, she gave birth to a son by Marx.

Demuth, Henry Frederick Lewis—illegitimate son of Karl Marx and Helene Demuth, he lived with a foster family in East London and became a machinist, trade union member, and activist who admired Engels and Marx but died uncertain which of the two men, if either, was his father. Known as Freddy.

De Paepe, César—Belgian journalist, physician, and young member of the International Working Men's Association, he briefly broke with Marx in 1872 and supported Bakunin during a battle for control of the International. He was a founder of the Belgian Workers' Party.

Dickens, Charles—Britain's most popular novelist, whose realistic description of nineteenth-century England came to define the difficult life of the underclasses and the exploitation of the mass of citizens in a booming industrial society.

Dmitrieff Tomanovskaya, Elizabeth, (née Kusheleva)—Russian-born revolutionary who appeared at the Marx home in London in 1870 at age nineteen and won the confidence of Marx and his daughters. She ran missions to Paris for Marx during the 1871 Commune, but eventually stayed in Paris and helped organize women on the barricades.

Donelson, Andrew Jackson—American minister in Prussia during the 1848 uprising, later special envoy and minister plenipotentiary to the federal government of Germany before returning to the United States in 1849.

Doucet, Ernest—Paul and Laura Lafargue's gardener in Draveil, France.

Doucet, Roger—son of Ernest Doucet.

Dourlen, Gustave—French physician who helped Charles Longuet escape from France after the Commune and later acted as doctor to the Longuet family in Argenteuil.

Dronke, Ernst—a writer who had escaped from prison in Germany, he became a member of the Communist League and editor of *Neue Rheinische Zeitung* in Cologne under Marx. He later emigrated to England and was a close associate of Marx and Engels.

Duff, Sir Mountstuart Elphinstone Grant—Liberal member of the British Parliament in the second half of the nineteenth century.

Dühring, Eugen—blind German socialist, philosopher, economist, and lecturer at Berlin University, he provoked Engels by threatening to inject utopian ideas into the growing German workers' movement. Engels's polemic *Anti-Dühring* became an important piece of Marxist literature.

Duncker, Franz Gustav—Berlin publisher who at Ferdinand Lassalle's behest agreed in 1858 to take a series of books by Marx. He published Marx's *A Contribution to the Critique of Political Economy* in 1859.

Dupont, Eugène—French working-class activist, participant in the 1848 Paris uprising, and member of the International General Council.

Eccarius, Georg—German tailor exiled in London, member of the League of the Just, Communist League, and International Working Men's Association. He was IWMA general secretary from 1863 to 1872.

Eichmann, Franz August—Prussian interior minister in 1848 and president of the Rhine province.

Ellis, Henry Havelock—British psychologist and close friend of Eleanor Marx. Impotent until the age of sixty, he made a career of studying sexual relations. He is said to have coined the terms "homosexual," "auto-eroticism," and "narcissism."

Engels, Friedrich—scion of a Prussian textile manufacturer, Marx's closest colleague, and coauthor of, among other things, the *Communist Manifesto*. Engels completed Marx's *Capital, Volumes II* and *III,* and wrote many of his own works. Known as the General, early in his career he used the pseudonym Friedrich Oswald.

Engels, Friedrich Senior—pious Barmen businessman and father of Marx's closest associate.

Epicurus — Greek philosopher who promoted the material basis of life as experienced by the senses, not superstition, with serenity achieved through simple living and virtue.

Ermen, Gottfried — Engels's partner in the Manchester firm of Ermen & Engels.

Ewerbeck, August Hermann — German doctor exiled in Paris and future member of the Communist League. A leader of the Paris League of the Just, to which he introduced Marx.

Favre, Jules Gabrièl Claude — French foreign minister in the Government of National Defense. He agreed to a tentative armistice in 1871 with Bismarck to formally end hostilities begun in the 1870 Franco-Prussian War. In France's elected government of 1871 he retained his position and fought against the Paris Commune and the International.

Ferdinand I — Austrian emperor from 1835 to 1848, said to be feeble-minded and under the control of Chancellor Clemens von Metternich.

Ferdinand II — king of the Two Sicilies, a region of southern Italy from Apulia to Sicily, which revolted in 1848, demanding food and a representative government. He regained control after a vicious campaign that earned him the nickname King Bomba and ruled until 1859.

Feuerbach, Ludwig — nineteenth-century German philosopher, Young Hegelian, and Marx's friend, whose writing, especially on religion, helped Marx move away from Hegel.

Fichte, Johann Gottlieb — German Romantic philosopher of the late eighteenth century who viewed the world subjectively, from a point of "I."

Flaubert, Gustave — nineteenth-century French novelist and author of *Madame Bovary,* later translated into English by Eleanor Marx.

Fleckles, Ferdinand — German doctor who treated Marx in Karlsbad.

Fleury, Charles (né Carl Friedrich August Krause) — Prussian spy and police agent, he posed as a newspaperman to gain entrée to the Marx circle in London. Also known as Schmidt.

Flocon, Ferdinand — French democrat, editor of *La Reforme* newspaper, and a member of France's provisional government in 1848.

Floquet, Charles — French Chamber of Deputies president in 1891, when Paul Lafargue entered the chamber from Lille.

Florencourt, Wilhelm von — Ferdinand von Westphalen's brother-in-law, and friend to Jenny Marx.

Flourens, Gustave — French natural scientist, academic, military adventurer, and revolutionary, he fought on the side of the Paris Commune and was killed by French national troops in 1871. A frequent visitor to the Marx home while exiled in London, he was apparently Jennychen Marx's first love.

Fox, Peter (né Peter Fox André)—British democrat and journalist, member of the International General Council from 1864 to 1869, editor of *The Commonwealth* newspaper.

France, Anatole (né Jacques Anatole François Thibault)—nineteenth-century French poet, novelist, and critic who dominated the French literary world in the later years of the century. He was a friend of Charles Longuet.

Freiligrath, Ferdinand—businessman and immensely popular German poet banned by Friedrich Wilhelm IV for the political tone of his writing. He and his family were close to the Marxes from 1845 in Brussels until a falling-out with Marx in London in 1860.

Freyberger, Ludwig—Austrian doctor and second husband of Louise Kautsky, he treated Engels as a live-in physician in London from 1894 until Engels's death in 1895.

Friedrich Wilhelm III—Prussian king from 1797 to 1840, whose reactionary policies ran counter to the wishes of an emerging class of men whose wealth and status was earned, not inherited.

Friedrich Wilhelm IV—Prussian king from 1840 to 1861, he reigned through the 1848 European uprisings and oversaw the counterrevolutionary triumph of reactionary forces in Prussia.

Fröbel, Julius—Zurich-based professor and publisher of radical literature who promised to fund a newspaper venture involving Karl Marx and Arnold Ruge in Paris.

Frye, Eva—London actress and second wife of Edward Aveling. Also known as Lillian Richardson.

Furnivall, Frederick James—British Christian socialist and ardent feminist, founder of numerous literary societies, including the Browning and Chaucer societies and most notably the New Shakespeare Society, early editor of the *Oxford English Dictionary*.

Gambetta, Léon—French statesman and republican agitator in the 1870 provisional government.

Garibaldi, Giuseppe—nineteenth-century Italian nationalist and revolutionary hero who participated in the 1848–1849 uprisings in Italy, he was instrumental as a military strategist and fighter in Italy's struggle for unification during the next two decades and also supported the Paris Commune.

Gentry, Gertrude—British maid of Eleanor Marx and Edward Aveling in their home in Sydenham, outside London.

George, Henry—United Labor candidate who came in second in the 1886 New York City mayoral election, an indication of the growing political power of the worker in the United States.

Gigot, Charles Philippe—Belgian librarian and radical who worked with Marx and Engels on the Communist Correspondence Committee in Brussels and joined the Communist League. Known as Philippe.

Gladstone, William—four-time British prime minister (first Tory, then briefly Peelite, and finally Liberal Party leader) during the nineteenth century, for periods beginning in 1868 and ending in 1894.

Goethe, Johann Wolfgang von—one of Germany's greatest poets, playwrights, and novelists. His work incorporated science, politics, social relations, romanticism, and classicism, and was absorbed by Marx and his colleagues partly because of Goethe's belief in the dynamic development of mankind.

Gottschalk, Andreas—Cologne doctor known for treating the poor, he was a working-class activist and communist. During 1848 he was president of the Cologne Workers' Association, but disagreed with Marx over tactics.

Grévy, François Jules Paul—French republican and president of France from 1879 to 1887, under his government amnesty was offered to exiled communards.

Guesde, Jules (né Mathieu Jules Bazile)—revolutionary socialist and close associate of Paul Lafargue in France, he was cofounder of France's first Marxist party, the French Workers' Party.

Guizot, François Pierre Guillaume—French prime minister under Louis-Philippe. Seen as a powerful hand behind the throne, he was forced out of office at the start of the 1848 Paris uprising.

Gumpert, Eduard—elderly German doctor based in Manchester who treated Lupus, Engels, Marx, and Jenny. He was the only doctor Marx trusted.

Hansemann, David Justus—Prussian businessman and future Prussian finance minister, financial backer of Marx's *Rheinische Zeitung* newspaper in Cologne.

Hardie, James Keir—Scottish miner, union organizer, and leader of the Independent Labour Party, in 1892 he became one of the first three workingmen to win a seat in the British Parliament. Known as Keir.

Harney, George Julian—British journalist, reform activist, and leader of the Chartist movement, his newspaper *The Red Republican* was the first to publish the *Communist Manifesto* in English and identify its authors, Karl Marx and Friedrich Engels.

Hartmann, Leo (né Lev Nikolayevich Hartmann)—Russian revolutionary and member of the *Narodnaya Volya* (People's Will), who fled St. Petersburg in 1879 after trying to assassinate Czar Alexander II. He was a frequent visitor at Marx's and Engels's London homes and eventually emigrated to the United States.

Hatzfeldt, Sophie von—German countess and socialite involved in a notorious nineteenth-century divorce case, which she won with the help of Ferdinand Lassalle. She made gestures toward socialism, mostly by supporting Lassalle's work.

Haussmann, Georges-Eugène—with the approval of Napoleon III and as part of his job as Prefect of the Seine, he redesigned Paris between 1850 and 1870, widening its boulevards, tearing down its warrens of poor housing, and building temples to culture, finance, and government. His designs also were aimed at making barricade fighting ineffective.

Hecker (first name unknown)—public prosecutor in Cologne in 1848.

Hegel, Georg Wilhelm Friedrich—German philosopher, considered one of the world's most important thinkers due in part to his work on the changing nature of life, which he called the dialectic. He was a major influence on Karl Marx.

Heine, Heinrich (né Chaim Harry Heine)—one of Germany's greatest poets, he was banned from publishing because of his political views and emigrated to Paris in 1831, where he remained for the rest of his life. He was Karl and Jenny Marx's closest friend in Paris.

Heinzen, Karl—radical German journalist who worked with Marx on the *Rheinische Zeitung* in Cologne and was part of his circle in Brussels, but fell out with Marx while in exile in London and emigrated to the United States.

Herwegh, Emma (née Siegmund)—daughter of a Berlin silk merchant and wife of German poet Georg Herwegh.

Herwegh, Georg—German poet expelled by Friedrich Wilhelm IV because he declared himself a republican. He worked with Marx in Paris but fell out with him over Herwegh's effort to lead a force of fighting men into Germany in 1848.

Herzen, Alexander—exiled Russian journalist who published the first Russian émigré journal, *The Bell,* which had influence inside Russia. He was an advocate of populism and friend of Mikhail Bakunin.

Hess, Moses—journalist and future socialist Zionist, he was the first avowed communist among Marx's early German friends. He would work with Marx in Cologne on the *Rheinische Zeitung* and *Neue Rheinische Zeitung,* as well as on journalism and propaganda in Paris and Brussels.

Hess, Sibylle (née Pesch)—German working-class woman who lived with Moses Hess in Brussels and Paris; they married in 1852.

Hirsch, Wilhelm—Hamburg-born Prussian police agent in London charged with infiltrating and reporting on Marx's group.

Hugo, Victor—nineteenth-century French novelist, poet, and elected official in two French governments. His work was among the first to be considered international, combining Romanticism with realism in language, character, and events.

Humboldt, Alexander von—German baron, scientist, naturalist, explorer, author, and a founder of the University of Berlin in 1810, he acted as messenger and gift-bearer from Friedrich Wilhelm IV in his attempts to have the staff of the radical German-language newspaper *Vowarts!* expelled from Paris.

Hume, David—eighteenth-century Scottish philosopher and economist who believed one can only know that which is seen or experienced (empiricism). The idea was incorporated by Marx into his own theories.

Hyndman, Henry—nineteenth-century British socialist and early Marx acolyte, he later founded the Social Democratic Federation in Britain, and though he had fallen out with Marx, he worked closely with Eleanor Marx on socialist and labor issues.

Ibsen, Henrik—Norwegian playwright who upended nineteenth-century theater by violating formal conventions, focusing on problems of daily life, and stressing characters over plot. His plays involving the oppression of women in society, especially *A Doll's House,* made public discussions that women had long had in private.

Imandt, Peter—German schoolteacher who worked with Marx in Cologne during the 1848–1849 revolts, he was a member of the Communist League in London.

Imbert, Jacques—French socialist, journalist, and member of the Democratic Alliance in Brussels, later governor of Paris during the initial days after the 1848 uprising in that city.

Isabella II—queen of Spain, overthrown in an 1868 revolt. The dispute over filling her throne was one of the factors that led to 1870 Franco-Prussian War.

Jaurès, Jean—French journalist, Second International delegate, socialist leader, and member of the French Chamber of Deputies. He was assassinated in 1914 for advocating peace on the eve of World War I.

Johnson, Samuel—eighteenth-century British poet, moral essayist, and scholar, he was famous for, among many things, his *Preface to Shakespeare.*

Jones, Ernest—British lawyer, journalist, working-class advocate, and Chartist leader. He was a defense lawyer during the Manchester Martyrs trial in 1867, and a longtime friend of Marx and Engels.

Jottrand, Lucien—Belgian journalist, lawyer, and president of the Democratic Association in Brussels, of which Marx was vice president.

Jung, Georg—German journalist and manager of the *Rheinische Zeitung* in Cologne, he raised money to support Karl and Jenny Marx during their lean years in Paris and Brussels.

Kant, Immanuel—eighteenth-century German philosopher whose work on the role of reason in world thought and development influenced Schiller, Fichte, Hegel, and, by extension, Marx.

Kautsky, Karl—German journalist, economist, historian, and leading Marx theoretician. He was asked by Engels to take over, with Ede Bernstein, editing Marx's writing after Engels's death. Kautsky's *Theories of Surplus Value* was based on his edit of Marx's material for *Capital, Volume IV.*

Kautsky, Louise (née Strasser)—Austrian socialist and close associate of the Social Democratic Party leadership in Germany and Austria, she became Engels's household manager in 1890, after divorcing Karl Kautsky. She later married Austrian doctor Ludwig Freyberger in London.

Kelly, Colonel Thomas—U.S. Civil War veteran and a leader of the Irish Fenian movement whose arrest in Manchester in 1867 and subsequent escape became a legendary event in the Irish independence movement. Three Irishmen were hanged for helping him flee.

Kératry, Emile de—French count and provincial police official in 1870 and 1871, he was prefect of the Haute-Garonne department. He arrested and interrogated Marx's daughters Jenny and Eleanor as part of France's anti-communard sweep.

Kickham, Charles—editor of *The Irish People,* whose mistreatment by English jailers was exposed by Marx.

Kinkel, Gottfried—German journalist apprehended in Prussia during the 1849 Baden uprising but freed from a fortress by his protégé Carl Schurz. He later appeared in London and was active among refugees who admired his story. He was reviled by Marx and Engels.

Kossuth, Joseph—Hungarian independence hero who fought the Austrian Empire in 1848, demanding separation for the Kingdom of Hungary. He was briefly head of a Hungarian revolutionary government.

Kovalevsky, Maxim—liberal Russian intellectual who befriended Marx in Karlsbad and the entire Marx family in London.

Kreuz, Marianne—Helene Demuth's younger sister, who came to live with the Marxes in London after the death of her employer Caroline von Westphalen in Trier in 1856.

Kriege, Hermann—German journalist and utopian socialist.

Krupskaya, Nadia—wife of Vladimir Lenin.

Kugelmann, Franzisca—daughter of Ludwig and Gertruda Kugelmann, whose written recollections of the Marx family helped supply personal details about their lives in London and abroad.

Kugelmann, Gertruda—wife of Ludwig Kugelmann and a special favorite of Marx, who appreciated her intellect.

Kugelmann, Ludwig—Hanover gynecologist, participant in the 1848–1849 revolt, and an early reader of Marx and Engels's writing, he was fanatically devoted to Marx. He joined the International and attended its congresses, but Marx grew to despise him, partly for the way Kugelmann treated his wife.

Lachâtre, Maurice—communard and French publisher of *Capital, Volume I.*

Lafargue, Charles Etienne—first child of Laura and Paul Lafargue; he died at the age of four. Known as Schnapps and Fouchtra.

Lafargue, François—wealthy, conservative father of Paul Lafargue. He owned vineyards in Bordeaux and property in Cuba and New Orleans.

Lafargue, Jenny—infant daughter of Laura and Paul Lafargue; she lived for only a month.

Lafargue, Jenny Laura (née Marx)—Karl and Jenny Marx's second daughter, and wife of Paul Lafargue. She lived most of her adult life in France and worked as a translator of her father's and Engels's writing. Known as Laura.

Lafargue, Marc-Laurent—third child of Laura and Paul Lafargue; he lived less than a year.

Lafargue, Paul—Cuban-born French socialist activist and propagandist, husband of Marx's daughter Laura, he helped introduce Marxism to France and Spain. Known as Tooley.

Lamartine, Alphonse Marie Louis de—French Romantic poet, political republican, and powerful orator, he was the recognized head of the provisional government in France after the 1848 uprising.

Lancaster, Edith—British member of the Social Democratic Federation, feminist, and friend of Eleanor Marx Aveling, she was committed to an insane asylum by her family for having an extramarital affair.

Lassalle, Ferdinand (né Ferdinand Leslauer)—German lawyer and socialist activist, he founded Germany's first working-class party, the General Union of German Workers, and was instrumental in getting Marx's *Critique of Political Economy* published, though Marx considered him more nemesis than friend.

Latour, Theodor—Austrian minister of war murdered by enraged workers in Vienna in 1848.

Lavrov, Pyotr—Russian-born journalist, math professor, and philosopher, exiled to Paris. He was a close Marx colleague, Commune sympathizer, and member of the International.

Lecomte, General Claude—led a brigade to Montmartre to recapture cannons from Paris insurgents in 1871, but lost control of his men and was captured and executed by furious Parisians. His death was used as an excuse for a brutal crackdown against the communards.

Ledru-Rollin, Alexandre—French republican and member of 1848 provisional government, he was part of a banquet campaign that precipitated the 1848 uprising in Paris.

Lee, H. W.—British socialist and journalist allied with Hyndman's Social Democratic Federation, he worked with Edward Aveling and Eleanor Marx Aveling.

Lees, Edith—British writer, feminist, and lesbian wife of Havelock Ellis. She was a friend of Eleanor Marx Aveling.

Lelewel, Joachim—Polish historian and veteran revolutionary, he participated in Poland's failed 1830 uprising and was an associate of Karl and Jenny Marx in Brussels.

Le Lubez, Victor—French exile in London who invited Marx to attend a meeting that would launch the First International Working Men's Association there. He was a member of the IWMA General Council and correspondence secretary for France.

Le Moussu, Benjamin—French engraver and member of the Paris Commune and the International General Council, he entered into business briefly with Paul Lafargue.

Lenin, Vladimir (né Ulianov)—leader of the October 1917 Revolution that overthrew a provisional government in Russia and ultimately allowed Lenin to establish the first communist state, based on some— but not exclusively—Marxist principles. He met Paul Lafargue twice and delivered a eulogy at the Lafargues' 1911 funeral in Paris.

Léo, André (née Léonide Béra)—Frenchwoman widowed at age thirty-one. She supported her children, André and Léo, by writing novels and became an advocate for women's rights. She defended the Commune, both during its fight against French national troops and, after its defeat, from exile in Switzerland.

Leopold I (né Leopold George Christian Frederick)—prince of Saxe-Coburg and Gotha, relatively liberal king of Belgium from 1831 to 1865.

Leske, Karl Friedrich Julius—liberal Darmstadt publisher who signed a contract with Marx in 1845 to publish his book on political economy.

Lessner, Friedrich—German tailor and Communist League member in London, he worked with Marx in Cologne during the 1848–1849 revolt, later traveled as a League propagandist, and was a defendant in the Cologne Communist Trial, where he was sentenced to three years in prison. He joined the First International and was one of Marx's and Engels's closest associates.

Lichnowsky, Felix—Prussian prince and rightist member of the Frankfurt National Assembly. In 1848 he was lynched during a mob uprising in Frankfurt.

Liebknecht, Ernestine—first wife of Wilhelm Liebknecht, friend of Jenny Marx in London, and later close correspondent when the Liebknechts returned to Germany.

Liebknecht, Natalie—second wife of Wilhelm Liebknecht, frequent correspondent from her home in Germany of the Marx women in London. She was especially close to Eleanor Marx at the end of her life.

Liebknecht, Wilhelm—lifelong Marx associate, member of the Communist League in London and later of the German Reichstag. He helped found one of the most important working-class parties, the Social Democratic Party of Germany. Known to the Marx family as Library.

Lincoln, Abraham—U.S. president from 1861 to 1865, he held office during the Civil War and signed the Emancipation Proclamation freeing slaves in the South and setting the nation on a course to end slavery in 1865.

Linnell, Alfred—English law clerk killed during the November 1887 police crackdown in London that followed the Bloody Sunday melee.

Lissagaray, Hyppolite-Prosper-Olivier—French aristocrat, journalist, and military man whose history of the 1871 Paris Commune was considered by Marx to be the best depiction of the insurgency. He was engaged to Eleanor Marx when he was thirty-four and she just seventeen, but, partly due to strong opposition from Marx, they never married. Known as Lissa.

Longuet, Charles—French socialist and journalist married to Marx's eldest daughter, Jenny.

Longuet, Charles Félicien Marx—first child of Charles and Jenny Longuet, he died shortly before his first birthday. Known as Caro.

Longuet, Edgar—son of Charles and Jenny Longuet, he was a physician active among the French working class, and a Socialist Party member. Known as Wolf.

Longuet, Félicitas—mother of Charles Longuet.

Longuet, Henry—son of Charles and Jenny Longuet, he did not live to see his fifth birthday. Known as Harry.

Longuet, Jean Laurent Frédéric—second son of Charles and Jenny Longuet, he was a lawyer and future leader among French Socialists, and was raised partly by Eleanor Marx. Known as Johnny.

Longuet, Jenny—daughter of Charles and Jenny Longuet, she was an opera singer, raised partly by Laura Lafargue. Known as Mémé.

Longuet, Jenny Caroline (née Marx)—Karl and Jenny Marx's eldest daughter and wife of Charles Longuet, she worked for her father as a correspondence secretary and briefly as a journalist whose crowning achievement was a series of articles that ultimately freed Irish political prisoners from English jails. Known as Jennychen, she used the alias J. Williams.

Longuet, Marcel—son of Charles and Jenny Longuet. Known as Par or Parnell.

Lorenzo, Anselmo—Spanish printer, working-class advocate, and member of the Spanish International.

Louis-Philippe—French monarch from 1830 to 1848, known as the Citizen King because he ascended the throne as a result of a popular uprising. During his reign moneyed interests thrived.

Loustalot, Elisée—eighteenth-century French journalist and Jacobin during the French Revolution.

Lyubavin, Nikolai—one of three Russian translators of *Capital, Volume I,* he was threatened by Sergei Nechayev for involving Bakunin in the project.

MacMahon, Marshal Marie Edme Patrice—military dictator of Algeria, head of Versailles troops in the fight against the Paris Commune in 1871, he was briefly military dictator of France during that period and the president of the Third Republic from 1873 to 1879.

Maitland, Dollie—English actress friend of Eleanor Marx, fellow Dogberry Club member, future wife of Ernest Radford.

Mann, Thomas—British mechanic, working-class political leader, and union organizer, he was a member of the Independent Labour Party and a future member of the British Parliament. Known as Tom.

Manning, Charles—Marx family friend and Laura Marx's rejected suitor.

Manteuffel, Otto von—baron, reactionary Prussian interior minister from November 1848 to November 1850, and Prussian prime minister from 1850 to 1858.

Martin, Alexandre—French worker who became minister in the provisional government after the 1848 uprising. Known as Albert.

Marx Aveling, Jenny Julia Eleanor (née Marx)—British-born socialist activist and labor agitator, translator of Flaubert and Ibsen, journalist,

Karl and Jenny Marx's youngest daughter, and common-law wife of Edward Aveling. Known as Eleanor and Tussy.

Marx, Charles Louis Henri Edgar—Karl and Jenny Marx's first son. Known as Edgar and Musch.

Marx, Franzisca—fifth child of Karl and Jenny Marx, she lived only one year.

Marx, Heinrich (né Heschel Marx)—first Jewish lawyer in Trier and Karl Marx's father, he became a Lutheran in 1817 in order to continue practicing law in the Prussian Rhineland.

Marx, Heinrich Guido—second son to Karl and Jenny Marx, he died after his first birthday. Known as Fawksy.

Marx, Henrietta (née Presburg)—Karl Marx's mother.

Marx, Jenny (née Johanna Bertha Julie Jenny von Westphalen)—daughter of a Prussian baron and wife of Karl Marx, she actively supported Marx's work and labored on behalf of socialists and workers.

Marx, Karl—Prussian economist, philosopher, journalist, and father of international socialism. Known as Mohr, he used the alias A. Williams.

Maürer, Germain—exiled German socialist writer, member of the early underground Paris workers' group League of Outlaws, later League of the Just. He lived near Marx in Paris and invited him to attend the group's meetings.

Mazzini, Giuseppe—Italian nationalist and founder, after the 1830 revolts, of the Young Italy society, whose goal was to unite various states, kingdoms, and duchies on the Italian peninsula into a country. He lived in exile in London and was a longtime nemesis of Marx.

Meissner, Otto—Hamburg publisher who signed a contract with Marx in 1865 to publish two volumes of *Capital, A Critique of Political Economy.*

Metternich, Clemens von—Austrian prince and foreign affairs minister from 1809 to 1821, chancellor from 1809 to 1848, and one of the most powerful reactionaries in nineteenth-century Europe, he was an early victim of the 1848 uprisings and resigned his post.

Mevissen, Gustav—Rhineland banker and financial backer of Marx's *Rheinische Zeitung* newspaper.

Meyerbeer, Giacomo (né Jacob Liebmann Beer)—Prussian opera composer who financed the radical German-language newspaper *Vowarts!* in Paris, reportedly at the behest of Friedrich Wilhelm IV, who wanted to expose and prosecute the opposition.

Michel, Louise—provincial-born French schoolmistress turned revolutionary during the buildup to the 1871 Commune, in which she participated. She stood trial for, among other things, plotting to assassinate government officials and participating in the arrest and execution of Generals Lécomte and Thomas.

Mill, John Stuart—nineteenth-century English philosopher and economist, member of Parliament, women's rights and peace advocate.

Millerand, Etienne—French politician, lawyer, and journalist, member of the Chamber of Deputies, head of the independent socialists, he defended Paul Lafargue against incitement to murder charges in the 1891 Fourmies trial and later defeated Lafargue in Parisian elections.

Millière, Jean–Baptiste—French lawyer and journalist, he participated in the October 31, 1870, revolt at the Paris Hôtel de Ville and was executed in May 1871.

Mincke, Paule (née Paulina Mekarska)—journalist and teacher who fought for women's rights in the years before the Paris Commune and was an active participant in the 1871 battle.

Miskowsky, Henryk—Polish refugee in London who accompanied Conrad Schramm as a second in his duel with August Willich.

Moll, Joseph—Cologne watchmaker and founding member of the League of the Just in London and the German Workers' Educational Association, he invited Marx and Engels to join the league. He died in 1849 fighting in the insurrectionary army in Baden.

Moore, George—British socialist who went into business briefly with Paul Lafargue in London.

Moore, Samuel—British lawyer, English translator of *Capital, Volume I* and the *Communist Manifesto,* he was a colonial official in West Africa, and Marx's and Engels's longtime friend.

Morris, May—daughter of William Morris, author, and advocate on behalf of the working class.

Morris, William—English architect, artist, poet, novelist, and social reformer, he was a founding member of the Socialist League with Eleanor Marx and Edward Aveling, and a working-class advocate.

Mulcahy, Dennis Dowling—physician and subeditor of Dublin's *The Irish People* newspaper, whose mistreatment at the hands of English jailers was exposed by Marx.

Napoleon I (né Napoleon François Charles Joseph Bonaparte)—French emperor from 1805 to 1815. Even in defeat he haunted the rulers of Europe, who were fearful of freedoms extended to French citizens under the Napoleonic Code and protective of borders created after his 1815 defeat at Waterloo.

Napoleon III (né Charles Louis Napoleon Bonaparte)—nephew of Napoleon Bonaparte and son of the king of Holland, Louis Bonaparte.

He was born in Paris, raised in Switzerland, and elected president of France from 1848 to 1851. He became Emperor Napoleon III in 1852 and ruled until 1870.

Nechayev, Sergei—Russian anarchist and conspirator, and close associate of Bakunin, he claimed to control a vast underground organization in Russia. He killed a student for questioning the group's existence and was later captured by the Swiss and imprisoned in Russia, where he died in 1882.

Nicholas I (né Nikolay Pavlovich)—Russian czar from 1825 to 1855, he presided over the reactionary period known as the Cruel Century and was on the throne at the start of the Crimean War.

Noir, Victor—French journalist for the republican newspaper *La Marseillaise*. He was killed by Napoleon III's cousin in January 1870.

Nothjung, Peter—German tailor and member of the Communist League in Cologne. He was arrested in Leipzig in 1851, the first of the Cologne Communist Trial defendants to be apprehended, and sentenced to six years in prison for attempted high treason.

O'Brien, James Bronterre—Dublin-born radical reformer, propagandist, and socialist, he worked against English domination of Ireland and for labor reform. He was known as the "Schoolmaster" of Chartism for his widely read writings declaring war on private property.

O'Donovan Rossa, Jeremiah—editor of the Dublin newspaper *The Irish People,* he was arrested in 1865 as part of a sweep against his newspaper, which was accused of stirring revolt and promoting socialism. His mistreatment while imprisoned by the English was exposed in a series of newspaper articles written by Marx's daughter Jenny. He was eventually freed and emigrated to the United States.

O'Donovan Rossa, Mary—wife of Jeremiah O'Donovan Rossa.

O'Leary—a sixty- or seventy-year-old Irish political prisoner whose real name was Murphy (but whose first name was unknown). His suffering at the hands of English jailers was exposed by Marx.

Orsini, Cesare—brother of Felice Orsini, he traveled to London with Paul Lafargue and worked with Marx to undermine Mazzini's influence in the International.

Orsini, Felice—Italian nationalist and republican, he was executed in 1858 for attempting to assassinate Napoleon III in a Paris bombing that killed eight innocent people.

Owen, Robert—first British socialist and manager of New Lanark, Scotland, where in the early nineteenth century he successfully ran a factory based on socialist principles. His later attempts at similar communities in the United States failed.

Panizzi, Anthony (né Antonio Genesio Maria Panizzi)—Italian-born keeper of the books at the British Museum Reading Room when Marx began using the facility in 1850.

Pannewitz, Karl von—Jenny von Westphalen's first fiancé.

Parnell, Charles Stuart—celebrated nineteenth-century Irish nationalist and member of the British Parliament representing County Wicklow, he was an outspoken advocate of Home Rule.

Perovskaya, Sofia—Russian revolutionary and Narodnaya Volya member engaged in an unsuccessful plot with Leo Hartmann to assassinate Czar Alexander II. A later attempt was successful, and she was executed for her role in the killing.

Petty, Sir William—seventeenth-century English philosopher, scientist, and political economist, he advocated a laissez-faire approach in his examination of the role of the state in the economy.

Philips, Antoinette—Marx's cousin in Holland and daughter of Lion Philips. Marx carried on a romantic if distant relationship with her for several years in the early 1860s. Known as Nanette and Netchen.

Philips, Jacques—Marx's cousin in Holland and son of Lion Philips, he was a lawyer in Rotterdam.

Philips, Lion Benjamin—Dutch businessman and brother-in-law of Karl Marx's mother, he handled the family's finances after the death of Heinrich Marx.

Pieper, Wilhelm—German refugee in London, a member of the Communist League, and a part-time journalist, he was a tutor to the Marx children and frequent secretary to Marx.

Pius IX (né Giovanni Maria Mastai-Ferretti)—head of the Roman Catholic Church (1846–1878) and Papal States of central Italy, who helped inspire the 1848 revolt in southern Italy by instituting social reforms.

Plater, Vladislaw—Polish count and participant in Poland's 1830 revolt, he was resident at Karlsbad during Marx's 1874 spa stay and mistakenly identified as "chief of the Nihilists."

Plekhanov, Georgy—Russian writer and philosopher, he emigrated to western Europe and founded the first Russian Marxist organization, the Emancipation of Labour, in 1883. He worked closely with Engels and Eleanor Marx, and was a strict Marxist who opposed revisionism in the years after Engels's death and during the Russian Revolution.

Plutarch—Greek biographer who lived from about AD 46 to AD 120, famous for chronicling the lives of early Greeks and Romans in almost novelistic form.

Proudhon, Pierre-Joseph—self-taught nineteenth-century French philosopher, economist, and author, whose work criticizing private property was called "epoch-making" by Marx. He abandoned social-ism to become one of the founders of anarchism.

Puttkamer, Elisabeth von—niece of Otto von Bismarck, she spent a day with Marx in London after sailing with him from Hamburg in 1867.

Quinet, Edgar—historian and veteran of the 1848 Paris revolt, he joined the French government as a National Assembly deputy in 1871.

Radford, Ernest—English lawyer, amateur actor, member of the Dog-berry Club, and a friend of Eleanor Marx.

Raspail, François—Writer, scientist, politician, veteran socialist of the 1830 and 1848 French uprisings, and an advocate of the proletariat.

Ricardo, David—English political economist, who believed in free trade, among other things. Marx studied him during his exploration of classical or "bourgeois" economists.

Rings, L. W.—German refugee in London accused, despite being nearly illiterate, of coauthoring minutes of a meeting of Marx's circle used as prosecution evidence in the Cologne Communist Trial.

Rochefort, Henri de—editor of the republican newspaper *La Marseillaise,* he joined the French provisional government after Napoleon III's defeat in 1870.

Roy, Joseph—French translator of *Capital, Volume I.*

Ruge, Arnold—German journalist and editor jailed for six years because of his liberal ideas. He collaborated with Marx on an unsuccessful French-German newspaper, which led to a permanent estrangement between them.

Rutenberg, Adolf—teacher banned from the profession by the Prussian government, likely for controversial newspaper articles, he was an early Marx colleague in Berlin and briefly editor of the *Rheinische Zeitung* in Cologne.

Saint-Simon, Claude Henri de—late-eighteenth-century/early-nine-teenth-century count, philosopher, and founder of French socialism.

Salt, Henry—assistant master at the prestigious British public school Eton, socialist activist, journalist, and member of the Fabian Society, he was an associate of Edward Aveling and Eleanor Marx Aveling.

Salt, Kate—Henry Salt's wife.

Sand, George (née Amandine Lucie Aurore Dupin, Baronne Dudevant)— celebrated and controversial nineteenth-century French novelist, she joined the 1848 revolutionary government in Paris as a propagandist.

Santi, Madame—family relation to Paul Lafargue's mother who helped Laura Lafargue in Paris after the birth of her first son.

Schapper, Karl—trained German forester, print compositor, and leader of the League of the Just in Paris. He was deported for his part in a

French uprising, helped reconstitute the group in London, and became a member of the Communist League Central Committee there. He worked with Marx on the *Neue Rheinische Zeitung* in Cologne and was a member of the General Council of the First International.

Schiller, Johann Christoph Friedrich von—German Romantic writer, historian, and figurehead for many members of the German Confederation seeking to make that loose grouping of states into a nation.

Schmalhausen, Sophie (née Marx)—Karl Marx's oldest and closest sibling.

Schneider, Karl II—lawyer and president of the Cologne Democratic Society. He stood trial with Marx and was acquitted on charges of inciting rebellion. He later defended Marx and Engels in a trial related to the *Neue Rheinische Zeitung* and Communist League members on trial in 1852 in Cologne.

Schöler, Lina—German friend of Jenny Marx and ex-fiancée of Jenny's brother Edgar von Westphalen.

Schorlemmer, Carl—one of the founders of organic chemistry. A German immigrant to England, he lived in Manchester, was a member of the International and German Social Democratic Workers' Party, and was a lifelong friend of Marx and Engels. Known to the Marx family as Jollymeier.

Schramm, Conrad—German émigré in London and a member of the Communist League, he worked with Marx on the *Neue Rheinische Zeitung, Politisch-ökonomische Revue* and fought a duel in his stead.

Schreiner, Olive—author, feminist, and Eleanor Marx's closest friend in London before Schreiner moved to South Africa, where she wrote *The Story of an African Farm* under the pen name Ralph Iron.

Schurz, Carl—German democrat and Marx detractor who later joined the insurrectionary army in Baden. He fled to Switzerland and London, and eventually emigrated to the United States, where he fought in the Civil War and became minister of the interior.

Scott, Sir Walter—Scottish historical Romantic novelist, one of the most popular of the early nineteenth century and a favorite of the Marx family.

Shakespeare, William—greatest playwright in the English language, whose plays began to appear in England at the end of the sixteenth century. The Marxes were Shakespeare devotees; Marx taught himself English by reading Shakespeare.

Shaw, George Bernard—Irish playwright, critic, author, and socialist reformer, he was an early convert to Marxism after reading *Capital, Volume I* in French, but gradually adopted his own brand of reform. He was an early friend to Eleanor Marx when he arrived in London, working with her on socialist newspapers and organizations, and in minor theatricals. His plays were considered too controversial to be performed in England before the twentieth century.

Shelley, Percy Bysshe—British Romantic poet and radical propagandist who inspired Marx's circle.

Skinner, Marian—English actress and frequent visitor to the Marx home as a Dogberry Club member and friend of Eleanor Marx. She later wrote recollections under her married name, Marian Comyn.

Smith, Adam—eighteenth-century Scottish political economist whose book *The Wealth of Nations* became the basis of classical economics and whose belief in the benefit of free markets gave rise to "laissez-faire" capitalism.

Staël, Madame de (née Anne Louise Germaine Necker)—eighteenth-century Swiss-French writer who some experts say wrote the first modern feminist novels with *Delphine* (1802) and *Corinne, or Italy* (1807).

Stanton, Edward—son of American woman's suffrage pioneer Elizabeth Cady Stanton.

Stanton, Elizabeth Cady—one of the founders of the U.S. woman's suffrage movement in 1848 and coauthor of *A History of Woman Suffrage*.

Stead, W. T.—crusading editor of the London newspaper *Pall Mall Gazette* and author of a controversial study on sexual commerce in London. He died on the *Titanic* in 1912.

Stepniak (né Sergei Mikhailovich Kravchinsky)—nineteenth-century Russian revolutionary and member of the Narodniks, he fled to western Europe after assassinating a military official in St. Petersburg in 1878. He was an apologist for terrorist tactics and a frequent visitor to Engels's home, and died after being hit by a train in London in 1895.

Stieber, Wilhelm—Prussian police spy, chief prosecution witness in the Cologne Communist Trial, and later head of the Prussian political police.

Sue, Eugène—nineteenth-century French doctor and author known for highly popular romantic novels.

Swinton, John—Scottish-born liberal newspaperman and editor of *The Sun* newspaper in New York.

Techow, Gustav—former Prussian military officer and democrat, he was a leader of the 1849 Baden insurrection.

Tedesco, Victor—Belgian lawyer and socialist, he was a member of the Communist League and Democratic Association in Brussels.

Tenge, Therese (née Bolongaro-Crevenna)—Italian married to a wealthy German landowner. Marx had a brief romance with her in Hanover while waiting for the proof sheets for *Capital, Volume I.*

Thomas, General Clément—killed along with General Lecomte by Parisians angry over their attempt to recapture cannons seized by insurgents in 1871. He was also loathed for his role in putting down the 1848 revolt in Paris and for the Buzenval massacre in January 1871.

Thorne, William James—Birmingham-born brick maker, working-class political leader, union organizer, and member of the Social Democratic Federation, he helped mount the London Dock Strike, and later became a member of the British Parliament. He was taught to read by Eleanor Marx. Known as Will.

Tillett, Ben—British shoemaker, navy man, dockworker, working-class organizer, and trade unionist, he helped run the London Dock Strike. In later years he became a member of Parliament.

Tocqueville, Alexis Charles Henri Maurice Clérel de—nineteenth-century French count, writer, historian, and social critic, he was elected to the French National Assembly after the 1848 revolt and remained in President Louis-Napoleon's government until Napoleon's coup in December 1851.

Trochu, General Louis Jules—Napoleon III's appointed military governor of Paris and, after Napoleon's capture by Prussian troops in 1870, head of France's provisional Government of National Defense.

Turgenev, Ivan—nineteenth-century Russian novelist who coined the term "nihilist," he was a friend of Bakunin. He managed to annoy both Russian radicals and conservatives in his writing, and found an early audience in the West.

Ulianov, Alexander—brother of Vladimir Lenin, he was executed in 1887 for attempting to assassinate Czar Alexander III.

Verlaine, Paul—nineteenth-century French Symbolist poet, he fought in the Franco-Prussian War and later supported the Paris Commune by working in its press office. He was imprisoned in 1873 after shooting his lover, fellow poet Arthur Rimbaud, and released in 1875.

Victoria (née Adelaide Mary Louise)—daughter of Queen Victoria, crown princess of Great Britain, and future empress of Germany after marrying Wilhelm I's son Friedrich, who lived only ninety-nine days as emperor.

Queen Victoria (née Alexandrina Victoria)—ruler of Great Britain and Ireland from 1837 to 1901. Her early reign was characterized by industrial, economic, and military superiority and growth, but class struggles and a changing society she did not understand tarnished her later years.

Vinoy, General Joseph—briefly head of the French Government of National Defense from January 1871.

Vogler, Carl—German bookseller in Brussels who agreed to publish *The Poverty of Philosophy,* Marx's attack on Proudhon.

Vogt, Carl—German democrat, geography teacher, and former member of the 1848 Frankfurt National Assembly, while exiled in Switzerland he accepted funds from Napoleon III to write and solicit articles favorable to France. He engaged in a public battle with Marx when details of the arrangement were published.

Wagner, Richard—nineteenth-century German composer, conductor, and nationalist, whose influence extended well beyond the world of music, into literature and politics.

Washburne, Elihu Benjamin—U.S. ambassador to France during the Franco-Prussian War and the 1870–1871 siege of Paris, he served in that position until 1877.

Webb, Beatrice (née Martha Beatrice Potter)—British sociologist and economist who along with her husband, Sidney, advocated a gradualist approach to social change. Author of works on socialism and trade unionism, she and her husband founded the London School of Economics in 1895.

Webb, Sidney James—British socialist and early member of the Fabian Society, he agitated on behalf of the British labor movement and with his wife, Beatrice, wrote a history of socialism and trade unionism in Britain. He and Beatrice founded the London School of Economics in 1895.

Weerth, Georg—German poet, journalist, and Communist League member, he worked with Marx in Paris, Brussels, and Cologne, and introduced Jenny Marx to her exile in London.

Weitling, Wilhelm—German tailor, author, and leading figure among socialist and communist workers in the first half of the nineteenth century, he advocated utopian socialism built on a cult of his personality.

Westphalen, Caroline von (née Heubel)—Ludwig von Westphalen's second wife and Jenny Marx's mother.

Westphalen, Edgar von—Jenny Marx's only full sibling. An early follower of Karl Marx, he would fight on the side of the Confederacy in the U.S. Civil War before returning to Prussia.

Westphalen, Ferdinand von—reactionary Prussian interior minister from 1850 to 1858 and eldest half brother of Marx's wife, Jenny, he thwarted much of Marx's work through his ministry.

Westphalen, Louise von—Ferdinand von Westphalen's wife.

Westphalen, Ludwig von—Prussian baron, ranking government official in Trier, and father of Marx's wife, Jenny. He was an early advocate of socialism, and introduced the concept to Marx.

Weydemeyer, Joseph—ex-lieutenant in the Prussian army and future member of the Union army in the U.S. Civil War, he was one of Marx's closest associates in Germany and later worked with Marx on publishing projects from Weydemeyer's base in New York. Known as Weywey.

Wilde, Lady (née Jane Francesca Agnes Elgee)—poet, writer, and Irish nationalist, mother of writer Oscar Wilde.

Wilde, Oscar Fingal O'Flahertie Wills—Irish-born playwright and novelist who challenged British society in the late 1800s with his work, appearance, and lifestyle. He served two years of hard labor in prison for homosexual practices.

Wilhelm I (né Wilhelm Friedrich Ludwig)—crown prince of Prussia, he became regent in 1858, when his brother Friedrich Wilhelm IV became incapacitated, and king in January 1861. In 1871 he became Emperor Wilhelm at Versailles after defeating Napoleon III and the French army in the 1870 Franco-Prussian War.

Wilhelm II (né Friedrich Wilhelm Victor Albert)—emperor of Germany from 1888 to 1918. Initially more liberal than his aged chancellor, Bismarck, who resigned under pressure, he became more conservative over time. He was commander in chief of the German armed forces in World War I, abdicated in 1918, and fled with his family to Holland.

Willich, August—ex-Prussian army officer, early communist agitator in Cologne, member of the Communist League, and a leader of the insurrectionary army in Baden in 1849. He emigrated to London and associated with Marx in 1849–1850, but they fell out over personal and political differences. He emigrated to the United States and fought in the Union army in the Civil War.

Wishart, George—Sixteenth-century Scottish religious reformer burned at the stake for his anti-Catholic preaching. His death spurred Protestant reformers and ultimately the victory of Protestantism, which was achieved in Catholic-dominated Scotland in 1560.

Wolff, Ferdinand—German journalist and close associate of Marx in Brussels, Cologne, Paris, London, and Manchester. Known as Red Wolff.

Wolff, Wilhelm—German journalist and teacher who escaped before being jailed in Silesia for violating press laws. Member of the Communist League Central Committee, he was among Marx's closest associates in Brussels, Cologne, London, and Manchester, and Marx dedicated the first volume of *Capital* to him. Known as Lupus.

Zetkin, Clara—member of the Social Democratic Party of Germany and activist for international socialism and German workers, she was highly regarded by Engels.

Zola, Emile—nineteenth-century French author whose naturalistic novels unflinchingly depicted French society under Napoleon III and advocated reform through detailed descriptions of suffering.

A Political Timeline

1837 — Marx joins the Young Hegelians in Berlin. After the death of German philosopher Georg Wilhelm Friedrich Hegel in 1831, some young followers built upon his dialectic theory that change was inevitable and began arguing for political and social reform. These Young Hegelians were based in Berlin.

May 1842 — Marx begins writing for *Rheinische Zeitung* in Cologne. The opposition newspaper was established in the most economically and intellectually advanced city in the Rhineland and backed by a spectrum of opposition figures, from middle-class businessmen seeking economic advances to socialists. Marx was made editor in October 1842.

February 1844 — Marx edits the first and only issue of the *Deutsche-Französische Jahrbücher* newspaper in Paris. Marx and Jenny had moved to Paris to join Arnold Ruge's newspaper, which was to give voice to French and German opposition writers. The newspaper failed to attract French writers, was banned in Germany, and resulted in arrest warrants for high treason in Prussia against Marx and three others associated with the paper.

Spring 1844 — Marx is introduced to the League of the Just in Paris. The secret conspiracy-propaganda society was formed there in 1836 by mostly German artisan refugees who adopted the principles of French worker communism espoused by Auguste Blanqui and Armand Barbes in their secret Société des Saisons.

August 1844 — Marx begins writing for *Vowarts!* in Paris. The weekly was known as the only uncensored opposition German-language newspaper in Europe. It was considered so radical that its editor was imprisoned and staff members, including Marx, were expelled from France.

Summer 1845 — Marx and Engels travel to England, meet League of the Just members and Chartists. Some German league members had fled Paris in 1839, after a failed revolt by French colleagues, and established a branch of the secret organization in London, along with a public recruiting tool called the German Workers' Educational Association. Marx and Engels also associated with veterans of the English reform movement, Chartism, which was looking for continental support.

January 1846—Marx, Engels, and Philippe Gigot form the Communist Correspondence Committee in Brussels. The committee's goal was to acquaint workers and socialists throughout Europe with events of mutual interest in order to prepare for and coordinate a future revolution. It was the first international organization Marx tried to form.

February 1847—Marx accepts an invitation to join the London-based League of the Just and opens a branch in Brussels. Marx and Engels agreed to join the league after its London leaders admitted they needed the younger men's help in attracting workers. It was the first proletariat organization Marx joined.

June 1847—League of the Just changes its name to the Communist League. Its members met in London to chart a new course. Under Marx and Engels's guidance, the league became the first international communist organization in history.

July 1847—Marx and Engels form a branch of the secret Communist League in Brussels and a public German Workers' Association. After the London Communist League meeting, Marx and Engels began recruiting members for a Brussels branch but were frustrated by a lack of participation by actual workers. They launched an educational and social society to attract workers for their clandestine group.

November 1847—Marx becomes vice president of the International Democratic Association in Brussels. The association was formed by professional men to counter Marx and Engels's influence among German refugees and Belgian radicals, but Engels managed to get Marx elected the group's vice president and make it yet another of his organizational tools.

February 1848—Marx and Engels's *Manifesto of the Communist Party* is published in London. Marx and Engels had been asked by the Communist League to produce a document to be used to recruit members. Engels and several other league members wrote versions, but Marx's is the one that came off the press in London in 1848. It was called by one colleague the most revolutionary document the world had ever seen.

March 1848—Communist League Central Authority is transferred to Paris. In 1848 Europe erupted in revolt from Berlin to Sicily, but its epicenter was Paris. Marx and his family moved there after he was expelled from Belgium amid heightened tensions over the presence of foreign radicals in Brussels.

Marx forms German Workers' Union in Paris. Paris was awash in refugee groups organizing to stir revolts in their own countries. Marx's union was to be an army of propagandists, not soldiers, who would secretly return to Germany to strengthen the burgeoning opposition there.

June 1848—Marx's *Neue Rheinische Zeitung* newspaper is published in Cologne. Marx and his colleagues reconstituted his earlier Cologne newspaper as a democratic organ reporting on previously secret government activities throughout the German Bund and on uprisings throughout Europe.

Marx dissolves the Communist League. After the brutal June Days uprising in Paris, in which counterrevolutionary forces battled civilians, Marx decided a secret society like the league was no longer necessary, because the fight could take place in plain sight and in the pages of his newspaper. The league leadership, nearly all in Cologne with Marx, voted to disband.

September 1848—Marx and Engels help form a Committee of Public Safety in Cologne. Tensions in Catholic Cologne, which was occupied by mostly Protestant Prussian troops, boiled over. Citizens, convinced the troops were their enemy, decided to form a militia to protect themselves, without the sanction of the government.

April 1849—Marx cuts ties with democratic associates in the Rhineland Democratic Union. By 1849's counterrevolution, Marx felt middle-class democrats had betrayed the working class to protect their interests. After 1849, Marx would never again work politically with the bourgeoisie.

May 1849—The *Neue Rheinische Zeitung* folds. The increasingly radical tone of Marx's newspaper resulted in an order for his expulsion from Prussia. The newspaper's final edition was printed in red ink.

September 1849—The Communist League is reconstituted in London, along with the German Workers' Educational Society. After the 1848 uprisings in Europe were quashed, political refugees from around the Continent descended on London. Among them were Marx and the league members, who reactivated the group and its recruiting tool.

Committee for the Assistance of German Political Refugees is established. Marx was elected to a committee that assisted the hundreds of German refugees streaming into London without food, shelter, or money. The committee was an offshoot of the German Workers' Educational Society, and as such was also used to attract members for the Communist League.

Early 1850—Marx and Engels join the Universal Society of Revolutionary Communists in London. The French-dominated, extreme radical group was composed mostly of followers of Auguste Blanqui, who was jailed in France for his role in the 1848 uprising.

March 1850—Marx's *Neue Rheinische Zeitung, Politisch-ökonomische Revue* is published in Hamburg. The German-language opposition newspaper was written in London by Marx and his colleagues in an effort to keep the 1848 revolt alive, at least in print. Due to a lack of money and what Marx called "official harassment" in Germany, the paper survived for only six issues.

September 1850—The Communist League Central Authority is moved to Cologne. Divisions arose among German refugees in London over whether they should support immediate revolution or, as Marx suggested, educate the workers to prepare for a changed state in the future. Marx bested his rivals by moving the Central Authority out of London and subsequently having his rivals ejected from the league.

Marx and Engels break with the Universal Society of Revolutionary Communists. While Marx supported Blanqui, he thought his followers reckless and feared they might provoke a revolt that would end in defeat for workers. He, Engels, and George Julian Harney quit the group.

August 1851—Marx begins writing for the *New York Daily Tribune*. Editor Charles Dana invited Marx to be a European correspondent for his liberal U.S. newspaper, submitting articles but also "leaders," or editorials. Marx could not write in English until 1852, so Engels penned his initial articles.

December 1851—Marx and his followers, calling themselves "the synagogue," begin meeting in London. The men around Marx distanced themselves from the rest of the German refugees and spent their time in the British Museum Reading Room and at "synagogue" meetings, drinking and discussing political economy and social theory.

November 1852—Marx disbands the Communist League. The arrest and trial of eleven league members in Cologne and the imprisonment of seven of them, in addition to the counterrevolutionary climate in Europe, led Marx to the conclusion that it was no longer productive to have a secret society, and he retreated into newspaper and theoretical work.

May 1859—Marx begins working with the German Workers' Educational Society's London newspaper, *Das Volk*. He dismissed the émigré newspaper as a rag, but used it to vent his anger against his rivals during the disappointing period surrounding the publication of his work on political economy.

June 1859—Marx's *A Contribution to the Critique of Political Economy* is published in Berlin. His friends and followers had long anticipated that the book would be his major political economic work, but it baffled and disappointed them, and went unnoticed in the press.

March 1860—Marx's *Contribution to the Critique of Political Economy* begins to sell in Russia, and a University of Moscow professor lectures on it. While the *Critique* was virtually ignored by Marx's target audience in Germany, the translation found a receptive audience in Russia, which was experiencing a rare burst of liberalism under Czar Alexander II.

March 1862—The *New York Daily Tribune* ends its relationship with Marx, saying it no longer needs the services of its London correspondent. As news of Abraham Lincoln's election as president and the subsequent Civil War dominated U.S. newspapers, the *Tribune* gradually eliminated its foreign coverage to focus on domestic turmoil.

May 1863—Ferdinand Lassalle founds the General Union of German Workers. In the early 1860s throughout Europe, workers had begun to recognize their strength. In Germany, Lassalle tried to organize them by publishing a pamphlet called *Workers' Program,* seen by many as the first step toward a modern German workers' movement. He next inaugurated a workers' political party.

July 1863—European workers come together in London to support an uprising in Poland. After Russia ended serfdom in 1861, Poles protested for more rights and, when their requests went unanswered, eventually revolted. European governments did not come to their aid, but workers expressed solidarity. They also decided to form an international society of workers to confront future challenges.

September 1864—The inaugural meeting of the International Working Men's Association is held in London. The First International was formed in St. Martin's Hall when English, Italian, French, Irish, Polish, and German opposition figures met to create an organization to counter the combined and growing power of government and business. Marx wrote the group's "Address to the Working Classes." Though his official role was merely correspondence secretary for Germany, he became the IWMA's leader.

September 1867—Marx's great book *Capital, Volume I* is published. The political economy Marx began working on in 1851 (if not 1844) finally appeared. Though Marx and Jenny both expected it to land like a "bomb" on the public and atone for all their sacrifice, it, like Marx's other economic works, was initially met with silence.

September 1868—Marx receives a request to allow *Capital, Volume I* to be translated into Russian. Economist and writer Nikolai Danielson alerted Marx that St. Petersburg publisher N. Polyakov wanted to publish a translation of *Capital*. It would be the first translation of *Capital* from the German.

August 1869 — The Social Democratic Workers' Party is formed. Marx's friend Wilhelm Liebknecht and his colleague August Bebel formed the workers' party during a congress in Eisenach, Germany. It represented 150,000 people and adopted the International's rules as its own.

November 1869 — Marx begins lobbying the International General Council to demand the release of Irish political prisoners and support Irish independence. He argued that in order to accelerate social change in Europe, one had to start in England, and that the key to change there lay in Ireland. English delegates to the International objected to his position, and the political challenge to the English government raised concerns about the IWMA and caused a crackdown on its members in France.

September 1870 — France declares a Republic after Napoleon III is captured by the Prussians during the Franco-Prussian War. French IWMA members were involved in the political maneuvering to establish a provisional Government of National Defense in France and continue the battle against the Prussians as a republican army. The International members believed, however, that the new government was populated with the same bourgeoisie who had abandoned the working class in the past and would do so again.

March 1871 — Parisians vote to elect their own government, a commune. National elections in February had resulted in a French government dominated by conservatives who approved a costly armistice with Prussia. Parisians, who had been under siege since August, felt betrayed and elected their own government of leftists — including members of the International — to ready a fight against French forces.

Marx is accused in press reports of orchestrating the Paris International and by extension the Commune. After French troops showed that they were reluctant to fight fellow Frenchmen, the government sought to make the Commune appear to be the work of foreigners. Topping the list of baleful influences was Marx, who was repeatedly identified in the press as the red puppet-master behind the Paris revolt.

May 1871 — Marx gives the IWMA General Council his thirty-five-page pamphlet called *The Civil War in France*. Before the Paris Commune, Marx was virtually unknown, but afterward, due in large part to his pamphlet praising the Parisians, he became known as the Red Terrorist Doctor, the evil architect of revolt, and was vilified in the press from Chicago to Vienna.

July 1872 — The New Madrid Federation is founded in Spain, the first Marxist organization in that country. Paul Lafargue's work there produced few results except the founding of a Marxist group in Madrid that became the parent of the still extant Spanish Socialist Party.

March 1872—The Russian edition of *Capital, Volume I* is published. Russian censors allowed *Capital* to circulate because, they said, it was so difficult to understand that no one would buy it. The first print run of three thousand copies sold out in less than two months.

September 1872—The Fifth Annual Congress of the International meets in The Hague. Marx had never before attended an International Congress outside London, but he used the event to facilitate his retirement by maneuvering to have the General Council moved to New York, essentially ending his leadership of the group.

Marx gives his last public address in a speech to the Amsterdam IWMA local. The speech was later regarded as one of his most controversial, because it fueled debate about whether Marx was a pacifist at heart or an advocate of violent revolution.

March 1875—The Socialist Workers' Party of Germany (SAPD) is formed in Gotha. German workers and socialists decided they would have more clout if they combined the two main workers' parties—the Lassallean General Union of German Workers, and Bebel and Liebknecht's Social-Democratic Workers' Party—into one organization. In 1890 it became the still extant Social Democratic Party of Germany.

November 1875—The French edition of *Capital, Volume I* is published. This translation sold through its first run of ten thousand copies quickly. Not only was the French-language version accessible to a wider audience than the German, but Marx had significantly reworked the book since its difficult first German edition.

July 1876—The First International is disbanded in Philadelphia. After the International was moved to America, its influence waned and splits began occurring throughout the organization. Its remaining ten members disbanded the IWMA to form their own groups, one of which would become the U.S.-based Socialist Labor Party.

October 1878—Anti-socialist laws are passed in Germany. Two assassination attempts on Emperor Wilhelm gave Chancellor Bismarck the support he needed for laws to curb the growing political power of the SAPD in Germany. As a result of the bill, Marx and other socialists could not publish their work in Germany.

October 1879—Jules Guesde establishes a French workers' party. The French left was split after the Commune, in part because its leadership was exiled. In Marseilles, socialist Guesde tried to form a party to unite laborers of all political affiliations. In 1880 it became the French Workers' Party, the first French Marxist party.

June 1881—Henry Hyndman forms the Democratic Federation in London and publishes *England for All*. Hyndman was one of the earliest

British "Marxists." His group was vaguely socialist, and said to be composed of workers and for workers. His book borrowed liberally from *Capital* at a time when Marx's work was not available in English, and Marx stopped just short of publicly accusing Hyndman of plagiarism.

March 14, 1883—Marx dies. His death, at his home in London, left the bulk of his life's work, *Capital,* unfinished, and his theories known and understood by very few people. Eleven mourners attended his funeral.

January 1884—The Fabian Society of middle-class intellectual socialists is formed. The group was derived from Hyndman's Democratic Federation and an earlier organization called the Fellowship of the New Life. Their approach to social reform was gradual. Their motto: "For the right moment you must wait, as Fabius did, most patiently."

March 1884—London Commemoration on the first anniversary of Marx's death. As many as six thousand people gathered in London to march to Highgate Cemetery to mark the first anniversary of Marx's death and the thirteenth anniversary of the Paris Commune.

August 1884—Hyndman changes his organization's name to the Social Democratic Federation. The new name indicated a shift in emphasis. The group went from being strictly a workers' organization to being a socialist association inspired by Marx. It was the first important British socialist group since the 1820s.

December 1884—Eleanor Marx and others leave the SDF to form the Socialist League. Claiming that the SDF was among other things too autocratic, some members formed a rival socialist organization to teach and organize along Marxist principles.

January 1885—*Capital, Volume II* goes to the press (eighteen years after Marx promised it to the publisher). In the period after Marx's death, Engels edited hundreds of pages of manuscript to produce the second volume of Marx's political economy, this one on the circulation of capital. He dedicated the book to Jenny Marx.

July 1886—Socialist leaders in France, Germany, and England begin discussing the creation of a Second International. The pace of capitalist expansion had accelerated in the 1880s, as did the expansion of state-business empires into colonies. Some socialists believed an international organization was needed to protect workers in this new and more threatening environment.

September 1886—Eleanor Marx Aveling, Edward Aveling, and Wilhelm Liebknecht tour the United States to promote socialism. The group traveled for twelve weeks, visiting thirty-five towns and cities as far west as Kansas City, and speaking at nearly every stop, sometimes at four different events each.

January 1887—The English edition of *Capital, Volume I* is published. British barrister Samuel Moore and Eleanor Marx's common-law husband, Edward Aveling, translated Marx's work, making it more widely available at a time of heightened labor tensions.

July 1889—The Second International Working Men's Association is inaugurated in Paris. French socialists hosted a congress that brought together 391 international socialists and trade union members, effectively launching the successor to Marx's First International. The event, also known as the Socialist International, called for the first global May Day demonstration in support of labor the following year.

August 1889—London dockworkers strike in an unprecedented action by organized labor and socialists. Sixty thousand dockworkers, among the most downtrodden and powerless laborers in England, brought the port of London to a standstill for the first time in a century. The strike lasted until mid-September, when they returned to work having won most of their demands.

May 1890—The first global May Day demonstration in support of labor. Rallies were held around Europe and in North and South America, calling for an eight-hour workday and labor rights. The largest demonstration occurred in London, where three hundred thousand people filled Hyde Park in a show of strength for workers, trade unions, and socialists.

July 1892—Three workingmen take their seats in the British Parliament. John Burns, J. Havelock Wilson, and Keir Hardie are elected to Parliament, the first workers to become members of the House of Commons.

January 1893—The Independent Labour Party of Britain is formed. Edward Aveling was on the committee to form the group and had Engels's approval for the endeavor. The ILP platform read as if Marx himself had written it: "collective ownership and control of the means of production, distribution and exchange" and an eight-hour day. Scottish miner Keir Hardie was made chairman of what would one day help form Britain's Labour Party.

May 1894—*Capital, Volume III* is sent to the publisher. For ten years Engels edited Marx's manuscripts for the third volume to produce a work on monopoly capital and the creation of the world market—and, most significantly, its downfall.

1894—Vladimir Lenin joins a Marxist group in St. Petersburg and travels to western Europe. Lenin set out to meet with Georgy Plekhanov, who spent much of his time in Zurich and London. Plekhanov had founded the first Marxist organization in Russia, the Emancipation of Labor group. Lenin also had a first encounter with Lafargue in Paris, where the young Russian surprised Marx's son-in-law with his knowledge of Marxist theory.

August 5, 1895—Engels dies at his home. Like Marx, Engels left much work unfinished, and though he had selected Karl Kautsky and Eduard Bernstein (as well as Marx's daughters), as his successors in editing Marx's works, battles over myth and theory began almost immediately among Marx's and Engels's followers.

January 1905—Rebellion erupts in Russia after the military opens fire on a workers' demonstration in St. Petersburg, killing about two hundred people. As in western Europe in 1848, an alarming uprising by the working class caused officials to promise concessions, including a legislative Duma, but as in 1848, the offers were hollow and meant only to calm the situation, not produce social reform.

Summer 1910—Lenin visits Paul and Laura Lafargue in Draveil. After participating in the 1905 revolt in Russia, Lenin, his wife, and his mother-in-law lived in western Europe. In Paris he spent his time studying and writing, and traveled to see Marx's daughter and son-in-law to discuss Marx's work.

December 1911—Socialist and workers' party leaders from France, Germany, England, Spain, and Russia pay last respects to Paul and Laura Lafargue. A who's who of twentieth-century socialist and communist leaders attended and addressed the Paris funeral of the Lafargues, who died in an apparent suicide pact in November. Among the mourners was Vladimir Lenin, who predicted that the triumph of the proletariat was near.

November 1917—Lenin and his Bolshevik followers seize power in Russia. Lenin had returned to Russia from exile in April 1917, after Czar Nicholas II abdicated in March and a provisional government was formed. He and his Bolshevik followers, determining not to support it, seized public buildings in November and arrested leaders of the provisional government who did not manage to escape. In January, Lenin declared a "revolutionary dictatorship."

Preface

I FIRST ENCOUNTERED the Marx family story in the back of a London magazine. The piece was about famous Londoners, and one sentence jumped out at me. It said that of Karl Marx's three surviving daughters, two had committed suicide. I paused in midarticle, realizing I knew virtually nothing about Marx's family or his personal life. To me he was a massive head atop a granite plinth at Highgate Cemetery and a body of theoretical work occupying hundreds of books. I had never given a thought to the women who nurtured him day by day as he struggled to create a theory that would revolutionize the world, nor to the life of the man whose ideas helped spawn European socialism, and spread communism from Russia to Africa, from Asia to the Caribbean.

I began to read in search of their story. What I found was that every aspect of Marx's philosophy, every nuance of his words, had been dissected, and that scores of Marx biographies had been written from every possible political perspective, but in English there was not one book that told the full story of the Marx family.* Not one text in the many volumes on Marx focused entirely on the lives of his wife, Jenny, and the children, and their extended family — Friedrich Engels and Helene Demuth. There were several biographies of Jenny Marx and the youngest Marx daughter, Eleanor, but no single text told the bittersweet drama that was their life story or put into context the impact their struggles had on Marx's work. I decided to try.

I began by gathering thousands of pages of letters that Marx family members wrote each other and their associates over more than six decades. Many of these were located in archives in Moscow and had never been published in English. I also used letters written by more distant relations

---

* I cannot speak for all non-English books, but I did not come across one that covered the story from Marx's boyhood to the death of his last surviving daughter.

and friends in which they discussed the Marxes. Reading this multitude of documents chronologically, contemporaneously, I began to hear the various characters speaking to each other as events unfolded around them. I was able to listen in on their daily dialogue — for twenty years Marx and Engels corresponded with each other nearly every day by mail, and the Marx women were equally prolific. The picture that gradually emerged was of a family that sacrificed everything for an idea the world would come to know as Marxism but which existed in their lifetimes largely inside Karl Marx's brain. Egress of his ideas was continually thwarted.

The story I discovered was of a love between a husband and wife that remained passionate and consuming despite the deaths of four children, poverty, illness, social ostracism, and the ultimate betrayal, when Marx fathered another woman's child. It was the story of three young women who adored their father and dedicated themselves to his grand idea, even at the cost of their own dreams, even at the cost of their own children. It was the story of a group of brilliant, combative, exasperating, funny, passionate, and ultimately tragic figures caught up in the revolutions sweeping nineteenth-century Europe. It was, above all, the story of hopes dashed against the bulwark of bitter reality, personal and political.

From the Marxes' own words I also found that details that had surfaced in biographies over the past 125 years were often changed or misinterpreted, sometimes for political, sometimes for personal, reasons. This is always the case for controversial figures, but I daresay none more so than Marx. Some of the examples are well known: immediately after his death in 1883 his followers tried to sanitize his resume — eliminate references to his poverty, his drunkenness, even the fact that he had a nickname, Mohr, by which he was known from his university days. Later, during the Cold War and again after the fall of the Berlin Wall, his biography became part of the ideological battleground between the East and the West. The details of his life, and by extension the lives of his family, altered according to whether one was describing a communist saint or a deluded sinner. Unless one knew which capital an author was writing from, it might not have been immediately apparent which version of Marx's life was on offer.

Marx's detractors often disparaged him as a bourgeois living in luxury while pretending to fight for the workingman. Those charges arose early — during Marx's lifetime — and followed him into the twentieth century as efforts were made to discredit him and his work. On the other hand, those who wanted to keep Marx perched atop a socialist pedestal fought for years to deny that he was the father of Helene Demuth's son, Freddy. Letters existed in the archives in Moscow in which party members discussed Freddy's birth, but Joseph Stalin, when told of them by

David Ryazanov, director of the Marx-Engels Institute, called it a petty affair and instructed Ryazanov to "let it be buried deep in the archives."[1] The letters were not published for some fifty years.

There are numerous other examples of mistakes and mischaracterizations that have occurred over the years, and many, like those above, have been discovered by Marx scholars and largely corrected. But others, unfortunately, continue to be repeated as fact by biographers of not only Marx, but also his associates. Going to the source, the words of the main actors themselves—especially the Marx women, whose letters seem to have been overlooked by many researchers—I have tried to clear up some of the remaining mysteries. (Of course, Marx himself was known to bend facts when necessary, meaning that his avowal of the truth did not necessarily make it so. In those cases I have tried to make clear that his version of events was not entirely trustworthy.)

As rich as the Marx family story is, I found it also shed light on the development of Marx's ideas, taking place as it did against the backdrop of the birth of modern capitalism. The capitalist system of the nineteenth century matured alongside Marx's daughters. By the end of the century, the battles they fought on behalf of the workingman looked nothing like those their father had fought in midcentury. His were relatively tame. Theirs had become savage. In fact, this aspect of the story became more important as I wrote.

When I began this project, the world looked quite different. Few questioned the capitalist system that dominated the globe—capitalism was in the midst of one of its periodic boom cycles. But as I moved from research to writing, belief in the infallibility of the system began to waver until, as a result of the financial crisis that reached its first peak in the autumn of 2008, academics and economists openly questioned the merits of free-market capitalism and pondered aloud what an alternative might look like. Marx's writing, in the wake of this turmoil, seemed all the more prescient and compelling. At the dawn of modern capitalism, in 1851, he had already begun anticipating just such an outcome. His predictions of impending revolution were inevitably wrong, his envisioned future classless society perhaps more than utopian (as much as he would have argued otherwise), but his analyses of the weaknesses of capitalism were eerily fulfilled. I therefore went beyond my initial mandate—to merely tell the Marx family story—by including more of Marx's theory and a fuller description of the development of the working-class and labor movements than I had planned. But, in the end, I don't think the Marx family story would have been whole without those elements. This was the life they lived; they ate, slept, and breathed political, social, and economic revolution. That, and a consuming love for Marx, was the steel mesh that bound them together.

Plutarch said, in writing the biographies of the great men of Rome and Athens before his death in AD 120, that the key to understanding such figures was not to be found in their battlefield conquests or their public triumphs, but in their personal lives, their characters, down to a gesture or even a word. I believe that through the Marx family story, readers might come to better understand Marx in the way Plutarch suggests. I would also hope that they come away with an appreciation for the women in Marx's life, who because of the society in which they were raised were assigned mostly supporting roles. I believe their courage and strength and brilliance have been relegated to the shadows for too long. Without them there would have been no Karl Marx, and without Karl Marx the world would not be as we know it.

In writing this book I made a few decisions toward which I would like to direct readers.

The Marx family wrote to each other in many languages. Their correspondence might be in English, French, or German—and often all three—with the odd smattering of Italian, Latin, and Greek. I chose to relieve the reader of the burden of frequently flipping to the chapter notes for translations and used English throughout, except in those cases where the language was critical to the drama of the letter or where its meaning was obvious.

Also, some of the correspondence contained racist remarks, which I have not included in this book because, first, they were not germane to the story, and second, they were entirely consistent with the norm at that period (slavery still existed in the United States). They would, however, have leaped off the page at contemporary readers. I felt that including racist words (which did not, in any case, appear more than a handful of times in thousands of pages) would have unduly distracted the reader. It is amply evident that Marx and Jenny were not racist, because they had no objection to their daughter marrying a young man of mixed race, and because of Marx's vociferous stance against slavery. If I had thought it necessary to include such phrases in order to understand the family I would have, but I truly believe they represented no adverse reflection on them, merely on the society in which they lived. Likewise, Marx, Jenny, and Engels used anti-Semitic phrases at times—usually about Ferdinand Lassalle. There have been numerous studies made about whether Marx was anti-Semitic. I decided to leave that debate to others and did not use those references. Marx himself was Jewish, and I believe the use of anti-Semitic language by Marx, Jenny, and Engels was, again, more a reflection of nineteenth-century culture than of any deep-seated prejudice.

Love and
Capital

Genius is accountable only to itself; it alone knew what ends were to be attained and it alone could justify the means.

—*Honoré de Balzac*

Prologue: London, 1851

~~~⌒~~~

*There must be something rotten in the very core of a social
system which increases its wealth without diminishing its misery.*
— Karl Marx[1]

IN THE IMPENETRABLE fog they appeared as ghosts. Haunting the doors and
alleyways along Soho's Dean Street, they had come to London by the tens
of thousands—Queen Victoria's London, the richest city in the world.
Generous, liberal, it had signaled like a beacon in the black and roiling
North Sea waters, offering sanctuary to the unfortunate and the friendless. The earliest among them had been the Irish fleeing poverty and famine, but after continent-wide revolts, Germans, French, Hungarians, and
Italians dressed in the outlandish costumes of their homelands disgorged
onto London's streets by the boatload. These were political refugees on
the run after failed attempts to topple monarchs and win the most basic
freedoms. Now, in the lashing rain and bitter cold, the very notion of battling for one's rights would have seemed preposterous. The beacon that
was London had proved a mirage; the city had opened its doors but offered
them nothing. They were starving.

Day and night a cacophony of anguished voices strained to be heard
amid the din of the capital. To survive, the newcomers sold what they
could—scraps of cloth, buttons, shoelaces. Most often, however, they sold
themselves, by the hour or by the day, in labor or prostitution. These men
and women wore their despair like a rough cloak, the misery driving some
of the industrious among them to crime. Carts ferrying steaming carcasses
of meat and pungent cheeses destined for richer districts picked up speed

5

through the neighborhoods of Soho Square and St. Giles to avoid their notorious thieves and cutthroats.[2] But in reality, most of the refugees were too weak to fight or steal. They had made the long journey to England brimming with hope; what remained of those dreams was all they had left to sustain them.

In a two-room attic three stories above Dean Street, an obscure thirty-three-year-old Prussian exile sat busily declaring war on the very system that condemned those below to their wretched existence. He made no attempt to conceal his purpose. Hunched over his family's only table, piled high with sewing, toys, broken cups, and other debris, he scribbled out a blueprint for revolution. He was oblivious to the domestic hubbub around him or the children who, having made his bulky figure part of their game, clambered up his back.

In rooms throughout England men of vision were similarly hard at work: Darwin was considering barnacles, Dickens had just given birth to his favorite offspring *David Copperfield,* and Bazalgette was imagining the vast underground sewage network that would flush away London's deadly waste. And in this room in Soho, cigar clenched in his teeth, Karl Marx plotted the overthrow of kings and capitalists.

Marx's revolution would not be the kind he mocked as beer-house bluster, advocated by émigrés in secret societies where they divided the spoils of a war won in their imaginations. And it would not be the utopian uprising expounded by French socialists who dreamed about a model society without any notion of the tangible steps needed to construct it. No, his revolution would be rooted in the basic premise that one man did not have the right to exploit another, and that history moved in such a way that the exploited masses would one day triumph.

But Marx fully understood that those masses did not even recognize themselves as having a political voice, much less power. They also had no conception of how the economic or political system worked. Marx was convinced that if he could describe the historical path that led to conditions in the midnineteenth century, and thus reveal the mysteries of capitalism, he would provide a theoretical foundation on which to build a new, classless society. Without that kind of foundation, the result would be chaos. In the meantime his own family would have to sacrifice; until he finished his book, *Capital,* they would have to do without.

In fact Marx's young family was already well acquainted with want. The distance between the Marxes and those less fortunate on the street was much less than the three stories that separated them. By 1851, when Marx began writing his book, disease resulting from deprivation had killed two of his children, their small bodies laid out in paupers' coffins in the very rooms where the other children ate and played. His wife, Jenny, a Prussian baron's daughter celebrated for her beauty, was reduced to pawning the family's belongings, from silver to shoes, to pay off creditors who hammered relentlessly at their door. And Marx's rascally son Edgar readily absorbed the lessons of the street from poor Irish children who taught him how to sing and then taught him how to steal.

But most worrisome of all for Jenny and Marx were their daughters. The men who visited their father day and night were nearly all fugitives. The children rarely had a place to play that was not crowded with exiles who fogged the room with cigar and pipe smoke, and filled their ears with coarse talk and revolutionary ideas. Edgar thrived in that environment. He relished the stories of drunken escapades and, to Marx's joy, bellowed at top volume the rebel songs his father's friends taught him. But both parents knew the girls' only hope of escaping a lifetime of poverty was a bourgeois upbringing in the company of genteel young women. No matter how committed they were to the cause, neither Marx nor Jenny wanted to see their daughters condemned to a life with the kind of men who climbed the narrow Dean Street steps, arriving at their door with empty stomachs but heads full of radical dreams.

Jenny cursed the fates that condemned her children to a life of indigence in a miserable flat full of someone else's broken furniture. But as bad as it was, she was also terrified that one more missed payment to the landlord might force the family onto the street below. There was but a vapor of income, a vacuum of savings; their very survival depended on the kindness of a friend or the mercy of a shopkeeper.

Marx assured Jenny that she and the children would not have to endure such suffering forever. Once his book was published, they would be flush and the world would thank them for their selflessness. In a rush of optimism in April 1851, Marx told his closest friend and collaborator Friedrich Engels, "I am so far advanced that I will have finished the whole economic shit in five weeks time."[3] In fact *Capital* was not finished for another sixteen years, and when it was published, far from sparking the revolt of the workingman, it caused barely a ripple.

The Marx family sacrificed everything for that ignored masterwork. Jenny buried four of her seven children, saw her three surviving daughters robbed of anything approaching a proper girlhood, had her once lovely face ravaged by disease, and suffered the ultimate betrayal when Karl fathered a child by another woman. She did not live to see her daughters' final sad chapters—two of the three committed suicide.

In the end, all the family owned—all it would ever own—was

Marx's ideas, which for most of their lives existed solely as a storm brewing inside his turbulent brain, and which almost no one else acknowledged or even understood. Yet as improbable as it might have seemed during those years of hunger, Marx did what he set out to do: he changed the world.

Part I

Marx and the Baron's Daughter

1

Trier, Germany, 1835

She required a true passion to relish, and above all some
interesting weakness to protect and support.
—Honoré de Balzac[1]

JENNY VON WESTPHALEN was the most desirable young woman in Trier.
There were others, to be sure, from much wealthier families, whose
fathers had attained higher ranking among the nobility. And no doubt
there were some who were considered more physically attractive. But it
was generally agreed there was no one who combined such rare beauty
with such a vibrant wit and intellect, as well as a respectably high social
standing among the local aristocracy—both those born to it and the new
class of men who had earned it. Her father, Baron Ludwig von Westphalen, was Trier's government councilor, which made him the leading
Prussian authority and highest paid official[2] in the town of twelve thousand, nestled like a fairy village on the banks of the Mosel. Ludwig's father
had been ennobled for his service in the Seven Years' War and had married the daughter of a Scottish government minister who was descended
from the Earls of Argyll and Angus.[3] It was to this Scottish grandmother
that Jenny owed her first name, her green eyes and dark auburn hair, and
also the rebellious streak that gave her features fire: Archibald Argyll was a
Scottish freedom fighter beheaded in Edinburgh, and another relative, the
reformer George Wishart, was burned at the stake in that same city.[4]

In 1831, however, far from being a political rebel, seventeen-year-old
Jenny was a fixture at the elaborate balls around Trier, where women dazzled
in their gowns and elegantly arranged coiffures while men attempted to

11

seduce them with finely cut evening coats and exquisite manners, but most of all with their most prized commodity, their wealth. It was a candlelit marketplace where young ladies were bought and sold, and Jenny danced from partner to partner, fully aware of the value of her appearance. The social expectations and boundaries were unmistakably clear—a velvet rope separated aristocrats like Jenny from other elements on the dance floor.[5]

In a letter to their parents in April, her half brother Ferdinand remarked on the numerous men who courted her but said Jenny exhibited appropriate reserve.[6] This changed, however, at a party that summer. There Jenny met a young lieutenant, Karl von Pannewitz, who ended an evening of intimacies in a fiery passion, asking for her hand in marriage. Jenny surprised her family, especially her father and the protective Ferdinand, by saying yes. It was a rash decision that she quickly regretted: within months she violated social protocol and broke her engagement.[7]

News of the scandal spread through Trier. Ferdinand's wife, Louise, described Jenny in December as shut off from the world, cold, uncommunicative, and withdrawn while her father negotiated an end to the affair.[8] But by Christmas Eve, Jenny's spirits had returned, and the entire family seemed happy to put the failed romance behind them. In a letter to her parents, Louise expressed shock and disapproval at what she called the strangely lavish festivities at the Westphalen home. "There must be no feelings at all in Jenny's nature, otherwise she would have strongly rejected such an inappropriate festivity, alone due to sympathy for her unhappy (former) fiancé.... How long will it take until the first successor that comes along will replace Mr. von Pannewitz...the possible candidates have been made a bit shy by the treatment that befell him."[9]

By first accepting and then ending the engagement, however, Jenny had in fact temporarily exorcised the demon marriage that possessed her peers. She returned to the social circuit, but there were now no special men to attract gossip or the notice of her family. Instead, under the tutelage of her father, she began a program of study—a heady mix of the Romantics and a new utopian philosophy from France called socialism. Jenny particularly immersed herself in the former, dominated as it was by German authors, musicians, and philosophers.[10] For them the highest good was to live for one's ideals, to reject all that impinged upon one's freedom, and—most important—to *create,* whether that creation be a new philosophy, a work of art, or a better way for men to interact with one another. It was not even necessary to succeed; the critical thing was to follow a dream to its conclusion, no matter the cost.[11] Light, previously seen as emanating from a distant deity, became internal; man's personal quest was now divine.[12]

For Jenny, attempting to recover from her seemingly tiny rebellion against her engagement (which at that time in that society would have been a major revolt), Romanticism was heroic and exhilarating. And beyond her immediate circumstances, she saw another reason to embrace the movement: some of the Romantics espoused equal rights for women. German philosopher Immanuel Kant had declared, "The man who stands in dependence on another is no longer a man at all, he has lost his standing, he is nothing but the possession of another man."[13] Applying Kant's statement to women, that possession was multiplied a hundredfold. The Romantics therefore offered nothing less than the prospect of true freedom for men and women—freedom not only to break rigid social bonds but to ultimately challenge the kings who had ruled virtually unchecked for centuries because they claimed to be God's emissaries on earth.

By her eighteenth birthday, in February 1832, Jenny had begun absorbing these lessons at the very time the world around her seemed to be dividing into two camps—those who wanted to force the kings and their ministers to better serve a changing society, and those who wanted to protect the status quo. That division was evident even in her family: though a Prussian official, Jenny's father admired Count Claude Henri de Saint-Simon, the founder of French socialism.[14] The father's passions would inspire his daughter, though he could never have foreseen how much.

Ludwig von Westphalen had long before been introduced to the French credo of equality and fraternity. He was eight years old when Napoleon won control of western Prussia, where Ludwig lived. With that conquest the lessons of the 1789 French Revolution and the Napoleonic Code were enshrined in the region, including equality before the law, individual rights, religious tolerance, the abolition of serfdom, and standardized taxation.[15] But the French influence in western Prussia went well beyond the way society functioned at that time; it spoke to a changed future. French Revolutionary and Enlightenment philosophers believed in the inherent goodness of men and held that they would create a better society if they were freed from leaders who kept them ignorant in order to retain control.[16] In this new order, achievement would be based on merit, not birth—a doctrine with enormous appeal to an emerging business class.[17]

As with the imposition of any foreign laws, however, the citizens of the occupied region grew resentful, and many worked to defeat the French. In 1813 Ludwig, who was among the agitators, was convicted of treason and sentenced to two years in a Saxon fortress. He was released soon after sentencing, however, when Napoleon was defeated at Leipzig, and though Ludwig had seemingly turned against the French, he, like many of his western Prussian countrymen, continued to practice their way of thinking.[18]

In 1830 trouble again emanated from France. An uprising that July overthrew King Charles X after he ignored the demands of the new grand bourgeoisie—bankers, bureaucrats, and industrialists whose power derived from money, not necessarily titles or land—and tried to undo steps his predecessor had taken toward granting the people a limited constitution.[19] Charles was replaced by the "Citizen King," Louis-Philippe, whom French historian Alexis de Tocqueville described as seeking to "drown revolutionary passion in the love of material enjoyment."[20] The bourgeoisie and educated classes throughout Europe were inspired by this French monarch, who saw the virtue in extending some freedoms in order to increase the flow of cash through France's economy. These admirers soon took to the streets clamoring for reform in their own countries.

The subsequent revolts that year were in the main put down quickly and savagely, most notably in Poland. But there were some lasting victories: Belgium won independence from Holland, and significant changes occurred below the state level, where important new players emerged. Leading the charge were the grand bourgeoisie, whose members believed a liberal, industrial society inevitable.[21] Also appearing was a previously unrecognized army of laborers, the proletariat, whose hands would actually build the new industrial world. And the French revolt was the first fought by socialists, then a middle-class movement that identified man as a member of a broader society, with all the responsibilities for his fellow man that this entailed.[22]

In this early manifestation, socialism was a benign philosophy, reassuringly Christian for Catholic Frenchmen. Outside France, however, it and the swelling chorus calling for change raised alarms. Fearful German leaders responded to events on their western border with brutal repression. Throughout the thirty-nine states, dominated by Prussia and Austria, that fell under the German Confederation (or "Bund"), doors to increased freedom, development, and opportunity slammed shut with an iron finality, the nobility unwilling to relinquish one bit of its privileged status.

Nevertheless a group calling itself Young Germany agitated for more rights, tapping into long-simmering resentment in a population that felt betrayed by Prussia's king Friedrich Wilhelm III, who fifteen years earlier had dangled the promise of a constitution if the people helped defeat Napoleon.[23] The people had answered his call to arms, the rising business class helped finance the battle for the perennially cash-poor aristocrats, and Napoleon was defeated. But the Bundestag that emerged after 1815 was a federal assembly of kings and princes—or, as one observer called it, "a mutual insurance society of despotic rulers."[24] They built statues to fallen liberation fighters but did not reward the living with reform.[25] Indeed, those rulers used their powers to further suppress dissent, instituting a crackdown on already limited freedoms.[26] Riots erupted and sporadic violence lasted for almost a year as agitators were hunted down and arrested.[27]

Jenny's half brother Ferdinand was fifteen years her senior and the son of Ludwig's late first wife, Lissette. He was as conservative as his father was liberal. In 1832 Ferdinand was building a career as a Prussian government official and a proud servant of the king. His father, however, was studying the very socialists the government wanted to suppress. In them Ludwig von Westphalen heard the familiar call of *fraternité et égalité* of his youth. He found merit not only in the coherence of the socialist ideal, but justification for its implementation in the street: the number of poor in Trier had grown dramatically, partly as a result of trade and tariff reforms. By 1830, one in four residents was said to be dependent on charity, and all the usual social maladies associated with extreme poverty surfaced—crime, begging, prostitution, and contagious disease.[28] Ludwig believed society could not simply let people fail, it had a responsibility to alleviate such suffering. He began proselytizing those beliefs to anyone who would listen. Besides Jenny, his most eager student was the son of a colleague. The boy's name was Karl Marx.[29]

In 1832 Marx was fourteen and attended the state-run Friedrich Wilhelm Gymnasium along with Ludwig's youngest son, Edgar. Though Karl had shown an aptitude for Greek, Latin, and German, he was weak in math and history, and did not stand out particularly among his classmates.[30] He had a lisp, which he struggled to overcome and which may have made him shy.[31] Under Ludwig's guidance, however, he developed a passion for literature, especially Shakespeare and the German Romantics Schiller and Goethe. Marx also began to absorb the early utopian socialist ideas, which in those days were as fanciful as the plays and poetry he devoured. Sixty-two-year-old Ludwig and his young friend roamed the hills above the wide and languid Mosel River, through forests of towering pines, discussing the latest thinking. Marx remembered those times as some of the happiest in his life. He was treated as a man and an intellectual by a learned and distinguished aristocrat.[32] Ludwig apparently also delighted in their talks, because they continued for years. Given Marx's middling academic performance, Ludwig may have been surprised at how quickly the boy at his side absorbed his lessons, but he shouldn't have been: for centuries—as far back as fourteenth-century Italy—Marx's family tree on both sides included some of the most prominent rabbis in Europe. If the Westphalens descended from Prussian and Scottish men of action, Marx descended from a line of Jewish thinkers whose authority in religion extended into politics.

In Trier the Marx family had included rabbis since 1693.[33] One, on Karl's father's side, was Joshua Heschel Lvov, who in 1765, several years before the American War of Independence and more than two decades before the French Revolution, wrote *Responsa: The Face of the Moon,* which advocated democratic principles. So great was his reputation that it was said no important decision was made in the Jewish world at that time without Lvov's opinion. Karl's grandfather, Meyer Halevi, who died in 1804, was known in Trier as Marx Levi and eventually adopted the surname Marx after he became the city's rabbi. And the family's rabbinical tradition continued into Karl's own boyhood: his uncle Samuel was senior rabbi of Trier until 1827, and Karl's maternal grandfather was a rabbi in Nijmegen in Holland.[34] These men's duties combined the spiritual and the practical; as their communities' rafts amid waves of social change, they were effectively the civic authorities for Jews.[35]

Before and after the French occupation of western Prussia, Jews were often looked upon with suspicion, if not open hostility, as outsiders in the Christian kingdom. But during the period from 1806 to 1813, when the region was under French control, a sliver of equality was extended to Jews. Heschel Marx, Karl's father, took advantage of the opportunity to get legal training and become the first Jewish lawyer in Trier, taking his place in civil society and even serving as president of the local bar association.[36] He, like Ludwig von Westphalen, was perhaps more French in his thinking than Prussian. He knew Voltaire and Rousseau by heart,[37] and no doubt saw his future through their rational lens, expecting it would be free of the fear and prejudice that had prevented Jews from entering a profession or government service. But with the defeat of Napoleon, the Prussian government repealed the rights given to Jews and in 1815 officially excluded them from public office. A year later the government banned Jews from the legal profession. Only three men in Prussia's westernmost province, the Rhineland, were affected by the ruling. Heschel Marx was one of them, and thus forced to decide whether to convert to Christianity and continue practicing law or remain a Jew.[38] He chose his profession. In 1817, at the age of thirty-five, Heschel became a Lutheran named Heinrich Marx.[39]

At that time Heinrich had been married for three years to Henrietta Presburg, who was neither educated nor cultured but came from a wealthy

Jewish family in Holland. The couple already had two children, and a year later, in 1818, they had another boy, this one named Karl.[40] Out of respect, Henrietta did not convert while her parents were alive, and the children did not do so until 1824.[41] Once again conversion was not a religious decision but a practical one: Karl, who was six that year, could not attend public school as a Jew.[42]

Thus, young Karl grew up in the crosscurrents of conflicting cultures. He was Lutheran in a Jewish household in an overwhelmingly Catholic city, raised by a father and tutored by a mentor, both of whom outwardly served the Prussian crown and abided by its repressive laws while secretly admiring the French philosophers who championed individual liberty — and, more treacherously in the case of Westphalen, their radical offspring, the socialists.[43]

Many biographers have said the Marx family and the Westphalens were neighbors. Heinrich's family did briefly live several streets away from the Westphalens the year Karl was born. But the Marxes then purchased a smaller home in 1819 on Simeonstrasse, just off Trier's bustling market square and yards from the massive Roman edifice the Porta Nigra, a dark concretion that seemed to groan under the weight of its sixteen centuries. The Westphalens lived south, across town, nearer the river on Neustrasse, in a tall house with elegant long windows that gave passersby a glimpse into the rich life inside.

The two households were divided by both distance and culture. The Westphalen home sparkled in a whirl of social activity, with Dante, Shakespeare, and Homer frequently introduced to the festivities by Ludwig (who could recite Homer from memory and the Bard in English), and Latin and French floated into conversation as naturally as if they were mere extensions of the family's native German. Guests were entertained with dramatic sketches and poetry as the household staff laid the table for sumptuous dinners that stretched late into the evening and spilled out noisily onto the street as guests rattled away in liveried carriages.[44]

By contrast the Marx home, which by 1832 had grown to include eight children, was still. Karl's father was a cautious intellectual, one who spent his time reading rather than reciting, while his mother spoke German poorly and with a heavy Dutch accent. She was not part of Trier society and appeared not to have any inclination to extend her world beyond the immediate needs of her family. The home was loving but not particularly joyous, moderately prosperous — Heinrich's hard work and the family's thrift had allowed them to buy two small vineyards — but without a sense of abundance. Marx respected his father, even if he often rebelled against his advice. But from an early age his relations with his doting mother were strained. He seemed to blame her for the gloom that pervaded the household.[45]

Despite the differences between the two families, however, their lives were intertwined. Ludwig von Westphalen and Heinrich Marx were among the city's mere two hundred Protestants and belonged to the same select social and professional clubs. Karl Marx and Edgar von Westphalen were classmates; in fact Edgar was the only lasting friend Karl made in school. And Sophie Marx, Karl's oldest and closest sister, was friends with Jenny von Westphalen.[46] The children roamed from one house to the other, and it may have been Karl's friendship with Edgar, rather than his relationship with Jenny's father, that first brought him to her attention. Edgar, who was five years younger than Jenny, was her only full sibling, and she confided to a friend many years later that he was "the idol of my childhood...my sole beloved companion."[47]

Edgar was fine featured and handsome with unruly hair that suggested poet, but he was not an intellectual; he was boyishly reckless and therefore protected (and spoiled) by his parents and older sister. The relatively studious Marx may have been seen as a good influence. Whatever the case, Karl was quickly absorbed into the family: by Edgar, who would become Marx's first disciple; by Ludwig, who was charmed by the young man's remarkable brain; and by Jenny, who could not have remained indifferent to this teenager who so impressed the two men she loved most.

In 1833 and 1834 the government's crackdown on dissent struck close to the two families. Up to that point, schools in Prussia had been left remarkably free of official interference as long as the debates therein were about German philosophy. (The government hoped to counter the influence of corrupt French ideas with healthy German ones.)[48] But after the death in 1831 of Germany's greatest living scholar, Georg Wilhelm Friedrich Hegel, some of his followers drifted into more dangerous territory, focusing on Hegel's theory that change was inevitable. Prussian officials began looking more closely at universities and schools to root out radicals who might interpret "change" to mean "political change."[49] A government spy's report on Trier identified some of the teachers at Marx's school as too liberal, saying their students read banned literature and wrote political poetry. Eventually one boy was arrested and a popular headmaster sidelined.[50]

In the midst of this, Marx's father brushed up against the government over a speech he delivered at a club to which he and Ludwig von Westphalen belonged. The Casino Club, Trier's most exclusive private association of professional, military, and business men, met in January 1834 to honor liberal members of the Rhineland diet (provincial assembly). Heinrich Marx had helped organize the gathering and addressed the group, thanking the king for allowing the diet to meet as a representative body of the people and applauding him for listening to the wishes of his subjects. But while his speech was sincere, it was interpreted as ironic and raised alarms among government officials. Weeks later the club met again, and this time the speeches (some in tribute to the 1830 French uprising) gave way to banned "songs of freedom," among them France's "Marseillaise," which monarchies considered an incitement to revolt tantamount to raising a red flag. What alarmed officials was not only who sang the rebel songs—the pillars of the Trier community—but that they knew the lyrics *by heart*. The "frenzy of revolutionary spirit" (as described by a military officer at the event) could not be dismissed as an aberration. The club was put under surveillance and Heinrich Marx regarded with suspicion by the government.[51]

Karl was an impressionable sixteen-year-old when his headmaster was demoted and his law-abiding father unjustifiably scrutinized. It is easy to imagine the impact the state's repression would have had on him. If the notions of freedom of speech and equality before the law were previously abstract concepts for him, they were so no longer. Marx now experienced at first hand the Berlin government's terrifying and seemingly arbitrary reach, and the anger and indignity a man felt when he realized he was powerless to confront it.

Marx scholar Hal Draper has noted that Prussia's heavy-handed control had the unintended consequence of making "revolutionaries of very mild reformers." Indeed, government efforts to suppress talk of democracy and socialism only ensured that the concepts were discussed—if sometimes in whispers—from the schoolhouse to the dinner table, across the social spectrum. And the more they were discussed, the less they were viewed as French imports; they became ideas that had relevance and representatives in Germany.[52]

In 1835 a pamphlet by the father of German socialism, Ludwig Gall, appeared in Trier. It described society as divided between laborers, who produced all the wealth, and a ruling class, who reaped all the benefits.[53] Heinrich Heine had become the most popular poet in Germany, despite a ban on his work. He had moved to Paris after the government issued a warrant for his arrest (one minister called for his execution),[54] and his lamentations on this forced exile were enthusiastically copied and read in schools and universities where students were awakening to the potential of organized dissent.

Not surprisingly the atmosphere at the Westphalen home was charged. Jenny, Edgar, and Karl had all been schooled not only in the Romantics, who screamed out to them to recognize and confront injustice, but also the socialists, who blamed the ills of society in part on an exploitative new economic system that drove farmers off their land and artisans into factories. Germany still lagged far behind Britain in industrial development, but the Rhineland was its most industrialized area, and the effects could be seen in the new wealth on display in Trier and the new poverty. Marx needed only to look around to see the shapes that cast the shadows.

In 1835 Karl, now seventeen, prepared to leave Trier for university. In a school essay on choosing a career he carefully examined the allure of ambition, the inadequacy of his own experience, and what he called "relations in society," which had already limited his aspirations to some extent because of his father's social position. Concluding, he wrote:

> The chief guide which must direct us in the choice of a profession is the welfare of mankind and our own perfection...man's nature is so constituted that he can attain his own perfection only by working for the perfection, for the good, of his fellow men....If he works only for himself, he may perhaps become a famous man of learning, a great sage, an excellent poet, but he can never be a perfect, truly great man....
>
> If we have chosen the position in life in which we can most of all work for mankind, no burdens can bow us down, because they are sacrifices for the benefit of all; then we shall experience no petty, limited, selfish joy, but our happiness will belong to millions, our deeds will live on quietly but perpetually at work, and over our ashes will be shed the hot tears of noble people.[55]

That was the Romantic rebel Jenny von Westphalen fell in love with. This provincial man-child, who dared to declare himself a tool for the improvement of all mankind, embodied the heroes in the books her father gave her—he was Goethe's Wilhelm Meister and Schiller's Karl von Moor, and he would be Shelley's Prometheus, chained to a precipice because he dared to challenge a tyrannical god. In the young man four years her junior who stood before her bursting with self-confidence and courage, absolutely convinced of the powers of his intellect (even if he wasn't sure where those considerable powers and that intellect would take him), she recognized her idol.

Despite scattered calls for gender equality, the most an early-nineteenth-century woman with Romantic aspirations could hope for was to bravely, and with much self-denial, provide emotional and domestic support to the man who chose to pursue his bold dreams. Such was the commitment Jenny made to herself and Karl. It is not known whether they declared their love for each other that summer before he left Trier for the university in Bonn, but within a year they had: in 1836 Jenny von Westphalen secretly agreed to marry Karl Marx.

2

Berlin, 1838

Set me at the head of an army of fellows like myself, and out of Germany shall spring a republic compared to which Rome and Sparta will be but as nunneries.

—Friedrich von Schiller[1]

MARX'S FIRST YEAR at university was drowned in alcohol. The seventeen-year-old who left Trier declaring himself ready to sacrifice all for the good of mankind rented the most expensive student apartment available in Bonn, joined the university's Poetry Club, and became president of the bourgeois Tavern Club. He grew a wispy beard, wore his black curly hair long and disheveled, and on one occasion was imprisoned overnight for drunken rowdiness. He was threatened with arrest for carrying a pistol and fought saber duels against members of a rival aristocratic club. He also spent freely amid his champagne-quaffing fellow students. The few letters he sent home were generally appeals for money as he sank deeper and deeper into debt.

That was not the start Marx's father had envisioned for his son. Karl was the first member of his family to attend university, and the day he left for school, on October 15, 1835, the entire clan went to the riverboat at four in the morning to bid him farewell. As the oldest boy, he represented the Marxes' future: he would be the support—moral and financial—for his five sisters and his mother, and the rock upon which Heinrich Marx's legacy would be built. He would also be the first man in the family to construct a life completely outside the confines of the Jewish tradition, and his father saw avenues of opportunity from law to literature to politics awaiting him.[2] This proud father told Marx shortly after the young man

22

arrived in Bonn, "I should like to see in you what perhaps I could have become, if I had come into the world with equally favorable prospects. You can fulfill or destroy my best hopes."[3]

But it is unlikely Marx was listening as he plunged into his new student life. He enrolled in the law faculty, signing up for ten courses for the year. He was drawn to philosophy and literature, and he had discovered his voice as a poet. His father worried that in addition to an overly active social life, he was taking on too much academically, and warned, "There is no more lamentable being than a sickly scholar."[4] He also frankly said he did not understand Marx's poetry: "In short, give me the key, I admit that this is beyond me."[5] And he wondered incredulously, "is dueling then so closely interwoven with philosophy?"[6]

Heinrich was at times terrified by the unbridled egotism that impelled his son. He struggled to comprehend as he watched Karl lash out in disparate intellectual directions—he wanted to be a lawyer, a playwright, a poet, a theater critic. Both he and Henrietta implored their son to show restraint, out of regard for his health, his and their reputations, the family's finances.

In the spring of 1836 Karl fought a saber duel and was cut above the eye. It was more a badge of honor than a serious injury, but it was enough to make his parents insist he leave Bonn and enroll at the more respected and serious University of Berlin.[7] School officials at Bonn released him on August 22, 1836, with a letter noting his excellent or very diligent attention to his studies, but said by way of character reference, "He has incurred a punishment of one day's detention for disturbing the peace by rowdiness and drunkenness at night.... Subsequently, he was accused of having carried prohibited weapons in Cologne." To Karl's credit, however, it was added that he had not engaged in any forbidden association—that is, political association—with his fellow students.[8]

Jenny von Westphalen had no doubt been kept abreast of Marx's antics by her friend Sophie Marx, whose postscripts to her father's letters sounded breathless in anticipation of the next installment from her beloved brother. Karl's adventures were wildly cosmopolitan and bold compared with life in Trier. If he was spending the family's modest fortune in the meantime, so be it—living vicariously did not come cheap.

It had been only ten months since he set off from Trier, but the boy who left returned an eighteen-year-old man—more physical, more intellectual, and more exotic. Jenny too had changed. She was twenty-two and at the height of her beauty.[9] The two who had known each other so well as family friends, and more intimately as students of Jenny's father, were shy when they rediscovered each other. In a letter to Karl, recalling their encounter, Jenny wrote, "Oh, my darling, how you looked at me the first time like that and then quickly looked away, and then looked at me again, and I did the same, until at last we looked at each other for quite a long time and very deeply, and could no longer look away."[10]

Sometime between August and October, when Karl left for Berlin, the two became engaged. They told Marx's family but not the Westphalens: there were so many possible objections on their side, from the difference in the couple's ages to the fact that Karl had no money and no clear future. The unspoken objection, however, was social. In the rigid hierarchy of Prussian society it was permissible to associate across the stratosphere of the higher classes, but condescending to marry outside the aristocracy was a sacrifice most parents would not want their daughters to make. There was also the question of religion. Karl reacted furiously years later to the suggestion that his having been born a Jew impeded his marriage. But throughout his life Marx was regarded by friend and foe alike as Jewish, and it was unlikely his father's conversion erased this heritage from the minds of Trier society. (In the Rhineland even marriage between Catholics and Protestants was controversial.)[11] Heinrich Heine, a Jew who did not change religions, called conversion an "entry card into the culture of Europe." It did not, however, guarantee acceptance.[12]

Karl and Jenny, with the connivance of the Marx family (Heinrich Marx said he felt like a character in a romance novel[13]), agreed to keep their engagement secret and not correspond directly until a way could be found to make the marriage palatable to Jenny's parents. Fueled with a passion he said consumed him, Marx set out on a five-day journey by coach for Berlin, resolved to study diligently, find a career, and establish himself as an independent man and worthy husband.[14] For her part, Jenny began her wait. She was no longer the seventeen-year-old who impetuously agreed to marry a military man, only to realize she had no interest in him beyond his appearance and skill on the dance floor. She was committed to Marx. Being forced to battle society to have him only made the affair more delicious.

Still, it would have helped considerably in persuading her parents to accept the match if Marx had distinguished himself at university, proving he was destined for the brilliant career Jenny knew awaited him. There is no doubt he understood that. But as would happen throughout their lives when Marx felt under pressure to produce or perform, he was paralyzed by distractions. There would always be one more book to study, some new data to digest, a language to learn in order to study crucial texts in the original. And in Berlin, Karl would find distractions to last a lifetime.

24

★ ★ ★

During his first term Marx succumbed to what one writer called the romantic "cult of isolated genius." Perhaps it was a response to the size of the school—at two thousand students the university was nearly three times larger than the one in Bonn. Or it could have been Berlin: the city had about three hundred thousand residents and was the Bund's second largest city after Vienna.[15] Or Marx might simply have absorbed the academic culture in which he'd been immersed: Berlin was one of the most distinguished universities in Europe, and emphasized individual study and original research.[16] Likely all of those factors, as well as Marx's longing for Jenny, turned him into the haunted figure his father described in a fit of pique: "Disorderliness, musty excursions into all departments of knowledge, musty brooding under a gloomy oil-lamp; running wild in a scholar's dressing-gown and with unkempt hair instead of running wild over a glass of beer; unsociable withdrawal with neglect of all decorum...in this workshop of senseless and inexpedient erudition."[17] Heinrich beseeched his son to straighten up. He tried to convince Karl of the poetry inherent in fulfilling one's duty. But by then his son was already well beyond the reach of his father's advice.

Marx explained what he called his "moment of transition" in a long letter to Heinrich written after his first year at Berlin, the only letter to his father from his university days to have survived.

> Dear Father,
>
> When I left you, a new world had come into existence for me, that of love, which in fact at the beginning was a passionately yearning and hopeless love. Even the journey to Berlin, which otherwise would have delighted me in the highest degree...left me cold. Indeed, it put me strikingly out of humor, for the rocks which I saw were not more rugged, more indomitable, than the emotions of my soul, the big towns not more lively than my blood, the inn meals not more extravagant, more indigestible, than the store of fantasies I carried with me, and, finally, no work of art was as beautiful as Jenny.

He described breaking off all personal relations in Berlin and throwing himself into study and creative experimentation. His first inclination was to write poetry, and he produced three volumes for Jenny, but he said they were inadequate in expressing the "extent of a longing that has no bounds." Next he devoured the law and the classics. He studied criminal, civil, and canon law, translated into German the first two books of ancient Roman civil law, the *Pandect,* and wrote his own three-hundred-page philosophy of law. He translated part of Aristotle's *Rhetoric* from the original Greek, the historian Tacitus's *Germania* and the poet Ovid's *Songs of Sadness,* or *Tristia,* from Latin. He also began to teach himself English and Italian, and wrote a humorous novel, *Scorpion and Felix,* and a Faust-inspired play, *Oulanem.* And yet, he said, despite these multitudinous pursuits, "at the end I emerged not much enriched."[18]

What in fact resulted was a physical and mental breakdown. A doctor ordered Marx to leave the city for a stay in the countryside. Taking his advice, Karl walked nearly four miles from the university southeast to the fishing village Stralau on the River Spree.[19] There he found accommodations, went hunting with his landlord, and, he offhandedly told his father, "While I was ill I got to know Hegel from beginning to end, together with all of his disciples."[20] The German philosopher had been dead for six years, and though his star had waned slightly among the younger professors and students at the University of Berlin (where he had been a professor), if Marx was going to advance on his intellectual quest, he had to pass through Hegel.

The most basic premise of Hegel's philosophy was that the history of mankind was the result of conflict. Two ideas clash and the result is a third idea, which in turn comes into conflict with another and gives birth to something new. The nature of life is therefore dynamic; change is at its very core. Hegel saw this as inevitable, and called it the dialectic. Though the root of the dialectical process was based on tension, this was actually reassuring, because it said, in effect, that conflict was not arbitrary but necessary to historical progress. Hegel's dialectic gave conflict meaning—or, as Engels would say, "mankind no longer appeared as a wild whirl of senseless deeds of violence."[21] Hegel also advanced the notion of the *Geist,* or Spirit, which he held pervaded a people grouped together by historical circumstances, and its alternative, alienation, which occurred when a man did not recognize himself in the greater world or his productive contribution to it.

Hegel's eloquent philosophy dominated the Romantic era in Germany and spawned dozens of "Hegelians" who discussed his theories until they, as he would have expected, produced something new. It is easy to see how exciting the hope inherent in his dialectic would have been to the generation studying in Berlin, where the movement was headquartered. They had witnessed initial calls for reform repressed and basic freedoms reversed in favor of stasis. And yet they could see beyond their borders to the west, in France, Belgium, and England, that political, artistic, and economic advances were being made because kings were not afraid to allow their people to speak, write, and, in some cases, vote. They saw steel being turned into rails that sent trains screaming deep into virgin countryside at previously unheard-of speeds of sixty miles per hour, and they heard the crackle of electric current, which had produced the first battery and stimulated the invention of a new and seemingly magical way of communicating called a telegraph. Applying Hegel's teachings to this new world, the Young Hegelians saw in his conflict theory the potential not just for change but for social revolution.[22]

Hegel had made Berlin a magnet for restless souls from within Germany but also countries east, most notably Russia, whose people strained under the feudal yoke of an even more repressive system. When Marx regained his health and returned to Berlin from Stralau, his romantic isolation was over. He joined a group of Young Hegelians in the bohemian Doctors' Club, where he combined two of his favorite activities — philosophical debate and drinking.[23]

Marx's difficult first months in Berlin were matched by Jenny's back in Trier. Because they had agreed out of deference to her parents not to correspond, she fell victim to jealousy and presumed neglect. Imagining that Karl in faraway Berlin had forgotten her, she became ill, exhibiting a lethargy her parents believed was physical but Heinrich Marx identified as depression. (Karl used the news of Jenny's illness as a partial excuse for his own breakdown.) Heinrich, who acted as epistolary go-between for the young lovers, was nearly as tormented as she. In letter after letter to his son he spoke of Karl's sacred duty toward Jenny and how only his efforts to win people's goodwill and favor would ensure that "she is exalted in her own eyes and the eyes of the world." He described the "priceless sacrifice" Jenny had made when she agreed to become his wife, and added, "Woe to you, if ever in your life you could forget this!"[24]

Karl answered with the three volumes of poetry he had written for Jenny, which he sent to her via his family at Christmas in 1836. The first two were called "The Book of Love," and the third "The Book of Songs." They were dedicated "To my dear, eternally beloved Jenny von Westphalen."[25] Years later Jenny, who kept the volumes, laughed at his adolescent expressions of passion, but that December, on receiving the verses as her first messages from Karl after months of silence, she wept tears of delight and pain. Karl's sister Sophie assured Marx of Jenny's love and said Jenny would gradually try to prepare her parents for the news of their engagement.[26]

That preparation, however, was only a new source of torment. No letters exist from Jenny during this period, so we hear of her struggles only through Heinrich, whose correspondence with his son increasingly included not only admonitions for him to set his sights on a career, but also advice on how to court and soothe the troubled Jenny. On the one hand, he was an exceedingly loving father trying to rescue and guide what he saw as an intellectually and morally dissolute son. On the other, Heinrich himself was not unlike a disappointed, if necessarily distant, suitor who saw the object of his love offering her youth and beauty to an unworthy rival. In one particularly poignant (and prescient) letter to Karl in March 1837, Heinrich wrote:

> At times my heart delights in thinking of you and your future. And yet at times I cannot rid myself of ideas which arouse in me sad forebodings and fear when I am struck as if by lightning by the thought: is your heart in accord with your head, your talents? Has it room for the earthly but gentler sentiments which in this vale of sorrow are so essentially consoling for a man of feeling? And since that heart is obviously animated and governed by a demon not granted to all men, is that demon heavenly or Faustian? Will you ever... ever be capable of truly human, domestic happiness? Will—and this doubt has no less tortured me recently since I have come to love a certain person like my own child—will you ever be capable of imparting happiness to those immediately around you?...
>
> I note a striking phenomenon in Jenny. She, who is so wholly devoted to you with her childlike, pure disposition, betrays at times, involuntarily and against her will, a kind of fear, a fear laden with foreboding, which does not escape me, which I do not know how to explain, and all trace of which she tried to erase from my heart, as soon as I pointed it out to her. What does that mean, what can it be? I cannot explain it to myself, but unfortunately my experience does not allow me to be easily led astray.

Heinrich told Karl he had long hoped to see his son's name held in high repute (and though he never mentioned it, he may have seen the alliance with Jenny as raising the entire family's social status), but now he wanted only to know that his son was capable of love. "Only then would I find the happiness that for many years past I have dreamed of finding through you; otherwise I would see the finest aim of my life in ruins." As for Jenny, he said, "only a lifetime full of tender love can compensate her for what she has already suffered....It is chiefly regard for her that makes me wish so much that you will soon take a fortunate step forward in the world, because it would give her peace of mind...you see, the bewitching girl has turned my old head too, and I wish above all to see her calm and happy. Only you can do that and the aim is worthy of your undivided attention."27

But Marx's attention *was* divided, between this romance—which he told his children years later made him a wild Roland in his desperation to

28

see and hold his Jenny[28]—and his new circle of friends among the Young Hegelians. It may have been the proximity of those friends, or the blind (one might say obsessional) dedication to things intellectual that he would exhibit all his life, but Marx seemed at least temporarily to have chosen his life in Berlin over his love in Trier.

Marx had been taken under the wing of Adolf Rutenberg, a geography teacher allegedly fired after being found drunk in the gutter but who was more likely relieved of his duties for writing provocative newspaper articles.[29] Karl also fell under the influence of the radical theologian Bruno Bauer. Bauer picked up where an earlier follower of Hegel, David Friedrich Strauss, left off in his 1835 book, *The Life of Jesus*, which argued Christianity was based on a historical myth. Hegel had held that God, a rational force, directed the dialectic of history. The Young Hegelians disagreed. Harking back to the Romantics, they argued that man was the author of his own destiny, that it was not imposed upon him by an unseen, however benevolent, being. And, if one followed that train of thought, the next logical but dangerous conclusion would be that if God was not the puppet-master, the king was not activated by his hand. Instead the king was a mere man whose authority could be—and should be—challenged by other men.[30]

This was political dynamite, and nineteen-year-old Marx was at the center of the debate. He had been quickly accepted as a leader among his peers, even though most of them were not peers at all but established professors and writers at least ten years his senior. (One of these elders said without equivocation that young Marx was Rousseau, Voltaire, Heine, and Hegel combined in one person.)[31] In these fervent and subversive discussions Marx was developing the uncompromising style that would earn him so many enemies, while also beginning to formulate, fragment by tiny fragment, the philosophy that decades later would come to be known as Marxism. Karl must have felt himself on fire. Ludwig von Westphalen's reading of the utopian socialists while he and Marx walked the hills of the Rhineland would have seemed like the recitations of fairy tales compared with the debate that rumbled like a storm through Berlin coffeehouses and beer halls.

The Karl Marx who was being hatched in that heady environment was known as Mohr. This was an allusion to his jet-black hair and dark complexion, but also a reference to Schiller's murderous but charismatic Robin Hood–like character Karl von Moor in *The Robbers*, who led a band of brigands waging war on a corrupt aristocracy. For the rest of his life, all of Marx's intimates would address him by that nickname.

Heinrich Marx, however, did not recognize this son, this Mohr, sensing only the growing distance between Karl, his family, and, he feared, Jenny. In August 1837 Heinrich wearily accused Karl of neglecting his home, where his eleven-year-old brother Eduard was gravely ill (he would die four months later), his mother was frantic with worry, and where Heinrich himself had been unwell for seven or eight months. He said he could not entirely rid himself "of the thought that you are not free from a little more egoism than is necessary for self preservation."[32] In December, still trying to get through to his distracted child, he spelled out Karl's obligations in numbered points. Under category number 1, "Tasks of a young man," it said regarding Jenny: "procure her a future worthy of her, in the real world, not in a smoke-filled room with a reeking oil-lamp at the side of a scholar grown wild." Heinrich said Karl owed a great debt to Jenny's father, who had consented that spring to the marriage despite much familial opposition. "For, in truth, thousands of parents would have refused their consent. And in moments of gloom your own father almost wishes they had done so, for the welfare of this angelic girl is all too dear to my heart."

Angrily, Heinrich declared that he and Karl had "never had the pleasure of a rational correspondence" and he blamed his son, whom he described as self-consumed to the point of irreverence. He rejected a letter from Karl that contained a few lines and an extract from a diary entitled "The Visit" as a "crazy botch-work which merely testifies how you squander your talents and spend your nights giving birth to monsters." And he accused "Herr Son" of spending more money in one year than the richest of men, mockingly asking how "a man who every week or two discovers a new system and has to tear up old works laboriously arrived at, how can he, I ask, worry about trifles?"[33]

Heinrich's fury was exacerbated by the knowledge that he was dying. He had pinned his life's hopes on his son, but he would not live to see them realized, and worse than that, could not imagine that they ever would be. In his last full letter to Karl, in February 1838, Heinrich did not apologize for his irritation and said he was only laying down his arms at that point because he was too tired to fight. But he wanted Karl to know that the source of his anger was love: "Always believe, and never doubt, that you have the innermost place in my heart and that you are one of the most powerful levers in my life.... I am exhausted, dear Karl, and must close. I regret that I have not been able to write as I wanted to. I would have liked to embrace you with all my heart."[34]

Marx had not planned to visit Trier for Easter. He had already spent more money in Berlin than his father earned that year, and his parents agreed the five-day journey by mail coach would be too costly. But his father's deteriorating health, reported in letters over the winter by his mother and sister, convinced Karl he had to return home. He did so in late April and stayed in Trier until May 7, shortly after his twentieth birthday.[35] Heinrich died of tuberculosis and inflammation of the liver three days later and was buried on May 13.[36]

Some biographers have accused Marx of inexcusable callousness toward his father, claiming he did not attend his funeral because he said he had better things to do. That is a misrepresentation of events. Having just left Trier, Karl did not return for the funeral because it would have been impossible to make it there on time, and in any case, he had said his good-byes. And while there are no letters from this period in which Marx described his loss, there is no doubt it was profound. Throughout his life Marx carried a daguerreotype image of his father in his breast pocket, and at Marx's own death forty-five years later, Engels would place the worn photo in Marx's grave.[37]

With Heinrich gone, there were no more appeals from the Marx family for its gifted but wayward eldest son to stop dabbling in dangerous philosophy and become a man worthy of society's respect. But a new, more critical voice emerged, this time from the Westphalen household, and it did not appeal, it threatened.

3

Cologne, 1842

Ah dear, dear sweetheart, now you get yourself involved in poli-
tics too. That is indeed the most risky thing of all.

—Jenny von Westphalen[1]

FOR THE THREE years after his father's death, Marx's family became the circle of Young Hegelians in Berlin. He abandoned the courses and lectures in which he was enrolled to pursue his studies in their company and on his own. From the summer of 1838 to the end of his university career in 1841, Marx took only two courses, and one of them was taught by his friend Bruno Bauer.[2] But it was not an easy path. His financial situation was dire, because his mother was not as willing as his father had been to allow him to exceed his budget—she had little money coming in and six children besides Karl to support. He was also under the scrutiny of Jenny's brother Ferdinand, who had led the opposition to Karl and Jenny's engagement. After he was overruled by the ultimate authority, Ludwig von Westphalen, Ferdinand had used his influence in Berlin to have his future brother-in-law's activities investigated. He discovered Marx was cavorting with atheists, liberals, democrats, and socialists—extreme radicals of every stripe—and taking no visible steps toward securing a career with which he might support a wife and children; his preferred classrooms appeared to be the beerhouses and cafés surrounding Berlin's most splendid square, the Gendarmenmarkt.[3] Karl defiled everything Ferdinand believed was right and good—church, state, and family—but as long as Marx had the baron's protection, the engagement was secure. All Ferdinand could do was store away incriminating information for a more auspicious day, when he might rescue his sister from what he believed was a terrible mistake.

Jenny and Karl, meanwhile, settled into their long-distance romance, tormenting each other in letters by describing their insecurities and jealousies, and melodramatic accounts of ill health designed to stir the lover's sympathy. Their correspondence overflowed with the ratcheted-up anxiety of unconsummated passion, and in the style of great tragedians, they seemed to relish each new injury; if they could not feel each other's love at first hand, at least they could feel pain. In one letter Jenny addressed Karl's fear that she had been flirting with someone else. Her response was meant to reassure him, but while withdrawing the dagger from his heart, she could not resist giving it a twist. She wrote: "It is curious that precisely someone was mentioned to you who has hardly ever been seen in Trier, who cannot be known at all, whereas I have been often and much seen engaged in lively and cheerful conversation in society with all kinds of men. I can often be quite cheerful and teasing."

But lest he think she was too cheerful, she continued:

I have tortured myself with the fear that for my sake you could become embroiled in a quarrel and then in a duel. Day and night I saw you wounded, bleeding and ill, and, Karl, to tell you the whole truth, I was not altogether unhappy in this thought: for I vividly imagined that you had lost your right hand, and, Karl I was in a state of rapture, of bliss, because of that. . . . I could write down all your dear, heavenly ideas and be really useful to you. All this I imagined so naturally and vividly that in my thoughts I continually heard your dear voice, your dear words poured down on me and I listened to every one of them and carefully preserved them for other people.[4]

Like her brother, Jenny was well aware of Karl's activities in Berlin, but unlike Ferdinand, she approved. Her romance had revealed the possibility of a deep and exciting life she could never have in Trier, where practical men made practical decisions and women raised their families to perpetuate the society they had always known. Through her father and her fiancé, Jenny had been introduced to the possibility of a better world, and she saw herself at the center of the fight to achieve it. She did not do things by halves, and so this new, much more serious Jenny asked Marx for books—"quite a special kind, a bit learned . . . a bit such as not everyone likes to read; and also no fairy-tales, and no poetry, I can't bear it."[5]

In 1840, after the death of his father, Friedrich Wilhelm IV took the throne as king of Prussia. The deceased had been a product of the old battles against the French—both the ideas of the Revolution and Napoleon himself. His son, however, represented a new generation. He was forty-five years old and regarded as intelligent, advanced, and free of the constraints brought on by the ghosts of that earlier era. The growing bourgeoisie looked to him for democratic reform to match the industrial and economic advances they had made, especially after the 1834 completion of the Zollverein customs union that freed trade between many German Confederation states. This nascent liberal opposition believed Friedrich Wilhelm IV would recognize that Prussia and greater Germany risked falling behind the rest of Europe unless those engaged in business were allowed to express their ideas to the crown as members of a constitutional government.[6] For the likes of Marx and his cynical colleagues, any throne was regarded with contempt, but it was hoped the new king would lift restrictions on the press and publishers, and allow a free-flowing exchange of ideas.

Though the calls for reform reached the king, he chose to ignore them. The nobility dominated the high posts and the army's officer corps, as they had during his father's reign. He made token gestures toward the bourgeoisie by convening provincial assemblies, but they were not given the authority to do anything meaningful. As for the masses, this new king viewed them as immoral, in particular because some had begun to question his God-given right to rule them as he saw fit. There would be no constitution, and, far from extending basic freedoms, he would silence the growing voices of dissent by imposing new restrictions on the press, speech, and assembly.[7] At the same time Austrian chancellor Prince Clemens von Metternich sought to suppress so-called dangerous thought throughout the German Confederation.[8] Universities came under intense scrutiny—one writer later said, "The university became an annex of the barracks."[9] The Young Hegelians took up the challenge, but they were no match for the government.

Fearing that the University of Berlin had become too reactionary to give him a degree, Marx submitted his thesis, "Difference Between the Democritean and Epicurean Philosophy of Nature," to the University of Jena. Located in the most liberal of the small German states, this university was something of a degree factory, awarding doctorates by mail. Marx turned in his thesis on April 6, 1841, and received his doctorate in philosophy just over a week later, on April 15.[10] He dedicated his dissertation to Ludwig von Westphalen, "as a token of filial love.... You... were always visible proof to me, that idealism is no figment of the imagination, but a truth."[11]

Bruno Bauer had moved to Bonn to teach and assured Marx he could find a lectureship there, too. But Bauer's own position was in increasing jeopardy over his vehement attacks on religion and its role in the state. In the summer of 1841 the Prussian minister of religion and education instituted a campaign against Bauer that condemned Marx by association. The result was that Marx had little hope of finding a teaching job anywhere in Prussia.[12]

Karl was twenty-three and Jenny twenty-seven. She had already waited nearly five years to marry him, but until he found employment that union would be impossible. Marx had entered university with the idea that he would be a judge or a lawyer, but he had strayed far from that legal path in his studies, and in any case the field was swamped with applicants. Germany in general was inundated with middle-class university graduates competing for too few jobs — enrollment in higher education had doubled in the previous twenty years.[13] The position of last resort for the educated unemployed was journalism.[14] On the professional scale it ranked near the bottom and was considered a refuge for what one historian called "the disreputable, the meretricious, the unstable."[15] It was also not a profession known for high pay — if any pay at all. Marx, however, had little choice, and besides, he argued, a journalist did not write to make money: newspapers were the educated classes' primary means of defiance. Marx had not had anything published except some poems in a review associated with the Romantics,[16] but he had defiance to spare — and ideas.

Throughout 1841 Marx traveled between Trier, Bonn, and Cologne, tracking possible writing opportunities. During that time he spent six weeks in Trier, his longest stay there since he set off for Berlin in 1836, when his engagement to Jenny was still secret.[17] Now able to be seen in public as an acknowledged couple, they set the town gossips' tongues wagging. No one, perhaps with the exception of Jenny, ever accused young Marx of being handsome. One Marx biographer quoted a resident of Trier as saying Marx was "nearly the most unattractive man on whom the sun ever shone." He was compact as a boxer, coarse featured, unshaven, unkempt. He wore a dark frock coat of relatively good quality but often failed to button it correctly.[18] His black beard had grown past the point of respectability and in the social code of midnineteenth-century Prussia it announced its bearer as an extreme radical, as did the cigars he smoked — in public. (Gentlemen smoked pipes in the privacy of their homes.)[19] Marx's very person confronted the conservative society around him without his having to utter a word. But at his side, as he strolled through Trier, was his physical opposite. Jenny was tall, lithe, and elegant. Topped by a flame of auburn hair, a single strand of pearls emphasizing her long neck, she was so naturally beautiful it mattered little what she wore — her figure did not require fine drapery to be admired — and yet fashionable she was. Jenny's father's position and her mother's taste insured that she was dressed in the best couture Trier had to offer. To the eyes watching from behind shop windows, she was as seductive as her fiancé was repellent (and suspect).

Jenny was immune to remarks about their incongruous appearance, but she was troubled by comments about the difference in their ages and Karl's unstable position. She would not, however, give their critics the satisfaction of seeing her discomfort. Karl, on the other hand, was oblivious; he was without prospects but full of hope nonetheless. Liberal men with money and democratic aspirations were growing tired of being treated like children by a paternalistic king. Marx saw in "the incapable noblemen and the lethargy of the servants and subjects who let everything be as God wills it" the makings of a catastrophic end to the old system.[20]

To get around restrictions on public political debate and political parties, writers often masked discussions in theological and philosophical terms, and met in groups they called literary or philosophical societies.[21] For Marx and his colleagues such attacks against religion were attacks on its role in the state structure: they argued that a myth involving a good man named Christ was used to prop up a rotten system and tyrannical rulers. Therefore religion, like the state it supported, was immoral. Marx and Bruno Bauer were hoping to start a journal they would call *Atheistic Archives* to give them a platform for these ideas, but they needed investors to provide funding.[22] Apparently Marx approached wealthy liberals in Trier. Jenny obliquely described the response of one such, a local doctor named Robert Schleicher — adding a caution of her own:

> Schleicher told me just now that he has had a letter from a young revolutionary, but that the latter is greatly mistaken in his judgment of his countrymen. He does not think he can procure either shares or anything else. Ah, dear, dear sweetheart, now you get yourself involved in politics too. That is indeed the most risky thing of all. Dear little Karl, just remember always that here at home you have a sweetheart who is hoping and suffering and is wholly dependent on your fate.[23]

Jenny teasingly called her traveling purveyor of dangerous ideas "dear little man of the railways"[24] and "my dear wild boar," and busily prepared herself intellectually for their life together as husband and wife. She chastised him for not commenting on her Greek, which she said was evidence

36

of her erudition, and described rising early to read three Hegelian articles in a newspaper and a review of Bauer's book *Criticism of the Synoptic Gospels*.[25] Jenny's activities had a new sense of urgency and edge about them. And no wonder. She had taken one of the most socially dangerous—and arguably reckless—steps a woman of her class could take: after years of frustrating sexual restraint, Marx and Jenny had finally consummated their relationship in July in Bonn.[26] During their visit, Caroline von Westphalen had designated Jenny's younger brother Edgar as chaperone to preserve her daughter's "outer and inner decency."[27] But he was a poor choice of guardian: Edgar was a freethinker, Marx's friend, and entirely sympathetic to the couple's desires. He left them alone. Jenny wrote to Karl afterward:

> I can feel no regret. When I shut my eyes very tightly, I can see your blessed smiling eyes... then I myself am happy with the knowledge that I have been everything to you—and can be nothing to others. Oh, Karl, I know very well what I have done and how the world would outlaw me, I know all, all of that, and still I am happy and overjoyed and would not give up even the memory of those dear hours for any riches in the world. That is my treasure and shall remain it forever....Each happy hour I lived through again, once again I lay close to your heart, drunk with love and overjoyed!...Karl, to be your wife, what a thought—maybe, oh God, it makes me dizzy!

According to the social mores of that time, Marx could walk away from their sexual encounter with little more by way of reprimand than denunciation as a scoundrel (unless Ferdinand wanted to make the insult public and challenge Marx to a duel). But if Marx and Jenny did not marry, she would be ruined. Anticipating the reaction in Trier if their relations became known, Jenny said, "My parents live there, my old parents who love you so much; oh Karl, I am bad, I am very bad and nothing is good in me except my love for you."[28] More than at any point in their courtship, Jenny's future now depended on her marriage to Marx. But at the very moment when she most needed it, she could no longer count on her father to protect their bond.

Ludwig von Westphalen had been fighting an illness that became serious in December 1841. Marx returned to Trier and moved into the Westphalen home to help care for him, which also allowed him to be near Jenny.[29] While he was there, a group of Prussian cabinet ministers issued a provocative censorship decree. Ostensibly the result of the king's desire to relieve writers of any undue constraint, it actually expanded restrictions first applied in 1819.[30] Under the new law, any writing seen as "frivolous or hostile" toward the Christian religion, any perceived attempt to confuse religion and politics, anything deemed by the government offensive or defamatory against individuals or whole classes—in fact, any "tendency" found to be pernicious—was to be censored. The Prussian government thereby gave itself, through its army of censors, ultimate and arbitrary control over the written word.

Marx used his months in Jenny's home to formulate a response. The result was a frontal assault on every aspect of the censorship law. He made no effort to hide his politics behind religion or philosophy; on the contrary, his first piece of journalism, in a state that brooked no dissent, was a declaration of war on the government's new law. Marx's controlled rage poured out in his twenty-two-page piece: "The law against a frame of mind is *not a law of the state* promulgated for its *citizens, but the law of one party against another party. . . .* It is a law which divides, not one which unites, and all laws which divide are reactionary. It is not a law, but a *privilege. . . .* The real, *radical cure for the censorship,* would be its *abolition.*"[31]

Marx sent the article, signed "A Rhinelander," to Arnold Ruge, editor of the *Deutsche Jahrbücher,* or "German Yearbook," in Dresden. Ruge, who was sixteen years older than Marx, had spent six years in jail because of his liberal ideas. Another academic exile denied university promotion because of his views, Ruge had begun a newspaper in Prussia but was forced to relocate after it was banned because of its political tone. Now he published in a more favorable location, but even there, Marx's piece did not make it past the censors.[32] It likely also did not get past Jenny's vigilant brother Ferdinand, who had been assigned to an important government post in Trier in 1838. It was clear the subversive document was written in his father's home.

Ludwig died a month after Marx submitted his article to Ruge, and with his death went Marx's staunchest male ally in the Westphalen household. Ferdinand, now head of the family, immediately went to work to try to break the engagement, enlisting Jenny's conservative uncle Heinrich George von Westphalen to pressure her. Though it is unclear whether Jenny's mother was aware of the extent of her daughter's relations with Marx, Caroline took Jenny's side and hurried her away from Ferdinand's influence to a home she owned in the resort town of Kreuznach, fifty miles east of Trier.[33] There the two women stayed to ride out the storm.

Marx also left Trier, eventually making his way to Cologne. He had joined a club there that included not only some old Berlin Doctors' Club colleagues but also Cologne businessmen who counted themselves among Prussia's opposition.[34] Marx's Berlin friend Georg Jung and a new acquaintance, Moses Hess, had persuaded a group of businessmen to finance a newspaper, the *Rheinische Zeitung* (Rhineland Gazette), which declared itself "For Politics, Commerce and Industry," a phrase readers would interpret to mean the cherished interests of the middle class.[35]

The mix of those involved in the *Rheinische Zeitung* showed how extraordinarily diverse the opposition in Prussia was—which was both its strength and its weakness. In addition to the Berlin crowd of Young Hegelians, socialists, nationalists, democrats, and intellectuals of various radical stripes, the newspaper's backers included liberal lawyers, doctors, and industrialists. Most notable among them were banker and railway baron Ludolf Camphausen, a future Prussian prime minister, and businessman David Justus Hansemann, a future Prussian finance minister.[36]

What brought these men together was opposition to a government they felt had not kept up with the times. Middle-class businessmen had become stronger as a result of the 1834 customs union that put them in touch with colleagues in other German states who had the same aim—to push development and trade as far and as fast as they could. They saw the German Confederation's loosely aligned states, with their separate rulers, laws, and currencies, as impediments to potentially limitless industrial growth. They wanted the Bund to become a nation, a united political and economic force. Coordination, however, was only part of it. Like many intellectuals, who felt strangled by a government that dictated what they could write and say, Prussia's middle classes believed further development impossible without profound social change. How could the nation advance without meritocratic structures, without freedom of speech and assembly, without equal rights under the law and fair taxation? (The last item was especially irksome for the middle class; it was heavily taxed by a government populated by noblemen who paid no tax at all.)

The Rhineland voices calling for reform were particularly powerful because the region was the most economically advanced in Prussia. Its center of intellectual activity was Cologne.[37] When he arrived in that city, Marx was twenty-three years old, with one unpublished article to his credit. Within a year he would become editor of one of the most influential opposition newspapers in Prussia.

The *Rheinische Zeitung* was launched on January 1, 1842, with four hundred subscribers. Marx began writing for it four months later. For his first article he returned to press freedom, prompted by a debate on the issue in the Rhineland diet.[38] Not only was the subject controversial, but writing about provincial diet debates at all was banned by a Prussian leadership fearful people might mistakenly think they had a say in government. For absolutists, diet deputies were "apprentices of the devil," and spreading their words risked making readers "even more foolish" than they already were.[39]

Despite the odds, Marx's article made it past the censors; his argument was complex enough to befuddle the guardians of political purity assigned by the government to review it. The piece was also funny, literary, and eloquent enough to enlighten his unofficial audience. His premise was simple: freedom is the essence of man, and laws are meant to enshrine and protect that freedom.

> No man combats freedom; at most he combats the freedom of others. Hence every kind of freedom has always existed, only at one time as a special privilege, at another as a universal right....
>
> Laws are in no way repressive measures against freedom, any more than the law of gravity is a repressive measure against motion....Laws are rather the positive, clear, universal norms in which freedom has acquired an impersonal, theoretical existence independent of the arbitrariness of the individual. A statute book is a people's bible of freedom.
>
> Therefore *press law* is a *legal recognition of the freedom of the press.*[40]

This, Marx's first published political writing, appeared on May 5, 1842, his twenty-fourth birthday, but it did not appear under his name. Marx remained safely anonymous, though his friends knew he was the author and praised him lavishly. Moses Hess, the paper's subeditor, declared Marx the "greatest, perhaps the only genuine philosopher in the current generation."[41] Ruge said it was the best article on the subject ever written. Jung called it superb.[42]

Triumphant, Marx returned to Trier. His reception there, however, was the opposite of the adulation he had received in Cologne. He quickly became embroiled in a major squabble with his mother over money and his future. She complained he was ignoring the family and that she had been given the cold shoulder by the Westphalens. The fight was so severe Marx took a room at a guesthouse for the remainder of his visit, staying just long enough to attend the wedding of his sister Sophie. But he was little moved by the histrionics; his attention was rooted in Cologne. "It is truly fortunate that scandals of a public nature make it impossible for a man of character to be irritated over private ones," Marx told Ruge.[43]

The *Rheinische Zeitung's* profile steadily grew, but its editorial department was increasingly in turmoil. After a succession of editors, by the summer of 1842 Marx's old friend Adolf Rutenberg was named editor in chief.

But it soon looked as though his time in that position would be short, too. Rutenberg was drinking heavily and had run afoul of Prussian censors.[44]

By then, Marx had submitted a number of articles heralded for their brilliance and his continuing ability to sufficiently obscure his meaning in order to pass government scrutiny. He also reassured investors, who feared the newspaper was falling under the sway of Berlin radicals who wanted to turn it into an organ for theoretical debates. Marx concurred, explaining that the *Rheinische Zeitung* should not engage in abstract theory but consider only "practical questions." He further said the newspaper should direct those who contributed their writings, not be directed by them, a surprising stance for a mere contributor who hoped to remain such.

But Marx did not intend to remain purely a correspondent. His remarks were understood and applauded by the newspaper's financial backers, and on October 15 he was named editor in chief.[45] On his first day he published a rebuttal to a rival newspaper's accusation that the *Rheinische Zeitung* espoused communism, then a philosophy virtually interchangeable with socialism, except that its adherents sought the abolition of private property (anathema to the businessmen who funded the *Rheinische Zeitung*). Marx wrote that his newspaper "does not admit that communist ideas in their present form possess even *theoretical reality,* and therefore can still less desire their *practical realization,* or even consider it possible."[46]

Gustav Mevissen, a Rhineland businessman and financial backer of the newspaper, described Marx as an intellectual and physical tempest, "a powerful man...whose thick black hair sprung from his cheeks, arms, nose and ears. He was domineering, impetuous, passionate, full of boundless self confidence, but at the same time deeply earnest and learned."[47] This enthusiastic editor was seen dashing around Cologne, dodging carts and carriages on its cobbled streets, with newspaper articles stuffed in his pockets,[48] or scouring coffee shops and dingy basement restaurants and beer halls for difficult-to-find newspapers from other German states and foreign countries. Marx absorbed it all, and using tips and documents from well-placed sources he had cultivated in Prussia and beyond, vanquished his press rivals and eluded those in government who sought to silence him. Under Marx's guidance the *Rheinische Zeitung* became the liberal voice of Prussia.

With its success and Marx's impressive leadership, the paper soon attracted gifted writers from around Germany—one contributor said, "All the young, fresh, free-thinking or revolutionary...talent that Prussia and Germany possessed took refuge here."[49] And yet if the newspaper attracted freethinkers, its editor held tight the reins. His earlier position on the role of contributors had been more than mere maneuvering. Indeed, Marx's reputation as a dictator stemmed from this era. Bruno Bauer said Marx was possessed of a "berserk fury" when crossed—and in the editor's chair he was crossed frequently.[50] Nothing made it into the paper without his approval, and that meant the Young Hegelians in Berlin, who now called themselves "The Free," were banned unless they refrained from "vague reasoning, magniloquent phrases and self-satisfied self-adoration" and included "more attention to the actual state of affairs, more expert knowledge."[51] The Free promptly accused him of being conservative, but Marx said he was willing to suffer the wrath of a "few Berlin windbags" rather than sacrifice his newspaper.[52]

His twenty-three-year-old brother Hermann had died on October 14, the day before Marx was appointed editor, and there is no indication he returned home for the funeral.[53] Instead Marx remained in Cologne, elbow deep in research on one of two articles he would later tell Engels "led him from politics pure and simple to economic conditions and thus to socialism." His research awakened in him the notion that men's relationships were fundamentally material, which is to say economic.[54]

The first article was about the gathering of fallen wood in private forests by peasants, which the Prussian government had begun to characterize as theft. The poor had traditionally been allowed to collect deadwood for heating, and this continued even after the end of serfdom in 1807. But by the 1840s the fires of industry claimed the wood and paid landowners handsomely for it. The government took the side of the landowners (not surprisingly, since landowners were the very nobility who peopled the government) and made unauthorized removal of fallen wood a crime. By the time Marx wrote about it, because of increased poverty and a population boom, wood "theft" had reached epidemic proportions, accounting for five-sixths of all prosecutions in Prussia.[55] Marx used the law's own language to undermine it, exposing the absurdity and hypocrisy of a system that allowed the landowner to lay claim to what Marx called "nature's alms." He declared the law so skewed in favor of the landowners that "we are only surprised that the forest owner is not allowed to heat his stove with the wood thieves."[56]

The second article concerned the poverty of Mosel wine growers as a result of taxation and free trade among German states.[57] The businessmen who financed the *Rheinische Zeitung* saw the virtues of free trade—it increased their profits by expanding their markets—but Marx had begun to see that their gain would always come at the expense of the smaller landholder and local grower, who did not have the means to compete in a wider market dominated by large-scale producers.

In his investigation of "practical questions" Marx was apparently unconcerned that his articles criticized the very system many in his audience championed and that his writing might cost him the support of shareholders. In fact, as Marx quickly matured as a journalist, the newspaper became more radical. The *Rheinische Zeitung* was relentless in its coverage of the Rhineland diet and the government in Berlin, meticulous in its presentation of the facts (as its editors saw them), probing in its analysis, and mocking in tone. It spoke to the educated classes in Prussia in a bold new voice, and subscriptions grew from four hundred to thirty-five hundred in the first year. Marx managed to outmaneuver authorities alarmed by his reports by wearing them down: one weary censor said, "Marx would die for his views, of whose truth he is absolutely convinced."[58] The fight was exhausting for Marx, too, as were his ongoing quarrels with writers over what constituted a newspaper article as opposed to a philosophical treatise or downright propaganda.

In December he traveled by coach to Kreuznach to spend Christmas with Jenny and her mother. He now had a position of relative respect among powerful liberals, a good annual income, and he had settled in one place. At long last he was able to be married, and he and Jenny decided they would do so in June.[59] But when Marx returned to Cologne, he learned that the government had banned the *Rheinische Zeitung,* condemning the enterprise as illegal, without permission to operate and exhibiting prohibited tendencies.[60]

Marx's newspaper had been an annoyance to the governments in the Rhineland and Berlin almost from its inception, and the notion of banning it had been floated as early as November. But some have suggested the last straw was a January 4, 1843, piece attacking Czar Nicholas I. The uproar from that assault prompted a face-to-face meeting between the czar and the Prussian ambassador to St. Petersburg during which the Russian monarch demanded Prussia rein in its liberal press.[61] On January 21 Friedrich Wilhelm himself convened a ministerial council that decided to ban the paper. The government gave the *Rheinische Zeitung* until the end of March 1843 to operate, and in the meantime ordered that it be scrutinized by two censors.[62]

Marx resigned from the paper on March 17. He hoped his departure might save it (it did not; the *Rheinische Zeitung* presses fell silent on March 31), but in any case he was ready to sever the connection. He told Ruge, "I had begun to be stifled in that atmosphere. It is a bad thing to have to perform menial duties even for the sake of freedom; to fight with pinpricks, instead of with clubs. I have become tired of hypocrisy, stupidity, gross arbitrariness, and of our bowing and scraping, dodging, and hair-splitting over words.... The government has given me back my freedom."[63]

43

4

Kreuznach, 1843

So everywhere, in every part,
My soul abides still in your heart;
It dreams its maddest dreams right there,
It leaps and somersaults in thin air.
—Heinrich Heine[1]

ONCE AGAIN MARX was without work or income. This was to be a theme in the decades to come; Marx would spend his life stressing the primacy of economics but was chronically irresponsible when it came to his own finances. (His reputation must have been known. At the instigation of Jenny's family, he signed an agreement that his future wife would not be responsible for any debts he incurred before marriage.)[2] Unable to wrest any money from his mother,[3] he traveled to Holland in March to see his uncle Lion Philips to discuss his inheritance. And though the records here are absent, it appears Philips gave him an advance because subsequently Marx had money for the rest of the year, and it is impossible to imagine he had managed to save anything from his job in Cologne.

During that period Marx also exchanged letters with Ruge, who was formulating plans to relocate, possibly to France, to begin a newspaper called the *Deutsch-Französische Jahrbücher,* or "German-French Yearbook," which would combine the voices of opposition from both countries. Marx was enthusiastic about the project, but Jenny had reservations. She feared that once Marx left Germany for France he would be seen as betraying his country and not be allowed to return.[4]

At about this time Marx did, in fact, receive two offers to stay in Prussia. One came from a family relation named Esser, who was chief privy councilor for the Rhine Court of Appeal in Berlin. Esser had been charged by Prussian authorities to offer Marx a government job, possibly as a way to co-opt a young critic before his following grew. Another government job opportunity may have been the work of Ferdinand, who, having failed to end the engagement, sought to at least keep his sister close and her politically wayward husband in check.[5] Civil service posts were coveted by university graduates because they brought security and prestige, but Karl rejected both offers.

Marx was increasingly convinced a move outside Germany was necessary, to, as Ruge said, launch a newspaper that operated free of restraint and "with merciless honesty."[6] In May, Marx went to Dresden to meet with Ruge and Julius Fröbel, a Zurich-based professor who ran an important publishing firm. Ruge and Fröbel agreed to put up the money for the paper, with Marx as coeditor at a salary comparable to what he earned in Cologne, plus royalties potentially worth about half that amount. Marx accepted and said he would begin preparing articles in Kreuznach so they would have a store ready.[7] Oddly, in the middle of a letter to Ruge about these arrangements, Marx inserted an uncharacteristically personal note.

> I can assure you, without the slightest romanticism, that I am head over heels in love, and indeed in the most serious way. I have been engaged for more than seven years, and for my sake my fiancée has fought the most violent battles, which almost undermined her health, partly against her pietistic aristocratic relatives, for whom "the Lord in heaven" and the "lord in Berlin" are equally objects of religious cult, and partly against my own family, in which some priests and other enemies of mine have ensconced themselves.[8]

Marx cited "unnecessary and exhausting conflicts" with both families and implied that he and Jenny had been actively trying to marry since their engagement in 1836. But in truth their plans were impeded by one person only—Marx. He apparently had found it necessary to make his intellectual journey through Bonn, Berlin, and Cologne alone, no matter what the delay might have cost Jenny emotionally or how much it may have put their engagement at risk. Remarkably, she never appeared to lose patience with him. Though her letters were filled with expressions of anxiety, they overflowed with love for her Karlchen. On the eve of their marriage she said she was prepared to accompany him anywhere. "I precede you and I follow you. If only I could level and make smooth all your paths, and sweep away everything that might be an obstacle to you."[9]

The German Romantic philosopher Johann Gottlieb Fichte believed a person only recognized his or her true self when that self—the

"I"—impacted on something or someone else. Marx and Jenny discovered their true selves through each other.[10] Their engagement ended on June 19, 1843, when they married at a Protestant church in Kreuznach. No one from Marx's family attended the wedding. The only family members on Jenny's side were her mother and her brother Edgar. Marx was twenty-five and Jenny twenty-nine.[11]

As a wedding gift Caroline von Westphalen gave her daughter a centuries-old and extremely valuable silver dinner service and linens, all with the Argyll family crest, and she provided the young couple with money for a honeymoon in Switzerland.[12] Jenny had been the image of thrift prior to her wedding, instructing Karl not to buy anything in advance—even flowers for her wedding dress—to save money.[13] But afterward, in the euphoria of their initial days as husband and wife, she adopted Marx's attitude and watched without regret as what little cash they had evaporated. On their return from a Swiss resort at Rheinphalz popular with newlyweds, she and Karl took a slow route by coach and allowed mendicant friends who visited them at inns along the way to help themselves to their wedding money, which they kept in an open strongbox on a table. By the time they arrived back in Kreuznach the box was empty.[14] It was a self-defeating act of liberation right out of the Romantics' playbook. Percy Bysshe Shelley himself would have approved.

The monetary loss was absolutely irrelevant to the high-minded pair. Marx's trunks, they believed, contained something much more valuable—forty-five volumes he hoped to study during his honeymoon, among them Hegel, Rousseau, Machiavelli, and Chateaubriand.[15] In the quiet security of Jenny's love, he would examine not just the texts but also the practical, political, and economic lessons he had learned in Cologne. The Karl Marx who would achieve historical preeminence appeared with his long-awaited marriage to Jenny. Their vows had been a mutual affirmation of faith; their marriage would be a mutual cultivation of flame. Her love enabled him. His honeymoon studies and reflections produced two of his most famous declarations: religion is the opium of the people, and the heart of the emancipation of mankind is the proletariat.[16]

The couple stayed in Kreuznach until October, making love surrounded by books, in a town where they had obligations to no one but each other. By July, Jenny was pregnant and Marx was tackling some of the most difficult questions he had yet encountered.[17]

Up to that time, Hegel was the single most important influence on Marx's thinking, and in a way continued to be so even after Marx rejected him for focusing on ideas and not (as Marx saw it) the real world. Yet the scaffolding remained: Hegel's dialectic became Marx's dialectic as Marx transformed Hegel's words from intellectual arguments into political action. Marx's revisionist approach was due in no small part to the influence of Ludwig Feuerbach.[18] Feuerbach was a friend of Marx and Bruno Bauer, and in 1841 published a book called *The Essence of Christianity,* in which he said God was the creation of man, who gathered all of humankind's virtues and projected them onto the image of a deity to be worshipped. Feuerbach argued that doing so had alienated man from what was best in his nature by essentially handing his good qualities over to someone or something else, leaving man feeling weak and unworthy. Next, in 1843, Feuerbach published a series of essays in which he argued that earlier thinkers, notably Hegel, were wrong to describe thought—like religion—as originating from somewhere outside man and coming to him like a thunderbolt, when in fact man generated thought and through his thoughts created God and philosophy.[19]

Marx applied that thinking to Hegel's notion of the state and found that Hegel had described a system in which the state functioned separate from man and imposed its sense of order on him. But Marx argued the state *was* man—the society of men—and that man should be the author of his own laws—a constitution—which would be the contract under which the state operated.[20]

Marx next scrutinized religion. Feuerbach held that religion was a vessel man constructed to carry his goodness. But Marx looked at religion and saw the reflection of man's suffering. He said religion was created by man and used like a drug to ease his pain in a world he felt powerless to change. "Religion is the sigh of the oppressed creature, the feeling of a heartless world and the soul of soulless circumstances," he wrote. "It is the opium of the people."[21]

Attempting to restore men to the rightful center of their universe, Marx began what he called a "reckless critique of everything that exists, reckless in the sense of a critique that fears neither its own results nor any conflict with the powers that be." He told Ruge that this was what they must do in their newspaper. Ruge and Fröbel said such a newspaper could operate in one city only.

Paris.[22]

Part II

The Fugitive Family

5

Paris, 1843

We are not, then, presenting the world, doctrine-like, with a new set of principles: here is the truth, kneel before it! We are developing a new set of principles for the world out of the old principles of the world.

— Karl Marx[1]

THROUGHOUT HISTORY THERE have been moments when Paris was the center of the creative universe—and 1843 was one of them. Everyone, whether of real or imagined import, was there, and everyone was politicized. French, German, Russian, Polish, Hungarian, and Italian reformers mingled with painters, poets, novelists, composers, and philosophers who had begun to celebrate the real rather than the ideal in their works.[2] Aristocrats with storied names met revolutionaries with checkered pasts in gilded salons or at secret society covens where plots were hatched to turn kingdoms into nations. Political fugitives surfaced on the velvet banquettes of Right Bank cafés, where they were feted like princes. Decorated soldiers, who traded the military for civilian life among the opposition, were heralded for their audacity—though the abandonment of their full-dress uniform was deeply lamented by women of fashion. This was King Louis-Philippe's Paris, a magnet for radicals from every social stratum throughout Europe.

During the French Revolution, an eighteen-year-old Louis-Philippe had briefly worked to overthrow the king and afterward traveled extensively through England and that wildly egalitarian frontier, the United States. He was thus exposed to the most advanced political thinking, and by the age of fifty-four not overly discomfited by a boisterous opposition, so long as it did not interfere with his passion for business. He had learned from the mistakes of his ousted predecessor and understood that a certain degree of liberality was necessary, not only for his own survival on the throne but in order for business to thrive and replenish state coffers. As a result, Paris was glorious in its wealth and flamboyance. One gown that was all the rage was made of 250 yards of Chantilly lace and Indian cashmere, and cost 10,000 francs—ten times the annual income for a working family.[3] Yet Paris was also home to radical prophets of the left (some accompanied by women dressed in that very haute couture), who sought to bring an end to such excesses. Wrote Friedrich Engels, Paris was quite simply the place where "European civilization had reached its fullest bloom."[4]

Jenny and Marx rumbled into town after a long coach journey and found themselves in the middle of this carnival. They'd come to Paris because it was free—because writers could say what they liked without threat of censure—but they may have been surprised at what freedom looked like. In Prussia it had been a mere concept to them, an article of faith, not something experienced. Now they could see it in the bustle of the bourgeoisie answering the government's challenge to "get rich" and hear it in the voluble, public, and undisguised debate of isms—liberalism, socialism, communism, nationalism—an exclamatory blizzard roaring out of the very city where these movements were born.[5] Neither Karl nor Jenny had ever been so far from home in a place so utterly foreign. And yet, both agreed, Paris was where they belonged.

Almost immediately they plunged into Parisian life. Jenny, who was devoted to the theater and who, like her mother, adored a crowd, especially loved the opéra bouffe that played out on the tree-lined boulevards of the French capital, where men postured in tight breeches and coats as richly textured and hued as women's finery, and the women, arrayed head to toe in extravagant styles designed to capture attention, feigned to disdain that notice once won. The streets featured a constant—and to an observer like Jenny, comical—courtship ritual; it was as if these upper classes had nothing to think about but love. And yet in the streets around them, and serving them in their homes, were the people who would one day achieve their downfall. These poor seethed with hatred, but the threat they posed went unnoticed by their social superiors, so secure were they in their delusion that society would always be at their command.

After watching her youth slip away year by dreary year while she waited for Karl at her parents' home in Trier, Jenny was finally living the life she had dreamed of, and with the promise of income from Marx's forthcoming newspaper, the future looked even brighter. Karl had ideas for books he would write and she would transcribe, she was going to have a baby, and they would do it together in Paris, where revolution was romantic and even its foot soldiers had style. This daughter of the Rhineland inhaled the great metropolis's air of possibility and found herself intoxicated.

Shortly before the couple's arrival, Ruge had pulled into town in a specially built carriage with his wife, a brood of children, and a large leg of veal. He was rich by marriage but tight with his money, and he proposed to the Marxes that they all economize by living in a communal arrangement with another couple, the poet Georg Herwegh and his wife, Emma. Ruge, who was quite proper and morally conservative, had taken two floors in a rather modest apartment building on the rue Vaneau between the Seine and the Boulevard Saint-Germain. All three men would be part of the *Deutsche-Französische Jahrbücher,* with offices across the street, and Ruge said the women could share the household duties.[6]

The notion might initially have seemed reassuring to Jenny and Marx, because they would be living with fellow Germans in a familial arrangement in a strange new city. But the plan quickly collapsed. Years later, the Herweghs' son Marcel said his mother had summed up the situation in one glance and recognized trouble: how could Frau Ruge, "the nice small Saxon woman, get on with the very intelligent and even more ambitious Frau Marx, whose knowledge was far superior to hers?" The Herweghs, sensing the potential for domestic discord, declined immediately,[7] while Karl and Jenny lived with the Ruges for just two weeks before moving up the street to a larger, more elegant building in which they could begin their married life alone.

Dr. Karl Marx and his wife mingled easily with Parisian radical and democratic circles where, for the first time, they were introduced to society as a married couple. Marx was proud of Jenny—proud of her beauty, which even amid the celebrated women of Paris was remarked upon, but also of her intelligence. From the earliest days of their marriage, he regarded Jenny as an intellectual equal, and that was no mere token sentiment: Marx was ruthless when it came to things of the mind, and he would not have relied on Jenny's judgment if he did not think she was in fact brilliant.[8] Indeed, throughout his life Marx held only one other person in a position of such high esteem and trust, and that was his alter ego and collaborator, Friedrich Engels. But where Engels understood and supported Marx intellectually, Jenny also humanized him.

In private Marx was warm, loving, kind, and generally described as excellent company when he was not plagued by sleepless nights or stricken by disease, both due to anxiety over his work. In public, however, he was most often fiercely argumentative, intellectually arrogant, and notoriously

impatient with anyone who disagreed with him. His frequent drinking episodes with colleagues throughout the years in Bonn, Berlin, and Cologne
often devolved into verbal if not physical fights. He had little time for social
niceties; for someone so conceptually fascinated by the alienation of man,
Marx routinely alienated those who encountered him. And while the arguments may have invigorated him, they also distracted him. He was happiest
buried in his books (which he called his "slaves"). Marx was an introvert who,
despite his best efforts to the contrary, attracted followers because he exuded
remarkable self-confidence and leadership. The rich Russian liberal Pavel
Annenkov called Marx "the embodiment of a democratic dictator" who
commanded respect in spite of his social clumsiness and shabby exterior.[9]

Jenny, however, was expert in the ways of society. In her quiet, refined
way, she reassured those who might have been intimidated by her slightly
strange species of a husband. On her arm, and only there, the public Marx
looked very much like the private Marx—relaxed, funny, at times even
frivolous. This cerebral wild man appeared positively tame when his wife
was at hand.

Jenny was twenty-nine and Marx twenty-five when they arrived in
Paris. His reputation as a writer from Cologne was known among the
German émigrés, but he was a relative lesser light among that group—
Paris was a refuge for some of Germany's most famous political and literary exiled sons. Herwegh was one of the more famous. Months earlier,
King Friedrich Wilhelm IV had called him in for a personal meeting after
his recent book was banned for political reasons. The king tried to persuade Herwegh to join him in creating a cultural rebirth in Prussia. But
the poet famously replied that he was a born republican and could not
serve a crown. Herwegh was then banished from Prussia, Saxony, and
Switzerland, and eventually made his way to Paris.[10] As would be
expected, his fame grew with each expulsion. Along the way he married
the daughter of a wealthy Berlin silk merchant (the best man at their wedding was the future anarchist Mikhail Bakunin) and dreamed of becoming the poetic voice of the new Germany.[11]

Like Marx, Herwegh was engaged to write for Ruge's newspaper. The
pair became close friends and the couples, both relative newlyweds, socialized. The Marxes soon learned, however, that their talented and extremely
handsome friend was notorious around the city for his free spending and
his love affairs. Herwegh's current mistress was the Countess d'Agoult,
who wrote under the name Daniel Stern and had had three children by
her previous lover, the Hungarian composer and pianist Franz Liszt. The
countess held one of the most famous salons in Paris. Among her intimates
were George Sand, Chopin, Ingres, and Victor Hugo.[12]

By the midnineteenth century, the line between artists such as these and political radicals such as Marx had blurred. The artists had been largely cut off from the rich patrons who previously paid them for their poems and songs.[13] Now the "head workers," as Marx called them, were free to starve just like the hand workers. Faced with the yawning abyss of penury, many such romantic, alienated geniuses became politicized. One writer said the artists were almost universally partisan, regarding themselves and their works first and foremost as political tools.[14] Swept up in that demimonde of creativity, Marx and Jenny appear to have taken Herwegh's indiscretions in stride, something Jenny especially may not have been willing to do in narrow-minded Germany. In any case, throughout his life Marx held poets to a different social standard. His daughter Eleanor said Marx called poets "queer fish who must be allowed to go their own ways. They should not be assessed by the measure of ordinary or even extraordinary men."[15]

At about the time Marx met Herwegh, a German doctor introduced him to Heinrich Heine. Heine had been exiled in Paris since Karl was a boy, but he had always been a presence in Marx's life, not only as a poet-idol but as a distant relation on his mother's side. Though Heine was twenty years older than Marx, and like Marx more inclined to make enemies than friends, the two bonded immediately. Heine would say they needed "very few signs in order to understand each other."[16]

Heine had been a beautiful young man — the overall impression he made was softness, from his gentle eyes to his long, slightly wavy hair — but he was a tragic figure by the time Marx and Jenny encountered him. He had been diagnosed with a type of roving paralysis, which in 1843 had struck the left side of his face, and he feared he was going blind. He had just married his paramour Mathilde (an illiterate Frenchwoman fifteen years his junior who did not know he was famous), on the eve of a duel he expected to lose. (He did not.)[17]

But while Heine existed as if on the verge of death, that only seemed to feed his poetic gift. Described by his critics as a "monstrous egotist," he was in fact so insecure that he wept over bad reviews in Marx's presence. (In such cases Marx turned him over to Jenny, who used both wit and kindness to soothe the troubled writer and restore his confidence.) Heine became family to the Marxes, and they visited each other's apartments daily.[18] Marx's relationship with Heine was one of his most important in Paris; it politicized the poet and helped Marx mature as an artist and a man. Marx, however, hated Mathilde and her friends, suspecting them of being pimps and prostitutes who preyed upon the weakened Heine.[19]

★   ★   ★

Ruge's newspaper, which was to be a monthly written in French and German, was supposed to begin publishing in November 1843, but there were funding problems. There was also trouble with contributors: Ruge had not been able to attract a single Frenchman. In fact, the only non-German to commit to the enterprise was the Russian Bakunin, who was now also in Paris. Ruge dispatched Marx to try to find French writers and wondered whether they should "serenade" the women authors George Sand and Flora Tristan. Marx knew both, but whether he approached them to write for the *Jahrbücher* is unknown. Ultimately, neither they nor any other French author appeared in the newspaper. While the Germans hungrily consumed French philosophy, the French seemed resistant to being associated with German ideas; the Germans, the French believed, were grappling with problems they themselves had overcome in 1789.[20]

As a result of all this stress, Ruge became ill and irritable, and the newspaper's publication was delayed until February 1844. When it did appear, under Marx's editorial direction, it was book length and contained poems by Herwegh and Heine; an exchange of letters critical of Germany between Ruge, Marx, Feuerbach, and Bakunin; essays by Bakunin, Moses Hess, and a former newspaper editor expelled from Bavaria named F. C. Bernays; and two articles each by Marx and a young German in England named Engels. A thousand copies were printed.

Ruge, a moderate democrat by nature, was angry over the radical direction in which Marx had taken the *Jahrbücher* and what he called the unpolished style in which Marx wrote.[21] (Ruge was merely the first of many who would criticize Marx's use of pages-long paragraphs, obscure literary allusions, rambling arguments, and apparent lack of regard for whether the reader understood what he was trying to say.) Jenny recalled that the newspaper she had counted on to secure their future "came to grief after the very first issue."[22]

The paper did not find a readership in Paris and was blocked at the German border. Ruge and Fröbel cut the funding, and Jenny's fears that her husband would not be allowed to return home were realized: Prussian governors were instructed to arrest Marx, Ruge, Heine, and Bernays as soon as they stepped onto Prussian soil, the charge against them high treason.[23]

Among the articles the Prussians found offensive were two that Marx had begun during his honeymoon. One was a critique of Hegel, and the other was titled "On the Jewish Question." Both incorporated lessons learned during his years in Berlin and Cologne but also displayed a new French influence, especially his discussion of the as-yet barely recognized proletariat. Derived from the Latin word *proletarius,* which meant the lowest class or those without property, the term as applied by Marx referred to victims of social change. These were not people who were historically poor; the proletariat of the nineteenth century had once been able to support themselves but had become casualties of so-called economic and industrial advances that, among other things, replaced men with machines and the cheaper labor of women and children, or cut their wages by either reducing the time they worked or increasing their hours without raising their pay.[24] In his critique of Hegel, Marx posited that theory alone could not create a revolution, but the proletariat, powered by the brute strength born of injustice and armed with the intellectual weapon philosophy, could.[25] "The *head* of this emancipation is *philosophy*," he said, "*its heart* is the *proletariat*."[26]

In tackling the "Jewish Question," Marx looked at religion not as a theological issue but as a social and political one. The Jew in early-nineteenth-century Germany functioned largely within the mercantile and financial trades, the unspoken but sanctioned areas allotted to him by the state that had helped shape how Jews were viewed by society and each other. Since 1816, when Marx's own father had been faced with the choice of remaining a Jew or entering society as a Christian, Jews in Prussia had not had equal rights. In the early 1840s, however, the rights and role of Jews in society were being examined anew.

In his treatise Marx considered how religion was used in day-to-day affairs in Germany, whether that be Christianity in the political arena or the Jewish dominance of the marketplace, and what freedom from religion would mean in nontheological terms. He argued in the case of Jews, their main activity, finance, had become integral to the state's very existence and concluded that liberating Jews from the confines of that commercial activity (which had, he felt, become the essence of Judaism), and thereby depriving the state of its benefit, would precipitate the German social revolution he sought. The state could not stand if one of its pillars — in this case finance — crumbled; the government Marx and his fellows despised would collapse.[27]

Marx's two *Jahrbücher* articles addressed entirely different subjects, but both concerned the future of the German Confederation and both ended with its dissolution. With them, Marx had gone well beyond anything he had written while gently jousting with censors in Cologne. In Paris the restrictions on his writing had been lifted, and through this French prism the tendency of his writing bent toward revolution.

By the time the *Jahrbücher* folded, Jenny was seven months pregnant and the couple's financial situation was precarious. Marx and Ruge's relationship had soured over the political tone of the paper, and they were also fighting over Herwegh. Ruge was disgusted by Herwegh's behavior. He called him a *lump*, or tramp, and said he had "succumbed to the delights of Paris, the shops, the carriages, the rich people's lovely rooms, the flower stalls, the girls." He expressed horror at Herwegh's relations with the Countess d'Agoult, and he accused him of being wanton and lazy. Marx heard him out during one of his tirades and left quietly, but at home he composed a letter in which he angrily defended Herwegh's genius and called Ruge a narrow-minded philistine.[28] The true root of their acrimony, however, may have been money: Ruge refused to pay Marx the salary he had promised and in lieu of cash offered him copies of his seemingly worthless newspaper. Ruge's refusal was irritating not only because Marx had no other income and was about to become a father, but also because he knew Ruge had just made a killing on railway stocks.[29]

Before Jenny and Karl's situation became dire, however, Georg Jung and former *Rheinische Zeitung* stockholders in Cologne sent them twice the amount Marx would have earned as *Jahrbücher* coeditor—a token of appreciation, they said, for Marx's work on their behalf.[30] That windfall in turn irked Ruge and prompted him to complain to Fröbel that Marx and Jenny had gone mad with spending. "His wife gave him for his birthday a riding switch costing 100 francs and the poor devil cannot ride nor has he a horse. Everything he sees he wants to 'have'—a carriage, smart clothes...in fact the moon."[31] A subsequent letter by Ruge complaining about another form of mania on the part of his estranged colleague sounded much nearer the mark. He described Marx as cynical and crudely arrogant, "a peculiar personality—perfect as a scholar and author but completely ruinous as a journalist. He reads a lot; he works with unusual intensity...but he finishes nothing, breaks off everything and plunges himself ever afresh into an endless sea of books."[32] The split between the two men that year was bitter and final. Over time, Marx would spare Ruge no insult. "Ferret-faced ignoramus" was among the shortest and least offensive.[33]

The first Marx child was born on May 1, 1844. Little Jenny, or Jennychen, was named after her mother but had the black eyes and hair of her father.[34] Neither Jenny nor Marx had any real experience with infants. Jenny had been raised in a house full of servants, where children were handed over to nurses as soon as they were born. And Marx was so disengaged from his family that he had long behaved as though he were an only child, despite seven siblings. Their bohemian friends in Paris, who rose at 5 p.m. and stayed awake until 5 a.m. at cafés, salons, and restaurants, were no help either, so Jenny and Marx struggled along with Jennychen as best they could until, at one point, the infant appeared gravely ill.

Help in that case arrived from an unlikely source: Heinrich Heine. The forty-six-year-old poet, still coping with partial paralysis, who had never had a child himself, climbed the stairs to the Marx apartment to find the young parents frantic because their daughter was having convulsions. Heine took charge, ordered hot water, and gave the baby a bath.[35] Jennychen recovered, but her traumatized parents did not: they decided Jenny should take the child to Trier, where her mother could help guide Jennychen through her dangerous first months.

Wearing a velvet cloak and feathered hat, the baby in her arms, Jenny reluctantly boarded a coach for the Rhineland in early June, leaving Karl alone in Paris. As mother and child headed east, Jenny worried. They had not been married a year, and she feared Karl would fall victim to "the real menace of unfaithfulness, the seductions and attractions of a capital city."[36] Jenny knew Paris was a place where desires, once expressed, were easily gratified.

She needn't have worried. Marx was indeed preoccupied during her absence, but it was not with other women. While she was away he descended into the subterranean world of secret societies, and began his first real exploration of economics.

6

Paris, 1844

Five men listened and did not understand and five
others did not understand and talked.
— Alexander Herzen[1]

JOBLESSNESS WAS LIBERATING for Marx—it meant he could go back to school. His classrooms were gaslit cafés and wine cellars, and small offices crammed with men rendered invisible to each other by dense cigar smoke. There were no lectures, there were discussions—boisterous gatherings that drew curious passersby who watched men from many nations shout at each other in languages they did not understand, bellowing about the relative merits of socialism, communism, nationalism, liberalism, and democracy, and whether governments should be taken by force and rebuilt from the ruins, or whether appeals should be made to the ruling class that fundamental social change was coming—one could see it all around!— and monarchies must adapt to meet it. There were those who argued in favor of increasing the political power of the bourgeoisie and industrialists, who saw hope for all mankind in the advances that had sped up production, cut the cost of basic goods, and opened new markets. Other voices, however, urged caution, saying those very advances posed a new and even greater threat to the masses than the kings the bourgeoisie hoped to render impotent. They argued that industrialists were fueled by greed alone and would willingly sacrifice generations of workers in their quest for greater wealth.

All sides of the debate saw the need for new forms of government in Europe; the nature of society had changed. Absolute monarchs with their obsequious courtiers and despots with their bloody henchmen seemed costume characters from another era, and yet they still had the power to impede social and economic progress. Yes, all the men in Marx's circle agreed, the monarchies must go. They could not agree, however, on how, or on what would replace them.[2]

In March, before Jenny left for Trier, Marx had attended a banquet where these issues were to be discussed. Around the table sat several men who would figure in nearly every major European revolutionary drama for the next thirty years. Their ideas were diverse and represented various degrees of sophistication, but their personalities were already well formed and larger than life.[3] Two would be of particular importance to Marx: Mikhail Bakunin and Louis Blanc.

Bakunin was the son of a Russian count with a vast estate that included five hundred serfs. His mother was from one of the country's most celebrated families, the Muravievs, members of which had been hanged in 1825 for their part in an uprising against the czar. Bakunin trained in the military but deserted the army when he was about twenty-one, and eventually landed in Berlin in 1840, where he joined the Russian circle of Young Hegelians that included his close friend the novelist Ivan Turgenev[4] (who coined the term "nihilism[5]"). Tall and lanky, Bakunin wore a dirty student's cap over a thick shock of equally dirty black hair. He was an utterly physical man of action, ferocious in his appetites and eager to throw himself into any fight to defend his ideas or his friends. He was oddly distant, however, when it came to women (he was even said to be impotent), but that did not seem to diminish his appeal: from one country to the next, women of all classes were mesmerized by him.[6]

By the time Bakunin arrived in Paris, he had acquired a reputation as a revolutionary, which he believed required instinct rather than thought.[7] He was four years older than Marx, but by his own admission less intellectually developed when they finally met. From the start their relations were strained. Observed one writer, "Between the Russian aristocrat and the Jewish lawyer's son there was not merely a clash of temperaments, but a lack of any common background of tradition and ideas."[8] Decades later Bakunin wrote of their time together in Paris: "We saw each other pretty often, for I greatly respected him for his learning and for his passionate and serious devotion—though it was always mingled with personal vanity—to the cause of the proletariat, and I eagerly sought his conversation, which was always instructive, and witty, when it was not inspired by petty hate, which alas! was only too often the case. There was, however, never any frank intimacy between us—our temperaments did not permit. He called me a sentimental idealist, and he was right; I called him vain, perfidious and sly, and I was right too."[9]

Louis Blanc, who in 1844 was thirty-three, was one of France's most celebrated socialists, especially among the country's enlightened workers. He was physically and intellectually the opposite of Bakunin. About the size of an eight-year-old, Blanc was tiny, but he had an authoritarian streak and intellect that propelled him to the leadership of the movement.[10] In 1840 he published two books, *Organization of Labor,* which called for worker control of a democratic state, and *History of Ten Years,* a critique of the reign of Louis-Philippe. In 1843 he cofounded the important opposition newspaper *La Reforme,* which advocated the abolition of the monarchy in favor of a republic, universal suffrage, guaranteed employment, and worker protections.[11] Blanc, like Bakunin, would cross paths many times with Marx over the years, and as with Bakunin, most of the encounters would be adversarial.

At the time the men met for their banquet, there were no international organizations under whose auspices they could gather, partly because the problems each confronted were unique to their regions, and partly because opposition groups as such barely existed outside the minds of their self-declared leaders. Gradually, however, in the melting pot of men and ideas in Paris, those who were at the forefront of the new ideologies began transcending the barriers of languages and customs to talk about common concerns. Several dominant strands were prominent among these European middle-class reformers: liberalism, radicalism, nationalism, and socialism.

Liberals wanted a broadly democratic government based on merit, not birth, with the vote extended to those with property and education. Liberals also wanted freedom of speech, press, and assembly, and protection of property rights. They were not opposed to a king as long as they also had a constitution. Radicals were liberals who did not want a king—they wanted a republic—with wider suffrage and social reform. Nationalists were usually liberals (notably Germans and Italians) who wanted a united country and a national culture that included a common language, history, and the arts. The socialists differed most from their fellows in the opposition. Socialism arose in France in direct response to the growing power of business. Its adherents opposed unequal property rights, which they believed were used as a social and political bludgeon to enrich the wealthy and ensure that those with only skilled hands or strong backs were excluded from the political system. Socialists generally supported democracy as a repudiation of monarchs and feudalism, but they believed it did not adequately protect workers from the injustices of industrialization.[12]

All of those isms, however, existed largely in the theoretical realm, topics of discussion that could not be applied because they had no mass support—no army. The reason for this was relatively straightforward: the working class, which Marx believed would form this army, was suspicious of middle-class reformers and consequently of their ideologies. Marx, too, was suspicious of these ideas. As much as the needs of mankind dominated the discussions of opposition intellectuals, the material needs of individual men were curiously absent. Also, the intellectuals' revolution in many cases merely substituted one dominant elite (the nobility) for another (the grand bourgeoisie), meaning the tyranny of wealth over work would continue. Finally, Marx did not recognize in any of the isms designed to cure society's ills a real *understanding* of the disease spreading through Europe's fledgling industrial economic system (monarchies and their problems, on the other hand, were obvious), and without that knowledge, no meaningful social change was possible. Fully admitting that he, too, did not completely understand, Marx set out in search of answers.[13]

He found some with the help of two Germans on the rue Vaneau. August Hermann Ewerbeck and Germain Maürer were both members of the secret League of the Just, formed in 1836 by extreme, mostly proletarian, German refugees in Paris.[14] The league, half a propaganda, half a conspiracy society, had adopted French communist ideas, which advocated the abolition of private property as the surest way to change society at its foundation.[15] Marx attended these German workers' meetings and those of their French counterparts, and came away impressed by their full-blooded commitment to a communist struggle, as opposed to the intellectuals' armchair socialism. He wrote: "The brotherhood of man is no mere phrase with them, but a fact of life, and the nobility of man shines upon us from their work-hardened bodies." He also saw in some of their faces the alienation of men whose labor—indeed, whose lives—had been exchanged for an inadequate wage, and who did not even have by way of ancillary compensation the pride of their production: what they made belonged to the factory owner.[16]

Inspired, Marx returned to the books he had been reading that year, specifically texts by French and English economists, filling notebook after notebook with scrambled jottings. These became the "Economic and Philosophical Manuscripts" or "1844 Manuscripts," which Marx left unfinished but which formed the basis for his life's work.

The study of what Marx called "bourgeois economists" led him to the conclusion that these men believed economic systems operated according to cold, immutable laws that carried men along and were beyond their control. These economists also believed that business, left to grow without government interference, would eventually produce a general benefit for all mankind. But Marx had seen and heard evidence to the contrary, and he set out to demythologize economics, to describe its real-world mechanics and, most forcefully, its consequences.[17]

In the manuscripts Marx worked his way through wage, rent, credit, profit, private property vs. communism, and the relations of capital to labor, and he took yet another look at Hegel. What he discovered was that acquisition of the glittering prize of the new economic system, money (and by extension the things that such capital could buy), had become *the* driving force in modern man's existence, perverting every aspect of his relations with other people, even how he viewed himself. It magically enabled the rich man to become whatever he chose:

> I *am* ugly, but I can buy for myself the *most beautiful* of women. Therefore I am not *ugly*, for the effect of *ugliness*—its deterrent power—is nullified by money...I am bad, dishonest, unscrupulous, stupid; but money is honored, and hence its possessor....I am *brainless,* but money is the *real brain* of all things and how then should its possessor be brainless? Besides, he can buy clever people for himself....Does not all my money, therefore, transform all my incapacities into their contrary?[18]

Meanwhile the labor that produced the rich man's wealth robbed the worker of his lifeblood: "It produces palaces—but for the worker hovels. It produces beauty—but for the worker, deformity. It replaces labor by machines, but it throws one section of the workers back to a barbarous type of labor, and it turns the other section into a machine. It produces intelligence—but for the worker, stupidity, cretinism."[19]

Marx sought to explain how this corrosive relationship had developed. He began placing man in a system in which the grand bourgeoisie, which controlled all the money as well as the means of production, dehumanized the worker by reducing him to selling his labor for a wage determined by the property owner or industrialist. It was as if a man had a bag of corn to sell, but instead of setting the price himself based on what he knew to be its value, he accepted whatever the buyer wanted to pay for it. Just as the seller lost control of the value of his crop, the worker in the new industrial relationship lost control of his worth. He became alienated, an object, laboring for a class of men who reaped all the benefits and gave him in return only the means to survive.

Marx's theories became spectacles; evidence was luminescent everywhere. Most immediately, he could see streets swollen with people driven to the city to seek work in the new industries but, once there, unable to find jobs that offered living wages. (The French had even invented a new word for the phenomenon—pauperism.) Wages had been falling for nearly twenty years while the cost of living during the same time rose 17 percent. In 1844 wide-scale food shortages began, even as the rich heaped their tables with ever more lavish fare.[20] A series of scandals exposed how French officials had helped create the economic imbalance by concentrating extreme wealth in the hands of a select few.[21] What Marx witnessed, therefore, was not the free market the economists so glowingly described in their treatises, but a market controlled by the rich for the benefit of the rich.

Though he had discounted communism as unrealizable just two years earlier in Cologne, Marx now saw it as the means to recalibrate society. Men would achieve wealth, but that wealth would not be private property but shared. Men would work, but their work would benefit themselves and the greater good, not the property owner. He described communism as "the genuine resolution of the antagonism between man and nature and between man and man. It is the true resolution of the struggle between existence and essence, between objectification and self-affirmation, between freedom and necessity."[22] His friend Heine said he feared communism would kill art and beauty, but he said, "If I cannot refute the premise that all men have the right to eat, then I must accept all of what follows from it."[23]

French and German workers in Paris who identified themselves as communists believed that the only way to destroy the corrupt new economic order was revolution; it was simply not possible to negotiate an end to such exploitation as long as its beneficiaries had so much to lose. Industrial feudalism (as some of them called it) would go the way of its agrarian predecessor only by acts of violence. Marx agreed, writing, "In order to abolish the *idea* of private property, the *idea* of communism is quite sufficient. It takes *actual* communist action to abolish *actual* private property."[24] And in the midst of Marx's economic musings, as if on cue, such violence occurred. Word arrived of an uprising in the Prussian region of Silesia. For the likes of Marx and the workers in Paris, this was electrifying as a portent of what was to come.

On June 4, 1844, driven mad by their misery, a group of weavers marched on the home of a pair of Prussian industrialist brothers, demanding higher pay and singing "You villains all, you hellish drones / You knaves in Satan's raiment! / You gobble all the poor man owns / Our curses be your payment!" The protesters were beyond desperate, beyond furious. Men, women, and children had been subjected to such low wages that some of the workers had starved. Their demands denied, the enraged weavers stormed the house and destroyed it, though the brothers escaped

unharmed. The next day, as many as five thousand weavers and their families staged a wider revolt. They burst into homes and factories, destroyed
machines, and looted and ransacked the comfortable residences and offices
of the men who denied them food. The industrialists called in the Prussian military, which fired on the crowd, killing thirty-five. Armed with
rocks and axes, the mob drove away the soldiers, but by the next morning,
military reinforcements arrived and the weavers were vanquished. Those
who could, fled; those who could not were arrested.

The weavers' revolt was the first of its kind involving industrial workers
in Germany, and though it failed, Marx recognized in it the connection
he sought between an impassioned proletariat, economics, and the state.
The driving force behind the rebellion was not an abstraction such as religion or ethnicity or a throne, as many had been in the past, but something
much more tangible: bread. Marx was also particularly heartened by the
target of the weavers' revolt—the enemy of the future, the bourgeoisie—
who, because they controlled the money, would ultimately control the
government, even the king, as they already did in France.[25]

Energized by events at home, as many as two hundred Germans at a
time, including Marx, Herwegh, and Heine (the latter two having written poems for the Silesian weavers), began meeting on Sundays at a Paris
wine merchant's shop near the Trône barrier on the Avenue de Vincennes.
French police informers reported they discussed killing kings, oppressing
the rich and religious, and other "words of horror."[26] Marx also met frequently with Bakunin and other liberal Russian nobles who spent part of
the year in Paris and might be persuaded to make some of their fortunes
available to the cause.[27] And in July 1844 Marx was introduced to France's
famed anarchist Pierre-Joseph Proudhon, a self-taught workingman who
famously asked in his 1840 book, *What Is Property?*, and answered, "Property is theft."[28] Proudhon declared that he was not proposing a new system, he was simply demanding an end to privilege; justice, he said, was all
he was after. But Marx called Proudhon's work "epoch making." He said
Proudhon was the first person to illustrate the social ills inherent in a system based on private property. Although the two men talked frequently,
sometimes all night, about communism, Marx said he mostly taught
Proudhon German philosophy, which the Frenchman was unable to study
properly because he did not read the language.[29]

The Marx who wrote for Ruge's *Deutsche-Französische Jahrbücher* earlier
that year and was charged with high treason for his articles was an uniniti-
ated choirboy compared with the Marx who in the summer of 1844 began
writing for the newspaper *Vowarts!* (Forward!). The Paris-based weekly

was known as the only uncensored opposition German-language newspaper in Europe.[30] In fact the newspaper was financed by a Prussian opera composer named Giacomo Meyerbeer, who was introduced to the socialists, communists, and their more timid liberal brethren through the Countess d'Agoult and reportedly instructed by Prussia's king Friedrich Wilhelm to draw out the rebellious Germans in Paris by giving them the editorial space to hang themselves.

Marx's friend Bernays was made editor in chief, but an editorial assistant, Adalbert von Bornstedt, was an Austrian spy and agent provocateur in the pay of Prussia's king. It is possible Marx and the other writers knew who Meyerbeer and Bornstedt worked for but took their chances anyway in order to get their ideas published. In any case, spies were as common in their circle as alcohol and cigars, and sometimes, because they made for good gossip, just as agreeable a diversion.[31]

Heinrich Börnstein, who founded the newspaper but did not finance it, recalled that twelve to fourteen men would gather for editorial conferences each week at his Right Bank apartment on the rue des Moulins, just north of the Tuileries. "Some would sit on the bed or on the trunks, others would stand or walk about. They would all smoke terrifically, and argue with great passion and excitement. It was impossible to open the windows, because a crowd would immediately have gathered in the street to find out the cause of the violent uproar, and very soon the room was concealed in such a thick cloud of tobacco-smoke that it was impossible for a newcomer to recognize anybody present." Those attending included Marx, Heine, Herwegh, Ruge, Bakunin, the poet Georg Weerth, and the communist Ewerbeck. None of the writers was paid for his work.[32]

Marx's letters from Paris to Jenny in Trier during this period no longer exist, but her letters to him indicated a creeping anxiety about their future—possibly the kind of dread Marx's father detected in her so many years before. In a letter dated June 21, Jenny seemed delighted to hold court from morning to night and fool residents by her apparent affluence. "I behave towards everyone in a lordly fashion and my external appearance fully justified this. For once I am more elegant than any of them and never in my life have I looked better and more blooming than I do now. Everyone is unanimous about that." After describing her unexpectedly warm encounters with Marx's mother and sisters, she wrote, "What a difference success makes, or in our case rather the *appearance* of success." But the question on everyone's lips remained whether and when Karl might get a reliable job, and she said in so many words that the thought had crossed her mind as well. "Dearest heart, I am often greatly worried about our future, both that near at hand and later on, and I think I am going to be punished for my exuberance and cockiness here. If you can do, set my mind at rest about this. There is too much talk on all sides about a steady income."

Jenny was evidently struggling to be strong as her husband traveled further along a dangerous road. The reason, no doubt, was her daughter. For the first time her loyalties were divided between her husband and the child she had come so close to losing in Paris. She called Jennychen "the most intimate bond of our love" and cried out in anxiety over their insecure state. "If we can only hold out for a time, until our little one has grown big."

Paragraph by paragraph Jenny alternated between news and fears, but in the end she seemed resigned that the path Karl had chosen was inevitable and correct, and all would be well if he simply wrote—although she suggested he do so without as much rancor or irritation. "You know how much more effect your other articles have had. Write either in a matter-of-fact and subtle way or humorously and lightly." Yet to those who doubted his course, perhaps including herself, she said, "O, you asses, as if all of you were standing on firm ground...where is there any firm foundation now? Can one not see everywhere signs of earthquake and the undermining of the foundations on which society has erected its temples and shops?"[33]

About a month after Jenny wrote those words, the Prussian earth shook indeed. Coming after the violence in Silesia in June, a failed assassination of Friedrich Wilhelm IV raised alarms throughout the kingdom. Again the perpetrator was motivated not by politics, according to Jenny, but by hunger. In a letter to Karl she described the would-be assassin: "For three days the man had been begging in vain in Berlin in constant danger of death from starvation—hence it was a social attempt at assassination! If something does break out, it will start from this direction...the seeds of a social revolution are present." And yet, she said, Prussians were oblivious to the danger. "All the bells were ringing, the guns firing, and the pious crowd flocking into the temples to convey their hallelujahs to the heavenly Lord for having so miraculously saved their earthly lord."[34]

Marx published Jenny's letter in *Vowarts!* on August 10, 1844, and signed it "A German Lady." Her first piece of published writing appeared three days after Marx's own initial contribution to this most radical of all German-language newspapers.[35] Soon *Vowarts!* attracted the attention of the Prussian authorities, who were on high alert after the assassination attempt. While their spies had had the men associated with the paper under surveillance, officials did not act against them until *Vowarts!* printed an article declaring regicide was the only way to convince the Prussian

68

people that the monarch was not divine but a weak and fallible man. The Prussian government pressured its French counterpart, which did not want to be seen harboring exiles who advocated the murder of kings.[36] Trumped-up charges involving the newspaper's license were brought against editor in chief Bernays, who was imprisoned for two months. The rest of the staff braced for more charges and possible expulsion.[37]

In that atmosphere Jenny prepared to return to Paris. She wrote to Karl between August 11 and 18 that she would soon be at his side, where "all hell is being let loose." Her note overflowed with love for the "dear father of my little doll" and her "good, sweet, little wild boar," and she asked him, "Karl dear, how long will our little doll play a solo part? I fear, I fear, that when her papa and mama are together once again, and live in common ownership, the performance will soon become a duet."[38] As she always would, Jenny rallied to her husband's side when he was under threat. If he were opposed, she would defend him; if he were in danger, she would protect him. Any fears she had about their financial security were swiftly deferred to the vanishing point. Within days of receiving her letter, Marx made the acquaintance of the man who would be his other lifelong protector, Friedrich Engels.

7

Paris, 1845

I simply cannot understand how anyone can be envious of genius; it's something so very special that we who have not got it know it to be unattainable right from the start; but to be envious of anything like that one must have to be frightfully small minded.

—Friedrich Engels[1]

ENGELS HAD BEEN traveling from England back home to Germany when he decided to make a slight detour in Paris. Marx knew him as the author of what he considered a brilliant piece on political economy written for Ruge's newspaper earlier in the year. Engels knew Marx as the tyrant who ran the *Rheinische Zeitung* in Cologne but whose writings he greatly respected. The two met on August 28, 1844, at the Café de la Régence and talked for ten straight days and as many nights.[2] The café near the Louvre was a fitting location for their first substantial encounter: it was famous throughout Europe as a salon where chess masters matched wits.

At twenty-three, Engels was tall, slim, blond, meticulous in his dress, and athletic. He loved women—as many as possible—and horses. At his factory-owning father's insistence, he had quit school when he was seventeen to learn the family trade. Calling himself a businessman and a Royal Prussian artillerist,[3] Engels was on the surface completely unlike the cerebral, squat, dark and disheveled family man Marx, except for what one colleague called his "penchant for boozing" and his biting humor.[4] If Marx was simply who he appeared to be, however, Engels was more complicated. On the one hand he was the man society recognized and enjoyed—the reckless bachelor who rode to the hounds and had a preternatural gift for discerning good wine. But he was also an impassioned revolutionary, one who took a radical Irish factory girl as a live-in lover and even as a teenager wrote trenchant newspaper articles on the social evils resulting from unregulated industrialization in his native Barmen. It was the revolutionary Engels who introduced himself to Marx that August in Paris, but Marx readily embraced both sides of this extraordinary character.

Engels was a rare combination, a man of ideas and a reformer who could write articles of great eloquence and immediacy, but also a man of business who knew the workings of industry from the owner's suite to the factory floor. He understood the social, political, and economic ramifications of the new industrial system because he had lived it. He was an envoy from the material world, arrived at Marx's door to fill the gaps in his theoretical studies.

On Engels's side, he recognized in twenty-six-year-old Marx a powerful personality and intellect unlike any he had known. The good soldier had been looking for someone or something to serve, and he found that person in Karl Marx. Engels later described their historic Paris meeting with great understatement, observing: "Our complete agreement in all theoretical fields became evident and our joint work dates from that time."[5] He would, quite simply, be the savior of the Marx family. He not only provided the material context for Marx's work but would provide the material sustenance for the family's very existence.

Engels was the oldest of eight children and the heir to a growing textile firm begun in Prussia's Wuppertal valley by his great-grandfather in the eighteenth century. By the time Engels was a teenager in Barmen, that area of the Rhineland was one of the most industrialized in Germany, its Wupper River polluted and discolored by factory waste. His family practiced the fundamentalist and intolerant Pietist strain of Christianity: any sort of public fun was condemned; scripture and the judgment of their small community were considered the ultimate authorities. Almost as soon as he had a discernible personality, Friedrich alarmed his parents by rebelling.[6] In a letter to his wife, Friedrich Engels Senior expressed concern over his fifteen-year-old son because he did not obey even after being severely punished. The father had also found in Friedrich's desk a "dirty book which he had borrowed from the lending library, a story about knights of the thirteenth century.... May God watch over his disposition... I am often fearful for this otherwise excellent boy."[7]

During his years at the Elberfeld gymnasium, Engels developed a real interest in and, unlike Marx, a talent for poetry. His first poems were published when he was seventeen, and he hoped to become a literary man.[8] His father, however, wanted him to go into business, so he forced his son to drop out of school. Engels was sent to the industrial town of Bremen to serve as an apprentice, and it was there that the son of a factory owner began his life as a revolutionary. Some of his early rebellious antics became well known around town.[9] He challenged his peers to grow mustaches, considered indecent in polite society. A dozen did and met for a "mustache jubilee."[10] He also boasted to his sister that he insulted the "philistines" by not only parading his mustache at a concert but wearing an ordinary coat and going barehanded while the young men around him wore tailcoats and kid gloves. "The ladies, incidentally liked it very much.... The best of it is that three months ago nobody knew me here and now all the world does."[11] But his real protest took written form. Engels's "Letters from Wuppertal," signed by his alias, the self-described philosophical commercial traveler "Friedrich Oswald," caused a sensation. Published in a Hamburg-based periodical in 1839, when Engels was eighteen, they were eventually picked up by liberal-leaning newspapers throughout Germany.[12] The letters described factory workers who, beginning as early as the age of six, toiled in low rooms and breathed in more coal fumes and dust than oxygen. Such conditions were "bound to deprive them of all strength and joy in life," he wrote, and those "who do not fall prey to mysticism are ruined by drunkenness."[13]

> Terrible poverty prevails among the lower classes, particularly the factory workers in Wuppertal; syphilis and lung disease are so widespread as to be barely credible; in Elberfeld alone, out of twenty-five-hundred children of school age, twelve-hundred are deprived of education and grow up in the factories—merely so the manufacturer need not pay the adults, whose place they take, twice the wage he pays a child. But the wealthy manufacturers have a flexible conscience, and causing the death of one child more or less does not doom a pietist's soul to hell, especially if he goes to church twice every Sunday. For it is a fact that the pietists among the factory owners treat their workers worst of all; they use every possible means to reduce the workers' wages on the pretext of depriving them of the opportunity to get drunk.[14]

"Oswald" also came out in favor of the liberation of women, which he said was a basic step on the path toward freedom for all people.[15] (Though Engels may have had a slightly less altruistic reason—he saw the sexual possibilities in freeing women from social strictures.)

As for politics, Engels declared in a letter to a friend that he hated the king, who at the time was Friedrich Wilhelm III. "If I didn't so despise him, the shit, I would hate him still more. Napoleon was an angel compared with him. . . . I expect anything good only of that prince whose ears are boxed right and left by his people, and whose palace windows are smashed by the flying stones of the revolution."[16] He dismissed the nobility as the result of "sixty-four society marriages."[17]

Engels returned home to Barmen in 1841 and then went to Berlin to do a year's military service. Unofficially, he also went to Berlin to be near the university and the Young Hegelians, whose works he had read in Bremen. Engels joined the new generation of Young Hegelians known as The Free. They greeted him warmly; he had already published at least thirty-seven articles, and everyone in their circle was aware of the legendary "Friedrich Oswald's" attacks.[18]

One of Engels's major influences at that time was Marx's friend Moses Hess, the first among them to espouse communism. Hess believed revolution was inevitable and would arise from France, Germany, and England together—France as the land of political revolt, Germany as the center of philosophy, and England as the seat of world finance.[19] As luck would have it, after Berlin, the last of these would be the next stop on Engels's journey of self-discovery.

In 1837 the Engels family had joined with the Ermen brothers in England to open cotton mills in Manchester, and Engels's father sent his eldest son there for the next part of his training. He would work in the Victoria Mills offices of Ermen & Engels in the city that was considered the industrial heart of the world. There was no better place for Engels to learn the business—or for the other Engels, the revolutionary, to learn how to overthrow the system.[20] On his way he stopped in Cologne to meet the editor of the *Rheinische Zeitung,* Karl Marx. But Marx dismissed him out of hand as a member of The Free, which he disdained, and the meeting was concluded quickly[21] (so much so that when the two reconnected in Paris, it was effectively the first time they had met).

When Engels arrived in Manchester in November 1842, on the eve of his twenty-second birthday, the town was recovering from a major workers' strike over wage cuts. The atmosphere was electric. The workers were some of the most downtrodden in the world, and yet under English law they had the freedom to assemble—and that gave them a glimmer of hope that they might be able to improve their lot.[22] But it would not be easy. One observer noted of Manchester at the time: "There is no town in the world where the distance between rich and poor is so great, or the barriers between them so difficult to be crossed."[23] Engels soon did so, however, with the help of a nineteen-year-old Irishwoman named Mary Burns.[24]

Mary worked in Engels's factory with her father and fifteen-year-old sister, Lydia (or Lizzy). It is unclear how Engels met Mary, whether it was at the factory or, as some biographers have suggested, after Engels spotted her selling oranges at the Hall of Science, a center for socialist lectures and events in Manchester. But wherever the meeting occurred, Engels was no doubt attracted by what friends described as Mary's wild beauty, wit, and native intelligence. The alliance was crucial for Engels. Mary introduced him to "Little Ireland" and other working-class districts in Manchester where gentry such as he would never travel, even to collect rent.[25] What he found there was no sanitation of any kind, a cesspool reeking of urine in which putrefied animals were left to rot, pigpens every twenty paces, and "mud so deep that there is no chance of walking without sinking ankle deep." The one- or two-room homes had mud floors. Engels said the filth and stench was so bad it would be "impossible for a human in any degree civilized to live in such a district."[26]

And yet, those were the homes where the workers in his father's factory, and factories like it, lived. And those were the workers whose labor would create the manufacturer's bright new future. Engels concluded that the only difference between slaves and factory workers was that slaves were sold for life, while the workers sold themselves day by day.[27] But like the workers, he saw some promise arising from the depths of such misery. Engels felt that the situation "brought home to their minds the necessity of a social reform by means of which machinery shall no longer work against them but for them."[28]

Mary also introduced Engels to numerous Irish and British radicals.[29] One, the Briton George Julian Harney, marveled at the "slender young man with a look of almost boyish immaturity who spoke remarkably pure English."[30] The rebel inside this seemingly harmless Prussian youth was on fire with indignation after his first weeks in Manchester. While working in his father's factory office, Engels began writing articles for British reform newspapers about conditions in Germany and sending letters to Germany about his findings among the workers in England. Marx published five of them in the *Rheinische Zeitung* in 1842, the author identified only as "X." The articles in Britain were generally signed "F. Engels."[31]

By 1843 Engels's education on the street had been augmented by a thorough reading of English economics, politics, and history. The result was his twenty-five-page "Outlines of a Critique of Political Economy," which was edited by Marx and published in Ruge's Paris newspaper in early 1844. That article was perhaps the earliest "Marxist" indictment of the still nascent capitalist system. In it Engels wrote that those who owned the machines created economic and social chaos by engaging in a cycle of overproduction followed by cutbacks, which forced wages lower, triggered social crisis, and inflamed class conflict. Labor-saving advances did not ease the plight of the worker, but were employed only to increase profits. Men were laid off because of the new machines, and those left on the job were expected to work just as hard—if not harder—to make up for the lost manpower. In that system, the capitalists' gains were dependent on the workers' losses.[32]

By the time they met in August 1844, Marx and Engels had reached the same conclusions but had arrived at them from different directions. At that point they agreed the best way forward was through propaganda. Engels planned to return to Germany to write a book on his time in England (it would become the classic *Condition of the Working Class in England*), while Marx would begin a book on political economy based on his studies that year. Before Engels left Paris in September, he wrote fifteen pages of a polemical pamphlet that he and Marx intended to author together, a document attacking the positions of some of their former associates. In their introduction Marx and Engels described the pamphlet as a kind of catharsis, after which they would undertake positive philosophical and social works. It would be their first joint publication. Marx called it *The Holy Family, or Critique of Critical Criticism.*[33]

Jenny returned to Paris to find Marx busily writing his portion of the pamphlet. She had not met the new friend who so energized her husband, but Marx was overflowing with Engels's stories of the Manchester factories and his inside description of how the industrial system operated. Marx was more convinced than ever that social theory could not exist apart from actual experience. Bruno Bauer made an easy target at just that moment, because he had argued in a recent publication that history was a force that directed men, and not the other way around. Bauer had also written that the involvement of the masses in the French Revolution had tainted the intellectual ideas upon which it was based and contributed to its failings. Finally, he had deigned to criticize Proudhon.[34]

Marx hoped to get the pamphlet published quickly, to counter Bauer and also to earn some money. That, in addition to more funds sent by Georg Jung from Cologne in July, would give him and Jenny enough to live on through the fall.[35] They would need it. At any moment Marx could be arrested or expelled if the Prussian government succeeded in persuading the French to extend punishment of the *Vowarts!* staff beyond Bernays. Marx was under intense pressure to finish his writing, which all but ensured that he would not. It took him until November to finish the first draft of his addition to Engels's fifteen pages.[36] When he had, Marx's section had grown to nearly three hundred pages, much of it rambling observations on a Gothic novel by the French author Eugène Sue.[37]

Marx had swerved wildly off course. This may have been caused by excitement over his association with Engels, whom he urged to return to Paris in November. (Engels said he could not: he was drowning in his book on the English working class, risked a falling-out with his family if he left, and had a love affair to clear up.)[38] Or it may have been a simple act of releasing steam. Over the past year Marx had built up a head full of ideas. *The Holy Family* reads in parts like an explosion.

By January Marx had still not completed the final draft, nor had he made any progress on his economic work. In a letter to him, Engels sounded very much like Jenny as he tried to coax his friend toward completion: "Do try and finish your political economy book, even if there's much in it that you yourself are still dissatisfied with, it doesn't really matter; minds are ripe and we must strike while the iron is hot... do as I do, set yourself a date by which you will definitely have finished, and make sure it gets into print quickly."[39]

That letter was dated January 20, 1845. Apparently Engels had not learned of the changes in Paris. Nine days earlier the French interior minister had issued an order giving select members of the *Vorwärts!* staff— Marx, Heine, Ruge, Bernays, and Bakunin among them—twenty-four hours to leave the city and slightly longer to depart France. Louis-Philippe had been persuaded to expel the "atheists" by noted Prussian scientist Alexander von Humboldt, who offered as tribute a rare porcelain vase from Friedrich Wilhelm. The French king—wanting peace so his government could prosper—gladly accepted the vase and tossed out the troublesome writers.[40] According to Jenny, a police commissioner came to their apartment on a Sunday armed with an expulsion order.[41]

The possibility that they would be forced out of France had been hanging over their heads for months, but nothing could have truly prepared them—especially Jenny—for the actual act. She had become a Parisian. Her world existed on the streets between the Place Saint-Germain and the Latin Quarter. Paris was where she and Karl had started their lives together as man and wife, it was where their daughter had been born, and it was where their friends lived. She wanted to stay, and the expulsion order offered just that possibility, if those named signed a statement promising they would engage in no further political activities. Everyone but Marx and Bakunin agreed to the conditions. An associate said Marx refused because "it conflicted with his pride to place himself voluntarily under police supervision."[42] Having tasted life outside repressive Prussia, Marx was not now inclined to surrender his freedom to write and speak.

Instead he tried to negotiate terms that would allow him and his family to remain in Paris, during which time the twenty-four-hour expulsion order was extended for nearly a month. But the government was adamant, as was Marx, and on February 2 he and the young journalist Heinrich Bürgers left Paris in a small stagecoach on a bumpy journey through the snow and sleet to Belgium. Bürgers described their lively conversation and his not entirely successful attempts to cheer up his traveling companion with song. The two arrived in Brussels on February 5, 1845.[43]

Jenny, her eight-month-old daughter, and a wet nurse who had come back with Jenny from Trier to care for Jennychen, stayed behind with the Herweghs. Streams of visitors came by to discuss the expulsions and their efforts to stop them, and to generally offer help.[44] She wrote to Marx that Bakunin, who was still trying to convince the government to allow him to remain in Paris, "came and gave me a lesson in rhetoric and drama in order to unbosom himself to me," and that the German journalist Alexander Weill made himself her "special protector." The main help she needed, however, was financial. Jenny was trying to collect enough money to cover debts and pay for the trip to Brussels. Karl had given her 200 francs, but the back rent alone was 380. She wrote him on February 10, "I don't know what we're going to do. This morning I traipsed all over Paris. The Mint was closed and I shall have to go again. Then I visited the carriers and the agent of a furniture auctioneer. I had no success anywhere." Sending "a thousand kisses from mama to papa, and a little kiss from the Munsterchen," she signed off, "Adieu my friend. I long to see you again.... Best greeting to our new fatherland."[45]

Within days she had sold their furniture for what she described as a ridiculously small sum and quit Paris. "Ill and in bitter cold weather, I followed Karl to Brussels," Jenny recalled.[46] She did not know that this would be only the first of many such moves. The Marx family's life on the run had begun.

8

Brussels, Spring 1845

I have seldom known so happy a marriage in which joy and
suffering . . . were shared and all sorrow overcome in the
consciousness of full and mutual dependency.

—Stephan Born[1]

TINY BELGIUM WAS an island of princely benevolence in a sea of repressive
monarchs. It had been an independent country only since it had broken
off from Holland fifteen years earlier, and though it had a king, it also had
a constitution, which was considered the most liberal in continental
Europe. What it lacked in excitement (Brussels compared with Paris felt
more like a town than a city), it made up for in freedom. All King Leopold I asked of refugees settling within his borders was that they refrain
from direct political activity and propagandizing that might annoy Belgium's much larger and more powerful neighbors.[2] Similar conditions had
not been acceptable to Marx in Paris, but for personal and professional
reasons he agreed to them in Belgium. Not only was another baby on the
way, but on the day he left Paris he had signed a contract to write a book
on political economy.[3]

Marx wrote Leopold two letters asking, as "your majesty's most humble and obedient servant," to be allowed to live with his wife and child in
Belgium, and agreeing "to pledge myself on my word of honor, not to
publish in Belgium any work on current politics."[4] Leopold accepted, and
the Marxes were allowed to establish residence in the Belgian kingdom.[5]
That did not mean, however, that they would be left entirely unsuper-
vised; Belgian authorities had been alerted by the French about the Prussian agitator in their midst. A note from the chief of police to the mayor of

Brussels read, "Should it come to your knowledge that he has broken his word and is taking any other action prejudicial to the Prussian government, our neighbor and ally, I request you to report to me forthwith."[6] The suspicion was soon justified. In the land where Marx vowed not to write anything political, he would produce arguably the most revolutionary treatise of the nineteenth century, the *Communist Manifesto*. But that was still a future endeavor. When he arrived in Belgium, Marx did try to keep his word.

For her part Jenny seemed to have anticipated a more settled existence in Brussels than she and Marx had had so far. Before he left France she had given her husband a detailed list of requirements for the accommodations she hoped he would find. It is amusing to imagine Marx, expelled for advocating the murder of kings, traveling through the countryside by stagecoach with a list in his pocket that instructed him to pay careful attention to cupboards—"they play an important role in the life of a housewife"—but not to worry overly about kitchen utensils. He should find a house with "four rooms and a kitchen, plus a room to hide all the objects and valises. Three rooms ought to be heated....Our room doesn't necessarily have to be elegant. It would be a good thing if this room, as well as that for your work, was furnished, however modestly." She left it to her "noble protector" to resolve how best to store the books.[7] In imagining such a home in Brussels, Jenny may have been reacting to the shock of expulsion. Perhaps by planting deep domestic, if not bourgeois, roots she was trying to protect the family from another knock at the door by another constable bearing an order for them to leave. Or, expecting her second child, she may simply have sensed that their bohemian life was ending.

But when Jenny reached Brussels in late February, she discovered that their rootless life was far from over: Karl still had not found them a permanent place to live. She, Jennychen, and the wet nurse joined Marx at the Bois Sauvage boardinghouse on the Place St. Gudule in the very heart of the city. Dwarfed by the Cathedral St. Michel, which towered above it as a constant reminder of the terrific power of Marx's enemy the Church, the Bois Sauvage was hardly the home Jenny had dreamed of, but it was a favorite stop for German refugees, who were not as numerous in Brussels as in Paris—only several hundred, compared with an estimated eighty thousand in the French capital.[8] In this smaller grouping bonds were easily established, fellow travelers quickly became friends.

In Paris the Marxes' social life had been full of high drama, both political and personal, as befitted that great stage. Their early days in Brussels were much quieter, but also much richer. Through the years the circle around Marx was often disparaged by his enemies as the "Marx party," a label that suggested an organization with significant numbers. But no such collection ever existed, and even those people who used the phrase knew they were really only referring to Marx's close associates and family. True, that inner circle shared a common ideology, but the men and women around Marx and Jenny were also bound by affection. Most of these so-called party members came together for the first time in mid-1840s Brussels.

The day after Marx arrived in the city he set out to find the poet Ferdinand Freiligrath, to apologize to him for the way he had been treated by the *Rheinische Zeitung* when Marx had been editing the paper three years earlier. At that time Freiligrath (who was also a businessman and thus an inspiration to the young Engels) was one of Germany's most popular poets. His initial following was based not on politics—as with Herwegh—but on the sheer beauty of his work. He argued poets should not be involved in social questions and had a public spat with Herwegh over the issue. In 1842 Freiligrath was awarded an annual pension from the Prussian king and subsequently denounced by the *Rheinische Zeitung* as a paid enemy of freedom.[9]

Over the next two years, however, as the Prussian government became more reactionary, Freiligrath's poems became politicized. In 1844 his book *Patriotic Fantasies* was banned. He renamed it *Confession of Faith* and in the preface renounced his royal pension. The king was furious, the book was deemed illegal, and Freiligrath fled to exile in Belgium. He and his wife, Ida, were living quietly in Brussels, trying to decide their next move, when the Marxes arrived. Immediately the families established warm relations.[10] Freiligrath, who was eight years older than Marx, called his new friend a "nice, interesting, unassuming, resolute fellow."[11]

The Freiligraths, however, soon moved to Switzerland, and the Marxes abandoned the Bois Sauvage for the house they had vacated. In May the Marxes moved again, to a suburb east of Brussels near the Porte de Louvain.[12] With nearly 1,000 francs sent to them from Engels, Jung, and other supporters in the Rhineland, they were able to pay a year's rent and settle into a home (owned by a Belgian democrat) on the rue de l'Alliance, in a working-class neighborhood that also featured a library.[13] The house was a dreary affair compared with their rue Vaneau residence in Paris. It was a soot-darkened, three-story building on a street dotted with market stalls and the workshops of small craftsmen. But Jenny did not seem discouraged by her humble quarters, a colony of friends having begun to form around them. Bürgers, the journalist who had traveled to Brussels with Marx, moved nearby,[14] as did another German journalist, Karl Heinzen, whom Marx had known in Cologne (and had once taken hostage during a drunken episode).[15] Moses Hess and his lover Sibylle Pesch, an uneducated working-class woman he'd met in Cologne, rented a house two doors down from the Marxes,[16] and the socialist-leaning ex-Prussian lieutenant Joseph Weydemeyer (whom Marx called Weywey) moved in with Jenny and Karl for a period.[17] But the two most important friends—who would in fact become family—arrived in April. One was Helene Demuth and the other, Engels.

Helene, known to the Marx family by many names but most often as Lenchen, was six years younger than Jenny and two years younger than Marx. She was from a village near Trier, one of seven children born to a baker and his wife. Lenchen had worked as a housemaid for the Westphalen family from the time she was a girl of about eleven and essentially grew up with Jenny, her brother Edgar, and Karl—albeit as a servant attending to the master's children, among her other duties.[18] In April 1845 Jenny's mother sent twenty-five-year-old Lenchen to Brussels to help Jenny because she was concerned about her daughter's ability to care for one infant with another on the way. She told Jenny she was sending the best she could, short of coming herself.[19] The blond-haired, blue-eyed Lenchen took over management of the house, giving Jenny more time to help Karl with his work and prepare for the baby. It is unclear what Lenchen's politics were when she arrived in Brussels, if indeed she ever expressed them, but she was quickly absorbed into the circle of communists and socialists around Marx and Jenny, and participated fully in their social life. From the spring of 1845 Lenchen was as much a member of the Marx family as those born into it. In return she offered them blind devotion. One colleague said though she had many marriage offers over the years, she always chose the Marxes over her suitors.[20]

The timing of Lenchen's arrival was fortunate: she was there to ensure the smooth running of the household just as Engels appeared to disrupt it. Engels had rented the house next door to the Marxes but by all accounts spent most of his waking hours in their home.[21] Since he'd left Paris eight months earlier, Engels had been with his family in Barmen, finishing his book *Condition of the Working Class in England* (in which, he told Marx, he accused the English bourgeoisie of murder, robbery, and other crimes on a mass scale in their factories) and fighting with his father. Everything the son had become was objectionable to the father, and to placate him, the younger man agreed to go back to work while he was home.[22] But, he wrote Marx, "I was sick of it all even before I began work; huckstering is too beastly, Barmen is too beastly, the waste of time is too beastly and most beastly of all is the fact of being, not only a bourgeois, but actually a manufacturer, a bourgeois who actively takes sides against the proletariat. A few days in my old man's factory have sufficed to bring me face to face with this beastliness, which I had rather overlooked."[23]

He quit his job, told his father he wanted nothing more to do with the factory, and with Moses Hess began agitating around the Rhineland on behalf of communism.[24] Engels's activities, however, soon drew the attention of police, who described him in a report as a "rabid communist who wanders about as a man of letters."[25] His father feared an arrest warrant would be issued and shame the entire family, so rather than suffer that fate, he gave his renegade son the funds to escape to Brussels—which worked out nicely, because that was exactly where he wanted to go anyway.[26]

Before he arrived, Engels declared in a letter to Marx that he was anxious to put "theoretical twaddle" aside and turn to real things and real men.[27] His book on the English working class was to be published in Germany in May, and he told Marx he would gladly give him his royalties to help ease the family's financial burden; he would have enough money from his father to live on.[28] In the meantime he was ready for work and rabble-rousing in equal measure. He had been so well behaved in Barmen, Engels said "I fear that the Almighty may overlook my writings and admit me to heaven."[29]

Marx was thrilled to have his high-spirited companion at his side, and Jenny was happy to finally meet this man six years her junior. (Engels had so far known her only as a rather forbidding-sounding "Madame Marx.") If Engels planned to work with Karl, he would also have to work with Jenny. She was truly the right hand she had hoped to be when she had fantasized that Marx would be wounded in a duel and lose his ability to write. And all of this was easier now that their home had become the center of activity for their friends, which meant that Marx no longer went out to meetings as he did in Paris—the meetings came to him, and her. Stephan Born, a twenty-three-year-old German typesetter they met in Brussels, noted, "I have seldom known so happy a marriage in which joy and suffering were shared and all sorrow overcome in the consciousness of full and mutual dependency. Moreover I have seldom known a woman who in outward appearance as well as in spirit, was so well balanced and so immediately captivating as Mrs. Marx."[30]

Their little colony lived together harmoniously and sympathetically, Jenny recalled, sharing their meager resources. The success of one, she said, was the success of all. They dined together, danced together, and drank together under the cascading chandeliers of Brussels's grand cafés.[31]

There the Germans also met political refugees from other countries, who told the same stories of growing want and despair back home.

There seemed to be a curse on Europe in 1845. Bad grain harvests and a potato blight that began in Ireland had spread to the Continent, devastating food supplies. Rural populations were faced with the wrenching decision of staying on land that could no longer feed them or leaving all they had ever known for strange new homes among strange new people. Either path could lead to starvation. Tens of thousands of Europeans who could afford a ticket chose to emigrate. More than one hundred thousand moved to the United States alone in 1845, the first in a series of record-breaking years for such immigration. But most of those who abandoned their fields did not travel as far; they descended by droves on Europe's increasingly overcrowded urban centers.[32] Roads connecting the countryside to the towns were clogged with cartloads of families and their belongings, or single stragglers carrying everything they owned on their backs. Food shortages increased as the number of these small farmers dwindled.[33] Disease was rife. Crime, vice, and child trafficking became boom industries, and the threat of riots grew as the agricultural depression deepened and spread.[34]

At the very time that agriculture was beginning to suffer, the gears of commerce shifted into overdrive. Europe's population had grown by nearly 40 percent since 1800, and industrialists worked as quickly as they could to supply that huge market. In the past, goods had been made to meet demand, but now the production process was so much cheaper and faster that profit-hungry manufacturers no longer waited for customers to ask for their goods. Instead they created their own markets, and if there were not enough local consumers to buy what they had to sell, they used the new railways and steamships to dispatch their products all over the world. There was no end, so they thought, to the potential for commerce. This mentality was especially prevalent in England, the most industrialized country in the world. There the question for those who could afford it was no longer "What do I need?" but rather "What do I want?"—and the gulf between those who asked that question and the rest of the population had grown alarmingly vast.[35]

Accelerated commerce did create jobs, but the new factories and expanded mines did not produce enough of them to satisfy the growing population, and they did not necessarily employ the men who had been forced by mechanization or competition to abandon long-held trades. Women and children were often the first to be hired, because they worked for a fraction of the cost of men. Further, the work created by the factories and mines did not provide the kind of security and stability families had always known. These families had worked for the same master or in the same trade or on the same land for generations. Their lives had been hard, but their very beings had been part of the fabric of their community, part of the soil. Now jobs were awarded and retained at the whim of a new creature called a foreman, often an outsider loyal solely to his employer. Conditions on the factory floor also had to be considered: workers were haunted by the very real prospect of injury or death. With twelve- to eighteen-hour workdays six and a half days a week, factory families lived to work and worked to survive.

These unfortunates, and the millions like them who had yet to make their way into the industrial system, were far more numerous than the people who enjoyed its riches. But they were the most easily ignored—they were downright invisible, a voiceless, powerless, leaderless, illiterate mass. There were some on the periphery, however, mostly artisans such as tailors, cabinetmakers, and printers, who witnessed the misery of these people whose lives, whose society, had been turned upside down. There were also intellectuals who did not know these workers—this proletariat—but knew of their plight. In coffee shops and taverns and halls throughout Europe, artisans and intellectuals debated a myriad of social changes aimed at alleviating it.

Indeed the same easy transport that had helped expand commerce also helped spread ideas of reform. Literacy levels still ranked below 50 percent in most of Europe, but there was a hunger for knowledge. Books had become international, and authors like Balzac, Victor Hugo, and Dickens, who described society—from the manor house to the gutter—in a new realistic style, were recognized as universal writers. Their works were discussed excitedly in drawing rooms and clubs that had previously known only local authors.[36] Newspapers, too, moved more quickly from one capital to another, evading local censors employed to ensure that nothing a particular king wanted to keep from the public made it off the printing press. Even in Russia, where the most repressive ruler in Europe, Czar Nicholas I, had established twelve censorship agencies, foreign newspapers made their way into the hands of average citizens.[37] Marx's friend Pavel Annenkov said of the phenomenon, "What had previously constituted a privilege of the highest aristocratic and governmental spheres now became a common practice."[38]

Perhaps most dangerous of all, however, were the traveling men and women who, like Trojan horses, carried revolutionary notions in their heads and hearts. Unlike the emigrants who uprooted themselves to begin a new life abroad, many others, members of Europe's educated class, traveled on business or to continue their studies. They left their homes for short-term stays elsewhere and in the process were introduced to new ideas and a wider worldview. A cross-pollination began that saw French and American lessons of democracy transported all the way to St. Petersburg and the intricacies of English business debated in Milan. Throughout Europe a buzz of excitement greeted the new concepts socialism and communism, which proponents said would correct social ills and rescue those left without food, shelter, or work due to disasters natural and manmade. And as leaders from groups exiled by their governments met in foreign capitals, one could detect in the tone of their talks a perceptible shift from national to international concerns.[39]

Demonstrations of discontent were rare in Europe at that time: workers seemed to have no idea how to contend with the insidious and mammoth force called industry. But there had been the Silesian workers' revolt the year before (which Engels felt marked the beginning of the active working-class movement), and in late March 1845, one hundred people were killed in Lucerne, Switzerland, when a simmering political-religious dispute erupted into violence.[40] To those calling for social reform such incidents were increasingly emblematic.

Crowned heads around Europe also took note. Society was changing for them, too. Previous threats had come from other monarchs, with wars fought over land or honor or religion. But since the eighteenth century's revolutions in America and France, and their more recent aftershocks in 1830, the danger was less predictable and the goal was often a pesky notion of human rights. The threat to a ruler might still come from a rival throne, but it could also arise from an enlightened nobility, a bourgeois intellectual, or a shopkeeper wearing a blouse and red sash.

Europe was headed into uncharted territory. The relatively simple social structure that had prevailed for centuries, in which the decisions of kings and princes went unchallenged and all members of a society were bound to (if not owned by) their betters, appeared increasingly battered. But what would replace it? In fact, it *was* possible to visit the future of continental Europe. All it took was a trip across the English Channel. Engels had been there, and in the summer of 1845 he brought along a companion: Karl Marx.

9

London, 1845

*We can't say what this luck of the world is. I'm obliged to strive
very hard—very hard indeed, sir, now, to get a living; and then
not to get it after all—at times, compelled to go short, often.*

—Street performer[1]

IN THE SPRING before he and Engels left for England, Marx began sketching out ideas for a book they would write together that would get them past the "theoretical twaddle" and illustrate once and for all that to have meaning, ideas—be they religious, political, or economic—must be rooted in the real world.[2] German intellectuals in particular had been confined to the loftiest realms of philosophy out of necessity, because the government banned them from discussing or publishing anything that might be recognizably pertinent to daily life. Even the socialists used vague words like "humanity" and "suffering" to obscure their intended meanings—man and starvation. But Marx and Engels argued conditions required that the theoretical veil be lifted and the material truth exposed. In his eleven-point *Theses on Feuerbach,* written at this time, Marx famously summed up the problem: "Philosophers have only *interpreted* the world in various ways; the point is to *change* it."[3] With that call to action, and a 1,500-franc advance Marx had received for his book on political economy (which he still hadn't started), he and Engels prepared to set off for England.[4]

Jenny decided to return to Trier with Lenchen and the baby while Karl was away. She was six months pregnant, which would make travel difficult, but her mother had been having a terrible time with Jenny's brother Edgar. After years of dithering, he had finally taken his law exams but seemed no closer to settling down or finding a job. While studying in Cologne he was caught up in radical circles and merrily drained his mother's purse for what he declared was the cause of the revolution and the sufferings of society, but in actuality funded a quite active social life and frequent nights at the opera. Jenny, who had loved her brother dearly when he was a boy, told Marx she found it difficult to be tender toward him now. Edgar was considering an extended visit to Brussels, which Jenny probably hoped would relieve some of her mother's burden by making this "scatterbrain" her responsibility.[5] She set off east by coach for Trier, saying good-bye to Karl and Engels, who departed in July in the opposite direction.

During most of their six weeks in England, the two men stayed in Manchester. Nearly five hundred thousand people worked in England's textile trade, and that city was its epicenter. For a social scientist, it was quite simply the laboratory of the industrial world. By the time Marx and Engels arrived, the full transformation from a home-based textile industry to a mass-scale factory system had occurred. The small artisan master—who by social tradition took care of his workers with varying degrees of benevolence until those workers became masters themselves—had been almost entirely replaced by a faceless company with no obligations to its employees beyond a wage set low enough to ensure maximum profit. Man was no longer a man, but an appendage to a machine. Indeed he was no longer even the head of his own family; that, too, belonged to the factory.[6]

Marx and Engels's studies involved days at the Chetham Library, the oldest public library in Britain, where they escaped the rain of black soot outside to sit in a wood-paneled alcove surrounded by stained-glass windows, reviewing the works of British economists such as David Ricardo, Adam Smith, David Hume, and Sir William Petty—all of whom surfaced in later Marx and Engels writings. At night they prowled the pubs where middle-class businessmen socialized, or met up with Mary Burns and visited crowded workers' districts[7] that pulsed with activity at all hours, especially on Saturday nights, when workers lined up to be paid. There was a madness then, when a week's hard labors were miraculously changed into silver and copper. For a moment the hand that held the coins also held the promise of freedom, but sometimes factories paid the workers in a pub, and their weekly earnings never made it past the door. Those men and women succumbed to the illusion that their work had earned them happiness. Others took their precious pence directly to the market, which operated from ten at night to midnight, to buy provisions. But even from a distance, the sprawling marketplace looked and smelled like hell on earth:

row upon row of stalls were lit by the smoky red flame of grease lamps, and all that was on offer was the rotting produce and spoiled offal that had been rejected by more prosperous shoppers earlier in the day. Mired in a carpet of mud and swill, it was yet another hideous reminder of the depths to which those who lived in these districts had sunk.[8]

In the workers' residential area, low cottages consisting of two rooms, a cellar, and a garret housed an average of twenty people each, with one outdoor toilet for every 120 residents. The stench of human and animal excrement was pervasive; houses were packed so tightly the wind could not reach the courtyards to blow away the foul odor.[9] Those who worked in the mills worked on cotton, and cotton was what they wore in all seasons, wool being too dear. Clothes that still bore a suggestion of color were considered evidence of wealth—most workers' garments had been washed so often they exhibited mere hints of their original hues. Workingmen could not afford hats to protect them from the perpetual cold rain, so they wore sodden paper fashioned into caps. Gloves, stockings—such accouterments did not even register in the vocabulary of the workers' districts. Shoes, too, were an extravagance; men, women, and children went barefoot year round.[10]

In this desperate world, family life disintegrated. Mothers who had to work but had no one to care for their youngest children gave the infants opium to keep them sedated until they returned. Girls as young as twelve were "married" off to ease the family's financial burden, and boys as young as six began their lives on the street for the same reason. Fathers who had once enjoyed the dignity of supporting their loved ones now competed against their teenage sons for work that earned them a pittance. Sickness was one more luxury the poor could not afford; death was considered preferable and more merciful than injury or disease, because a hurt or ill worker meant another burden on already broken families.[11] Indeed, funerals for the poor, especially the Irish poor, were raucous affairs in honor of the lucky one who'd passed on. The frantic fiddles and crush of bodies dancing jigs and reels inside the house of mourning helped the living briefly blot out the wretchedness of their own continued existence.

If it was reality Marx sought, he found it in Manchester. Before this trip he had never actually witnessed proletarian life, and it is unlikely that anything he had experienced thus far could have prepared him for the debasement of humanity he saw there. He had met workers in Paris, but had only heard their stories. Now he was knee-deep in industrial waste, both physical and spiritual. The sights, smells, and anguished sounds of that place would have been shocking. Marx was, after all, a middle-class intellectual married to an aristocrat, who traveled in cultured circles. Though he had long criticized those who led with theory, the truth was that he had done the same. No longer.[12]

The two friends left Manchester after about a month and a half and traveled to London to witness yet another face of this new industrial society. They found the capital so crowded it was difficult to walk, and yet, Engels said, one had the sense of being alone and surrounded by indifference.[13] In Manchester the rich took pains not to see the poor—the city was laid out in such a way that the wealthier classes could live without actually having to encounter poverty.[14] In London no such effort had been made. Rich and poor shared the same streets, but it was as if they were two different species, so far apart socially they did not exist for each other except as objects of exploitation. The poor stole what they could from the rich, and the rich stole what they could from the working poor—one act called crime, the other, industry.

London's already teeming slums had swelled that year because of the Irish famine, and many of the diminished new arrivals hardly appeared human. The old women sitting on wet ground in London's alleyways looked more like heaps of rag; only the pipe smoke rising from under their hoods indicated that a person inhabited the space. The children, dressed in tatters, were so covered in grime it was often impossible to tell their age or sex.[15] The more prosperous of the Irish immigrants had come from stone cottages, but most knew only dirt huts, their skin thickened and grooved by their native land's bitter weather and colored brown from washing in the tannin-dyed waters that rushed down Ireland's hills. They were resented even by fellow countrymen who had already carved out an existence in London, because they worked for wages that even the most desperate among them would not consider, and because they took up precious space.[16]

In Manchester the workers' districts spread like weeds along the length of the river, but in London the slums were vertical, and the poor crammed the four-story houses from cellar to garret. Every inch, including the staircase, was occupied.[17] Some people rented only a place in a bed, not even the whole bed. Others rented space on a rope strung along the wall, where they could sleep sitting up. Boys and girls, men and women, strangers piled together in a mass of humanity each night, looking for the warmth and rest that the upper classes took for granted.[18] Because of that crowding, and because more people were competing for even less work, the level of depravity in London was immeasurably worse than in Manchester. The sex industry where the poor congregated in Soho Square, St. Giles, and the Strand, was legendary. Young children mimicking adults uttered vile propositions to any passerby who might give them a farthing.[19]

Those children, whose families had been driven off their farms or out of their villages for lack of food and work, had learned how to survive in the street. They were the resilient proletariat of the slums. Society asked what they had to sell, and they answered, like those in the factories in Manchester, with the only thing that belonged to them—their bodies.

Marx and Engels toured the city and met up with Germans and Britons working on behalf of these poor. Some were members of the secret League of the Just, which Marx had first encountered in Paris and which operated in London at the Red Lion Pub in Soho, under the benign name German Workers' Educational Association.[20] Its leaders were Karl Schapper, Heinrich Bauer, and Joseph Moll. Engels, who had originally encountered them in 1843, said they were the "first revolutionary proletarians whom I met...I shall never forget the deep impression that these three real men made upon me who was then still only wanting to become a man."[21]

The league used the Educational Association as a cover to recruit members. There were branches in Switzerland and Germany as well, and as suspicion fell on the Educational Association, the Germans started choral societies and athletic clubs, anything they could do to attract additional members for their underground league.[22] By 1845 membership had reached only about three hundred. Little by little, however, the organization had begun to include non-Germans, so the overarching group was now called the Communist Workers' Educational Association. Its membership cards, printed in twenty languages, read "All men are brothers." However, Engels noted, these branches were composed almost entirely of artisans—the aristocracy of the labor force—many of whom aspired to be masters themselves.[23]

The English radical or reform movement, by contrast, had included a healthy mix of workers and artisans as far back as 1792, when a shoemaker founded the London Corresponding Society to press for voting rights. (For his efforts Thomas Hardy was charged with high treason, disemboweled while still alive, and then hanged.) Because England had industrialized earlier than other nations, the study of this new system was most mature there.[24] In 1820 Robert Owen, the first British socialist, had argued that workers possessed a form of currency—labor—that was woefully undervalued, and since then, English radicals had conceived of labor in both qualitative and quantifiable terms.[25] They held manufacturers directly responsible for the exploitative system, but they also looked to the source of their capital and found the same wealthy landowners and provincial merchants who had long controlled Parliament. These men were financing the new industry with an eye toward lucrative monetary returns while ensuring the continuation of their power. So far they had succeeded on both counts, but not without challenges.[26]

In 1830, when Europe was experiencing uprisings in France and Poland, workers in Manchester attempted to gather all laborers under an umbrella union to push for political reform—including universal male suffrage—to end the stranglehold of the upper class. But two years later, when the Reform Act was passed, Parliament sidestepped them, expanding suffrage only to select members of the middle class. Workers were effectively cut out of the political bargain.[27] Far from spelling defeat, however, the setback accelerated union formation. By 1833 one organization had at least half a million members.[28] Workers also awakened to the fact that they as a group had a distinct place in society, that they formed a class of men, the *working class*. Bronterre O'Brien, a radical propagandist, sounded their note of defiance: "From the laws of the few have the existing inequalities sprung; by the laws of the many shall they be destroyed."[29]

In 1837 British labor agitators presented the House of Commons with six demands, which came to be known the following year as the People's Charter, calling for top-to-bottom political reform ultimately aimed at making Parliament accessible to all male British citizens.[30] But within five years the Charter movement was dying, the six points repeatedly rejected. By 1845 Chartists were looking for increased cooperation with workers in France and Germany in order to survive.[31]

It was at that moment that Marx and Engels met in London with leaders of the English workingmen's movement, most notably George Julian Harney, a Chartist leader and editor of the London-based *Northern Star* newspaper, and Ernest Jones, also a Chartist, who would remain Marx's and Engels's friend for life.[32] Engels, who acted as translator for Marx, recalled that those involved in the talks came away convinced that the various movements—Chartism, socialism, and communism—were manifestations of the same historical struggle by the proletariat against the bourgeoisie.[33]

Marx and Engels learned much from these German and English veteran revolutionaries, who instructed the two younger men not only on the history of their movements but on the practical aspects of organizing. The pair returned to Belgium fired up with ideas for radicalizing the workingman in Brussels and beyond.

Behind his severe and notoriously scornful public facade, Marx had a depth of feeling for his fellow man that his detractors may not have recognized. Many of his contemporaries would remark that Marx had more hate in him than love. Looking at his life, however, it is clear he had a healthy dose of each, and it is impossible to imagine that both passions weren't stirred mightily by what he saw in England. Marx came away from his trip a changed man. The words he knew so well from the texts he had read, words he himself had repeated, had new meaning. The words had faces.

One other important aspect of the trip worth mentioning is that it solidified Marx and Engels's friendship. They had spent ten days together in Paris a year before, but since then had communicated mostly in letters and seen each other as part of a larger group. Traveling together in England, they found they were entirely sympathetic not only intellectually but also personally. Most of those Marx had worked and socialized with to that point were many years his senior. Except for Herwegh and Bakunin, he had largely been surrounded by men from another generation. But he and Engels spoke the same language, their historical starting points were similar, and their outlooks were based on common, though far from identical, experiences.

As intellectuals they were brilliant, incisive, prescient, and creative (but also elitist, cantankerous, impatient, and conspiratorial). As friends they were bawdy, foulmouthed, and adolescent. They loved to smoke (Engels a pipe, Marx cigars), drink until dawn (Engels fine wine and ale, Marx whatever was available), gossip (mostly about the sexual proclivities of their acquaintances), and roar with laughter (usually at the expense of their enemies, and in Marx's case until tears streamed down his cheeks).

Now the best of friends, the two men traveled back to Brussels with new focus and energy. Marx brought with him the ferocious clarity that tends to accompany revelation. Engels brought something more earthly: his "wife"—Mary Burns.

10

Brussels, 1846

Life involves before everything else eating and drinking, housing, clothing and various other things. The first historical act is thus the production of the means to satisfy these needs, the production of material life itself.

—Karl Marx[1]

JENNY RETURNED TO what she called their "colony of paupers" in Brussels in late September, just in time to have her second child. She had put off her return journey from Trier until the last minute because she did not want to abandon her mother. Edgar had finally left home for Brussels, where he planned to stay for several months before heading to the United States to try his hand at business, and Caroline von Westphalen was now very much alone.[2] Jenny discovered that this woman who so loved company had retreated deeper and deeper into her home and her memories. Her finances had long since been depleted, and she rarely went out into society. With neither wealth nor a husband of rank, she was relegated to the shadows of the world that had once embraced her. She was a sixty-year-old widow, discarded like so many others.

Jenny was intensely devoted to her mother and may have feared she too would be discarding her if she left Trier. Angrily, she wrote Karl about the plight of women in society, defending women against men, even against her and her husband's own radical ideology. Rights were discussed endlessly in their circle, but they were first and foremost the rights of men. The equal rights for women the Romantics had advocated were apparently a fight for another day. In her broad indictment she also revealed frustration over their expulsion from France and their insecure position in

93

Brussels. And while she was at it, Jenny defended the homeland they both reviled.

I feel altogether too much at ease here in little Germany! Though to say so in the face of you arch anti-Germans calls for a deal of courage, does it not? ... One can live quite happily in this old land of sinners. At all events it was in glorious France and Belgium that I first made acquaintance with the pettiest and meanest of conditions. People are petty here, infinitely so, life as a whole is a pocket edition, but there heroes are not giants either, nor is the individual one jot better off. For men it may be different, but for a woman, whose destiny is to have children, to sew, to cook and to mend, I commend miserable Germany.[3]

There was never any doubt Jenny would return to Brussels, nor any evidence she truly believed Germany was the place where she could be most fulfilled as a woman, mother, and wife. On the contrary, when the possibility arose years later for the Marxes to return to Berlin, Jenny was adamantly opposed to the idea. If anything, her letter displayed the frustration she felt in having to choose between her duty as a daughter and her duty as a wife. But circumstances cut short any extended internal debate. When she wrote Karl in August, she was eight months pregnant. If she wanted to have her child in Brussels, she had to leave Trier quickly.

Karl's socialist friends in Germany offered to accompany her along the way, handing her off like a delicate parcel to the next escort at various coach stops and inns on her journey through the forests and fields of western Prussia. Her main concern, she said, was to have as many breaks as possible "for the joggling might well have unpleasant consequences." She asked Karl to meet her, Lenchen, and Jennychen about fifty miles into Belgium at Liège and accompany them on to Brussels.[4] The travelers thus arrived at the rue de l'Alliance two weeks before Jenny gave birth, on September 26, to another daughter. The child was named Laura after Jenny's sister, who had died as a toddler.[5]

Before the baby's delivery, Jenny had been concerned the commotion might disrupt Karl's work. She wrote, "If only the great catastrophe did not take place at the very time when you are finishing off your book, the publication of which I anxiously await." She arranged to have the infant on the top floor of the house, and the children were eventually quartered downstairs so Karl could write undisturbed on the middle floor in his study and what she jokingly called their immense—though unheated—salon.[6] There were many reasons Jenny wanted to see his book (known among them simply as his "political economy") published, from the long-overdue praise she believed it would bring her husband to its ability to advance debate and speed political reform. But perhaps most immediately, their finances depended upon it: she and Karl had no other income, and while their friends had been generous so far, the couple could not (nor did they want to) rely on future kindness.

Throughout his life Marx was a great dissembler when describing the progress of his work. In response to questions about writing he should have completed, he would often say he was a week or two from finishing, or busy polishing the final draft, or that he had encountered a financial or personal setback that delayed him but was now back on track. Most often he was nowhere near completion. New ideas clashed with existing ones to produce something he was convinced was wonderfully unexpected and important. Under such circumstances how could he tell his mind to simply stop so that he could sit down to write? Imagine what he might be missing if he did! In this case it seemed that Marx hadn't told Jenny his book would not be published anytime soon because it was still in the conceptual phase—that is, in his head. Over the years Jenny would learn that for her husband, the much cherished and sought after book contract was in fact debilitating. She could quite literally see his mental torment as his body erupted in painful boils because of the pressure. But those discoveries would come much later. In 1845 Jenny still believed a deadline meant that the work would be completed on time and that they could rely on its resulting income.

Marx was in fact writing, but not on his political economy. At about the time of Laura's birth, with the cries of the newborn filling the house, he and Engels began work on a book they called *The German Ideology.*

Marx had actually started considering *The German Ideology* in the spring, in his *Theses on Feuerbach.* But by the fall, fresh from their English trip, the two men were prepared to finally consign all German philosophy to the trash heap, and along with it German socialism as it was being propagated at that time. Karl told his anxious publisher, Karl Leske, who was waiting for the overdue economic book, it would be impossible to produce that text without first demolishing all that had gone before it, especially the Young Hegelians.[7] It might seem that Marx had slain that dragon countless times already, but he thought otherwise, and he and Engels set out to do it together.

The German Ideology laid out for the first time, in basic terms starting with the advent of man, Marx's notion of the material basis of human history. Marx and Engels argued that contrary to what Hegel and his progeny believed, history was not guided by a force separate from man, it *was* man, the story of man, a chronicle of his actions. To believe otherwise, to make man a mere player in a drama directed by a greater power (whether movement, God, or king), was to render him impotent and obscure his ability to see himself as a capable actor in the society of his fellow man. They argued that all life, all death, all change—political, economic, and social—arose from very tangible circumstances. There was no mystery, no need for mankind to look elsewhere for answers.[8]

Addressing the problem "scientifically," which is to say assessing evidence found in real life, they determined that man's existence was rooted in the process of *production,* that indeed, man distinguished himself from animals as soon as he began to produce his means of subsistence.[9] (They also proclaimed, cries from Marx's top floor surely in mind, that the first division of productive labor was between a man and a woman for child breeding.)[10] Subsequently, they wrote, each generation stood on the shoulders of the previous one by using improvements in the methods of production to develop itself and modify society according to changed needs.[11] But at a certain stage "destructive forces" are introduced, when machinery and money are consolidated under the control of a few men as private property. That elite in turn gives rise to its opposite, a class "which has to bear all the burdens of society without enjoying its advantages...a class which forms the majority of all members of society, and from which emanates the consciousness of the necessity of a fundamental revolution, the communist consciousness."[12]

Marx and Engels concluded that all revolutionary historical change was the result of clashes between those who controlled production at any point and the mass of people subjected to their control.[13] Presaging Marx's future emphasis on education and understanding as necessary precursors to revolution, they suggested that real, lasting change could not occur as a result of violence alone: simply eliminating the ruling elite by force would not erase the "universal truths" its members had enshrined—their laws, their art, their hallowed institutions.

> The ideas of the ruling class are in every epoch the ruling ideas; i.e., the class which is the ruling *material* force of society, is at the same time its ruling *intellectual* force. The class which has the means of material production at its disposal, consequently also controls the means of mental production, so that the ideas of those who lack the means of mental production are on the whole subject to it.[14]

Therefore, in order to reach the point of revolution, the masses had first to recognize that the system under which they lived—no matter how entrenched or supposedly divine—was entirely the creation of a ruling class whose goal was to retain power. Secondly, they had to have developed an intellectual foundation upon which to build a new society out of the one they hoped to replace.

The two men worked on *The German Ideology* from the end of September 1845 until August 1846. It grew to two volumes and more than five hundred pages. Like their first joint work, *The Holy Family,* the bulk of the book singled out for ridicule several personalities in the radical circles in Germany. Years later, Lenchen recalled Marx and Engels howling with laughter and waking everyone in the house as they wrote. Those nights of hilarity were in fact all the recompense the family ever got from the book.[15] They and their friends in Germany tried to interest eight publishers in it without success. In the end, Marx said, they surrendered the manuscript to the "gnawing of the mice all the more willingly as we had achieved our main purpose—self-clarification."[16]

In the fall of 1845, shortly after Laura's birth, the Marx family was thrown into a panic by news that Prussia was trying to have Marx expelled from Belgium. The German refugee population in Brussels was growing, and no doubt some were paid by the government in Berlin to keep an eye on the troublemakers among them. There was no particular provocation on Marx's part for the fresh diplomatic pressure; it could simply have been that he was reported by spies as being at the center of the radical refugees, and Prussia wanted him relocated farther away from its borders.

Marx tried to bluff his way out of his predicament. He wrote to Trier's chief magistrate and asked for documents to allow him to emigrate to America, which, if granted, would have effectively meant he was no longer a Prussian citizen and presumably no longer of interest to its authorities. There is nothing to suggest that Marx had any intention of moving to the United States and every indication that he used this request as a ploy to deflect Prussian attention. In any case, his plan failed: permission to emigrate was granted, but the pressure from Berlin continued. In December 1845, to shield himself from further meddling, Marx renounced his Prussian citizenship.[17]

Although that left him officially stateless, this represented a mere administrative change in his status, since he could not return to Prussia anyway without being arrested. But the notion of no longer being bound to a state he thought illegitimate may have been liberating. In the beginning of 1846, Marx, Engels, and Philippe Gigot, a young Belgian librarian, began organizing a Communist Correspondence Committee. The aim was to break down national barriers among workers and socialists, and to be ready "when the moment for action comes."[18] Newsletters could be written without regard to newspaper censors; the only threat came from the less systematic *cabinets noir,* which were established by European monarchies to inspect the mail for political dynamite.[19]

The committee's membership was minuscule and its correspondence equally so, but it was the first international organization Marx had ever tried to form and as such the seed of his entire political movement. Jenny assumed secretarial duties, copying Marx's indecipherable handwriting (during Marx's lifetime only Jenny, Engels, and Marx's daughters could ever truly master it). Engels continued to work with Marx on their joint writing, and all three participated in Communist Correspondence Committee meetings. Soon the house at 5 rue de l'Alliance was alive with activity around the clock, though its residents tried to work quietly so as not to attract the attention of Belgian officials. Marx said he managed only about four hours' sleep a night during that period, and those were in the early morning.[20] George Julian Harney's wife, writing from England, suggested that Jenny institute an "Anti-3 or 4 o'clock-in-the-morning Association" banning revolutionary activities in the wee hours for the sake of the family's rest.[21] It might have been a good idea: nerves had begun to fray within the Marx and Engels households, a situation that was exacerbated when Jenny returned to Trier in March to attend to her ailing mother. Marx was "working" on two books, had a new political organization and a growing number of refugees gathered around him, and was responsible for two children under the age of three. Lenchen no doubt took charge of the children, but there was no one to take charge of Marx.

In Jenny's absence the committee scheduled a meeting on March 30 and invited a tailor named Wilhelm Weitling to speak. Weitling, the illegitimate son of a German laundrywoman and a French military officer, was a legendary figure among socialists and communists, and had a strong following among working people suspicious of middle-class intellectuals. He had cofounded the League of the Just in Paris and was author of the popular underground book *Mankind as it is and as it ought to be.* Early on, Marx had compared him favorably with Proudhon, but as Weitling's career as an agitator continued, he seemed to become increasingly unhinged, his ideas at best utopian. Many attributed this unraveling to time spent in prison in Prussia and Switzerland. Weitling had been jailed in the latter for his book *The Gospel of a Poor Sinner,* in which Christ, like himself, was depicted as a communist and illegitimate son of a poor girl. Some said Weitling truly believed he was a messiah.[22] According to Engels, he "carried a recipe for the realization of heaven on earth ready-made in his pocket...and [was] possessed with the idea that everyone intended to steal it from him."[23] Among his treasured proposals was the creation of an army of forty thousand criminals to wage guerrilla war against the ruling class.[24]

The Marxes greeted Weitling warmly when he arrived in Brussels in February (Engels described his reception as an act of "almost superhuman forbearance"[25]). Joseph Weydemeyer recounted an all-night card game at Marx's home involving Marx, Weitling, Edgar von Westphalen, and himself, followed by a day of vagabonding with Jenny. This occurred "in the most agreeable manner imaginable. Early in the morning we went to a café, then we took the train to Villeworde, a nearby village, where we had lunch. We were madly gay, and came back on the last train."[26]

But after Jenny left for Trier and the committee met, the conviviality ended. Seated around a small green table in Marx's salon, the men turned their attention to politics. The Russian Annenkov, who was fascinated by the theater of politics but did not commit to any particular cause, was in Brussels at the time and vividly described the meeting during which the leader of German communism past was confronted by the leader of German communism future. Annenkov said Weitling did not look like a crazed revolutionary. At thirty-eight he was ten years older than Marx, fair haired, handsome, with an elegantly cut coat and a "coquettishly trimmed small beard." He had the air of a polite businessman. Marx, by contrast, was wild in his appearance, awkward in his movements, but utterly confident. "He looked like a man with the right and power to demand respect, no matter how he appeared before you and no matter what he did....His ways defied the usual conventions in human relations, but they were dignified and somewhat disdainful." Annenkov described Marx's voice as sharp and metallic, and said he spoke in the imperative as if to make disagreement (for those who dared) impossible.

Engels opened the meeting, attended by a handful of colleagues, saying it was necessary for those who wanted to transform labor to agree on how that might be done. In his memoirs Annenkov described Marx's leonine head bent over a piece of paper, a pencil in his hand, while Engels spoke. But Marx couldn't sit quietly for long. He demanded that Weitling, whom he accused of making "so much noise in Germany with your preaching," explain his activities. Weitling offered vague ideas about acquainting workers with their plight and rallying them to communism and democracy, but Marx interrupted angrily. He said raising fantastic hopes on the part of the workers was mere dishonest sermonizing, which "assumes an inspired prophet on the one side and on the other only gaping asses." It was not enough, he argued, for men to know that they were miserable, they had to understand why, and rousing the workers without offering them a clear plan or doctrine could lead only to failure. Weitling tried to defend himself, but Marx slammed his fist on the table so hard it shook the lamp and shouted, "Ignorance never yet helped anybody!" Everyone scattered. Marx was left angrily pacing the length of the room.[27]

Marx was only beginning to unleash his fury. (One colleague described him as the "sort of man who brought up heavy artillery in order to smash a window pane.")[28] Within days he attacked another member of his group, a German journalist named Hermann Kriege, whom he pilloried as a sentimental utopian who used the word "love" thirty-five times in one article.[29] He then went on to print pamphlets attacking other French and German "sheepish socialists" he thought insufficiently scientific—those unable or unwilling to discuss ways to alleviate real need and real injustice in the real world.[30] His mind branded by the images he'd seen in industrial England, Marx no longer had patience with men who turned their backs on the hard evidence of existence in favor of abstract theories. There was no time for obfuscation; the revolution, he believed, was imminent.

For Marx, Poland—where peasants in Galicia had revolted in February and slaughtered hundreds of nobles—provided the latest proof of the coming tidal wave. The uprising had spread to Cracow, where a Polish revolution and an end to serfdom was declared, but after ten days the effort failed, in part because the insurgents lacked organization or plan. And that was exactly Marx's point: a sustained and successful revolution was impossible without a clear understanding of the history that had brought man to that juncture and a blueprint for the future once the old system was obliterated.[31]

The Galicia revolt was a reminder of Europe's cancerous condition, and its reverberations were felt in every capital where rulers were being pressured by food shortages and related financial crises that threw workers out of jobs and left governments short of cash. Understanding that like-minded men should at the very least be aware of events in each other's countries at such a critical juncture, Marx was trying without much success to attract writers for his correspondence committee. So far only a handful of men in Germany and the circle around Harney in England had answered his letters; once again he was finding it difficult to engage the French. In May, Marx, Engels, and Gigot wrote to Proudhon, Marx humbly asking him to be the committee's correspondent from France because no one else was as fit for the task.[32] But Proudhon may have heard of Marx's recent outbursts against fellow socialists, especially from Weitling's friends in Paris; he replied by suggesting strongly that he feared Marx risked becoming a leader "of a new intolerance." "Let us not pose as the apostles of a new religion," Proudhon explained, "even if it be the religion of logic, the religion of reason." If Marx could guarantee a free and full exchange of ideas in the correspondence, Proudhon said, he would join it, "otherwise — no!"[33]

Marx had nothing but problems with his committee while Jenny was away, and he was also in trouble at the Engels home. Mary Burns had been living with Engels for six months, and while the two households socialized — in fact practically lived together — Marx and Jenny never seemed to care much for Engels's companion. Some biographers have suggested Jenny did not approve of the fact that Engels and Mary weren't married, but that was unlikely: Moses Hess was not married to his partner either (though many Marx chroniclers have mistakenly referred to Sibylle at this time as Hess's wife), and Marx and Jenny had encountered and condoned numerous such arrangements in Paris. Others have hinted that Jenny felt socially superior to Mary and could not warm up to her for that reason, but throughout Jenny's life, acquaintances remarked that she exhibited no class prejudice whatsoever. It seemed more likely that she and Marx simply did not like — or understand — Engels's lover. The cultural gulf between Mary, the twenty-three-year-old daughter of an Irish factory worker, and Jenny, a thirty-two-year-old Prussian aristocrat, was enormous. In a March 1846 letter to Marx from Trier discussing a "radical breach" at the Engels house involving Mary, Jenny wrote that she was happy she had been absent from Brussels because she, as an "ambitious Lady Macbeth" long critical of Engels's relationship, would have been blamed. She suggested that Engels could find another companion. "There is an abundance of lovely, charming, capable women," she noted, "…waiting for a man to liberate and redeem them." Whatever occurred that spring, Mary returned to England soon afterward.[34]

Other personal fireworks were exploding in the small refugee community in Brussels: the bonhomie of the first year was evaporating. Hess told Marx he wanted nothing more to do with his "party" because of his treatment of Weitling (he later accused Marx of demanding the personal submission of those around him).[35] And everyone in their circle was broke, none more so than Marx himself. In March the publisher of his long-overdue economic book suggested he try to find someone else to bring it out, and when it was finished return the 1,500-franc advance.[36] (Again, Karl seemed not to have mentioned any of this to Jenny, because at the same time she informed him that his book's imminent publication was greatly anticipated in Germany.)[37] Even Engels was uncharacteristically short of funds — he wrote his new brother-in-law that he had 150 francs' worth of goods in pawn and needed that amount by return post.[38]

Marx told Weydemeyer, now back in Germany and trying to get *The German Ideology* published, that he was in a serious predicament. "In order to make ends meet for the time being here, I recently pawned the last of the gold and silver as well as a large part of the linen." But the worst of it was that the family had to leave the rue de l'Alliance—their year's lease was up, and they did not have the money for another. They were forced to move back into the Bois Sauvage, where Engels had also taken rooms. Marx described a general state of financial collapse among their friends, saying, "As you can see, *misère* on all sides! At this moment I'm at a loss what to do."[39]

None of these setbacks, however, caused Marx to deviate from the radical path he had chosen. Nor would they ever. And in any case the situation for Marx and Jenny was bad but not dire. There were still sources of money they could likely tap if necessary among the businessmen in Cologne (though for political reasons Marx preferred not to). As for friends, even as ones like Hess fell by the wayside, others appeared to take their place. In April 1846 one such appeared out of the blue. A short, stocky, thirty-seven-year-old man who Engels said looked like a German peasant in provincial bourgeois clothes, knocked at Marx's door. His name was Wilhelm Wolff. He had been sentenced to prison for violating press laws but escaped before being jailed in a Silesian fortress. Known by the Marx circle as "Lupus," Wolff, was quickly followed by German journalist Ferdinand Wolff ("Red Wolff"), the German poet Georg Weerth, the Belgian lawyer and journalist Lucien Jottrand, the Belgian lawyer Victor Tedesco,[40] and the aged Polish historian and revolutionary Joachim Lelewel (Jenny fondly remembered him wearing the blue blouse of the common laborer during their evening outings at Brussels cafés).[41] As Marx was alienating many of his early socialist acquaintances, the growing reputation of his circle attracted new ones.

In August, Engels volunteered to go to Paris and set up a correspondence committee there, hoping to find recruits among the French if they could not be drawn by letters from Brussels.[42] But he had no more success in Paris than Marx had had from Belgium, and by November he had been denounced to the police by informers who heard him declare in workers' meetings that the aims of communism could not be achieved without a "democratic revolution by force."[43] Engels told Marx that since he was being dogged by police and an expulsion order was hanging over his head, he planned to give political agitation a rest and instead devote his time to fun. He would subsequently report that he had the zealous Paris police to thank for some "delicious encounters" with young women and "a great deal of pleasure."[44]

* * *

Marx's uncle Lion Philips and Jenny's mother gave Karl and Jenny enough money to move out of the Bois Sauvage in December and into a small house in another Brussels suburb, Ixelles. Jenny was seven months pregnant. She did not want to have her third child in a boardinghouse, but they had lacked the funds to finance a move themselves, and there was no money on the horizon from Karl's writing.[45] Marx claimed he had finished a draft of his economic work but said it had been set aside so long he would have to rewrite it.[46] The publisher Leske had essentially washed his hands of the project, and Marx could not find anyone else to take it or *The German Ideology*. He wearily wrote Annenkov,

> With this letter I should have liked to send you my book on political economy, but up till now I have been unable to have printed either this work or the critique of German philosophers and socialists which I mentioned to you in Brussels. You would never believe what difficulties a publication of this kind runs into in Germany, on the one hand from the police, on the other from the booksellers, who are themselves the interested representatives of all those tendencies I attack. And as for our own party, not only is it poor, but there is a large faction in the German communist party which bears me a grudge because I am opposed to its utopias and its declaiming.[47]

Yet in this same letter Marx demonstrated he did not fear being ostracized by the Germans (or anyone else). No doubt Marx had been harboring a grudge against Proudhon since the Frenchman's letter setting conditions for his participation in the Communist Correspondence Committee; Marx would have despised the tone of that letter, which condescendingly scolded him like a schoolboy. But his December revolt against the man whose work he had once called epoch-making exceeded mere pique. During the past years, especially in 1846, Marx had systematically demolished all the theorists he had studied while he struggled to construct his own system. Proudhon was the last of the big men still standing, and he gave Marx an opening for attack in his new two-volume book, *The Philosophy of Poverty*. Marx received it in December 1846 and told Annenkov his first impression was that it was "very poor," and evidence that Proudhon did not understand the relevant historical or economic developments. According to Proudhon, he said, man did not build on the past activities or productive gains of those who came before him, because history existed "in the nebulous realm of the imagination and soars high above time and place.... The evolutions of which Mr. Proudhon speaks are presumed to be evolutions such as take place in the mystical bosom of the absolute idea."[48] As Marx so often expressed it, such abstraction was useless—and dangerous.

He also criticized Proudhon's lack of understanding of what the French writer coldly called "economic categories" such as slavery. Marx wrote: "Direct slavery is as much the pivot upon which our present-day industrialism turns as are machinery, credit, etc. Without slavery there would be no cotton, without cotton there would be no modern industry. It is slavery which has given value to the colonies, it is the colonies which have created world trade, and world trade is the necessary condition for large-scale machine industry."[49]

But Marx had not finished. He quickly wrote his own book, *The Poverty of Philosophy*. A tight hundred pages, it was a work of significant weight and passion. In it he used Proudhon as a vehicle to detail his own theories of history, economics, and revolution. In this, the first book Marx had written alone and the first in which he called himself an economist,[50] he concluded:

> From day to day it thus becomes clearer that the production relations in which the bourgeoisie moves have not a simple, uniform character, but a dual character; that in the selfsame relations in which wealth is produced, poverty is produced also; that in the selfsame relations in which there is a development of the productive forces, there is also a force producing repression; that these relations produce *bourgeois wealth,* i.e., the wealth of the bourgeois class, only by continually annihilating the wealth of the individual members of this class and by producing an ever-growing proletariat.[51]

Proudhon's book was enthusiastically received in France and translated into German.[52] Marx, however, could not find a publisher for his retort. He paid for the printing of eight hundred copies in Paris and Brussels out of his own extremely limited funds.[53] The book was not a success, but it was an important milestone for Marx. He had knocked off the last of the intellectual giants. His long battle with the old socialism, communism, Hegelianism, Christianity, and Judaism was finished, and it had produced something new—the starting point of a political-economic-social system that required not just theory but action and would change society at its core.

Marx said it was time to become part of the historical revolutionary process, and with that in mind he, Jenny, and their Brussels cohorts joined the League of the Just.[54]

11

Brussels, 1847

Give a little thought to the Confession of Faith. I think we
would do best to abandon the catechetical form and call the thing
Communist Manifesto.

—Friedrich Engels[1]

THE LEAGUE OF the Just had been headquartered in Paris, but by the fall of 1846 police harassment had intensified and most of its strongest members fled France. In London the league could operate without fear of official interference, partly because it was seen as so insignificant. Thus the organization moved its central committee to the British capital, coalescing around the German communists and English Chartists with whom Marx and Engels had met the year before.

Marx had approached these men early in 1846 about uniting with his correspondence committee, but that was at the height of his assault on fellow socialists and communists, and they may have been reluctant to join ranks with such a volatile character. The league declined his offer. By the fall, however, Marx's letters had convinced them the times demanded that the vague, utopian goal of a future ideal society be abandoned in favor of "scientific" communism, which sought to understand and materially support the modern oppressed class, the proletariat, who were already engaged in a revolutionary struggle even if they did not recognize it as such.[2] In February 1847 a Cologne watchmaker named Joseph Moll arrived at Marx's door in Belgium and asked him to join the league. Moll then went to Paris to see Engels. He told them that members wanted the two younger men to help reinvigorate the group. Marx and Engels accepted the challenge.[3]

Evidence to support Marx's argument that the league needed to evolve beyond its utopian roots could be found in the economic and agricultural crisis then raging across the continent, which had triggered widespread unrest among the very people the league existed to help but had so far failed to attract. The bad potato and grain harvests that began in 1845 had continued, and this, coupled with new trade policies that had forced small growers out of business while allowing large producers to ship food to lucrative foreign rather than domestic markets caused the price of many staple items to double between 1845 and 1847.[4] The number of bankruptcies during this period was unprecedented, as the high cost of food reduced the amount of money people could spend on other items. Businesses closed; starvation began appearing in the cities.[5] That winter one-third of Paris's million inhabitants relied on charity administered by local officials, the Catholic Church, or aid societies. Soon food riots erupted, followed by workers' strikes, and the portentous barricade again made an appearance. Some provincial governments tried to tame restless cities by directing grain away from villages and towns, but that only exacerbated dire conditions in the countryside.[6]

One writer proclaimed this the moment in history that signaled the end of the ancient agricultural order, when fortunes rose or fell based on harvests and seasons. The new order would be tied, for better or worse, to trade and production. But in 1847, Europe and its people were the unfortunate victims of the worst of both worlds.[7]

The League of the Just was the first proletariat association Marx had consented to join. In general he did not like organizations and public politics. He was a writer and thinker utterly lacking in the diplomatic skills or patience needed for group endeavors (even though throughout his life he was not only drawn into them but in almost all cases became their leader). It is not known whether Marx hesitated before joining (his earlier approach had been to ally, not immerse), but Moll may have caught him at a moment when he was feeling unusually warm toward his fellow man: he arrived in Belgium immediately after the birth of Marx and Jenny's first son. Born on February 3, the baby was named Edgar, after Jenny's brother,[8] and from infancy it was clear from Marx and Jenny's correspondence that Edgar was their favorite child. Jenny said the little boy with the big head would never be an Adonis but she loved the wildness in him, describing him with pride as her "little monster."[9]

Yet such joy also meant increased financial pressure. There were now three children and five adults in the Marx home, counting Lenchen, the baby's wet nurse, and Edgar von Westphalen. There was also the not insignificant postage for a growing correspondence (parcels to Paris could cost as much as six francs[10]), and meals of brisket and potatoes for the men who had no families and so spent their time at the Marx table. In letters to friends Jenny and Marx never begrudged the expense when describing their financial straits, even when one of the men taking lunch with them daily was Weitling *after* his very public falling-out with Marx. Marx always said the movement was bigger than the individual and sacrifice inevitable. Through Engels, Marx tried to collect money owed to him by friends in Paris, but even if that came in, there was still the question of their next few francs.[11] They would not come from his political economy: in February the publisher formally canceled Marx's contract. That source of income had now become another debt.[12]

Sacrifice was inevitable, but in letters Engels seemed oblivious to the personal and professional pressures on Marx and displayed even less sensitivity toward Jenny. Engels was still in Paris trying to make contact with socialists and politicized workers. While there he saw several old friends. Moses Hess showed up with syphilis.[13] Bernays, who had gone to jail for publishing *Vowarts!*, emerged traumatized and was in semihiding in rural France, coming up to Paris only occasionally.[14] And Heine was living in a tiny apartment that overlooked a dreary courtyard, one of his eyes permanently closed due to a stroke.[15] Even the notorious cad Herwegh, now a father of three, had settled down — at least temporarily.[16] Engels associated with these and a handful of league members, but he made few new friends (except among French ladies).

In a letter in March, Engels wrote Marx that the political situation was getting tense. "The police here are in a very ugly mood just now. It would seem that, by hook or by crook, they are determined to exploit the food shortage to provoke a riot or a mass conspiracy." Some communists had been arrested and were to stand trial. Engels tried to persuade Marx to get out of "boring" Brussels and come to Paris to cheer him up. His reasons for asking had almost nothing to do with revolutionary subversion; if subversion of any kind came into Engels's picture, it was mostly the sort that ruins marriages. He told Karl he would have money in April. "So for a time we could enjoy ourselves famously, squandering our all in taverns. . . . I for my part have a great desire to go carousing with you. . . . If I had an income of 5,000 fr. I would do nothing but work and amuse myself with women until I went to pieces. If there were no French women, life wouldn't be worth living. But as long as there are *grisettes,* well and good!" Perhaps realizing that Marx might not take that bait, he added, "Still that does not prevent one from sometimes wishing to discuss a decent topic or enjoy life with a measure of refinement, neither of which is possible with anyone in the whole band of my acquaintances. You must come here."[17]

Marx did not. He had neither the money nor the time. The political situation in Belgium was also tense. The Prussian government had alerted Belgian officials that the refugees were, contrary to their promises, engaged in political activity. The German bookseller Carl Vogler, who was part of their Brussels circle and whom Marx had asked to publish his *Poverty of Philosophy,* was arrested in April.[18] Marx had begun writing for the Brussels opposition emigrant newspaper *Deutsche-Brüsseler-Zeitung,* and while his articles were not necessarily political, they drew attention to him that he could ill afford. He wrote Herwegh to say the Prussian embassy was shadowing the newspaper's editor, giving Marx every reason to fear that he, too, was being watched.[19]

In June members of the league were to gather in London for a first congress to discuss the group's reorganization. Marx told Engels that as much as he would have liked to attend, he could not afford to go[20] (he had to pay for his *Poverty,* which was to come out that month). There was also the question of a passport; though Marx could take the risk of crossing borders without proper documentation, he may have thought it unwise given the greater police scrutiny. He said Lupus would go instead as representative of the Brussels branch. Engels would be the French delegate. The presence of these two men ensured that Marx's ideas for transforming the league would be ably represented.

Dozens of league members gathered in a private room at a London pub during the week of June 2 and agreed to major changes that sharpened the group's focus, beginning with its name: the League of the Just became the Communist League, and its slogan changed from the vague but reassuring "All Men Are Brothers" to the more muscular "Working Men of All Countries, Unite!" In its new incarnation the league became the first international communist organization in history. Engels, Moses Hess, and Karl Schapper were asked to draw up a Communist Credo to be made available to potential recruits.[21] A first draft was written in London, its question-and-answer format explaining who the communists were, their aim, the history of the proletariat, and the path to revolution.[22] The group also issued a circular full of grand rhetoric to be distributed to those league members who did not attend the June meeting.

> Brothers! We represent a great, a wonderful cause. We proclaim the greatest revolution ever proclaimed in the world, a revolution which for its thoroughness and wealth of consequences has no equal in world history. We do not

know how far it will be granted us to share in the fruits of this revolution. But this we know, that this revolution is drawing near in all its might; this we see, that everywhere, in France as in Germany, in England as in America, the angry masses of the proletariat are in motion and are demanding their liberation from the fetters of money rule, from the fetters of the bourgeoisie, with a voice that is often still confused but is becoming ever louder and clearer. This we see, that the bourgeois class is getting ever richer, that the middle classes are being more and more ruined and that thus historical development itself strives towards a great revolution which will one day burst out, through the distress of the people and the wantonness of the rich.[23]

Communist League members charged out of London on their historic mission to change the world. But it was truly a case of the mouse that roared: their numbers were tiny. A former Berlin police official sent to London to check on the group estimated its membership that summer at a mere eighty-four agitated souls.[24] When Marx formed his branch of the league in Brussels that summer, it had eighteen members. First on the list was Jenny, and since the group also included her brother Edgar and Engels, that meant there were only fourteen members outside Marx's innermost circle.[25] Such were the shock troops of the communist revolution circa 1847.

The Brussels league, with few exceptions, was composed of the Germans and Belgians who lived near the Marxes. It was very much a close-knit, almost family affair, which was likely the source of its strength. There was little if any dissent, and everyone took directions from Marx, who was not surprisingly elected branch president.

The German typesetter Stephan Born recalled Karl and Jenny's home in Ixelles as extremely modest and poorly furnished, but it nevertheless served as the "spiritual center of communism." Marx and Jenny had both welcomed him kindly when he was introduced to them by Engels, but Born seemed particularly struck with the warmth shown by Jenny, whom he described as a committed communist. "Throughout her life she took the most intense interest in everything that concerned and occupied her husband.... Marx loved his wife and she shared his passion."[26] Each had one hand clenched in a fist and the other clutched together.

Everything was speeding up in Brussels. The publisher of the *Deutsche-Brüsseler-Zeitung* had virtually turned over control of the newspaper to Marx,[27] and Marx and Engels had also founded a German Workers' Union to attract and educate workingmen, who were underrepresented in the league. On Wednesdays it met at the incongruously opulent wood-paneled

Café au Cygne on Brussels's famous Grand-Place. Marx lectured on historical materialism and the exploitation of capital, while others taught courses in language, science, and culture. Sundays were family affairs with recitations (sometimes by Jenny), popular theatricals, and dances.[28] Improbably, Marx was also made vice president of the International Democratic Association, a small organization of professional men from several countries that had been established by Marx's rivals to counter his influence among the workers. Marx was out of town at the time the group was formed, so it was left to Engels to cleverly co-opt it and turn the group into a vehicle for Marx.[29] It was one of the earliest examples of a lifetime of such battles, in which Marx and Engels swiftly and often ruthlessly destroyed their enemies with razor-sharp intellectual argument backed up by political skulduggery. They relished such fights, and were nearly always successful. One had the sense their opponents never fully understood what had hit them.

That whirl of activity and the newspaper drew the attention of the police, who wrote in a confidential report:

> This noxious paper must indisputably exert the most corrupting influence upon the uneducated public at whom it is directed. The alluring theory of the dividing-up of wealth is held out to factory-workers and day laborers as an innate right, and a profound hatred of the rulers and the rest of the community is inculcated into them.... The circumstance that the number of members [of the Workers' Union] has increased from thirty-seven to seventy within a few days is worthy of note.[30]

Marx told Herwegh that this number soon reached one hundred and was growing.[31]

In September, Marx was obliged to go to his uncle's home in Holland to discuss his inheritance.[32] He and Jenny had managed to live with virtually no income since his advance from Leske in the summer of 1845 (which Leske, of course, was now demanding back). The year before his uncle Lion and Jenny's mother had given them money to move, but aside from trifles Marx was able to collect from friends, they were penniless and expenses were mounting. A year's rent would be due in December, and Marx wanted to travel to London for the next league meeting in November; Engels said it was essential that he attend to solidify gains in the face of new threats.[33]

Bakunin had arrived in Brussels that fall and had immediately begun to stir up trouble. His relations with Karl had long been strained, but by 1847 he harbored new grudges against him for his treatment of Weitling and

Proudhon. Bakunin credited Weitling for his transformation from philosophy student to revolutionary and Proudhon for taking him one step further—from revolutionary to anarchist.[34] While Bakunin joined the Democratic Association at Marx's behest, it was too organized for his taste. He told Herwegh, "In such company you cannot breathe freely."[35] He added that Marx was carrying on his usual "evil work" and ruining laborers with his theories.[36] And he excoriated Karl and his followers as rebels sunk into well-upholstered armchairs: "Vanity, malice, tittle-tattle, theoretical arrogance...theorizing about life, action and simplicity and a complete absence of life, action and simplicity.... The word bourgeois is repeated ad nauseam as a catchword—but they themselves are all head to foot small town bourgeoisie."[37]

Marx returned from Holland with a promise of money though without any actually in hand. But such was the importance of the league meeting, in light of increasing challenges to his ideas and leadership, that he made the trip to London anyway, though that meant leaving Jenny to face all their financial difficulties alone. He wrote Pavel Annenkov in Paris for help.

> My economic situation just now is so critical that my wife is being veritably harassed by creditors and is now in the most wretched financial straits....In this situation, which I am not ashamed frankly to disclose to you, you would in truth save me from the worst if you could arrange to let my wife have a sum of between 100 and 200 francs. I shall, of course, be unable to repay you until my money matters have been settled with my family.

If Annenkov agreed, he should send the funds to Ixelles: "However my wife must not be able to deduce from your letter that I wrote to you.... Another time, I trust, I shall be able to send you more cheerful news."[38] Other than such pleading, Jenny was left to fend for herself.

On November 27 Marx, Engels, Georg Weerth, and Victor Tedesco met in Belgium's North Sea port city of Ostend and caught a steamship for Dover the next day. The stream of radicals headed to the English capital was impressive, as several organizations had planned events at the end of November. The first was a celebration in honor of the brutally quashed Polish revolt of 1830, from which that divided country had yet to recover. Poland had become a unifying cause for the opposition across Europe, and French, Belgian, Italian, Polish, Danish, and English sympathizers gathered at a pub on Soho's Great Windmill Street to remember its martyrs.[39]

Marx, who was not known as a public speaker, delivered an address in

German on the lessons of the Polish conflict (it was then translated into English by Schapper). He described the world as a place where the bourgeoisie of all nations were united against the proletariat of all nations—the "brotherhood of the oppressors against the oppressed, of the exploiters against the exploited." But, he said, while the proletariat so far had no such united front, they had a shared experience upon which to build a new world.

> The old Poland is lost in any case and we would be the last to wish for its restoration. But it is not only old Poland that is lost. The old Germany, the old France, the old England, the whole of the old society is lost. But the loss of the old society is no loss for those who have nothing to lose in the old society, and this is the case of the great majority in all the countries at the present time. They have rather everything to gain by the downfall of the old society, which is the condition for the establishment of a new society, one no longer based on class antagonisms.[40]

Speaker after speaker reaffirmed their solidarity with Poland and the workingman, and the evening ended with hats off for the singing of the "Marseillaise."

The next day the Communist League congress commenced at the same site and was attended by many of the same faces. For most, these events marked the first time they had actually seen Marx, who was notorious in their small circle for his vitriolic essays against fellow socialists and governments alike. Just as he broke down the world into black and white, there was seemingly no middle ground in people's opinions of him. He inspired fear and loathing as often as love and admiration. The league members who had agreed to make him their ideological leader were curious to see this human lightning rod.

The German tailor Friedrich Lessner, who lived in London, described Engels as slim and agile, "more like a smart young lieutenant of the guard than a scholar."[41] But he was struck by the force of Marx's presence, both physical and mental. "Marx was still a young man, about twenty-eight years old, but he greatly impressed us all. He was of medium height, broad-shouldered, powerful in build and energetic in his deportment. His brow was high and finely shaped, his hair thick and pitch-black, his gaze piercing. His mouth already had the sarcastic line that his opponents feared so much." He said Marx never uttered a superfluous word and had nothing of the dreamer about him. Lessner came away from his first encounter with Marx thinking of him as a born leader who "represented the manhood of socialist thought."[42]

For ten days league members met in a large room above a pub. Sitting on benches at tables laden with pots of beer, they debated in German, French, Italian, and English the principles first discussed in June. Their clothing proclaimed their social positions, from the worn cotton uniform of the workingman to the shabby dignity of the middle-class intellectual's black frock coat to the traditional costumes and bizarre hats of visitors from distant provinces in even more distant lands. Marx, Engels, and their followers tried to steer this diverse grouping away from utopian ideas and hoped to erase such flights of fancy from the league's program. The league had to be made relevant to workers if it was to grow, and that meant it had to aggressively address the workingman's needs and desires.[43]

By the end of the meeting the Rules of the Communist League stipulated membership requirements and established a multitiered organizational structure for the group.[44] Also agreed was a revised aim. Previously the league's goal was a mere suggestion: "The emancipation of humanity by spreading the theory of the community of property and its speediest possible practical introduction."[45] The new aim was pure Marx: "The overthrow of the bourgeoisie, the rule of the proletariat, the abolition of the old bourgeois society which rests on the antagonism of classes, and the foundation of a new society without classes and without private property."[46] The rules specified that the group would remain secret, because while it might operate freely in places like London, its members in Prussia faced arrest if discovered. But the league needed a document that explained its program to those who might want to join. At the end of its December meeting, the group asked Marx and Engels to write it quickly.

Engels had already written a new version of the communist "catechism" that he had begun in June, but he was having second thoughts about the format even before they arrived in London. In a letter to Marx he had said, "Give a little thought to the Confession of Faith. I think we would do best to abandon the catechetical form and call the thing Communist *Manifesto*."[47]

12

Brussels, 1848

*I am told that there is no danger because there are no riots; I am
told that because there is no visible disorder on the surface of
society, there is no revolution at hand. Gentlemen, permit me to
say that I believe you are mistaken.*

—Alexis de Tocqueville[1]

JENNY AND MARX danced their way into 1848. The German Workers'
Union held a New Year's Eve celebration at the Café au Cygne, which
Jenny helped organize. The *Deutsche-Brüsseler-Zeitung* called the event a
step toward strengthening democracy in several countries,[2] but for Jenny,
it was primarily a step toward strengthening her spirit. The previous year
had been difficult. She told a friend, "My time is always meagerly divided
between the big and small sorrows and troubles of daily life, [and] the
concern for the affairs of my dear husband." On top of that, she said, while
Karl was in London "we all, great and small, men and mice, got sick so
that I had to stay in bed for fourteen days."[3] But by New Year's they
appeared to be turning the page on domestic misery. The children were
well; she said baby Edgar had "lost some of his awfulness." Even their
financial situation was looking up: Karl's mother had finally said that she
would advance him some of his inheritance.[4]

So on December 31 they celebrated by putting the revolution aside for
the evening. It was the first ball Jenny had attended in years. For the occasion, she and the other upper-class women in their circle wore full evening
dress, from their jeweled necks to their gloved fingers. Indeed a rainbow of
blue, yellow, green, and red silk gowns rustled across the Grand-Place
toward the Cygne that night, illuminated by gaslights reflecting from a

thousand diamond-shaped windowpanes on the surrounding guild halls and the Hôtel de Ville. On any given day the square bustled with dark-coated merchants and aproned marketeers, but that night Grand-Place was magical.

The newspaper reported that inside the café a "folly of elegant women" applauded vigorously during a series of speeches,[5] including one given by Marx that eerily echoed his father's speech in Trier in 1835, in which his praise of the king was misinterpreted as sly criticism. (In the son's case it most probably was the latter.) Marx praised Belgium for its liberal consti-tution, which he said allowed a "humanitarian seed" to flourish for the good of all Europe.[6] For her part Jenny participated in a dramatic perfor-mance, which the *Deutsche-Brüsseler* not surprisingly said displayed her "brilliant talent for recitation. It is very impressive to watch exceptionally gifted ladies trying to improve the intellectual faculties of the proletar-iat."[7] Such business concluded, an orchestra sounded the note for dancing, and couples took to the floor. The music could still be heard by weary passersby well into the morning of the new year.

Despite Marx's oft described physical awkwardness, he loved to dance and displayed some agility while doing so. He and Jenny glided through waltzes and the more formal quadrilles, which required particular coordi-nation with their fellow dancers. The crowd was much changed from ear-lier days at Rhineland balls. Ropes no longer separated the aristocracy from the lower classes, and not all the men and women wore evening clothes—in fact, some of the men had caps tucked into their pockets, a fashion offense that would have inspired eviction in more formal settings. But the woman in Marx's arms, though thirteen years older now, had not changed; she was still the eighteen-year-old who had dazzled Trier.

Since their marriage Jenny had suffered financial insecurity and the inconvenience of forced exile. She had been distressed by the serious ill-ness of her infant daughter and the political persecution of her husband, and yet she seemed remarkably untouched by it all. It was as if she still felt herself protected by a shield of aristocratic privilege. Her class might have debts and heartache, but the nineteenth-century social net—at least for a Prussian—was designed to prevent its members from falling through. Those of the ruling class did not fail unless they wanted to. Jenny joked about being queen at the court of "high miserable grandeur,"[8] and yet she did see it as a court, as a sort of heraldic assembly obsessed with a jesterless world. One has the sense that at this point she saw herself as part of a socially aware, politically active bohemian crowd—young and experi-menting, their futures uncertain but without question bright. It was a thrilling environment for a woman of intelligence and convictions. There is no doubt she was committed to her husband's ideas, but her letters are less clear on whether she recognized that she was moving inexorably away from the protected world she was raised in and into a political and social maelstrom.

That night in Brussels, none of their group seemed to have a sense that tomorrow held anything but promise. All of their friends had joined the celebration. Engels had fetched Mary Burns when he was in England, and she was among them dancing at the Cygne. But Mary's presence cast one of the few shadows on the otherwise splendid evening. The strain between her and the Marxes was still apparent. Stephan Born said Marx had made it clear Jenny did not want to talk to Mary, which Born took as evidence of Jenny's noble character.[9] Yet it was not that Jenny was too arrogant to speak to Mary; she was angry with Engels for being insensitive toward the workingmen and -women attending the event. "By bringing his mistress to this group of mostly working-class people," Born explained, "Engels risked reproach often made that the rich sons of the manufacturers used the young girls of the people for their pleasure."[10]

Engels was soon to face an even more serious accusation in that regard: at a meeting of the Workers' Union in Brussels, Moses Hess accused him of raping Hess's partner, Sibylle. Red Wolff took the minutes of the meeting but artfully avoided recording Hess's allegations—a delicate maneuver that Engels (who did not attend) told Marx made him split his sides with laughter. "Moses brandishing his pistols, parading his horns before the whole of Brussels...must have been exquisite....If, by the by, the jackass should persist in his preposterous lie about rape, I can provide him with enough earlier, concurrent, and later details to send him reeling." Hess, who was eight years older than Sibylle, had put her in the care of Engels, who was Sibylle's age, asking him to help her cross the border into Belgium. Engels told Marx that Sibylle confessed she was in love with him, and, after Engels did not reciprocate, she apparently told Hess that Engels had made her drunk and raped her. "Her rage with me is unrequited love, pure and simple.... The *strong wine* proves to be no more than 1/3 bottle of Bordeaux." Engels said Hess was "perfectly at liberty, by the way, to avenge himself on all my present, past and future mistresses."[11]

In early January Engels left Marx alone in Brussels to finish the *Manifesto*. By that time there had already been three drafts, two by Engels and one by Hess. Marx started from scratch, though he used Engels's last draft as inspiration and outline. Jenny worked as his secretary to help speed the project. Their handwriting intertwined on the page as he scribbled his thoughts on paper and she followed in an elegant, feminine hand, patiently copying out and making legible her husband's blistering indictment of the bourgeoisie and his belief that revolution was right, inevitable, and imminent. Imminent it might be, but as always, Marx was distracted by other commitments. He was writing for the *Deutsche-Brüsseler* and preparing economic lectures for the German Workers' Union that he intended to turn into a pamphlet. He also had to attend to duties for the International Democratic Association, which included opening a new branch in the industrial textile center of Ghent, Belgium's own little Manchester. And in January he addressed the association on a free-trade theme he had begun writing about in September.[12]

Some proponents said free trade was like the monarchs who ruled by divine right—that is, God's will. Trade would bring people together, advance spiritual and social well-being, and, as one historian described it, multiply the blessings of civilization. (That argument had even been used to lift trade restrictions in England.)[13] But Marx said free trade simply meant the "freedom of Capital to crush the worker." He nevertheless came out in favor of such trade, because only then, he said, could industry flourish, which would in turn hasten social change, including the cleaving of the world into two distinct classes—the moneyed bourgeoisie and wage laborers.[14] (Engels later described them as "hereditary wealth on one side, hereditary poverty on the other.")[15] Marx envisioned this system spinning out of control, leading to an economic meltdown and social revolution.

Some might have accused Marx of cynicism for embracing rather than battling a system of trade that he predicted would cause suffering among the workers. But one of Marx's revelations was that however difficult restraint, premature attempts at revolution would be doomed to failure. Until conditions were such that a vast majority of the people recognized the need for rebellion (and he counted on free trade to help create just those conditions), attempts to raise their lot through violent action would amount to nothing more than the grasping for power by a small band of elitists.

Marx had hoped to present his free trade theory to a gathering of economists in Brussels in September but was barred from doing so. His ideas would not, however, go to waste: portions of his argument would ultimately appear in the *Communist Manifesto*.

Engels, who was in Paris, told Marx he was frustrated by a lack of action among league members in France. Part of the problem, he said, was that they had seen nothing from the London congress as yet and were "naturally growing completely supine," even though the political temperature on the Continent was rising.[16] While Engels's comment may have been a gentle prod to get Marx working on the *Manifesto,* on January 26 an even more frustrated league leadership sent Marx an unequivocally blunt letter stating that if the *Manifesto* did not arrive in London by February 2, "further measures will be taken against him."[17]

In fact Marx was nearly finished. At the end of January he mailed the twenty-three-page document to London.[18] The tailor Lessner took the manuscript to a German printer named J. E. Burghard, who ran a shop on Liverpool Street in the City of London. Burghard placed a dark green cover on the pamphlet, titled *Manifesto of the Communist Party* even though no such party existed. No author's name appeared on the eight hundred copies that came off the press at the end of February 1848.[19] The English Chartist George Julian Harney called the pamphlet, written by Marx at his small suburban home and copied out by his wife at their dining table, the most revolutionary document the world had ever seen.[20]

As Marx wrote it, the *Manifesto* was less dramatic than Engels's question-and-answer credo, but in its quiet control much more powerful. Marx's pamphlet read like an opening statement in a legal case (evidence perhaps of the lawyer he might have become). He began with the melodramatic "A specter is haunting Europe—the specter of Communism," then set out to put that "nursery tale" to rest by describing communism and the corrupt system it hoped to replace.[21]

Synthesizing ideas from other intellectuals and economists until they became his own, Marx described crimes committed by the bourgeoisie, who, he said, "left remaining no other nexus between man and man than naked self-interest, than callous 'cash payment.'" He said the system had reduced traditional occupations of respect—doctors, lawyers, priests, poets, scientists—into paid wage laborers, and turned "the family relation to a mere money relation." Marx described a state of turmoil unlike anything in history in a world dominated by capital, because of its need to constantly revolutionize production and raise profits, which in turn required new markets around the globe: "It must nestle everywhere, settle everywhere, establish connections everywhere." Its system of trade brought raw materials from far-flung places to producers across oceans so products could be sold to consumers a steamship or rail line away. Old national industries were destroyed; old civilizations were, too, as they were drawn into the new web. Of this system Marx said, "In one word, it creates a world after its own image."[22]

But, he explained, this society also created the seeds of its own destruction, and "is like the sorcerer, who is no longer able to control the powers of the netherworld who he has called up by his spells."[23] Commercial cri-

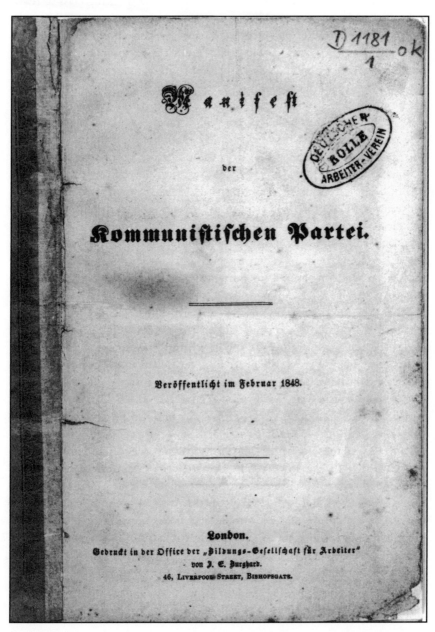

Cover of the first edition of the *Manifesto of the Communist Party,* which rolled off the press in London in February 1848, just as Europe ignited in an unprecedented revolt. (IISG, Amsterdam)

ses would accelerate with overproduction, and the army of workers required to run industrial society's machines—the working class or revolutionary proletariat—would turn into a force for its demise. "What the bourgeoisie, therefore, produces, above all, is its own grave-diggers. Its fall and the victory of the proletariat are equally inevitable."[24] For Marx, such class conflict was a fact of historical progression as surely as the product or discovery of one generation formed the basis of an improvement in the next.

Marx declared that at the core of communism was the abolition of private property. He answered possibly alarmed critics by noting that nine-tenths of the population at that time did not possess property, so the only people standing to lose would be the minority who had made their gains through exploitation: "Communism deprives no man of the power to appropriate the products of society; all that it does is to deprive him of the power to subjugate the labor of others by means of such appropriation."[25] Why should an industry whose operation depends upon the work of one hundred people, perhaps even one thousand, enrich only a handful? Why should the earth's bounty—its minerals, land, and seas—come under the exclusive control of any man for his own gain?

Marx answered critics who charged that communism threatened the fabric of the family by accusing them of hypocrisy. He pointed out that under the bourgeois industrial system, children were already deprived of childhood. They were not educated but treated as mere "articles of commerce and instruments of labor." As for marital relations, those too had already been destroyed by the moneyed class, which sexually exploited working wives and daughters—either through intimidation or prostitution—and considered seducing one another's wives a sport.[26]

"In place of the old bourgeois society, with its classes and class antagonism, we shall have an association, in which the free development of each is the condition for the free development of all."[27] But he said that could only be achieved by the "forcible overthrow of all existing social conditions. Let the ruling classes tremble at a Communistic revolution. The proletarians have nothing to lose but their chains. They have a world to win.

"Working men of all countries, Unite!"[28]

13

~⌒~

Paris, 1848

They did not despair of themselves nor of their fate, they did not despair of their king nor of their God. And then at last despair was aroused among them by hunger.

—Prince Felix Lichnowsky[1]

THE COMMUNIST MANIFESTO would eventually be translated into as many as two hundred languages, but when it was published it went virtually unnoticed. Europe was already on fire. In the third week of February 1848 rumors circulated in Brussels of a political earthquake in Paris, rumors too fantastic to believe: *Louis-Philippe abdicated the throne and fled into exile. A provisional government declared in France. France, a Republic!* On Thursday the twenty-fourth, the railway station in Brussels was packed with people waiting for the delayed train from Paris to arrive with the news. Even the French ambassador was there to learn what, if any, government he served. At half past midnight on Friday the train finally arrived. Stephan Born, who was in the crowd, recalled that the engineer jumped from the train while it was still moving and shouted, "The red flag flies over the towers of Valenciennes. The Republic is declared!" A roar went up from the crowd, *"Vive la République!"* The French ambassador and his wife scurried away from the platform as mostly German voices kept up the chant.[2] Within weeks that cry echoed in capitals across Europe as, one by one, leaders who had once seemed invincible fell like flicked dominoes. More remarkable still, they did not fall before armies; they fell before common men whose only real weapon was their plentiful number.

One historian has written, "History does not eliminate grievances; it lays them down like land mines."[3] That was certainly the case in 1848.

The grievances that exploded that year could be traced directly to the 1815 Congress of Vienna, which carved up Europe in such a way as to erase any trace of Napoleon's conquests. The borders imposed by the leaders who made up the congress had never, however, quite fit the populations they were meant to contain. And the monarchs who emerged from the meetings believing themselves cloaked in new strength were actually weakened as a result of the Napoleonic wars. Their people had made blood sacrifices in battle, but in peace received nothing in return. Taxes did not fund improvements; they filled treasuries that financed a lavish court life. Rights that had been dangled as a reward for driving out the French did not materialize; they were more strenuously denied by newly empowered police forces. Crops failed but governments provided no relief; unemployment soared but there was no attempt to create jobs. Between 1815 and 1848, however, the discontented had found their voices, and in 1848 they had finally risen up. That year's revolt became known as the Springtime of the Peoples. It was the first—and is still the only—Europe-wide rebellion of the people against their rulers.[4]

Paris in February was the dramatic high point of the outbreak of the 1848 revolts, yet they actually began in the fall of 1847. The first occurred in Switzerland, when a freshly installed government went to war against seven Catholic regions that had chosen to secede rather than abide by a new liberal constitution. In neighboring Austria, powerful Chancellor Metternich saw the war as a threat to the conservative monarchs of Europe and tried to rally support against the "Godless radicals." But after twenty-six days of fighting, the liberals won: Switzerland was unified. News of their triumph spread throughout Europe.[5] One radical sent the Swiss a message: "The clock of the peoples marked midnight; the Swiss people advanced the hands several hours toward the dawn."[6]

That Swiss revolt was quickly followed by one in Palermo. Italy did not in fact exist at that time; it was broken up into two principalities, three kingdoms, three sovereign duchies, and the Papal States controlled by the pope. In Piedmont the ruling class spoke French; in Lombardy and Venice they spoke German; and throughout the peninsula the people communicated in dialects incomprehensible to their neighbors a few miles away.[7] In the 1830s nationalist Giuseppe Mazzini had formed the Young Italy movement to unite his country, but the region seemed hopelessly divided, without the benefit of rail or communications links that had helped insurgents organize elsewhere in Europe.[8]

In early January 1848, however, a rebellion sparked by a food crisis erupted in Sicily, the poorest part of what would become Italy. Aided by criminals looking to expand their authority and liberals inspired by reforms instituted by Pope Pius IX in the Papal States, Palermo residents caught King Ferdinand off guard and within two weeks established a provisional government. By the end of January the king known for his absolute power had lost control of all his territories from Sicily to Apulia. In February, in a last-ditch effort to retain his throne, Ferdinand proposed a constitution,[9] and that constitutional contagion spread swiftly north. Mazzini, who was in London, summoned his followers to rush home, their dream of a nation seemingly within reach.[10]

The events in Switzerland and Italy, however dramatic, were mere warm-ups in the battle against monarchical rule. The prizefight would occur in France, where European revolutions had traditionally been born. Like King Ferdinand, Louis-Philippe was surprised by the events of 1848—though of all who occupied a throne, he should not have been. Louis-Philippe had had adequate warning signs had he cared to look around him, but from the isolation of his palace he haughtily wagered, "Parisians won't start a revolution in winter. They storm things in hot weather."[11] How little he knew his people.

For nearly a year French opposition parliamentarians had been agitating for electoral and political reform, partly in response to 1847 election laws that made a mockery of voting rights.[12] A voting tax of 200 francs was instituted in a country where even the aristocrats among the workers—the artisans—earned on average just 600 francs a year. That meant that out of nine million potential male voters, only about a quarter of a million could afford to cast a ballot.[13]

In order to circumvent strict new rules on political association that did not allow more than six people to meet for a political discussion without permission, a series of grand banquets was organized.[14] The first took place in July in Paris in an open-air dance hall under a tent with a seventy-piece orchestra. The Château Rouge banquet attracted more than twelve hundred people, and that gathering of moderate optimists was followed by more than twenty-two others around the country, some attracting as many as six thousand people. With each feast the tone became more radical, building to a banquet in Lille in November during which a republican leader, Alexandre Ledru-Rollin, toasted the sacred but unrecognized rights of the majority of Frenchmen: "Political rights to the people, it is said, is madness. How entrust them with them, in their state of incapacity, of ignorance, of moral depravity?" But, he declared, "I say that those who pay the taxes of blood and sweat and silver have the right to participate in the government which disposes of all these riches."[15] By that time, Engels wrote in an article for London's *Northern Star,* the majority of France's lower bourgeoisie was prepared to join the opposition; they had concluded that the king and his loyalists in government were the "obedient servants of a small number of bankers, stock jobbers, railway-speculators, large manufacturers, landed and mining proprietors."[16]

A massive banquet was scheduled in Paris's twelfth arrondissement for February 22, to be preceded by a march to the event by those who could not afford the price of entry. Until then the king had not been overly concerned about the banquets, but Prime Minister François Guizot, who was despised as the evil architect behind Louis-Philippe's rule, feared that this one could be a catalyst for trouble, so the gathering was banned. Guizot's order persuaded eighty out of ninety-nine organizers to abandon the event, but the crowds who had been summoned to march were in no mood to capitulate.[17] Despite a cold, persistent rain on the morning of February 22, they gathered at the Place de la Madeleine and shouted, "Down with Guizot!"[18]

The next day the weather was worse—sleet and rain stung bare heads and hands like icy needles—but the demonstration was even larger. The eighty-thousand-strong National Guard had been dispatched to control the mob, but they too were tired of the monarchy. They turned their guns butt side up and joined the protest. A wild cheer erupted. The call was again raised for Guizot to go.

By the afternoon Louis-Philippe, who was too old and perhaps too tired for a fight, gave in and dismissed his powerful minister. He might have assumed that this sacrifice would satisfy the crowd, but come evening the streets swelled with demonstrators who wanted more. As they noisily marched down the Boulevard des Capucines, men and women arm in arm, they met a police line that opened fire. Fifty (some reports said as many as eighty) people were killed. The demonstrators loaded sixteen of the bodies onto carts and marched in a solemn torchlit procession through the darkened city.[19] The clatter of metal wheels on wet paving stones and the thud of hundreds of feet echoed through the otherwise empty streets. There were no more shouts or rebel songs. The seething mob was terrifying in its silence.

It is safe to say few people slept in Paris that night—certainly neither the protesters nor the king. All through the night barricades were built. More than one million paving stones were torn up and more than four thousand trees cut down to build fifteen hundred structures to counter army and police attacks. But by morning the army, too, had begun to come over to the opposition.[20] On February 24, no doubt haunted by visions of the French Revolution and the guillotine that dispatched Louis XVI, Louis-Philippe abdicated, donned a disguise, and fled to England, declaring he did not want to spill the blood of the French people. Before he left he gave his nine-year-old grandson his crown. He wanted to make the child sovereign ruler of France, with his mother as regent until he came of age, but the situation had moved well beyond such farce. The boy and his mother escaped, too, and a provisional government was formed.[21]

Alexis de Tocqueville, an aristocrat not overly sympathetic to the opposition, was nonetheless one of the more eloquent observers of the Paris revolt. In a speech to France's elected lower house, the Chamber of Deputies, nearly a month before tensions flared, he had pleaded with political leaders to open their eyes and see that a rebellion driven by want was at hand. "Can you not see that their passions, instead of political, have become social? Do you not see that they are gradually forming opinions and ideas which are destined not only to upset this or that law, ministry or even form of government, but society itself?...Believe me, the real reason, the effective reason which causes men to lose political power, is that they have become unworthy to retain it."[22]

The United States quickly recognized the new French government.[23] Around Europe, the response was more apprehensive. Absolute monarchs saw a certain poetic justice in Louis-Philippe's fall. He had ascended the throne as a result of the revolt in 1830 and was now toppled by one. But they would not be allowed to savor the moment for long.[24]

About a week before news of the Paris revolt reached Brussels, Marx had been given a warning that something was about to break. French socialist Jacques Imbert, a member of the Democratic Association and a refugee in Brussels, told him to get ready. But rather than flee to safety in case violence spread to Belgium, Marx and Jenny moved the family from the security of suburban Ixelles back to the Bois Sauvage, to the center of Brussels.[25] Engels was already there: on January 29 French police had broken into his Paris apartment and given him twenty-four hours to leave France or face extradition to Prussia. Two conflicting explanations exist for his expulsion.[26] One was that the French were alarmed by a speech he gave to German emigrants hostile to the government.[27] The second was that he was expelled because of a dispute over a woman. Stephan Born said Engels had threatened to expose a "Count X," who had discarded his mistress without any means of support, in which case she would have been condemned to life as a concubine for a series of men, if not a prostitute. This version involved a duel. The real story must remain a mystery.[28] The Democratic Association simply published a note in the *Deutsche-Brüsseler* saying that it was completely satisfied with Engels's account of the events that led to his abrupt departure from France.[29]

After the joyous initial news of the Paris revolt, the Marx household and Engels waited expectantly for more information. But the day was eerily quiet. It was as if all sides were assessing the situation and plotting their next move. Belgian authorities had long been aware of the various clubs and associations radical refugees had formed in Brussels, but they had not seen them as any real threat. Now things were different. Unemployment in Belgium's textile factories was rising, and throughout the small country there were pockets of famine. One historian of Belgium's workers' movement said not a day passed "without a starving worker breaking a shop window for the sake of appeasing his hunger in prison."[30] Authorities feared that foreign elements would use their links to the Paris rebels to foment violence in Brussels, and there was the possibility that Belgian workers would see their grief reflected in the face of the Paris mob and decide that Belgium, too, would be better off without a king.[31]

By Saturday, February 26, the Belgian government had drawn up a list of foreigners to be watched and if necessary expelled.[32] Marx and other leaders of the Democratic Association had meanwhile begun alerting members and friends about a demonstration to be held the next night to "obtain through the ways proper to Belgian political institutions the advantage which the French people have won."[33] Victor Tedesco went from café to café, standing on tabletops, summoning people to the protest.[34] By Sunday evening the Grand-Place in front of the Hôtel de Ville, as well as surrounding taverns and cafés, swelled with the committed and the curious.

Citizens had turned out for a peaceful demonstration, but as their numbers grew they became increasingly agitated and the situation more chaotic. The "Marseilleise" rang out alongside shouts of *"Vive la République!"* The civil guard (comprised largely of middle-class volunteers), the police, and army infantry units bolstered by reserve troops from the provinces, ringed the massive square on foot and horseback, visibly nervous as the crowd grew more boisterous and physical. Engels, Stephan Born, and Lupus were among other Germans watching from a café as the crowds spilled off into side streets chanting, *"Li-ber-té, é-gal-i-té!"* Suddenly the gendarmes in the square moved against the crowd. Demonstrators were knocked to the ground and beaten, and police fanned out along the periphery, grabbing those who fled.[35] Lupus was stopped, and when a knife was found on him was taken into custody along with thirty-four Belgians and four other foreigners. He was interrogated, transferred to a detention facility, and then sent to prison.[36] Marx later claimed that Lupus was beaten by drunken police guards who "tore off his glasses, spat in his

face, kicked him, punched him, abused him....They tortured him."
(Lupus's right eye was so badly damaged his sight was threatened, though
in the end he suffered no permanent injuries.)[37]

Leopold's government was in some ways far shrewder than others in
Europe. Authorities in Brussels thought that if they could identify the
miscreants behind the Grand-Place melee as German, they might be able
to delude the Belgian populace into thinking their fellow countrymen
were not agitating against their government. At the very least this could
buy them time to take steps to head off revolt. In addition word was spread
that the king would abdicate if the people so wished, that at heart he was
a republican. That clever whispering campaign bolstered Leopold's support
among the people without his actually having to do anything.[38]

By Monday rumors had circulated throughout Brussels that disreputable Germans who had been thrown out of their own countries were
responsible for the Sunday night violence. In an article for the *Northern
Star,* Engels wrote, "In less than a day the whole mass of the shopocracy...
raised one unanimous outcry against the German rebels....The Germans
had fixed a place of meeting in a coffee house, where every one of them
was to bring the latest news from Paris. But the outcry of the shopocrats
was so great, and the rumors of the government measures against the Germans so manifold, that they were obliged to give up even this innocent
means of communicating with each other."[39] Jenny noted that the police,
the military, and the civil guard were all called out against the Germans,
who decided it was time to arm themselves. "Daggers, revolvers etc were
procured. Karl willingly provided the money, for he had just come into an
inheritance," she matter-of-factly recalled in her autobiography years
later.[40]

Indeed, in early February Marx had received the promised 6,000 francs
from his mother.[41] The money was desperately needed to pay debts and to
set aside for the months ahead, because there was no other income for the
foreseeable future. But Marx rarely thought of the future where his own
finances were concerned. Money in his hand one minute was gone before
the next—in most cases it had already been spent several times over. Jenny
knew what prematurely spending his inheritance meant: creditors, insecurity, deception. Yet she did not seem to quibble over whether Marx
should buy firearms for insurgents rather than food for his family. In fact
she seemed naively surprised at the Belgian government's alarm over her
husband's actions. "In all this," she proclaimed, "the government saw
conspiracy and criminal plans: Marx receives money and buys weapons,
he must therefore be got rid of."[42]

Jenny's point may have been, as some Marx biographers have suggested, that the Belgian government had nothing to fear from him or his fellow Germans because they planned to take their fight home, across the border to Prussia. But even if that had been the case, Belgium still would have considered it within its rights—at the very least—to expel armed rebels who were bent on overthrowing an ally. Jenny's somewhat bizarre response appeared to be an indication that she still may not have fully realized that the revolutionary theories she so admired in her husband's writings had a distinct material reality in the form of guns.

By March 1, Lupus and the other foreigners arrested that Sunday had been taken in black police carriages to the train station and expelled to France. Time was running out for Marx, too. On Monday, February 28, a police spy had spotted him exchanging 2,100 francs in banknotes with two men.[43] If it could be proved that Marx was arming rebels in Belgium, he might be hanged. He told Jenny to take the children to Trier, but she refused. As Marx's wife she faced harassment there, too.[44] (Even Marx's elderly mother was questioned by Trier authorities about the money she'd sent her son and forced to sign an affidavit that it was to support his family.)[45]

The Communist League, meanwhile, had transferred its Central Authority from London to Brussels to be nearer the revolt in Paris. But by March 3, Marx had decided the authority should be transferred again, to Paris itself.[46] It could be that he had already decided to go there, too: Ferdinand Flocon, editor of Paris's opposition *La Reforme* newspaper, was now a member of France's provisional government, and in this capacity invited "Good and Loyal Marx" to return to France. In a letter dated March 1 but probably received by Marx at least a day or two later, Flocon told him, "Tyranny exiled you, now free France opens its doors to you and to all those who are fighting for the holy cause, the fraternal cause of all the peoples."[47] The timing of Flocon's letter could not have been better. On March 2, King Leopold I signed an order expelling Marx from Belgium and forbidding him to ever return.[48]

Marx, Engels, and Born had been sleeping at a friend's home outside Brussels to avoid arrest, but on March 3, Marx was at the Bois Sauvage at five in the evening when the expulsion order was handed to him. It included the now familiar twenty-four-hour deadline for his departure.[49] While Jenny and Lenchen began getting the family's things together—a not insignificant task because they had lived in Brussels for more than three years— Marx called five members of the Communist League, including Engels and Gigot, to his second-floor rooms. They formally agreed to move the Central Authority to Paris and to give Marx power to constitute a new authority there.[50]

Police had been watching the boardinghouse and reported that they saw several people visit Marx between nine and eleven at night. At one in the morning, police pushed into the darkened Bois Sauvage past sleeping staff and mounted the stairs to the first floor, where the Marxes had rooms.[51] A report said a police agent, followed by four officers and a chambermaid, first burst into a bedroom where Jenny and Lenchen were sleeping. They searched the room for half an hour before going to the second floor, where they found Marx in a dressing gown, arranging his trunks for departure. On a table nearby were half-empty glasses of wine and beer, evidence to the police of the meeting that had taken place there earlier. Officers searched the room and found league documents, including the one transferring its authority to Paris. They then demanded official papers from Marx, and he produced his original expulsion order from France and his new expulsion order from Belgium. The police scoffed that neither document constituted proper identification or a passport, and he was promptly arrested. He was allowed to dress and then, surrounded by uniformed officers, was marched to a waiting police vehicle.[52]

Terrified, Jenny left the house to find their friend the Belgian lawyer Lucien Jottrand. She knew the possible consequences for a German arrested in Brussels. The police could, probably would, charge her husband with treason if they could confirm that he had provided money for arms. Jenny instructed Jottrand to take whatever steps were necessary to find Karl and free him. Still desperate, she rushed from house to house, through the darkened streets of central Brussels, velvet cloak trailing behind her, trying to rouse sleeping friends and find help. Along the way she met Philippe Gigot, who offered her his arm to steady her mentally and physically. Together they returned to the Bois Sauvage, where a police sergeant politely offered to take Jenny to see her husband.[53]

Gigot and Jenny followed him to the station, only to be told Marx was not there. She was then interrogated as to why she had gone to see Jottrand and whether she herself was carrying proper papers. Gigot protested that the questions were absurd and insolent. He was thrown into a cell. (A police report later called him a victim of his gallantry.)[54] Jenny, meanwhile, was arrested for not having proper identification, charged with vagabondage, and placed in a dark cell with three prostitutes.[55] "As I entered sobbing, an unhappy companion in misery offered to share her place with me. It was a hard plank bed. I lay down on it."[56] Police said they left Jenny there only for a short time before moving her to a cell with two beds, the other occupied by a woman arrested for assault. In this account Jenny was so thankful for the transfer that she gave her jailer half a franc.[57]

The next morning was dull and cold. Jenny said she looked out her window and saw, behind the iron bars of the window opposite, a "cadaverous, mournful face." It was Gigot. "When he saw me he beckoned to me, pointing downwards. I looked in that direction and saw Karl being led away under military escort." Not knowing whether that escort was taking Marx to his death, she remained in her cell in a state of wretched anxiety for another hour before being taken before a magistrate and questioned. For two hours he grilled her about her and her husband's activities, but she said he got little out of her.[58] "The interrogation was naturally a sham," Marx wrote later. "My wife's only crime consisted in the fact that although belonging to the Prussian aristocracy, she shares the democratic opinions of her husband."[59]

In the end no charges were brought against Marx (who said he spent the night in a cell with a madman[60]) or Jenny, and they were released at three in the afternoon, just hours before their expulsion deadline. Marx had asked that Jenny be allowed to stay in Brussels for three more days to collect herself and prepare the children for the journey, but Jenny refused to remain without him.[61] She and Lenchen quickly packed their things, and Jenny sold what she could. She left their treasured silver plate and all her Argyll linens with the bookseller Vogler.[62]

Many of the couple's friends gathered at the Bois Sauvage to say farewell. Stephan Born, who treated Jenny so tenderly in his written recollections that he seemed to be slightly in love with her, said, "A deep sadness lay on her pure features. We shook hands and said goodbye when she reached her provisional home. Everything had been provisional for her, a real home for herself and her children she had never known."[63]

On March 4 Marx, Jenny, Lenchen, and the three children, accompanied by Red Wolff, left Brussels for Paris. They could see in the flickering candlelight inside their carriage that the train was full of Belgian soldiers heading south to reinforce the border with France.[64] Marx and his family were traveling farther, toward the very epicenter of the revolt, but instead of being alarmed by the prospect they were filled with excitement. Jenny recalled thinking, "Where could we feel more at ease than under the rising sun of the new revolution? We had to go there, we just had to!"[65]

14

Paris, Spring 1848

The great appear great in our eyes
Only because we are kneeling.
Let us rise!

—Elisée Loustalot[1]

KARL AND JENNY did not arrive in Paris until the next day. The journey was cold, and it was difficult to keep the children warm despite piles of hay thrown onto the carriage floor as insulation.[2] Jenny held one-year-old Edgar, and the girls snuggled inside the heavy coats of the men to keep their small bodies from freezing. The trip took longer than usual because some of the tracks had been torn up in protest against rail companies that had been seen as facilitating the industrial demon. In the dead of night the passengers were forced to switch to horse-drawn omnibuses until an intact rail line could be found. At dawn, however, their enthusiasm returned; they could see along the way that stations were festooned with red flags and the French tricolor. From the countryside it appeared the government had been overthrown in a great festival, but as the small party drew closer to the capital, the battle scars became clearer: locomotives, rail cars, and trestles were burned, smashed, and disabled. The last station before reaching Paris, in the factory town of St.-Denis, was burned out entirely.[3] In Paris the devastation was everywhere. Stones that had helped build the barricades were strewn over streets once neatly paved. Roads were blocked with burned-out bread carts, broken furniture was piled as high as housetops, and carriages had been overturned. The windows at the Palais Royal were smashed, and the guardhouse opposite stood a charred ruin, the guards inside incinerated.[4] In the magnificent halls of the Tuileries, the

131

ragged wounded lay sprawled on the palace's thick carpets beneath portraits of former royal occupants now torn to shreds. And from the palace windows white curtains could be seen fluttering through broken panes like tattered flags of surrender.[5]

This was no longer the Paris Jenny and Marx had left in 1845. The glorious city was broken, but it was free, at least for men—universal male suffrage was declared in France on the day they arrived. Paris was also peopled by Marx's friends and associates, and the couple no longer had to live in fear of arrest. Jacques Imbert, who had tipped off Marx to the pending revolt, was now governor, and his office was in the Tuileries.[6] Another close friend, Marc Caussidiere, was police prefect in Paris, and he was busy forming a civil guard of newly released political prisoners.[7] Engels called the period a "republican honeymoon." By day civilians, who had only dry bread and potatoes to eat, planted what they called "liberty trees" along the boulevards to replace those cut down for barricades. After sunset the narrow streets echoed with revelry and song.[8]

The night of their arrival it was difficult for Karl and Jenny to find lodgings because so many people had flocked to Paris to celebrate. The Marxes finally found a spot in a small Right Bank rooming house near the Bastille, on the rue Neuve-Ménilmontant, run by a woman who catered to German socialists.[9] Once installed, Marx left the family almost immediately to attend a meeting led by French veteran revolutionary Armand Barbes (newly freed from prison, where he'd served time for conspiring against the king), visit members of the new provisional government, and renew acquaintances with émigrés[10] who had remained in Paris and many others who had streamed back since February 24. Bakunin was among them. He had returned on February 28, and was thrilled to find that young dandies in carriages and idlers with canes were no longer the main attractions on the boulevards.[11] Instead the streets were crowded with men of the revolution—the *"quarante-huitards,"* or "48ers"—with their beards, flowing cravats, and broad-brimmed hats.[12] They were hardened fighters, but at that moment they reeled like romantics drunk on sunshine.

This was a Paris not seen since the 1830 revolt, perhaps not even since the first heady days of the 1789 Revolution. Gustave Flaubert left his home in Rouen and traveled to Paris to observe the "artistic aspect" of this latest uprising.[13] George Sand set to work writing bulletins for the Interior Ministry, and Victor Hugo was asked to be education minister (he declined).[14] Political clubs seemingly sprouted wherever there was a table and a sufficient number of chairs. Women's groups advocating divorce, an end to workplace discrimination, and day care to free women to work emerged. Yellow posters colored the city's walls in an exuberant declaration of women's rights. The advocates leading that charge were mostly female intellectuals who enjoyed scant support from the men behind the wider revolt.[15] (French socialists were notoriously antifeminist.)[16] There was also an explosion of newspapers—within a month 171 of them appeared in Paris alone.[17] Indeed, on that first day Flocon offered Marx money to start a journal, but Marx refused, explaining that he wanted to remain independent of any government, even a republic.[18] In any case he was entirely focused on organizing his German comrades to take their fight back home. League leaders from London were already in Paris, and colleagues from Brussels were en route. Said Engels, "The tidal wave of revolution pushed all scientific pursuits into the background; what mattered now was to become involved in the movement."[19]

Far from ending in Paris, the "Springtime of the People" was still spreading, and one of the places it spread fastest was the German Confederation. The Bund's thirty-nine regions had suffered the same calamitous agricultural and business setbacks as their neighbors in Europe. Food prices had risen by more than half since 1844, and there were hunger riots in almost every state. Germany was still largely an agricultural nation, but those industries that had developed had hurt artisans badly. These craftsmen were bitter that they were forced to work in factories alongside less skilled men, women, and children—if they had work at all.

The most pressing problems were in Prussia, the largest state in the Bund and, with sixteen million residents, its most populous.[20] The immediate crisis there had begun the year before, when Friedrich Wilhelm IV needed a favor from the United Diet, the body of representatives from the provincial diets that was composed of mostly Prussian gentry. The United Diet held the purse strings of government, and Friedrich Wilhelm, who had squandered the surplus he inherited from his father on court activities, wanted a loan to build a railroad. Perhaps surprisingly to him, the diet (whose loyalty he should have been able to count on) was not willing to rubber-stamp his request. Members were nervous about being perceived as indulging the spendthrift and increasingly unpopular king at that moment.[21] Tens of thousands of people had died of hunger or related causes in East Prussia and Upper Silesia in the previous twelve months, and the usually passive countryside was in an uproar; about a third of all antigovernment, antigentry protests occurred there. During that diet session in April 1847 alone, there were 150 food riots.

The diet said it would not approve the king's loan until he approved the constitution promised by his father more than thirty years before.[22] Friedrich Wilhelm refused, vowing that he would not allow a piece of paper to come between him and the people who loved him. The king then disbanded the diet, but not before its debate (which grew increasingly bold) had been reported in newspapers throughout Prussia. An observer noted, "There was a feeling in the air as if this United Diet...was not at all unlike the French Assembly of the year 1789."[23] Still, it would take almost a year for anything resembling revolt to occur in Prussia, and then only after the Paris upheaval and, more dramatically, the fall of the powerful Prince Clemens Wenzel von Metternich of Austria.

At seventy-four, Metternich was, to reformers of every stripe, the embodiment of all that was wrong with European governments in general and monarchies in particular. He was the architect of the Congress of Vienna and of the Holy Alliance of reactionary Prussia, Austria, and Russia, which existed primarily to maintain its own powerful position and to keep Poland divided and subjugated. Though he was not a king, merely Austrian chancellor, Metternich spoke for all of Germany and was considered by many to be continental Europe's chief diplomat.[24]

After the revolt in France, news of which reached Vienna during a carnival on February 29, all classes in Austria looked at one another with suspicion and expectation. The rebellion was sure to come, but from where? A short time before, a group of Viennese medical students had petitioned Austrian emperor Ferdinand. Describing themselves as liberal, not radical, they asked for the usual reforms—free press, free speech, a constitution, and academic freedom. When the petition was ignored, several thousand students organized a demonstration, which grew to include workers, to coincide with a March 13 session of Austria's diet. But when the protesters marched, troops opened fire, killing fifteen people. The protests spread, and so did support for the demonstrators. Even the national guard turned on the government and joined opposition ranks.[25]

So great was the uproar that by the end of the day, after forty years in power, Metternich resigned. (Like Louis-Philippe, he fled in disguise to England.)[26] Two days later Ferdinand promised a constitution, and the self-proclaimed Academic Legion of student victors took control of Vienna. The carnival that greeted news of the Paris revolt was once again in full swing. Throughout the empire—Budapest, Prague, Venice—regions broke free.[27] For five days Milan erupted in a glorious revolt against Austrian rule. Artisans and laborers manned fifteen hundred barricades built in a matter of hours out of sofas, pianos, mahogany tables, and pews contributed by Milan's finest households and churches. The Milanese had only six hundred muskets, so they improvised with clubs, pikes, and swords taken from museums and La Scala opera house. Before the week was over the city was theirs.[28]

★   ★   ★

News of the events in Vienna reached Berlin on March 16. The city had already been the scene of riots and street fighting since word arrived from Paris, but the early protests were not organized; they were spontaneous manifestations of frustration arising from a population in which only one person in ten had regular work, and half of those were apprentices earning a pittance. Eighty-five percent of Berlin's four hundred thousand people belonged to the lower classes, and more than half of those relied on poor relief to survive. These masses struck out against authority, looting what they could, fighting whoever tried to stop them. By the time the Vienna revolt occurred, middle-class organizers, students, and radical intellectuals had joined the effort, and it began to assume a more coordinated—and threatening—character. Another appeal was made to the Prussian king to approve the traditional liberal freedoms. This time he listened.[29]

At ten in the morning of March 18, Friedrich Wilhelm issued a proclamation: censorship was abolished, and reforms would be instituted. The Prussian cabinet would resign, the king had summoned the disbanded diet to return, and together they would work toward a united Germany. The king appeared on his balcony before a jubilant crowd that gathered to thank him for his concessions. The square teemed with mostly lower-class Berliners and students, and at the periphery mounted troops were stationed. The king's voice was drowned out by the mob. They heard what they chose to hear—they believed they had gained everything they wanted. A drumroll sounded, and it seemed the troops might be withdrawn, but instead they rode their horses into the crowd to disperse it. In the confusion two shots were fired, and the joy that had prevailed just moments before turned to terror and then rage. The king, the people thought, had signaled his troops to open fire.[30] A witness said the cry went up, "We are betrayed! We are betrayed!" followed by the shout "To arms!"[31]

The witness continued: "In all directions the thoroughfares were soon blocked with barricades. The paving stones seemed to leap from the ground and to form themselves into bulwarks surmounted by black, red and gold flags and manned by citizens, university students, tradesmen, artists, laborers, professional men, hastily armed with all sorts of weapons from rifles and shotguns down to pikes, axes and hammers."[32] A white banner was lowered from the palace bearing one word—"Misunderstanding"—but it was too late.[33] At four in the afternoon church bells rang as if to mark the start of the horrible battle. All through the night government cannons pounded their targets as civilian fighters screeched vengeance. Perhaps most terrifying of all was the echo of a single shot followed by a sharp cry, the unmistakable sound of execution.

The next morning, Sunday, the church bells tolled again. The king ordered the shooting to stop.[34] After that fearsome night, the sounds of which would have been inescapable even inside the royal palace, Friedrich Wilhelm had determined that the only way to save his throne was to throw himself on the mercy of his people and trust in their loyalty. He ordered the army out of Berlin and opened the doors of his arsenal to the people, who would secure the capital.[35] By three o'clock troops began to withdraw and the barricades were dismantled.[36] By noon Monday peace had been established.[37]

At sunset nearly every light in Berlin was lit and virtually every street was crowded with people as the soldiers marched, regiment by regiment, out of the city.[38] Then, from all around, silent processions began toward the palace. During the fighting hundreds of people had fallen before the estimated hundred thousand cartridges fired by the military. Litters of those dead were carried aloft by men still covered in blood and gunpowder, and placed row upon row in the palace courtyard. The crowd called out for the king, who appeared on the balcony with his wife.[39] A voice shouted "Hat off!" and the king, who had previously bowed to no man, removed his hat in tribute to the dead below.[40]

The fight for freedom in Berlin was far deadlier than anywhere else in Europe at that point, but just three days after it began, the king was able to ride on horseback unmolested among the people, who now, fully armed, were in control of the city. Friedrich Wilhelm ordered a general amnesty for political prisoners and enemies of the state, allowing Prussian exiles to return home. He also said his kingdom would have a constitution. Improbably, centuries of absolute rule appeared to be over; Prussians were no longer subjects, they were citizens. All around Berlin the words "People's Property" were boldly inscribed on public buildings.[41]

The American minister in Berlin, Andrew Jackson Donelson, had kept an hour-by-hour diary of the battle. On March 30, before sending his report to Washington, he wrote:

> The king in the meantime is powerless. Disarmed as if by magic of his guards and of the ceremonies which gave so much apparent splendor and dignity to his court, he sees disappear as a dream all that mystic inheritance which he has received from his fathers, and by which he has believed that his authority was of divine right.... He has been still unable to comprehend the force of the great moral truth that all men are born free and equal—and that they can confer no political distinction or power which is divine.... He cannot comprehend that these virtues...are designed by providence to illustrate the advent of a reform which is to give Europe better governments and a better

people — an era in which absolutism falls, not that kings are bad men, but that the system is no longer suited to the wants of society.[42]

In Paris, German socialists and communists knew of the events in Berlin and were plotting ways to return, in order to ensure that rights extended to the middle classes also applied to the workingman. Herwegh (who was celebrating the euphoria of revolution by having an affair with the wife of Russian writer Alexander Herzen[43]) was outfitting a so-called German Legion to march into southern Germany and fight for a republic there. Herwegh's wife, Emma, backed the plan as a way to burnish his revolutionary credentials and also renew interest in him as a poet.[44] Thousands of recruits eagerly signed on to the adventure, which the new French government helped finance.

Marx believed the French assistance was actually a cynical attempt to rid Paris of German laborers in order to make room for the French in a tight job market.[45] While that was true, the support was also partly in response to the absolute mania among revolutionaries of all nationalities crowded together in Paris. Faced with that restless bunch, the French encouraged the emigrants to leave, all except the Poles and the Irish, who'd been adopted by France as victims of foreign rule.[46] However, Flocon did think Poland needed stirring up, so he sent Bakunin there, giving him 2,000 francs and two passports to go to Posen and see what havoc he could wreak.[47]

Marx and Engels were deeply opposed to Herwegh's legion, which they predicted would quickly be defeated, revive fears of French invaders, and strengthen conservatives in government. When Marx expressed these concerns at a meeting of the Democratic Association, which was helping Herwegh, he was heckled as a coward and a traitor, even by some members of his reconstituted Communist League. He responded by expelling the dissenters and establishing a separate organization, the German Workers' Union, which met at a café on the rue St.-Denis. That group included the league leadership from London — Schapper, Moll, and Bauer — as well as the Brussels circle.[48] Marx proposed that Union members wear red ribbons. Schapper suggested blood red. The uncharacteristic flourish was agreed.[49]

Next, Marx organized his own infiltration into Germany. Instead of a legion of fighters, his men would be propagandists. They would return with no fanfare, in small groups or as individuals, and plant the seeds of communism quietly throughout the Confederation.

In fact, the propaganda had already begun. On March 17, Jenny wrote Weydemeyer, who was in Germany, asking that he publish a notice about the differences between Marx's German Workers' Union and Herwegh's group, which she described as using retired Prussian officers to conduct military drills. Engels had said one of the strikes against Herwegh's legion was that it would be betrayed before it reached Germany. Jenny's letter blithely seemed to do just that. She continued:

> Try to have this circulated as widely as possible in the German press. I should like to write you much more about the interesting movement under way here, which is growing from minute to minute (four hundred thousand workers marched past the Hôtel de Ville tonight). The masses of demonstrators are growing and growing. But I am so overburdened with housework and caring for my three little ones that all I have left is time to send you and your dear wife cordial greetings from afar.

She signed her letter *"Salut et fraternité, Citoyenne et Vagabonde Jenny Marx."*[50]

Herwegh's legion left for Germany on April 1, following a colorful parade of a thousand proud insurgents, their sabers and bayonets gleaming, and dozens of eloquent tributes befitting a warrior-poet's troops. Twenty-five days later the corps was almost annihilated in its first battle.[51]

Marx's Union had four hundred members (out of the estimated eighty thousand German exiles in Paris), and with a subsidy from the French government they began leaving Paris in early April. Engels went to his favorite recruiting ground, Wuppertal, Lupus to Breslau, Schapper to Wiesbaden, Born to Berlin. Marx went to Cologne.[52]

They returned undetected,[53] armed with the *Communist Manifesto* and a handbill Marx and Engels had written, titled "The Demands of the Communist Party in Germany." It stipulated a united Germany, universal male suffrage, paid legislators (to make it possible for those other than the very rich to serve), universal arming of citizens, abolition of all feudal debts and burdens, nationalization of all princely and feudal estates, establishment of a central bank and paper currency, separation of church and state, limitation of inheritance rights, the right to work, and free education for all.[54] That document, though hardly radical today, would have been heretical to the thrones of midnineteenth-century Europe.

Marx, Jenny, the three children, Lenchen, Engels, and Ernst Dronke (a writer who had earlier escaped from prison in Germany) left Paris on April 6. The family had a one-year visa for Mainz, but they stayed there only two days before splitting up. Engels and Dronke went to their assigned cities, while Jenny, Lenchen, and the children went to Trier and Marx headed to Cologne.[55]

Engels called this the second act of the struggle.[56]

15

Cologne, 1848

*Radical revolution, universal human emancipation is not a
Utopian dream for Germany. What is Utopian is the partial,
the merely political revolution, the revolution which would leave
the pillars of the house standing.*

—Karl Marx[1]

MARX HAD NOT been in Cologne for five years but found little changed.
The businessmen who were frustrated with the government in 1843 were
still frustrated. The workingman who believed himself doubly victim-
ized—by the state and the bourgeoisie—was still a victim. The only real
changes had come in the past month. Censorship had been lifted since the
March 18 uprising in Berlin, and at long last writers could say what they
pleased. Three of Marx's colleagues, Moses Hess, Georg Weerth, and
Heinrich Bürgers, had been trying to start a successor to Karl's earlier
Cologne newspaper, to be titled the *Neue Rheinische Zeitung,* or "New
Rhineland Gazette."[2] Marx's weapon of choice being a newspaper, he was
heartened that efforts to establish one were already well under way. He
was equally heartened when he discovered that in the month before his
arrival, seeds had been planted for a communist organization in Cologne.

On March 3 Andreas Gottschalk, a doctor popular for treating the
poor, and two former Prussian lieutenants, August Willich and Fritze
Anneke, had organized a communist uprising, attracting five thousand
people to Cologne city hall to make their demands. The effort ended prematurely with the arrests of the organizers, but the network had been
established, and when the three men were released from jail in Friedrich
Wilhelm's general amnesty, they returned to Cologne to begin a new

working-class group there. By April it had eight thousand members.³ Almost immediately Marx disagreed with its leader Gottschalk over tactics. Gottschalk preferred explosive rhetoric about workers' rights and arming a people's militia, communist notions that terrified the middle classes of Germany, who were afraid the rights just won would be lost with a revolt by the more numerous lower classes. Marx, however, believed that although the pace of change was frustrating, historical development was slow, and before there could be proletariat rule, there had to be middle-class rule. In any case, a proletariat "class" barely existed in Germany. The number of people who labored with their hands was great, but they were disorganized and did not as yet recognize their own strength. To support the ultimate goal of that group, Marx believed one had to work for middle-class democracy. Viewing upcoming elections as just such an opportunity, he encouraged participation to ensure victories by democratic candidates over reactionaries who would roll back on reforms. Marx further believed that any newspaper he and his associates published in Cologne had to be democratic, not communist, because in Germany democracy was the ideology with the greater immediate potential.⁴ If they had chosen to produce an ultraradical newspaper, Engels said, "there was nothing left for us to do but to preach communism in a little provincial sheet and to found a tiny sect instead of a great party of action."⁵

The pragmatic approach was not unlike the one Marx had taken during his tenure as editor of the earlier *Rheinische Zeitung,* when he refused to publish The Free's communist ideas because he believed they were too impractical—too theoretical—for the paper's middle-class readership. He had returned to Prussia intent on working quietly and broadly to steer the kingdom, and ultimately the German Bund, along the path of reform. He understood the delicacy of the moment: too much change would spark a middle-class flight to the safety of the bad old, but reassuringly familiar, order.

Some former colleagues felt Marx had taken too moderate a path. Others, including the government, saw him as a dangerous radical, and that perception complicated his efforts to regain his Prussian citizenship, which he tried to do as soon as he arrived in Cologne in April.⁶ Without it, liberalization or not, he was under constant threat of expulsion. Jenny had planned to wait in Trier until Karl's application was filed and approved. But with no action imminent, she packed up the family—four-year-old Jennychen, two-year-old Laura, and one-year-old Edgar—and moved to Cologne in June.⁷ By that time Marx had won a battle of wills with Hess over control of the *Neue Rheinische Zeitung* (partly by making up for a funding shortfall at the newspaper with his own money) and staffed the paper with Communist League members from Brussels and Paris. He was named the newspaper's editor.[8]

Roland Daniels, a Cologne doctor, helped Marx and Jenny find an apartment at 7 Cecilienstrasse, near the newspaper's editorial offices.[9] The location was convenient; a few blocks from the Rhine, it was in the center of Cologne's commercial district. It was also lovely; a nearby square—Heumarkt—was surrounded by the pseudo-palaces of the mercantile class. It was not, however, entirely reassuring or safe: both the apartment and editorial offices sat in the shadow of a Prussian garrison of eight thousand troops. Cartloads of materiel clattered noisily into the garrison from dawn to dusk. Crates of ammunition were brought in and rifles with bayonets distributed to the artillerymen.[10] All around, soldiers busily extended and reinforced their vantage points. It was clear the garrison was preparing for war; the question was, against whom? The government claimed it was reinforcing in case of attack from without, but Engels was convinced that troops were preparing to fight the new order within.[11] In a somewhat pathetic attempt to counter the threat, the newspaper staff kept eight rifles with bayonets and 250 live cartridges on hand. Engels described the office as a fortress. But if the staff's firepower was dwarfed by that of the surrounding troops, their courage was undiminished. Marx began carrying a gun.[12]

Such was the state of the free press in Prussia when, on June 1, 1848, the *Neue Rheinische Zeitung* published its first issue, proclaiming itself an "Organ of Democracy."[13] It would have been more accurate to have called it an "Organ of the Birth Pangs of Democracy." Often using reports from colleagues at the scene of battle, the daily paper offered blow-by-blow descriptions of the changing face of European society as governments fell and opposition parties struggled to install suitable replacements. Marx believed one of the newspaper's roles was to educate the less progressive Germans about the state of affairs in countries where the quest for democracy had progressed further, in order to prepare them for the next phase in their own political and social development. But already the news from the rest of Europe was discouraging. It told a story of retreat rather than advance.

Between February and June the euphoria of the early days of revolution had vanished, and in its place appeared antagonisms largely based on class mistrust. The middle classes saw the revolts as their victories, but feared the outcome if lower classes, who had provided the muscle in the fight, were denied a share of the spoils. The nobility feared a loss of political power and economic privilege under middle-class governments that promoted voting rights. And the peasants in the countryside were afraid the middle class would tax them to raise funds to pacify hungry masses primed for revolt in the city. It turned out that toppling governments had been the easy part. Restoring order was proving extremely difficult—in most places, impossibly so.

In France the presidency of the provisional government had gone, in a symbolic gesture, to an eighty-year-old veteran of the Revolution. But the aristocratic poet Alphonse Marie Louis de Lamartine was in actuality the new regime's voice and guiding spirit. Lamartine was a republican whose oratory was so impressive it was considered by many a weapon as effective as a rifle. It fell to him to try to control the exuberant men leading the provisional government.[14] Among his partners in the attempt were the socialist Louis Blanc, journalist Flocon, Ledru-Rollin (who had radicalized the banquets in the lead-up to February 24), and a worker known simply as Albert (alias Alexandre Martin).[15] The result was chaos. None of the men had governed before, and each had a different vision of what the new government should look like.[16]

The list of the provisional government's accomplishments between February 24 and general elections on April 23 was, however, impressive: the abolition of slavery in the colonies, universal male suffrage, freedom of assembly and press, the establishment of national workshops to guarantee employment, a shortened workday, and the abolition of the death penalty for political offenses, to name but a few.[17] But no matter how long the list of decrees, someone's concerns went unanswered. Tensions and resentment grew.

In the countryside, for example, where people harbored a deep suspicion of Paris, the peasants were disappointed that the provisional government did not overturn decisions dating from 1827 that deprived them of some communal rights—including the old question of fallen timber. That disappointment turned to outrage when this same government then imposed a 45 percent surtax on land to ease the strain of a business crisis brought on by the revolt. When Ledru-Rollin as interior minister sent civil servants into the countryside to campaign for republicans, in order to secure what he called a revolutionary National Assembly in the upcoming elections, the countryside was horrified: the dreaded liberals and socialists in the capital were not content with robbing their purses; now they wanted to impose their political will on the provinces. Peasants, landowners, and of course the nobility fled in droves to conservative candidates.[18] The process in Paris was no less divisive and far less orderly. France had no real structure in place for a poll in which every one of its more than nine million men could vote.[19]

Turnout on election day was massive; 84 percent of those eligible to vote did so. When the results were counted, out of 876 deputies elected, fewer than 100 were radical or socialist. The overwhelming majority were conservative or moderate, and many were the very men who had ruled under Louis-Philippe. Parisian workers did not see themselves represented in the new government; they saw the moneyed class they thought they had just overthrown.[20]

Tocqueville, who was elected to the National Assembly from the provinces, reported that when he returned to Paris after the vote he was horrified.

> I found in the capital one hundred thousand armed workmen formed into regiments, out of work, dying of hunger, but with their minds crammed with vain theories.... I saw society cut in two: those who possessed nothing, united in a common greed; those who possessed something, united in a common terror. There were no bonds, no sympathy between these two great sections; everywhere the idea of an inevitable and immediate struggle seemed at hand.[21]

On May 15 disgruntled workers led by veteran extremists assaulted the newly elected National Assembly. They had attended the session ostensibly to listen to a debate on Poland, whose latest independence bid had just been put down. But soon the crowd was immense and threatening, and demands were made—including several by the anarchist Auguste Blanqui, whose mere presence terrified moderate assemblymen. Blanqui had spent much of his life in prison for political crimes, periodically sending out venomous statements directed at the ruling class.[22] When he appeared in the assembly, he had been free for about two months but still wore his prison pallor: he was emaciated and had chalk white lips. His worn frock coat fit tightly over withered limbs. Tocqueville said he looked like a molding corpse.[23] He embodied what the middle classes dreaded, the future they most feared—a second reign of terror.

Former government minister Louis Blanc entered the room and was literally picked up by Blanqui's followers. "They held him by his little legs above their heads; I saw him make vain efforts to extricate himself, he twisted and turned on every side without succeeding in escaping their hands, talking all the while in a choking strident voice," Tocqueville recalled. The boisterous insurgents declared the National Assembly stillborn, placed a red cap on the empty president's chair, and instituted a new provisional government. Their reign lasted only a few hours before Blanqui and his cohorts were arrested.[24]

The French government had successfully met its first challenge. And though it can be dismissed today as political theater, at the time it was a frightening example of the threat the extreme left posed to the new order. As with the voters in the French countryside, the outburst drove liberal sympathizers in the capital toward moderate and conservative leaders. Many began to think the greater enemy was not those higher up the social scale, but those below.

In Prussia, too, the tide was turning away from the workers as the middle and upper classes' fear of disorder eclipsed their desire for truly democratic reform. Immediately after the March 18 uprising in Berlin, Friedrich Wilhelm IV made good on his promise to pick a more liberal cabinet. The prime minister was Marx's old *Rheinische Zeitung* backer Ludolf Camphausen, and the finance minister was another Marx associate from Cologne, David Hansemann. Next, elections were called to select a new assembly to guide the massive changes on the horizon in Prussia, and a separate Confederation-wide vote was scheduled to pick men who would be charged with creating a new nation called Germany. But as in France, the German electorate had no experience in wholesale politics. Factions got to work to try to sway novice voters—conservatives who wanted to restore the old stability, constitutionalists who wanted progress but not at the risk of disorder, and democrats who believed in the liberal promises of the March revolt. Communists like Gottschalk were instructing their followers not to vote at all, and many peasants and workers wanted action even before an election, their needs too great to wait for votes to be cast and counted.[25]

In late March there were uprisings, this time by artisans who wanted an immediate return to trade guilds, which would control competition and thereby ensure their employment. In scenes reminiscent of the Silesian weavers' strike, they attacked the homes of the rich as well as factories. Peasants in the countryside, meanwhile, also rioted. Their targets were large landowners who had bought up and consolidated small plots, leaving the peasants empty-handed.[26]

Political reforms were difficult in the best of times, but infinitely more so during an economic crisis triggered by civil unrest. The newly empowered liberal bourgeoisie pragmatically assessed the alternatives, and, as one writer nicely put it, discovered "revolution was dangerous and that some of their substantial demands (especially in economic terms) could be made without it. The bourgeoisie ceased to be a revolutionary force."[27] They could be liberal concerning all things financial without having to be so politically or socially.[28]

The new government stabilized the economy, using its powers to secure a loan to free credit and take the steps necessary to get business moving again. (It also finally approved the king's loan for the railway he wanted to build.) The moneymen taken care of, the government next tried to calm the restive artisans and peasants by assuring them that their concerns would be dealt with in good time. But that promise was not enough — from the artisans' perspective, Camphausen's government was no better than the old one.

The injury was compounded when ambiguous wording in much-bally-hooed elections managed to disenfranchise many in the lower classes.[29] The election law stipulated that any man who had reached his legal age was *eligible* to vote; it did not guarantee that he had the right to do so. In some cases men who received salaries were not allowed to cast ballots because they were not "independent." Those without fixed residence because they traveled as seasonal laborers or journeymen were not allowed to vote in the cities. In one region bachelors and Jews were excluded.[30] By the time the vote was counted, fewer than half of the eligible electorate had cast ballots, and in some regions no more than 30 percent. Of those who did *not* vote, the majority were workers or members of the lower classes. It was no surprise, then, that the victors were seen by many as puppets of the ruling and middle classes who had turned their backs on the men and women of the Berlin barricades.[31] Disgusted, the *Neue Rheinische Zeitung* declared the newly elected German and Prussian assemblies incompetent.[32]

The German National Assembly, which met in Frankfurt, was especially disappointing. It had not existed before, and its sessions were consumed by structural matters. It was supposed to be the ultimate legislative authority in a united Germany, but because Germany did not yet exist as a nation, it was not clear whether it could enact laws. Engels called it "the parliament of an imaginary country.... It discussed imaginary... measures of an imaginary Government of its own creation, and... passed imaginary resolutions for which nobody cared."[33]

Understaffed and underfinanced, the *Neue Rheinische Zeitung* sought to explain the complicated goings-on. Colorful placards advertising the paper dotted the walls of Cologne's narrow streets. Subscription lists were posted in beer and wine shops.[34] But quite apart from those efforts, what drew readers was the scope of the newspaper's coverage and the audacity of its reportage in a country that had scant experience with a free press. Using a web of correspondents around Europe and clips from foreign papers traded in an informal exchange system, Marx published more news from abroad than any other newspaper in Germany. The *Neue Rheinische Zeitung*'s circulation quickly grew to five thousand subscribers (and no doubt it had many more readers as it changed hands in coffeehouses and taverns), making it one of the most widely read in the thirty-nine German states.[35] Its notoriety began attracting visitors to its offices, some from as far away as America.

Many of these travelers were eager to see the audacious organ in operation and also to meet the man described by police as the soul of the paper and by Engels as its dictator.[36] Albert Brisbane, an American socialist, was in the Rhineland reporting for the *New York Daily Tribune*. He said he found Marx at once moderate and reserved but also possessing "the passionate flame of a bold spirit."[37] Others were less generous. Carl Schurz, a German who would one day become U.S. secretary of the interior, was a nineteen-year-old tasting rebellion for the first time. He was in Berlin during the height of the March 18 fighting and traveled to Cologne later in search of another face of revolt. He attended a meeting and heard Marx speak. "He could not have been much more than thirty years old at the time, but he already was the recognized head of the advanced socialistic school. The somewhat thickset man, with his broad forehead, his very black hair and beard, and his dark sparkling eyes, at once attracted general attention." But Schurz said Marx's speech was intolerable. "Everyone who contradicted him he treated with abject contempt; every argument he did not like he answered either with biting scorn at the unfathomable ignorance that had prompted it, or with opprobrious aspersions upon the motives of him who advanced it." Schurz concluded that Marx repelled many who might otherwise have become his followers.[38]

Those closest to Marx, especially Jenny and Engels, saw in his anger only the frustration of a man who believed to his core that he was right. Marx was utterly without self-doubt when it came to things political, and it was difficult for those who did not know him to see the difference between that complete self-assuredness and arrogance. He did not help his own cause. He was a journalist, a philosopher, and an economist, and though all those occupations were ultimately concerned with political questions, he was not a politician. Marx exhibited little interest in being loved, or even liked. If he was appreciated, well and good, and he returned the sentiment with fierce loyalty. If not, well and good also; he had no time to ponder such inconsequentialities as an individual's wounded feelings or hurt pride.

Marx's list of detractors grew during his time in Cologne. Unfortunately for the newspaper, some of them were the very businessmen needed for its survival. Fearful that he was moving too far to the left when on June 5 he attacked Prime Minister Camphausen for his suggestion that the March 18 revolt be officially downgraded to a riot, those stockholders would soon abandon Marx altogether. This time the catalyst would not be a local crisis, but a bloody battle in Paris.[39]

16

Paris, June 1848

On opening my eyes, I heard a sharp, metallic sound, which shook the window-panes and immediately died out amid the silence of Paris.
"What is that?" I asked.
My wife replied, "It is the cannon."

— Alexis de Tocqueville[1]

IT HAS BEEN said that by June 1848 every man and woman in Paris was armed. The gulf between the classes had become unbridgeable. The government was ineffectual. The people were starving. Crowds gathered in the streets each night, idle, agitated, explosive.[2] By late May a rumor began to circulate that the working classes were planning a banquet of their own in June. It did not take a leap of imagination to assume that the feast, if held, would launch a workers' rebellion. In the end, however, it was not a banquet that precipitated the revolt, but government action.[3] On June 21 a decree came before a National Assembly committee calling for a reversal of the guaranteed-work pledge approved by Lamartine's ministers. Victor Hugo, now a member of the assembly, warned that doing so would create an "army of paupers" and a future "praetorian guard of a new dictator." But the government was running out of money, and it looked to make cuts in a costly jobs program that many feared had turned into a haven for antigovernment radicals.[4]

National workshops had been established to provide men with employment on state and municipal projects and, if such work wasn't available, a minimum amount of money needed to survive. Given the feeble French economy, the program was all that stood between hunger and one hundred thousand men and their families. As word spread that it might be amended or dissolved, protests erupted. Shouts of "Bullets or bread! Bullets or work!" arose, and barricades reappeared in the city.[5] By June 23 a portion of Paris was under the control of the workers.[6] On June 24 General Louis Eugène Cavaignac, minister of war and former military dictator of Algeria, and the fifty thousand troops at his command began a counteroffensive.[7]

A terrible thunderstorm broke that day, flooding Paris, but it did not douse the fighting. From six in the evening on, cannons bombarded buildings and barricades. Men and women fell where they stood. Blood streamed between wet paving stones. Building facades exploded and reappeared as piles of rubble. Shopwindows shattered, the merchandise inside available to anyone who dared venture out into that infernal night.[8] By the end of the first day the newly elected National Assembly had voted to turn over all its executive powers to Cavaignac. France's democratic leaders found the prospect of a dictator less terrifying than an armed, desperate working class bent on even greater revolution.[9] But far from frightening the workers by extending Cavaignac's powers, the legislative cowardice only increased their fury. Each day the battle grew.

Tens of thousands of men and women fought street by street. Tocqueville had little sympathy for the civilian militants but he said they fought "with marvelous harmony and an amount of military experience that astonished the oldest officers." Women made the ammunition and men fired it, and when the men tired or were killed, the women mounted the barricades and the children made the charges for their guns. At the Faubourg St. Antoine, the Panthéon, the Place de la Madeleine, the Hôtel de Ville, and throughout the city, the revolt raged for four days as the Parisians tried to hold out against the military and its heavy weapons.[10]

The fighting ended on June 26. The toll was staggering: an estimated fifteen hundred people died. But the killing did not stop when the last barricade fell. Insurgents were hunted down and executed, three thousand in all. Up to fifteen thousand more people were arrested and forty-five hundred of those deported in packed convoys to Algeria.[11] For many that trip amounted to a death sentence. The loss of life, however, apparently did not overly disturb the tremulous assembly.

Having defeated the workers as he had been asked to do, Cavaignac declared martial law and posted fifty thousand troops along the Champs Elysées, where their horses dined on the greenery that had once been the pride of Paris. Radical clubs were closed and press freedoms revised—only newspapers paying a good-conduct pledge of the enormous sum of 24,000 francs could publish. Soon Cavaignac punished all workers for the actions of the June fighters by eliminating newly enacted limits on the length of the workday.[12] The democratic experiment was over. Louis Blanc fled to England to escape the fate of fellow reformers thrown into jail for having preached the politics of rights, work, and equal representation.[13]

Marx reported on the June Days, as they were known, with constant updates beginning on June 24. Thanks to his network of colleagues, no one else in Germany was reporting the action so quickly, and this raised concerns at the highest levels. It had taken days for news about the February revolt to reach Berlin; now it took just hours for accounts of the much bloodier June Days to arrive. The government feared the latest Paris violence would again trigger a follow-on rebellion; the same class antagonisms existed in Paris and Berlin, and the same tensions could easily be brought to a boil.

On June 26 Marx dedicated the entire newspaper to the Paris story. His reports were breathless: *"Paris bathed in blood; the insurrection* growing into the *greatest revolution that has ever taken place,* into a *revolution of the proletariat against the bourgeoisie."*[14] Engels added: "What distinguishes the June revolution from all previous revolutions is the *absence of all illusions and all enthusiasm.* The people are not standing on the barricades as in February singing 'die for the party.' . . . The workers of June 23 are fighting for their existence and the fatherland has lost all meaning for them."[15] Marx said the conflict laid bare the social reality in France that the bourgeoisie had been trying to hide and that the worker may not have fully comprehended: France was two nations—one a nation of owners and the other a nation of workers.[16] He said the *fraternité* declared in February and written on every prison and barracks wall in France was a fraud.[17] February, he said, was the "*nice* revolution," because it aroused universal sympathy, and the social struggle appeared only in poetic phrases. The June revolution was the "*ugly* revolution, the nasty revolution because the phrases have given place to the real thing."[18] June was a civil war between capital and labor. Engels called its victims the "martyrs of the first decisive battle of the proletariat."[19]

Just like that, everything had changed. The February revolution was dead, and the counterrevolution—the fight waged by reactionary forces trying to undo reforms they had been forced to make earlier that year— began, not only in Paris but throughout Europe. Engels reported that after Marx wrote a tribute to the fallen French insurgents, the *Neue Rheinische Zeitung*'s last remaining middle-class shareholders deserted them, and they were left scrambling for funding.[20] "But we had the satisfaction of being the only paper in Germany, and almost in Europe, that had held aloft the banner of the crushed proletariat at the moment when the bourgeois and petty bourgeois of all countries were trampling the vanquished in the ground with a torrent of slander."[21]

By the end of June the Communist League leadership from London and Brussels was in Cologne and ready for action, yet Marx wanted the organization dissolved. For Marx the league had become an outdated burden, a secret society at a time when men were shouting their grievances in the street, weapons in hand. In his seemingly paradoxical way, Marx saw in each revolutionary defeat the seed of revolutionary triumph, but he was certain that conspiratorial societies would have no part in that victory. There was no more need for shadows: the fight had to take place in plain sight. The league voted on its future and, though not without dissent, decided to disband. Members now busied themselves with the *Neue Rheinische Zeitung*—a much better propaganda tool than any pamphlets the league might publish—and organized against conservative forces strengthening once again in Germany.[22]

By July 2 Prussia had yet another new government, the one led by Marx's former colleague Camphausen having fallen. Though still liberal, its successor declared that the best way to counteract poverty was to "restore the weakened confidence in the preservation of law and order and to establish soon a firm constitutional monarchy."[23] The constitution still remained a distant goal, but the law and order crackdown began immediately. On July 3 the *Neue Rheinische Zeitung* reported the arrests of Gottschalk and Fritze Anneke, the latter for a speech he had given on uniting workers' groups. Police accused him of inciting civil war. Marx's newspaper reported that six or seven police had burst into Anneke's home at sunrise and four of them had entered the bedroom where Anneke and his pregnant wife were sleeping. They did not show a warrant but demanded that Anneke leave with them. The account said one of the policemen, who pushed Anneke down the stairs and smashed a glass door, was drunk, and mentioned that a public prosecutor identified only as Hecker arrived at the scene later.[24] Within two days the *Neue Rheinische Zeitung* published Hecker's objection to the report and what he called the "defamations and insults" against the police. He said legal action might be taken.[25]

On July 6 Marx was interrogated by authorities about the unsigned article.[26] By July 10 eleven compositors at the newspaper were called in to testify concerning the identity of the author.[27] A month later Cologne police began targeting the *Neue Rheinische Zeitung*'s editorial staff. Karl Schapper, who had a wife and three children, was ordered to leave Prussia because the government declared him to be a foreigner — even though he was a German citizen — and Marx knew that, given his still unsettled citizenship application, authorities considered him a foreigner, too.[28]

Cologne became dangerous for the circle around Marx. Homes were broken into. Families were at risk of harassment or expulsion. Arrests were increasingly random, and those making them did not necessarily follow legal procedures. Such niceties no longer seemed to matter. The Prussian assembly was busily undoing the rights that had paved the way for its very existence. But they could not do so fast enough to satisfy the king. After yet another political crisis, a third new government was formed — this one by royal order in September — which Marx called a counterrevolutionary triumph led by "crack-brained jackasses."[29]

Everywhere he looked Marx saw political and social chaos. While newly elected assemblies stood paralyzed, the so-called forces of order were battling the forces of democracy in the streets of Paris, Berlin, and Vienna, and the hunger and deprivation that had triggered the unrest in the first place had only worsened. Before February the lower classes had merely been neglected; after the June Days they were recognized, but with mistrust and fear, and thus were shunned by the higher classes, who now lacked all sympathy for their misery. The workers, too, were changed. They had learned they could not count on anyone else to defend their rights. They had also seen their strength in battle, and though they had lost nearly every contest, they now realized their own violent potential.

In Cologne on September 11, 1848, drunken soldiers who had made unwanted advances toward a young woman clashed with angry members of the local civic guard. Some civilians were cut by sabers in the skirmishes, which ended only when commanders ordered the military men back to their base.[30] The violence was the culmination of mounting tensions between the majority Catholic locals and the majority Protestant Prussian military, long seen as occupiers by the city's residents (the soldiers were so convinced the population hated them that they refused to eat in restaurants for fear they would be poisoned).[31] By the time of the September incident there was one soldier for every fourteen citizens in the city and an untold number of weapons at the military's disposal.[32] The episode persuaded many in Cologne that they needed to form a protective militia.

Two days later as many as six thousand people — some said ten thousand — met on the Frankenplatz, in the shadow of the Cologne Cathedral, to form a Committee of Public Safety.[33] To some extent the size of the crowd was Marx's doing: that morning the *Neue Rheinische Zeitung*'s editors had traveled through Cologne's warren of cobbled streets ringing a bell to call citizens to the evening meeting.[34] A sea of people carrying torches and straining to hear the speakers shouting from the back of a cart expressed overwhelming support for the committee. When it was formed, it included Marx, Engels, and five other *Neue Rheinische* editors. Its thirty members also included a pharmacist, a merchant, a shoemaker, a butcher, a roofer, and a grocer, evidence of the widespread concern among Cologne's citizenry about the Prussian military presence.[35] But the dominance of the newspaper staff on the committee and the name of the organization, which conjured up ghosts of the Jacobin dictators of the French Revolution, raised concerns.[36] Posters appeared on Cologne's walls warning of a future red republic. Though such alerts frightened the middle class, the workers and peasants were not unduly concerned.[37] They were hungry for action, and the only action on their behalf was coming from the extreme left of the political spectrum.

The following Sunday the type of violence the upper and middle classes feared erupted in Frankfurt, where the fledgling German National Assembly was seated. The spark was a humiliation inflicted on Germany when Prussia signed an armistice to end a war with Denmark over two dukedoms Denmark and Germany each claimed. The deal ceded the states of Schleswig and Holstein to Denmark.[38] German citizens saw the armistice as a terrible blow that, if not rectified, would undermine hopes for a powerful and united Germany. On September 5 the Frankfurt Assembly refused to approve the armistice — a meaningless gesture, since it could not force Prussia to resume the war it had shouldered on behalf of all Germany. Faced with an impossible task, the national government effectively admitted its impotence and resigned.[39]

By September 16, with no new government willing to form, the assembly reversed its earlier decision and voted to accept the armistice. The next day the streets of Frankfurt around St. Paul's Church, where the assembly met, rang with the disappointed cries of an angry mob.[40] Rightist national assemblyman Prince Felix Lichnowsky and a friend were caught by protesters while out riding and lynched. Troops were called in to put down the demonstration, and the fighting lasted for forty-eight hours before those manning the barricades were defeated.[41]

The *Neue Rheinische Zeitung* expressed sympathy for the insurgents and took up a collection for them and their families. On September 19 and 20 Engels wrote that though the protesters were defeated, they would not put down their weapons until their liberation had been won, and he warned that the next targets might be "petty princely residences" and "manorial estates."[42]

There can be no doubt that this call to arms disguised as reporting raised alarm bells from Frankfurt to Cologne and all the way to Berlin. Four days after Engels's remarks were published Cologne authorities responded with what Marx called an "almighty appetite for arrests." Before dawn police arrested two members of the newspaper staff, and warrants were issued for others.[43] Wrote Marx, "If these gentlemen go ahead with their plans, it will soon be a mystery how the editorial work of our newspaper is to be carried out.... It is merely a question of who will first lose their sense of humor: the gentlemen from the Public Prosecutor's office or the editors of the *Neue Rheinische Zeitung*."[44]

As news of the Monday morning arrests spread, violence erupted—looting, clashes with police, and broken gaslights and cut gas lines in parts of Cologne.[45] Most workers were idle on Mondays, and Marx feared the timing of the arrests was planned so that the maximum number of workers might be provoked into a fight, in which case the government would have an excuse for a crackdown. He went from gathering to gathering that day to try to urge workers not to be baited by police, explaining that to do so would mean certain defeat by the thousands of troops stationed in Cologne. By evening, however, passions freshly fueled in taverns had reached a pitch, and men once again poured out onto the streets. As many as forty barricades were built and gun shops and hardware stores looted for scythes, axes, anything that could be used as a weapon.[46]

At noon the next day, however, a state of siege was declared in Cologne: the workers did not have a chance to fight. Officials disbanded the civic militia, ordered taverns closed at 10 p.m., and banned all public meetings and the publication of the *Neue Rheinische Zeitung* and three other Cologne newspapers.[47] Marx issued a leaflet to subscribers saying, "The pen has to submit to the saber," but he did not expect the interruption to last long.[48]

The interruption did not in fact last long—just long enough to imperil the paper's existence. It had always operated in debt, but now that subscriptions had halted, there was no money with which to publish. On top of that, arrest warrants were issued by public prosecutor Hecker for Lupus, Engels, and Bürgers. The charge: plotting to overthrow the government.[49]

Lupus fled southwest, to Bavaria's Palatinate province, but returned quickly to Cologne and went into semihiding.[50] Engels and Bürgers left and stayed away, because police had published their descriptions. Engels's mother wrote him from Barmen, "Now you have really gone too far.... I was trembling when I picked up the newspaper and saw therein that a warrant was out for my son's arrest.... Dear Friedrich, if the words of a poor, sorrowing mother still mean anything to you, then follow your father's advice, go to America and abandon the course you have followed hitherto."[51]

Engels did not go to America, he went to Brussels. But as he sat down to eat with Dronke at a hotel on October 4, the two were arrested by police on the lookout for Engels. The pair was held for several hours before being deported to France.[52] Engels also faced arrest there, and so he dared not stay. Besides, he said, he was heartbroken by what he found.

> Cavaignac's shells had blown Paris' irrepressible gaiety sky-high; the sound of the "Marseillaise" and the "Chant du Départ" had ceased.... the workers, who had neither bread nor arms, ground their teeth in suppressed resentment...Paris was dead, it was no longer Paris. On the boulevards, no one but the bourgeoisie and police spies; the dance halls and theaters deserted....In brief, it was the Paris of 1847 again, but without the spirit, without the life...I had to leave it, no matter whither. So first of all to Switzerland. I had not much money, that meant going on foot. Nor was I set on taking the shortest route; one does not readily part from France.[53]

Engels embarked on an enforced break from revolution. He was now twenty-eight years old, and the boyishness Harney had remarked on in London was gone, replaced by a more weathered soul toughened by life at the front lines of intellectual revolt and years of living on less than he needed. But his enthusiasm and joie de vivre had not diminished one bit. His clear blue eyes sparkled at the prospect of adventure — whether it be revolutionary or, perhaps even better, sexual. He had been neck-deep in the former, and while he strolled across the country he indulged in all he could of the latter, proclaiming *"La belle France!"*[54]

"And what wine!" Engels declared in his journal titled "From Paris to Berne," which recorded (with an excessive number of exclamation points) his travels, along with a hand-drawn map of his route. In the "red republic" of Burgundy, so christened by Engels not because of its politics but because of its wine-colored streets and people, he said he wished he had pockets full of money. "The 1848 harvest was so infinitely rich that not enough barrels could be found to take all the wine. And what is more, of such quality — better than '46, perhaps even better than '34!...At every step I found the gayest company, the sweetest grapes and the prettiest girls....It will therefore readily be believed that I spent more time lying in the grass with the vintners and their girls, eating grapes, drinking wine, chatting and laughing, than marching up the hill."[55] He made friends with locals by drawing caricatures of Cavaignac and Ledru-Rollin, and along the route met wanderers like himself who had left the upheaval of Paris for the bucolic countryside. Politics played little if any part in his travels as he made his way toward Geneva, where he arrived tanned and rested, and wrote Marx to say he needed money.[56]

But money was one of the things Marx had least of—along with time, help, and peace of mind. He was furiously trying to keep the *Neue Rheinische Zeitung* operating. He had begun publishing again on October 12, more than a week after the state of siege was lifted in Cologne. He could not start any earlier because shareholders—those very few who would even consider backing it—were reluctant to support a publication that had so many fugitives on its editorial staff.[57] Adding to these woes, the fall subscriptions had come due while publication was suspended, and with no guarantee the paper would reappear, existing subscribers had not paid for renewals.[58]

Georg Weerth and Ferdinand Freiligrath (who had just been acquitted in Düsseldorf on charges of publishing a revolutionary poem[59]), had joined the newspaper to try to make up for the shortage in writing manpower.[60] Meanwhile, Jenny had moved her base from the couple's comfortable apartment to the filthy editorial offices, which reeked of printer's ink, oil lamps, and cigars, to take care of the sundry tasks involved in running a newspaper and the personal requests from party refugees like Engels and those in jail seeking help for their families.[61]

Somewhat curiously, at no time during these rising tensions in Cologne did Marx and Jenny appear to think it prudent for her to leave the city and take the children to Trier. Marx's arrest seemed imminent, and there were warning signs that the thousands of soldiers in the garrison and the armed civilians in Cologne were looking for an excuse to do battle. But neither Marx nor Jenny displayed any real anxiety over her safety. The reason may have been Jenny's brother Ferdinand, who had protected her so ably at the balls in Trier when she was a girl and was now rising quickly in the Prussian government. Stephan Born noted rare disharmony between Marx and Jenny over Ferdinand. He overheard Marx tease Jenny, saying, "Your brother is so stupid that he will become a Prussian minister yet." The remark, Born noted, made Jenny blush,[62] for while Marx freely expressed his disdain for Ferdinand, Jenny harbored familial affection for him. Their letters were warm and their mutual regard evident. Theirs was a loving relationship complicated by politics.[63] Ferdinand had been invited to the king's court at Potsdam,[64] and was on intimate terms with government leaders—especially Interior Minister Franz August Eichmann, who was also president of the Rhine province, and soon-to-be interior minister Baron Otto von Manteuffel.[65] It therefore seemed that his sister, though the wife of a well-known agitator, could count on the protection of his position. Others would not be so lucky.

17

Cologne, 1849

The revolution is dead!—Long live the revolution!
—Karl Marx[1]

THE STORY THE *Neue Rheinische Zeitung* told when it resumed publication
was of a European counterrevolution nearing victory. An ugly episode on
October 6, 1848, had turned the tide. Viennese workers, students, and
national guard, already angered by months of reversals and the realization
that they could not sustain their March triumph, were outraged when the
Austrian minister of war, Theodor Latour, tried to enlist the guard to help
imperial forces put down an independence movement in Hungary. Workers captured Latour, bludgeoned him with hammers and iron pipes,
stabbed him repeatedly, and then hung his mutilated body on a lamppost.
The emperor immediately left Vienna, making concessionary promises as
he did so in order to ease his flight. Most of the bourgeoisie, however, had
no choice but to stay. From behind closed doors they feared Vienna was
slipping into anarchy and that the romantic student-led revolution of the
early months had turned into a workers' reign of terror. Imperial forces
were called back from Hungary. Thousands of troops headed to Vienna to
retake it for the king and the propertied class.

As many as fifty thousand workers, students, and national guard members inside the city readied for conflict, distributing arms and building barricades.[2] An estimated seventy thousand Austrian troops bivouacked
outside, awaiting the command to enter. It came on October 28. The army
unleashed its heavy weapons on Vienna, and the battle was over in four

days. Rage had proved no match for cannons. Three thousand Viennese and thirteen hundred soldiers died in the fighting. There were twenty-four hundred arrests and twenty-five executions. The battle ended the Austrian revolt, and word of the defeat resounded through a stunned Europe as had the fall of Metternich in that same city seven months earlier.[3]

Marx was furious over the ruthlessness with which the European governments responded to that year's revolts and seethed about the silent acquiescence of the cowardly middle class in the face of such brutality. In uncharacteristically incendiary language he wrote in his newspaper: "The purposeless massacres perpetrated since the June and October events, the tedious offering of sacrifices since February and March, the very cannibalism of the counterrevolution will convince the nations that there is only one means by which the murderous death agonies of the old society and the bloody birth throes of the new society can be *shortened,* simplified and concentrated—and *that* is by *revolutionary terror.*"[4]

But even as Marx used those provocative words, it was becoming clear to him that violence was *not* the answer. If nothing else had been learned from the preceding months, it was that a man and a barricade were powerless against a king and his army. Those who worked and fought with their hands could not defeat through battle alone a well-equipped, well-trained military backed by the wealth of the state and supported by men of property. So, rhetoric aside, at the end of October, Marx the realist began looking for a new weapon. He found it in taxes. Examining a people's relationship with their government, he saw mutual dependencies. But he took issue with the conventional interpretation of those dependencies. Kings had promulgated the notion that citizens were wholly dependent on the government, when in Marx's view it was the other way around. Rulers needed their people to keep the farms operating, the plants manufacturing, the shops stocked with merchandise, the ships and railways loaded with cargo. They needed their people to work. But in addition to that, kings also needed their people to turn over to the government the money they had earned. Taxes financed palaces, parliaments, the military—in short, they funded a kingdom's very existence. Thus, in a kingdom with a repressive government, the people paid their jailer to keep them in chains.

Marx claimed that monarchs miraculously became disciples of constitutional government when their people discovered the "economic secret" that if they turned off the tax spigot they could bring down the realm. He made this case in an October 20 article in the *Neue Rheinische Zeitung,*[5] and surprisingly, this theme was picked up by the Prussian assembly, which had been thoroughly emasculated by the king after the fall of the third post–March 18 government.

The new prime minister, Count Brandenburg, was a conservative and the illegitimate son of Friedrich Wilhelm II. On November 9 he transferred the Prussian National Assembly against its will to the small city of Brandenburg, thirty-five miles west of the capital. And, to ensure that support for the assembly did not spill out onto the street, forty thousand troops were stationed in Berlin and a state of siege was declared.[6] Seemingly unable to help themselves, assembly members turned to their electorate, instructing them to withhold taxes until the assembly was allowed to return to Berlin.[7]

From November 17 on, Marx enthusiastically repeated the phrase *"No More Taxes!!!"* in a banner headline in his newspaper. He also repeated the call in an appeal from the Rheinische District Committee of Democrats.[8] Within days the three men who had signed that document—Marx, Schapper, and Karl Schneider II, a lawyer and president of the Cologne Democratic Society—were summoned to appear before a magistrate on charges of public incitement to rebellion.[9] There was evidence to support the charge: from Bonn to Düsseldorf, insurgents had adopted the antitax mantra, attacking and burning anything resembling a tax collection center (though the effort never gained enough momentum to seriously threaten the government).[10]

The legal pressure against Marx intensified on all fronts. In early November the *Neue Rheinische Zeitung*'s offices were raided and Marx was charged with treason for a letter his newspaper had published.[11] In early December he was summoned again to the magistrate's office, this time on charges filed by the imperial ministry accusing the newspaper[12] (which it called the worst of the "bad press"[13]) of libel. Rumors circulated that Marx would be arrested. Nevertheless, he told Engels, who was still in Switzerland, that he would not stop publishing articles offensive to the government. "This *fort* had to be held and the political position not surrendered."[14]

While Marx was busily fighting his numerous court battles, Friedrich Wilhelm IV effectively killed the government born nine months earlier by dissolving the Prussian National Assembly on December 5 and imposing a "constitution" that gave him the power to suspend all rights and declare war. He magnanimously ordered new elections (not that he had to abide by an elected assembly's rulings, but it must have seemed a nice gesture after what his people had been through). Marx called the actions nothing short of a coup d'état.[15]

Surprisingly, the "coup" seemed to have a salutary effect in Prussia, however briefly. The king was restored to what he saw as his rightful place. Now it was just a matter of tying up loose ends, which is to say eliminating once and for all what remained of the opposition.

★   ★   ★

By mid-January 1849 conditions were safe enough for Engels to return to Cologne to help Marx through what the latter called "an atrociously bad patch."[16] Most of their colleagues who had left Prussia under threat of arrest in the previous months had now returned and were again at the offices of the *Neue Rheinische Zeitung*. In the case of some, charges had been dropped; others were acquitted while in exile. Engels chose to take his chances in court alongside Marx.

On February 7 Marx, Engels, and the newspaper's publisher appeared for trial on charges of libeling police in the article on Anneke's arrest the previous year and of insulting Chief Prosecutor Zweiffel in the piece. Marx and Engels both addressed the packed courtroom. Marx took on the Zweiffel charge of calumny by arguing that the newspaper would have been guilty if it had reported what he *was*—a traitor to the people—but in fact it had merely stated what Zweiffel *said*—that he promised to roll back freedoms won in March—and therefore no insult or defamation had occurred.[17] Marx relied heavily on the Code Napoleon in his argument and also on the duty of a free press. "It is by profession the public watchdog," he declared, "the tireless denouncer of those in power, the omnipresent eye, the omnipresent mouthpiece of the people's spirit that jealously guards its freedom." He pointed out that the article in question showed that the paper was merely fulfilling this duty of denunciation, and he ended his statement with a review of the past tumultuous months, putting the trial in that larger context to argue that the case could not be considered outside its historical setting.[18] "What caused the defeat of the *March revolution?* It reformed only the highest political summit, it left all the groundwork of this summit intact—the old bureaucracy, the old army, the old boards of prosecuting magistrates, the old judiciary which had been created, had developed and grown gray in the service of absolutism. The first duty of the press is now *to undermine all the foundations of the existing political state of affairs*." Applause rang out in the courtroom. Marx sat down.[19]

It was next Engels's turn to dispute the charges that police had been libeled by the report that one of its officers was drunk when arresting Anneke. No policeman was libeled, he said, because no policeman was named. In addition, witness testimony backed up the report.

If the press is to be forbidden to report what occurs before its very eyes; if in every complicated case it has to wait until a judicial verdict has been passed on it; if it must first ask every official, from the minister down to the policeman, whether he would feel his honor or delicacy impugned by the facts of the case being mentioned, irrespective of whether these facts are true or not; if the press is faced with the alternative of either falsifying events or remaining completely silent—then, gentlemen, freedom of the press is at an end, and if that is what you want, then pronounce us *"guilty"*!

The jury did not: the three defendants were acquitted on all charges.[20]

The next day Marx was back in court for his "no more taxes" treason case. Alongside him were Schapper and the lawyer Schneider. Marx again addressed the court, and this time his speech took nearly an hour. In making the case that he and his codefendants had the right to use taxes as a weapon against the government, Marx reminded the second jury of the history of the past year. Absolute monarchy, aristocratic privileges, guilds, enthralled peasants—Marx said that the elected National Assembly had sought to abolish that system to make way for economic progress, basic freedoms, a modern society.[21] The king, the army, and the powers behind the old society, threatened by the assembly, had staged a coup. "If the crown makes a counterrevolution," Marx said, "the people have the right to reply with a revolution." And he cited historical precedents for using taxes as a revolutionary tool, noting that the U.S. Declaration of Independence was born out of a tax revolt against England. "The National Assembly, as such, has no rights; the people have merely entrusted it with the defense of the people's rights. If the assembly does not act in accordance with the mandate it has received, then this mandate lapses. The people then takes the stage itself and acts on its own authority."[22] The jury agreed the defendants had been within their rights, and the three were acquitted, the jury foreman personally thanking Marx for his informative address.[23]

Despite its efforts to take Marx and his colleagues out of circulation through the courts, the government had been repeatedly frustrated by hostile Rhineland juries that produced only dismissed charges or acquittals. But there was another card to play. The commandant of Cologne wrote to Rhine provincial president Eichmann stating that Marx was becoming "increasingly more audacious now that he has been acquitted by the jury and it seems to me high time that this man was deported." He accused Marx of "befouling everything with his poisonous tongue." A formal deportation request was sent to the police superintendent the morning of February 17 asserting that since Marx had arrived in Cologne the previous April, his behavior had become dangerous and intolerable: "He takes the liberty to insult in any way he thinks fit our Constitution, our King, and the highest government officials in his increasingly popular paper, constantly seeking to promote even greater feelings of discontent and indirectly calling upon the people to revolt."[24]

Several days later a report on Marx went all the way to the desk of

Prussian interior minister Manteuffel. It said Marx had indeed ridiculed "all that men normally respect and hold sacred," but cautioned that deporting him might provoke unrest. Manteuffel approved Marx's expulsion in principle but left its enactment up to the discretion of local authorities, who decided to wait until Marx gave them "direct cause" to expel him.[25]

Compared with others who had been ejected from Prussia, Marx seemed to have had an even greater role in stirring up antigovernment sentiment. But once again Marx was shown a curious deference, which may have been due to his wife's influence on her brother. Ferdinand, now head of the district government at the Silesian town of Liegnitz, had the attention of the very men who could determine his brother-in-law's fate, and by extension his sister's. During the past critical months he had worked and socialized with the king, Count Brandenburg, Crown Prince Wilhelm, Eichmann, and Manteuffel.[26] But whatever the reason that Marx was allowed to remain in Cologne, his life there was one of constant harassment. Hate mail poured in to the newspaper, and there were other, more personal threats.[27] Two armed noncommissioned officers appeared at Marx and Jenny's apartment demanding retribution for an article about an officer convicted of selling army materiel. The pair told Marx that Prussian troops in Cologne felt slandered by the piece. They wanted the author named and warned that if he was not handed over, they would "no longer be able to restrain their men." Marx responded coolly, explaining what legal recourse the officers had and pointing out that threats would achieve nothing. He then let them see the butt end of a gun sticking out of his dressing-gown pocket. The meeting ended with a standoff, neither side willing to initiate violence.[28]

Marx had learned to shoot as a boy around Trier, where hunting was common, but he is not known to have ever fired a weapon at another person. In later years frustration and personal problems would drive him to challenge his enemies to duels, but it was never clear whether he relished the prospect. He valued his life (that is, his work) too much to lose it on a misty field at twenty paces. Though he advocated revolution, Marx thought individual violence mostly counterproductive. After tensions in Cologne had cooled and Marx no longer feared for his family, he filed an official complaint, describing the officers as a "robber band" and wondering at the new legal authority that extended their jurisdiction to the doorsteps of civilians.[29]

After months of debate, at the end of March 1849 the Frankfurt National Assembly had finally come up with a constitution that would turn the

German Confederation into a nation. In early April the Prussian king rejected it, not because it was too liberal, he claimed, but because he was not sure the other German princes would agree with its stipulation that he become emperor of all Germans. The king's final betrayal of the previous year's Berlin promises was met with scorn from Germany's more liberal states and once again roused even members of the middle class to consider the possibility of revolt.[30] On April 15, with these tremors rumbling throughout the Bund, Marx left Cologne on a tour of Germany to assess the situation, raise money for his newspaper, and make contact with workers' groups.[31] He entrusted Engels with his family's safety.[32]

The day before he left Marx took an important step in the history of the communist movement, formally cutting ties with his bourgeois democratic associates. Early on, he had been criticized for pragmatically aligning himself with democrats, but after a year in which these liberals, who had espoused support for the workers, repeatedly turned their backs on them in order to secure their own political and economic gains, Marx had had enough and quit the Rhineland Democratic Union.[33] Marx biographers Boris Nicolaievsky and Otto Maenchen-Helfen identified this as the moment when Marx aligned himself completely with the proletariat. Never again would he seek political accommodation with the bourgeoisie.[34]

Marx was away from Cologne for three weeks. During his trip this advocate of the working man, who had just declared a permanent rupture with the middle class, raised eyebrows by spending two weeks at a first-class hotel in Hamburg.[35] Often while traveling, he took holidays from his poverty and treated himself (nearly always on someone else's coin) to the best hotels and spas. It was a peculiar weakness—he seemed to love luxurious surroundings—and it provided ammunition to his enemies, who throughout his life (and even after his death) would accuse him of being a closet elitist while publicly championing the downtrodden. Those critics misunderstood Marx: he did not begrudge anyone comfort, he just insisted that they earn it and that they not exploit anyone else in the process. Judging from his letters, Marx also mischievously appeared to enjoy inserting himself among the upper classes to play the devil and watch their reactions as, little by little, they found themselves enjoying his company, which they invariably did. In Hamburg, however, there may have been another reason for his self-indulgence. He knew the psychology behind begging: when one wants a little money, an outstretched hand will do; when one wants a lot, it's best to look as though one doesn't really need it. But beggar he was. Marx and Jenny had spent nearly all they had, much of it to pay the newspaper's expenses. In addition, Marx was singularly unsuccessful in his panhandling. He returned to Cologne on May 9 poorer than when he left and had to borrow funds to pay his hotel bill.[36]

There was also bad news awaiting him: his order to leave Prussia had finally been written. It was dated May 11 but was not delivered to Marx until May 16. The *Neue Rheinische Zeitung*'s reporting on the last gasp of revolution in Germany had apparently given the authorities the excuse they were looking for to expel him.[37]

In the wake of the Prussian king's rejection of a united Germany, skirmishes had broken out around the Bund. South of Berlin, in the Saxon capital of Dresden, street fighting lasted for nearly a week. Bakunin, who had arrived in April to hear his friend Richard Wagner conduct Beethoven's Ninth at the Dresden opera house, stayed on and manned the barricades with Wagner in early May in one part of the city while the opera house burned in another. Bakunin proposed that he and his fellow insurgents use all their explosives to blow up the town hall, with themselves in it.[38] (He abandoned this plot and fled the city. He was arrested three nights later, an erotic novel he had written while on the run through Prussia found among his possessions.)[39]

As soon as Marx returned from his fund-raising trip, Engels, who had drafted plans for uprisings in the Rhine River valley as he watched the fighting from the editorial offices in Cologne, retrieved two chestloads of ammunition confiscated by workers who had stormed an arsenal in nearby Solingen, and went to Elberfeld to join the insurgency.[40] Engels helped build barricades and then set off to inspect the uprisings in the area. On the bridge between Elberfeld and Barmen, as Engels directed gunners, his father spotted him. Engels was wearing a red sash, and there was no denying that he was there to stir up revolt. He and his father quarreled bitterly.[41] Meanwhile, some of the middle-class organizers of the Elberfeld uprising began expressing concern that the notorious "red" from Cologne would give their revolt a more radical face than it deserved. They asked him to leave.[42] Engels agreed, but not before undertaking what he called one more "reconnaissance" mission. Armed with sabers and pistols, Engels and two colleagues rode on horseback to a military arsenal near Elberfeld and robbed it, making off with weapons and equipment they brought back to the street fighters.[43] This exploit earned Engels yet another arrest warrant.[44]

Despite the setbacks, Engels left Elberfeld no less enthusiastic than when he'd arrived. He hoped the disparate fights breaking out around the Rhineland under the black, red, and gold flag of German unity might coalesce into a final battle against the crown, and wondered in the *Neue*

Rheinische Zeitung "whether the people will leave it at '**Hats off!**' this time!"[45] Engels bemoaned the fact that Berliners had not risen up against the king, even if it meant certain defeat, because at least they would have "left behind themselves, in the minds of survivors, a wish for revenge, which in revolutionary times is one of the highest incentives to energetic and passionate action."[46]

The newspaper's staff worked overtime to churn out special editions on the uprisings. In its crowded offices, presses noisily thumping out double-sided pages of print, men frantically wrote the latest reports before handing them to compositors who painstakingly set the copy letter by letter. Working late into the night beside a dim oil lamp, Marx finally threw caution to the wind: he openly urged the people to move against the king,[47] who after a year of pretended reform had just revealed his true feelings by saying that the only remedy for democrats was soldiers.[48] In his newspaper Marx now referred to Friedrich Wilhelm as Herr von Hohenzollern, publicly stripping him of the title the king said had been bestowed on him by God.[49] Marx's expulsion order was issued two days later.

With this deadline looming the newspaper rushed out a final issue. It appeared on May 19, 1849, and was defiant from beginning to end. Marx wrote: *"We have no compassion and we ask no compassion from you. When our turn comes, we shall not make excuses for the terror."* The editorial board's farewell admonished Cologne residents not to revolt, because they would surely lose. They thanked their readers and proclaimed that their "last word everywhere and always will be: **emancipation of the working class!**"[50] The issue was printed first page to last in red ink and became an instant classic. It sold twenty thousand copies—more than triple the number of subscribers—and some copies went for ten times the original price.[51] Engels recalled with pride, "We had to surrender our fortress, but we withdrew with...band playing and flag flying, the flag of the last, red issue."[52] A journalist unsympathetic to the newspaper later admitted that the issue had become a collectors' item: "One hears again and again of instances of the paper being expensively framed."[53]

None of that adulation helped Marx, however. Once again he and Jenny scrambled to pack up their family and leave town before they were forcibly escorted across the border. Jenny gathered all their belongings and the only thing of value still left, her silver plate, which she put in a borrowed suitcase. She entrusted three hundred books belonging to Karl to Roland Daniels, the doctor who had helped them find their apartment, and she sold bits and pieces of furniture to fund their escape.[54] Meanwhile, Marx wrapped up affairs at the newspaper. He owned all the equipment and sold it to pay off shareholders, printers, and employees. Remaining supplies and equipment were given to another democratic newspaper in the city, the *Neue Kölnische Zeitung* (New Cologne Gazette), which was published with a black border in honor of its sister paper's demise.[55]

Most of the newspaper staff scattered quickly. Engels said there were twenty-three legal cases still pending against them, so there was every reason to leave while they still could.[56] As soon as the final issue hit the streets, Marx, Jenny, Lenchen, the three children, and Engels fled Cologne by Rhine river barge, first to Bingen and then to Frankfurt.[57] Jenny stayed there briefly—just long enough to pawn her silver, or, as she said, "convert into ready money the silver plate I had just redeemed from the pawnbroker's in Brussels"[58]—before separating from Marx and taking the children to Trier. Though on the run again, Jenny confidently told a friend: "All the pressures we now feel are only the sign of an imminent and even more complete victory of our views."[59] She was merely parroting Marx's optimism. Despite setbacks all around, he remained, at least outwardly, convinced that the government would be overthrown.

Marx and Engels stayed in Frankfurt and appealed to insurgents around Germany to coalesce in the National Assembly's shadow in order to concentrate their forces and coordinate planning in the revolt against Berlin. Having no luck, they traveled to Baden to make the case to hard men fighting there that they should move their operation to Frankfurt. But no one seemed interested in saving the hapless assembly, and so the two headed back to Bingen.

At the very moment when Marx had given up on Germany and decided to leave, he was arrested. On reaching Bingen, Marx and Engels were picked up by troops and taken to Frankfurt, where they were held for several days before being released. The two then decided to split up. Marx would travel with Red Wolff to await Jenny in Paris,[60] where delegations from various rebellious German states were already busily seeking support and recognition. Engels went to Baden to join the battle, the artilleryman in him again craving action. Above all, he believed it necessary that the insurgents continue to be seen as the aggressors. "The defensive," he observed, "is the death of every armed uprising."[61]

But in truth the fight was already over. Government forces were merely mopping up scattered pools of resistance. The kings and princes of Europe were once again settled comfortably on their thrones—everywhere, that is, except in France.

18

Paris, 1849

Hegel remarks somewhere that all facts and personages of great importance in world history occur, as it were, twice. He forgot to add: the first time as tragedy, the second as farce.

—Karl Marx[1]

SOMETIMES THE CHARACTERS arising from the ashes of grave events are so bizarre they almost seem like accidents. One such emerged in France in the midst of the chaos of the spring of 1848. He was announced simply as *"Lui"*—"Him"—on medals and lithographs distributed free of charge in a surprisingly modern advertising campaign suggesting that, at long last, there existed someone who would set things right. At a time when Parisians were slaughtering each other in cold blood and the countryside cowered in horror, fearing, quite legitimately, that the crimes of that revolutionary city would spill out into the towns and villages, this would-be savior was in London, waiting for the opportune moment to return. But his presence was already everywhere, the walls of Paris covered in posters of this unknown man with the reassuringly familiar name.

"Him" was Charles Louis Napoleon Bonaparte, nephew of Napoleon Bonaparte, and he believed that he, too, was destined to be emperor of France. Just in case the crowds needed convincing, a compatriot hired organ grinders and street singers who roamed the boulevards predicting the imminent return of another Napoleon. For many French that name, no matter who bore it, meant stability, work, food, even wealth—in short, everything they lacked.[2]

Louis Napoleon, who though born in Paris had been raised in Switzerland and had no real ties to France except history, had tried twice before

166

to take part in French politics.[3] Both forays ended in failure, the second spectacularly so. In that instance he arrived in France in August 1840 dressed as an emperor. An eagle hovered majestically above his head (inspired less by the preeminence of the man below than by the piece of bacon Louis Napoleon had concealed in his hat). He declared that he had come to lead France and planted an imperial flag in Boulogne. The national guard promptly arrested him for trying to stage a coup.[4] Sentenced to life in prison in northern France, he remained there for six years—his longest period in the country—before escaping to England dressed as a workman. There he continued to plot the reconquest of his uncle's throne.[5]

By May 1848 the time was right. Virtually unknown in France, Louis Napoleon's name created a stir when it appeared on ballots in elections for the National Assembly: he won seats representing four districts.[6] The government was horrified by the prospect that this escapee with a famous name might take a seat in the assembly, and officials contested his election. Louis Napoleon graciously resigned and returned to England, where he waited for French politicians to awaken to the possibility that a weak Napoleon—which is how he portrayed himself—might be a powerful but malleable symbol around which to build a recovery. He had no power base of his own and would have to rely on current government leaders. As he expected, politicians saw the light. He returned to France in September to take his seat in the National Assembly.[7]

Louis Napoleon was inelegant in the extreme—he had a huge head and torso but tiny legs—and was blessed with the placid face of a dimwit. On top of that he spoke French badly, and with a heavy foreign accent. Nevertheless, the same strategists who welcomed him back to the assembly began to maneuver him into position for even greater things. He was the perfect tool to lull the people into a false sense of security while in fact leaving control of France in the hands of the same men who had pulled the levers of power for decades.[8] When presidential elections were held in December, Louis Napoleon won more than five million votes compared with his nearest competitor Cavaignac's one million.[9]

But this new Napoleon was not the dimwit he pretended to be. He initially allowed himself to appear to be a blank slate on which the French could inscribe their hopes and dreams—their futures—and while he had his own ideas, he mostly kept them to himself for the first year. Indeed, his immediate task was to get to know the country he had been elected to lead. That country was racked by political jealousy, mistrust, and hatred. The wounds of the past year were far from healed, and while the extreme left and the workers had been defeated, they were not dead. Louis Napoleon needed to solidify the government in order to stave off their seemingly inevitable challenge. It would not be imminent: if the government was splintered, the opposition was more so; the workers had not recovered from the June Days of the previous year.

Marx arrived in Paris on June 9 in the midst of an Asiatic cholera epidemic and an early-summer heat wave. He had traveled under the alias Monsieur Ramboz because he no longer had friends in government who could ensure his safety.[10] The differences between February 1848 and June 1849 could not have been greater, but the arc of revolution and counter-revolution in France was a familiar one. It mirrored the dramas throughout Europe, where the initial euphoria of revolt gave way to political uncertainty, violence, a realignment of loyalties that left the working class to fight its battles alone, and finally the installation of a reactionary government comprised of a ruling class that included a new breed—the industrialist and his financiers.

Marx was disgusted but not surprised that the middle class, the bourgeoisie, the men of property, had abandoned the proletariat when it came to a choice between their private interests and the good of a class they neither knew nor understood. He was frustrated, though again not surprised, that this massive proletariat could not unite to successfully confront the powers above them. Still, Marx had faith that the French working class—the "four million men who have no secure wages"[11]—would rise up. He wrote Engels: "Paris is dreary. On top of that the cholera is raging mightily. For all of that never has a colossal eruption of the revolutionary volcano been more imminent than it is in Paris today....I consort with the whole of the revolutionary party."[12]

That expectation of immediate revolution was pitifully realized on June 13. Ledru-Rollin, who was now among the liberal minority in the National Assembly, led the opposition to Louis Napoleon's invasion of Rome to restore the pope as head of the Papal States.[13] The pope, whose democratic leanings had helped precipitate the 1848 uprising in Sicily, had fled Rome amid political chaos that included the assassination of a close associate, and in his absence a Roman Republic was declared.[14] Louis Napoleon thought that coming to the aid of the pope would win him favor among French Catholics, put him in a better position to negotiate for territory, and show that the Napoleonic tradition of European intervention had returned—but not as an army of aggression.[15]

When the assembly rejected the Ledru-Rollin–led motion to impeach the president over the Rome invasion, his followers stormed out and took their fight to the citizens.[16] Despite Marx's optimism, however, the political and social temperature had cooled significantly from its peak in June 1848. The rebels took over a school and issued a call for barricades, but, reported Marx, all anyone could muster was a few chairs thrown into the street.[17] The protest achieved nothing beyond revealing the impotence of the so-called revolutionaries and strengthening Louis Napoleon's hand in further crackdowns: a state of siege was extended and new restrictions on refugees were imposed. Above all, the government did not want Paris to once again become a sanctuary for foreign rabble-rousers.[18] Police paid special attention to the Germans, who, they feared, were leaders of an international revolutionary committee. An early Marx biographer described this sinister cell as existing only in the fertile imagination of the security forces[19]—and, one might add, of Marx himself. His rhetoric did absolutely nothing to make governments revise their visions of catastrophe.

Jenny, Lenchen, and the children arrived in Paris on July 7. Usually Jenny had a difficult time leaving her mother in Trier, but that summer she was eager to do so. She told her friend Lina Schöler, who had been engaged to Jenny's brother Edgar before he left for America, that her mother's financial worries and old age had made her hard and selfish. "I did not feel at ease there. Everything has changed too much there and one does not, of course, always remain the same oneself." In any case, she said, she had an intense nostalgia for Paris.[20]

Jenny, who was pregnant again, and her band of tiny travelers had conducted all the baggage they had accumulated in their year in Cologne through Brussels by coach and then by train down to Paris. On arrival she described herself as fit and well, which may have been less a reflection of the ease of her journey than of her rapture at being in Paris again. After a year in the shadow of a military garrison under the heavy hand of Friedrich Wilhelm, she found life in Louis Napoleon's reactionary Paris wonderfully liberating. "At this moment Paris is splendid and luxurious.... The aristocracy and the bourgeoisie suppose themselves safe since the ill-starred 13th of June.... On the 14th all the grandees, together with their carriages and their liveried retainers, were already creeping out of the holes in which they had been hiding and thus the marvelous streets are awash with magnificence and splendor of every description.... The children...can hardly open their eyes wide enough to take in all these marvels."

This was the city she loved and the home she wanted. Paris was where she had lived as a new bride and from which she had been driven against her will. Now, she described for Lina a six-to-ten-room cottage in Passy, about an hour outside Paris, which they had been offered at a reasonable rent. It was near Heine's new home, was elegantly furnished, and had a garden.[21] In the meantime, she said, they lived in a salubrious district near Les Invalides, in a pretty, cozy apartment. Red Wolff lived with them, too, and she invited Lina (whom that gentleman, dubbed "red Orlando *furioso*" by Marx, fancied) to visit her in their city of beauty and ease.[22]

But at the very time Jenny was happily detailing their situation, Marx was desperately writing letters trying to find money to support his family. He evidently kept the full dimensions of the bad news from Jenny, who seemed unaware that their usually tight financial position was now nearly impossible. Before Marx left Cologne he'd spent the rest of his inheritance advance on keeping the newspaper afloat. He told Joseph Weydemeyer that he was without a sou and asked him to try to find him money until he started receiving funds from the redistribution and sale of his old attack on Proudhon, which he overoptimistically (if not disingenuously) assured him was imminent: "If at all possible, pursue this matter, but without mentioning it to anybody. I tell you that, unless help is forthcoming from one quarter or another, I am lost, since my family is also here and the last piece of my wife's jewelry has already found its way to the pawnbrokers."[23] He also appealed to Engels, who was fighting with insurgents in Baden, "*raise money for me somewhere*. . . . In the present *circumstances,* I cannot live a completely retired life, still less get into financial difficulties."[24]

Money, however, was not the worst of their problems. Five days after Jenny wrote to Lina about her future in the city of all cities, there was a knock at the door. Jenny's vision of a secure and happy life in Paris was shattered. "The familiar police sergeant came again and informed us that Karl Marx and his wife had to leave Paris within twenty-four hours," Jenny recalled in her unfinished memoir.[25] Marx had been classified an undesirable foreigner no longer welcome in the French capital. He tried to convince authorities that he was a benign presence and would only be working on a book on economics,[26] but the line that had gained him entry into Brussels in 1845 did not work in 1849 Paris. Marx had earlier warned correspondents that his mail was being opened by French police, and if that was the case there was no credible way he could have claimed to be anything but a rebel poised for what he himself called "an early revolutionary resurrection."[27]

The expulsion order said the family could move to Morbihan, in Brittany, three hundred miles west of Paris, but Marx deemed it the equivalent of a death sentence, because its marshes were breeding grounds for disease. He appealed and, thanks to a slow bureaucracy, won a month's reprieve, though the period was by no means easy.[28] He said he felt as though the "sword of Damocles" hung over his head.[29] In addition, Jenny and the children were ill, leaving Marx to play "male nurse."[30] In letters he attributed Jenny's condition to her pregnancy, but it was likely that she was depressed over being forced to change countries for the fourth time in four years. Throughout her life Jenny retreated into illness when the weight of their personal problems became too great. In those cases Lenchen became mistress of the house, and Karl (himself no stranger to stress-induced maladies) publicly maintained the facade that her affliction was physical.

For his part, Marx used his intellectual and party pursuits as a shield against looming personal catastrophe. He had a remarkable facility for separating his business from his personal life. (One writer said Marx considered giving in to such suffering a bourgeois self-indulgence, which was unpardonable in time of war.)[31] In a letter to Freiligrath in July, describing a controversy involving his finances, he suggested they should talk politics to distract him from this private unpleasantness.[32] And even in the despair of that July, with no money and no idea what the future held, he wrote Weydemeyer, "Awkward though the present state of affairs may be for our personal circumstances, I am nevertheless among the *satisfied*. Things are going very well." He believed that the conflicting self-interests of those who had defeated the workingman of Europe during the past year had surfaced and that the players were now viciously turning on one another.[33]

Throughout the summer, in an effort to keep his family afloat financially, Marx considered a number of moneymaking schemes, from writing pamphlets on economic issues to publishing a new newspaper in Berlin. He even turned to his old publisher Leske, whom he still had not repaid for the advance on the economic book he had failed to produce, to see if he might be interested in publishing his work. But all schemes remained just that, and by mid-August, when France finally rejected his appeal and told him to either settle in Brittany or leave the country immediately, his prospects were bleaker than they had been when he left Cologne.[34]

Out of desperation Marx wrote to a young German lawyer and fellow socialist, Ferdinand Lassalle, looking for financial help to move his family out of France. He asked Lassalle to keep the request quiet, but Lassalle apparently discussed his financial situation publicly, which infuriated Marx. Marx could not tolerate being viewed as weak or vulnerable, and he was loath to have his enemies privy to the details of his personal travails.[35] He told Freiligrath he found the situation "unspeakably annoying" and said the "direst straits are better than public begging."[36] Despite his pride, however, he accepted Lassalle's money. There was nothing else to be done.

Marx had asked the French for a passport to move to Switzerland, but the government refused; the only place for which they would issue a travel pass was England.[37] Marx wrote Engels in Switzerland on August 23 to say he was leaving France for London but that Jenny would be allowed to remain briefly to settle their affairs.[38] In an earlier letter to Engels, Marx had declared that it was essential that they begin a literary or commercial venture.[39] With his departure for England imminent, he entreated Engels to join him, stating that he was assured of the money to start a German newspaper there. "I count on this *absolutely*. You *cannot* stay in Switzerland. In London we shall get down to business.... I confidently count on you not to leave me in the lurch."[40]

Marx left Paris the next day and crossed the English Channel on August 26.[41] Jenny, Lenchen, and the children remained in Paris for two more weeks, though they were harassed by police who had only reluctantly agreed to let them stay on.[42] If Jenny had experienced the thrill of political drama the first time she and Marx were hounded out of Paris, among so many friends caught in the same government net, this time she felt only dread. She was seven months pregnant, and the Paris heat made it difficult for her to move around. There were few friends to assist her. Heine, who was the closest thing to family she had in Paris, was still there, but he had only limited use of his arms and legs, and his weight had dropped to a skeletal seventy pounds. He took three different kinds of morphine to ease his pain and never left his room, though he continued to write poetry by dictating his verse in a near whisper through a partially paralyzed jaw.[43] This man who had once saved Jennychen could not help her now.

In just over a month the brilliant future Jenny had envisioned for herself and her family in Paris had evaporated. Now she was headed to England, a cold, wet country she did not know. With a generous 100-franc subsidy from Freiligrath, Jenny, Lenchen, and the children (who were now five, three, and two) traveled to Calais on September 15 and then took the steamer to England.[44] Many people they knew had taken that same route, and she tried to find strength in their journeys. She said the men "who fought with sword and pen for the reign of the poor and oppressed were glad to be able to earn their bread abroad." She, however, went to England with only one immediate goal after six years of uncertainty: she wanted a place to rest.[45]

Part III

Exile in Victoria's
England

19

London, 1849

Hell is a city much like London...
Small justice shown, and still less pity.
—Percy Bysshe Shelley[1]

IN 1849 the two-day journey across the Channel from France to England was difficult for the heartiest souls, but for Jenny it took all the strength she could muster to survive it. She was thirty-five, more than seven months pregnant, and had been on the move since May, when the family had been forced out of Cologne. Drenched, cold, weakened by seasickness, and exhausted from caring for the children (who were equally wet, cold, and sick), she finally traveled up the Thames by steamer in the expectation that she would soon join her husband. Marx, however, was not at the dock when they arrived. Laid up with what he described as a choleralike illness, he instead sent his poet friend Georg Weerth to retrieve his family. Thus it was Weerth who introduced Jenny, Lenchen, and the children to their new and strangely forbidding home, conducting them by hackney coach through the fog to a boardinghouse run by a German tailor in Leicester Square, in the heart of London's West End. She was instructed to remain there until her husband was fit enough to find permanent lodgings. Marx, meanwhile, was staying in tony Grosvenor Square with Karl Blind, a German friend who had married into money.[2]

It is not difficult to imagine Jenny's utter desolation as she sat in their small room, with its inadequate coal fire, pondering the future. Once again she had been wrenched from Paris—luminous, opulent, and gay—and dropped into a city she did not know and whose language she barely understood. But this transition was more difficult than the others, because her family was larger, because they had even less money and fewer prospects, and because London was the terminus at the edge of Europe for thousands of desperate travelers like them. Queen Victoria's England had become a virtual repository for banished monarchs, rogues, and rebels, offering the illusion of liberty to victims of revolt or repression. One Italian visitor gaily wrote: "From the despotic ruler of fifty millions to the starving organ grinder and broom girl the land of refuge is open equally to them all."[3] But English reformer George Julian Harney more accurately described what such liberty meant for most exiles: they were "free to land upon our shores and free to perish of hunger beneath our inclement skies."[4]

As with Marx's journey to Manchester, nothing in Jenny's experience could have prepared her for the filth, noise, and misery she found in this, the biggest and richest city in the most industrialized nation in the world. There were parts of London where she would have felt at home, Grosvenor Square being one of them. There, the warmth of a fire in every room and the enveloping comfort of silk dresses sunk into cushioned settees exuded the security she had known in her family's home in Trier. There were even parts of the city where one might settle into a genteel poverty, retaining the trappings of respectability while being well short of the normally accompanying wealth. But there was not a trace of gentility in Leicester Square and little that could be mistaken for respectability. Jenny, whose trunks still contained exquisite dresses from her first days in Paris and whose calling card still identified her as Baroness von Westphalen, was an alien in the hard gray world around her. Despair seemed to hang in the gritty air she breathed.

Indeed, the Marxes arrived in London at the start of the season when the city's fog was so impenetrable the sun did not appear to rise. Even during the day it was nearly impossible for a stranger to find her bearings along streets illuminated by the yellow glow of gas jets or bobbing lanterns held aloft by boys hired to light a pedestrian's way. One foreigner said the fog was so thick you could shake a man's hand and not be able to see his face while doing so.[5] Add the stench of the place to that oppressive atmosphere, and the overall sense was one of suffocation.

Thousands of horses plied London's muddy streets, pulling carts, carriages, and omnibuses, and in the process they deposited a hundred tons of manure each day. That animal smell mixed with the choking odor of human waste that arose from the cesspools in cellars where Londoners disposed of their "night soil."[6] In overcrowded areas like the West End and Soho, some cellars could be three feet deep in excrement.[7] The year

Jenny arrived, that waste was beginning to be diverted into the Thames, but rather than eliminate the problem, it simply made it more mobile. The fetid sludge moved back and forth with the tide through London's rudimentary drainage system; this river that might have cleansed the city instead cut like a great open sewer through its heart, spreading not just stench but, more dangerously, disease.[8] In 1849 London was just coming out of one of its periodic cholera epidemics. Soho and the area around Leicester Square had been hit particularly hard by the outbreak, partly because the poor nestled there like vermin in every available crevice.[9]

In the post-1845 world, when the potato blight and growing economic crisis triggered mass migration, the West End and Soho were the destinations for thousands of refugees arriving from the Continent to the east or Ireland to the west. They made their way to these districts because previous émigrés had carved out small territories of French, German, Italian, or Irish, where one need not speak a word of English or adopt English ways. Too often those already settled exploited the newcomers, demanding exorbitant rents and robbing them of the small amounts of money they had in reserve. That in turn forced the friendless unfortunates out onto the street, where they vied for space with London hordes so notoriously intent on their trades that they would as soon trample a refugee in the gutter as slacken their pace. Desolate and cold, the refugees were forced to find shelter in the area's network of alleys, which grew so crowded with the arrival of more and ever poorer asylum seekers that they evolved into virtual cities within a city. They had their own laws and, some would argue, their own languages.[10]

Perhaps not surprisingly, the blocks around Leicester Square were home to more than a hundred gin palaces—dazzling, cavernous, beckoning saloons where those lucky enough to have a shilling in their pocket could buy a glass of liquid comfort.[11] In fact, an antic, dark, carnival atmosphere existed in the district: vendors lined the streets selling potatoes, coffee, hot eels, pea soup, tarts, and nuts. Men known as standing patterers shouted out lurid details of the violent or obscene pamphlets they offered for sale (though both the violence and obscenity were usually vastly overstated). Poets and dramatists stood on corners reciting their works with great pathos. But it was the Italians who dominated the thoroughfares. About eight hundred Italian boys, many imported to England by child traffickers, worked the streets as organ grinders. Carrying a pet monkey or a trained mouse, they cranked out tunes barely discernible as Rossini or Bellini in order to earn enough money to satisfy the padrone who kept them in tenements in nearby Clerkenwell and Saffron Hill.[12]

There was a Saint Vitus's Dance aspect to all that noise, all that life. It was not joy that inspired the frenzied activity, but fear. All around her Jenny saw refugees like herself driven to near madness in their struggle to survive. This, then, was to be their new home.

Like so many other exiled '48ers, Marx had arrived in London still charged with adrenaline from the past year and intent on reinvigorating the revolutionary forces that had nearly changed the face of Europe. If anything, his passion had only increased as a result of the revolt's collapse at the hands of the monarchies and moneymen. The middle class had gained some political rights, business had been awarded more freedom to operate, but the workingman was in many ways worse off than he had been before. He was still the exploited hand that produced the goods pouring out of industrial factories. He was still largely invisible, because he had no political power. And when he was acknowledged, it was with alarm and suspicion, because the memories of the barricades in Paris, Vienna, Milan, and Berlin were still fresh.

Marx ached to finish the fight he believed had ended prematurely, and he looked expectantly toward the next uprising. He predicted it would be led by the petite bourgeoisie—the small shopkeepers, tradesmen, and bureaucrats—whose livelihoods were threatened by the avaricious grand bourgeoisie and who had gone home empty-handed after the dividends from the recent revolt were distributed. These small bourgeois would try to seduce the workers into joining them in battle against the ruling classes. Marx grudgingly saw the union as inevitable but brief: "For us the issue cannot be the alteration of private property but only its annihilation, not the smoothing over of class antagonisms but the abolition of classes, not the improvement of the existing society but the foundation of a new one."[13]

Yet how to reach the workers on the Continent to prepare them for this social earthquake, especially from as far away as England? That required an organization, a newspaper, and a program to win their trust, so Marx plunged once again into politics. He reestablished ties with old Communist League associates in order to resurrect the organization in London and helped establish a refugee aid committee. Marx's real fixation, however, was starting a newspaper. His goal was a German-language monthly of about eighty pages that would eventually become a weekly or daily paper. It would be distributed in exile communities around Europe, but most important, it would be read deep in enemy territory—in Germany itself. The league's public organ as the revitalized group tried to expand, the paper would also maintain pressure on reactionary regimes by speaking freely from London for those unable to do so on the Continent.[14]

Marx had no money for the paper, and neither did the other league members, most of whom were refugees like him, but he was optimistic the funds could be found. He told Freiligrath he expected the first few weeks would be the most difficult. In the meantime he began a series of economic lectures such as "What Is Bourgeois Property?" for the German Workers' Educational Society,[15] which he delivered in a room above the Red Lion Pub. If the lectures were successful, he figured, they could be reprinted in his newspaper.

Now thirty-two, Marx looked every bit the university professor. He wore a shabby, dark, knee-length frock coat and stiff shirtfront, but over this traditional gentleman's garb he draped a loose artists' scarf around his neck. His uncombed blue-black hair showed hints of gray, but his beard retained its uniform raven color. He did not wear spectacles, only a monocle in his right eye, which he inserted for effect, to magnify his penetrating stare.[16] Using a blackboard, he patiently explained the formulas and theories that, in years to come, would be recognizable as the building blocks of his book *Capital*. Marx's students were mostly younger colleagues; as appreciative as they may have been of this brilliant teacher with his strong Rhineland accent, they were artisans and intellectuals, not the workers the league needed to recruit. The latter could, however, be found among the newly arrived refugees, and during the day Marx traveled from one end of the city to the other trying to raise money to help them and thereby earn their trust.[17]

Surprisingly, the competition for such philanthropy was stiff. At the time there were dozens of émigré factions in London whose leaders had briefly risen to a position of some power in 1848, only to be sent running for safety to England. Once there they created a small but aggravated pool of sharks competing for scraps of funding, attention, and political support. The Germans were the most notoriously obstreperous — with each other and when interacting with other refugee groups — and in many ways the most colorful.[18] The comparatively monochrome English viewed the artisans and workers among them as fantastical creatures, in their lederhosen, green hooded coats with bright trim and tassels, and peaked hats topped with a spray of human hair, their fingers and thumbs covered in rings that signified status or profession.[19] Pub patrons watched in awe as these men sat down to a night of drinking, their constitutions seemingly able to absorb limitless quantities of beer. The Germans were earnest and strong, and, certain their stay in England would be brief, saw little need to adapt.

The various émigré faction leaders saw themselves as head of *the* new movement that would successfully complete their revolution. They formed committees, plotted strategy, and even created provisional governments unrecognized by anyone but themselves and their usually minuscule gang of followers. They stomped about with great bluster, parading their power and stature, and at times battled each other to keep their supporters' fighting spirits alive. But opportunities to expand what they saw as their constituency were seriously limited, the only ready source of recruits being the hapless hordes spilling onto London's docks. Accordingly, the German factions vied to help the newcomers, such solicitude inspired partly by concern but also by a self-interested desire to enlist troops for the next round in the great revolutionary struggle.

Marx did not consider himself one of these faction heads, mocking them as aspiring "democratic dictators" who chose new ministers nightly from the men gathered around them at their favorite pub. Despite being accused throughout his life of despotic ambitions, he claimed to have no desire to be head of any country, real or imagined, and did not want praise from the great masses, whom one colleague said Marx considered at that point a "brainless crowd whose thoughts and feelings are furnished by the ruling class."[20] No, he did not want to lead them, but he did want to *teach* them, because if his theories on the progress of history were correct, those masses represented the future.[21] He believed that only they, armed with knowledge and bolstered by the strength of their numbers, could defeat the ruling classes. If the system he thought fair and just—a communist system—was to be born, it would have to be the child of a proletarian revolution fought by the kind of men who had made their way to London's docks. Marx knew the quickest way to create a base among them was to provide what they needed most at that point—not theory but material assistance (man needed to eat before he could dream). He and his colleagues distributed an appeal to reformers in Germany to help the thousands arriving desperate in England.

> They do not know in the morning where they will lay their head that evening, nor in the evening where tomorrow's food is coming from.... Whether liberal, democrat, republican or socialist: supporters of the most varied political doctrines and interests, they are all united in the same exile and the same misery. Dressed in rags, half a nation is begging at the doors of foreigners. Our fugitive compatriots are also wandering on the cold pavement of the resplendent metropolis, London.... In every street of the city one can hear the grief of an exile lamenting in our tongue.[22]

The appeal reassured potential donors that none of the committee members would be allowed to draw assistance from the fund, and it promised to publish monthly spending accounts. By mid-November the fund had enough money to help fourteen families. Soon sixty families depended on committee aid, and that number would grow to five hundred.[23] The group also set up a communal lodging and eating house in Soho, and a workshop where émigrés could practice their trades.[24]

To help with the refugee work a small clique formed around Marx that included Weerth, Red Wolff, Karl Blind, the Communist League's Heinrich Bauer, and former Prussian officer and aristocrat turned communist August Willich. Jenny, as always, worked as a kind of secretary, and soon Engels, too, arrived to help.

Engels had been in touch with Marx and Jenny only sporadically since they had left Cologne together the previous May. Engels had, as he described it, "buckled on my sword-belt" and headed straight into the fight in Baden, becoming adjutant in an all-volunteer force of about eight hundred men under Willich. Baden would be the last big clash of the German revolt, and Engels was exhilarated by the experience.[25] In the heat of June uniforms were exchanged for blouses and social distinctions in the grand insurgent army disappeared.[26] Engels told Jenny, "I was in four engagements... and discovered that the much-vaunted bravery under fire is quite the most ordinary quality one can possess. The whistle of bullets is really quite a trivial matter... I did not see as many as a dozen men whose conduct was cowardly in *battle*."[27]

The insurgents in Baden numbered between 6,000 and 13,000, but they faced up to 60,000 Prussian and Bavarian troops.[28] Among the many rebels killed was Moll, the giant from the Communist League who had persuaded Marx and Engels to join the group in 1847.[29] Soon after Moll's death, and facing certain defeat, Engels's unit crossed the border into Switzerland, where an estimated 10,000 men had already sought refuge. Engels wanted to join Marx in England, but he could not travel the most direct route through France because the borders were closed. Instead, in early October he went south to Genoa and then from Italy by a long (and by all accounts pleasurable) sea journey via the Straits of Gibraltar to England.[30]

The Marxes had stayed in Leicester Square only a short time after Jenny's arrival. With the help of English-speaking friends they found a two-room apartment off King's Road in Chelsea. It was not the fashionable area it is today (most of Chelsea's inhabitants were as desperate as the Marxes), but it was an improvement over Soho, and the move allowed them to escape to private quarters in time for Jenny to deliver another son.[31]

As Jenny cried out in childbirth on November 5, 1849, the entire city seemed to roar back in response. A raucous crowd had gathered on the streets below. From the window the family could see the flash of fire-crackers and hear shouts they did not understand: "Guy Fawkes Forever!" and "Please to Remember the Fifth of November!" It was Guy Fawkes Day, and the English were recalling the successful foiling of a seventeenth-century Catholic plot to murder the king and members of Parliament. Boys in masks rode wooden donkeys through the streets, and "Guys" dressed in rags stood on the back of carts and raised broomsticks topped with enormous masks up to second-floor windows to frighten those inside. Marching bands played while people danced, sang, and drank in honor of a distant victory over the forces of disorder.[32]

Marx and Jenny thought it auspicious that their fourth child, Heinrich Guido Marx, should be born on the anniversary of an antigovernment plot, and in honor of the great conspirator they nicknamed the child Fawkes-chen.[33] From the start, however, Fawksy was unwell. Marx and Jenny could not afford a wet nurse, so Jenny tried to nurse him herself, but he was in constant pain. The baby cried night and day, a condition Jenny attributed to the "many anxieties and unspoken sorrows" he absorbed along with her milk.[34] One colleague told another that the "young communist who has installed himself *chez* Marx...is getting on everyone's nerves with his bawling; however, he will no doubt become more reasonable in due course."[35] He did not, and Jenny's first months in London were ones of constant worry as, unable to do anything to help him, she watched her child weaken.

Engels reached London on November 12, a week after Fawksy's birth, and took a room in Soho. His influence was immediately recognizable; his presence seemed to embolden Marx. Just days after his arrival, the refugee committee was reorganized to exclude so-called petit bourgeois members.[36] Even if Marx believed a union with them in a future battle inevitable he would not work with these men by choice. Marx had still not forgiven—nor would he ever—the betrayal of the 1848 revolt, and certainly for Engels that betrayal was more stinging still, because it had cost the lives of friends he had fought beside. No matter how great the refugees' immediate needs, the two men would not work with the more prosperous bourgeoisie on their behalf.

Marx, however, exhibited no such scruples when it came to his own entrepreneurship. He was eager to accept funding for his newspaper from businessmen or anyone else who would help raise the five hundred pounds needed for its operation.[37] Marx once wrote, "In politics a man may ally himself with the devil himself—only he must be sure that he is cheating the devil instead of the devil cheating him."[38] He was confident, as he had been with the *Neue Rheinische Zeitung,* that no matter who put up the cash, he would write whatever he pleased in his newspaper.

By mid-December Marx let Weydemeyer know that he had found a publisher and distributor in Hamburg for the *Neue Rheinische Zeitung, Politisch-ökonomische Revue* (New Rhineland Gazette, Political-Economic Review). A notice published by the *Revue*'s board (whose address was Marx's Chelsea apartment) announced that the newspaper would appear in January.

Time was of the essence: Marx was almost feverishly optimistic about the future, telling Weydemeyer, who was still in Germany, "I have little doubt that by the time three, or maybe two, monthly issues have appeared, a world conflagration will intervene."[39] But the *Revue*'s publication was—predictably—delayed by money problems. Out of desperation Marx prepared to send someone to the United States to pluck "golden apples" as other socialists and democrats had successfully done.[40] American towns and cities, some of which were renamed in honor of '48ers (Lamartine, Pennsylvania, for example[41]), were fertile territory for antimonarchy radicals, but Marx and his friends could not even find the money to finance the trip. The plan was abandoned.

January passed without the *Revue*'s appearance, and then February, and then, as was his wont when financially squeezed, Marx became sick. Not only was his newspaper being held up by money problems, but he was being dunned at home by bill collectors. Of particular annoyance was the German doctor Ludwig Bauer, who had attended Fawksy's birth. Marx accused him of plotting to "fleece" him and prematurely sue for payment.[42] The dispute had serious ramifications for Jenny and Marx. It meant they could no longer turn to Bauer for medical care despite Fawksy's continued illness, and also that their personal financial problems would become fodder for London's thriving refugee gossip mill. This was an unbearable position for Marx, especially because he had no way to counter it. They were destitute; his only weapons were his increasingly acerbic attacks on his fellow Germans and his writing.

The *Revue* finally appeared in March, after Marx reached a deal with the publisher giving the latter a healthy share of future earnings to make up for Marx's shortage of ready cash. The paper contained the start of an important series by Marx titled "The Class Struggle in France."[43] In assessing the recent French revolt, Marx for the first time used the phrase "dictatorship of the proletariat" (later to be radically reinterpreted by, among others, Lenin), which he described as a station on the turbulent road to a pure communist state.

This Socialism is the *declaration of the permanence of the revolution,* the *class dictatorship* of the proletariat as the necessary transit point to the *abolition of class distinctions generally,* to the abolition of all the relations of production on which they rest, to the abolition of all the social relations that correspond to these relations of production, to the revolutionizing of all the ideas that result from these social relations.[44]

In the *Revue*'s first edition, Marx also linked the relative calm on the Continent in 1849 to the previous year's discovery of gold in California, which he said had created a revolution of its own that helped spark an economic recovery in Europe. But gold or no gold, he asserted, another economic crisis was certain—it was after all the flawed nature of the new economic system—and that next crisis would trigger a comprehensive uprising.[45]

In his language there was no moderation that might comfort a bourgeois backer or reader. The Marx who wrote in the *Revue* was an unequivocal communist. He spoke for and to the proletariat, who, he said, had launched the first great class battle of modern society, in June 1848 in Paris. If no one was willing to carry on that fight in the street for the moment, he and his handful of colleagues in London would do so in print.

The *Revue* was a valuable outlet for Marx as an intellectual platform, but from the start it was evident that it would not be the thriving venture he had imagined. The newspaper was written and edited in London, but because it was published in Hamburg, where press laws were restricted, the proofreader and publisher (who would be liable if a report ran afoul of the government) wanted to pass it by the censors. That, however, would have meant certain suppression. Those in Hamburg were overruled and the paper was published,[46] but its appearance raised more alarm than support: German authorities were alerted to the reconstituted Communist League and its efforts to agitate in Germany. Moreover, the newspaper was so subversive that finding investors was practically impossible. There were also distribution snags, and while some subscriptions were sold, the proceeds were not sent regularly enough to Marx to defray his costs.[47]

Marx, Engels, and Jenny all frantically solicited funds and chased payments to try to keep the enterprise alive. But the so-called Marx party was in an extremely difficult position: they needed money for the newspaper at the same time they were appealing for refugee aid. Add to that Marx's personal financial crisis, which was known more generally than he would have liked, and it is not surprising that his rivals in London began spreading rumors that he and his cohorts were misappropriating refugee money for their own use. They also suggested that the funds Marx collected went exclusively to communists, leaving others (literally) out in the cold.[48] The whispers were particularly damaging because they were spread not only in

London but by letter to newspapers in Germany. The rage these reports engendered in Marx, Engels, and even Jenny was matched only by their frustration, for at that point they had no currency beyond their reputations.

In a confidential letter to Weydemeyer in May, Jenny fairly screamed in pain and anger over their situation.

> I beg you to *send us as soon as possible any money that has come in or comes in* from the *Revue*. We are in *dire need of it*. No one, I am sure, could reproach us with having made much ado about what we have been obliged to renounce and put up with for years; the public has never, or hardly ever, been importuned with our private affairs, for my husband is very sensitive about such matters and would sooner sacrifice all he has left rather than demean himself by passing round the demo-cratic begging-bowl.... But what he was entitled to expect of his friends, espe-cially in Cologne, was active and energetic concern for his *Revue*.... Instead, the business has been utterly ruined by the negligent, slovenly way in which it was run, nor can one really say which did most harm—the bookseller's procrastina-tion, or that of acquaintances and those managing the business in Cologne, or again the whole attitude of the democrats generally.
>
> Over here my husband has been all but crushed by the most trivial worries of bourgeois existence, and so exasperating a form have these taken that it required all the energy, all the calm, lucid, quiet self-confidence he was able to muster to keep him going during these daily, hourly struggles.[49]

If Weydemeyer needed an illustration of those struggles, Jenny detailed a day in their life: Fawksy, who was now six months old and had not yet slept more than two hours at a time since he was born, was experiencing convulsions. He hovered between life and death. "In his pain he sucked so hard that I got a sore on my breast—an open sore; often blood would spurt into his little, trembling mouth." She reported that as she was feed-ing him one day, their landlady came in, demanded five pounds she said they owed, and, when she did not immediately receive it, raised the alarm that Jenny must be forced to pay. "Two bailiffs entered the house and placed under distraint what little I possessed—beds, linen, clothes, every-thing, even my poor infant's cradle, and the best of the toys belonging to the girls, who burst into tears. They threatened to take everything away within two hours—leaving me lying on the bare boards with my shiver-ing children and my sore breast." Jenny summoned a friend, Conrad Schramm, who made an attempt to get help, but the horses pulling his cab took fright, and he was forced to jump out. He was brought bleeding back to the Marx apartment, one more thwarted creature in need of attention.

The next day, Jenny said, Marx tried to find other lodgings, but when he mentioned that he had four children, no one would take the family. Finally, a friend helped them rent two rooms at a hotel in Leicester Square, but as they began to move their things out of the Chelsea flat they were stopped, because English law forbade moving after sunset. "The landlord bears down on us with constables in attendance, declares we might have included some of his stuff with our own, that we were doing a flit and going abroad. In less than five minutes a crowd of two or three hundred people stands gaping outside our door, all the riff-raff of Chelsea." Marx and Jenny had been in tight spots before but had never sunk to this level of humiliation. All their possessions were out on the street and now had to be moved back inside until dawn.[50]

The Marxes eventually managed their return to Leicester Square but were there for only a week before that landlord, too, ejected them. Once again it was no doubt a question of payment, possibly combined with the distress of the other hotel residents due to Fawksy's incessant crying. At last Jenny's mother came to the rescue, giving them enough money to rent two rooms (one of which was actually no more than a large closet) at 64 Dean Street.

As for Marx's *Revue*, he published just six issues before folding it. He attributed its failure to lack of money and official harassment. Jenny accused the Prussian government of blocking the *Revue*'s sales by bribing the bookseller contracted to distribute it.[51]

The house on Dean Street, in Soho's French district, was owned by a Jewish lace dealer who had earlier rented a room to league member Heinrich Bauer. A shoemaker by trade, Bauer had been sent that spring to Germany to reconstitute the league there. A statement he carried from the Central Authority declared, "As in France in 1793 so today in Germany." It described the next chapter in the revolution and the need to prepare the proletariat by ensuring that everyone was armed. In the future, it warned, the workers would not stoop "to serve as the applauding chorus of the bourgeois democrats" and pledged that once the government in Germany had been overthrown, the league's Central Authority would return.[52]

According to Engels, Bauer's work was beginning to bear fruit, but an unfortunate incident about a month after he arrived derailed his efforts.[53] In May a madman had tried to assassinate King Friedrich Wilhelm.[54] Bauer's agitation, coupled with the Central Authority's radical address and the *Revue*'s incendiary articles, ensured that the finger of blame would be pointed at the league. Conservative newspapers in Prussia said the attack had been prepared in London by Marx's circle, and one royalist paper charged that Marx himself had recently been spotted in Berlin.[55]

As they had in France and Belgium, Prussian officials began pressuring the English to deport the dangerous extremists. The British ambassador in Berlin received a confidential report from the Prussian interior ministry saying that Marx's group was not only plotting against Germany but against the queen of England, possibly in collusion with British soldiers. The document stated that Marx's group "formally taught and discussed" the murder of princes and had up to twenty trained men in reserve for such actions. Evidence that Queen Victoria was in danger was clear, the report said, from a phrase picked up by a spy at a supposed meeting of German exiles in London: "The English moon calf will likewise not escape its destiny. The English steelwares are the best, the axes cut particularly sharp here, and the guillotine awaits every crowned head."[56]

To avoid the police harassment that Marx and Jenny had come to know so well, they considered relocating to the English countryside, where they might be forgotten, but they couldn't afford the move.[57] The only alternative was to fight press report by press report, slander by slander. To do that, they turned to mainstream London newspapers. In letters to the editors of the *Sun,* the *Spectator,* and the *Globe* (some only slightly changed from newspaper to newspaper), Marx, Engels, and Willich (who proudly identified himself as a colonel in the insurrectionary army in Baden) described the absurdity of linking them and Friedrich Wilhelm's would-be assassin, who was an ultraroyalist.[58] They also appealed indirectly to the British public by declaring themselves the victims of close—and unwarranted—surveillance by English police agents:

> Really, Sir, we should have never thought that there existed in this country so many police-spies as we have had the good fortune of making the acquaintance of in the short space of a week. Not only that the doors of the houses where we live are closely watched by individuals of a more than doubtful look, who take down their notes very coolly every time anyone enters the house or leaves it; we cannot make a single step without being followed by them wherever we go. We cannot get into an omnibus or enter a coffee-house without being favored with the company of at least one of these unknown friends.... Now, of what use can be, to any one, the scanty information thus scratched together at our doors by a lot of miserable spies, male prostitutes of the lowest order, who mostly seem to be drawn from the class of common informers, and paid by the job?[59]

The English were not necessarily fond of the refugees in their midst, especially the poor, bearded variety they equated with atheism and immorality. But they were more inclined to ignore than expel them. The English were convinced that their social and political system was so sound they had nothing to fear from foreign radicals, and it was a point of pride for many that their country, unlike the continental monarchies, did not deprive people of their rights simply because they did not agree with their politics.[60]

Whether this public appeal influenced the English government is unknown, but no action was taken against Marx and his colleagues, and there was no official reply to the Prussian government's request that they be deported.

Who *was* Marx that he attracted so much attention? In the greater scheme of things in 1850 the answer was: no one. His name would not have been familiar outside European opposition circles and probably not widely known within those. He was an obscure philosopher and journalist. In the former occupation, he had had virtually no impact on the wider public even when he was attached to a university, and now he had none at all. With regard to the latter, he was easily discounted as a roaming practitioner of a particularly disreputable art.

Of course Prussian officials knew him from his years of agitating, and he was a thorn in the side of his brother-in-law, who was about to be named interior minister. But he was not an immediate threat—even he would likely have admitted as much at that point. More than anything Marx was a handy bogeyman for the Prussian government. After 1848 governments across Europe had tried to blame the uprisings on the press, which they said exaggerated social discontent and stirred the passions of otherwise law-abiding citizens. Marx was easily targeted by Prussians looking for culprits behind that upheaval—or any subsequent violence— partly because his name was associated through his paper with communists, who were seen as the most radical actors in the unrest, and partly because he was so obscure that few people would rise to his defense.

For his political rivals in London's feuding and competitive émigré world, Marx was also a convenient target for accusations and gossip, not so much because of his beliefs but because of his acerbic temperament. In an age when some rebels were viewed as romantic heroes—especially the Italian Giuseppe Mazzini and Hungarian Joseph Kossuth—Marx was, by comparison, unlovable.[61] He came across as isolated, contemptuous, aggressive, and arrogant. Some of Marx's bitterest critics were former followers. (One mocked him as "the omniscient, the all-wise, young Dalai Lama Marx.")[62] The philosopher Isaiah Berlin has suggested that Marx's miserable living conditions and thwarted ambitions during his first years in England only exacerbated whatever negative characteristics he had. "The petty humiliations and insults to which his condition exposed him, the frustration of his desire for the commanding position to which he thought himself entitled, the repression of his colossal natural vitality, made him turn in upon himself in paroxysms of hatred and rage....He saw plots, persecution and conspiracies everywhere."[63] All of that made criticizing Marx easy. What made criticizing him necessary was his obvious potential.

Gustav Techow was a former Prussian officer who had fought alongside the insurgents in the 1848 revolt. He considered joining the Communist League in London in 1850 and met Marx and Engels to discuss the group. Techow said Marx gave the impression not only of intellectual superiority but of genuine significance. "If he had had as much heart as intellect and love as hate, I should have gone through fire for him even if he had not just occasionally hinted at his complete contempt for me, which he finally expressed quite openly. He is the first and only one amongst us all whom I would trust to have the capacity for leadership and for never losing himself in small matters when dealing with great events."[64]

Techow perfectly described the core of Marx's intellectual strength and personal weakness. In Marx's mind he was always dealing with great events, which made it nearly impossible for him to find time for the small matters that absorbed the mere mortals around him or to understand the ramifications of his actions on the people he loved most.

A disturbing example had occurred the day after Jenny arrived in London on September 17. A refugee organization listed Marx as one of five board members elected on September 18,[65] and one would assume this meant that he had attended the meeting. It is possible he was elected in absentia, but if not, Marx was guilty of true callousness toward his family: he had been too ill to meet them at the pier when they arrived, distraught and disoriented, from France, but apparently well enough the next day to join colleagues at a pub to be elected to a refugee aid committee. If Marx was on hand for the vote that night, it was merely one occasion in a lifetime of such occasions when he disregarded his family's welfare and focused on the needs of the party or his theoretical work.

Marx undoubtedly cherished his family, but he preferred to operate on a plain above the quotidian affairs that made Jenny's and the children's lives so difficult. He was prepared to make whatever personal sacrifices necessary in order to advance his ultimate goal of creating a more just society, but that relentless battle against institutional cruelty resulted in a private cruelty of its own. A decade earlier Marx's father had worried about his son's excessive "egoism" when Marx was in Berlin grappling with the Young Hegelians and blithely bankrupting his family in the process.[66] Like an artist single-mindedly dedicated to his work, Marx expected his family to fall into place behind him because they, too, recognized its importance. This certitude about the correctness of his vision may have blinded him to his family's needs.

And what of Jenny? Did she give any indication that she was less committed to Marx's goals and philosophy because of the toll it was taking on her and her children? All we have to go by are her letters, her unfinished autobiography, and the testimony of her friends, but it does not appear, at least in the early months of their lives in London, that she wavered in her loyalty. Of course, as a nineteenth-century wife coming from an aristocratic tradition she had no real choice other than to support her husband, and no doubt she did not want to give their enemies—or her family—ammunition with which to attack Marx if she complained. But even bearing those caveats in mind, it appeared that Jenny *was* fully committed to Marx's work and truly did recognize and understand the needs of the rare genius she had chosen as a husband. For all his faults, Jenny loved Marx deeply and trusted him completely, and like the young Romantic who defied society and family by marrying him, she saw his life's work as her own. In her letter to Weydemeyer listing their domestic miseries in excruciating detail, she added, "Do not suppose that I am bowed down by these petty sufferings, for I know only too well that our struggle is not an isolated one and that, furthermore, I am among the happiest and most favored few in that my beloved husband, the mainstay of my life, is still at my side."[67] Any anger she harbored was directed at those she felt had betrayed Marx. Any complaints she reserved for the ruling classes her husband challenged. Jenny's life was difficult, infinitely so. But she did not blame Marx for her woes. All she demanded was his fidelity.

At the start of their life in London, Jenny was outwardly shaken but her core was firm. Even if she had dared to gaze into the future, she could not have imagined the ways in which her strength and commitment to her husband would be challenged as he careened from one political or financial failure to another. The real tragedy, however, would be personal.

20

Zaltbommel, Holland, August 1850

I really want to act as a deadly arsonist and stroll through
the country with a torch in my hand when I see this idyll here,
which is simply based on coffee bags, tea boxes, herring tins
and oil bottles!

—Jenny Marx[1]

IN THE DRY heat of June 1850, when the spring's mud and manure had
turned into a dust cloud kicked up by a multitude of horses' hooves, Marx
discovered an escape hatch, a portal to his idea of heaven. After convincing staff that his research was significant and securing a recommendation
for admission, Marx obtained a reader's ticket for the British Museum
Reading Room.[2] If it can ever be said that Marx attended a church, the
Reading Room would be that sanctuary. Beginning that June and continuing for the rest of his life, this facility was his refuge.

In 1850 the Reading Room was not the magnificent circular library
under a domed ceiling it would become, but rather a kind of woody gentleman's club with row upon row of oblong tables surrounded floor to
ceiling by books. The man in charge was himself an immigrant, an Italian
named Anthony Panizzi, who had arrived in England in 1823 as another
penniless conspirator who could not speak the language. By the time
Marx made his acquaintance in 1850, Panizzi had worked his way up to
become the Reading Room's Keeper of Printed Books.[3]

It is difficult not to come to the conclusion that moving in off the street
had a salubrious effect on Marx. He was away from the din and the dust
(both inside and outside his apartment) and away from the political bickering
that surrounded him at the German Workers' Educational Society, the

league, and the refugee committee. From the start of his work at the museum, his relief was apparent. Marx had always been happiest in quiet study. Indeed, his greatest immediate source of frustration was that he could not afford to devote all his time to the library. The reason was a familiar one: debt. Marx had signed an IOU worth twenty pounds with a London merchant that was due to be repaid at the end of July, but he did not have the money. He appealed to Karl Blind, with whom he had stayed when he arrived in London but who was now in Paris, to try to find someone to help, saying, "If I were unable to pay it, I would lay myself open to a public [scandal] which, given the present state of the parties here, and [my] relations with the Prussian Embassy and the English Ministry, [could] have most disagreeable consequences." Even if he did receive this loan to repay the previous one, it would be only a patch on a bad situation. There was no publishing opportunity on the horizon, no paid work to be had, and no one to turn to for money except possibly his uncle in Holland. But, Marx told Blind, personal complications made that impossible for the foreseeable future.[4]

Engels, meanwhile, had been under pressure from his family to abandon his dangerous and bohemian friends, especially Marx, who they believed poisoned young Friedrich's mind. His sister Marie, with whom Engels was close and who had married a socialist, suggested he go back to work until his party had a reasonable chance of success.[5] Engels's father had a more drastic suggestion: he wanted him to go to Calcutta, where Britain's East India Company was busily exporting huge quantities of cotton.[6] Engels was considering New York, because he thought he might be able to entice Marx to join him, but in the end he chose neither. He knew the situation in London was untenable. The streets were crawling with refugees struggling to earn a living, and many among them were writers also trying to start newspapers or sell articles to publications abroad. Engels decided the only sensible option was to work at his father's mill, to support not just himself but also the Marx family. Given a chance, Engels believed, Marx would produce a groundbreaking book on political economy that would go far toward educating the proletariat and preparing them for revolt. Marx, too, felt he was poised to do so; all he needed was time, which meant that all he needed was money. Of the two men, Engels had had the more successful writing career up to that point—as poet, author, and journalist—but he regarded Marx so highly that he volunteered to put his own aspirations aside so his friend could write.[7]

Of course Engels's father did not know the real reason behind his son's decision, but he was happy that Friedrich had reached it. Competition was fierce in the cotton trade, and he wanted a family member in Manchester to keep an eye on his English partners.[8] Engels, now thirty, was to begin in November and within a year would be paid a healthy annual salary of £200 plus expenses for entertainment. (By comparison, bank employees received about £70 a year, and a lower-middle-class family with three children was able to live on £150 a year.)[9] In the meantime, however, debts were mounting that could not wait for Engels's first paycheck.

Perhaps inspired by his sacrifice, Jenny was determined to do something, too, to lighten their burden, and made up her mind to go to Zaltbommel, in Holland, and talk to Karl's uncle. She said she was desperate about their future—and she had a new reason for concern. Marx was correct when he said he was a "strong-loined paterfamilias" whose "marriage is more productive than his industry."[10] Jenny had discovered she was expecting another child.

In an August letter to Marx from Holland Jenny described her journey— "fifteen hours of swaying at sea and fifteen hours of dreadful sickness," followed by a cold reception and then "creepy hugging" when Lion Philips finally recognized the bedraggled woman at his door. Perturbed that none of the women of the house would be there during her stay, Jenny said she had wasted no time in coming to the point and suggested their only alternative, if they could not use some of Marx's inheritance, was to move to America. Much to her dismay, Philips thought that a good plan— until, that is, Jenny explained it, too, would require money. The "little man" then became intensely negative, Jenny said, attacking all they believed in. Philips was particularly bitter because he and his sons had lost money due to the 1848 revolts. Recalled Jenny:

> I just did not succeed in bringing him round, wherever and however I tried, it was in vain...yesterday evening I collapsed into bed with a heart like lead, breathing heavily and all in tears....Alas, my beloved, dear Karl, I am afraid I have done the big effort in vain, and will not even bring the production costs of the trip back home. What I have suffered here since yesterday in terms of inner grief, anger I cannot express in this few lines.

Fuming, she wrote that what she really wanted to do was "act as a deadly arsonist and stroll through the country with a torch in my hand when I see this idyll here which is simply based on coffee bags, tea boxes, herring tins, and oil bottles!" Jenny's degradation was complete—she was a beggar refused by family—and still she did not blame her husband:

> I believe dear Karl I will return back home to you with no results, fully deceived, mauled, tortured in mortal fear. If you knew how I yearn for you

and the little heads. I cannot write of the children—my eyes start to quiver and I have to remain brave here. Thus kiss them, kiss the little angels a thousand times from me. I know how well you and Lenchen will take care of them. Without Lenchen I would have no calm here at all. . . . Farewell, Karl of my heart.[11]

As Jenny was in Holland humiliating herself, Marx was in London betraying her; while she pleaded with his family for assistance, he was having sex with Lenchen on Dean Street.

It would be easy to blame Marx alone for such an unforgivable act of betrayal, but that would ascribe a timidity and vulnerability to Lenchen that were not reflected in her character. Now thirty, Lenchen was known as the dictator of the house, the only one in the family who dared confront Marx when he was boiling mad and needed to be brought into line.[12] It was unlikely that Marx forced her to do anything against her will. Perhaps Marx and Lenchen were drinking (a favorite recreation for them both), or he was in need of consolation because Jenny was away and Engels was preparing to leave, so he simply turned to Lenchen. A less likely scenario was that Marx the master took proprietary advantage of Lenchen the servant. Such relations were not uncommon; they were considered no more than aristocratic mischief. But Marx was not an aristocrat, and Lenchen was considered one of the family. She was the closest thing Jenny had to a sister, and she and Karl were the people Jenny trusted most besides her mother. It isn't known whether this was the first or the last time the two had intercourse, but it was the only one with such a disastrous result: Lenchen became pregnant, which meant that she and Jenny would both give birth in the spring of 1851.

Marx could not have known about Lenchen's condition; mercifully, neither did Jenny. When she returned from Holland with nothing from Lion Philips except a toy for one of the children, she experienced the full joy of reunion. She recalled, "My poor little Edgar came leaping towards me . . . and Fawkeschen stretched his tiny arms out to me." Jenny wrote in her memoirs that she had been anxious to return to their life, no matter how small, no matter how difficult.[13]

Among the characters who attached themselves to Marx during his first year in London, one of the most flamboyant was August Willich. He was born von Willich, but abandoned that sign of high breeding when he became a communist. He hailed from one of the oldest, most distinguished families in Prussia and was rumored to have descended from the Hohenzollern stock that produced Prussia's kings. Engels, who fought under Willich at Baden, told Jenny he was "brave, cool-headed and adroit" in battle but a tedious ideologue and socialist dreamer otherwise.[14]

August (as befitted his name) looked the part of the dashing warrior hero. He was neat and polished, with piercing blue eyes, chiseled cheekbones, and a full, curly blond beard. He had aligned himself with the radical doctor Andreas Gottschalk in Cologne and was one of the authors of the first attempted communist revolt there in early 1848. But Marx had not had much to do with him until he turned up in London with a recommendation from Engels.[15] From that moment on, Willich attached himself to Marx's side, involving himself in all party matters, clandestine and public, in England and back home in Prussia. While the Marxes were still living in Chelsea, Jenny described his exuberant appearance in their bedroom early one morning, saying he entered "like a Don Quixote, dressed in a gray woolen doublet with a red cloth round his waist instead of a belt, roaring with laughter in real Prussian style and ready to expatiate in a long theoretical discussion on so 'natural' communism."[16] Marx cut Willich short, but that was by no means the last of his intimate encounters in the Marx household. It appeared the natty dresser had designs on Jenny.

How could he resist? She was a sister in the aristocracy, reduced to dire circumstances by her beliefs and marriage, who still managed to hold her head high, retain her sensuous charm, and inspire the respect and devotion of those around her. Willich may have believed that it was his duty as a true German Romantic to come to her rescue. His intentions were hardly obscure; Jenny said, "He would come to visit me because he wanted to pursue the worm that lives in every marriage and lure it out."[17] He did not succeed in this, but he did awaken Marx's fearsome jealousy.

Marx, Engels, and Willich worked together on league and refugee matters through the summer of 1850, but a rift began developing over strategy that was surely sharpened by what Marx obliquely called "personal matters." Although Marx had put aside all theoretical work since 1848 in favor of political agitation and opposition journalism, it was becoming apparent to him that a revolution was *not* imminent. Willich, however, was a man of action who reveled in secret societies. He believed the league, despite its small numbers, could through sheer force of will trigger an uprising, and he disagreed with Marx's dawning conclusion that massive social change was more than likely years away. For his part Marx argued that certain things were necessary for a successful revolution, but the Willich doctrine of impetuous violence was not one of them.

The dispute was revealing. Marx was in many ways more social evolutionist than revolutionist; his ideas were revolutionary but his methods evolutionary. A revolution, according to Marx, could occur only as a result of definite historical processes and could not be prematurely launched by force. One expert explained that for Marx, two developments were necessary before the old society could be replaced by a new: First, there must be greater class consciousness among the masses and increased participation in the sociopolitical process through trade unions and by employing freedoms of speech, assembly, and press. Second, before the proletariat could produce a classless society—a communist society—there had to be a period of petit bourgeois rule.[18] Such talk was heretical to Willich. He accused Marx of abandoning the battlefield of revolt for the safe terrain of theory.

Willich was a man who did not like to travel without an army, so he began looking for allies against Marx's intellectualizing. Though he was born an aristocrat, most of Willich's support came from working-class German refugees. He lived with them, ate with them, and used the familiar form of "you" reserved for friends when speaking with them. He was thus much more popular than Marx, who lived with his family in conditions that were whispered to be bourgeois and paid for by funds diverted away from the workingman.[19]

Earlier that year Marx, Engels, and their colleagues had aligned themselves with a London organization called the Universal Society of Revolutionary Communists. The Frenchmen who dominated this group were followers of Auguste Blanqui (he of the jailhouse pallor and parched lips who had so terrified the French National Assembly in 1848).[20] Marx had an appreciation for Blanqui, who was still in prison in France, but he quickly soured on his fellows in the Universal Society, considering them mere "alchemists of the revolution." He also thought they might foolishly provoke a conflict, which would undoubtedly result in another defeat.[21]

Willich, however, began working more closely with this group, which included a criminal named Emmanuel Barthélemy who had just escaped from prison in France after being sentenced to forced exile for his part in the June Days.[22] Barthélemy frequented a fencing parlor on Rathbone Place near Oxford Street that was popular among the French émigrés as well as Marx and his friends. (A colleague described Marx as "lustily" giving battle to the Frenchmen: "What he lacked in science he tried to make up in aggressiveness.")[23] Barthélemy in turn began visiting Marx's flat. Jenny, however, did not like him. Barthélemy was no more than thirty, with a black mustache and goatee that made his face appear more ashen than it probably was, but she thought him strange and found his gaping black eyes—the eyes of the void—repulsive.[24] Unknown to the Marxes was the fact that Barthélemy was a violent man who used politics as an excuse for crimes, including murder. The revolution that interested him most was the twist of a knife in someone's back.

According to Wilhelm Liebknecht, a twenty-four-year-old communist convert who also arrived at Marx's doorstep that summer, Willich and Barthélemy began plotting against Marx: "They called Marx a traitor and said traitors must be killed."[25] At the same time Willich was turning to extremists for support, he also made overtures to the petit bourgeois democrats Marx and Engels had thrown off their refugee committee the previous year. Willich lobbied the committee to once again join with the democrats, arguing that a unified position would strengthen their efforts. When his idea was rejected, he resigned in a huff from the Communist League's Central Authority. Several days later, however, apparently looking for a fight, Willich attended a league meeting, where he proceeded to insult Marx and finally challenge him to a duel.[26] The root of the problem may indeed have been political, but it was acted out against the backdrop of any designs Willich may have had on Jenny and under the venomous influence of Barthélemy.

Though Marx dismissed the very notion of a duel, which in any case was illegal in England, Conrad Schramm, the impetuous young gallant ever eager to come to the aid of Marx and his family, threw himself into the dispute by insulting Willich. The duel then became one between twenty-eight-year-old Schramm and forty-year-old Willich.[27] Schramm ignored Marx's pleas to abandon the fight, and took a night boat to Belgium with his second, a Polish army officer named Henryk Miskowsky, as well as Willich and Barthélemy.[28] Liebknecht reported that they agreed to duel with pistols even though "Schramm had never fired one and Willich never missed his target."

Liebknecht was at Marx's apartment the next day, September 12, counting the minutes with Jenny and Lenchen. Jenny was not the cause of the duel, yet she no doubt felt in some way responsible because of her history with Willich. Liebknecht said they waited all day for word, but not until evening, after Liebknecht and Marx had left, did the door open and Barthélemy enter. The Frenchman bowed stiffly and, in response to Jenny and Lenchen's question "What news Schramm?" he answered, "Schramm has a bullet in his head." Barthélemy bowed again, leaving the women to grieve over their friend's fate. Said Liebknecht, "You may imagine the fright of the insensible lady; she now knew her instinctive dislike had not deceived her."

An hour later a distraught Jenny related the news when Marx and Liebknecht returned. Liebknecht said they had all given up Schramm for lost.

But the next day, while they were talking about him, "the door opened and in comes with a bandaged head but gaily laughing the sadly mourned one, and relates that he had received a glancing shot which had stunned him. When he recovered consciousness, he was alone on the seacoast with his second and his physician."[29] Schramm survived, but Marx and Willich's relationship could not. Four days after the duel a formal split occurred during a Central Authority meeting.

The minutes of the meeting reveal none of the preceding drama. Marx, his mind as hard and brilliant as a diamond, knew he would emerge the victor in any battle of wits. While he could be absolutely volcanic in more private settings, in such meetings he seemed to enjoy frustrating his opponents by appearing as calm and as rational as possible. Such was the case when the Central Authority met to discuss and vote on his proposal that the executive body of the Communist League be moved from London to Cologne, that the league's rules be declared null and void and rewritten, and that the London league be split into two groups, or "districts," both reporting directly to Cologne but having little to do with each other.[30] These steps were necessary, Marx said, to avoid a scandalous public rupture and to ensure that the league survived whatever disagreements had arisen among its members. He explained that the London group was divided not just by personal issues but over its position vis-à-vis the next revolution. "Whereas we say to the workers: You have fifteen, twenty, fifty years of civil war to go through in order to alter the situation and to train yourselves for the exercise of power, [the other League faction says] we must take power *at once,* or else we may as well take to our beds." Marx said he wanted no more than twelve people in his "district"; the other London league could take the remaining members.[31]

Karl Schapper was an original league member and Marx's close friend, but he was on the opposite side on this issue. He did not agree with Marx's go-slow approach, and though he said he fully expected to be "guillotined," he would go to Germany to fight anyway. If Marx wanted to split the London league he could do so, but "in that case there should be two leagues, one for those who work with the pen and one for those who work in other ways."[32]

Willich remained silent. Marx had even tried to draw him out at one point, but he and another member showed their disdain for the proceedings by walking out. A vote was taken, and only Marx's group cast ballots. Not surprisingly, they unanimously backed the split.[33] Within two days Marx and his colleagues also resigned from the German Workers' Educational Society, and shortly after broke with the Blanquists of the Universal

Portrait based on a drawing of eighteen-year-old Karl Marx during his first year of university at Bonn. (International Institute of Social History [IISG], Amsterdam)

Jenny von Westphalen in Trier, circa 1836, the year she secretly agreed to marry Karl Marx. (David King Collection, London)

Ferdinand von Westphalen, Jenny Marx's eldest brother, was Prussian interior minister during Marx and Jenny's first decade in London. His reactionary policies resulted in the incarceration of Marx's friends. (Friedrich–Ebert-Stiftung Museum / Studienzentrum, Trier)

Edgar von Westphalen was Jenny Marx's younger brother and closest sibling, and one of Karl Marx's earliest followers. He left Europe for America in the mid-1840s and, much to Marx and Jenny's surprise, joined Confederate forces during the U.S. Civil War. (Friedrich–Ebert-Stiftung Museum / Studienzentrum, Trier)

Friedrich Engels at twenty-five, shortly after he and Karl Marx met in 1844 to begin their lifelong collaboration. (IISG, Amsterdam)

Helene Demuth lived with the Marx family for nearly forty years, suffering grinding poverty alongside them. She left the family briefly in the summer of 1851 after giving birth to Marx's son. (David King Collection, London)

Rue de l'Alliance, Brussels, where the Marxes lived beginning in 1845, was a working-class district of artisans and shopkeepers. It was here that many of Marx's friends first assembled and where the "Marx party" was born. (David King Collection, London)

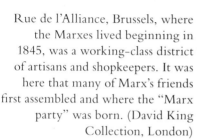

Wilhelm Wolff, known as Lupus, joined Marx's circle in Brussels. When he died in 1864, this bachelor tutor left Marx and Jenny nearly a thousand pounds. Marx dedicated *Capital, Volume I* to him. (Friedrich-Ebert-Stiftung Museum / Studienzentrum, Trier)

Edgar Marx in a drawing by family friend Roland Daniels from 1848, when Marx and his family were in Cologne amid a tumultuous rebellion that eventually saw them forced from three countries because of Marx's activities. (IISG, Amsterdam)

Some of the Marx family's greatest tragedies occurred in their top-floor apartment at 28 Dean Street, Soho, London. The Marx flat was a refuge for revolutionaries and bohemians of all nationalities. This undated photograph was taken decades after the family had moved. (IISG, Amsterdam)

Frederick Demuth was born in 1851, the son of Karl Marx and Helene Demuth. He was raised away from the Marxes by a foster family in East London, but in later years was one of Eleanor Marx's closest friends. (David Heisler, London)

In 1856, thirty-six-year-old Friedrich Engels worked at his father's textile factory in Manchester, England, using funds from the firm to finance Marx and his family. He lived a double life, both businessman and revolutionary. (IISG, Amsterdam)

Marx turned to Ferdinand Lassalle in 1857 to try to find a publisher in Germany for an economic work, but his relations with Lassalle were acrimonious and competitive as Lassalle rose to the top of the socialist and workers' movement in Germany. He died in 1864 in a duel over a nineteen-year-old woman. (IISG, Amsterdam)

Marx in 1861, after being feted in Berlin by Ferdinand Lassalle and the Countess von Hatzfeldt, and pampered by his cousin Antoinette Philips in Holland. (David King Collection, London)

Laura Marx at about age sixteen, in 1862, when she received a reader's ticket for the British Museum Reading Room, where she helped her father with his research. (IISG, Amsterdam)

Marx (standing left), Friedrich Engels, and Marx's daughters (left to right) Jenny, Eleanor, and Laura in 1864, after the family moved into their grand new home at 1 Modena Villas in London. (David King Collection, London)

Russian anarchist Mikhail Bakunin was Marx's adversary from their earliest days in Paris. In 1869, Bakunin plotted to wrest control of the International Working Men's Association from Marx. (IISG, Amsterdam)

This photograph has been repeatedly identified as a portrait of Marx's wife, Jenny, but a Russian historian discovered it was actually a Marx family friend, Gertruda Kugelmann. The photo was taken in Hanover, where the Kugelmanns lived. (IISG, Amsterdam)

Society of Revolutionary Communists. Engels, Marx, and George Julian Harney wrote a letter to the group inviting them to come to Engels's apartment off Dean Street to witness the burning of the society's contract.[34] There was one last act in Marx's scheme to demolish the likes of Willich and his associates: he asked the new Central Authority in Cologne to expel the London dissidents, saying they were in a state of rebellion and violating all league agreements and laws. Cologne approved his request.[35]

Marx's sweet victory over his enemies came just as Harney published the *Communist Manifesto* in his newspaper the *Red Republican*. It was the first English translation of the work and also the first to identify its authors: "Citizens Charles Marx and Frederic Engels."[36] But Marx did not have time to savor either triumph. In destroying his league rivals he had created a monster army of enemies (who called the *Manifesto* reactionary) as Engels was preparing to leave for Manchester. With his friend's departure Marx would be left in London with a pack of young followers barely dry behind the ears. Aside from Jenny he would have no real intellectual companion and no one to help fend off the inevitable backlash from his Communist League coup. There were also nagging financial problems. In late October Marx had written to Weydemeyer (who since May had faithfully made payments to keep Jenny's silver in pawn in Frankfurt) to sell the silver and send him the money; the family could not survive without it. The only items he specifically did not want sold were a small silver mug, a silver plate, and a small knife and fork. Those belonged to his five-and-a-half-year-old daughter, Jennychen.[37]

The children were among the few bright lights in the Marxes' lives. Despite the trauma of moving, the dramas over money and politics, the cold and the hunger—not to mention the terror of being surrounded by people who spoke a language they did not know—Jenny described the girls as "pretty, blooming, cheerful and in good spirits." She said their "fat boy," three-year-old Edgar, was the "paragon of comical humor and full of the drollest ideas. All day the little imp sings funny songs with tremendous feeling and at the top of his voice, and when he sings the verse from Freiligrath's Marseillaise, *'Come, O June, and bring us deeds / Fresh deeds for which our hearts do yearn'* in a deafening voice, the whole house reverberates."[38]

The only child truly suffering in their first year in London was the one born there, but he did not suffer long. Heinrich Guido died from complications caused by pneumonia on November 19, not long after his first birthday. Marx wrote Engels in Manchester to let him know the "little gunpowder-plotter" had died that morning after a convulsion. "A few minutes before, he was still laughing and joking. . . . You can imagine what it is like here. Your absence at this particular moment makes us feel very lonely."[39] Four days later Marx described Jenny to Engels as "in a really dangerous state of excitation and exhaustion. She had nursed the child herself and had fought for its existence under the most difficult circumstances and at the greatest sacrifice."[40]

Fawksy, whom Jenny called "my poor little child of sorrow," was buried at a Quaker cemetery off Tottenham Court Road.[41] His tiny coffin did not have far to travel when the family carried it in a funeral procession. Along Soho's teeming back streets, funerals were a familiar sight, and it is likely the Marxes attracted little attention, which would have made their grief all the more bitter. They were merely one among a multitude of beleaguered families gripped in the maw of poverty while a few streets away fortunate others flourished amid incalculable wealth.

21

London, Winter 1851

With this general prosperity, in which the productive forces of the
bourgeois society develop as luxuriantly as it is at all possible
within bourgeois relationships, there can be no talk of a real
revolution.

—Karl Marx and Friedrich Engels[1]

IN 1851 Queen Victoria proudly declared that her beloved husband, Prince Albert, had successfully united the world behind peace and prosperity. Albert was president of the commission of notables who created the world's first Great Exhibition, a triumph of trade, industry, and inventiveness. On opening day, May 1, one-quarter of London's population gathered in Hyde Park to witness the event. The thirty-two-year-old queen, awestruck by the marvels around her, was among them. Inside the Crystal Palace, which was built to hold the expo and whose dome was larger than that of St. Peter's Basilica in Rome, some hundred thousand exhibits displayed the wonders of the age, from Foucault's Pendulum to the flush toilet, from the cotton spinning machine to a daguerreotype of the moon. The exhibition marked the birth of the shopping mall, with multistory shops that moved merchandise with exceptional ease. It also included the world's largest indoor greenhouse, demonstrating man's dominance over nature. With Handel's "Hallelujah Chorus" sung by a thousand-member choir swelling in the background, the queen said, "One felt...filled with devotion, more so than by any service I have ever heard."[2] Thus the head of the Church of England declared industry to be the new religion. Britain's Golden Age of Capitalism—a word that had just begun to be used among the cognoscenti, along with its glorious counterpart, imperialism[3]—was born.

In fact throughout Europe King Capital had ascended the throne. An economic boom had begun not long after 1849, when the last of the revolts were quashed and reactionary powers reinstated. Governments had learned the lesson intrinsic in Marx's preaching that joblessness, hunger, and related disease were much more threatening to their stability than any ideology or even an enemy's army, because if the bottom layer of society—its foundation—rose up, the entire house of cards collapsed. To avert that, works programs had been instituted to build railways, housing, factories, anything that could employ a lot of men and, more crucially, produce a hefty profit.[4] In London alone in 1851, construction employed more than sixty-six thousand people, making it the capital's biggest industry. Needless to say, they were not building homes for those packed together in overcrowded slums. The rush to build occurred in Belgravia, Kensington, and newer suburbs in north London, where villas were erected for the suddenly cash-rich middle class.[5]

All this industry had the blessings of Europe's kings and their acquiescent parliaments, which had been infiltrated by businessmen who owned railways and played in that exciting and expanding arena called the stock market. These men argued that success and prosperity would continue if a simple formula was followed: business must be privately owned and competitive, and it must purchase commodities (including labor) at the cheapest price possible, while selling its products in a free market at the highest price possible. The formula was capitalism.[6]

Railways, steamships, and the telegraph had accelerated the pace of business, shattering restrictions once set by time and distance, but it was gold that inspired a new boldness, and in some cases recklessness, in the marketplace. European businessmen watched their counterparts in California amass mountains of money in the freewheeling, unregulated environment of America's frontier. European governments looked at their own comparatively empty treasuries and acknowledged that continental businessmen were losing out because they were shackled by outdated rules.[7] Mining was subsequently deregulated, trade rules were liberalized, banks were established to fund commerce, and laws were rewritten to encourage business growth.[8]

The exhibition in London reflected this mercantile dawn, and just as there was no way for the average worker to avoid the new economic imperative, there was no way for the average Londoner to avoid the grand show. Parts of the city were transformed for the many heads of state and other dignitaries expected to arrive: manure was scooped up almost as soon as it was dropped; painters freshened building trims with splashes of green, burgundy, azure, and yellow; shop owners scrubbed soot-covered windows to a sparkle; and most important, the hundreds of homeless who slept in Hyde Park each night were driven out to infest more remote pastures. The dowager that was London was rouged and powdered, and made ready to receive.

There seemed no end to English self-congratulation over not only the exhibition but the country's singular standing on the globe. By 1851 Britain owned half the world's oceangoing ships as well as half the world's railway tracks.[9] Its success was a triumph of philosophical rationalism, political pragmatism, and commercial ingenuity, all of which the exhibition would showcase.

The event would also be a global tribute to the power of private wealth, which was particularly galling to Marx. Where before he had had to contend with the fantasies of would-be revolutionaries, who created imaginary monuments to themselves without having taken a single step to earn them, now Marx was surrounded by capitalist dreamers, for whom traders were peace envoys traversing a world made harmonious because manufactured goods could be sold from China to Brazil, from Canada to the Boer Republics. For Marx and Engels the exhibition was nothing less than modern Rome's pantheon, a temple to "cosmopolitan-philanthropic-commercial...bourgeois megalomania."[10] What capitalists championed as the benefits of free trade—the breaking down of national boundaries and character, the blurring of local methods of production and social relations—Marx and Engels saw as contributing to the next major financial crisis, which they predicted would occur the following year.[11]

In a way neither Jenny nor Engels could, the exhibition seemed to goad Marx back to work. In his estimation there was nothing wrong with the industrial or technological advances on display; history was built on them. Indeed, he was as excited as a child by a model electric engine featured in a Regent Street window, declaring the electric spark was a "far greater revolutionist" than steam and that "the consequences are indefinable."[12] But it fell to Marx to explain how humanity's marvelous advances came under the control of such a small number of capitalists, and why it was wrong that those stupendous strides, though benefitting many, enriched so very few.

That spring, 1851, before most people had even heard of capitalism, Marx began wrestling with this massive and evolving economic, political, and social system, which would one day extend its reach across the globe, impacting every aspect of human existence. At capitalism's infancy, Marx set to work chronicling its rise and predicting its fall.[13] Over the next sixteen years, he would write thousands of pages before producing the first volume in his magnum opus, *Capital.* His young followers would see in it a blueprint for an alternative to capitalism, which they called Marxism.

★   ★   ★

Marx did nothing by half measures, and so his submersion into economics was complete. A young colleague named Wilhelm Pieper, who occasionally acted as Marx's secretary when not exploring the inner sanctums of a brothel, jokingly complained to Engels, "Whenever one goes to see him one is welcomed with economic categories in lieu of greetings."[14] Engels was likely unsurprised; Marx's letters were also full of economic theories that he wanted to test out on his able friend. It was at this time that the two men began a vibrant, near daily correspondence that would last almost two decades, until 1870, when Engels moved back to London. One of Marx's daughters recalled the highlight of the day at their home was the arrival of the letter carrier, dressed in his red military-style frock coat and gold-banded top hat. The double rap of his stick on the door sent the children flying down the stairs, because they knew how happy a letter from "Uncle Angels" would make their father.[15] Not only did it represent the latest entry in their epistolary conversation, but it usually contained money the family could not do without.

After moving to Manchester in December, the Marx children's "angel" had installed himself at two addresses. One was a respectable flat where a businessman might be expected to live and entertain associates. The other was a house on the outskirts of town, where he registered as Mr. and Mrs. Boardman and lived with Mary Burns and her younger sister, Lizzy. Their associates were often Irish radicals. The famine that had decimated their island was over, but Ireland's weakened state militated against any immediate hope of independence from England; there was simply not enough energy in the counry at that moment to wage such a fight. But the anger among the Irish in Manchester was raging, not only over Westminster's rule of Ireland, but over its treatment of Irish working men, women, and children living in England.

Engels may have assuaged his conscience over capitalist "huckstering" by gleefully using its proceeds to finance his rebellious friends. From the start of his career as a textile merchant he underwrote the Marx family— even if it meant dipping into the factory cash box to do so—and he supported the Burns family in Manchester. Engels certainly put on a good show of being a factory owner's son. He appeared at all the right clubs and was considered a genial companion there, but his real friends were those this society would as soon send to the gallows. He swam, fenced, and rode to hounds, and while he enjoyed the exercise for its own sake, it was also aimed at hardening his body in the event he was called back to arms.[16] Jenny teasingly called him a "great cotton lord." He was that, but he had a rebel's heart. She said she was glad he was the same old Fritze.[17]

Engels did not know how long his father would want to keep him in Manchester, but while he was there he eased Marx and Jenny's worries considerably. His letters often contained a pound or two to cover their basic needs. In fact, for the first time since they arrived in London, things were looking up. Marx was working on his economic studies and planning to try to sell his writings from Cologne in pamphlet form.[18] He even envisioned restarting the *Revue* in Switzerland.[19] The children, too, seemed to have rebounded after Fawsky's death. To be sure, not all was smooth — bitter disputes still existed among the émigrés: Red Wolff had been beaten up by Willich's followers in December, and Conrad Schramm and Pieper were viciously manhandled when they turned up at a banquet honoring the Paris revolt.[20] But rather than engage in such brawls, Marx now tried to insulate himself from his rivals, dismissing their propaganda as the work of "apes" who "bombard their enemy with their own excrement." To which he sarcastically added, *"Each according to his abilities."*[21] (The phrase, used in mockery here, would be expanded upon in the future and become a cornerstone of Marx's communist theory.)

By the end of January, whether because Fawksy had died at 64 Dean Street or because they were told to leave for nonpayment (Marx had asked Engels for money earlier that month because he was behind on his rent[22]), the family moved again. Their new address was 28 Dean Street, Soho, which, while just several doors away, was in fact a slight improvement over their previous lodgings. The three adults and three children now had two full rooms to themselves on the top floor of a narrow, four-story, century-old Georgian building that housed a shop on the ground level. The building was home to three other families, two Italian — one was the landlord — and a teacher of languages from Ireland, who sublet part of his space to Marx.[23]

The garret apartment was far from commodious. Its front room, with three windows facing the street, was at most fifteen by ten feet: it served as a reception room, dining room, parlor, and study. The back room, which had a corner fireplace and a sloping roof, was even smaller, but it was where the family and Lenchen cooked, slept, and bathed.[24] Running water did not reach more than ten feet above street level, so the Marxes had to fetch theirs from the ground floor. Likewise there was no toilet connected to the central water supply; their choices were a communal water closet (the deposits went into a cesspool in the cellar) or a chamber pot in their apartment.[25] Nevertheless, from their lofty heights they may have considered themselves lucky. Looking out the windows, across the rooftops and chimneys of other decaying buildings, they could imagine themselves closer to the sky than the street. Liebknecht called the apartment a "pigeon loft where a multitude of various bohemian, fugitive and refugee folks went in and out," and for the next five years it would be the "house of Mohr," a center for all the men gathered around him. For their refugee friends, Liebknecht said, it was the most settled abode they could find in London, short of a graveyard.[26]

In the new apartment the Marx family settled into a reassuring routine. The girls went to school. Jenny split her time between her husband's affairs and those of her children, and Lenchen ran the household, which meant trying to stretch the money Engels sent them (or Marx borrowed) far enough to make sure they had enough to eat. When that was insufficient, she turned to the pawnshop, where the children believed another "uncle" like Engels gave them money in exchange for whatever household items or clothing they could temporarily do without.

For his part Marx spent every day at the British Museum Reading Room, dragging his young colleagues along with him.[27] Liebknecht recalled that while other refugees in London busily plotted the overthrow of the world, "we, the scum of humanity, were sitting in the British Museum and trying to educate ourselves and to prepare arms and ammunition for the battles of the future. . . . Sometimes we would not have had a bite, but that would not prevent our going to the Museum. . . . There were at least comfortable chairs to sit down on and in winter a cheering warmth which were missing at home, if one had any house or home at all."[28]

At night there were political meetings, nearly all of which occurred in private rooms over a pub. There, shining pewter pots of dark brown stout were served and long clay pipes offered to those who cared for a smoke.[29] If no one had money—which was most of the time—the young exiles who had been with Marx all day would return to Dean Street to bask in a homely albeit poor family atmosphere they sorely missed. Whatever little the Marxes had, they offered the men who considered Marx their leader, as much as he may have protested that designation.

Friedrich Lessner, the tailor, said Jenny greeted them with such ease that they felt they were in the presence of their mother or sister. He described her as tall, very beautiful, and distinguished, but entirely free of the pride or stiffness her class might have been expected to exhibit in such low company. Rather, he said, she was lovable and witty.[30] Liebknecht admitted that Jenny may have exercised an even greater sway over them than did Marx himself. "This dignity, this loftiness, that kept aloof not familiarity but everything unbecoming, acted with magic power on us wild or even a little rude fellows."[31] Years later Liebknecht wrote of Jenny that she was "the first woman who made me recognize the educational strength and power of women. . . . Mother, friend, confidante, adviser, she was to me the ideal of a woman and she is my ideal even now."[32] She even managed to charm a Prussian spy who had infiltrated Marx's circle; he reported back that Jenny "accustomed herself to this gypsy life out of love for her husband and seems to feel quite at home in this misery."[33]

And in the midst of that activity were the three Marx children. They were never excluded from the company of their elders, not because Marx thought they could learn from the adults, but because he believed the adults could learn from the children. (Marx liked to say, "Children must bring up their parents.")[34] Marx's authority over them was exerted not by way of orders but by suggestions—to which they invariably agreed. According to Liebknecht, in the presence of women and children Marx displayed a gentleness that "an English governess might have envied."[35]

The first wave of refugees arriving in London after 1848 had included many continental lesser lights, but by 1851 the veterans of revolution had begun to appear, and their arrival set off a fresh and almost comical competition among the less distinguished radicals seeking to prove their worth.[36] Marx and Engels described these men as "a mutual insurance club of the heroes to be."[37]

Marx had known all the important players in Paris in 1848, and now that Louis Napoleon's government had made dissent nearly impossible, those men had fled to London and began paying courtesy calls to 28 Dean Street. Among the first to visit was Louis Blanc, who appeared early one morning. Lenchen led him to the front room while Marx, who was still in bed, got dressed in the back. Liebknecht described the scene later related to him by Marx, who with Jenny spied on Blanc through a partially opened door. Marx said Blanc looked around the poorly furnished room before discovering an "extremely primitive mirror, before which he at once took his place, struck a pose and stretched his dwarfed frame to the utmost—he had the highest heels on his boots I ever saw—and salaamed like an amorous rabbit in March." Jenny could hardly keep from laughing out loud. When Marx finished dressing and washing, he announced his entry by clearing his throat, "enabling the coxcount of a popular tribune to retreat a step from the mirror and receive his entering host with a proper bow."[38]

In truth, Marx had no interest in forming alliances with Blanc or any of the other men whose names were associated with the revolutionary movements of the past twenty years. He thought the veterans of 1830, including the formidable Mazzini, who was beloved by the English and seen as incorruptible, were "experienced swindlers" who took advantage of the younger generation by allowing them to do all the work while they collected the money and basked in the glory.[39] These men and the lesser radicals formed new alliances, split off from each other, and mutated yet again into new groupings at a dizzying pace, but all the intrigue left no time for real work. The focus of these refugees was entirely on themselves and each other. All Marx needed, he believed, was his small band of associates, though he would have preferred that Engels were with them in London. In early February he told him, "I am greatly pleased by the public, authentic isolation in which we two, you and I, now find ourselves. It is wholly in accord with our attitude and our principles. The system of mutual concessions, half measures tolerated for decency's sake, and the obligation to bear one's share of public ridicule in the party along with all these jackasses, all this is now over."[40]

Engels agreed, replying: "One comes to realize more and more that emigration is an institution which inevitably turns a man into a fool, an ass and a base rascal unless he withdraws wholly therefrom, and unless he is content to be an independent writer who doesn't give a tinker's curse for the so-called revolutionary party. It is a real SCHOOL OF SCANDAL AND MEANNESS in which the hindmost donkey becomes the foremost savior of his country." Indeed, he suggested their position gave them a new freedom. "From now on we are only answerable for ourselves and, come the time when these gentry need us, we shall be in a position to dictate our own terms. Until then we shall at least have some peace and quiet. A measure of loneliness, too, of course — *my God,* I've already had a three months' spell of that in Manchester." The main thing was to get something published. "What price all the tittle-tattle the entire émigré crowd can muster against you, when you answer it with your political economy?"[41]

Marx was eager to finish his book. Politics had descended into farce, and theory was the only area worthy of attention. But a series of personal crises occurred to derail his plans. Marx had a debt bearing down on him that even Engels could not erase. He owed more than forty pounds to various people, and the situation was causing a scandal from London to Brussels to Trier. At his wits' end, Marx even threatened his mother, saying that if she did not give him enough to cover his obligations, he would come back to Prussia and have himself thrown in jail. Apparently she had no qualms about seeing her son locked up, and offered him nothing. Marx then told Engels he had not a farthing in the house, "so that tradesmen's bills — butcher's, baker's AND SO FORTH — keep mounting up. . . . You will admit that this is a pretty kettle of fish and that I am up to my neck in petty-bourgeois muck. And at the same time one is also said to have exploited the workers! and to aspire to dictatorship! What horrors!"

In the midst of that turmoil, on March 28, 1851, Jenny gave birth to a baby girl. She was named Franzisca. Although Marx said the delivery had been easy, Jenny remained in bed, "the causes being domestic rather than physical." At that time Lenchen would have been about six months pregnant, and Jenny may have finally discovered her condition, though not the identity of the father—that was something Marx wanted to discuss with Engels. He wrote: "Finally, to give the matter a tragi-comic turn, there is in addition a *mystère* which I will now reveal to you in very few words." Here he was interrupted in his writing by Jenny. Marx promised to continue but apparently never did.[42] (No letter has survived—if one ever existed—in which Marx admitted he was the father of Lenchen's child.) In his next letter to Engels, on April 2, Marx vowed that no matter the cost, he would come to Manchester to explain. "I must get away from here for a week. The worst of it is that I now suddenly find myself hampered in my work at the library. I am so far advanced that I will have finished with the whole economic shit in five weeks' time."[43]

There could not have been a worse time for Marx to be embroiled in a personal scandal, especially one of such magnitude. The whole of the European opposition was descending on London for the Great Exhibition. The refugee communities were alive with excitement because the visitors arrived with money to spend, in return for which they wanted news on the various revolts being cooked up in London. "Never has the emigration drunk more and cheaper than during the period when the solvent masses of German philistines were in London," Marx and Engels wrote of what they called that year's "public house politics."[44] Finally in the spotlight, those who had been exiled to London did not want to disappoint. Fresh conspiracies were hatched, dates set for revolution, and bonds sold to finance the fight (redeemable after insurrectionary governments were installed).[45] And, of course, most delicious of all was the gossip, which spread from pub to pub and was cleverly embellished at each tipsy juncture. The possibility that Karl Marx was living with two women who were both mothers of his children would have been irresistible to that crowd, not only a tale worth the price of the ticket to London but a means of discrediting this arrogant tyrant who was so eager to criticize (if not destroy) his enemies, this champion of communism who said his ideology had nothing to do with free love and posed no threat to the sanctity of marriage.

In the months leading up to the exhibition's May opening, a wild story had circulated that Louis Blanc and Ledru-Rollin (who by this time were adversaries) were organizing a worldwide rebellion from a Haymarket pub. It would involve ninety thousand foreign refugees, who would simultaneously set fire to the houses they lived in, aided by two hundred thousand

Irish and their dreaded Catholic priests disguised as match sellers.[46] The rumors were preposterous, but that did not stop continental authorities from pressing London police to arrest subversives and investigate suspected plots. Governments that had suffered the brunt of the 1848 violence thought the English insanely reckless for mounting the exhibition so soon after that upheaval. The British ambassador to Vienna wrote, "England is looked upon as the focus from which not only every revolutionary movement in other countries is propagated but murder and mutiny fomented and encouraged."[47]

Jenny's brother Ferdinand von Westphalen was one of the most outspoken on the threat posed by extremists in London. He had been named Prussian interior minister the previous December and was thus in charge of the kingdom's domestic security. In a January 1 proclamation he announced a severe crackdown: no political meetings could be held without police supervision, the book industry was placed under state control, and newspapers were required to pay a large fee to be deposited with the police in order to publish.[48] Commented Engels to Marx, "Your brother-in-law is confiscating books with praiseworthy zeal. My only fear is that like a *Prusso-bureaucratic Brutus* he will soon be laying violent hands on your stuff, and that might put an unwelcome stop to the payment of fees."[49] As England began its Golden Age of Capitalism, Prussia began what became known as the Decade of Reaction.[50]

Among Westphalen's goals was to keep revolutionary materials out of Prussia. Guards were placed at train stations, surveillance was increased, and traps were set to catch the men carrying banned writings into the kingdom. Nor was he content to limit the campaign to Prussian or even German territory. Ferdinand was convinced that the heart of revolution beat in London, so in the spring of 1851 he sent spies and agents to England to root out the conspirators, one of whom he no doubt suspected he knew quite well.[51] (For his part Marx publicly called Ferdinand a "weak-minded and fanatical reactionist.")[52] Westphalen believed the queen would agree to expel the agitators only if they were caught red-handed in treasonable activities. The incriminating material had to be convincing—it did not necessarily have to be true.[53]

At this time a Prussian spy named Wilhelm Stieber turned his attention to Marx's circle. He employed a man named Charles Fleury who pretended he was a newspaper editor named Schmidt in London to cover the exhibition. Fleury's actual job was to report on German radicals in the British capital and on the Marx household in particular. The ultimate recipient of his information would be Jenny's brother.[54]

All of this meant that just as Lenchen's pregnancy became undeniable,

Marx would be under intense scrutiny—from rivals in the opposition, from the Prussian government, and, most immediately and most dangerously, from his wife and her family. He had to do whatever he could to make sure he was not exposed as the child's father. News of his infidelity would ruin him politically and make him the laughingstock of his opponents. Personally, it could not have had greater consequences. His act of disloyalty would crush Jenny, who had already suffered so much for his sake. Worst of all, Marx risked losing his family altogether. Her extreme distress might help Ferdinand (who addressed his sister as "my dear cherished Jenny"[55]) convince her to return to her mother in Prussia, where she could raise her children in comfort and security. It is likely that Marx gave no thought to the child about to be born to Lenchen; that was a future concern, and there were many more immediate problems bearing down on him.

At the end of April, Marx took a train to Manchester to see Engels. It is easy to imagine the discussion between the two men. Engels would have been entirely sympathetic to his friend's predicament. But what could the situation have been for the two women left alone at Dean Street? Jenny and Lenchen had been close since they were children. Now they would be utterly alienated, suspicious and deeply saddened. For Lenchen the only alternatives would have been to have the child and leave the Marxes, or abandon the child but by necessity also leave the Marx household. There must have seemed no scenario under which she would have been allowed to stay, or felt comfortable doing so. For Jenny's part, if she believed Marx was the father of Lenchen's child, their life together would be ruined. She had asked him for nothing but love and loyalty, in return for which she gave him everything.

Jenny remained in bed, taking brandy and port by the spoonful nearly every hour to steady her nerves. She boarded Franzisca out to a wet nurse, probably out of fear the child would suffer Fawksy's fate if she nursed her under such distress.[56] Lenchen took care of the other children. Laura and Edgar were likely too young to detect any unusual strain in their small household, but Jennychen would be six in May, old enough to recognize tension but too young to understand it. From her earliest photographs, she had the worried look of a child overburdened by the troubles of the adults around her. She was thin and pale, with large dark eyes that seemed to apprehend more than they should. Years later she told Laura that from the time she was a child she "always kept that which was disagreeable to me to myself. Of that which pains me I cannot speak."[57]

Marx was back in London for Jennychen's birthday on May 1. There is not a word in any existing letters from that time about a solution to the question of Lenchen's pregnancy, but it is generally understood that during Marx's trip to Manchester, Engels agreed to say he was the father.[58] The two men must have seen that as the most logical option. Engels cared not a whit about his reputation, especially with regard to women. And, given that reputation, the story of Lenchen's pregnancy would have been plausible to the émigré community. It would even save Lenchen from shame; like so many other women, the whisperers would say, she had merely been seduced by an expert. It was a fiction she was apparently willing to accept.

Did Jenny believe it? It is impossible to say. But is it logical that in the intimacy of their lives together with Lenchen, she could not have known the truth? This was a marriage of substantial duration. In rooms small and cluttered, Jenny and Karl had been closer than close. Offenses committed while one party was absent might be momentarily disguised, but the surreptitious glance, the ducked head—these were accretions of confession she could not have failed to recognize. Jenny would have seen the truth in Marx's every false move. Under those circumstances a woman would know if her spouse was lying, no matter how much she wished it to be otherwise. The only reference Jenny ever made to Lenchen's pregnancy was cryptic. In her memoirs she wrote: "In the early summer 1851 an event occurred which I do not wish to relate here in detail, although it greatly contributed to increase our worries, both personal and others."[59]

Marx prided himself on being able to put aside personal travails and focus only on the greater goal, but that May he would have to have been made of steel not to be shaken to his core. Just as his domestic drama reached a crescendo, he learned that his Communist League colleagues in Prussia were being arrested. One by one the crackdown ordered by Jenny's brother was netting his friends back home. First to be detained was the Elberfeld tailor Peter Nothjung, on May 10. Police used documents found in his possession to make more arrests eight days later. Among those were Lessner, who under an assumed name had gone from London to Mainz for a propaganda trip; Hermann Becker, who had begun publishing a series of Marx's collected works in April; Roland Daniels, the Cologne doctor who had helped Marx and Jenny find an apartment in 1848; and Heinrich Bürgers, who had traveled with Marx when he fled Paris for Brussels so many years before. In all, twelve Marx associates were accused of high treason and trying to subvert the state. Eleven were arrested.[60] The only one who managed to leave Prussia before being apprehended was Freiligrath, who arrived in London the third week in May.[61] Soon others, fearing arrest, also fled. By late June most of the so-called Marx party were either in jail in Prussia or in exile in London.

In a letter to Engels, Marx blamed the men around Willich for the arrests. He said their playing at revolution and scheming about the exhibition had alerted authorities in Prussia. "These gasbags know that they are neither conspiring, nor pursuing any real goal.... All they want is to *seem* dangerous.... Has there ever been a party like this, whose avowed aim is simply to show off?"[62]

Before Daniels was hauled away by police he had managed to send an unsigned letter to Marx instructing him to get rid of all incriminating material, because houses in England were going to be searched. Marx told Engels to burn everything they didn't need and to store important items with Mary. Engels did, and then left for London to be with Marx and their newly arrived colleagues.[63] He visited from May 31 to June 15, and while without doubt the men's focus was political, his presence would have helped calm the Marx household in the days before Lenchen gave birth. It also may have reinforced the notion that Engels was the child's father, because he was in the home when the baby was due. But he did not stay long enough to see it born. By the time another newborn's cries rose from the attic on Dean Street, Engels had returned to Manchester.[64] Lenchen delivered a son on June 23, 1851. She named him Henry Frederick—Freddy for short.[65]

Marx tried to escape to the Reading Room to work on his economics—that year he would fill fourteen notebooks with his studies[66]—but he admitted to Engels that domestic turmoil and extreme financial distress made any progress nearly impossible.

> At home everything's always in a state of siege. For nights on end, I am set on edge and infuriated by floods of tears. So I cannot of course do very much. I feel sorry for my wife. The main burden falls on her and, fundamentally, she is right. Industry must be more productive than marriage. For all that, you must remember that by nature I have very little patience and am even somewhat hard, so from time to time I lose my equanimity.[67]

Lenchen did not register Freddy's birth until August, six weeks after his delivery. When she did, she listed herself as mother but provided no father's name. It is unclear whether she lived at Dean Street with her baby that summer.[68] Jenny wrote Stephan Born that Lenchen had moved out, but it appeared to have been only briefly.[69] In any case, the period would have been torture for everyone involved. Whether Lenchen stayed in the apartment with her child or left abruptly after its birth, either move would have aroused suspicion. The émigré community, which Marx had attacked unmercifully over the league arrests, was already abuzz with rumors. And then there was the personal tragedy for Lenchen and Jenny. If Lenchen left the Marxes, she would abandon the only family she had known and be adrift in a country whose language she did not speak, or she would be forced to return to the Rhineland in shame. For Jenny, Lenchen was irreplaceable as a cherished friend and helper. Besides, who but Lenchen would share their miserable life without complaint?

In a letter to Weydemeyer on August 2, a day after Freddy's birth was registered, Marx bemoaned his circumstances, projecting all blame outward:

> As you can imagine, my circumstances are very dismal. My wife will go under if things continue like this much longer. The constant worries, the slightest everyday struggle wears her out; and on top of that, there are the infamies of my opponents who have *never yet* so much as attempted to attack me as to the substance, who seek to avenge their impotence by casting suspicions on my civil character and by disseminating the most unspeakable infamies about me.... I, of course, would make a joke of the whole dirty business; not for one moment do I allow it to interfere with my work but, as you will understand, my wife, who is poorly and caught up from morning till night in the most disagreeable of domestic quandaries... is not revived by the exhalations from the pestiferous democratic cloaca daily administered to her by stupid tell-tales. The tactlessness of some individuals in this respect can often be colossal.[70]

The sad chapter of Lenchen's pregnancy ended with as little clarity as it began. Sometime in August she gave Freddy over to the care of a family named Levy who lived in East London, an area notorious for its poverty, even by comparison with Soho.[71] The family would have required a stipend, and it is believed that Engels provided it.[72] Freddy was raised away from his mother and the Marx family, while Lenchen remained at Dean Street. A tacit understanding must have been reached between Lenchen, Jenny, and Marx that their interdependence was too great to be riven by her pregnancy. The agreement made their lives tolerable, but it did not heal the wounds or stop the rumors that, contrary to what Marx told Weydemeyer, *were* affecting his work.

In mid-August a new calumny was published. A London-based German weekly suggested that Marx wrote for a reactionary newspaper in Prussia and was a spy for his brother-in-law Ferdinand.[73] Marx sent a letter intended for publication to a German journalist, explaining that the charge was absurd and that the only professional connection Ferdinand von Westphalen had with Marx was incarcerating his publisher and blocking the sale of his *Revue*. But even this effort did not bring Marx relief.

The journalist who received the letter was an Austrian spy, and the only people who read it were police. Marx's side of the story remained untold.[74]

Raging over the incident, Marx, accompanied by Freiligrath and Lupus, went to the London weekly to challenge its publisher to a duel. Presumably the publisher did not wish to acknowledge this wild foreigner's attempt to restore his honor, because the showdown did not occur.[75]

Just as it seemed their lives could not be more wretched, a rare ray of mercy arrived. Marx received a letter from the *New York Daily Tribune* asking him to work as one of eighteen paid foreign correspondents. His beat would be European affairs. Marx had met the *Tribune*'s editor, Charles Dana, at the *Neue Rheinische Zeitung* in 1849, when the American was in Europe to witness the counterrevolution. Perhaps Dana's memory of the encounter was jogged by letters Marx had sent out earlier that year to U.S. newspapers asking if they needed a London-based reporter. The *Tribune*'s circulation was about two hundred thousand, the largest of any paper in the world,[76] and while Marx disparaged it as a rag, he was eager to work for it.[77] But there was a problem: Marx could not yet speak or write in English (though he was trying to learn by memorizing Shakespeare).[78] Once again he turned to Engels, explaining that he was so busy with his economics he wondered "if you could possibly let me have an article in English on conditions in *Germany* by *Friday morning* [in seven days]."[79] Marx instructed his friend to feel free to be "witty and uninhibited" in his name.[80] At that moment he was anything but.

22

London, 1852

*Men make their own history, but they do not make it just as
they please; they do not make it under circumstances chosen by
themselves, but under circumstances directly encountered, given
and transmitted from the past.*

—Karl Marx[1]

ENGELS WAS DILIGENT in writing for the *Tribune,* but the one-pound-per-article
fee was not nearly enough to keep the Marx family fed and clothed, even with
frequent supplements from the Ermen & Engels cash till. Marx frantically
tried to find someone to publish collections of his past writings or buy copies
of the *Revue*—in short, anything to earn money quickly and easily. Joseph
Weydemeyer had settled in New York and was looking for journalism work,
but Marx encouraged him, "after mature consideration with Lupus," to
become a publisher of political tracts.[2] The list of offerings from Marx alone
would keep a future Weydemeyer Inc. busy for a year, if not longer.

Engels suggested a better course would be for Marx to get to work
immediately on a book on economic history—the first of several volumes—to be sold in Germany.

> The main thing is that you should once again make a public debut with a sub-
> stantial book, and preferably with the most harmless, the history....It's abso-
> lutely essential to break the spell created by your prolonged absence from the
> German book market and, later, by funk on the part of the booksellers. But
> once one or two instructive, erudite, well-grounded and withal interesting
> things of yours have appeared, *then it will be quite a different matter,* and you can
> snap your fingers at booksellers who offer you too little.

He added by way of rare chastisement, *"Do be a little businesslike this time!"*[3]

But Marx was isolated and impotent. He could not write what he wanted to because he needed to earn money, his colleagues were rotting in jail in Cologne without trial and his movement was therefore on hold if not dead, and he was the object of derision by his critics, not just in London and Germany but among opposition rivals touring America as well. A rumor was spread there that "Marx's party presents prizes for vice in order not to become moral heroes."[4] What made the libels especially annoying was that they occurred at the same time so many other exiles of 1848—whom Marx now considered charlatans—were being rewarded handsomely for their heroism. They had amassed piles of money by selling bonds for their future governments, soliciting loans to be used to mount their revolutions, and delivering speeches after which collection plates were passed and filled. A speaking tour of America could raise twenty thousand dollars.[5]

Joseph Kossuth, the hero of Hungary who had faced off against the Hapsburg monarchy and come very close to victory, arrived in London that October as if he had been one of the queen's own warriors returning from battle. He was the guest of the Lord Mayor of London at the close of the Great Exhibition, which by its last day had attracted six million people. Multitudes lined the street to see him, and they were not disappointed. In native Hungarian garb, with a saber at his side, Kossuth stood up in his carriage to receive the accolades of the crowd.[6] Despite what some critics have said, Marx never expressed the slightest interest in that sort of adulation. He disdained such exhibitions of vanity. But the differences between his situation and Kossuth's did not escape him. He told Engels, "Like the Apostle Paul, Mr. Kossuth is all things to all men. In Marseilles he shouts *Vive la République!,* in Southampton, GOD SAVE THE QUEEN." Marx charted Kossuth's fund-raising efforts and gloated that they were not as successful as one would expect.[7] But all of that was just a distraction for Marx. It mattered little to his family whether Kossuth left London with his pockets full of coin. They had none.

On December 2, 1851, an event more significant than the Marxes' seemingly inescapable personal and financial misfortunes occurred, one that diverted the attention of the entire family, from Marx down to his young son Edgar. Louis Napoleon staged a coup d'état and officially closed the book on the uprisings of 1848. Backed by the army, this pretender, who had been a stranger to France just three years before, effectively tore up the constitution of France's Second Republic, dissolved the National

Assembly, and proclaimed himself president for life. The coup, timed to occur on the anniversary of the 1804 coronation of his uncle, followed a prolonged dispute with the assembly over the approaching end of his four-year term in 1852.[8] "In one night," Victor Hugo said, "liberty was struck down by a hand sworn to support it, the inviolability of the law, the rights of the citizen, the dignity of the magistrate, the honor of the soldier all disappeared, and there arose the despotism of a personal government founded on the saber, perjury, murder and assassination."[9]

Republicans, socialists, and democrats took to the streets, not just in Paris but in south and central France as well, to protest. But their ranks crumbled before the military, which fell on them with overwhelming force. In just two days of fighting, on December 3 and 4, an estimated five hundred people were killed and twenty-six thousand arrested.[10] Carl Schurz, who had chronicled the Berlin uprising in 1848, was in London at the time of Louis Napoleon's coup. According to his account, the news caused an uproar among the exiles. Everyone gathered at the French clubs, where the mood was "bordering on madness."[11] No matter the London passion, however; the fight on the Continent was over.

Marx said the coup completely undermined the émigrés who had lived with the dream of a glorious return to battle.[12] One immediate benefit to Marx was that they were now—at least temporarily—too demoralized to demonize him. And to some extent he had the satisfaction of knowing that his prediction that armed uprisings would prove futile had been borne out.

Weydemeyer was planning to publish a weekly German communist newspaper, *Die Revolution,* in New York beginning in January, and Marx got to work on an article on the French coup for the first issue.[13] By the time he sat down to write, the French people had shown that, far from objecting to Louis Napoleon's bold gesture, they were thrilled by it. A plebiscite on his government was supported by a staggering 92 percent of the voters.[14] Also approving were France's moneymen, who viewed Louis Napoleon's success as their own—a gleeful stance vividly described by Marx: "The crimes are his," was their mirthful assessment, "but the fruits are ours."[15]

The urgency of the news from France seemed to be just what the Marx family needed to shake off the effects of the previous terrible year. Marx's work for Weydemeyer's newspaper would earn him no money, but it consumed him intellectually and brought him and Jenny together again. As she had with the *Manifesto,* she copied his writing as he turned out page after page. On December 17 Jenny wrote Engels that her dear Karl was "burning his fingers over the French stuff" and would have the article done by the end of that week, when Engels was due for a holiday visit. Marx's enthusiasm and industry were contagious. Jenny said even four-year-old Edgar, who was now called Colonel Musch, wrote three letters a day to Engels, "sticking used stamps thereon with the utmost conscientiousness."[16] Years later Jenny recalled those days spent copying Marx's "scrawly articles" as among the happiest of her life.[17] As was the case for Marx, work on behalf of the revolution numbed her most grievous personal pain.

Predictably, Marx was not finished with the article by the end of that week, and his work was further disrupted by Engels's arrival. Christmas at the Marx household was by necessity a modest affair, given their financial situation, but Engels's appearance ensured that at least they would have enough to drink and eat, thanks to his money and Lenchen's cooking.

Most of Marx's circle now met outside Soho, in a wine shop on Farringdon Street, near the heart of London's newspaper district, Fleet Street. Marx called his club "the synagogue."[18] It is likely that the young bachelors who loyally followed Marx to the library and synagogue also partook of the family's Christmas and New Year's festivities, because on January 1 Marx sent Weydemeyer a letter explaining that neither he, Lupus, nor Red Wolff had anything ready for his paper. He attributed the delay to private issues on his part, illness for Lupus, and the need to rewrite Red Wolff's piece,[19] but the real reason may have been what Engels called an "almighty binge."[20] Engels apologized to Jenny for the outing, which landed Marx in a "bed of pain and penance" for two weeks.[21] She replied, "How can you imagine that I would have been angry with *you* over that little drinking spree?...Besides, such interludes often have quite salutary effects, but this time father Marx must have caught a bad chill during his nocturnal philosophic excursion with 'the archbishop's nephew,'" by which Jenny meant Engels.[22]

Marx finally recovered enough to get back to his writing on January 20, but he could do so only from the comfort of his apartment. His problem was no longer the side effects of alcoholic excess, but hemorrhoids. Marx told Engels he could not return to the Reading Room because his piles had "afflicted me more grievously than the French Revolution."[23] In the meantime Jenny kept his correspondence alive with gusto, apologizing for her infirm husband and offering, in letters to associates including Engels and Weydemeyer, journalistic news and political views just as Marx would.

Most prominent in these missives were updates on those arrested in her brother's crackdown. Marx and Jenny had learned that after nine months of detention, their friends in Cologne would not stand trial for treason in January as expected, because authorities declared the investigation so complex that it had to be started all over again. Little had been said in the press about the eleven detained men and even less about the machinations of prosecutors who looked as though they were delaying their trial because they did not have enough evidence to convict.[24] Jenny wrote Weydemeyer that their comrades would have to remain "in the jug" for three more months, hideously treated by the authorities and ignored outside of Marx's circle.[25]

With Jenny acting as his correspondence secretary, Marx began working nearly around the clock to organize a propaganda campaign designed to keep the fate of these fellow league members alive in the newspapers. Marx claimed that the liberal and democratic press in Prussia were staying away from the story because the parties they represented saw the prosecution as a way of eliminating a political rival.[26] Marx therefore turned to English newspapers to try to draw attention to the case. He was also rushing to finish his report on Louis Napoleon's coup, which he called *The Eighteenth Brumaire of Louis Bonaparte,* a reference to the 1799 date on the French revolutionary calendar on which Napoleon I staged a coup that established his dictatorship.[27]

Marx worked at the family's only table, surrounded by more than the usual household commotion. The children had created a new game that involved harnessing Marx to chairs they lined up behind him to form a stagecoach. The seated Marx was the horse, who had to pretend to pull his exuberant passengers or face a whipping. His daughter wrote years later that "several chapters of the *Eighteenth Brumaire* were actually written in this capacity as steeple chaser of his three small children."[28] When he really needed to concentrate, Marx sought refuge in the quiet of the night. He stayed up until dawn in the apartment's cold front parlor, smoking the only cigars he could afford, those known as "cheap and nasty." In the mornings he collapsed on the sofa while family life continued all around him. Such practice took a toll on his health and, in particular, his eyes.[29] Oil lamps or candles were most often used for reading, but their light was dim. Paraffin lamps burned the brightest, but they had a strong smell in such a confined space.[30] None of the solutions was good, and yet—lacking others—he resorted to them night after night, and even during the day, because the sun rarely penetrated the gloom that engulfed London in winter.

Despite Marx's focus, the initial *Brumaire* articles did not appear in Weydemeyer's paper: before Marx could finish, the newspaper folded. The problem was in part that the "article" had grown[31] (Marx said of its own accord[32]) into a small book. Marx seemed to thoroughly enjoy—and was at his best in—this kind of reportage, where he combined the weight of his erudition and grasp of current events to put what appeared of a moment into a greater historical context. Where others saw waves, Marx recognized tides. Of Louis Napoleon's improbable rise he wrote:

> The tradition of all the dead generations weighs like a nightmare on the brain of the living. And just when they seem engaged in revolutionizing themselves and things, in creating something that has never yet existed, precisely in such periods of revolutionary crisis they anxiously conjure up the spirits of the past to their service and borrow from them names, battle cries and costumes in order to present the new scene of world history in this time-honored disguise and this borrowed language....
>
> The social revolution of the nineteenth century cannot draw its poetry from the past but only from the future.... In order to arrive at its own content, the revolution of the nineteenth century must let the dead bury their dead.[33]

One would never imagine that the author of the *Eighteenth Brumaire* was a dray horse tied to a chair while writing it, or that his eyes were so inflamed he could barely see. Rather, one is struck by its beautiful clarity. It is succinct and eloquent; superior in its analysis as well as its style. None of that, however, ensured Marx would find a publisher, and Marx needed *something* to earn money. He had once again floated the idea of recycling his attack on Proudhon, and also tried to interest a publisher in his still-conceptual economic book. Neither produced a positive response.[34] At the end of February he told Engels, "A week ago I reached the pleasant point where I am unable to go out for want of the coats I have in pawn, and can no longer eat meat for want of credit." The only bright spot on his horizon was the ill health of one of Jenny's reactionary uncles. "If the cur dies now I shall be out of this pickle." The cur, however, did not die, and Marx's lack of coat and cash meant he was unable to attend an 1848 anniversary banquet. He sent Jenny, who did not have to pay an entrance fee because she went as the companion of a Frenchman.[35]

Spies seemed to have a sixth sense when it came to invading the Marx household at vulnerable moments, and Marx received an anonymous tip that he and his friends were under the surveillance of an infiltrator.[36] Marx thought he knew the man. Wilhelm Hirsch had suddenly appeared among Marx's group in December, when it began its Thursday night meetings on Farringdon Street. Marx's hunch was right: Hirsch had been hired by Prussian police to find the evidence prosecutors needed to finally convict league members jailed in Cologne.[37] In their first year in London, Marx and his associates had indeed sounded like the brimstone gang they were accused of being—revolution, assassination, all manner of antigovernment activity was discussed. But by the time Hirsch attended their gatherings, their immediate concerns had turned to propaganda and their own survival. From the start the group was suspicious of Hirsch, and without telling him moved the "synagogue" to Wednesday night at the Rose and Crown Tavern in Soho.[38] But this was far from a solution. Hirsch was paid by the piece—if he produced evidence he earned his fee—so, rather than come up empty, he forged minutes of fictitious meetings. Marx did not know at that point about Hirsch's inventions, nor did he know that another spy, Stieber, had obtained a stack of documents from rival émigré meetings that he intended to use against Marx's friends. Most dangerously of all, Marx did not know that yet another police agent was working his way into his small circle, a man whose betrayal would cost Marx and his friends dearly.

Engels was in London over Easter, but the visit was not the gay romp his Christmas trip had been. Marx and Jenny's youngest child, Franzisca, suffered a severe attack of bronchitis and died shortly after her first birthday, on April 14.[39] The death of a child of that age was common in nineteenth-century England; an estimated 15 percent died before they had turned one.[40] But that harsh statistic was no comfort to anguished parents, and certainly not to Jenny, whose sorrow was compounded by their poverty. The family did not even have the money to buy Franzisca a coffin.

Unable to properly bury her daughter, Jenny put the child's body in the back room of the apartment and moved all the bedding into the front, where the family slept until the needed funds could be found. She wrote in her memoirs, "Our three living children lay down by us and we all wept for the little angel whose livid, lifeless body was in the next room." Jenny and Marx tried without success to borrow money from German and English friends (even Engels was short of cash). Finally, Jenny turned to a French emigrant who lived nearby, and he gave her two pounds to buy a coffin. "She had no cradle when she came into the world and for a long time was refused a last resting place," Jenny recalled. "With what heavy hearts we saw her carried to her grave!" Franzisca joined Fawsky at the cemetery a few blocks away.[41]

Marx and Jenny did not have time to mourn their daughter before they were assailed by more bad news. Weydemeyer had been trying to arrange publication of Marx's *Brumaire,* but on the day of Franzisca's funeral a letter from him arrived saying that this was unlikely.[42] Marx told a friend the effect of the letter was devastating. "For two years now she [Jenny] has seen all my enterprises regularly come to grief."[43] Marx confided in Engels, "You cannot imagine what a wretched time I had last week. On the day of the funeral, the money I had been promised from various quarters failed to arrive, so that I was finally compelled to go to some French neighbors in order to pay the English vultures. And on top of this, alas, a letter arrived from Weydemeyer giving reason to suppose that in America too all our hopes have been dashed.... Although by nature tough, I was, on this occasion, very hard hit by the wretched business."[44] Later he admitted, "I assure you that, when I consider my wife's sufferings and my own impotence I feel like consigning myself to the devil."[45]

In a way Marx did. A Hungarian journalist named Janos Bangya had made Marx's acquaintance and by that spring had become a central figure in his life. Bangya was the spy Marx had not detected, and his treachery would be not just political but personal. Judging by Marx's letters to Engels and colleagues in America, he appeared to trust Bangya completely, and by the end of April had fallen into a trap laid for him by his new friend. For his own amusement Marx had written satirical sketches describing several German opposition exiles in London, depicting their associations, enthusiasms, and goals. Bangya told Marx a publisher named Eisenmann in Berlin would pay twenty-five pounds for a short book of similar pieces, which Marx could write anonymously.[46]

Engels, whom Marx wanted as coauthor, was uncertain. He wondered whether the price was worth the scandal when those they attacked found out who was responsible. He also worried whether, appearing during the investigation of their Cologne friends, the book would be viewed as disloyal to the wider German opposition, if not reactionary.[47] But Marx was drawn irresistibly to the project because of the money Bangya offered. The Hungarian said he would deliver the funds as soon as he received the manuscript. In late May, Marx went to Manchester to work with Engels on the project.

Each time Marx left London, he left Jenny behind to confront angry creditors alone. In this case there was at least the possibility of future income: while Marx was away, Bangya gave Jenny a contract said to be from the Berlin publisher, agreeing to Marx's terms.[48] But this didn't buy the milk, bread, potatoes, and coal the family needed immediately to survive. The timing of Marx's trip was particularly difficult because it came only a month after Franzisca's death, and Jenny was still suffering the pain of her loss and the guilt that they may have been able to save her and Fawksy had they lived a life that offered their children the basic comforts they deserved.

Earlier that month Marx and Jenny had sent Jennychen, Laura, and Musch to stay in Manchester. The visit coincided with one by Engels's father, so it is likely the children stayed with Mary and Lizzy Burns. Each of the children sent Marx a note attached to a letter from Engels, in which they described their joy over a good meal of rump steak, peas, and potatoes. Laura wrote for Musch, who said, "After a comfortable dinner we will have a splendid supper. Bread and butter, which you like so very much, cheese and beer. We will drink on your and Mr Fred health and if we are tipsy it will be for your health. Farewell my best Papa."[49] The children wanted so little to be happy, but Marx and Jenny were unable to provide it.

After the children returned and Marx had replaced them in Manchester, Jenny wrote him an anguished letter: "Meanwhile I sit here and go to pieces. Karl, it is now at its worst pitch....I sit here and almost weep my eyes out and can find no help. My head is disintegrating. For a week I have kept my strength up and now I can no more."[50] Marx's reply was 90 percent business and 10 percent sympathy. It could have been that he was having such a good time with Engels (he said they laughed till they cried over their exile sketches) that he could not empathize with Jenny's plight. Or it could have been that he knew the best way to help his wife, short of sending her money, was to focus her mind on work. Marx frequently described Jenny as resilient, able to rebound with only the slightest encouragement, and perhaps with that in mind he wrote on June 11: "Dear heart...you must never have any qualms about telling me all. If you, my poor little wretch, have to endure bitter reality, it is only fair that I should share that torment, at least in my thoughts." He then gave her a veritable to-do list of party-related tasks and briskly complimented her handling of another bit of political business.[51]

For the Marx children, the political activity in their household, the assorted characters who met there nightly, and the ongoing dramas with creditors no doubt seemed normal. They had nothing, in any case, to compare it to, because their friends were children of men and women like their parents—largely poor German refugees engaged in opposition politics. But Marx and Jenny could claim no such innocence or ignorance about how very different their lives would have been if they had decided to raise a family within the normally acceptable sphere of their class. By the time they reached London they were well aware of the difficulties arising from their choices, and each year those difficulties mounted. But the period they were entering would be one of their darkest. Truly nothing seemed to go their way.

Jenny and Ernst Dronke alternated copying out Marx and Engels's hundred-page émigré sketch, *The Great Men of the Exile,* as Marx stood by dictating their words. When it was finished, Bangya promptly handed over the fee, minus seven pounds (which he had likely loaned Marx), leaving Marx with eighteen.[52] By the time Marx paid Dronke he did not have enough to meet expenses, and Bangya would not say when the pamphlet might be published, despite Marx's high hopes for its sales.[53] Engels, too, was strapped, and told Marx in August that he did not know whether he could send him any funds for the next six weeks.[54] Marx's *Brumaire* had at least finally been printed in New York, in a revived edition of Weydemeyer's newspaper made possible with forty dollars from a German émigré there, but the funding was not sufficient to pay for the paper's distribution, and so it sat in piles, unread.[55] Furthermore, Wilhelm Pieper botched the English translation, thus postponing any possible London sale, and still no publisher in Germany had expressed interest in the work.[56] The delays were critical, because with each passing day the article's relevancy diminished and others were free to publish their accounts of France's presidential coup. To his annoyance Marx learned that his nemesis Proudhon's critique of Louis Napoleon had earned him more than one hundred thousand francs.[57]

Marx's anxiety over money was all too evident in his distressed letters from that period, which dealt obsessively with the finances of his rivals. He was also uncharacteristically focused on attacks against himself and Engels. One that especially galled him came from a German exile traveling in Cincinnati, who said, "Marx and Engels are no revolutionaries, they're a couple of blackguards who have been thrown out of public houses by the workers in London."[58] Marx often declared himself immune to gossip, but his dire financial situation in the second half of 1852 and the utter lack of recognition of his work amplified the sting, no matter how distant.

In the case of the Cincinnati insult, when its author, Gottfried Kinkel (whom Marx called "Jesus Christ Kinkel" because of his messianic political fantasies), returned to London, Marx confronted him by mail, but Kinkel did not respond. Believing that Kinkel would not open a letter postmarked Soho for fear it was from him, Marx had Lupus send a note from Windsor on the type of paper normally used for love letters. If Kinkel indeed opened it, he would have found lurking amid the perfumed roses and forget-me-nots a rambling indictment by Dr. Karl Marx.[59]

Marx was at the end of his tether. He told Engels his entire household was ill, but he could not afford a doctor. "For the past eight–ten days I have been feeding the FAMILY solely on bread and potatoes, but whether I shall be able to get hold of any today is doubtful.... The storm is breaking out on all sides," with the baker, greengrocer, and butcher all clamoring to be paid. "You'll have seen from my letters that, as usual, when I myself am in the shit and not just hearing about it secondhand, I plow through it with complete indifference. Yet, what to do? My house is a hospital and so worrying is the crisis that it compels me to devote all my attention to it. What to do?"[60]

The last option was the pawnshop, where items fetched at most a third of their value—and in the end even less, because of the high interest charged. Marx tried to pawn some of Jenny's silverware with the Argyll crest, but the shop owner, alarmed to see such remarkable valuables in the hands of a wild and obviously impoverished foreigner, smelled a thief and wanted to have Marx arrested. Perhaps because of his shame, Marx never recorded the outcome. One surviving version of the story has Marx successfully convincing the pawnshop owner that, improbable as it might seem, he was married to a descendant of one of Britain's most historic families. Another has Marx arrested on suspicion of theft and held overnight by police, until Jenny provided proof of her Argyll connection.[61] Whichever scenario was true, the result was the same: utter humiliation for Marx. He had sunk so low that he was considered disreputable even in the eyes of a pawnshop owner in one of the most fetid districts in all of London.

By the fall of 1852 the Marx family's cramped apartment had become a command center for exiles busily rooting out spies and trying to exonerate their colleagues in Cologne. Jenny told Marx's friend Adolf Cluss in Washington that a complete office had been set up in their Dean Street flat. "Two or three people are writing, others running errands, others scraping pennies together so that the writers may continue to exist and prove the old world officialdom guilty of the most outrageous scandal. And in between whiles my three merry children sing and whistle, often to be harshly told off by their papa. What a bustle!"[62]

After seventeen months the case against Communist League members in Prussia had finally come to trial. The evidence against them was ludicrous, but that did not ensure their acquittal—their conviction was a matter of pride for the government. Marx and friends concluded that the jury was stacked against the defendants. It included three members of the upper middle class, two city patricians, two landowners, two advisers to the government, and a Prussian professor.[63] On the positive side for the defense, however, was the disappearance of two principal prosecution witnesses—one of whom fled to Brazil—and shocking evidence of police malfeasance.[64]

The prosecution's case was based on a seventy-page indictment that painted an alarming picture of the radical German opposition gathered in

London, which was said to be under Marx's direction. And while the long road from the first arrest in May 1851 to trial in October 1852 was twisted indeed, the government's lawyers went back even further, presenting evidence from 1831 and the beginnings of the league.[65] Some of the material had been gathered from interrogations of the accused during their long solitary confinement and after forced marches — one for eleven days — that, not surprisingly, had taken a toll on them.[66] Among the battered were the publisher Becker, said to be going blind, and Doctor Daniels, who was showing signs of consumption.[67]

Marx was emphatic that while the evidence obtained directly from the accused was indeed proof of antigovernment sentiments, it did not show that they were, as alleged, engaged in an antigovernment *plot*. The so-called proof for that charge was based, he said, on evidence gathered by spies in London and designed to convince the public that it was not political opinions that were on trial, but rather dangerous men acting at the behest of a more dangerous leader. Though Marx was not in the dock with the other eleven men, it was clear he was the prosecution's main target.[68]

One cache of documents, presented to prosecutors by Stieber, was actually based on surveillance of the Willich group, which *did* plot antigovernment violence. A police report acknowledged that Marx's group had split from that cadre, but, fixated as officials were on Marx, they chose to ignore that detail.[69] "The Marx Party stands head and shoulders above all the émigrés, agitators and central committees.... Marx himself is personally known and it is evident that he has more brains in his little finger than all the rest have in their heads."[70] As a result, the government duplicitously used the documents as evidence, wagering that there were enough areas in which the Marx group and the Willich group overlapped that jurors might not notice the differences.

But while that sleight of hand worked for the Stieber file, it did not for evidence submitted by the spy Hirsch, which was so patently false it was discredited almost immediately. The Dean Street defense committee proved that the minutes he'd claimed came from meetings of Marx's synagogue — which Hirsch swore he'd attended, and during which plots were discussed — were amateurish forgeries. The committee assembled handwriting samples to show that, contrary to Hirsch's claims, the minutes had not been written by Liebknecht and another member named L. W. Rings (who, unfortunately for Hirsch, was nearly illiterate and so would have been an unlikely note taker in any case). The committee also obtained testimony from publicans that the group met on Wednesdays, not Thursdays, and at a different location than Hirsch indicated. Faced with overwhelming and well-publicized proof of fraud, the court had no choice but to throw out Hirsch's minutes.[71]

The loss of that evidence, however, made the prosecution more intent than ever on retaining its most inflammatory item against the defendants. (The top law enforcement official in Berlin had written to the Prussian embassy in London, "The whole existence of the political police depends on the result of this trial!")[72] An unsigned letter that an expert witness testified was written by Marx was discovered to have accompanied a batch of fifty "Red Catechisms." It declared, "The revolution is closer than many people think. Long live the revolution!" and instructed whoever received the Catechisms to slide them under the doors of revolutionary sympathizers before midnight on June 5, 1852. Even though the letter had supposedly been written after the defendants were incarcerated, it was used against them.

This evidence was greeted with howls of incredulity in London, where anyone who knew Marx understood it to be false: not only would he never engage in such melodrama as sliding a document under the doors of supporters as the clock struck twelve, but its contents contradicted his beliefs. Marx had earned the wrath of fellow exiles for saying that revolution was *not* imminent.[73] He went before a British magistrate and swore under oath that he had nothing to do with the letter or the Catechism, and this declaration was sent to the defense in Cologne, as well as published in British newspapers. The prosecution was, however, unmoved. It did not allow a comparison of Marx's handwriting with that in the incriminating letter.[74]

On the witness stand Stieber had described an elaborate network in London in which each "secret agent" was watched by another spy—one presumably a local hire working by the job, and the other a professional overseeing him.[75] In October, Marx told Engels that suspicious characters had once again been posted outside his house while the defense committee worked upstairs. Both Engels and Marx also thought their mail was being read.[76] But they did not let the surveillance impede their work: for five weeks exiles defiantly marched up and down the long flight of stairs at Dean Street assembling evidence to undermine the state's case against their friends. The visitors arrived early and stayed late, filling the flat with cigar smoke and alternating between laughter and outrage as news of the case came in. The children grew so used to the men crowding the room, eating meals and drinking beer, that they considered them part of the household. One morning a committee member arrived before Jenny was dressed, which sent her scurrying for her clothes. But Colonel Musch shouted not to worry, "It's just Freiligrath."[77]

During this period Jenny represented her husband at public functions unrelated to the trial, including a tribute to a colleague executed in Vienna in 1848, because Marx was absorbed in the case to the exclusion of all else.[78] He wrote an article on it that grew to nearly fifty pages, and was intent on publishing it quickly to draw attention to the trial. "Needless to say, I myself am incapable of contributing so much as a centime to the thing," he told Engels. "Yesterday I pawned a coat dating back to my Liverpool days in order to buy writing paper."[79] At just that moment his landlord threatened to evict the family for nonpayment of rent. Marx said the man made a terrible scene, but he countered with such ferocity that the landlord sheepishly backed down.[80]

The league trial ended on November 7, and even Berlin newspapers predicted that the defendants would be acquitted because the case against them had not been proven.[81] But the jury returned mixed verdicts: four defendants were acquitted, including Daniels, while the seven others were convicted. Three were given six years in prison, including the journalist Bürgers; three were given five years, including the publisher Becker; and the tailor Lessner was sentenced to three years in jail.[82] Jenny said the verdict showed that the jury was torn between "hatred of the dreadful incendiaries" and "HORROR inspired by the villainy of the police."[83]

Less than two weeks later Marx officially disbanded the league. The trial's outcome, the extremes to which Prussian officials were prepared to go to quash the group, the general reactionary spirit in Europe, and Marx's belief that the time was right for reflection and study but not organizing, led him to the conclusion that for the moment, the league was no longer useful.[84] Two events illustrated the prescience of Marx's reasoning. On December 2 that bastion of republicanism, France, once again became an empire. President-for-life Louis Napoleon was declared Emperor Napoleon III. The little man who once used bacon to entice an eagle to fly above his head had outmaneuvered the savviest government ministers and hoodwinked a populace into believing that he would restore French glory and stability. It was as if every gain between 1815 and 1848 was wiped out in one wave of an ermine-covered arm.

Closer to home, Marx and Engels finally learned the real fate of their tell-all pamphlet, *The Great Men of the Exile*. There had never been an interested publisher—the police had requisitioned the manuscript and, in return, Bangya received payments from Berlin twice a month (which was why he was able to pay Marx so promptly). Marx and Engels had planned for the document to be made public, which would have put it in police hands eventually, but Bangya's double-dealing made it available *only* to police, allowing them to gain insight into the exile community at the very time they were prosecuting the Cologne case.[85] Roland Daniels's brother blamed Marx for Roland's arrest, claiming that it would not have occurred if Marx had not associated with Bangya.[86] (That charge was unfair; Daniels was arrested a year before Marx met Bangya.) Bangya, meanwhile, fled to Napoleon's Paris to become a special agent in the French police ministry.[87]

Marx was surprisingly philosophical about both Napoleon and Bangya, perhaps because at just that moment a Swiss publisher had enthusiastically praised his pamphlet on the Cologne trial and promised to rush it into print. Marx was thrilled that his *Revelations Concerning the Communist Trial in Cologne* would be published.[88] Jenny calculated, based on the publisher's estimates, that they could count on thirty pounds from initial sales alone.[89] Marx sent Adolf Cluss in Washington a copy and suggested that he try to bring it out in America:

> To appreciate to the full the humor of the thing, you must know that its author, for want of anything decent to wear on his backside and feet, is as good as interned.... The trial dragged me even deeper into the mire, since for five weeks, instead of working for my livelihood, I had to work for the party against the government's machinations. On top of that, it has completely alienated the German booksellers with whom I had hoped to conclude a contract for my Economy.[90]

The Swiss opportunity, however, would turn into yet another disappointment. The publisher had smuggled nearly the entire consignment of two thousand copies of Marx's *Revelations* into Baden, where it was to be picked up for distribution throughout Prussia. It was not: all the copies were confiscated in the village where they were dropped and burned on orders of the Prussian government.[91] Marx was beside himself with anger and declared in exasperation, "It's enough to put one off writing altogether. This constant toil *for the king of Prussia!*"[92]

And that was not the final insult. Within months the publisher's partner was demanding that Marx pay the 424-franc printing cost. One more moneymaking venture had turned into a debt.[93]

23

London, 1853

*We had grounds enough for melancholy but we were charmed
against it by our grim humor. Whoever started to complain was
immediately most forcibly reminded of his duties to society.*

—Wilhelm Liebknecht[1]

THE PRUSSIAN GOVERNMENT having won that round, Marx decided to
declare publicly that he wanted nothing more to do with party politics.
He felt abused by his opponents but more bitterly by those he had called
friends: "I no longer feel inclined to allow myself to be insulted by any old
party jackass on so-called party grounds."[2] The Communist League
defense committee had one last task. It sent out an appeal for funds for the
families of those imprisoned in Prussia.[3] That done, members packed up
and left the Marx apartment for what Engels hoped would be paying jobs.
Engels was worried that the men around Marx were turning into loafers
and could easily become full-time drunks.[4] He had helped finance the
committee's operations, and between that and his own expenses, he said
he had "gobbled up half of my old man's profits." He and his colleagues
would have to cut back—not that he minded eating into his father's earnings, but he was afraid he might be found out.

So Engels set an example: he moved into cheaper lodgings and drank
cheaper liquor.[5] For his part Marx began the new year by sending off his
first English-language article to the *Tribune*. He was now promised two
pounds per piece and planned to try to write at least two each week.[6]
Jenny expected the income would be enough to cover daily expenses,
though not enough to finance a move out of what she called their "poky
Dean Street flat." That said, she did not seem to be in a hurry to leave it.

By 1853 the Marxes had been living in Soho for nearly three years, and their horrified first impressions had softened. Even Jenny had grown accustomed to the poverty, filth, and chaos. She had found favorite pubs and coffeehouses where she could meet friends and nestle by a fire or, if she was lucky enough to get a free ticket, go to the theater. She also liked to take long walks through the district.[7] This woman who loved the stage had come to appreciate the show going on all around her, the colorful display of the very best and worst of London life.

Oxford Street, with its canopied windows and dry-goods stores, was crammed with omnibuses, liveried carriages, and well-dressed women out for a day of shopping. The Haymarket bustled, too, with working women and girls who filled baskets that they carried on their heads or suspended from their necks as they walked the streets selling produce or flowers or herbs. And then there was the Irish district, where a meal often meant only a cup of coffee. Ruddy-faced women, their heads covered in hoods, sat on the ground with their knees and feet tucked up inside their dresses to form a warm ball of their bodies; they displayed only a hand when a rare customer stooped to buy whatever meager offerings they had to sell.[8] Everyone had a signature song or phrase to attract customers, and those shouts of commerce, combined with the chatter of many voices speaking many languages, created a spontaneous opera out of Soho street life. Tragic and rambunctious by equal measures, for a passerby it was ever changing and, because of that, consistently amusing—as long as one did not look too closely.

During her walks Jenny glided through the crowd, her face obscured by a dark veil. She appeared every bit the elegant figure she had been raised to be, and more likely would be assumed to be visiting the quarter than resident there. Once while out walking, Jenny caught the attention of Red Wolff, who was notoriously nearsighted as well as amorous. Not recognizing her, he sidled up and in the style of a Parisian boulevardier tried to seduce her. Jenny was known to be able to make a man freeze by a mere look if he showed any sign of boldness. But in Red Wolff's case she laughed heartily at his mistake, perhaps pleased that after all she had been through she could still inspire such passion by her appearance alone.[9]

For the Marx children Soho was quite simply home, the most settled life they had known. The girls were not allowed out in the late afternoon or evening without escort, due to the many entertainments in the district that attracted unsavory types. The Soho Theater on Dean Street, for example, was a ramshackle affair known as a favorite among thieves and prostitutes.[10] Just as dangerous was Caldwell's dance house, also on Dean, which was frequented by young clerks and apprentices of the German middle class who were out to capture a wife—or at least a companion—from among that set.[11]

Jennychen and Laura were still very young—Jenny nearly nine and Laura seven—but both were gregarious. Jennychen was described as the image of her father, with black hair, black eyes, creole complexion, and the same intensity, while Laura was graceful and fair-haired like her mother. Liebknecht said Laura had roguish eyes even as a child.[12] While the girls were relatively sequestered on Dean Street, the indomitable Musch was allowed to roam. He knew many of the poor Irish children on the street, who taught him songs in return for his paltry supply of weekly pocket money.[13] The Marx family spoke German at home, but the children had picked up English easily, and Musch spoke it like a true Soho urchin. Jenny described one incident after the baker warned he would cut off their bread supply. The man showed up at the door where six-year-old Musch was standing and asked, "Is Mr. Marx at home?" Musch replied, "No he a'nt upstairs," and, tucking three loaves under his arm, ran off to tell his father.[14] No doubt he picked up such artful deception on the street: one observer said that Soho children were taught to steal when they were barely able to walk.[15]

There was little real risk, however, that the girls or Musch would fall in too deeply with the Soho crowd. Like their parents', their social lives revolved around other German refugees—they even attended picnics at the so-called Communist Laborer's Educational Camp outside London, an informal arcadian gathering for the families of Communist Laborer's Educational Club members.[16] Musch was especially close to Karl Blind's stepson Ferdinand Cohen.[17] But the Marx children's best playmate—their preferred playmate—was their father. Sometimes they called Marx Papa, but most often he was Mohr or Challey to them. The children allowed him to work every day, but on Sunday they demanded his full attention, and by all accounts he willingly gave it (though he kept a pad in his pocket and surreptitiously made notes from time to time).[18]

When the weather was fine, the family and any of Marx's associates who happened to be at Dean Street would walk an hour and a half from Soho to Hampstead Heath for a picnic. Lenchen carried a basket she had brought from Germany and filled it with lunch treats; beer was purchased on the Heath. After lunch the adults dozed or read newspapers, and Marx played with the children.[19] Liebknecht recalled that Marx once tried to knock chestnuts out of a tree for so long he couldn't move his right arm for eight days.[20] On other occasions there were games for which Marx's friends were roped into service as horses, each man carrying a child on his back who did battle until the two-legged steed cried out that he'd had enough. There were also donkey rides, which Marx insisted on taking, unaware of the comical figure he cut on the shambling beasts.[21] On the long walk back to Soho someone sang or Marx recited passages from *The Divine Comedy* or played the part of Mephisto in Goethe's *Faust* (which Liebknecht said he did not do very well, because he exaggerated considerably). And then there were Marx's original stories. He invented tales "by the mile," and if he dared stop, the children cried out, "Tell us another mile!"[22]

Marx had begun instilling a love for literature and language in his children at the earliest age, and, like Jenny's father, he made Shakespeare a treasured guest in their house.[23] He and Jenny magically transformed their cluttered attic salon into a sumptuous palazzo at Verona, a thundering battlefield in France, or the chilling Tower of London by reciting acts from Shakespeare's plays until the little ones had memorized the lines enough that they could join in, too. Marx also read the children Dante, Cervantes, Sir Walter Scott, James Fenimore Cooper, and Balzac — whenever possible in the original language. The children's letters showed them to be as familiar with the characters in those books as with the family's friends, and the young scholars often made precocious literary references and puns. The Marx household was rich in things intellectual, which likely helped make its complete lack of material comforts bearable.

Ironically, the best description of Marx family life on Dean Street came from a Prussian spy's report. He had been invited into the apartment and found there a man whose genius and energy were immediately impressive but whose personal life was utter chaos. "He leads the existence of a real bohemian intellectual. Washing, grooming and changing his linen are things he does rarely, and he likes to get drunk. . . . He has no fixed times for going to sleep and waking up." The report said the three Marx children were truly handsome, and, despite Marx's wild and restless character, as a husband and father he was "the gentlest and mildest of men." But the household was such as to make a gentleman shudder:

> Marx lives in one of the worst — therefore, one of the cheapest — quarters of London. He occupies two rooms. . . . In the whole apartment there is not one clean and solid piece of furniture. Everything is broken down, tattered and torn, with a half inch of dust over everything and the greatest disorder everywhere. In the middle of the living room there is a large old-fashioned table covered with an oilcloth, and on it there lie his manuscripts, books and newspapers, as well as the children's toys, and rags and tatters of his wife's sewing basket, several cups with broken rims, knives, forks, lamps, an ink pot, tumblers, Dutch clay pipes, tobacco ash — in a word, everything topsy-turvy; and

all on the same table. . . . To sit down becomes a thoroughly dangerous business. Here is a chair with only three legs, on another chair the children are playing at cooking—this chair happens to have four legs. This is the one which is offered to the visitor, but the children's cooking has not been wiped away and if you sit down, you risk a pair of trousers.

Remarkably, none of that seemed to embarrass either Marx or Jenny: "Eventually a spirited and agreeable conversation arises to make amends for the domestic deficiencies, thus making the discomfort tolerable. Finally you grow accustomed to the company, and find it interesting and original. This is a true picture of the family life of the communist chief Marx."[24]

Beginning in 1853, after the émigré skirmishes, after the Cologne trial, after the deaths of two children and the birth of one he could not claim, Marx temporarily set aside his economic writing and his political life, and became a quiet observer. He was a journalist for a New York newspaper, doing what a nineteenth-century husband and father might be expected to do—support his family. And while there is nothing to indicate that he did this well (the family was chronically in debt), there is also nothing to indicate that he resented it. Marx the revolutionist was on a sabbatical of sorts, observing and documenting the life around him rather than working to change it.

The Marx byline appeared frequently on the front news page of the most popular daily paper in America at this time. He might be censored and persecuted when writing in his own language in his own country, but in the freewheeling press and boisterous political dialogue of the United States at midcentury, Marx would have found an eager audience. Many readers of the liberal *New York Daily Tribune* would have agreed with Marx's criticisms of political and social inequality in Europe and his outspoken articles against slavery and capital punishment. Often the editors used Marx's pieces as the leaders, or opening editorials, that set the *Tribune*'s tone on any given day. Marx did stir controversy with some of his reports—notably when he cynically attacked independence heroes like Kossuth or Mazzini—and occasionally he complained that his articles were edited to tone them down. But after one controversial report the *Tribune* added a note of endorsement for its man in London: "Mr. Marx has very decided opinions of his own, with some of which we are far from agreeing, but those who do not read his letters neglect one of the most instructive sources of information on the great questions of current European politics."[25]

Marx and Engels both understood that this period was a mere holiday from active participation in politics. Engels even imagined that in the future they would be back in Germany, working and recruiting new party members and—that consistent desire—publishing a newspaper.[26] He believed that the next time the Marx party was called to the world stage, it would be in a much better position to act, partly because so many weak hangers-on had left Europe for America, but also because a new generation would have been introduced to the party through the injustices of the Cologne trial. Finally, he said that they had matured in exile. In an April 12, 1853, letter to Weydemeyer, Engels looked deep into the future and described what he imagined lay ahead.

> I have a feeling that one fine day, thanks to the helplessness and spinelessness of all the others, our party will find itself forced into power, whereupon it will have to enact things that are not immediately in our own, but rather in the general, revolutionary and specifically petty-bourgeois interest; in which event, spurred on by the proletarian *populus* and bound by our own published statements and plans—more or less wrongly interpreted and more or less impulsively pushed through in the midst of party strife—we shall find ourselves compelled to make communist experiments and leaps which no one knows better than ourselves to be untimely. One then proceeds to lose one's head—only *physically speaking* I hope—, a reaction sets in and, until such time as the world is capable of passing *historical* judgment of this kind of thing, one will be regarded, not only as a brute beast, which wouldn't matter a rap, but also as *stupid,* and that's far worse. I don't very well see how it could happen otherwise.... The main thing is that, should this happen, our party's rehabilitation in history will already have been substantiated in advance in its *literature.*[27]

Engels's letter could be seen as a prescient description of the vicissitudes, if not egregious excesses, of twentieth-century communism. But when he wrote it, its nineteenth-century cofounders had not yet produced the works they hoped would vindicate their theories and provide guidance for another age. Marx and Engels were determined to do so, but both were kept from the task by the immediate needs of the Marx family.

Since their arrival in 1849 the Marxes, like tens of thousands of London poor, had been forced to watch the city's annual Christmas pageantry with wonder and sad regret. Across the town grimy shopwindows were brightly polished, the warm glow from inside suddenly penetrating the fog so passersby could see the colorful toys, fabrics, and jewelry within. Windows displayed ball dresses, kid gloves, and satin boots—unspeakable luxuries in a city carpeted in mud. Food emporiums and markets on every corner swelled with meat, fowl, and fish. Vegetables were piled into green, red, and white mountains, joined by fresh fruit and berries and a dazzling assortment of sweets. The bustle began early and continued into the night, as carts and vans clattered to and fro, delivering fresh provisions to the shops and parcels to expectant households. At night the rhythmic clopping of horses' hooves on paving stones provided a background beat for the holiday carolers and fiddlers who drove all other singers and musicians off the streets.[28] It was impossible to ignore the festivities, and yet, without money, the Marxes had had to. But that year, 1853, the family decided to indulge at least some of its fantasies.

For the Marxes, Christmas was an entirely secular event. In answer to his children's questions about its origins, Marx explained the story of Christ as the tale of a poor carpenter killed by rich men. In general he had no time for religion, but he said that one could "forgive Christianity much, because it taught us the worship of the child."[29]

The Marx children were not allowed into the apartment's front room during the week before Christmas, while the adults decorated and prepared gifts. Many years later in a letter to Laura, Jennychen recalled Christmas on Dean Street: "I see, as if it was happening now, how you, Edgar and me would strain our ears, impatient to hear the ringing of that bell that would invite us to enter the room where the tree was standing. When that long-awaited sound did ring out in the end we were nearly startled.... Timidly you stayed behind while I rushed forward with extraordinary boldness—to hide my own timorousness. How splendid did that living-room seem to us, how elegant and new looked that old dusty furniture."[30]

Engels and other friends had arrived to help decorate the tree and bring the children gifts—dolls, guns, cooking utensils, a drum. Jenny remembered it as the family's first truly merry Christmas in London.[31] And, as with other such visits involving Engels and the crate of wine he contributed, Marx became ill afterward. In fact the entire family was sick, especially Musch, who, according to Marx, was raving and thrashing with a high fever. He wrote Engels, "I hope the little man will soon recover."[32]

Despite Marx's wish for good health, the year 1854 would be plagued by family illness. Disease moved from one to the next, but, said Marx, mercifully never struck them all down at the same time. The children's illnesses were simple cases of measles or colds, but Jenny and Marx both suffered longer bouts of a variety of ailments.[33] Marx was incapacitated at one point for nearly three weeks by rheumatism and a boil between his nose and mouth that grew so large he could hardly speak or laugh. He also continued to suffer from a hepatitis-like liver complaint he had first contracted in the spring of 1853 (and which would plague him for the rest of his life).[34] According to Jenny, her husband was unable to sleep until they resorted to opium and Spanish fly, a topical ointment that, if ingested, was rumored to be an aphrodisiac. Under the circumstances Marx could not write, and so the family's cash box was depleted. Jenny told their trusted friend in Manchester, "Karl was tremendously pleased when he heard the postman's portentous double knock. '*Voila!* Frederik [*sic*], 2 pounds, we're saved!' he cried."[35]

Jenny's malady began soon after Marx recovered, and may have been worsened by mental strain. Now forty, she discovered she was pregnant again. It had been nearly four years since Jenny carried Franzisca, the longest period she had gone since her marriage without being pregnant. Perhaps she had taken steps to avoid conception following Franzisca's and Fawksy's deaths, or perhaps she had not recovered enough emotionally to be intimate with Marx after his betrayal with Lenchen. Whatever the reason, the prospect of another child must have seemed like a curse. Just when they had begun to manage to live poorly but with some hope of survival, they would have more doctor bills, more nurses to pay, and—worst of all—the worry that another child born in poverty in London would have a brief and bitter existence.

Marx tried desperately to find other writing work to supplement his *Tribune* income. In a deal arranged by his sister's husband he agreed to write for a South African newspaper published in English and Dutch, but that fell through in March when the editor said that Marx wanted more money than his paper could pay.[36] Marx also negotiated with a Swiss newspaper to produce articles he dismissed as "miniature dunghills." He did not agree with the paper's politics but told Engels he would take the work purely for Jenny's peace of mind.[37]

Marx described his house as a veritable hospital, and he worried that the pittance he earned did not allow him to buy the kind of food his family needed to stay healthy. He was especially concerned because cholera had broken out in London again, and its epicenter was Soho.[38] On Broad Street alone, a minute's walk from Dean Street, 115 people had died of the disease (nearly 11,000 would die of cholera in London that year).[39] Like many others, Marx believed the cause was new sewer pipes that had been laid through ground where victims of the 1665 plague were buried.[40] The real cause, discovered by Soho doctor John Snow, was sewage leaks into wells from which Londoners drew their drinking water. One such well was on Broad Street.[41]

Though just three months pregnant, Jenny was confined to bed in June. The doctor insisted she get out of London for her health, and so Marx arranged for her, Lenchen, and the children to stay at a friend's house in the country. Jenny would then go to Trier.[42] But all of that required money Marx did not have: the doctor had sent him a bill for twenty-six pounds for services rendered over the winter and demanded regular payment or else he would cease treating the family; in addition, there were apothecary bills and regular household expenses. If Marx had been healthy and able to work through the winter, he might have kept the most aggressive creditors at bay. He told Engels he was in a fix and that his *misères* had turned him into "A VERY DULL DOG. *Blessed is he* that hath no family." He asked Engels whether any of their friends could be leaned on for a loan, but they, too, were broke.[43] The immediate drama of refugee life was over, and they were now forced to earn a living in whatever wretched quarter they inhabited. With the prospect of political upheaval conferring relevancy on their lives now remote, they spent their time focused on crumbs instead of crowns.

Even Engels, who had the good fortune and temperament to be able to glide through most crises, was depressed and angry. On the Continent tensions were rising over a territorial dispute between Turkey and expansionist Russia, and it looked as though a war might break out that would drag in France and England. The prospect of following the movements of great armies as a journalist, not to mention fatigue with his father's business, inspired Engels to write to the *Daily News* in London and offer his services as a military correspondent.[44] The initial response was positive: the editor praised Engels's work and asked for an article as a trial run.

"If all goes well," Engels eagerly told Marx, "in the summer, when my old man comes over, I shall chuck up commerce and move to London."[45] But within two weeks the newspaper politely rejected Engels on the grounds that his articles were "too professional." Engels told Marx that he suspected one of their enemies connected with the paper may have learned of his approach and informed the editor that Engels was "no more than a former one-year volunteer, a communist and a clerk by trade, thus putting a stop to everything. . . . The whole affair has put me terribly out of temper."[46] A final irritant was that Engels's business colleagues discovered he was living with Mary (he had briefly given up his other lodgings to save money), and the potential social and political complications required that he take another apartment, which he could not afford.[47] He wrote Marx, "Of all the band there's nobody we can rely on except each other."[48]

Indeed, thanks to poverty, alcohol, and women, the rest of their friends were swirling down the drain. The Pole who had been Schramm's second in the duel against Willich had died when the Whitechapel shack he lived in with six other refugees burned to the ground.[49] Pieper, who had briefly lived with the Marx family when he was struck by a bad case of syphilis, landed on Marx's doorstep again, twice. First he was thrown out of his lodgings because he ran out of money. He became solvent again by giving German lessons, but was soon back with Marx, having spent all his earnings living for two weeks with a prostitute he described as a "jewel."[50] Weerth, meanwhile, had gone all the way to California prospecting for a wife.[51] Liebknecht had been considering two possible wives from among their circle in London, one English and the other German, and finally settled on the German. But after the wedding, he lost his job.[52] As for Lupus, drink made a victim of him. After an evening with Engels in Manchester, he staggered off alone to another pub, where he met up with six pimps and two prostitutes. He claimed the pimps followed him out of the pub and proceeded to beat him up and steal his money. But Engels said there was more to the story than that, because instead of going home, Lupus had spent the night with a strange Englishman who charged him a shilling for keeping him in his room not two hundred feet from Lupus's own flat.[53]

Lupus's bizarre tale fired the imagination of the Marx children, who were privy to all the sordid details of their father's friends' lives. Laura, who was home sick when Marx first learned the news, wrote Jennychen and Edgar at school to say that Lupus was attacked by highwaymen.[54] Musch then wrote Marx, describing the event as if his father had not been the one to tell them about it in the first place: "My Dear Devil, I hope you are quite well because I am coming to see you and forgot to tell you that Lupus went out to drinks like he generally does and got quite drunk and as he's going along the streets there came some thieves and stole his [illegible] and his spectacles and five pounds . . . and beat him dreadfully. . . . I am your friend Musch la Colonel."[55]

Amid so much personal turbulence, on July 8 Marx sent Jenny off to Trier alone. This resulted in even more debt because, as he told Engels, for pride's sake she had to maintain what she called an "appearance of affluence" and could not arrive there looking shabby. "These extraordinary expenses again brought me into conflict with my permanent and 'decent' creditors AND SO FORTH. 'It's the old, old story,'" he said with resignation, quoting Heine.[56] But there was even more to the old story than he described. The *Tribune* wanted to cut Marx's salary, partly because of an economic crisis in America but also because he had had disputes with the editors over the *Tribune*'s habit of using bits of his writing in other copy without crediting him.[57]

Now alone with his children and Lenchen, Marx tried to lift his spirits by indulging in what Liebknecht called "mad revelry."[58] The most infamous episode involved Liebknecht and Edgar Bauer, who, despite Marx's attacks on him and his brother Bruno in *The Holy Family,* had remained his friend. One night the gang proposed taking a drink in every pub they could find between Oxford Street and Hampstead Road—a distance of about a mile and a half. "We went to work undaunted," Liebknecht recalled, "and managed to reach the end of Tottenham Court Road without accident." There, however, a verbal scuffle involving phrases like "damned foreigners" and "English snobbery" threatened to get physical, so Marx and friends beat a retreat. On the way home Bauer spotted some paving stones and began throwing them at streetlights. Marx and Liebknecht joined in, and four or five lamps were broken. It was two in the morning, however, and the noise raised alarms. Liebknecht reported that three or four police gave chase as he, Marx, and Bauer dodged into side streets, an alley, and a backyard before losing them. Liebknecht understatedly recalled that during their flight, "Marx showed an activity that I should not have attributed to him."[59]

That was not the last bout of drinking for Marx while Jenny was away, and though the binge may have lifted his spirits, it did further damage to his household budget. Laura wrote her "Momchen" to say her father lay in bed all one Sunday "because the day before he had drunken lots of gin."[60] But not all was stupor. While Jenny was away, Marx and his friends kept the children busy with multiple adventures around London, and on one occasion Marx, Lenchen, and the children went to Camberwell, a favorite summer retreat for Londoners, to stay with a Cologne friend, Peter Imandt.[61] Imandt's brother, who was in Germany, had been given a letter to give to Jenny, but reported that he had been unable to deliver it. "This sent us into a great fright," Jennychen told her mother, "because we thought you were in prison."[62]

Jenny was not. She returned to London in late August, well, rested, but heavily pregnant. She would need that store of strength to survive the devastating darkness that lay just ahead.

24

London, 1855

*Bacon says really important people have so many relations to
nature and the world, so many objects of interest, that they
easily get over any loss. I am not one of those important people.*
—Karl Marx[1]

ON JANUARY 17 an infant's cry once again rang from the attic apartment
on Dean Street. Jenny gave birth between six and seven in the morning.
Marx, who believed the years ahead would be ones of political struggle
requiring an army of intelligent men, was only half joking when he
announced the birth to Engels saying, the child was "unfortunately of the
'sex' *par excellence*. If it had been a male child, well and good."[2] The baby
was named Eleanor, and from the moment she was born she was critically
ill. Jenny was beside herself at the thought of a third child struggling for its
life. As if to make that struggle even more difficult, the winter was unusually harsh. A sharp wind sliced through their drafty apartment, making
a mockery of what they called shelter.

The period was bleak all around. The Frenchman Barthélemy, who said
he kept a bullet in reserve to kill Marx for betraying the cause, was hanged
that month.[3] Since he had left the refugees around Soho and stopped visiting Marx's apartment, Barthélemy had been traveling with a posh émigré
set in northwest London's St. John's Wood neighborhood, and his self-
regard had grown accordingly.[4] In 1853 he was tried and received just two
months in prison for killing a fellow refugee in a duel. (He convinced the
judge that he did not know it was illegal to settle scores with pistols in
England.)[5] But in December 1854 he was involved in two murders, and he
could not talk his way free. The killings stemmed from a plot to assassi-

nate Napoleon during a ball at the Tuileries. Barthélemy had obtained a ticket to the event and a weapon, but, needing money to travel, he stopped to see his former employer. Apparently the man was unwilling to give him the funds, so Barthélemy shot him. He next killed a policeman during his escape.[6] A jury convicted him of manslaughter on January 5, 1855. Seventeen days later, he was executed at Newgate Prison,[7] where penal law had once been literally written in blood.[8]

Neither Marx nor Jenny mourned his death, but his hanging was a horrible footnote to an unfortunate early chapter in their London life and a reminder of just how far some among them had strayed from the ideals for which they fought and sacrificed so much.[9]

By March Eleanor was worse still, and like Fawsky, her shrill cries so disturbed the household that an Irish wet nurse was hired in hopes the change might ease her distress.[10] Marx, who had a severe eye inflammation he thought was caused by reading his own economic manuscripts, was also swallowing bottles of medicine to try to cure a cough. But his beloved eight-year-old Musch, Marx told Engels, was sickest of all. Marx took charge of caring for the boy, who had a severe gastric fever he could not shake, staying with him night and day during his illness.[11] By March 8, he told Engels, the doctor was very pleased that Musch had made great strides toward recovery, in fact so much so that Marx considered visiting Engels as soon as he could do so with a clear conscience.[12]

Throughout March, Musch's condition fluctuated: the doctor was pleased with his progress, then disturbed when new symptoms developed and old ones returned. On March 16 Marx told Engels he feared Musch would not recover,[13] but eleven days later he said he had been improving visibly, and the doctor saw every reason to hope. The main thing was that Musch was very weak, and it was not clear whether he could withstand the treatment needed to make him strong enough to travel to the country—far from the foul London air—where the doctor said he must go to get well.[14]

Marx kept vigil with his son, staying at his side and carrying him whenever he left his bed. Lenchen was also continually with the boy. Jenny, however, was so distraught at the prospect of losing this child whom she called her pride and joy, her angel, her heart's darling, that she tried to stay in the front room, away from her son, while he lay in the back, by their only fire. She was afraid her tears would frighten him. But Musch, that little boy with the expressive eyes and large head, was too wise. He told his sisters, "When Mummy comes to my bed always cover my hands and arms so she doesn't see how thin they are."[15] He knew what his mother feared.

While Edgar was sick, the girls took care of Eleanor and kept a close eye on the Irish nurse, who was cheerful and good natured but had a predilection for gin and brandy. Jenny said the girls "watched her like a hawk," and eventually Eleanor grew stronger.[16] Engels took care of Marx's writing for the *Tribune,* so at least a trickle of money came into the household.

On March 30 Marx told Engels that Musch's health was changing by the hour. Yet the fluctuations involved more steps backward than ahead. The boy's disease appeared to have turned into abdominal consumption, a form of tuberculosis, and though he did not say so outright, the doctor seemed to have given up hope. Wrote Marx: "For the past week emotional stress had made my wife more ill than ever before. As for myself, though my heart is bleeding and my head afire, I must, of course, maintain my composure. Never for one moment throughout his illness has the child been untrue to his own good-natured, and at the same time independent, self."[17]

On April 6 Marx wrote Engels: "Poor Musch is no more. Between five and six o'clock today he fell asleep (in the literal sense) in my arms.... You will understand how I grieve over the child."[18] His son, his wonderful rascal the Colonel, whose imagination, vitality, and humor had been the very lifeblood of the family, was gone, his color faded, his flesh cold to the touch. Left behind, in their small rooms under the eaves of a dilapidated building, in a shabby hive of a neighborhood, in the largest city in the world, was an agonizing loneliness.

Liebknecht described the scene at the Marx home immediately after Musch was pronounced dead. Jenny and Lenchen wept side by side over his body, along with the girls whom Jenny held so tightly it was as if she wanted to defend them against the death that had taken her boy. Marx angrily rejected any consolation[19]—this was not a loss; no, this was theft.

And yet, who was the thief? Musch had died of intestinal tuberculosis, a disease not uncommon, but one exacerbated by poor nutrition and unhealthy living conditions.[20] No parent under similar circumstances could help but question what might have been done to change the tragic outcome, and we can have no doubt that Marx and Jenny did so as well. There is also no doubt that this descent into the darkest corner of their souls could have led them to only one conclusion—the revolutionary path they had chosen had killed him. He was the third child Jenny and Marx had lost, but his death was so much more profound. Jenny confessed that the day of his passing was the most dreadful in her life, worse than all her previous pain and suffering combined.[21] One family friend said Musch's death caused Marx's gray-flecked hair to turn white overnight.[22]

★   ★   ★

Musch was buried two days later at the same Quaker cemetery on Totten-ham Court Road where Fawksy and Franzisca were interred.[23] Marx sat dumbly in his carriage, his head in his hands, as the glass-sided hearse took Musch's body to the cemetery. Liebknecht stroked Marx's head and tried to reassure him by reminding him of the family and friends who loved him. But Marx shouted, "You cannot give me back my boy!" and groaned in pain. The rest of the short journey to the cemetery was made in heavy silence. Liebknecht said when Musch's small coffin was finally lowered into the ground, he so feared Marx would try to follow that he jumped to his side to prevent it.[24]

If the funeral was sorrowful, Dean Street in the days immediately after-ward was infinitely worse. Marx told Engels the house was desolate. "I cannot tell you how we miss the child at every turn," the prostrated father wrote. "I've already had my share of bad luck but only now do I know what real unhappiness is. I feel BROKEN DOWN. Since the funeral I have been fortunate enough to have such splitting headaches that I can neither think nor hear nor see. Amid all the fearful torments I have recently had to endure, the thought of you and your friendship has always sustained me, as has the hope that there is still something sensible for us to do together in the world."[25]

Part IV

The End of
La Vie Bohème

25

London, Fall 1855

If yet your gentle souls fly in the air
And be not fixed in doom perpetual,
Hover about me with your airy wings
And hear your mother's lamentation!
— William Shakespeare[1]

LESS THAN TWO weeks after Musch's death, Marx and Jenny boarded the cheapest train available and headed north through the loamy English countryside toward Manchester and Engels.[2] They knew they could count on him to help restore their spirits. Both were physically and mentally shattered by the thought that if they had been able to get Musch out of London early enough, he might have survived. Now they sought just such a refuge for themselves. Marx parceled out his writing responsibilities for the *Tribune* and a German newspaper in Breslau to friends[3] and focused entirely on caring for Jenny, whom eleven-year-old Jennychen poignantly described as "thin as a small candle, as a half-pence candle, and dry as a herring."[4] Marx feared his wife might not survive their latest tragedy. Jenny herself said the pain had taken root in the deepest, quietest portion of her heart, a merciless inhabitant that would never age or stop bleeding.[5]

Jenny and Marx stayed in Manchester for nearly three weeks, but if Jenny was soothed while she was away, the balm did not last when she returned to Dean Street. In the first week of May she fell into a deep depression and stayed in bed. The girls and Lenchen were also still traumatized by Musch's death.[6] Marx called their situation agony, observing that even the "unremittingly awful" weather seemed one with the family's consuming grief.[7] But there was one bright spot. They had learned

249

that Jenny's uncle, the "cur" Marx had hoped would die earlier, finally did. With his passing they anticipated an inheritance of at least one hundred pounds, enough to see them through the year if they stayed within a budget.[8] The inheritance, though, was bittersweet. Had it come earlier, who knows what could have been done to save Musch?

In early July Marx told Engels that when the money arrived, he would take the family out of London. "The memory of our poor, dear child torments us, and even interposes itself in his sisters' play. Such blows can only be mitigated slowly, with the passage of time. To me the loss is as poignant as on the first day."[9] In fact they did not have to wait for the inheritance to leave the city. Peter Imandt, their schoolteacher friend from Cologne, was going to Scotland for a month and offered the Marxes his cottage in Camberwell.[10] The family jumped at the chance to flee from their sorrow and the legion of angry creditors that had grown in size and vehemence while the family mourned.[11] Some Marx biographers have attributed the family's flight entirely to Marx's efforts to dodge bill collectors, but from their letters it is clear that the primary reason for their departure was grief for Musch.

Shortly after they arrived in Camberwell, Jenny wrote a relation in Prussia describing Jennychen and Laura's sense of loss: "All their lovely little games have stopped, their songs have fallen silent. The third person in their circle was missing, their loyal, inseparable comrade left with his happy jokes and games, with his wondrous ringing voice which used to sing Scottish and Irish folk songs." Of the two older girls, her mother said that Jennychen was most affected.[12] Gradually, however, she and Laura turned their attention to baby Eleanor, who after a difficult few months was now flourishing. "It is as if they passed on all the love they had for their beloved brother to this little soul which appeared as a little godsend to them . . . when this house was a place of distress."[13] By September, Marx could pronounce that the healthy country air, far away from Soho[14] (which a decade later Marx said he still approached with dread[15]), suited his family. Even Jenny's spirits had improved somewhat. And as luck would have it, Imandt decided to make his stay in Scotland semipermanent. This meant that the family could remain in Camberwell until Jenny's inheritance arrived, and they could find lodgings away from Dean Street.[16] Jenny said they would look for a place closer to the British Museum, so Marx could continue his work there. In the meantime they kept the Dean Street flat against the dreadful event that they might have to return.[17]

If Marx's interest in world affairs was any indication of his state of mind, he appeared to have partially regained his equilibrium (at least enough to be able to escape into politics in order to forget his sorrow) about the time the family decamped to Camberwell. The balance of information in his letters to Engels tilted from the personal to the professional, and the focus in that area was almost entirely on the Black Sea and Russia's southern Crimean Peninsula, which by the summer of 1855 had become a theater of conflict involving Turkey, Russia, France, and England. It was the first momentous clash between European powers since 1815 and the first modern war, in which steamships moved troops, cameras documented the fighting, and reports were telegraphed by journalists from the scene of battle.[18] Those reports described battlefield horrors in a way readers had never before encountered, and drew back the curtain to expose the reckless decisions that had cost their loved ones' lives.[19]

Like nearly all international conflicts, the Crimean War was rooted in an earlier fight. A century before, Ottoman rulers had thanked France for help in their wars against Russia and Austria by giving it authority over Christians in the Holy Land, the majority of whom were not Roman Catholic, as in France, but Orthodox as in Russia and Greece. That act led to decades of tension as the "gift" was revoked in favor of Orthodox Christian nations. In 1852, to bolster support among French Catholics and backed up by military force, Napoleon III asked the weakened Ottoman leadership to once and for all honor its vow to give Roman Catholics control of the Christian holy sites. The Turkish sultan agreed, but Russia did not. Russia invoked another treaty that it said gave it dominion over Orthodox Christians throughout the Ottoman Empire, including the Holy Land.

Turkey was caught in the middle of the dispute between powerful rivals who still bore enmity resulting from the Napoleonic Wars, an enmity heightened by Western European fears of Russian expansion. Turkey assessed the situation and sided with France. A series of military moves and countermoves between the unhappy giant Russia and the comparatively weak Turkey drew the attention of Britain and France, which sailed their fleets into the Black Sea to try to forestall a greater conflict. Instead they became mired in it themselves, and in March 1854, Britain and France declared war on Russia. Within weeks British forces were landing at Gallipoli, in Turkey.[20]

Engels would later write that he and Marx relished whatever outcome of whichever war would hasten worldwide revolution.[21] In the case of Crimea, they hoped for the defeat of Russia. The two men had long regarded the czarist state as the greatest threat to reform in Europe because it was the most powerful reactionary government on the Continent. Russia had emerged from the Napoleonic Wars with an aura of military invincibility and sat as a massive spoiler at the edge of Western Europe. In 1848 it had helped Austria quash the independence uprising in Hungary, and when its services were no longer needed elsewhere during that turbulent period, it turned its reactionary zeal against its own citizens, launching what would be known as the Cruel Century.[22] Many of Russia's intellectuals, who had once come exclusively from the nobility but now included the sons of merchants and professionals, had been exposed to ideas considered dangerous by Czar Nicholas I, who was determined to eradicate them.[23] (He even demanded that the word "progress" be struck from the official Russian vocabulary.)[24]

During the course of the Crimean War, in the spring of 1855, Nicholas died suddenly and was succeeded by his son, Alexander II. Soon afterward, peace talks began in Vienna and Napoleon III made a triumphant visit to England. (Marx witnessed Napoleon—whom he called a "monkey in uniform"—crossing Westminster Bridge.)[25] But negotiations faltered, and men continued to fall on all sides. The reports coming into London from the battlefront described shocking ineptitude. The British army was commanded by aging or inexperienced aristocrats and largely made up of young Scots and Irishmen forced by poverty to enlist.[26] *The Times* of London's groundbreaking reports described inadequate provisions for the troops (including summer clothes during winter battles), the deaths of thousands from cholera, and needless slaughter, accompanied by powerful descriptions of the sickening smell of death rising from battlefields slippery with the blood of fallen soldiers. By the time peace was concluded in February 1856, six hundred thousand men had died, the vast majority from disease.[27]

With so much death it was hard to imagine that anyone could claim victory, and yet France and England were seen as the winners. Russia's defeat greatly minimized the threat it posed and opened the way for liberalization under Alexander II. The war also popularized a concept coined in 1853: "realpolitik."[28] In the new world of interconnected markets nurtured by diplomatic ties and guarded by military might, ideals seen as impediments to material gains were easily ignored and quietly abandoned. For Marx and Engels, the Crimean War exposed what they called the self-serving alliances of the leaders in London and Paris, who on the commercial front gained favorable terms for a new trade market in Turkey and on the diplomatic front realigned the balance of power in Europe to France's benefit.[29]

Marx and Jenny spent the fall of 1855 in Camberwell waiting for her inheritance. Marx, however, was anxious to get back to London and work, spurred on in part by the war and in part by anger over the death of one of the Cologne trial defendants, thirty-four-year-old Roland Daniels. Daniels had been acquitted of all charges, but the harsh conditions in which he was held for seventeen months before trial proved an effective death sentence. Marx told Daniels's widow, Amalie, that he was inconsolable over the loss of such a friend and would write an obituary of him for the *Tribune*. "It is to be hoped that circumstances will someday permit us to wreak upon those guilty of cutting short his career vengeance of a kind sterner than that of an obituary."[30]

But first, Marx had to go into hiding—not for political but for financial reasons: the doctor who had treated Musch and was pursuing Marx for payment had traced him to Camberwell. Marx wrote Engels an uncharacteristically cloak-and-dagger letter explaining that the family would remain at Imandt's but he would flee incognito to Manchester.[31]

Marx remained with Engels until December, before returning surreptitiously to Dean Street, where he shut himself up in his flat, fearful of running into the doctor or his bill-collecting henchmen.[32] This self-imposed incarceration ended when Jenny received £150, her portion of her late uncle's fortune. Marx had not found other lodgings, so when Imandt returned to Camberwell, Jenny and the children reluctantly moved back to Dean Street[33] and Marx paid off the "hostile forces" who besieged them as soon as the family's arrival was noticed.[34]

Also awaiting them was Pieper. While they were away, the hapless lover had discovered the music of Wagner, who had been in London earlier that year,[35] and he may have thought he could lift the family's spirits by playing some of the composer's work. Marx told Engels he was horrified by this "music of the future."[36] But if Pieper's attempt to cheer the family with music failed, his presence was the perfect tonic. Those initial weeks back in London, during their first Christmas without Colonel Musch, might have been far drearier if not for Pieper's escapades.

One day while he was tutoring the girls, a note arrived for him. The unfamiliar hand inviting him to a rendezvous was obviously a woman's, and it made Pieper wild with anticipation. He handed Jenny the note, and she recognized the writing at once as that of the Irish wet nurse employed after Eleanor's birth. She was hardly the woman Pieper had conjured up in his imagination, and the family laughed uproariously at his expense. But, ever the gentleman, Pieper kept the rendezvous. He was apparently unwilling to disappoint a lady.[37]

Pieper had, in fact, become more practical during the previous sobering year. The man Jenny called a "Soho Byron"[38] had concluded that he could be truly happy only if he found a wife with enough money to tide him over during difficult times. With that in mind he set out to seduce a greengrocer's daughter whom Marx described as "a tallow-candle in green spectacles...without any meat or flesh whatever." She had long been in love with Pieper, so he approached her father, declaring his love for the daughter and, more important, his need for a loan to secure the future he would at some point no doubt offer her. He asked his would-be father-in-law for twenty to forty pounds, and said he would marry his daughter at a propitious moment.[39]

The greengrocer's response came in the form of a letter addressed to 28 Dean Street: he forbade Pieper ever to set foot in his house again. The distraught young lady then showed up at the Marx flat proposing that she and Pieper elope. Pieper, however, was less interested in his love-struck fräulein now that she was poor, and so the affair ended quickly.[40] Throughout, however, Jennychen and Laura had been highly amused by the romantic comedy that played out in their salon, Jennychen describing Pieper as "Benedick the married man" from Shakespeare's *Much Ado About Nothing,* until Laura, now ten, corrected her, pointing out that Benedick was a wit but Pieper was a mere clown, and a penniless clown at that.[41]

The inheritance from Jenny's uncle had left the Marxes relatively debt-free all winter. Now money barely featured in Marx's letters to Engels, and when it did, it was most often linked to trade and finance, not his personal problems.

With the help of Ferdinand von Westphalen, Jenny received a passport to travel to Trier with the children and Lenchen in the spring of 1856.[42] The reason for Jenny's trip was twofold. Her mother was ill, and Jenny and the children wanted to get away from Dean Street. They left on May 22 and planned to be gone for three or four months.[43] One might have assumed that, left alone with Pieper, Marx would have relished the chance to work unencumbered by Jenny and the children, but after just one day, he decided he could not stay there either, and began plotting his escape. He told Engels the doctor had recommended he get a change of air to combat a return of his recurring liver ailment.[44] His letters indicate that he also required a change of location for his mental health. Indeed, a May 23 letter to Engels showed just how quickly Marx went to pieces without the bustle of the family to distract him. He had buried himself in Shakespeare, and told Engels he was mystified by the word "hiren" in *Henry IV.* He questioned whether Samuel Johnson was correct in interpreting "hiren" as "siren," or could it not, Marx asked, be a play on "hure" — or whore — and siren? Or perhaps "heoren," a reference to hearing? He concluded, "You can see TO WHICH LOW STATE OF SPIRIT I am DEPRESSED today from the great interest I show in this matter."[45]

To be able to work (which is to say, to be able to live), Marx needed the anchor that Jenny and the children provided. He ordered his thoughts only in the midst of their disorder. Throughout his life, theirs was the society he craved. This man, who from age seventeen committed himself to the work of humankind, apparently could not rise to the task in the absence of the women who made up his small household. He longed particularly for Jenny. She was not only his friend and lover, but had been his most trusted intellectual sounding board since their honeymoon thirteen years earlier. Neither his heart nor his head functioned without her.

By the beginning of June he could stand his solitude no longer, and traveled with Pieper to Hull, and then on alone to Manchester to stay with Engels, who had just returned from a tour of Ireland with Mary.[46] From Dublin to Galway Engels had encountered a desolate land defeated by famine and occupied by England—armed constables were everywhere. He described the population as demoralized, "crushed, politically and industrially," from the peasant to the bourgeois landowner. Blaming Westminster, he declared, "The English citizen's so-called freedom is based on the oppression of the colonies." In a show of solidarity, Engels now sported the enormous mustache popular among impoverished Irish aristocrats. To that he added, in defiance of his relatively clean-shaven English commercial colleagues, a beard so long and thick it completely covered his cravat and collar.[47] (At this time Marx's beard was short and trimmed.)

But even the company of his cherished friend could not satisfy Marx's longing. It may have been the still-fresh wound of Musch's death or simply that Marx had not been away from his entire family for such a long period since their arrival in London six years earlier. Whatever the reason, he felt their absence profoundly. Marx wrote his wife on June 21, 1856, two days after their thirteenth wedding anniversary: "Mere spatial separation from you suffices to make me instantly aware that time has done for my love just what the sun and the rain do for the plants—made it grow. My love for you, as soon as you are away from me, appears for what it is, a giant, and into it all the vigor of my mind and all the ardor of my heart are compressed.... My darling sweetheart, I am writing to you again because I am alone and because it is irksome to converse with you all the time in my head without you knowing or hearing or being able to answer me." His eyes, he said, were spoiled by poor lamplight and tobacco smoke, but he could imagine Jenny vividly in his mind.

There you are before me, large as life, and I lift you up in my arms and I kiss you all over from top to toe, and I fall on my knees before you and cry: "Madame, I love you." And love you I do.... You will smile, my dear heart, and wonder "why this rhetoric all of a sudden?" But if I could press your sweet white bosom to mine, I would be silent and say not a word....

There are, indeed, many women in the world, and a few of them are beautiful. But where else shall I find a face of which every lineament, every line even, reawakens the greatest and sweetest memories of my life? In your sweet countenance I can read even my infinite sorrows, my irreplaceable losses, and when I kiss your sweet face I kiss away my sorrow. "Buried in her arms, revived by her kisses"—in your arms, that is, and by your kisses.[48]

Unfortunately, Jenny's response to Marx's letter apparently no longer exists, but she too described their painful separation, in a letter to Liebknecht's wife, Ernestine, in mid-July. Jenny detailed the joy she derived from her children,[49] baby Eleanor (who was now known as Tussy, from the French verb *tousser,* because of her persistent little cough[50]) and the older girls, who drew admiring crowds when they went out walking in Trier. But, Jenny said, "all over the place there is something missing.... The separation from 'Mohr' is difficult for me; the girls miss him very much, too: even Tussychen has not forgotten daddy and mentions him remarkably often." Jenny also admitted that she could not master her sadness over Musch. "The longer I am without the dear child, the more I think of it and it gets ever more distressing."[51]

Jenny's trip to Trier was cut short by another death, this time her mother's, on July 23. Caroline von Westphalen had been ill for some time, and Jenny was at her side for the last eleven days of her life. Such a loss would have shaken her to the very core at the best of times, but coming so soon after Musch, it affected her gravely. Jenny wrote Marx that she planned to leave Trier as soon as she settled her mother's affairs with Ferdinand. She then proposed going with the children to Paris, which had always represented solace and comfort to her, and on to the island of Jersey off the coast of Normandy, partly to recover, partly because Jersey was cheaper and more pleasant than London, and partly so the children could learn French. Jenny also announced that Lenchen's sister Marianne, who had worked for Jenny's mother, would be returning to live with them in London.[52]

Marx scrambled for a response to his wife. In Jenny's absence, he was supposed to have found a house or apartment away from Dean Street and, of course, to have earned money. He had done neither. Furthermore, the inheritance of the previous year was all but gone. Marx told Engels that, given Jenny's fragile mental condition, he had to agree that her scheme was splendid, but in reality he could not see how it was financially possible.[53] He said Jenny had no idea what had been happening in London while she was away. "As you can imagine, I am like a cat on hot bricks. I shall have to do something about lodgings when the FAMILY arrives, but have no idea how to get out of the old ones or move into new, having neither the MEANS nor any immediate prospects."[54]

Marx did the mature thing: he tried to delay the inevitable. He wrote

Jenny, "Much though I hanker after you and the children—and this *QUITE indescribably*—I should like you to stay on *in Trier for another week*. It would do you and the children no end of good." To paint as bleak a picture as possible he added, "I have Pieper sleeping with me in your stead. HORRIBLE. In the same room, at any rate. . . . For three weeks I've been as hypochondriacal as the devil."[55]

There was in fact one truly good reason for Jenny remaining in Trier: the heat in England that August was unbearable. Engels said he was "sluicing and bathing" his outer man with water "and the inner man with a variety of other fluids."[56] In that atmosphere Marx set about frantically, from morning to night, to find a new home for his family.[57] Finally, on September 22, he announced to Engels that he had found one, in an area called Haverstock Hill, near Hampstead Heath in north London.[58] It was the destination favored by stockbrokers, merchants, and commercial men aiming to move their families out of the city.[59] The area was still under construction—neither roads nor sewage lines were completed, and there were no gaslights to penetrate the night and the fog (Marx described the region as "somewhat unfinished")—but he was tremendously relieved at having found it.[60]

Nine Grafton Terrace was a seven-year-old, three-story brick house located in a row of nearly identical attached homes. With eight rooms, it was four times larger than Dean Street, and the rent was nearly twice as high.[61] Marx might not have chosen such an expensive house if he hadn't been eager to leave Soho, but he may also have been blinded to the cost by expectations of Jenny's inheritance from her mother. Looking at their expenses, he may have calculated in his singularly delusional way that her money, plus his earnings, would suffice to keep them in their pricey abode.

Jenny's younger brother Edgar was in the United States, working as a farmhand in New York State, when he learned of his mother's death. Though he had no money of his own (he had taken out a loan using Ferdinand's name as surety that May), Edgar said in a letter to his brother in August, "I cede my claim to my mother's furnishings and to her possible assets to my sister Jenny."[62] It was known that Caroline von Westphalen had relatively little money and some stocks when she died, but Jenny and Marx anticipated that whatever they inherited would be significant compared with what they had—about fifty pounds—out of which they had to pay debts and make a down payment on the rent for their new house.[63] Even Jennychen recognized their plight, writing her father a note to say that her mother had paid the back rent: "I think tomorrow we will again be in our old hole." Marx asked Engels for help, which of course he provided.[64]

Part of the Marx family's fiscal trouble at this time was due to market turmoil. The first tremors from a financial earthquake in America were being felt across the Atlantic and were beginning to affect European banks and stocks. The shares Caroline had invested in had fallen sharply, and Ferdinand did not want to sell them at a loss.[65] Many people would find themselves victims of the plunge. The economic boom that began in 1849 and continued through the 1850s had been built on speculation. Countless investors had joined the stock craze, acquiring shares in firms that barely existed and railways that went nowhere. The formerly secure banking industry had joined the circus by adopting risky new policies: banks began accepting paper payment in the form of personal checks and approving loans based on personal credit, not bills guaranteed by individuals on solid financial footing. In many cases finance had become tantamount to gambling.[66] It was a heady time for those wanting to increase their wealth and willing to bend the rules to do so.

In 1856 some experts began to recognize that this soaring capitalist system was built on weak foundations—in some cases air—and they anticipated a financial crash of global dimensions. These soothsayers were correct: what they were witnessing was the start of the first modern economic crisis to hit the capitalist world. It began with the collapse of a bank in New York, and because all advanced economies were now intertwined, a crisis in one became a crisis in all.[67] The British government declared finances in the queen's realm to be sound,[68] but Marx and Engels were giddy with the certainty that not only was England unsound, but France and the rest of Europe were as well. Engels declared that at some point in the following year, he expected a "day of wrath such as has never been seen before; the whole of Europe's industry in ruins...all the propertied classes in the soup, complete bankruptcy of the bourgeoisie, war and profligacy to the nth degree."[69] Marx, too, saw social storm clouds and expected that he and Engels would be dragged back into revolutionary action. "I don't suppose we'll be able to spend much longer here merely as spectators," he told Engels, adding jokingly, "the very fact that I've at last got round to setting up house again and sending for my books seems to me to prove that the 'mobilization' of our persons is AT HAND."[70]

At the beginning of October, Jenny received ninety-seven pounds six shillings from her inheritance, and the family moved into Grafton Terrace. The will's execution and the distribution of funds were arranged by Ferdinand's brother-in-law, Wilhelm von Florencourt,[71] who though not a blood relative was treated as such by Jenny. She thanked him for his help and also told him to "express to Ferdinand once again my deepest gratitude for all the love and loyalty."[72] Jenny had had disputes with her brother over other parts of the family's legacy, but by the time she was settled in

Grafton Terrace she seemed ready to move beyond hard feelings over per-sonal—and apparently party—matters. Without doubt her graciousness toward Ferdinand was motivated partly by necessity; he held the family purse strings. But she also seemed to value her extended family more after her own losses in London and her mother's death in Trier. She had com-municated with him during her recent stay in Prussia, and perhaps during that period of mourning they had recognized the personal ties that bound them were deeper than the politics that drove them apart.

In a letter to Florencourt that might have been depicting a German Romantic landscape painting rather than her new London residence, Jenny described Grafton Terrace as a palace compared with Dean Street. The new home was "airy, sunny, dry and built on gravelly soil. It is surrounded by dewy green meadows where cows, horses, sheep, goats and chickens graze in cozy harmony. In front of us, the huge city of London extends in misty silhouettes, but when the view is clear, we can precisely distinguish the cupola of St. Paul's Cathedral." The back rooms, she said, looked up toward Hampstead Heath and Highgate.[73] In fact, the area around Grafton Terrace was actually much less grand. Jenny told another correspondent, "One had to pick one's way over heaps of rubbish and in rainy weather the sticky red soil caked to one's boots so that it was after a tiring struggle and with heavy feet that one reached our house."[74] And although the house was spacious, it would have been described at the time as a quite modest middle-class residence.[75] The work areas—kitchen and laundry room—were located belowground. The first floor had two parlors, a bedroom, and small cloakroom; the second floor three more rooms; and there was an attic where Lenchen and Marianne slept.[76] The house did have two water closets,[77] and, Jenny was pleased to say, space in the garden for chickens.[78]

The family's main problem was that the home was unfurnished, and the Marxes had nothing of their own with which to fill it. They could not afford anything new, so Jenny said they scoured sales at fifty houses for secondhand rubbish to fill the place.[79] Still, she told Florencourt, even those retrievals were a joy: "All my old sufferings and burdens fall victim to this marvelous palace....The children are very happy with the many new rooms, and the small delighted Eleanor is constantly kissing the nice carpets and the 'bow-wow' who cowers on the felt hearth rug."[80]

The family spent a quiet first season in their new quarters. But quiet did not bring tranquility. While Jenny occupied Dean Street, she had longed to be away from the memories there. But as she sat in seclusion on Grafton Terrace she was still burdened by them, and now had none of the distrac-tions to which she had previously turned to help her forget. She missed her long walks through the West End. She missed chats in the pubs in

Soho and St. Giles—the Red Lion on Great Windmill Street, the White Hart Inn on Drury Lane. And she missed the friends who popped in and out of their apartment at all hours as if it were their home, too.[81] For most of those friends, the trip to Grafton Terrace was too long and difficult for a casual visit. Freiligrath, for example, could no longer stop by as he had in Soho; he was now manager of the London branch of a Swiss bank, and his duties kept him too busy to make the trek to north London.[82] Even Pieper, who had turned up as regularly as a stray cat on the family's Soho doorstep, no longer visited. And others had left the city entirely. Lupus was now permanently ensconced in Manchester with Engels, and Red Wolff had found work as a schoolmaster in Lancashire.[83] Finally, some of their dearest companions had died. Georg Weerth, who had introduced Jenny to London, died in Havana while on business. He was thirty-four when claimed by an illness he had picked up in one exotic locale or another.[84] Also dead was their old friend Heine. He, of course, had been dying as long as they had known him, but his final years were extremely difficult. His brother said, "Seven years of bodily misery had alienated him from the external world, he seemed totally unfamiliar with the routine of ordinary life on this planet."[85] Jenny and Marx had both loved Heine deeply. His passing was a sad coda to a wondrous time, a desecration of their cherished Paris memories.

Jenny spent the first months at Grafton Terrace depressed and surrounded by medicine bottles, including opium. "It was a long time," she confessed, "before I could get used to the complete solitude."[86] In addition, despite Marx's financial calculations, they were once again out of money. All of Jenny's inheritance had gone toward setting up the place.[87] At the same time, the *Tribune* was failing to print two of Marx's articles each week as agreed, and *Putnam's,* another American publication that had solicited his work earlier in the year, still had not paid, even though he'd sent them the articles they'd requested. Before Christmas 1856, Marx wrote Engels yet again—the count was now approaching the countless—asking for money. "If I'm late with the first payment to my LANDLORD, I shall be *entirely discredited.*"[88]

Although the family had left Dean Street, their most intractable problems followed them. They were sick and broke, and now they were also alone. "*La vie bohème* had come to an end and instead of openly carrying on the struggle against poverty in exile, we now had to maintain at least the *appearance* of respectability," Jenny wrote years later. "We were sailing with all sails set into bourgeois life. And yet there were still the same petty pressures, the same struggles, the same old misery, the same intimate relationship with the three balls of the pawnshop—what was gone was the humor."[89]

26

London, 1857

*In these hard times, you must be plucky and keep your head
unbowed. The world belongs to the brave.*

—Jenny Marx[1]

BY LATE JANUARY the family's financial situation was even worse. The *Tribune* had rejected all but one of Marx's articles, and Marx suspected the
paper might be trying to starve him out. "So here I am," he told Engels,
"without any prospects...completely stranded in a house into which I
have put what little cash I possessed and where it is impossible to scrape
along from day to day as we did in DEAN STREET. I am utterly at a loss what
to do, being, indeed, in a more desperate situation than five years ago. I
thought I had tasted the bitterest dregs of life. *But no!* And the worst of it is
that this is no mere passing crisis. I cannot see how I am to extricate
myself."[2]

Marx and Engels, politically and intellectually, were as close as ever—
Marx called Engels his alter ego.[3] But by 1857 the differences in their
personal lives were extreme. Engels had begun receiving a share of the
profits from Ermen & Engels,[4] and his father had come to see him as a
competent, perhaps even talented, businessman. He no longer worried
overly about his son's communist views; as long as he performed so well as
a capitalist, he could call himself whatever he liked in private. From that
comfortable vantage point, Engels wrote:

> Your letter arrived like a bolt from the blue. I had believed that everything
> was going splendidly at last—you in a decent house and the whole BUSINESS

261

settled; and now it turns out that everything's in doubt. . . . I only wish you had told me about the business a fortnight earlier. For my Christmas present my old man gave me the money to buy a horse and, as there was a good one going, I bought it last week. If I'd known about this business of yours I would have waited a month or two and saved the cost of its keep. . . . I'm exceedingly vexed that I should be keeping a horse here while you and your family are down on your luck in London.

Engels told Marx he would send him five pounds each month, but Marx should feel free to ask for more. Engels's increased sense of responsibility may have been due to his decision "to turn over a new leaf." He told Marx, "I've been leading far too frivolous an existence of late."[5]

Marx, meanwhile, once again fell victim to liver troubles that he said left him unable to do much of anything except teach himself Danish[6] (such was his idea of sickbed leisure). Jenny was also ill, but her problem was an all too familiar one: she was pregnant. Their financial situation was so bad, however, that neither could afford to give in to their condition.[7] Marx continued to write for the *Tribune,* and Jenny acted as his secretary until she was finally confined to bed, at which time thirteen-year-old Jennychen and eleven-year-old Laura began their long careers as their father's assistants. Jenny told Engels the two girls had ousted her "altogether with the *chi-i-ief* of the household" while their forty-three-year-old mother waited for her latest child to enter the world.[8]

In the spring of 1857, perhaps because he was using fewer of Marx's newspaper pieces, the *Tribune*'s Dana offered Marx a job as a contributor to the *New American Encyclopedia,* a multivolume dictionary of general knowledge being written by U.S. and European scholars. Marx was admonished by the *Encyclopedia*'s editors not to allow his "party's" point of view to creep into his entries. Despite the restrictions, Marx was excited by the project, which promised a steady and generous income and would require less work than the articles he and Engels wrote for the *Tribune.*[9] Engels even suggested that Marx tell Dana he could write the entire *Encyclopedia* alone, though in reality Engels, Lupus, and Pieper would help. "We can easily supply that amount of 'unalloyed' erudition," he crowed, "so long as unalloyed Californian gold is substituted for it." Uncharacteristically optimistic, Engels saw the project as Marx's financial salvation. "Now everything is going to be all right again and even though there's no immediate prospect of payment, it's still a very secure berth."[10] Marx quickly forgot about his liver and returned to the British Museum to begin research for the encyclopedia entries.[11]

The Reading Room that Marx returned to that spring had been transformed. Books still covered the walls from floor to ceiling, but now twenty arched windows soared upward toward a massive round window at the apex of a dome. (There was no artificial light in the library. Readers depended on not very reliable sunlight, and often the library was closed due to fog.) The long tables had been replaced by adjoining desks positioned in concentric circles. The effect was more privacy for the researcher, who could disappear into his thoughts from the comfort of a now-cushioned chair. Marx's trek to the museum was at least twice as long from Grafton Terrace as it had been from Soho, but he walked there almost daily, health permitting. Engels had suggested that Marx rent an office for his encyclopedia work, but Marx already had a free one—a desk between rows K and P in the Reading Room. For the next quarter century he was a fixture there.[12]

The work from Dana had come just in time to distract Marx from his latest family tragedy. On July 6 Jenny gave birth to a son who died almost immediately.[13] Marx told Engels, "In itself, this was no disaster," but he hinted at circumstances surrounding the birth that "have branded themselves on my mind" and made it "agonizing to look back upon"—so much so that he said he did not wish to discuss them in writing.[14] Jenny remained in bed for several weeks and, according to Marx, was "extraordinarily out of temper." He did not blame her, but he told Engels he found it wearisome.[15] In her correspondence, however, far from being piqued, Jenny seemed sanguine. She told Ferdinand's wife, Louise, that her newborn boy (whose name she did not mention, if he had been given a name at all) had survived slightly over an hour before dying: "Again a silent hope of the heart was buried in the grave."[16] Jenny's dead children now outnumbered those living.

For more than a year Marx and Engels had been keeping a keen eye on the creaks and groans issuing from the financial markets, especially in France and America. Engels had wagered that a massive economic failure, which would precipitate social revolution, would occur before the end of 1857. By October Marx declared it well under way: "The American crisis... is BEAUTIFUL and has had IMMEDIATE repercussions on French industry, since silk goods are now being sold in New York more cheaply than they are produced in Lyons."[17] Engels agreed, calling the crash "superb and not yet over by a long chalk... for the next three or four years, commerce will again be in a bad way. *Now we're in luck.*"[18]

As a result of the crash the *Tribune* fired all its European correspondents except Marx and one other man, but cut Marx's earnings in half. Yet even with that blow to his own finances, Marx's joy over the economic crisis was undiminished.[19] Marx told Engels, "Never, since 1849, have I felt so COZY as during this OUTBREAK."[20] Jenny told a colleague, "Though the American crisis has touched our purse all too appreciably...you can nevertheless imagine how HIGH UP the Mohr is. He has recovered all his wonted facility and capacity for work, as well as the liveliness and buoyancy of a spirit long since blighted by great sorrow, the loss of our beloved child [Edgar].... By day Karl works for his living and by night at the completion of his political economy."[21]

Just as the Great Exhibition and accompanying capitalist triumphalism goaded Marx back to his study of economics, so, too, did the possible fall of the moneyocracy. He had not focused on his economic work for years; he was too busy trying to make money to write about it. But the crisis once again instilled in him a sense of urgency to finish his book. Watching the bank failures, the stock and commodity market calamities, the contagion of bankruptcies, the joblessness and homelessness and hunger, Marx feared that the system would tumble down around him before he had a chance to explain it and provide guidance for a postcapitalist world. Marx told an associate in Germany that he "frittered away" his time writing for the *Tribune* and the *Encyclopedia* and living like a hermit, and at night he worked on the outlines of his "political economy," generally until four in the morning and sustained by copious amounts of lemonade and tobacco. It was essential, he said, "TO GET RID OF THIS NIGHTMARE,"[22] adding later, "even if the house should come tumbling about my ears," this time he would finish.[23]

Engels, who kept Marx up-to-date on market rumors from Manchester, gleefully noted that his commercial colleagues were infuriated by his good spirits in the face of collapse. He said their desperation could be seen in the clubs, where liquor consumption was on the rise.[24] As for himself, Engels told Marx, "the bourgeois filth of the last seven years has undoubtedly clung to me to some extent; now it will be washed away and I shall become a changed man. Physically, the crisis will do me as much good as a bathe in the sea. I can sense it already. In 1848 we were saying: Now our time is coming, and so IN A CERTAIN SENSE it was, but this time it is coming properly; now it is do or die." The new Engels planned to confine his extracurricular activities to fox hunting.[25] (Describing one seven-hour hunt, he said, "That sort of thing always keeps me in a state of devilish exhilaration for several days; it's the greatest physical pleasure I know.")[26]

As the economic meltdown spread across the Continent—affecting even railway operations in Russia—Marx and Engels tracked its progress. Marx chuckled that the same firms that were normally against works programs for the unemployed now demanded government financial support and invoked their "right to profit" at public expense.[27] The two men watched for signs that the crisis had spread to agriculture, at which point, they believed, it would become "spectacular."[28]

Marx had been corresponding for years with a socialist in Düsseldorf named Ferdinand Lassalle, who in 1848 had made a name for himself as a reformer but was best known at the time for representing the Countess Sophie von Hatzfeldt in her twelve-year divorce suit. Lassalle presented the case as a fight for the emancipation of women, but it captivated the public (even the Prussian king) with its salacious details about the private lives of the upper echelon of German society. After its successful resolution, which left the countess and Lassalle rich for life, Lassalle moved in with his client, who was twenty years his senior.[29] Marx accused him of being a kept man who coquetted with the aristocracy while declaring himself a champion of the workingman.[30]

Despite their suspicions about Lassalle, Marx and Engels valued him as a useful contact with party members in Düsseldorf and Berlin. He also had connections with publishers. By 1857 Marx had been out of the German book market so long it would be difficult to find a publisher without someone local working on his behalf. He told Lassalle he was in the final stages of writing what he described as a "critical exposé of the system of the bourgeois economy." The book was entirely scientific, Marx said, and would pose no problem with censors. "You would, of course, oblige me by trying to find someone in Berlin prepared to undertake this." Marx suggested that the book be published in installments and without rigid deadlines, and also stressed that the author must be paid for his work.[31]

He was too proud to confide his financial woes to Lassalle, but he told Engels that because his *Tribune* earnings had been halved, his situation was unbearable and he would "sooner be miles under the ground than go on scraping along in this way. Always to be a burden on others while constantly tormented oneself by beastly trifles."[32] It was the end of a frigid January, and Jenny had pawned her shawl to get the few pence needed to buy food.[33] "Fortunately," Marx mused, "events in the outside world offer a good deal of solace just now. Otherwise, in private I THINK I lead THE MOST TROUBLED LIFE THAT CAN BE IMAGINED. NEVER MIND!" Then, almost as an afterthought, he added, "What could be more asinine for people of wide aspirations than to get married at all, thus letting themselves in for the *little miseries of domestic and private life*."[34]

On Dean Street the children had been too young to understand the family's poverty, but on Grafton Terrace they were old enough to recognize the difference between their position and that of the middle-class families around them. Marx's neighborhood peers were largely neat, predictable, churchgoing English businessmen with thriving young families. He, on the other hand, was a disheveled atheist immigrant scholar incapable of making ends meet. The neighbors could not have failed to see the creditors lined up at the Marx family door, and surely heard whispers from local shopkeepers that they did not even pay their most basic bills.

Jennychen was especially sensitive to their plight, and a visible example of it. When she was thirteen she grew so quickly that Jenny and Lenchen could not alter her clothes fast enough to keep her in dresses.[35] The disparity between her situation and that of her schoolmates was impossible to hide and deeply shameful. Yet she exhibited no anger. Quite the contrary, Jennychen considered herself one more burden on her beleaguered parents. In working-class families, daughters Jennychen's age would already have been employed outside the home.[36] Her parents would not allow that, and so she tried to contribute by working around the house. For all her efforts, however, she was not a convincing domestic. The clothes she sewed for Tussy were too flashy (one outfit was silver and red), and at the table she was, in her mother's words, "clumsy." "When it is her turn to set the coffee table," Jenny wrote, "all the cups are constantly in mortal danger; but then one is always recouped with a very good cup of tea, for all the fear for the pedantically arranged chinaware, since the little profligate cannot help exceeding the prescribed amount of tea with a couple of spoons."[37] While Laura—rosy cheeked, blond, delicate, musical—seemed the embodiment of a Victorian girl, Jennychen was dark, strong, and intellectual.[38] For her thirteenth birthday she had received a diary from Laura, but instead of filling it with girlish daily observations and dreams, she used its pages to write a long essay on Greek history.[39]

Jenny had hopes that, despite their poverty and politics, she could turn her daughters into proper—if not bourgeois—young ladies, and she was determined to educate them in such a way that they could find a cultured husband (preferably English or German) and raise their own families free of financial and political concerns. She confided to a friend that sometimes she wanted to be an "amateur" herself and turn away in disgust from things political (an impossibility for her and Karl, for whom, "unfortunately, it always remains a vital question"). Whatever the cost, she did not want revolution to be the driving force in her daughters' lives.[40] Their futures, however, like those of most young women in the midnineteenth century, depended on their father's fortunes. And regrettably for the Marx daughters, *their* father was thwarted at nearly every turn.

★   ★   ★

In the spring of 1858 Lassalle found a publisher for Marx's book.[41] Berliner Franz Gustav Duncker (whose wife was one of Lassalle's mistresses[42]) agreed to Marx's proposed installments and wanted the first one at the end of May. Despite having specified that he needed to be paid, Marx was so excited by Duncker's interest that he said he was prepared to write the first installment without remuneration,[43] but Duncker offered him more than Berlin professors usually received for similar work. The publisher looked for additional installments every few months and said he was quite prepared to commit to an ongoing economic series by Dr. Karl Marx.[44]

At long last the book Marx had been carrying in his head would become a reality. But from the moment the contract was signed, Marx's mind and body rebelled: his liver troubles intensified to the point that he was "incapable of thinking, reading, writing or, indeed, of anything SAVE the ARTICLES for the *Tribune.*" He told Engels, "My indisposition is disastrous, for I can't begin working on the thing for Duncker until I'm better and my fingers regain their VIGOR and GRASP."[45]

Marx eventually sent his friend in Manchester an outline of the first installment, but Engels found it "A VERY ABSTRACT ABSTRACT INDEED." He apologized for not being able to understand it, implying that his factory work had deadened the theoretical part of his brain.[46] Marx, however, was so fragile that Engels's mildest criticism sent him reeling; he could not even write a letter in response. That task fell to Jenny:

> For the past week Karl has been so unwell as to be quite incapable of writing. He believes you will already have deduced from the labored style of his most recent letter that his bile and liver are again in a state of rebellion.... The worsening of his condition is largely attributable to mental unrest and agitation which now, of course, after the conclusion of the contract with the publisher, are greater than ever and increasing daily, since he finds it utterly impossible to bring the work to a close.[47]

Jenny and Engels had known that the contract would be torture for Marx. During the previous fifteen years, stretching back to their days in Paris, Marx had never met a deadline, adhered to length limits, or completed an assignment in the manner requested (the sole exception to this last was the *Communist Manifesto*). The problem was not lack of initiative but his inquisitive mind. Marx simply could not set aside research and begin writing; he was enthralled by the unknown and felt he could not commit his theories to paper until he understood every angle of his ever-evolving subject. But that, of course, was impossible—the halls of knowledge are infinite and mutable, and though he would have been happy to wander through them for the rest of his days, a contract required that he stop. And that was when the torment began, traveling swiftly from his mind to his body. Marx recognized the importance of the work at hand, telling Weydemeyer, "I have got to pursue my object through thick and thin and not allow bourgeois society to turn me into a MONEY-MAKING MACHINE."[48] There was, in fact, little real risk of that happening; Marx simply needed to look for someone or something to blame.

On April 29, twenty-seven days after he sent Engels his outline, Marx finally wrote him again. "My long silence can be explained in one word—inability to write. This existed (AND TO SOME DEGREE EXISTS STILL) not only IN THE LITERARY, but IN THE LITERAL SENSE OF THE WORD. The few obligatory articles for the *Tribune* were dictated to my wife, but even that was only possible by APPLYING STRONG STIMULI. Never before have I had such a violent *attack* of liver trouble and FOR SOME TIME there was a fear that it might be sclerosis of the liver." He said his doctor wanted him to travel, stop all work, and "gad about."[49]

Engels told Marx to come to Manchester immediately. He should buy a first-class train ticket, which Engels would pay for, and Engels would also send money to Jenny to cover any expenses associated with Marx's absence.[50] The next day Marx wrote to say he would arrive within five days. He added guilelessly, "Since yesterday I have been feeling much better."[51]

Jenny, too, seemed relieved that Engels had intervened. In fact the family marveled at Marx's transformation under Engels's care. They shouldn't have: Engels offered Marx a complete escape from himself and his responsibilities—both debt and deadline—plying him with good food, good wine, and fine cigars in the hope that enforced relaxation would unblock the genius within. Engels told Jenny he had Marx out riding horses for two hours and that Mohr was now "waxing quite enthusiastic about the thing."[52]

Marx stayed with Engels until the end of May, when the first installment of his book was supposed to be in the publisher's hands. Instead he wrote Lassalle a letter filled with half truths and nearly ludicrous excuses. He explained that he had been sick, pumped full of medicine and ordered by his doctor to "DROP ALL INTELLECTUAL LABOR FOR SOME TIME and, finally, engage in riding as the main form of treatment. . . . With the utmost reluctance I eventually gave way to the insistence of doctor and family, and joined Engels in Manchester." He asked Lassalle to kindly explain his situation to Duncker. He failed to mention when he might expect to deliver his manuscript.[53]

* * *

Back in London, Marx proclaimed himself well and working. "The damnable part of it is that my manuscript...is a real hotchpotch, much of it intended for much later sections," he told Engels. "So I shall have to make an index briefly indicating in which notebook and on which page to find the stuff I want to work on first." In other words, on the day Marx was to have completed his work he was actually only beginning to organize his notes. That was no mean undertaking: Marx had accumulated eight hundred pages.[54]

By mid-July there was still no manuscript, and Marx's financial situation, which had suffered while he was in Manchester, required that he spend all his time trying to raise money. London was experiencing a record heat wave as Marx trekked into the city by foot or omnibus to try to borrow money from one acquaintance on the assurance that another guaranteed its repayment. The heat was so intense and the drought so severe that most of the liquid flowing along the Thames was sewage, and the stench made it impossible to breathe.[55] Marx told Engels the situation was unbearable. Jenny was a particular concern: "The general unpleasantness has made a nervous wreck of my wife, and Dr. Allen, who, of course, suspects where the shoe PINCHES but doesn't know the real state of affairs, has now told me repeatedly and positively that he cannot rule out brain fever or something of the sort unless she is sent to a seaside resort for a longish stay." Marx described Jenny's problem as twofold—daily pressures and "the specter of final and unavoidable catastrophe."[56]

Out of desperation Marx went to a loan society, which advertised loans from five to two hundred pounds without security, on the strength of references alone. Freiligrath and a grocer gave Marx references, and Marx spent two pounds he could ill afford on fees to have his request processed, but in the end the loan was denied. Again he turned to Engels. He composed three long lists of expenditures and debts, and asked his friend whether he could see any way out of the financial mess in which he found himself. Marx's biggest expenses, according to his accounts, were the pawnshop, taxes, school fees, the doctor, and the newspaper vendor. Marx estimated that even if he tried to reduce expenses drastically by taking the children out of school, moving to a working-class lodging house, sending Lenchen and her sister away from the family, and living on potatoes, he would still not have the money to pay his creditors.

The SHOW OF RESPECTABILITY which has so far been kept up has been the only means of avoiding a collapse. I for my part wouldn't care a damn about living in Whitechapel, provided I could again at last secure an hour's peace in which to attend to my work. But in view of my wife's condition just now such a metamorphosis might entail dangerous consequences, and it could hardly be suitable for growing girls....

I would not wish my worst enemy to have to wade through the QUAGMIRE in which I've been trapped for the past two months, fuming the while over the innumerable vexations that are ruining my intellect and destroying my capacity for work.[57]

Engels estimated that Marx needed fifty to sixty pounds urgently, and he said he could arrange to get his hands on about forty. But, he said, it was time for Marx to "have a go" at his mother or his uncle.[58] Marx attempted an approach to his mother, using a portrait of Eleanor as an excuse to resume the contact he had let lapse for years. Though her initial response was somewhat positive, she quickly went cold.[59] In the end it was Engels's money that once again saved Marx, with intervention by Freiligrath, who arranged the complicated transaction.[60]

Marx paid off what debts he could and then packed Jenny off to the coastal town of Ramsgate, a favorite among the English gentry and known as the "lung" of London for its healthy air.[61] She settled in among what Marx derisively called refined and clever Englishwomen: "After years during which she has enjoyed only inferior company, if any at all, intercourse with people of her own kind seems to agree with her." Within days Jenny sent for Lenchen and the children.[62] Their term at the South Hampstead College for Ladies had ended triumphantly: Jennychen won the school's top general prize in her class as well as the top French prize, and Laura took the second-highest class prize.[63]

Meanwhile Marx sent his *Tribune* articles to Jenny in Ramsgate to be copied out and forwarded to New York, and Lenchen's sister Marianne stayed in London to see to the house. All of this was designed to make sure that Marx had the time and space he needed to finish his manuscript, the completion of which he acknowledged was urgent.[64] Instead of working, however, Marx became sick again. On September 21, after not corresponding with Engels for weeks, he told him the reason was his liver. Any writing cost him tremendous effort, and because of that, he expected his manuscript would not go off to Duncker for two weeks.[65] A month later, on October 22, he said it would still be weeks before he would be able to send it to Berlin.[66]

By November, Lassalle was also wondering about the manuscript. A friend had visited Marx and Freiligrath, and reported back that, contrary to what Karl described in his letters, he was living in "splendid circumstances" with a beautiful wife. Marx quickly explained that he and Freiligrath had painted a bright picture of his situation for the visitor because Marx did not want "this average German bourgeois" to have the "malicious satisfaction" of knowing the truth. He then tried to offer a plausible explanation for keeping Duncker waiting. True, he had health and domestic problems, he said, but the real reason for the delay was his concern over form: "To me the style of everything I wrote seemed tainted by liver trouble. And I have a twofold motive for not allowing this work to be spoiled on medical grounds." The first was that it was the product of fifteen years' labor, which Marx called the best years of his intellectual life, and also that his work contained an important view of social relations that would be described scientifically for the first time. "Hence I owe it to the party that the thing shouldn't be disfigured by the kind of heavy, wooden style proper to a disordered liver." Once again he appealed to Lassalle to intervene with Duncker and explain his position. "I shall have finished about four weeks from now, having only just begun the actual writing."[67]

Weeks of fabrications and evasions followed in letters to Engels as Marx struggled to finish his book:

November 29: Jenny was copying out the manuscript.[68]

December 22: The manuscript must go to the publisher by the end of the year. "There is, quite literally, no time to lose."[69]

Mid-January: He had not yet mailed the manuscript, and though it amounted to three installments for a total of 192 pages, and though it was titled *Capital in General,* it contained nothing as yet on capital.[70]

January 21: The "ill-fated manuscript" was ready to be sent, but he did not have the money for postage and insurance.[71]

Finally, on January 26, 1859, Marx wrote a three-line letter to Engels saying the manuscript, *A Contribution to the Critique of Political Economy,* had gone off to Duncker.[72]

Marx wondered, if the book was a success in Berlin, whether he should approach a publisher in London about an English translation.[73]

27

~~~~~

London, 1859

*Alas, 'tis terrible to be wise when it brings the
wise man no reward.*

—Sophocles[1]

As MARX WORKED on his manuscript, the global financial crisis that he
and Engels had expected would precipitate revolution ended without
destroying the capitalist system, provoking social upheaval, or toppling
any governments. Prussia had a new ruler, but the cause was entirely natural. King Friedrich Wilhelm had gone insane in 1858, and his brother,
Wilhelm, took over as regent. Wilhelm had once been a lightning rod,
because it was believed he ordered troops in Berlin to open fire on the
crowd in March 1848, thereby triggering the deadly revolt in that city.[2]
But Regent Wilhelm soon pleased those who might have opposed him by
purging government of the men behind the previous decade's repression.[3]
Among them was Jenny's brother Ferdinand.[4]

It was as if dawn had finally broken over reactionary Prussia. Wilhelm
looked to England and the West rather than Russia for alliances, and
appointed moderate liberals to his cabinet.[5] Political, cultural, and professional groups were to some extent allowed, and there were rumors of an
amnesty for political exiles. Heightening the sense of celebration accompanying these new freedoms, the year also marked the hundredth anniversary
of the birth of Germany's great poet, dramatist, historian, and philosopher
Johann Christoph Friedrich von Schiller. Throughout the Bund and German communities in Europe and America, festivals commemorated the
man who was seen as the embodiment of German cultural identity.[6]

Though Marx and Engels had not witnessed the revolution they'd so hoped for, what transpired instead was encouraging—a changing climate in their native land that made their goal of working-class political parties and organizations increasingly possible. After years of surreptitious gatherings, such groups could now work aboveground, preparing the way for an end to monarchical-capitalist-bourgeois rule, the reign of the proletariat, and, ultimately, the abolition of classes. It was also an environment in which Marx's writings might be published, if for no other reason than that his nemesis, Ferdinand von Westphalen, was no longer in a position to thwart him.

Throughout the early months of 1859 Marx waited anxiously for signs that his book was moving toward publication. Jenny, too, waited, boasting to family in Prussia of the imminent publication of a large work by her husband, who she said had ruined his health the previous year in intense study.[7] Not only did the pair view the book as important for the "party" and Marx's reputation, but they also expected it to be a major source of income: once released in Germany it could be translated and published in England, a much more lucrative market.[8]

Though Marx had been eight months late getting his book to the publisher, he expected no delays from Duncker. As he awaited news from Berlin, his anxiety was evident in every letter he wrote to Engels. One can almost feel his agitation as he paced his study, waiting for the postman's knock. Two weeks passed, then a month. Six weeks after receiving the manuscript, Duncker sent Marx only one proof sheet to review. Marx was beside himself with frustration.[9] He felt that his work needed to be published immediately to have any relevance, and more practically, he wanted to be paid. Yes, his contribution had been much delayed, but that was *creation;* all Duncker had to do, the exasperated author may have contended, was typeset the thing.

Marx saw Lassalle as the problem. He was sure that Duncker had set aside his economic book in favor of a work of fiction by Lassalle.[10] In the meantime, Duncker had also published an anonymous pamphlet by Engels called *Po and Rhine* on military tensions between Austria, France, and Prussia.[11] After nine weeks Marx had received only three proof sheets, or about 48 pages, of the 192-page work. Marx wrote Lassalle to say it appeared to him that Duncker was regretting having undertaken the book, and that was why he was handling it in such a dilatory fashion.[12]

With no publication in sight, Marx finally told Lassalle of his financial situation and asked him to back him on a short-term loan.[13] Lassalle demurred. Instead he contacted a cousin, who offered to employ Marx in a news service, telegraphing reports from London.[14] Despite complicated and costly logistics, and the fact that Marx did not agree with the news service's political slant, Marx jumped at the chance and excitedly described his expected earnings to Engels. But within weeks that scheme, like countless others, collapsed. Marx again blamed Lassalle.[15] He said Lassalle had criticized his cousin over the conservative bias of his news service and had made it appear that he spoke for Marx as well. Marx growled, "Thus the blockhead has frustrated the best prospect I had for the summer."[16]

Everywhere Marx turned, he met with frustration. By mid-May the first installment of his economic book was supposed to be ready, but the date came and went without word of its publication. Instead, Duncker had published a pamphlet by Lassalle on military matters along the lines of Engels's work.[17] Marx's suspicion that Lassalle's writing was getting preferential treatment was heightened when he learned that Lassalle had moved out of the Countess von Hatzfeldt's home and now lived in Duncker's house.[18]

On May 21, 1859, four days after returning the last proofs to Berlin, Marx used a transparent ploy to press Duncker to set a publication date, by telling him he had one hundred orders for the book from America and needed to know a price.[19] But that attempt apparently met with no response, and Marx sent off a blistering letter to Duncker accusing him of deliberate procrastination. "I hereby demand, and indeed categorically, that you desist from these machinations, the purpose of which seems to me exceedingly suspect. All my acquaintances in England are of the same opinion." (That is to say, Engels, Lupus, and Jenny.)[20]

At about the time Marx was ready to explode, the German Workers' Educational Society in London began publishing a newspaper, *Das Volk*.[21] Marx had not had anything to do with the Workers' Society or exile politics since 1851. He associated regularly with fewer than a dozen people beyond his family, and while in letters he and Engels ridiculed exiles outside their small circle, they did not do so publicly, and so they did not draw the kind of fire they had during their first years in London. But Marx seemed to be looking for a fight. He was angry and frustrated, and saw the potential for mischief-making through the press. (He wrote, "Life here in London is too tough for one not to indulge in distractions of this kind every eight years or so.")[22] He told Engels that *Das Volk* was a "dilettante rag" but it could be used to torment their longtime rival Gottfried "Jesus Christ" Kinkel, who had his own newspaper.[23]

Liebknecht and *Das Volk* founder Elard Biskamp had actually asked Marx to collaborate with them on the paper. Though he had initially declined, it seemed that he could not withstand the temptation of having a newspaper at his disposal, and he soon began offering what he called "'pointers' about this and that."[24] His influence grew; at Marx's prodding

Das Volk began printing broadsides at Kinkel and his allies, and at critics on the Continent. That in turn reawakened all the animosity against the "Marx party" lying dormant in exile circles.

Marx went to Manchester in June to see Engels and Lupus. Far from steering him away from a reckless course, they encouraged his rage, believing that his groundbreaking economic work was being kept from the world by a publisher too ignorant to recognize its value. On June 22 Marx wrote Duncker another letter scolding him for breaking his promise to publish and pay for the book in early June. Marx threatened to put a notice in newspapers explaining why his book was delayed. No doubt exaggerating again, he said the step was necessary because he had received so many inquiries about it that he could not respond to each one individually.[25] Marx's letter to Duncker proved doubly embarrassing. Unbeknownst to Marx, a thousand copies of his *Contribution to the Critique of Political Economy* had come off the press eleven days earlier, and he had gravely insulted the man he hoped would publish his next work.[26]

The volume's release caused Marx more anxiety as he awaited reaction to his book. Engels declared that he liked it,[27] which was a subdued response compared with his usual praise for Marx's writing. Others in their circle were frankly perplexed. Liebknecht said he had never been so disappointed in a book, and *Das Volk*'s Biskamp told Marx he didn't understand its purpose.[28] It was no surprise that the work was mystifying for Marx's associates: the *Contribution* read like a man theorizing for himself, Marx in midthought, somewhere between his "1844 Manuscripts" and the future *Capital*. The preface laid out Marx's argument for the material basis of history, but the subsequent sections read like fragments, raising questions but failing to answer them.[29]

In the wider press there was no reaction at all, aside from a review Engels wrote for *Das Volk,* which was picked up in some German-language newspapers, most notably in America.[30] Jenny and Marx called the lack of response a "conspiracy of silence,"[31] and it nearly drove Marx mad. He told Lassalle, "You're mistaken, by the by, if you think that I expected glowing tributes from the German press, or gave a rap for them. I expected to be attacked or criticized but not to be utterly ignored, which, moreover, is bound to have a serious effect on sales. Considering how vehemently these people have, at various times, railed against my communism, it was to be expected that they would now unleash their wisdom against the theoretical argument in support of the same."[32] Fuming, Marx wrote Engels to say his émigré rivals were rejoicing over his apparent failure.[33]

In July, Marx developed an illness he blamed on the heat.[34] In August he was still vomiting.[35] In addition to disappointment over his book, Marx's family was in full financial meltdown. They had pawned everything they could, and Jenny was forced to appear in county court to defend the family against creditors' demands, but she arrived too late to make her case for a more liberal repayment schedule. The debts remained unchanged and pressing.[36] In the midst of these personal calamities, Marx had assumed editorial control of *Das Volk,* which meant that he was financially responsible for it, too. Its finances were in worse shape than his family's, but he was optimistic, telling Engels, "I am convinced that, within six weeks, the thing will be on a solid footing."[37] On August 26 he announced, " '*Das Volk' is no more.* . . . The FACT is that as the paper improved, losses increased and readers fell off."[38] Soon afterward the paper's printer sued Marx for twelve pounds.[39]

The pit Marx found himself in was deep. And worst of all, he was viewed by his enemies as defeated, which he found intolerable. Isolated and bereft, he told Engels in September, "There is absolutely no-one to whom I can freely unburden myself."[40] But Engels had his own problems. He had been insulted by an Englishman at a drunken gathering and hit him with an umbrella. Unfortunately the man's eye was struck, and while there was no permanent damage, the Englishman demanded compensation that Engels feared could amount to two hundred pounds. "On top of which there would be a public scandal and a ROW with my old man, who would have to put up the money," Engels said. "The worst of it is that I'm completely in the hands of this swine and his SOLICITOR. . . . Needless to say these blasted English don't want to deprive themselves of the pleasure of getting their hands on a BLOODY FOREIGNER."[41] What this meant for Marx was that he could expect nothing from Engels until the case was settled.

With friendship but also funds in mind, Marx suggested that Engels skip town and go to the Continent,[42] but given his social and business position in Manchester, Engels dismissed that possibility out of hand.[43] With no other money on the horizon, Jenny took the drastic step of approaching her brother Ferdinand for a loan behind her husband's back. Marx would have never approved—not only out of pride but because if his enemies learned of the source, it would revive all the old rumors about collaboration between the two. Perhaps luckily for Jenny, Ferdinand pleaded poverty now that he was out of work, and so she did not compromise Marx with the transaction. She, however, felt sullied by what she called the "unpleasant step" she had been forced to take.[44]

Marx had seemingly done all he could to alienate Duncker and ensure that his firm did not publish the next installment of his economic work,

276

but by October Marx appeared to realize that Duncker still represented the best chance he had for getting it into print in Germany. Hoping he would again approach Duncker on his behalf, Marx told Lassalle he had considered another publisher (though there is no indication that was the case) but decided it would be best if the first two installments came out under the same imprint. "I shall now be obliged to remodel the thing completely, as the manuscript for this second installment is already a year old." He thought he could have it done by December at the very latest. He also informed Lassalle that he was translating the first installment into English (though there is no evidence that was the case either). "At any rate I am assured of a better reception in England than in Germany where, so far as I am aware, nobody inquires after the thing or gives a straw for it. All I want is to place the whole of this *first* section, at least, before the German public. Should the latter continue to pay no heed to the work, I intend to put all subsequent sections straight into English."[45]

Marx told Engels he felt confident that the second installment would proceed easily, but within a month he admitted he was making very little progress.[46] "In some ways I envy you for being able to live in Manchester, cut off as you are from the war between mice and frogs. Down here I have to wade through all this ordure and do so in circumstances which already consume too much of the time I should be devoting to my theoretical studies."[47]

By December, Marx was drowning. He told Engels he had been cited in county court for nonpayment by small creditors, paid five pounds to settle the *Das Volk* suit brought by the printer, and had fed Biskamp for three months because he was ill and had no income.[48] Marx wanted Engels to come to London for Christmas. In addition to his own peace of mind and that of his wife, he said, "it's absolutely essential for my girls to have a 'human being' in the house again for once. The poor children have been too early tormented by domestic misery."[49]

Indeed, it is hard to imagine how Jennychen and Laura, now fifteen and fourteen respectively, coped in their tumultuous household. They witnessed their father's creative torment, heard him rage against the conspiracy of his enemies, and felt the humiliation of creditors banging at the door. In a letter to Ferdinand's wife, Jenny painted a gloriously rose-tinted picture of her daughters' existence: "Both our tall girls continue making us happy with their lovely, friendly and modest nature. They use all the rare spare time they have left beside school and the many private lessons to pamper their little sister to their heart's content. In exchange the small, graceful, brown curled girl always runs toward them with opened arms, and when the girls come home over the fresh, smiling, evergreen meadows charged with their satchels and drawing folders, there is always a reunion ceremony as if the girls had been on a trip around the world."[50] This was the same spot Jenny had earlier described as so muddy that when they returned home they carried the weight of a village on their shoes.[51] The truth, inevitably, lay somewhere between the two descriptions.

What was clear was that the girls were thriving intellectually. Again in 1859, Jennychen took the top general prize at her school and Laura took two second prizes.[52] They could speak English, German, and French; read and write in English, German, French, and Italian; and knew a smattering of Spanish (at least parts of *Don Quixote*).[53] They played piano, sang duets, painted portraits. They had the upbringing any middle-class girls might be expected to have at that period in England. But in addition, thanks to their father, they had an intensive education in politics.

In late December, Jenny reported that her eldest daughter had all but put her out of business as Marx's copyist for the *Tribune*. In a Christmas letter to Engels (who despite Marx's entreaties did not come to London for the holiday) Jenny was philosophical about her changing role (she said teasingly she was mainly dismayed that she could not get a pension for having served so long as Marx's secretary) and their latest year of misery. "Had we been 'BETTER OFF' this year," she wrote, "I'd have seen the funnier side of all this trouble, but humor goes by the board when one is constantly having to struggle against the pettiest *misère;* never have I found it so oppressive as now, when our dear little girls, who are blossoming so sweetly, have to endure it too. And then, on top of that, the secret hopes we had long nourished in regard to Karl's book were all set at naught by the Germans' *conspiracy of silence.*"[54]

Jenny often observed that no matter how bleak their situation, Marx managed to remain optimistic, such was his confidence in the ultimate success of his ideas. At times she almost apologetically portrayed herself as the realist of the two, as if seeing their lives clearly was an act of betrayal. At no time did Jenny express doubt in Marx's brilliance, but she did doubt the reception his works would receive. She had no faith in the public's ability to comprehend his ideas. Like a hardened revolutionary, she believed the only way to get its attention was a bigger bomb, and Jenny believed Marx's *next* work would be that explosion. She told Engels, "The second installment may startle the slugabeds out of their lethargy and then they will attack its line of thought the more ferociously for having kept silent about the scientific nature of the work. *We'll see.*"[55]

Jenny may have been hopeful because the previous month, a difficult work of science by another writer in England had made its obscure author instantly famous. Charles Darwin had burst on the scene on November 22 with his book *On the Origin of Species by Means of Natural Selection.*[56] Of their circle, Engels read it first and declared it "absolutely splendid.... Never before has so grandiose an attempt been made to demonstrate historical evolution in Nature, and certainly never to such good effect."[57] Marx said it was "the book which, in the field of natural history, provides the basis for our views."[58] Marx and his friends spoke for months of Darwin and the revolutionary power of science. Liebknecht came to the conclusion that Darwin, in his English country home, was "preparing a revolution similar to the one Marx was initiating himself at the turbulent center of the world—only that he inserted his lever at a different place."[59]

Darwin's book had sold out in a single day, and Jenny may have consoled herself that a breakthrough of such proportions awaited her husband. She clung to that belief as to a life raft.

But instead of working on his all-important second installment, Marx spent the next year continuing a war of words with a former member of the defunct Frankfurt National Assembly who now worked as a geography teacher, journalist, and provincial politician in Switzerland. Marx believed the fight was for the very future of the party, but his friends watched in dismay as he spent all his time and a staggering amount of money on legal and literary battles over an insult he should have ignored.

The episode had begun with a bit of gossip exchanged at an event in May 1859. At the time, France and Austria were at war over Austria's hold on Northern Italy. Marx's old friend Karl Blind told him that the German democrat Carl Vogt had received money from Napoleon in exchange for pro-French propaganda—both of his own creation and from any writers he could bribe. Vogt and his friends had started a newspaper in Switzerland and used it to promote the position that France should be favored in the fight against Austria.[60]

Marx loved gossip, and he passed this tidbit along to Engels in a letter on May 18, saying Vogt had sold himself to Bonaparte.[61] He also mentioned the rumor to *Das Volk's* Biskamp, who published the unsourced accusation in the paper and sent Vogt a copy for a response.[62] The insular and insecure world of German exiles was a mesh of connection and affinity, more often spiderweb than safety net. Marx was deeply involved with *Das Volk,* so Vogt, who had an antagonistic history with Marx dating back to the *Neue Rheinische Zeitung,* named Marx as the source of what Vogt called scandalous lies.[63]

The affair was the proverbial tempest in a teapot, confined to small-circulation newspapers read by German exiles. But it flared up when Liebknecht got hold of a pamphlet titled *A Warning,* which contained the same charges against Vogt but in greater detail.[64] Liebknecht sent a report on the scandal to the *Augsburger Allgemeine Zeitung,* which had the widest circulation of any German newspaper in the first half of the nineteenth century.[65] Vogt sued the paper, though the case was dropped for technical reasons. He emerged vindicated, however, because the *Allgemeine Zeitung* had not been able to prove he was an agent of Napoleon or even identify the source of the rumor. Marx came out the loser.[66] Nearly everyone outside his immediate circle believed he was the author, even after a friend of Blind's stepped forward to say he had written the pamphlet against Vogt.[67]

Were there not greater battles worth fighting? Of course. But the drama reached a pitch at the end of 1859, amid Marx's disappointment over his economic book and during an acute phase in his chronic personal financial crisis. Because he was incapable of ordering any other aspect of his life, Marx fixated on the Vogt affair with maniacal intensity. He turned the full force of his fury on Vogt and those associated with him, and in the process strained relations with some of his most valued friends, including Freiligrath and Liebknecht, whom he accused of a range of crimes that all amounted to a single transgression: Marx believed they took sides against him.

Freiligrath was especially wounded by Marx's attacks and announced that he would withdraw from all party activities as a result.[68] The loss was personal for Marx, because Freiligrath had been one of his closest companions since 1844, but it was also financial: he often relied on Freiligrath's position as a banker to negotiate deals that kept the Marx family afloat. This in mind, Marx sent Freiligrath a long apology, though privately he did not forgive him.[69] Jenny went so far as to break off all relations with the Freiligrath family, saying simply, "I am not fond of half MEASURES."[70]

Thus, 1860, which was supposed to be the year Marx was recognized for his erudition, instead became a year of ignominy. In January he learned Vogt had published a book called *My Action Against the Allgemeine Zeitung* that named Marx as the source of libels against him.[71] Vogt then went into colorful detail about Marx's alleged history as the head of a gang of ruffians who engaged in blackmail, extortion, and counterfeiting while plotting acts of violence—all in the name of the proletariat. Marx's real allegiance, Vogt declared, lay with his aristocratic brother-in-law, Ferdinand von Westphalen.[72]

The book sold out its first printing of three thousand copies, and a second was ordered.[73] It was also excerpted in Berlin's popular liberal *National-Zeitung,* which identified Marx as leader of a group of blackmailers called the "Brimstone Gang" that threatened to denounce people in Germany as enemies of the state unless they paid a specified amount of money. It further claimed that Marx and his cohorts worked with the secret police in Germany and France. Marx was portrayed as a scoundrel and a thug who conned the workingman and ruled his gang "with a rod of iron."[74]

Marx did his best to keep news of Vogt's pamphlet and the *National-Zeitung* from Jenny, but he discussed it repeatedly with Engels as he awaited copies to see exactly what slanders they contained.[75] Engels understood his friend well enough to know that the antagonism with Vogt would consume him, and he tried to remind Marx that the only real way to disarm Vogt and all their critics was to complete the next installment of his own book. "I hope that you won't let the Vogt affair stop you from getting on with it," Engels pleaded. "Do try for once to be a little less conscientious with regard to your own stuff; it is, in any case, far too good for the wretched public. The *main* thing is that it should be written and published; the shortcomings that catch your eye certainly won't be apparent to the jackasses."[76] Marx assured Engels he was working and could finish the next installment within six weeks, but he had decided in the meantime to sue the *National-Zeitung.* "This lawsuit will be the peg on which we can hang the whole of our riposte to *the public at large* in court. Later on, we can turn our attention to that bastard Vogt."[77]

Marx began writing letters to former colleagues asking for testimonials concerning his work—theoretical and political—but the recipients would have been unable to read them unless Jenny copied them out in her legible hand. By early February it therefore became necessary that she be informed of the Vogt affair so she could transcribe his letters and legal documents.[78] Jenny later described this as the start of a year of sleepless nights. She was worried not only about her husband, but about her daughters, who would be exposed to the calumnies against him.[79] Adding to the family's torment, the reports were not confined to Germany, but also appeared in New York and, worse, London, where the girls' friends might read them.[80] The *Daily Telegraph* picked up the story and ran what Engels called "two columns about Vogt's shit."[81]

Marx declared in public statements that he was preparing legal action against the *National-Zeitung,*[82] and in private told Engels he had threatened the "dogs" at the *Daily Telegraph* with libel.[83] In a letter to the *Telegraph* Marx demanded the editors apologize for "vilifying a man of whose personal character, political past, literary productions, and social standing, you cannot but confess to be utterly ignorant."[84] The *Telegraph* responded by printing an article by its Berlin correspondent that, far from apologizing, accused Marx of attacking a British newspaper because he could not refute the accusations circulating against him in Germany.[85]

Though Marx believed the press had the right to insult writers, politicians, actors, and other public figures, in this case, he said, the *National-Zeitung* had picked out all the slanders from Vogt's book and strung them together like "dry bones." Newspapers, he was certain, pandered to a public whose political prejudices led them to believe the worst. And, he said, because of his long absence from political life, that public had no basis upon which to judge the truth or falsehood of Vogt's statements. "Quite apart from any political considerations," Marx wrote, "I therefore owed it to my family, my wife and children" to bring the case to court.[86]

During his first burst of activity preparing ammunition for a Berlin lawyer who agreed to represent him in a libel case, Marx dispatched more than fifty letters. He contacted all his associates from the early days in Berlin, Paris, Brussels, Cologne, and London, who were now spread across the globe. His goal was to describe his career, such that it was, and counter the Brimstone Gang accusations.[87] If necessary, he was even prepared to have Ferdinand called as a witness, though Jenny wanted to avoid the family scandal that would ensue.[88]

Explaining that his own house was in a state of utter pandemonium, Marx went to Manchester and set up, with help from Engels and Lupus, a smaller version of the defense committee formed during the Cologne Communist League trial.[89] Marx's lawyer sent him encouraging signals about the case, and testimonials from old friends arrived verifying Marx's side of the story. Marx told one ex-comrade, "I ought to account Mister Vogt's attack a blessing, if only because it has brought me into closer contact with the doyen of our revolution and our emigration."[90] A vote had even been taken at a gathering of workingmen in London censuring Vogt and backing Marx.[91] If nothing else, said Jenny, the case was helping Marx distinguish "true and loyal friends from shams. What a difference between the lesser folk and the GRANDEES."[92]

Some of these friends, though still strangers to Marx, could be found in Russia, which continued to benefit from the relatively liberal policies of Alexander II. Marx's *Contribution to the Critique of Political Economy* was beginning to sell there, and a University of Moscow professor had lectured on it.[93] "Russia has always been good ground for you," Jenny wrote Marx excitedly.[94]

Marx's Manchester stay appeared to do them both good. With Marx's departure went the raging storm that emanated from the first-floor room where he worked—smoking, cursing, pacing, and talking aloud to the letters he received. When Marx was home, the household was thoroughly engaged in his needs and activities; his work was their work, his moods affecting them all. In this the Marx family was typically Victorian — the man was the sun around which all the women in the home were duty-bound to revolve. That is not to say the Marx women and Lenchen did so unwillingly — their life's mission was to protect Marx and his ideas. But the job was exhausting, and so Marx's visits with Engels were often holidays for the women left behind. This time they used his absence to redecorate. Jenny had unexpectedly received money from an old family investment and decided to use it frivolously.[95] Lenchen, Marianne, Jenny, and the girls — except four-year-old Tussy, who was mainly a source of entertainment — painted walls, moved worn carpets, and rotated furniture from one room to another to give the house a new look. They even managed to "buy" some new furniture by exchanging their old pieces for items in the pawnshop (Jenny called the pawnshop owner her "right hand man"), including a fashionable, machine-made wool Brussels carpet of vibrant colors and cane chairs to replace leather ones that were missing legs.[96] Jennychen had done some pastel copies of Old Master paintings during the past year. These were hung on the walls in gold frames.[97]

The renovation was completed just before Jennychen's sixteenth birthday, on May 1. There is no letter describing the event, but doubtless, even given the Vogt imbroglio, they celebrated. The Marx family was an embattled, miniature world unto itself, and each of its milestones was marked like a national holiday. Marx especially would have wanted to honor Jennychen, and would not have allowed his troubles, no matter how grave, to disrupt it. He had a special bond with his eldest daughter, who even as a teenager had a deep understanding of his work. He had also watched with appreciation as she nurtured her siblings when he and Jenny were incapacitated by personal or financial distress or illness. Without complaint she had voluntarily made sacrifices unusual for a child, and they told on her face and figure. She was warm and pretty, and had an easy laugh and a wit to match her parents', but she never looked particularly young. Worry shadowed her eyes and etched lines across her forehead. She instinctively drew some of the sting felt by her parents in order to free her younger sisters to be lovely and gay. Her efforts were noble but costly. From the time she was a teenager she suffered respiratory problems that left her physically delicate.

Of all his children, Marx said, Jennychen was most like him.[98] At sixteen she was earnest and cerebral, and not at all preoccupied with romance. She wanted an occupation. And while she valued the one she had, working with her father, Jennychen also wanted one of her own, and she believed she had found it in drama. The Marx family loved the theater and went whenever they could to see Shakespeare performed at the nearby

Sadler's Wells Theatre or in Shoreditch, in East London (they stood during performances because they could not afford seats[99]). The family's conversation sparkled with lines from plays, but Jenny and Marx did not want their daughter to become an actress. For a young middle-class woman in Victorian England, when even table legs were covered out of a sense of decency, a life of exposure on the stage was a most disreputable aspiration. Still, her mother recognized Jennychen's talent, her beautiful voice (which she described as low and sweet), and her excellent elocution. She told a friend that neither she nor Marx would have held Jennychen back from the stage had she really set her heart on it, except for concerns over her health. Quietly, Jennychen began a campaign to change their minds.

Marx's Manchester trip ended abruptly when Engels got word that his father had died of typhoid fever. Engels received permission from the Prussian government to return home.[100] It was his first visit there since being expelled from Cologne in 1849, and he stayed for several weeks before returning to Manchester to begin negotiations on restructuring his father's firm.[101] But even before the details were agreed, Engels came into money and astonished Marx by sending him one hundred pounds. Marx called the windfall a "glorious surprise.... The whole family was filled with glee."[102]

The money may have helped blunt the impact of a barrage of bad news. The public prosecutor in Berlin rejected Marx's criminal libel suit against the editor of the *National-Zeitung,* contending that "no issue of public importance is raised by this matter."[103] Next, on June 26, Marx learned that his criminal libel suit against the paper itself had been thrown out for lack of indictable offense,[104] and in late July his appeal was rejected by the high court in Berlin.[105] He and Engels knew it was hopeless, but Marx told his lawyer to take the case to the supreme court to see if he could file a civil suit[106]—more of Engels's money down the drain. In the meantime Marx set to work writing a polemical pamphlet against Vogt.

Jenny and Engels had watched the year slip away without any progress on Marx's important work—his life's work—on economics. He also let slide nearly all his writing for the *Tribune,* which he depended on Engels to supply in his stead so he could continue to draw money from the paper. Jenny and Engels expressed their anxiety and frustration to each other. She wrote Engels in mid-August to say she hoped to start copying out the Vogt pamphlet that week. "The thing is taking ages, and I'm afraid Karl is making too *thorough* a job of it." She also reported that Marx had taken no steps toward finding a publisher.[107]

Engels rarely lost his temper with Marx, but he did over Vogt. He had seen this pattern from their first days together writing *The Holy Family,* which was supposed to be a pamphlet but grew into a three-hundred-page book. Engels had been carrying Marx's journalistic load and trying to find a publisher for the Vogt polemic, but Marx was apparently so immersed in his writing that he ignored Engels's letters and advice. Engels angrily wrote Jenny that at the rate Marx was going, his pamphlet would not appear until 1861, "and there'll be no one to blame but Mr. Mohr himself. . . . We're forever producing truly splendid things, but take care to see that they never appear on time, and so they are all flops. . . . Insist for all you're worth on something being done—and *done immediately*—about a publisher, and on the pamphlet being finished at long last. Otherwise we shall wreck all our chances and ultimately find ourselves without any publisher *at all.*"[108]

Another month passed and Marx was still not finished, but he was preparing to strike a deal to publish his anti-Vogt work in London. The firm had never before produced a book and wanted Marx to pay fifty to sixty pounds up front, money Marx hoped to collect from friends.[109] Engels was vehemently opposed to the arrangement, saying he had no confidence in a publisher who wanted money in advance. He also said publishing in London would ensure that no one would ever read it: "The experience is one we have been through hundreds of times with émigré literature. Always the same ineffectuality, always money and labor gone down the drain."[110] Marx was not listening. He wrote Lassalle, "I have come to the conclusion that *printing in London* is the only possibility."

Marx told Lassalle the Vogt pamphlet could be paid for with ease and printed quickly. He seemed almost to have lost touch with reality and was full of grand plans for the future: "The time is approaching when our 'small' if, in a certain sense, 'powerful party' (inasmuch as the others do not know what they want, or do not want what they know) must devise its plan of campaign." He predicted that his second installment on economics would come out before the next Easter, in a "somewhat different form, more popular TO SOME DEGREE. Not, of course, as a result of any impulse from within myself, but, first, because Part II has an expressly revolutionary function, and, second, because the conditions I describe are more concrete."[111]

At about this time Marx sent Jenny and the children to the coast for a week.[112] It is not hard to imagine how much they would have needed a break from the Vogt madness, but they did not find much relief in Hastings—it rained their entire holiday. Jennychen described the party of women as covered in mud and looking like seaweed.[113]

By September 25 they were back in London, and Marx was at the point of selecting a title for his now two-hundred-page book. He suggested *Da-Da-Vogt,* an obscure reference to an Arab writer who was used by Napoleon in Algiers as Vogt had been used in Geneva. Marx said the meaning would become clear about halfway through the book,[114] and in a letter to Engels defended the title, saying it "will PUZZLE your philistine, pleases me and fits in with my SYSTEM OF MOCKERY and CONTEMPT." He said he would discuss it with Jenny, his "critical conscience."[115] One can imagine Engels tugging at his voluminous beard in exasperation. If Marx must give Vogt a nickname, he said, it should be one that is comprehensible without having to read half the book! "Your system of MOCKERY AND CONTEMPT is unlikely to produce anything but a title that is affected or contrived."[116] Marx gave way—perhaps because he had ignored all of Engels's wishes up to that point and needed his friend to finance the work. But Marx did not concede the point easily. He said that despite Jenny's most learned remark that even Greek tragedy used mystifying titles, he would defer to Engels and simply call his book *Herr Vogt.*[117]

In October, Marx learned his last legal hope in the *National-Zeitung* suit had come to naught. His case was rejected by the supreme court in Berlin, which ruled it lacked foundation.[118] The decision forced Marx to revise his Vogt book in order to include what he called his "spree with Prussian justice."[119] Jenny had painstakingly copied and recopied the manuscript as Marx wrote and rewrote it. She soon became ill. In late November she developed a fever and other symptoms, but refused to see a doctor. Marx let several days pass, but her condition worsened and he called a physician, who immediately ordered the children out of the house; though he had not identified the illness, he feared it was contagious.[120] The girls packed up that afternoon and went into exile to the Liebknecht home in nearby Kentish Town. (Marx had offered to send them to a boarding school, but he told Engels they did not want to go because of the religious rites.)[121]

Within two days the doctor diagnosed Jenny with smallpox.[122] Months later Jenny wrote a friend, "You can imagine the horror and distress of the household on hearing this pronouncement."[123] There had not been a smallpox epidemic of any significance in England since 1830, and since 1853 vaccinations for newborns had been mandatory, so the death toll had diminished each year. However, those unfortunate enough to be exposed to even a minor outbreak of the virus would find no consolation in those statistics—at its most merciful, smallpox could mean disfigurement from the pustules that covered its victims; at its worst it meant death. The disease was such an effective killer, in fact, that it had been used as a weapon by colonizers invading the Americas. In England at the time Jenny was diagnosed, thousands of people still died each year from the disease.[124]

As he did when Musch was ill, Marx stopped all work and concentrated on his wife. He wrote Engels, "It's a ghastly disease. Should Lenchen catch it, I shall at once send her to hospital. So far, I have done the nursing (the bulk of it) myself.... For many weeks my wife had been in an exceptionally nervous state owing to our many TROUBLES, and was thus more liable TO CATCH the contagion in an omnibus, shop or the like." For himself, writing was out of the question: "The only occupation that helps me maintain the necessary QUIETNESS OF MIND is mathematics.... Last night was dreadful—indeed at the moment, I myself am SICK as well. The devil alone knows what misfortunes we suffer." Soon exhausted, Marx hired a nurse to help with the care.[125]

Each day he had food sent to the Liebknechts' and went there to dine with the family and the girls, but his visits were brief. The danger of Jenny's illness had not diminished. Though she remained conscious, she lost control of her limbs and bodily functions. She was racked with pain, on fire with fever, and unable to sleep. "All the time," she recalled, "I lay by an open window so that the cold November air must blow upon me. And all the while hell's fire in the hearth and ice on my burning lips, between which a few drops of claret were poured now and then. I was barely able to swallow, my hearing grew ever fainter and finally, my eyes closed up and I did not know whether I might not remain shrouded in perpetual night!"[126]

The acute phase of the disease lasted seven days, but the doctor advised that Jenny would be ill for a much longer period, and it was not safe to bring the children home. The course of the disease rendered the danger of infection greater than ever. Marx was vaccinated with cowpox against the virus, as was Lenchen, but they would have to remain quarantined in the house for ten days. Marx wrote Engels on November 28 to say the children were very frightened. They had only seen their mother from the street, when they looked up through her open window at the ghostly sight of her lying in her sickbed. Marx, meanwhile, found comfort in a massive toothache, which he said helped distract him from worry about his wife.[127]

Amid this family turmoil, *Herr Vogt* was finally published. Engels received his copy on December 5, and much to Marx's satisfaction declared it the best polemical work Karl had ever written.[128] Indeed, *Herr Vogt* was an alternately biting and hilarious refutation of the claims made against Marx, with Vogt presented as a Falstaffian purveyor of "cock-and-bull stories," as well as a swine, a fat rascal, a buffoon, and a skunk.[129] It was also an entertaining travelogue through the radical opposition in the first half of the nineteenth century, less an autobiography of Marx—though there were revealing anecdotes—than a biography of a movement replete with letters by the men at the center of it.

Perhaps if Marx had published his book in Germany immediately after Vogt's version sold out, he might have had a better reception. He tried to put a positive spin on sales—forty-one copies sold in London, then eighty. He even mused that "things are going so well Pesch [the publisher] is 'contemplating' a second edition."[130] But there would be no second edition. The publisher went bankrupt, and in addition to the initial publishing costs and legal fees, which had reached one hundred pounds, Marx was sued by the printer for twenty pounds.[131]

Jenny blamed the "base, cowardly, venal press" for condemning *Herr Vogt* to the same graveyard in which Marx's other recent works lay buried and all but forgotten. Marx may have anticipated that outcome when he wrote *Herr Vogt*. In his preface he observed: "I know in advance that the same astute men who shook their heads sagely at the importance of Vogt's 'revelations,' when his concoction first appeared, will now be unable to comprehend why I am wasting my time refuting his childish allegations; while the 'liberal' pen-pushers who gloatingly took up Vogt's commonplaces and worthless lies and hastened to hawk them around the German, Swiss, French and American press will now find my mode of dealing with themselves and their hero outrageously offensive. But never mind!"[132]

The Vogt story briefly resurfaced in Marx's circle in 1870, when records unearthed in the archives of the French government proved that the rumor at the core of the case was true. Vogt had received money from Napoleon, forty thousand francs, to be exact, in 1859—the very year Marx first passed along the rumor to Engels.[133] But that vindication of Marx would not occur for another decade, and when it did, it barely registered as a footnote. For Marx and Jenny it was merely a reminder of a distant and costly struggle, and in the meantime there would be so many more damaging personal and professional defeats.

28

London, 1861

Hitherto I have always found that, once they set out on a revolu-
tionary course, all men of really reliable character . . . constantly
draw fresh strength from their setbacks and become ever more res-
olute, the longer they swim in the stream of history.

—Karl Marx[1]

JENNY GRADUALLY STRENGTHENED, but she emerged from her illness disfigured, her lovely face covered in a reddish purple mask of coarse flesh.[2] The children were finally allowed to return home on Christmas Eve,[3] a dry and sunny day so uncharacteristic of December in London[4] that it seemed ordered up for the happy occasion. They ran into the house they had been barred from for weeks and up the stairs to see their mother. But cheer turned to horror when the girls saw her. All three burst into tears. The woman seated in their mother's bedroom was unrecognizable. Jenny confided to a friend that the change in her appearance was truly dramatic: "Five weeks before, I didn't look too bad alongside my blooming daughters. Since I was by some miracle still without a gray hair in my head and had still kept my teeth and figure, I was habitually considered to be well preserved—but how changed was all this now! To myself I looked like a rhinoceros, a hippopotamus, which belonged in a zoological garden rather than in the ranks of the Caucasian race."[5] Jenny and Marx had both taken pride in her beauty. Now that, like everything else they valued, was threatened. Marx told Engels the doctor believed that Jenny would eventually heal, but he said in parentheses—almost a written whisper—"my wife's complexion is still far from smooth and probably won't be for some time to come."[6] Jenny was not a shallow woman, but she attached much importance to her looks. Her weakened state, plus the added worry that she was repulsive, made her impatient and emotionally labile. Her daughters' homecoming was overshadowed by the physical and mental strains of her disease.[7]

Marx eventually succumbed to the stress, which he blamed on weeks of sleepless nights and worry. The family's debt had grown immeasurably over the past year, thanks to the Vogt affair and Jenny's smallpox[8] (which, he said, produced a "hair-raising DOCTOR'S BILL"[9]). Then came word from the *Tribune* that Marx had drawn payment for nineteen more articles than he had written, and he was ordered not to submit any for six weeks.[10] Furthermore, the encyclopedia project was suspended. Engels and Marx had made it only as far as the letter *C*.[11]

These decisions were not—or at least not entirely—indictments against Marx so much as a reflection of the fact that U.S. newspapers at that time were almost exclusively concerned with domestic news. Abraham Lincoln had just been elected president, and Southern states had begun seceding from the Union. Marx and Engels cheered Lincoln's election and also the turmoil in the South. Politically they saw the advantages of both, but for Marx personally, the American events threatened the only steady income he had, however inadequate. He told Engels, "As you can see, I am tormented as Job, though not as god-fearing."[12]

On January 12, 1861, after the death of Friedrich Wilhelm, Prussia's regent Wilhelm became King Wilhelm I and issued a decree granting amnesty to some refugees.[13] The wording of the clemency was vague. Some German exiles in London would be allowed to return, though the door would remain closed to others under threat of prosecution. Marx felt he fell into the latter category, but Lassalle, in Berlin, believed Marx would be welcome and suggested they revive the *Neue Rheinische Zeitung* there with funds from the Countess von Hatzfeldt.[14] Marx initially dismissed the idea, but as his financial troubles mounted, he warmed to the notion of a well-funded organ in the Prussian capital. The main impediment for both Marx and Engels was Lassalle's involvement, and also the issue of whether Marx would or could return to Prussia to work on it.[15] Reservations aside, Lassalle's proposition was the only one on the horizon that offered Marx the means to earn a living, and by then Marx was desperate. He gave himself credit for "real ingenuity" in preventing the breakup of his household by arranging payment schedules with his legion of creditors. But that was all he could do—shuffle debt, not pay it.

As he often did when a situation was beyond his control, Marx retreated into study. He told Engels that for fun he was reading Appian's *Civil Wars of Rome* in the original Greek, and found Spartacus a "capital fellow," Pompey a "real shit," and believed Caesar made "deliberately crazy" military blunders to confound his opponents.[16] Marx's companion during his evening escapes was his daughter Tussy. She had turned six that month, and for her birthday Marx gave her her first novel, a nautical tale titled *Peter Simple.*[17] The little girl with the curly brown hair and phenomenal memory was, in fact, already deeply immersed in literature. She knew scene upon scene of Shakespeare by heart[18] (her favorite was a soliloquy by Richard III, because she could hold a knife while she recited it[19]), had learned German in part by reading and hearing *Grimm's Fairy Tales,*[20] and in general conducted herself intellectually as if she were a contemporary not only of her sisters, who were ten years her senior, but of her forty-three-year-old father. She and Marx would read the same books and then sit in his study and discuss them. For example, while discussing *Peter Simple* Tussy confided to her father that she was plotting to dress up as a boy and run away to sea to join a man-of-war. Marx agreed that it was a fine idea but suggested that they shouldn't tell anyone until her plans were "well matured." Tussy also composed letters to Lincoln offering him advice on the war, which she entrusted to her father (he pledged to mail them to the White House but in fact kept them as treasures).[21] Jenny said Tussy helped relieve Marx's cares with peals of childish laughter.[22]

Despite such pleasant diversions, Marx finally concluded he could hide from his problems no longer. After years of avoiding the step, he determined his only option was to take a steamship to Holland to ask his uncle for a portion of his inheritance.[23] Since he could not travel under his own name, he used a passport made out to a cabinetmaker named Karl Johann Bühring. As he prepared to leave, Marx put Jenny and the family's needs in Engels's hands. His trip would be open-ended, first to Holland and then possibly to Berlin to meet Lassalle and discuss the proposed newspaper. In the meantime Jenny needed to pay the grocers, bakers, and butchers weekly.[24] (Marx also relied on Engels to supply the family with wine. He said Jenny greatly appreciated it, as did the children, who "would seem to have inherited their father's fondness for the bottle.")[25] He promised to write Engels from Holland and added an uncharacteristically candid closing: "You will know without my telling you how grateful I am for the outstanding proofs of friendship you have given me."[26]

Lion Philips was sixty-seven and stubborn. A merchant who had built a good business with his sons[27] (thirty years later it would become Philips Electronics), he was not prone to charity. Furthermore, his relations with his nephew Karl had been strained by politics. But when the younger man arrived in Holland, Marx poured on the charm. He transformed himself from the communist his uncle believed him to be to a bohemian—but bourgeois—writer. He enlisted Lassalle to help in the ruse by asking him to mail him a letter mentioning the "success" of his anti-Vogt pamphlet and their joint plans for a newspaper. Marx wanted the "confidential" letter written in such a way that he could show it to his uncle without seeming a fraud.[28] He also, perhaps with a great deal more relish, enlisted the help of his cousin Antoinette in softening up her father. Twenty-four-year-old Antoinette, known as Nanette, quickly fell in love with Marx, and he courted her without moderation during his visit.[29] He described her as charming, witty, and with "dangerously dark eyes."[30] Danger indeed: Nanette gave him her undivided attention, and after his harrowing year with the Vogt affair and Jenny's illness, Marx could not entirely resist.

He stayed in Zaltbommel more than two weeks before traveling on to Berlin. During his stay in Holland, Marx sent Jenny only one letter and Engels none at all. At times Jenny had no idea where he was, or whether he was safe. His travel documents were false, his position with the Prussian government uncertain at best. On top of her worry over Marx, Lenchen had fallen ill: she was delirious, raving, singing, weeping. Her leg was inflamed, and there was fear she might be hemorrhaging or gangrene would set in. Unable to reach Marx, Jenny turned for help to the only other person she could count on. Engels provided much more than she requested, including money for a doctor for Lenchen and the coal, food, and wine needed to speed her recovery.[31]

Some Marx biographers have suggested that Jenny and Engels were never close, because in letters they addressed each other as "Mrs. Marx" and "Mr. Engels." But Jenny greeted her most intimate female friends with such formality—"Mrs. Liebknecht" or "Mrs. Weydemeyer," for example. There was absolutely no correlation between the salutation Jenny used in letters to Engels and the depth of her appreciation for him. Some have also suggested that Jenny was jealous of Marx's relationship with Engels. That, too, is baseless. Jenny and Engels each had roles to play in Marx's life that were separate and distinct. It is quite clear that neither of them would have wanted sole responsibility for the force of nature known as Karl Marx without the help of the other. Finally, some have written that Jenny resented being dependent on Engels. No doubt that is true, but she did not blame Engels; Jenny would have wanted her husband to be able to support them without his friend's constant intervention. No, the man in Manchester had been their salvation, and Jenny was only too aware of his selflessness in shielding Marx from disasters personal and financial, almost from the moment they had met. This moment was no different. Jenny wrote Engels on March 16, "How can I thank you for all the love and devotion with which you have stood by us for years now in our sorrows and afflictions? I was so happy when I saw there was five times as much as I had expected, that it would be hypocritical not to admit it, and yet my joy was as nothing compared with Lenchen's! How joyously her almost lifeless eyes lighted up when I ran upstairs and told her, 'Engels has sent 5 pounds for your COMFORTS.' "[32]

In late March, Marx sent Jenny a brief note telling her he was in Berlin with Lassalle. He did not offer details except to say prospects were good and he would not come home empty-handed. He also sent her about seven pounds.[33] Marx still had not written a line to Engels, but on arrival in Berlin he sent Nanette Philips a multipage letter describing his activities in colorful detail. He may have written in part for the benefit of her father, but his letter seemed primarily designed to keep alive the flirtation he had begun in Holland with a woman nearly half his age.

Marx told Nanette that Lassalle lived on Bellevuestrasse, one of the finest streets in Berlin, and was joined there each evening by the Countess von Hatzfeldt. At fifty-six she was still beautiful, with penetrating blue eyes and blond hair swept back from her face into cascades of flowing locks, though her beguiling appearance required an assist from generously applied cosmetics. Marx described her as good company — vivacious, not at all stuffy, and, most favorably, interested in the revolution.[34] During his first days in Berlin, which had been transformed by gaslight[35] and seemed a different city from the one he had inhabited as a student, Lassalle and the countess feted Marx as a visiting dignitary. They held grand dinners in his honor attended by society figures and took him to the theater and the ballet, where they sat next to the royal box. Lassalle even intervened directly with the head of police to try to have Marx's Prussian citizenship restored. Marx contentedly agreed to extend his stay until the issue was resolved. In the meantime he settled into a life of luxury, unperturbed by the king, known in Prussia as Handsome Wilhelm, or his security forces.[36]

After more than two weeks in Berlin, Marx said in a letter to a friend in Barmen that he found being a social lion and meeting so many "wits" tedious.[37] He seemed in no hurry to leave, however. Marx wrote Jenny only cursory letters with the "driest of facts," she told Engels. By April he had still not written his friend in Manchester, which alarmed Engels because he read in a German newspaper that Marx and his family might move to Berlin. Jenny found it incomprehensible that Marx hadn't written him, and wanted to assure Engels there was no truth to the report. She did not even know why Marx wanted Prussian citizenship; she had no longing to return to Germany, and her daughters were horrified by the notion: "The idea of leaving the country of their precious Shakespeare appalls them; they've become English to the marrow and cling like limpets to the soil of England."[38] In any case, Jenny did not want her daughters falling under the influence of the countess and her circle.[39]

Marx's letters to Nanette, meanwhile, were abundant and increasingly intimate. He called her "my sweet little cousin," "my little charmer," and "my cruel little witch" (because she had not written). In one long letter he provided a transcript of a teasing conversation he said he had had with the Countess von Hatzfeldt, who had hoped to keep him in Berlin:

> *She.* "This, then, is the thanks for the friendship we have shown you, that you leave Berlin so soon as your business will permit?"
> *I.* "Quite the contrary, I have prolonged my stay at this place beyond the due term, because your amiability chained me to this Sahara."
> *She.* "Then I shall become still more amiable."
> *I.* "Then there remains no refuge for me but running away. Otherwise I should never be able to return to London whither my duty calls me."
> *She.* "This is a very fine compliment to tell a lady, her amiability is such as to drive you away!"
> *I.* "You are not Berlin. If you want to prove me the sincerity of your amiability, do run away with myself."

Marx signed his letter to his cousin "Your knight-errant."[40] Responding, Nanette called Marx "Pacha" and admitted her attachment to him was not entirely philosophical.[41]

The contrast between Marx's life in Berlin (not to mention his fantasy life) and Jenny's in London could not have been more extreme. She was struggling to keep a household running with cash from friends and loans from the pawnshop. She described herself as a member of the "progressive party of the league of boots," which meant she spent hours every afternoon in the city, tromping around trying to keep the family's life and finances in order.

Jenny detested Lassalle, but she wrote him a letter while Marx was in Berlin thanking him for the friendship he had shown her "lord and master," though she pleaded with him not to keep Marx too long: "That is the point where I become possessive and egoistic and envious." As for her traveling to Berlin, whether permanently or for a visit, she said no. Politically, Jenny explained that she had searched all the corners of her heart and discovered that she no longer had a fatherland. Personally, she said she could not return because she did not want friends to see her smallpox-scarred face. "At this moment I am still the highly fashionable color magenta so that you would all be scared by me. I have become so ugly and ravaged."[42]

Marx must have recognized Jenny's distress in her letters, no matter how much she tried to conceal it with humor. He would also have known that while he was surrounded by beautiful women—or at least women with fortune enough to make themselves beautiful—his wife spent what she called "sad hours" imagining her face as a "battlefield" he would not love.[43] Yet Marx appeared to show no sympathy for her position. He stayed nearly a month in Berlin, rarely communicating with his family. Perhaps their correspondence reminded him of the familiar troubles awaiting him when he returned, and he wanted to keep his head in the clouds for as long as possible. Still, as the days slipped by without any word on his citizenship or any resolution on the newspaper front, Marx began to grow anxious to leave. He seemed to have soured on Berlin; he told Nanette he would never leave England for Germany, much less for Prussia, where boredom reigned supreme.[44] In fact, during a brief trip to Elberfeld, Marx found the company so dull he had a friend lie and say he had lost his voice and couldn't speak.[45]

Marx's mother had invited him to stop in Trier, and so he left Berlin on April 12 to visit what remained of his family in the Rhineland. He had not seen his mother for at least thirteen years. She was now seventy-four and ill. It is unlikely that any deep thaw in their relations occurred, but in her own way she did show some warmth toward her prodigal son by tearing up IOUs that Marx had given her in years past, thereby relieving him of that debt against his inheritance.[46] Marx's next important stop was in Holland, to conclude business with his uncle and, as he told Lassalle later, pay court to Nanette.[47] He was successful on all fronts. He received £160 from Lion Philips[48] after convincing that gentleman he was an enterprising writer with prospects from Berlin to Vienna to New York. As for Nanette, that flame stayed alive even after Marx left Holland for home.

Marx boarded a steamer in Rotterdam on April 28 and arrived in London on April 29.[49] He had been gone since February 28. Apparently he had not told his family he was returning, because Jenny said they burst with joy—cheering, hugging, and kissing—when he opened the door at Grafton Terrace and surprised them. Everyone stayed up late into the night to hear his stories and rummage through gifts from Lassalle. The women, who each received an elegant cloak, modeled them in the parlor, with the girls laughingly peeking out from behind the deep collars and Jenny parading in full splendor—so much so that Tussy shouted, "Just like a peacock!" In thanking Lassalle, Jenny said she was anxious to take the "coat for a walk" to impress the local philistines.[50]

The day after Marx's return, Lion Philips's son Jacques arrived in London to stay with the family.[51] Jacques was a young lawyer in Rotterdam who had come ostensibly to talk politics with Marx but who Marx thought was more interested in meeting his daughters.[52] His timing was perfect. Jennychen's seventeenth birthday occurred on Wednesday, May 1. The celebration was joyous in the extreme. Her father was home, they had money in their pockets, beautiful clothes on their backs, and a young man to dance and sing with.[53] For once the storm clouds that shadowed every moment of their lives had receded.

The respite would not last long. By June the young man was gone, as was all the money Marx had received from his uncle. The familiar knock of the creditor resumed with even greater urgency. By the fall Marx was again busily borrowing from one friend by promising that another would pay, but his machinations were so swift and without the necessary consultations that he found he had promised what was not there to give. In a *mea culpa* to Engels over some loose transactions Marx had conducted in his name, he ended by saying, "May I wish you in advance every happiness for the New Year. If it's anything like the old one, I, for my part, would sooner consign it to the devil."[54]

29

London, 1862

If only I knew how to start some sort of BUSINESS! All theory,
dear friend, is gray, and only BUSINESS green. Unfortunately,
I have come to realize this too late.

—Karl Marx[1]

THE GLOOM AT the end of 1861 was not confined to the Marx household.
Black crepe bordered all the shops and covered brass doorplates along
Regent Street, Oxford Street, every commercial center in London, and
every village throughout the countryside. Prince Albert had died in
December, and England was engulfed in mourning.[2] In London, Christmas came and went without festivities; one Victorian writer explained
that celebrations would have seemed treasonous.[3] Equal to the sense of loss
was the public's fear for Victoria. Albert's death caused the queen to retreat
from public life. The once vibrant and enlightened English throne seemed
vacant.[4]

At the same time there was a pervasive feeling of apprehension that the
country might go to war with America. Two representatives from the
Confederacy, on a mission to win European recognition of the South, had
been seized by Union troops while traveling aboard the British mail
steamer *Trent,* because British maritime law forbade neutral vessels from
ferrying belligerents in time of war.[5] London newsboys shouted the headlines—"We must bombard New York!"[6]—as members of the British
government debated whether to respond to what many saw as a violation
of a sovereign British vessel by U.S. forces.

Despite England's strong antislavery stance, politically powerful
English textile merchants feared their supply of cheap cotton would be

eliminated if the U.S. slave system was abolished.[7] Critics accused government ministers of using the *Trent* episode as an excuse to enter the U.S.
conflict against the North and thereby help the cotton oligarchy in the
South.[8] The English working class sided with the North (they saw a Union
victory as a triumph of democracy by workingmen like themselves), and
there were fears that British entry into the war would tear the fabric of
English society, since those who would be enlisted to fight would come
from the groups most opposed to the battle.[9]

The day after Christmas the *Trent* affair ended. The United States backed
down and agreed to free the two Southerners—not because their detention was illegal, but because the captain who seized them had not followed
proper procedures.[10] The news did not reach London's streets until January
8, but when it did, it spread quickly. Newspapers worked overtime printing three evening editions. In the bitter cold people crowded outside news
offices to watch the story being posted, the headlines so fresh that the ink
was still wet.[11]

Marx and Engels followed events on American battlefields and discussed them as if they were sitting in Washington, listening to the cannons firing across the Potomac. Many German immigrants who had
moved to the United States had joined the fight. Weydemeyer was in the
Union army, as was their old foe Willich, while Jenny's younger brother
Edgar had joined the Confederates.[12] Marx considered slavery the basest
form of capitalist exploitation, and both he and Engels saw ending it as a
major step in the global march toward revolution.[13] But in the meantime
the war was having an immediate impact on their livelihoods. The price
of cotton soared, causing profits at Engels's firm to decline in obverse tra-
jectory. Marx's income from the *Tribune* was cut by half, then by two-
thirds, because of the war.[14] Finally, in March, the *Tribune* wrote to say it
wanted no more articles from its London correspondent.[15]

The Marx family's plight had been so bad for so long that there were no
longer crises: financial free fall was a way of life. Marx had been able to
earn, borrow, and shuffle debt in such a way that the family remained just
barely afloat, year after year. His twelve years of appeals to Engels for cash
had what a cynic might see as a trace of the professional beggar in them.
But that was not how Engels saw it: he thought of the money he earned
communistically, that is to say, it was no more his than it was Marx's or
that of any "party" member who needed it. As far as Engels was concerned, Marx earned the money because he was writing his economic
book to further the party's goals. If that project was repeatedly delayed or
Marx's output so far disappointing, it was a source of frustration for Engels

but no reason to stop the flow of cash. The American war, however, threatened to do what Engels would not have done. The timing could not have been worse. Marx had tapped his fund of last resort, his uncle, and could not go back to him anytime soon. He had sold himself to this pragmatic businessman as a successful writer only temporarily short of cash.

By 1862 Engels's cotton mill had no orders and had cut its hours of operation by half. Engels calculated if there was no end to the U.S. war, his annual income would be a mere hundred pounds, less than he usually sent the Marx family. That spring Engels told Marx he could not advance him much of anything until July.[16] He summed up their situation for Marx crudely but succinctly: "Unless we can discover the art of shitting gold, there would hardly seem to be any alternative to your extracting something from your relations by one means or another. Think about it."[17]

Jennychen turned eighteen that year and was far from flourishing; over the past year she had become extremely thin. Part of the reason was simply poverty, but there was also frustration. She considered herself an adult who should no longer be dependent on her parents. For her contemporaries this meant finding a husband, but she had no urge to do so. Instead, behind her parents' backs she approached an American actress turned drama coach to see about a career on the stage.[18] Before any progress could be made, however, she became seriously ill.[19] Marx, who had learned of her attempt to get an acting job, blamed her ill health and rash decision on the "strain and ... stigma" of their financial distress. He told Engels, "TAKE ALL IN ALL, leading such a dog's life is hardly WORTH WHILE."[20]

In lieu of money Engels sent the family eight bottles of claret, four bottles of 1846 Rhine wine, and two bottles of sherry. Then both men got to work cutting expenses and seeking new sources of cash. Engels moved in with Mary and Lizzy to consolidate costs, though he had to keep his town apartment for appearances' sake.[21] Marx sent Jenny to the loan office to see if she would have better luck than he had, and the Marxes put everything they could in pawn, including all the children's possessions as well as Lenchen and Marianne's things, down to their boots and shoes.[22]

Until some light appeared on their financial horizon, Marx "disappeared" in order to avoid the gas company (which had threatened to turn off the supply), the piano teacher ("a most ill-mannered brute"), the school fees ("I do my utmost to spare the children direct humiliation"), and sundry other "sons of Belial."[23] Jenny told the men looking for money that her husband was away and she did not know when he would return. When Marx left the house, he told Engels, he did so incognito[24] (though, sadly, he did not describe the disguise he assumed to avoid detection).

★   ★   ★

Unfortunately for Marx, in May 1862 his city hosted the Great London Exposition, which like the fair in 1851 attracted visitors from around Europe.[25] Lassalle announced he would be coming in July and expected to stay at Grafton Terrace, apparently looking for reciprocation of the generosity he had showed Marx in Berlin the year before.[26] Marx did not have enough money to feed his own family, let alone Lassalle, who feasted on venison and mountains of ice cream.[27] But though Marx had not earned a single penny for seven weeks, he could not say no. He related his litany of gloom to Engels: "Every day my wife says she wishes she and the children were safely in their graves, and I really cannot blame her, for the humiliations, torments and alarums that one has to go through in such a situation are indeed indescribable. . . . I feel all the more sorry for the unfortunate children in that all this is happening during the EXHIBITION SEASON, when their friends are having fun, whereas they themselves live in dread lest someone should come and see them and realize what a mess they are in."[28]

Lassalle arrived in London on July 9 and revealed that he would stay for several weeks.[29] From the start the family was aghast at the pomposity of this thirty-seven-year-old lawyer, who believed himself at the center of historical events. Melodramatic in his gestures, he spoke in a loud falsetto voice and issued proclamations as if he were an oracle,[30] producing such a racket, Jenny said, that he alarmed the neighbors. Jenny recalled a Lassalle-style question addressed to his bemused audience: "Should I astonish the world as an Egyptologist or show my versatility as a man of action, as a politician, as a fighter, or as a soldier."[31] As if Lassalle's fantasies of grandeur were not enough, he also imagined himself a Don Juan.[32] The Marx women were appalled. They viewed him as a gluttonous lecher, a Priapus masquerading as an idealist.[33]

During his visit Lassalle spent money on himself lavishly and announced, with scant regret, that he had lost £750 in a speculation gone awry. But he did not seem inclined to lend Marx even a trifle.[34] Instead, he asked whether Marx and Jenny would be willing to send one of their daughters to Berlin to be a companion to the Countess von Hatzfeldt. Incensed, Marx told Engels, "Had I not been in this appalling position and vexed by the way this parvenu flaunted his money bags, he'd have amused me tremendously. Since I last saw him a year ago, he's gone quite mad."[35]

After listening to Lassalle pontificate for weeks, Marx and Jenny could take it no longer and decided to enjoy themselves by poking fun at his plans, which Marx said left Lassalle raging: "He shouted, blustered, flung himself about and finally got it fixed in his mind that I was too 'abstract' to understand politics."[36] Jenny reported that Lassalle hurried away when he discovered they had little sympathy for such a great man.[37] But his parting was not without drama. Marx had tried to keep the full truth of his impoverishment from his unwelcome guest. On the last day of Lassalle's visit, however, the landlord arrived, claiming he would accept no more delays and would now put a broker into Marx's house to sell all the family's possessions unless he was immediately paid. On the same day Marx also received final demands for taxes and letters from various merchants who threatened to cut off provisions and prosecute unless Marx cleared his debts. He suspected they all knew the landlord was making his last stand and had decided to join him. His situation no longer a secret, Marx finally laid it out in humiliating detail. Lassalle sympathized but said he, too, was stretched and could offer Marx only fifteen pounds in January. In the meantime, Marx could use his name as insurance to obtain money from others.[38]

Engels commiserated with his friend when Marx recounted the story; his own situation was worse by the day, though a look at his quarterly expenses showed he was not quite being forced to pawn his boots. Engels complained that he had to pay out £15 to stable his horse, and £25 for his tailor, shoemaker, shirts, and cigars. But his biggest expense remained Marx: he had either given Marx or paid Marx's bills in the amount of £60,[39] and he assured Marx he would not leave him in the lurch now. "We shall, I think, go on giving each other as much mutual aid as we can, it being quite immaterial so far as the cause is concerned which of us happens to be the 'squeezer' at the moment and which the 'squeezed,' roles that are, after all, interchangeable."[40]

Engels appealed to Marx, however, to stage some kind of "financial coup," either by getting money from his family or by finishing his book, which Engels estimated could bring in £70.[41] In the meantime Engels went to great trouble to arrange payment to Marx of an additional £60 above what he had given him the previous quarter, using Lassalle's name as surety for repayment.[42] That transaction made Lassalle furious; either he had forgotten his parting offer to Marx, or Marx had intentionally misinterpreted it in his own favor. In any case the transaction was completed, neither Marx nor Engels giving a damn how Lassalle felt.[43]

With this money Marx paid off his most insistent creditors and, in late August, sent the family to the coast at Ramsgate. Marx was alarmed by Jennychen's continued ill health. In addition to losing weight, she had a persistent cough that indicated a disease more serious than a mere cold.[44] "She's the most perfect and gifted child in the world," he told Engels. "But here she had to suffer twice over. Firstly from physical causes. And then she was afflicted by our pecuniary TROUBLE."[45] While they were away Marx went again to Holland to try to talk his uncle out of more money, but it turned out that Philips was traveling himself. Marx next went on to Trier to see his mother. As usual she was unwilling to help, and he returned from his trip poorer than when he left, though refreshed by another encounter with Nanette.[46] Through her, he could imagine himself to be what she saw—an elegant philosopher and writer—instead of what he knew himself to be, a hunted pauper with family obligations he was incapable of meeting.

Marx described himself as a "man on a powder barrel," and when he returned to London in September he took a step he had apparently never before considered: he applied for a job. Marx told Engels it was possible that he would start work at an English railway office at the beginning of 1863.[47] Now the "squeeze" was on both of them. Their hoped-for quick resolution of the U.S. war did not appear imminent. The fighting that had littered American fields with dead and dying men had also nearly killed England's cotton industry. Engels said by the fall of 1862 the price of cotton had soared fivefold. Unwilling to pay such exorbitant prices for material they had come to rely on as cheap and plentiful, customers fell away.[48] By November, Engels declared himself "very broke."[49]

Now accompanied by Laura,[50] Marx followed the war in newspapers and government documents at the British Museum. He also read U.S. newspapers (both from the Southern states and the Northern abolitionist press) at an American coffeehouse, because he said the English press suppressed some details about the course of the conflict.[51] As the war progressed, Marx's admiration for Lincoln—whom he called a "unique figure in the annals of history"—grew. Marx declared that though couched in lawyerly phrases, Lincoln's Emancipation Proclamation (which Marx called his "manifesto abolishing slavery") was "the most important document in American history since the establishment of the Union," and if Lincoln's style lacked drama, it was a refreshing change from the ceremony European leaders attached to mere trifles: "The new world has never achieved a greater triumph than by this demonstration that, given its political and social organization, ordinary people of goodwill can accomplish feats which only heroes could accomplish in the old world!"[52] Marx said of the United States at that moment, "events over there are such as to transform the world."[53]

Marx did not get the railway office job because his handwriting was so poor. The sixty pounds Engels had helped arrange for him over the summer was gone, and the approach of the new year meant fresh demands for money—most immediately the rent, which was due in January.[54] Out of options, Marx sent Jenny to Paris in December to see "literary gentlemen" about his work, as well as a banker friend to whom they had lent money when he was poor. From the start her trip was plagued by mishaps that Marx said would have been comical had they not been so tragic.

The boat Jenny took to France was caught in a storm so serious that another vessel sank nearby. She made it to Paris to catch a train to the banker's home, but the train had engine trouble and was delayed by two hours. Next an omnibus she was traveling in overturned.[55] And when she finally reached the banker's house, she discovered he had had a massive stroke the day before her arrival. Jenny left Paris with little more than a promise from a journalist friend that as soon as the next installment of Marx's economic work appeared, it would be published in French.

That was not the end of her misadventures. In London the cab Jenny was riding in collided with another and became entangled, which forced her to walk home through the sleet and mud with two boys carrying her luggage and the Christmas gifts she'd brought back from her journey. Expecting the warmth of a family greeting on her return from such an arduous trip, Jenny instead found the house conspicuously silent. Only two hours before, Lenchen's sister Marianne had died of rheumatic fever. She wrote a friend, "Jenny and Laurachen came towards me, pale and perturbed, and Tussychen I found drenched in tears. . . . You can also imagine Helene's suffering, the sisters loved each other so much."[56]

Marianne was laid in a coffin at the Marx house on Christmas Eve and buried three days later.[57] There was no Christmas tree, no plum pudding, no mistletoe. Instead, the dark coffin sat in the family's parlor throughout the holiday. Said Jenny, "The whole household was silent and sad."[58]

There were many instances in Marx's life in which he showed himself to be a deeply self-centered man. Even in respect to those he loved most, he was at times maddeningly blind to their feelings and needs. January 1863 was one such occasion. On the seventh of that month, Engels wrote Marx a brief note to say that Mary Burns, his companion of two decades and the woman he called his wife, had died: "Last night she went to bed early and, when Lizzy wanted to go to bed shortly before midnight, she found she had already died. Quite suddenly. Heart failure or an apoplectic stroke. . . . I simply can't convey how I feel. The poor girl loved me with all her heart."[59] Marx responded the next day. The first two lines of his letter expressed his surprise and dismay about Mary, and then he devoted the next thirty-one lines to his own financial problems—unless one counts as a tribute to Engels's loving companion Marx's hope that by unburdening himself he would be delivering a "homeopathic remedy," because "one calamity is a distraction for another." Or perhaps Engels was to have found solace in Marx's similarly compassionate sentence in which he said, "Instead of Mary, ought it not to have been my mother, who is in any case a prey to physical ailments and has had her fair share of life?"[60]

Engels waited nearly a week before he responded, and when he did, it was in the imperious Prussian tone that terrified his adversaries. "You will find it quite in order that, this time, my own misfortune and the frosty view you took of it should have made it positively impossible for me to reply to you any sooner. All my friends, including philistine acquaintances, have on this occasion, which in all conscience must needs afflict me deeply, given me proof of greater sympathy and friendship than I could have looked for. You thought it a fit moment to assert the superiority of your 'dispassionate turn of mind.' So be it then!"[61]

Marx waited even longer to respond to Engels. Eleven days passed before he wrote a letter full of contrition, an effort to redeem himself in the eyes of the man he most respected and most needed. In explaining his coldness, he in essence blamed Jenny. On the day he received the news of Mary's death, he explained, a broker had finally been put on the house. Marx also had not sent the girls back to school, because he could not pay the bill and in any event they did not have presentable clothes. Jenny had wanted him to explain their dire straits to Engels, and Marx had regretted the letter as soon as it was mailed. Engels's second letter had been an eye-opener, he admitted, and he had now decided to act on a conclusion he had reached months before. The only way for the family to survive would be for Marx to file for bankruptcy, send his two eldest girls out to be governesses, send Lenchen into service elsewhere, and move with Jenny and Tussy into a city-operated lodging house where Red Wolff had once lived when down on his luck.[62]

Engels forgave Marx. Like Jenny, Lenchen, and countless others, he recognized Marx's personal flaws but he, like they, loved him too much to allow those flaws to overshadow the brilliant qualities—his mind, his wit, even his capacity for love and loyalty (as hard as it must have been to remember those at such moments). Like the others, Engels also felt it was his role to protect this man, from whom he expected great things. He told Marx that although he was obsessed with his response to Mary's death, he wanted to put the matter behind them: "One can't live with a woman for years on end without being fearfully affected by her death. I felt as though with her I was burying the last vestige of my youth....I'm glad that, in losing Mary, I didn't also lose my oldest and best friend." Engels then described a transaction that amounted to graft (he took a bill intended as payment to Ermen & Engels and made it payable to Marx) and sent one hundred pounds so the family could stay in its home and the girls return to school. For himself, he said he was trying to relieve his sorrow by studying Slavonic languages, "but the loneliness was unbearable."[63]

The winter of 1863 took its toll on the Marx family as well. By April, Jennychen was ill again, Jenny was confined to bed and almost deaf (the likely cause a residual effect of her smallpox),[64] and Marx was suffering from the worst bout of liver trouble he had yet experienced. But he continued to slog through his economic manuscript, telling Engels in May that he expected to make a fair copy of "the beastly book" and take it to Germany to try to find a publisher.[65] He said he was confident the second installment would be "one hundred percent more comprehensible" than the first.[66] Marx explained that he did not work at home during the day, instead dragging his aching body to the British Museum to get out of the house where the "nagging" caused by mounting bills had reached a crescendo.[67] Perhaps hearing in his friend's description a cry for relief, Engels found enough money to allow Marx to pay his creditors and, with additional help from a friend of Jenny's in Germany, send the Marx women to the seaside for a holiday.[68]

They had been busily running the house while Lenchen was in Germany attending to a sick sister. Laura had proved herself a talented cook, making exquisite pies, cakes, and sauces. Jennychen called herself a "boot-jack" because she was in charge of the cleaning and sweeping. Jenny took care of the washing up, because she did not want her daughters to ruin their hands. They even turned their attention to what Jenny called the "clothing department": dyeing, turning, and patching worn clothes to give them the appearance of being new.[69] (The regeneration of clothing was not always a success. The year before, little Tussy had been teased by some neighbor children because of a bizarre homemade hat she wore.)[70]

The girls had enough of a social life now that they had to look respectable. (Jenny told a friend she was secretly surprised they had no sense of vanity, "the more so since the same could not be said of their mother in her earlier days.")[71] The friends visiting their home would soon include young men, and it was particularly important, so Jenny thought, that the family make a good impression on them, even if the girls seemed less than concerned about finding husbands.

Laura had grown into a beautiful young woman, with the same light auburn hair and green eyes that had made her mother the envy of Trier. She also had a reserve and nobility that belied the poverty in which she was raised. She was proud and dignified without being haughty, a talented writer and linguist whose eyes sparkled with a fiery joy. She was as comfortable in the kitchen as in the museum Reading Room, as poised in a ballroom as she was skillful swimming in the sea. Of the three girls Laura was fondest of "things."[72] One of her nicknames was Kakadou, a reference to a fashionable tailor in an old novel, which she had earned because she was the most stylish dresser among the Marx women.[73] Jennychen, on the other hand, was more complicated, at once stronger than her sister and yet more fragile. The eldest Marx daughter was aching to move beyond her role as sister and daughter. Intellectually, she had been raised like a middle-class boy, and she hungered for a challenge and to strike out on her own. Jennychen was lovely, but she was not classically beautiful like Laura. She was tall and shapely, but her features were not as regular as her sister's, and her mother said her nose was too snubbed.[74]

No matter their physical differences, however, Jennychen and Laura were more alike than not, and they were the closest of friends. As children they had shared the vision of the family, as they understood it, and now that they were young women who recognized that that vision left them estranged from the society their friends embraced, they relied on each other for support in subtle ways their parents may have missed. (Once when Jennychen was ill, for example, while Lenchen, Jenny, and Marx were preoccupied with getting her food and medicine, Laura wrote her a poem each day to lift her spirits.[75] She understood that her sister's symptoms were physical but were rooted in a spiritual malaise.) The two young women had depended on each other throughout the family's countless dark moments, and depended on each other still.

After Lenchen's return, the Marx women spent four weeks in Hastings, renting an apartment with three large windows and a garden. But the main attraction was the sea. Jenny took the girls rowing, they bathed, ate oysters, watched fireworks in the garden of a member of Parliament, and walked the hills until even Jennychen once again had rosy cheeks.[76] And, back in London, they found that in their absence Marx had made great progress on his book. It had grown to more than seven hundred pages, and Jenny warned her friends that it would "drop like a bomb" on German soil.[77]

All seemed to be finally moving ahead when Marx's work was interrupted by a new complaint: he had developed two boils, one on his cheek and the other on his back, the latter assuming frightful dimensions, eventually growing into a carbuncle the size of a fist.[78] Doctors blamed the carbuncle on poor hygiene and generally poor health, but Jenny attributed it to Marx's intense work habits over the past months, during which he "smoked twice as much as usual and took three times as many pills of various kinds." She expressed her frustration in a letter to Engels: "It seems as though the wretched book will never get finished. It weighs like a night-mare on us all. If only the LEVIATHAN were LAUNCHED!"[79] Meanwhile, Marx, in intense pain, retreated to bed.

A doctor instructed the family to apply hot poultices to Marx's back every two hours and to force him to eat and drink as much as possible. Marx had never had much interest in food, but the drink helped ease the pain, and for the next two weeks his daily diet included one and a half quarts of stout, three to four glasses of port, as well as a half bottle of Bor-deaux. Jenny sat up night after night by his bed or slept alongside it on the floor. Miraculously, she remained well, but Lenchen, who also helped with the nursing duties, fell ill with worry and exhaustion.[80]

Marx had barely recovered enough to be able to walk half an hour a day when he received a letter in late November from Germany announcing that his mother was dead.[81] (She had long before correctly predicted the date and time of her death—four in the afternoon of November 30, the day and hour of her marriage.)[82] Even though he was still light-headed and weak, he had to go to Trier. Armed with two enormous bottles of medicine, Marx counted on the "good Samaritanesses" he would find along the way to plaster his still-seeping wound.[83]

Marx made it to Trier without difficulty and found that the real business concerning his mother's affairs would have to be conducted in Holland. His mother's will was in what he called a confused state, and his uncle Lion was one of two named executors. But while in Trier, perhaps because of his mother's death or his own recent illness, he sent Jenny another mov-ing love letter in which he tried to erase all the torment of the previous years, as if their many sorrows had never happened and they were back in their Rhineland youth. On December 15, 1863, he wrote,

Dear sweet darling Jenny...
If I have been so long in writing to you, this was certainly not out of for-getfulness. Quite the reverse. I have made a daily pilgrimage to the old West-phalen home (in the Neustrasse), which interested me more than any Roman antiquities because it reminded me of the happiest days of my youth and had harbored my greatest treasure. Moreover, every day and on every side I am asked about the "most beautiful girl in Trier" and the "queen of the ball." It's damned pleasant for a man, when his wife lives on like this as an "enchanted princess" in the imagination of a whole town.[84]

Marx left Trier a week later for Holland. But while he was there, a car-buncle—or, as he said, a "second Frankenstein"—appeared exactly beneath the site on his back of the previous one. Once again he was debilitated by pain, and he thought he would likely not be able to return to London until January. He told Engels that his uncle tended to the poultices himself, and his charming and witty cousin, twenty-seven-year-old Nanette, "nurses and cossets me in exemplary fashion."[85]

Though Marx was in pain, he was warm and well fed during the holiday season, while Jenny and the children were in London, again reliant on Engels. Icicles hung from the windows outside, and the family needed a mountain of coal to keep the rooms in Grafton Terrace warm.[86] In winter it was not unusual for a ton of coal, stored in the cellar, to be used each month to heat a Victorian home. The horse-drawn cart making the much-needed delivery represented one more bill at a time when the family was stretched to the limit.

Marx did not write Jenny over Christmas, so after the New Year she sent him what she called a "rose-colored initiative" in the form of a letter to try to end an eight-day drought in his correspondence. Somewhat disingenuously, she said she would have felt "very, very deserted" during that festive season if she had not known he was well and taken care of in Holland. She then went on to describe their rather bleak celebration in London, which Marx could not have failed to interpret as a signal that she had felt very, very deserted indeed. Lacking a tree or any other holiday decorations, she said, Jennychen and Laura tried to cheer up Tussy by dressing more than twenty dolls in various costumes—including one they turned into a Chinese elder by using a lock of Tussy's hair, which they glued to the doll's chin. The landlord did not come demanding money because he understood Marx was away, and he and the "very involved neighborhood" knew Marx had been ill. But as soon as the holidays ended, the landlord appeared.

There had been some bright spots. The family spent New Year's Eve at home with a French family, the Lorimers. They welcomed the stroke of midnight with dancing and singing, their guests staying until two in the morning. The highlight of the holiday, however, came courtesy of Lupus, who gave the girls three pounds, with which they treated the entire household to the theater. Jenny said the evening was a great pleasure for their "tragedienne" Jennychen, and was topped off by a ride home in a cab. Everyone, she said, was highly satisfied. But her tone indicated that she was not. Rather than her usual sign-off of a thousand kisses, she ended her letter with, "Now good bye old boy! Let's hear from you soon."[87] And as January turned into February and Marx was still not back in London, her despair grew. In a letter to a friend, she starkly described her feelings: "Far from him, tortured by fear and worries, almost crushed by a starkly swollen burden of debt caused by long and expensive illnesses...we sat there, sad, lonely, with little hope."[88] Jenny felt utterly abandoned as she celebrated her fiftieth birthday with her daughters, amid record low temperatures and a hard frost[89] that matched her mood.

Jenny looked back on that period as one of her worst. Marx, on the other hand—despite being plagued by a fresh outbreak of pea-sized boils known as furuncles, oozing carbuncles the size of golf balls, and the pain and fever associated with both—told his uncle that the two months he lived in Holland were among the happiest of his life.[90] He returned to London on February 19,[91] fatter than when he left, and far fitter in mind and body than the women who greeted him at home.

Marx inherited about a thousand pounds from his mother's estate (though not all of it was immediately accessible, and about three hundred pounds would go to pay off debt),[92] and he used a portion of it, as Jenny had in 1856, to move the family to a new and better abode. Grafton Terrace was not haunted by death as Dean Street had been, but it was a scene of near constant domestic misery. From the moment they had moved in, the overall experience had been colored by extreme loneliness, illness, and want that had strained even Marx and Jenny's marriage.

The Marxes did not go far to find a new residence; they remained in reach of Hampstead Heath. But the home at 1 Modena Villas, Maitland Park—sunny, expansive, and quaintly situated near a chapel—was grander by several degrees.[93] The three-story suburban villa had a fireplace in every room, a garden in the back, a park in front, and a greenhouse off the main parlor. Each girl had her own bedroom,[94] and there was plenty of space for the animals Tussy had collected, which by that time included two dogs, three cats, and two birds.[95] Marx chose the first-floor room overlooking the park as his study, and the women had the run of the rest of the place. Here, Jenny felt, they could begin life anew. It was a home their daughters could display with pride and where their mother could preside as she was raised to do—a convincing respectability, the facade only partial.

Apparently oblivious to the lesson offered by Grafton Terrace, that having enough money initially to rent a place did not mean he would have the wherewithal to maintain payments, Marx signed a three-year lease for the whopping sum of sixty-five pounds a year.[96] As always, the family followed him joyfully into the extravagant new venture.

At the end of April, Engels alerted Marx that he was increasingly concerned about Lupus's health. He was fifty-five and suffered from debilitating headaches, but his doctor seemed content to treat him only for gout in his toe. Though Engels brought in a second doctor, Lupus's condition continued to deteriorate. His problem seemed to be either a brain hemorrhage or brain fever.[97] Marx, too, was alarmed, and went to Manchester on May 3. Six days later he wrote Jenny to say that Lupus had died. They had known this man since 1844 in Brussels, when he'd turned up at their door a stranger. Since then he had been a loyal party member—as loyal as family. Said Marx, "In him we have lost one of our few friends and fellow fighters. He was a man in the best sense of the word."[98]

The next day Marx learned just how true a friend Lupus had been. He had worked as a tutor during his years in Manchester, and as a bachelor had few expenses aside from drink. His will revealed that he had saved up about a thousand pounds, and of that he left one hundred pounds each to Engels, his doctor, and the Schiller Institute (a German social and cultural club in Manchester). The remainder, as well as his books and other effects, he gave to Marx and Jenny.[99]

Astounded by Lupus's gift, Marx gave an oration during the funeral, his voice failing him as he recalled his friend.[100] But for Engels, Lupus's death was particularly hard, because like Mary, Lupus had been a friend of his youth and a constant reminder of the greater struggle that was sometimes lost amid what Engels called the "bourgeois filth" in Manchester. He had seen Lupus almost daily, and sadly acknowledged, "With him Marx and I lost our most faithful friend and the German revolution a man of irreplaceable worth."[101]

Engels was so bereft he could not bear to stay in Manchester, so Marx invited him to London. For the first time in two decades, from a rare position of comfort and wealth, the Marx family would be caring for Engels instead of Engels caring for them.

Part V

From *Capital* to the Commune

30

London, 1864

*The lords of the land and the lords of capital will always use
their political privileges for the defense and perpetuation of their
economical monopolies. . . . To conquer political power has therefore become the great duty of the working classes. . . . One element of success they possess—numbers; but numbers weigh only
in the balance if united by combination and led by knowledge.*

—Karl Marx[1]

THE YEAR 1864 was transformational not only for the Marx family, but for
the European working class. Engels wrote, "the modern state, no matter
what its form, is essentially a capitalist machine, the state of capitalists."[2]
In the early 1860s that was becoming clear to workers, who saw industrial
and financial interests take control of the political system throughout
Western Europe and spread capitalism's reach into Europe's vast colonial
network. In England alone by the mid-1860s, there were 148 heads of
railway companies in the House of Commons, or nearly one-quarter of
that chamber.[3] After failing to open doors with reasoned political and
social arguments, in the end all it had taken for the bourgeoisie to co-opt
the ruling (and in many cases crumbling) aristocracy was money. That
was especially evident in England and France, and increasingly so in
Germany.

But the impact of the shift of power away from the landed aristocracy
was felt most dramatically outside Western Europe, in Russia and the
United States. In 1861 Czar Alexander II had sounded the death knell of
feudalism in Europe by abolishing serfdom. The next year Abraham Lincoln had signed the Emancipation Proclamation, which initiated the end

to slavery in the United States.[4] The practical result of those two actions meant that from the mid-1860s on, all men in Europe and America worked for some form of wage; no longer was there a social structure in place that allowed one man to force another to work against his will without remuneration.

Many industrialists and liberals congratulated themselves for laying the groundwork for a new era of labor freedom and helping to end the barbarous practices of the past. But intellectuals and working-class leaders argued that the new liberty had little value for the man with no food, no money, no education, and poor health, who watched his family being ground up in the industrial machine for which they "freely chose" to work. The Russian Nikolai Chernysevsky, who was arrested in 1862 for revolutionary activities, said freedom and legal rights had value only when men had the material means to take advantage of them. He feared laissez-faire liberalism in Russia would produce an even worse system than the feudalism it replaced, because it would be based entirely on self-interest without social safety nets—such as communal living and land—to catch those too poor, too old, or too weak to make it on their own.[5] Some European and American workers felt that same insecurity. In Russia the changed reality would spawn generations of revolutionaries. In Western Europe and America it would create trade unions and workers' political organizations.

During the earlier periods of revolt in Europe, in 1830 and 1848, opposition movements were led largely by enlightened members of the upper classes and intellectuals. By the early 1860s, however, the working class had grown in size, strength, and cohesion. And, perhaps most important, its members were better educated, which meant there were many more leaders with many more ideas about how to fight for workers' rights. The choices were no longer revolution or capitulation; the activist menu now included strikes, peaceful demonstrations, and political and industrial organization on a mass scale.[6] The mood was calm but determined; solidarity was seen as key.

In England a major umbrella organization of workers was formed under the banner of the London Trades Council. It was the first real attempt at such a broad-based organization since the demise of Chartism in the 1840s. In Germany, Lassalle published a pamphlet called *Workers' Program.* Marx dismissed it as a poor substitute for the *Communist Manifesto,*[7] but it was seen by contemporaries in Germany as the first step toward a modern workers' movement there. With his program as a springboard, Lassalle founded the General Union of German Workers in 1863. In France, too, the movement was growing, though less well organized in part because of lagging industrial development there. Yet because it was less organized, it was also more combustible.

Against that backdrop, in July 1863 European workers came together in London to support an uprising in Poland, one of the rare revolutionary events in the post-1848 period. The end of serfdom in Russia had been misinterpreted in Russian-controlled Poland as the start of a trend toward greater freedoms. Peaceful protests were staged in Warsaw for two years to try to press Russia to allow a constitution in Poland, but by January 1863 frustration at the lack of response boiled over and violence erupted. Western European governments—even self-declared champions of basic rights—did not offer to help the Poles,[8] but the workers meeting in London did. Delegates also agreed to create an international association of workers. Its inaugural meeting would be held in September 1864 in London.[9]

Marx and Engels were aware of these gatherings, and Marx solicited funds for the Poles in the name of the German Workers' Educational Society. But through the summer of 1864 Marx largely shunned politicking. His inheritances had bought him freedom, and he used the time to work on his book, study anatomy and physiology (inspired, he said, by Engels's knowledge of the subjects), and dabble in the stock market (also following Engels's lead).[10] Marx told his uncle he had made four hundred pounds on one speculation and declared trading to his liking. It made "small demands on one's time, and it's worth running some risk in order to relieve the enemy of his money."[11] (Again, this was an Engels stratagem: he had spent more than a decade in Manchester diverting funds from the factory system he loathed in order to support the man he hoped would destroy it.)

In fact the summer of 1864 was one of uncharacteristic harmony and ease for the Marx family.[12] Jenny attended auctions to find furnishings for their home, and the girls indulged in the bourgeois occupation of decorating their bedrooms.[13] Jennychen made a Shakespeare gallery of hers, decorating it with images of the Bard and famous Shakespearean actors, and making a bookshelf-shrine of her favorite plays.[14] She also took control of the greenhouse, which became a floral refuge for this young woman whose health had been ruined by poverty and who had never been surrounded by so much beauty.[15] Then, once settled into Modena Villas, Marx packed up his three daughters in mid-July for a seaside holiday. A new train line between London and Ramsgate had opened the year before, carrying travelers southeast, out of the sooty capital, and depositing them several hours later onto the strand at the sea's edge. Perhaps not surprisingly, Ramsgate's beach in midsummer was soon as crowded with

Londoners as Oxford Street at Christmas. Women in billowing dresses sat on chairs in the sand, elegantly dressed men strolled the beach smoking cigars, and all manner of entertainment amused the visitors, from acrobats to dancing troupes to singing minstrels. For the first time the Marx daughters plunged into the social life without concern for the cost. Marx used the time to recover from another carbuncle, which forced him to remain mostly in bed.

Meanwhile, back in London, Jenny delighted in a life she had probably thought she would never know again. In a letter to her vacationing family she said in their new home she didn't suffer from the heat because she was able to escape the sun by flouncing from one room to another. She made eighty jars of jellies and jams, had friends over for sumptuous dinners topped off by plenty of beer, and went out herself for evenings wearing what she described as her "finest costume"—fake diamonds and a white opera cloak.[16] When Marx and the girls returned from Ramsgate, Jenny set off on her own to Brighton for a two-week holiday as a "parlor boarder" with a private family.[17] That summer was more carefree than any since she had married Marx twenty years before. The only shadow was Marx's warning that Jenny not resort too often to the card identifying her as "Mme Jenny Marx, née Baroness von Westphalen," because some of Marx's enemies were also in Brighton and could use it against him.[18] But that was a minor concern compared with the traumas they had suffered and the humiliations they had endured. That summer Jenny had her picture taken in Brighton.[19] Her face no longer showed the scars of smallpox. She was relaxed, lovely, and elegant, the image of a woman who had never known anything but ease. The family's fortunes had changed swiftly and dramatically in the course of just a few months.

Engels's fortunes, too, had changed. At forty-four he was named a full partner in Ermen & Engels, with—despite the turbulent cotton market—all the wealth attached to that position.[20] He and Lizzy Burns celebrated by moving into a larger home. Now thirty-seven, Lizzy had lived with Engels and her older sister Mary since she was a girl. During that time, Lizzy had matured into a high-spirited Irish nationalist who turned their home into a safe house for the new breed of anti-English Irish radicals known as Fenians.[21] Their house provided the perfect cover. It was outside Manchester's Irish ghetto, and since Mary's death she had become the "wife" of one of the city's most important businessmen.

In September, Marx received the shocking news from Freiligrath that Lassalle had been shot dead in Geneva. Lassalle's friends said he had fallen in love with a nineteen-year-old woman, but she was already engaged to a

Romanian nobleman who challenged Lassalle to a duel. He had been no match for this man, who was described alternately as a "pseudo prince" and a "swindler,"[22] and was wounded in the lower stomach near the genitals.[23] He suffered a slow and painful death.

Marx and Engels had ridiculed Lassalle without mercy over the years, but the turn of events shook them both deeply, especially Marx. Lassalle had been at the height of his career. However improbably, he had become the leader of the German workers' and socialist movements. And, though he was also rumored to be negotiating behind the scenes for an alliance with Prussian prime minister Otto von Bismarck, he had advanced the workers' cause in Germany far more than anyone else.[24] Marx announced Lassalle's tawdry end to Jenny in a letter to Brighton, saying, "Whatever one may say, L. is too good to go under in this way."[25] Several days later he told Engels his thoughts had been "damnably preoccupied with Lassalle's misfortune. After all, whatever else he may have been, he was one of the *old stock* and the foe of our foes. And then the thing came so unexpectedly that it's hard to believe so noisy, STIRRING, PUSHING a person is now dead as a door-nail and compelled to hold his tongue ALTOGETHER. . . . Heaven knows our ranks are being steadily depleted, and there are no reinforcements in sight."[26]

As had happened before, however, when the ranks around Marx appeared to be thinning, reinforcements did appear. Two weeks after he wrote to Engels about Lassalle, Marx was asked by a French exile, Victor Le Lubez, to represent Germany at a meeting of international workers in London on September 28. Marx had not attended the earlier meeting in 1863, when delegates had decided to hold the event, but he had a sense that the men gathering at St. Martin's Hall were engaged in something important. He waived his usual objection and agreed to attend.[27]

Throughout Europe, workers had so far built only local or national organizations to fight for labor rights, but these parochial efforts were no longer sufficient. Governments had eliminated nearly all international barriers to commerce, causing trade to soar by 260 percent between 1850 and the late 1860s.[28] Industry, too, ignored territorial boundaries when looking for scab labor to break strikes, and security forces no longer considered borders a barrier in their efforts to combat antigovernment movements. Given that climate, the workers traveling to London were agreed that it behooved them to expand internationally in order to meet these new challenges.

The gathering proved a bigger success than its organizers could have imagined; the cavernous hall was filled to capacity. The event drew English workers from the London Trades Council, Italian nationalists allied to

Giuseppe Mazzini, Proudhonists and Blanquists from France, Irish nationalists, Polish patriots, and of course Marx and his tailor friend Georg Eccarius representing Germany.[29] (One writer described the gathering as a United Nations of radical citizens.)[30] Those attending agreed to form an International Working Men's Association, based in London, to liaise with and organize workers' groups in Europe and the United States. A panel was selected to write the International's rules and a declaration of principles: Marx was asked to serve on it.

In Germany meanwhile, members of the General Union of German Workers were scrambling to find a new president in the wake of Lassalle's death. Liebknecht asked Marx if he would become the party's leader, and other party members asked Marx for advice on possible candidates.[31] It was curious that these men in Germany turned to Marx in London for direction. He had not been involved in any political movement there for nearly fifteen years and had not had anything published except his *Contribution to the Critique of Political Economy,* which did not sell widely enough to have had a real impact. In many ways Marx had Carl Vogt's well-read and widely reproduced polemic against him to thank for his continued presence and popularity in Germany at that crucial moment.

Marx told Liebknecht he could not accept the presidency because he could not take up residence in Prussia. (His citizenship application had been rejected.) From his study in Modena Villas, however, Marx was intrigued by the possibility of such a maneuver, and he once again opened his political chess board, telling another party member it would be a good gesture if he *were* elected president—he would then be able to publicly explain why he could not accept, and it would appear to be an endorsement of the International.[32] In the end Marx was not elected, but he had, as it were, come in from the cold by reestablishing himself as a leader and major theoretician for German socialists and workers just as he began trying to win recruits for the International.

In late October, Marx was given draft copies of rules and principles written during International meetings he had not attended. He promptly dismissed them out of hand as the work of his old rival Mazzini—cliché ridden and so vague as to be impracticable. Rather than openly fight to impose changes, however, he resurrected a technique he had used with censors in Cologne: he wore down his fellow committee members. At a meeting at his home Marx kept the group talking about minor issues until one in the morning. At that point the exhausted delegation decided to call it a night, leaving the drafts with Marx until their next meeting. While they rested, Marx worked. In the solitude of his vast study, he unilaterally wrote an "Address to the Working Classes," tossing out the Mazzini-inspired declaration of principles and reducing forty proposed rules to just ten. When the committee met again, members accepted Marx's changes unanimously (and with relief), asking only that he add two minor sentences.[33]

Marx's ten-page address was a masterpiece of moderation. It chronicled what he called the "adventures" of the working class and described its advances against great odds. Since 1848, European countries had experienced unprecedented economic development and growth. "In all of them, the augmentation of wealth and power entirely confined to classes of property was truly 'intoxicating,'" he said, while at the same time during this epoch of commercial progress "death from starvation rose almost to the rank of an institution." Yet from that position of defeat, Marx said, the working classes arose with new strength. He lauded English laborers who had won a ten-hour workday, observing, "It was the first time in broad daylight the political economy of the middle class succumbed to the political economy of the working class."

But, Marx said, only when workingmen of different countries stood side by side, joined in a common struggle for emancipation—which only they could achieve—would they successfully counter the ruling classes and win the right to benefit from their own labor. He said this belief had prompted the formation of the International Working Men's Association, which would agitate not only for workers' rights but also for just foreign policies. Workingmen of one land must not be pitted against workingmen of another to fight and die in wars whose only result was to advance capitalist interests. He ended with the familiar refrain, "Proletarians of all countries Unite!"[34]

It is difficult to overestimate the impact of the International and that short address, even if the number of people aware of the new group at the time was small. Marx's words became the basis of a new working-class movement. Within weeks his piece was reproduced in opposition newspapers throughout Europe and as far away as St. Louis, Missouri, where Weydemeyer and his colleagues in the Union army read it while waiting to move against Confederate troops.[35]

In the wake of the International, the Marx home became the "Emigration Medina," according to Engels.[36] Among the first of Marx's visitors was Mikhail Bakunin, whom Marx had not seen for sixteen years. By now the Russian bear of a man was a near mythical figure for generations of revolutionaries, anarchists, and their more extreme offspring, the nihilists.[37]

After being arrested in 1849 outside Dresden, where he had proposed a suicide attack on the town hall, Bakunin had been sentenced to death for treason. Within six months, however, that sentence was commuted to life in prison, and he was handed over to Austria. There he was chained to the wall of his cell until, in May 1851, a military court found him guilty of treason and sentenced him to death by hanging. But on the same day his sentence was once again commuted, and he was turned over to Russia, where he was placed in St. Petersburg's notorious Fortress of Peter and Paul.[38] Years of incarceration under torturous conditions, especially his confinement in Russia, had caused Bakunin's teeth to fall out and his muscular body to turn into a wall of sagging flesh. He was a grotesque giant compared with the man who had once made women swoon and men pledge their loyalty.[39] His strength was sapped, as were his convictions. In 1858, through the intervention of Bakunin's mother, the czar gave him the option of staying in jail or spending the rest of his life in Siberia. The condition was that he sign a humiliating petition begging the czar for his release. Bakunin signed the petition and set out under escort on a long trip east.[40] In Siberia, Bakunin, now in his midforties, married the eighteen-year-old daughter of a Polish merchant. It was an odd marriage by all accounts: Bakunin was believed to be unable to perform sexually, and he was obsessively jealous regarding his young wife, Antonia.[41] Then, three years later, in 1861, he escaped Siberia, leaving his wife and boarding a series of ships between the Russian coast and Japan. He traveled to San Francisco, New York, and finally on to England, reaching Liverpool on December 27. From there Bakunin headed to London to stay with the Russian writer Alexander Herzen.[42]

Bakunin had been out of circulation since 1849, and his politics had remained frozen. He had not experienced the maturing process that calmed his earlier comrades-in-arms, and so, having regained his strength, he rejoined the fray with the lust for battle he'd exhibited on the barricades in Dresden. He knew no law but action. Said Herzen, "At fifty he was still the same wandering student, the same homeless bohemian [of his Paris days] caring nothing for the morrow, despising money, scattering it on all sides when he had it, borrowing indiscriminately right and left when he had none."[43] Marx described him as a "monster, a huge mass of flesh and fat" who was barely able to walk under the burden of his 280 pounds.[44]

Bakunin had been in and out of London since his arrival there in 1861, but Marx had not apparently learned he was in town until Bakunin asked the tailor Lessner to replenish his wardrobe for a trip to Italy.[45] Marx thought Bakunin might be an effective ally there against Mazzini, so he invited him to visit.[46] Bakunin's huge frame, topped off by a hat rakishly perched on the side of his head, filled the Marx family doorway the night before he and Antonia (who had joined him in London) were to leave for Florence.[47]

In the 1840s relations between Marx and Bakunin in Paris and Brussels had been tense. But when they met again in London, Marx told Engels, "I must say I liked him very much, more so than previously.... On the whole, he is one of the few people whom after sixteen years I find to have moved forwards and not backwards." With his characteristic all-or-nothing passion, Bakunin promised to dedicate himself entirely to socialism and the International.[48]

Marx might have saved himself an enormous amount of grief if he had recognized Bakunin's allegiance as a threat rather than a sign of support. As one Marx biographer wrote, Marx dreamed of building a better society out of the old one. Bakunin was the master of annihilation. He dreamed of destroying society and starting the process all over from the smoldering embers.[49]

By now the Marx family's long years of solitude were over. Marx was actively participating in politics again. He was also nearing completion of his economic work, which would no longer be an installment in his series for Duncker. It would be a book called *Capital*. Even the Marx daughters were freed from their self-imposed isolation. In October 1864 they gave their first ball[50] — or so Jenny described it, though by English standards a ball was attended by hundreds of people and the Marx guest list numbered only fifty. The event was also held long after the close of the fashionable "season,"[51] but that did not dampen the family mood or the preparations. The invitations read:

> *Dr. Karl Marx and Frau Jenny Marx born von Westphalen*
> *invite the pleasure of your company*
> *at a ball given at their residence*
> *1 Modena Villas, Maitland Park, Haverstock Hill, London NW*
> *on October 12, 1864.*[52]

Jenny told Ernestine Liebknecht that the girls had often been invited to such gatherings but had never been able to reciprocate, and out of embarrassment stopped accepting invitations. This ball was to be grand enough and lavish enough to make up for all the years the girls had had to shut themselves off from society for fear their friends would discover that their "doctor" father was a revolutionary and their lives steeped in miserable poverty. The upper parlors were cleared for musicians and dancing, while downstairs a table overflowed with extravagant platters of food. Through the huge windows of Modena Villas, a passerby could see fifty young men and women in full evening wear dancing by gas- and candlelight until four in the morning, with the proud mother and father and Lenchen joining in the festivities. Marx loved to dance, and his daughters' friends were among his favorite partners. Jenny, who was an expert judge of such events, declared it "glorious" and a "real success." There was so much food left over, the family was able to throw a children's party for Tussy's friends the next day.[53]

The final act of that pivotal year occurred when Abraham Lincoln won reelection as president. Marx excitedly wrote Lincoln a letter of congratulations on behalf of the IWMA.

> From the commencement of the Titanic-American strife the workingmen of Europe felt instinctively that the star-spangled banner carried the destiny of their class.... The working men of Europe feel sure that, as the American War of Independence initiated a new era of ascendancy for the middle class, so the American Anti-Slavery War will do for the working classes. They consider it an earnest of the epoch to come that it fell to the lot of Abraham Lincoln, the single-minded son of the working class, to lead his country through the matchless struggle for the rescue of an enchained race and the reconstruction of a social world.[54]

Marx was thrilled (he spoke of it in letters for months afterward) when Lincoln responded through the U.S. ambassador to England, Charles Francis Adams.[55] Adams said that Lincoln had expressed a "sincere and anxious desire that he may be able to prove himself not unworthy of the confidence" extended to him by his fellow citizens and those around the world.

> Nations do not exist for themselves alone, but to promote the welfare and happiness of mankind by benevolent intercourse and example. It is in this relation that the United States regard their cause in the present conflict with slavery-maintaining insurgents as the cause of human nature, and they derive new encouragement to persevere from the testimony of the working men of Europe that the national attitude is favored with their enlightened approval and earnest sympathies.[56]

Laura had become her father's full-time assistant at the British Museum,[57] working with him when he was well enough to make the walk to Great Russell Street or on her own when he was not. In fact this nineteen-year-old woman with the long auburn locks and stylish dress that emphasized her curvaceous figure went to the Reading Room every day. It is amusing to imagine the stir she caused in that staid preserve of academic gentlemen. She did so just about everywhere she went. One love-struck admirer asked friends of the Marx family to pass a message to Laura: "Tell her that I have three-hundred-fifty pounds a year, also forty acres of land and that I shall call on her one of these days. I passed their house yesterday but I did not go in because I was afraid of the Papa."[58] In Berlin, Ernestine Liebknecht said a young man who had merely seen Laura's picture fell in love with her.[59] Though younger than Jennychen, Laura had blossomed first, and Marx's return to party politics propitiously coincided with her maturation. The Marx daughters were used to their father's hoary old friends, but now a younger generation of Frenchmen began appearing on the scene.

The French revolutionary tradition had not died even after the defeat of 1848 and the return of empire—far from it. The men who fought on those earlier barricades were looked upon as heroes by many of those who were in their twenties in the mid-1860s. Those young men had been raised on stories of rebellion the way English children might dream of chivalrous knights; indeed, they proudly believed revolt was in their blood. The two luminaries this younger generation most admired were Marx's contemporaries Proudhon and Blanqui. Their ideas were discussed endlessly in the Latin Quarter, where all young radicals—students, journalists, artists, lawyers, doctors—met, drank, smoked, and, when they remembered to do so, ate.

Charles Longuet was one of those who neglected his plate. Tall and thin and sporting a scraggly beard, he was called by one contemporary "the most perfect example of a bohemian one could meet."[60] Longuet was born in an old bourgeois family in Normandy and had studied classics and law with the intention of getting a doctorate of law in Paris. But once in the French capital, he was drawn to radical journalism, politics, and Proudhon. Longuet's favorite café was the Latin Quarter's Brasserie Glaser, where he met with his friends Anatole France, Charles Baudelaire, and Georges Clemenceau.[61] It was with Clemenceau that he launched his initial journalistic venture and earned a four-month prison sentence.[62] Undeterred, when released Longuet founded the newspaper *La Rive Gauche* (The Left Bank), which soon became the most influential socialist journal in the country.[63] It was the first French publication to reprint Marx's Inaugural Address of the IWMA—not since 1847 had Marx's writings appeared in France.[64] Shortly after its publication, Longuet visited London. The month was February 1865; he had just turned twenty-six.

Another young potential comrade also arrived that month (according to his own recollection, though the timing has been disputed by scholars). He was a twenty-three-year-old Cuban-born Frenchman named Paul Lafargue, whose family had plantations in the Caribbean.[65] Lafargue's ethnicity reflected the eclectic island culture: he was black, white, Jewish, Cuban, and French, and liked to say that the blood of all oppressed people ran through his veins. When the Lafargues had returned to France, they settled in Bordeaux, where the family owned vineyards. Paul moved to Paris in 1861 to study medicine but was quickly swept up in the growing student movement. He and Longuet were acquainted through *La Rive Gauche* and the Paris International,[66] and though they were deadly earnest, their temperaments were quite different. This meant that they would never be close, even when, in years to come, they would both become Karl Marx's sons-in-law.

Longuet did not record his first impressions of Marx, but Lafargue did. He recalled that Marx was at work on *Capital* when he arrived at Modena Villas to deliver a message from the Paris IWMA. Though ill[67] (Marx told Engels he had had a new attack of carbuncles in February[68]), Marx welcomed the newcomer warmly, as he always did young people. (Lafargue quoted him as saying, "I must train men to continue communist propaganda after me.")[69] It was not Marx the political agitator who received him, Lafargue wrote, but Marx the theorist, alone in his study:

> It was on the first floor, flooded by light from a broad window that looked out onto a park. Opposite the window on either side of the fireplace the walls were lined with bookcases filled with books and stacked up to the ceiling with newspapers and manuscripts. Opposite the fireplace on one side of the window were two tables piled up with papers, books and newspapers, in the middle of the room, well in the light, stood a small plain desk (three by two feet) and a wooden armchair.[70]

That small desk was where Marx wrote. There was also a leather sofa where Marx napped every afternoon, and on the mantel were books, cigars, matches, tobacco boxes, paperweights, and photographs of Jenny, Engels, Lupus, and his three daughters.

Lafargue left "dazzled" by his first encounter with Marx.[71] But both his visit and Longuet's in 1865 were short. Longuet returned to France to continue his work on *La Rive Gauche,* Lafargue to deepen his involvement in radical politics.

In February the Marx girls threw a party for their mother. Her fifty-first birthday was an uproarious affair compared with the bleak day the previous year when she'd been left alone to contemplate a half century of misery while Marx was being nurtured by Nanette in Holland. Ten-year-old Tussy wrote "Dearest Frederick" on February 13, 1865, to ask if he'd supply a few bottles of Rhine wine and claret: "We are going to give the party ourselves without any help from Mama and we want it to go off very grandly."[72] Engels responded the next day, sending a case.[73]

But if the Marx women were carefree, the man of the house described himself as "infernally harassed" by ill health and the demands of the International, which required his attention every evening and well into the early hours of the morning.[74] Marx was technically only a member of the IWMA's Central Council, but he was the de facto head of the organization, which was growing by thousands of members at a time as whole unions signed up.[75] By April, Marx told one correspondent, England alone had twelve thousand members.[76]

True to Marx's bad luck, his International responsibilities were expanding just as he signed a contract to publish two volumes of *Capital, A Critique of Political Economy*. In January, Marx had authorized a friend to negotiate with Otto Meissner, a publisher in Hamburg.[77] The book was not ready, but since 1861 Marx had honed his theories to the point that he believed it was merely a matter of polishing the writing before the work he had been struggling with since 1851 — if not 1844 — would finally be finished.[78] Engels was ecstatic. He told Marx, "Get on with it quickly now. The time is really ripe for the book, and our names again command respect in the public eye.... Do not miss the moment — it may make an enormous difference to the impact it produces."[79]

Meissner wanted the book at the end of May and promised to publish it by October.[80] But Marx was overwhelmed by activism. He employed Jennychen as his IWMA secretary because, of his daughters, she was fluent in the greatest number of languages.[81] He used Laura as his researcher, and Jenny and Lenchen saw to the household. This assistance was still not enough to keep Marx on schedule. In May, when the book was due at the publisher's, he told Engels, "I'm hoping to put the finishing touches to my book by September 1 (despite numerous interruptions)."[82]

Those interruptions were many and varied. Marx was paralyzed by news in *The Times* of London on April 27 that Abraham Lincoln had been shot. The report was published twelve days after the U.S. president had died.[83] Marx called the assassination the "most stupid act" the South could have committed.[84] As he did for Lincoln's election victory, Marx cleared his desk of other work and crafted a letter on behalf of the IWMA, this one to Lincoln's successor, Andrew Johnson. It was a beautiful and impassioned remembrance of a man Marx greatly admired. He wrote, "The heart of two worlds heaves with emotion" over the death of a man who quietly and humbly pressed on with his difficult work, "tempering stern acts by the gleams of a kind heart, illuminating scenes dark with passion by the smile of humor... in one word, one of the rare men who succeed in becoming great, without ceasing to be good."[85]

As Marx was finishing his letter to Johnson (whom Marx soon vilified as a "dirty tool of the slaveholders"[86]), preparations began for Jennychen's twenty-first birthday. Marx used the opportunity to his political advantage — he invited five International members over for supper and told Engels it would be a "political birthday party."[87] It may not exactly have been the company Jennychen wanted at that important celebration. Marx was aware of her desire for independence, but he seemed in no hurry to help her cut ties to him, his work, or the family. Laura, on the other hand, was making great strides in that direction. On the day of Jennychen's birthday, a young man named Charles Manning asked Laura to marry him. Marx described the incident to Engels saying, "He's rich and generally a nice fellow, BUT LAURA 'DOES NOT CARE A PIN FOR HIM.'" Marx expressed some sympathy for the lad, saying it was a disagreeable case because Laura was a friend of his family and young Charles was "frightfully IN LOVE."[88]

Then, quite unexpectedly, in mid-May Engels telegraphed Marx to say Edgar von Westphalen had arrived in Manchester and would be in London the next day.[89] Jenny's younger brother was now forty-six, and they had not seen him since he was thirty, when in 1849 he had broken his engagement to one of Jenny's friends, given up his law career, and abandoned his family to seek his fortune in America. The man who left had been handsome, vigorous, and overflowing with notions of his own potential. When he knocked on the door at Modena Villas in May 1865, Jenny said, the joy she had felt at the prospect of a reunion turned to horror: she did not recognize him. The man who stood before her was beaten, old, gray, and stooped. It was days before she could find any trace of her brother in this stranger's face and deadened eyes.[90]

Before appearing in London, Edgar had fought for three years on the side of the Confederates in the Civil War and suffered the fate of many soldiers when the South was no longer able to resupply its troops. He had no provisions and no clothes, and when he reached a point of exhaustion such that he could no longer wield his weapon, he was released from the army. Returning to Texas, where he had purchased property, he learned it had been forfeited due to debt.[91] Next he lost a private teaching job and was finally forced to turn to friends in San Antonio for help.[92] But during the last year of the war too many men with families were looking for assistance. A single man had only two real choices, fight or leave. Before the war Edgar had written to Ferdinand asking for his portion of his father's estate, but his brother said he would give it to him only if he returned to Germany.[93] Edgar's appearance in London was a step along that path, but he was in no condition physically or mentally to travel on to Berlin just then.

Jenny immediately set about nursing her brother with the help of her daughters, who had heard stories about their uncle but were not old enough when he left Brussels to truly remember him. They called him "Robinson," because to their minds this man who appeared out of nowhere bearing the scars of war and wilderness was as exotic and mysterious as Defoe's *Robinson Crusoe*.[94] Marx, too, was puzzled by Edgar. He had been one of his earliest political disciples and one of the first members of the Communist League in Brussels, yet he had fought on the side of the Southern oligarchs. Marx told Engels, "It is a most strange irony of fate that this Edgar, who never exploited anyone other than himself and was always a WORKMAN in the strictest sense of the word, went through A WAR OF and WITH STARVATION for the slave-owners."[95]

Amid all this activity, Marx again experienced an eruption of carbuncles. He told Engels he was "working like a horse" to complete his book— and for fun, doing differential calculus[96]—but Jenny reported to Engels that her husband was tormented and did not sleep for two straight weeks in May because of the pain. She suspected the attack was brought on by many things—writing, the situation in America, and, once again, financial distress.[97] In July 1865 Marx confessed to Engels that all the money he had inherited the previous year from his mother and Lupus was gone.

"For two months I have been living solely on the pawnshop, which means that a queue of creditors has been hammering on my door, becoming more and more unendurable every day." The news that he had inherited funds had caused creditors dating back to his Cologne days to surface, and his local debts and furnishing the house had cost a staggering five hundred pounds.

I assure you that I would rather have had my thumb cut off than write this letter to you. It is truly soul-destroying to be dependent for half one's life. The only thought that sustains me in all this is that the two of us form a partnership together, in which I spend my time on the theoretical and party side of the business. It is true my house is beyond my means, and we have, moreover, lived better this year than was the case before. But it is the only way for the children to establish themselves socially with a view to securing their future, quite apart from everything they have suffered and for which they have at least been compensated for a brief while. I believe you yourself will be of the opinion that, even from a merely commercial point of view, to run a purely proletarian household would not be appropriate in the circumstances, although that would be quite all right if my wife and I were by ourselves or if the girls were boys.

Marx appeared to be in the mood for full disclosure, because in the same letter he told Engels the true status of *Capital*. "There are three more chapters to be written to complete the theoretical part (the first three books). Then there is still the fourth book, the historical-literary one, to be written." But yet again, postponement: "I cannot bring myself to send anything off until I have the whole thing in front of me. WHATEVER SHORTCOMINGS THEY MAY HAVE, the advantage of my writings is that they are an artistic whole, and this can only be achieved through my practice of never having things printed until I have them in front of me *in their entirety*."[98]

In order to be left alone to work on his book, Marx said he lied to IWMA members and told them he was leaving London. That summer the city was beastly hot; Marx told Engels he had been vomiting nearly every day for three months, and because of the heat he had worked by an open window and now had rheumatism in his right arm and shoulder blade.[99] Still, he promised to spare no effort to complete *Capital*: "The thing is a nightmarish burden to me."[100]

Engels agreed. "The day that manuscript is sent off, I shall drink myself to kingdom come."[101] But the book had already missed its deadline, and the prospects for its completion looked dim with each passing month. In August, Marx's "bilious" troubles and the heat made him incapable of thinking.[102] A week later he announced he had the flu and was forced to dabble "in irrelevancies, including astronomy."[103] Meanwhile, Laura became ill, Tussy had measles, Jenny lost two front lower teeth and ultimately had to have four replaced, Jennychen contracted diphtheria, and Edgar had begun to recover and was eating them out of house and home. Marx complained that all Edgar thought about was the needs of his stomach and his clothes — even his sex drive had gone to his belly.[104] On top of this, IWMA colleagues had discovered that Marx had not left London but was trying to avoid them. The organization once again insisted on his attention.[105]

By mid-January 1866 Marx had twelve hundred pages, and he said he was working twelve hours a day writing a fair copy of the book because Meissner was grumbling about the delay; Marx now hoped he could get it to him by March.[106] London was covered in an ankle-deep blanket of snow[107] as Marx sat at his desk near the fireplace copying the book and polishing the style — or, as he said, "licking the infant clean after long birth pangs."[108] But then a carbuncle appeared, followed by "all kinds of little progeny." Because of their location, he could not sit to write, and because of the pain and medication, he could not think to theorize. Doctors blamed the outbreak on excessive night work, which Marx said was unavoidable given the demands he faced during the day.[109]

By mid-February Marx felt he had lost so much ground that the book was no longer ready for publication. He told Engels there had been new developments in agricultural chemistry in Germany and France that he had to take into consideration, as well as new information on hereditary fees applied to rented land since he had last studied the subject, and finally new information on Japan that he was obliged to study in travel books. He said he could not send his manuscript to Meissner until he had included all this material.[110]

Under the care of a German doctor, Marx began an arsenic cure, ingesting small doses of the poison three times a day. Jenny told a friend he rarely slept and when he did, he was delirious and "forever talking of the various chapters which are going around and around in his mind."[111] Jenny and Engels had been through years of such physical crises with Marx, the most severe of them nearly always coinciding with writing deadlines. During the early months of 1866, however, his condition was more worrying than they had ever seen. Engels was normally the first to prod Marx on in his writing, but this time he told his friend he must stop all intellectual work and take care of his health, even if it delayed the completion of *Capital* by three more months.[112] He instructed Marx to go to the seaside to recuperate. "Do me and your family the one favor of *getting yourself cured*. What would become of the whole movement if anything were to happen to you, and the way you are proceeding, that will be the *inevitable* outcome."[113]

Marx agreed to go to the coast in March. But before he left, he had to pull himself together sufficiently to hold a "council of war" at his home.[114] The French section of the International was in turmoil, and moves were afoot to "rebel against the absent 'tyrant'" Marx.[115]

31

London, 1866

But women, good Lord women! What a sad destiny is theirs!
— Madame de Staël[1]

MARX'S NEGLECT OF IWMA activities during his illness and his efforts to hide in order to complete his book gave his opponents an opening against him. Again it was Mazzini who caused him problems, this time under the pretense of seeking to minimize the "German" influence on a supposedly "international" organization. But Marx had loyal followers willing to fight on his behalf. Five of them arrived at Maitland Park in early March. Three were old family friends; the two others, however, were young newcomers from France, neither of whom spoke English.[2] After their initial visits the previous year, Charles Longuet and Paul Lafargue were back in London and were now accepted by Marx as part of his inner circle. Both had burnished their revolutionary credentials in France amid the growing unrest over Napoleon's rule.

The changes wrought on France by Napoleon III were most evident in Paris, where he and Georges-Eugène Haussmann had launched a renewal project that transformed the city. Streets of small shops were cleared to make way for grand department stores—Printemps, Samaritine, and Bon Marché; working-class districts of narrow winding streets were destroyed and replaced by elegant boulevards lined by apartments for the rich or temples to culture and government. Other poor neighborhoods were torn down to make way for railways and their elaborate stations. The plan was partly designed to allow Napoleon to leave a permanent architectural imprint on the city, but also to rob rebellious citizens of the terrain they needed to effectively use barricades. Haussmann's broad, straight boulevards gave government forces the advantage in any uprising, because they could confront insurgents with a veritable wall of manpower, standing shoulder-to-shoulder and armed with glistening steel. Their cannons were also now able to fire straight down a boulevard and into a crowd.

Yet, as with every discharge, there was a recoil. The city's transformation had caused rents to soar beyond the reach of workingmen and -women, who were already coping with higher food prices. And while new transport systems made it possible for them to live outside central Paris, the cost of travel was too high to make such commuting generally feasible.[3] Discontent was widespread among the lower classes, and in the 1860s students took up their cause and began to agitate against the government. Lafargue and Longuet were among them.

In October 1865 an international students' congress was held in Liège, Belgium, to discuss educational reform. Lafargue and a group of French students decided to use the event to protest against the French government.[4] Their arrival was tantamount to a troupe of circus performers entering a small village: they paraded into the center of town, shouting anti-Napoleon slogans and dressed in bohemian attire—beards, broad-brimmed hats, knapsacks. Instead of the French flag, Lafargue and some of the other students carried a black crepe banner to depict a nation in mourning over liberties trampled by the emperor.[5]

Lafargue was immature, vain, and unable to resist a grand gesture when the opportunity arose. At times he seemed to act thoughtlessly, heedless of the meaning of his actions and their consequences. He tried to rally French students watching cautiously from the sidelines, arguing, "Is it not better to move in one direction or another than to remain indifferent?" and convinced some to replace the tricolor on their vests with the red ribbon of revolt.[6] Emboldened, he next climbed onto the speaker's tribune and declared war not on Napoleon but on God, proclaiming that science rendered God useless, that God was the devil and property was theft.[7]

The handsome young man with thick brown hair, long mustache, and exotic almond-shaped eyes went from being an unknown on October 27 to being recognized as a reckless radical on October 28. He was suddenly under the scrutiny of the French government. Standing taller (at least in his own mind) as a result, he met his idol Blanqui, who was also at Liège. For longer than Lafargue had been alive, Blanqui had had the reputation of being a dangerous and unrepentant fire-breathing revolutionary. Lafargue found him at sixty to be a small man with white hair and beard, and deeply sunken eyes, his hands like small birds, always in motion, his voice gentle and sympathetic. Blanqui spoke of revolution and admonished the group of twenty students straining to hear him not to listen to their elders—even to himself—when they suggested actions or ideas that ran counter to their beliefs. Lafargue was mesmerized, and later credited Blanqui with turning him to revolution.[8]

When Lafargue returned to Paris in early November his French medical studies were over—though not necessarily by his own choosing: the Academic Council of Paris met in December and voted to expel seven students, including Lafargue, for profaning the national flag and attacking the principles of social order at the Liège event. The student opposition in Paris was outraged by the decision to punish Frenchmen for words spoken outside French borders, arguing that no law existed rendering such actions a crime. Riots erupted. Students disrupted classes and clashed with police in the Latin Quarter. Ultimately eight hundred people were arrested. Two weeks later, despite the show of anger, the expulsion order was upheld. Lafargue was banned from the University of Paris for life and for two years from all other French universities.[9]

Lafargue's father did not want his son's studies interrupted, so he sent him to work with a French doctor at St. Bartholomew's Hospital in London. Lafargue left for England in mid-February along with Cesare Orsini, brother of the Italian Felice Orsini, who had been executed in 1858 for one of the most notorious crimes of that decade, the attempted assassination of Napoleon III in a bombing that did not hurt the emperor but killed eight innocent people.[10] It is unlikely that Orsini was the traveling companion Lafargue's father would have wanted for his son, and equally unlikely that the elder Lafargue would have wanted Paul to continue his radical associations in London. But within days of their arrival, Lafargue and Orsini met with members of the International and Lafargue was nominated as a member. Approved on March 6,[11] four days later he attended the war council at Marx's home.

The chronicle of Longuet's revolutionary history between February 1865 and the spring of 1866 was shorter. After Longuet had left London the previous year, *La Rive Gauche* lasted just seventeen issues before being censored. Longuet was sentenced to prison again—this time for eight months—but fled France before he could be arrested. His travels were not unlike those of the young Marx. He went to Belgium, where he tried to reconstitute his newspaper, but was expelled. He landed in Frankfurt and was expelled again. Eventually, like countless fugitives before him, in late 1865 he arrived in London.[12] There, he became a member of the International's Central Council on January 16, 1866.[13]

★　★　★

The IWMA members meeting at Marx's home on March 10 devised a strategy to reinforce in the minds of their English comrades, and anyone else on
the council who doubted it, that Marx was the undisputed head of the continental section of the International.[14] The group enlisted Orsini to describe
his fellow Italian Mazzini as ineffectual on behalf of the workingman, downright reactionary when it came to "science," and incapable of understanding
the "new movement."[15] (There was no love lost on either side: Mazzini called
Marx a "destructive spirit," "extraordinarily sly," "vindictive," and "impla-
cable.")[16] With the plan agreed, three days later Marx dragged his carbuncle-
plagued body to a meeting of the IWMA Central Council. As he did
whenever he was actually present to defend himself, he carried the day.
When face-to-face with those who challenged him politically, Marx fought
with the precise aggression he used when armed with a saber. He and his
associates were helped by the fact that few of their main opponents attended
the gathering, and the English ranks were diminished because a meeting on
universal manhood suffrage was under way elsewhere. But the outcome was
all that was important: the Mazzini backers were crushed.[17]

With relative peace of mind on the International front, Marx made his
way alone to the English coastal town of Margate on March 15 to try to
recover physically. He registered at a small inn but left after only one night
because, bizarrely, he was deeply disturbed by the presence of a motionless
man in the dining room who he thought was blind but turned out to be
deaf.[18] Marx next moved to private lodgings facing the sea and commenced a
vigorous, self-designed cure that involved miles of walking and sea baths. He
described himself as a "walking stick, running up and down the whole day,
and keeping my mind in that state of nothingness which Buddhism considers
the climax of human bliss."[19] Among his excursions was a sixteen-mile walk
to Canterbury, a town he found sadly lacking any trace of poetry.[20]

Marx's retreat to Margate meant that his home was free of his growling
presence (Tussy had taken to calling her father "Dr. Karl Marx of bad philosophy"[21]), which had the effect of separating the young Frenchmen from
the Marx daughters. Not that the continentals ignored the father—Marx
had been away only five days when he told Laura "that damned boy Lafargue" had already written him numerous pestering letters.[22] In fact Marx
thought he was the reason the men came to the house. Without doubt he
was the initial draw, but their attention had quickly shifted elsewhere.
Longuet was immediately attracted to Jennychen, who, though five years
younger than he, was as serious and discreet. But his reserve and his first
love—politics—prevented him from expressing any interest in her at that

point.[23] The demonstrative Lafargue, however, exhibited no such scruples. He fell desperately in love with Laura and made sure everyone was aware of his feelings. The medical student turned revolutionary became in Laura's presence a poet: "Her rich curly hair had a golden shimmer as if it had caught the rays of the setting sun . . ."[24] He also promptly made himself handy around the Marx household, thereby earning the nickname Tooley.[25]

On March 22 the Marx daughters gave a party. Lion Philips had sent them five pounds for Christmas, but Jenny and Marx had promptly borrowed it to keep the household running and only managed to reimburse their children that spring. All three girls were in on the planning. The event was not a ball, as their mother had arranged in 1864, but an "annual party," as Marx described it to Engels. They insisted Marx return from Margate for the evening, which he did.[26]

Karl and Jenny considered all three of their daughters to be very upright and English, much less bohemian than they had been—or indeed still were. So it was with relief that Jenny watched as those children began to share a social life with young men of comparable political beliefs, even though she positively rebelled at the thought of her daughters marrying revolutionaries. She confided to Ernestine Liebknecht that she had long worried that the "peculiar direction" of her elder daughters' education would lead to clashes with their peers, presciently writing, "The girls have been brought up with ideas and views which make up a complete partition for the society in which they move. . . . Would they be rich, they could get by without 'Baptism, Church and Religion,' but like this they both will have to go through arduous, difficult struggles and I often think that when one can't offer assets and complete independence from others, one is not doing right to bring them up in such a violent opposition to the world." Their predicament worried and depressed her: "The girls believe that I am often in a bad mood or irksome but it is nothing but the awareness that they cannot claim as much happiness as they would have the right to in their lives due to exterior and interior gifts."[27] In a letter to Ferdinand she was even more candid. Jenny said she feared she and Marx had sacrificed their daughters' future for the movement. "Everything that we do for others we take away from our children."[28]

But the house on Maitland Park and the influx of young men, with whom the girls could discuss politics freely and act as boldly as they liked, heartened Jenny. She was especially pleased with Lafargue, because he let slip remarks that led Jenny to believe his family represented old and abundant wealth. Laura, however, did not return—or even particularly notice—Lafargue's amour. It could have been that Laura did not know what to make of this suitor, who seemed ready to deliver himself heart and soul after knowing her only a month. Indeed, for all their political sophistication, the Marx daughters were sheltered and naive when it came to the opposite sex.

Jennychen and Tussy, now twenty-two and eleven years old respectively, followed their father to Margate immediately after the party, but Laura remained behind with her mother. She wrote Jennychen that a Mr. Faraday had come by for a *"tête-à-tête"* one evening. "We both made ourselves as agreeable as we could and I was as much delighted with him as I dare say he was with me." However, during their exchange (which she insisted was not flirtatious) her mother entered the room in a state of undress. Jenny was shoeless and, according to Laura, wearing "just so much of drapery as to relieve her from the charge of trusting entirely to nature for effects, and that drapery just so disposed as to show more than it concealed." The young man blushed crimson. Laura remained calm only by closing her eyes "to escape the sight of what I could not look upon." The next day, while home alone, Laura had another caller—her father's friend Peter Fox.

How frightened I was! The man who had recognized at first sight that I was wanting in that spark for which nothing can atone and who had never yet spoken half a dozen words with me.... He had a weight of grievances on his heart and head which were so overpowering as to be impossible to hide. Out came his skeletons—Poland—Ireland—Reform League—"Feudal aristocracy"—"British Ministry"—not one by one but all in a lump, till the room actually darkened with what I suppose were living incarnations of dead things invoked by his wild words and till his stammering and stuttering increased to that extent which rendered further *exposition* impossible.

The one-sided exchange lasted for an hour and a half, during which time, Laura said, she was "scarcely able to suppress my laughter."[29]

Jenny no doubt suspected Laura's immersion in the game of love would soon lead to marriage, but she may have thought her eldest daughter needed a bit of prodding in the romance department. Jennychen was still plotting a career in the theater but was also deeply involved in the International, corresponding with her father's friends and the many new associates who sought his advice. While Jennychen was in Margate, Jenny sent her a copy of Madame de Staël's novel *Delphine*.[30] It was a massive epistolary tale of a woman's life of torment because she repeatedly counted virtue and familial commitment as more important than love. But the effort seemed wasted on Jennychen; there was no one on her horizon. Even Longuet, whom she regarded solely as her father's protégé, had returned to Paris to serve his prison sentence.

As for Marx and his daughters, the Margate trip was not the jolly affair

they'd expected. The weather was terrible ("As if it had been made especially to order for the COCKNEYS who have invaded this place for the Easter holiday,"[31] the defender of the workingman wrote condescendingly of
London's laboring East Enders). And Marx, who had by then been on the
coast for a month, was increasingly worried about the International. In his
absence quarrels had erupted again, even as the group successfully intervened in a number of strikes, winning accolades from workers and new
members as a result. *Capital,* too, weighed on him. He told a friend, "It is
enough to drive one out of one's mind."[32]

Father and daughters returned to London in mid-April, whereupon
Marx was struck down by a toothache, vomiting, and rheumatism, which
resisted repeated doses of opium and treatments involving ether.[33] Marx
was back at home, but he was not back at work.

Marx and Engels had been watching the situation in Germany closely.
Bismarck, the prime minister who since the summer of 1863 had restored
reactionary rule to Prussia—silencing critics by banning political discussions, censoring the press, restraining liberal politicians under threat of
reprisal—now appeared to be trying to provoke war with Austria. Bismarck wanted a united Germany dominated by Prussia and viewed Austria as the main impediment to that goal.[34]

As in Paris against Napoleon, there were rumblings among students in
Berlin against Bismarck. In May 1866 a twenty-four-year-old student
tried to kill the prime minister as he traveled along the Unter den Linden,
firing five shots but missing his target. The student was Ferdinand Cohen,
stepson of Karl Blind, and had been Musch's boyhood friend during the
Soho days. Cohen was arrested immediately and supposedly committed
suicide in jail the next day.[35]

Engels mocked the assassination attempt, saying that Cohen had done
Bismarck a favor with his rash act. But Marx was moved to sympathy.[36]
He told Engels, "Cohen was a very good lad (although not particularly
gifted) for whom I have a special regard as he was an old friend of my
Musch."[37] Cohen's death could not have failed to give Marx pause to consider what a twenty-four-year-old Musch might have done with his life,
whether he would have tried something as reckless after a lifetime of
ingesting his father's radical ideas. Indeed, in the same letter to Engels,
Marx angrily blamed Blind for "his idiotic regicidal blather" that sacrificed this boy "on the altar of freedom."[38]

Prussia went to war with Austria in June, as Bismarck wanted. Marx
decided to use the conflict as an opportunity for the International to stress
the importance of neutrality among workingmen of all countries when

faced with a war between governments out to gain territory and increased power: he did not want to see workers sacrificed on the altar of capitalism. A meeting of the IWMA Central Council was called in mid-June to discuss an official response to the conflict. The group's policy had long been agreed upon—workers would not fight other workers. But now that an actual war was under way, the delegates' nationalistic prejudices rose to the surface. Lafargue took the podium and declared that any talk of nationalities or nations was reactionary, and that states should not exist but rather be broken down into communes, or local self-governing municipalities. In a long-winded speech he implied that the world was waiting for France to spearhead such a revolution, which would then be adopted universally. Marx got a roar of laughter from the crowd when he chastised Lafargue for abolishing nationalities in an address delivered in *French,* a language nine-tenths of those gathered did not understand. He then said sarcastically that Lafargue's very denial of nationalities carried with it the implication that the only way out of nationhood was to be absorbed by "the model French nation."[39] In the end, the Central Council advised workers to be neutral vis-à-vis the Austria-Prussia War,[40] which ended quickly, on July 3, after a decisive eight-hour battle from which Prussia and Bismarck emerged victorious.

Marx's fun at Lafargue's expense may in fact have been a sign of affection. He appreciated Lafargue's commitment to the International (even if he thought his notions confused), and he liked having a doctor around (even if Lafargue was still a student). And by August, Lafargue appeared to have gained Laura's attention and broken down her resistance. Marx told Engels in a letter dated August 7, "Since yesterday Laura is half promised to Monsieur Lafargue, my medical Creole. She treats him like the others, but the outbursts of feeling these Creoles are subject to, a slight fear that the young man (he is twenty-five) might do away with himself, etc., some fondness for him, undemonstrative as always with Laura (he is a good-looking, intelligent, energetic lad of athletic build), have more or less led to a semi-compromise."[41]

Jenny, too, seemed pleased if a bit surprised by the development, given Laura's previous disinterest in Lafargue.[42] Even Engels did not know whether he should offer congratulations under the circumstances but did so anyway.[43] Actually, the only one involved in the affair who seemed to embrace it with full fervor was Lafargue himself. He showed such a lack of restraint toward Laura that he earned a second and much less playful rebuke from Marx.

If you wish to continue your relations with my daughter, you will have to give up your present manner of "courting." You know full well that no engagement

337

has been entered into, that as yet everything is undecided. And even if she were formally betrothed to you, you should not forget that this is a matter of long duration. The practice of excessive intimacy is especially inappropriate since the two lovers will be living at the same place for a necessarily prolonged period of severe testing and purgatory. I have observed with alarm how your conduct has altered from one day to the next within the geological period of one single week. To my mind, true love expresses itself in reticence, modesty and even the shyness of the lover towards the object of his veneration, and certainly not in giving free rein to one's passion and in premature demonstrations of famil- iarity. If you should urge your Creole temperament in your defense, it is my duty to interpose my sound reason between your temperament and my daugh- ter. If in her presence you are incapable of loving in a manner in keeping with the London latitude, you will have to resign yourself to loving her from a dis- tance. I am sure you will take the hint.[44]

Marx's admonition included what sounded very much like a description of his and Jenny's own long courtship, and this may have put him in a reflec- tive mood, because he followed it with a rare admission of personal failure. After telling Lafargue that he needed clarity about his financial situation before agreeing to any engagement, Marx said: "You know that I have sacri- ficed my whole fortune to the revolutionary struggle. I do not regret it. Quite the contrary. If I had to begin my life over again, I would do the same. I would not marry, however. As far as it lies within my power, I wish to save my daughter from the reefs on which her mother's life was wrecked."[45]

Marx told Lafargue that he did not have confidence in his industrious- ness, and that his position as a student thrown out of one country and try- ing to restart his career in another was not overly promising. He said he also did not know whether Lafargue's family supported him, how it would feel about the marriage, or whether Lafargue could in any way promise Laura a secure life. He added,

Had it not been for my direct intervention (a weakness on my part) and the influence that my friendship for you exerted on my daughter's conduct, this affair would never have progressed to its present point; for this reason I bear a heavy personal responsibility.

To preclude any misinterpretation of this letter, I would like to state that— were you in a position to enter into matrimony today—it would not come about. My daughter would refuse. I myself should object. You must have achieved something in life before thinking of marriage, and a long period of testing is required of you and Laura.[46]

Within days Lafargue had a character reference sent to Marx by a famous French doctor, and his father had written Marx promising a large financial settlement when the young couple was married. He also requested that his son be allowed to consider himself Laura's fiancé.[47] Marx confidentially wrote to Engels that Lafargue had a "heart of gold but is a spoiled child and too much a child of nature." In a sign of his deep respect for his friend, he added that Laura would not accept Lafargue's marriage offer without Engels's approval.[48] Finally, just in case Lafargue could not restrain himself when in proximity to Laura, Marx temporarily sent her and Tussy to a boarding school in the coastal town of Hastings.[49] It was not unlike the South Hampstead College for Ladies, where Jennychen and Laura had attended classes in London, but it had the added advantage of distance. As to Lafargue, Marx reported to Laura after her departure, "*The knight of the woeful countenance* left me at the corner of his house. His heart having been considerably shaken before, he seemed to bear his separation *from me* with a rather heroic indifference."[50]

With Laura away, Marx absorbed Lafargue into the family business, keeping the young man busy preparing instructions for delegates to the first International Congress, which was scheduled for Geneva in September. Jennychen recalled Lafargue working one day from ten in the morning until ten at night translating Marx's directives into French. "The unfortunate youth looked fearfully woebegone.... He was neither shaved nor *combed,*" she told her mother, who was in Dover.[51] (Adding to his load, Lafargue, perhaps hoping to win Tussy as an ally in his pursuit of Laura, built her a swing set in the yard.)[52] Though Lafargue did everything in his power to insinuate himself into the family, he did not seem to fully insinuate himself into Laura's heart. While in Hastings she dreamily wrote to Jennychen about an earlier visit there, when she had walked and talked with a music teacher named Banner and had drunk milk with him from the same cup. "I hope I am not sentimental, but to forget is an art I have not learned and with me memory of that which is no more, is regret."[53]

Despite whatever hesitation she may have had, however, the wheels of marriage were in motion. Laura and Lafargue became officially engaged on September 26—her twenty-first birthday. There is no description of Laura's reaction, but her mother seemed happy and relieved on many counts. She told Ernestine Liebknecht that Paul was kind and generous and devoted to Laura, and, most fortunately, the young couple was of like mind on religion and politics. "Laura is thus spared of inevitable struggles and agony to which every girl is exposed with her views. Because how exceptional is it to find men who share these views and who have at the same time education, social position, etc." The wedding was not expected for another two years, after Lafargue finished his medical studies in England. In the meantime he took rooms nearby but was a virtual resident at the Marx home—with, unfortunately for Marx, all the added expense that entailed.[54]

Everything in Marx's life came to a head that fall. He had worked assiduously preparing for the International's first congress, which he would not attend but whose fate was in his hands until the moment the delegates left for Geneva. That actually made the event more difficult for Marx, because he could not control actors once they were out of sight, no matter how thoroughly he had prepared the ground. Moreover, he was finally ready to send *Capital* to Hamburg. He had decided he could not wait until he was satisfied with all projected volumes—or even the two volumes he had promised Meissner in his contract. Instead, he planned to send the publisher only the first volume of what he expected would be a four-volume work.[55] Finally, in the midst of all that labor and creative turmoil, Marx was absolutely penniless, once again hunted by the landlord and tradesmen who lined up at the door trying to collect overdue bills. On one occasion when a creditor appeared, Marx did not have enough money to pay in full. To keep both Lafargue and the creditor in the dark, he told his caller to wait a moment while he changed some money. He then slipped out the back and scurried to the baker's shop to borrow what he needed before anyone noticed he was gone.[56] He believed his daughter's immediate happiness was in jeopardy if Lafargue—or worse, his family—found out that the aura of respectability at Modena Villas was a sham. And there was a real risk of that: one brazen Frenchman to whom Marx owed money threatened to tell the elder Lafargue if he was not paid.[57] If that happened Laura might find herself in the unfortunate position of many young nineteenth-century women, who had discovered to their sorrow that a lack of funds trumped an abundance of love in negotiations involving the institution called marriage.

Marx wrote Engels that he had turned to his family in Holland and Germany for money, but to no avail. Jenny had now pawned so many of her things that she could scarcely go out of the house, and Marx had run from one end of the city to the other "begging small loans left and right, as in the worst refugee days. . . . On the other hand, I am being threatened by tradesmen, some of whom have withdrawn their credit and threatened to take me to court. This state of affairs was all the more critical in that Lafargue (until his departure for Bordeaux a few days ago) was constantly in the house and the REAL STATE OF THINGS had to be anxiously concealed from him." Shameless in his requests and his attempts to gain sympathy when strapped, he added, "Not merely has my work been frequently interrupted by all this, but by trying to make up at night for the time lost during the day, I have acquired a fine carbuncle near my PENIS."[58]

Engels heard the familiar cry for help and responded immediately. Given Marx's litany of woes, he likely also expected Marx to tell him that his manuscript would be delayed. But Marx surprised him, sending off a portion of his book, *Capital, Volume I,* to Hamburg in the second week of November 1866.[59] There was an audible sigh of relief from Manchester. Wrote Engels, "The news that the manuscript has gone off is a load off my mind. . . . To that end I shall drink a special glass to your particular health. The book has greatly contributed to wrecking your health; once you have got it off your back, you'll be quite a different fellow again."[60]

Jenny, too, expressed relief, but this woman who had known a lifetime of dashed hopes and shattered dreams with Marx also expressed foreboding. In a Christmas letter to Engels she said:

> If the publisher in Hamburg really can print the book as fast as he says, it is certain to come out by Easter in any case. It is a pleasure to see the manuscript lying there copied out and stacked up so high. It is an enormous weight off my mind; we have enough troubles and worries left without that. . . . I wish I could see everything in rosy colors as much as the others do, but the long years with their many anxieties have made me nervous, and the future often looks black to me when it all looks rosy to a more cheerful spirit. That is between ourselves.[61]

Soon a series of setbacks seemed to confirm Jenny's fears as the months slipped by accompanied by delays and indecision. Meissner refused to print only *Volume I,* instead wanting to wait until Marx had sent him *Volume II* as well. Next, Marx was debilitated by insomnia and carbuncles on his buttocks, which he admitted were directly connected to his state of mind.[62] (He mischievously told Engels later, "I hope the bourgeoisie will remember my carbuncles until their dying day.")[63] Finally, there was the old bugbear, money. Marx told Engels in early April 1867 he could not take the remainder of his manuscript to Hamburg as planned because his clothes and watch were in the pawnshop.[64] Engels, whom Jennychen described as "frantic with joy" over the book's completion,[65] provided the funds for their retrieval.

Years before, Engels had told his sister he dared not indulge in wishes, because if he ever allowed himself to be weak enough to do so, the thing he wished for always turned out to be something he could not have.[66] But that April, with *Capital* nearly two years late but finally moving toward publication, he allowed himself to wish and dream and, as he told Marx, imagine a more propitious future at last.

32

London, 1867

"Do you see anything?" Poussin whispered to Porbus.
"No. Do you?"
"Nothing."
"The old fraud's pulling our leg."

—Honoré de Balzac[1]

WHEN MARX FINALLY reached Hanover, where he awaited proof sheets from Hamburg, he received a long letter from Engels in which he expressed what he had perhaps left unsaid during the nearly two decades he had supported the Marx family while waiting for Karl to produce his great work.

> I always had the feeling that that damn book, which you have been carrying for so long, was at the bottom of all your misfortune, and you would and could never extricate yourself until you had got it off your back. Forever resisting completion, it was driving you physically, mentally and financially into the ground, and I can very well understand that having shaken off that nightmare, you now feel quite a new man....I am exceedingly gratified by this whole turn of events, firstly, for its own sake, secondly, for your sake in particular and your wife's, and thirdly, because it really is time things looked up.

Engels said in two years his contract at Ermen & Engels would end and he would leave the world of business. "There is nothing I long for so much as for release from this vile COMMERCE, which is completely demoralizing me with all the time it is wasting. For as long as I am in it, I am good for nothing else." This would, of course, mean a drastic reduction in income, but Engels felt that "if things go as they are now beginning to, we shall be able to make provision for that all right, too, even if no revolution intervenes and puts an end to all financial schemes. If that does not happen, I have a plan up my sleeve to have a fling for my deliverance and write a light-hearted book entitled: *Woes and Joys of the English Bourgeoisie.*"[2]

Marx, too, allowed himself to dream. In Hamburg, Meissner greeted him with enthusiasm and pledged his commitment to publish his works.[3] Overflowing with expectations, Marx told a Geneva friend that *Capital* "is without question the most terrible MISSILE that has yet been hurled at the heads of the bourgeoisie."[4] He wrote another friend in New York that (though he had only finished one volume) he expected three volumes would be published within a year, and he was using every moment to complete the work "to which I have sacrificed my health, happiness, and family.... I laugh at the so-called 'practical' men and their wisdom. If one wanted to be an ox, one could, of course, turn one's back on the sufferings of humanity and look after one's own hide."[5] Finally, he wrote Engels, "I hope and confidently believe that in the space of a year I shall be made, in the sense that I shall be able to fundamentally rectify my financial affairs and at last stand on my own feet again."[6]

Marx received the first proof sheets for *Capital* on his forty-ninth birthday, and the publisher was already putting notices about the book's imminent publication in newspapers. Things appeared to be moving in exactly the right direction, and Marx was bursting with confidence.[7] It would have been difficult not to be. While in Hanover he lived in the house of a veritable groupie (or as Marx described him, a fanatical supporter). Dr. Ludwig Kugelmann was a gynecologist who had discovered Marx and Engels as early as their first joint book, *The Holy Family,* and collected all their works. It is not clear what Kugelmann saw in socialism, communism, or Marx for that matter—he was bourgeois to the core. Whatever the attraction, Marx was shocked to find in Kugelmann's library a better collection of his and Engels's works than they themselves possessed.[8] With the weight of *Capital* lifted from his shoulders and his every need attended to by the Kugelmanns, Marx declared his health extraordinarily improved.

Also contributing to Marx's good spirits were the attentions of a thirty-three-year-old woman named Madame Tenge, née Bolongaro-Crevenna, who was married to a wealthy German landowner and who stayed with the Kugelmanns during Marx's visit.[9] He described her to Jennychen as "a really noble nature, of a peculiar suavity, frankness and simplicity of character. Nothing of the sham education. She speaks English, French and Italian (she is of Italian descent) perfectly.... She is an atheist and inclines to Socialism, although rather little informed on that point. What distinguishes her above all is a spontaneous kindness and the absence of all pretensions." Marx sent Jennychen a picture of Madame Tenge hidden behind his own, but she appeared not to have shared it with her mother or sisters.[10] (In a letter to Laura, Marx wondered that she had to ask what Madame Tenge looked like; Laura had not seen the picture.)[11] Jennychen may have kept the image to herself because she was aware of the effect Marx's associations with other young women during earlier trips had had on her mother. Marx, however, seemed positively chatty in discussing his "admiration" for Madame Tenge, which he hinted was reciprocated. He described this "superior woman" to his daughters as if they were his confidantes in matters of the heart.[12]

That outpouring of information came only after Madame Tenge had left Hanover. While she was in residence there, the Marx women complained they had heard little from him for nearly a month. Jennychen said she feared he had been arrested by Bismarck.[13] Laura told her father she "began to think that you had taken French leave and stolen out of our company for good and all." Laura perhaps best understood his silence.

I am sure there must be something delightful in the mere temporary "riddance" of that conventional "rubbish" one's "family"...to say nothing of the society you are in. There is a certain lady, I have noticed, occupies a large portion of your letters: is she young? is she witty? is she pretty? Do you flirt with her or suffer her to flirt with you? You seem to admire her very much and it would be *too silly* to suppose all the admiration was on your side. If I were Möhme I should be jealous.[14]

In each letter to Marx the family asked when he planned to come home. He finally did so shortly after Madame Tenge left Hanover. Without her as a distraction Marx soon became bored by Kugelmann. Earlier he told Engels he would remain in Hanover until he had read all the proofs, but after Madame Tenge's departure he said it was impossible to wait there until the book was complete, and in any case he had to get home to work on *Volume II*. He was reconciled to returning to London despite what he said awaited him—"torments of family life, the domestic conflicts, the constant harassment, instead of settling down to work refreshed and free of care."[15]

Marx had left London on April 10 and arrived back in England on May 19, after once again briefly stopping in Hamburg to see Meissner and collect portions of his book. While he might have been anxious to get back to work, he appeared to be in no hurry to return to Modena Villas. On the steamer from Hamburg to London he met a young German woman whose military bearing caught his attention. It was her first trip to London, and she would be traveling onward by train to friends in the country. Marx valiantly offered to escort her to the station. They arrived in London at two in the afternoon but her train did not leave until eight o'clock that evening, so rather than go home to his waiting family, Marx spent six hours with this stranger walking in Hyde Park, sitting in ice cream shops, and passing the time with other diversions. He described her to Kugelmann as cheerful and educated but aristocratic and Prussian to her fingertips. It turned out that the woman, Elisabeth von Puttkamer, was Bismarck's niece, and Marx said she was not a little alarmed to discover she had fallen into "red hands."[16] (Bismarck had, in fact, sent an envoy to see Marx while he was in Hanover to say he wished to make use of Marx's talents in the interests of the German people. Marx told no one but Engels about the absurd proposition.)[17] As for Marx and Bismarck's niece, they parted at the train station as friends. With no other young woman to detain him, Marx finally returned to his wife, daughters, and possibly most anxious of them all, Lafargue.

He stayed in London for only three days before going to Manchester to deliver proof sheets to Engels. Engels had not read any of the work as yet, and Marx was nervous about his reaction. He considered Engels his most important critic and also one of his most difficult, if for no other reason than Engels knew the subject as well as Marx himself. Marx had made a very revealing recommendation to Engels before leaving for Hamburg, suggesting he read Balzac's short novel *The Unknown Masterpiece,* which he described as "full of delightful irony."[18] The book was about a painter who, after years of labor and amid great anticipation, produced a masterpiece that only he could see or understand.

Engels's first response to Marx's work was mixed. He received the book in parcels of sixteen pages and said by way of gentle criticism that the difficult second batch "in particular has the marks of your carbuncles rather firmly stamped upon it." He said the "dialectic" had been sharpened since Marx's earlier *Contribution to the Critique of Political Economy,* but there were some things Engels liked better in that work than in *Capital.* Otherwise he declared himself delighted with what he had read.[19] Marx apparently chose to ignore his friend's partial misgivings, expressing great relief over Engels's approval and promising to reward Lizzy Burns with a dress from London if he found a generous English publisher for *Capital*—a prospect he felt certain was imminent.[20]

From the time of Laura and Lafargue's engagement, a good deal of the Marx family's attention had been devoted to them. In the spring of 1867 the young couple had caused a sensation in Haverstock Hill while taking riding lessons on the Heath. Laura looked beautiful and sat comfortably in the saddle, but Paul seemed less sure of himself and was given to grabbing the horse's mane instead of the reins. (Tussy made him a cushion to comfort his post-riding bruises.)[21] Marx's focus centered, however, on Jennychen. He worried privately about his eldest daughter, who was in the awkward social position of watching her younger sister prepare for marriage while she had no suitor in sight. Marx had even tried to persuade her to go to Germany while he was there for a much-needed change of scenery. But she had declined, saying, "On the contrary, I can assure you, I am very comfortable where I am....Really there isn't the slightest demand for fantastic smiles of pity...although there is a plentiful supply of them."[22]

Jennychen had long been less interested in things of the heart than of the intellect, and during this period she was especially so. With her acting prospects diminished—partly because of poor health, but also because as a Marx daughter that career would be a step too far—she tried her hand at playwriting. A drama she wrote during this period was part personal, part political tragedy, and greatly inspired by Shakespeare and her own family. (One line read, "My dear papa, your words have rent my heart, your people weep, if you resign who will protect their cause?")[23] She also busied herself transcribing page upon page of poetry in English, French, and German, and essays in French on the 1848 revolts, while simultaneously monitoring IWMA-supported strikes in England and France.[24] In her own quiet way, she daily grew more political and more literary.

In the summer of 1867 Lafargue's family invited the three Marx daughters to accompany Paul to Bordeaux for a visit. Jenny and Marx did not want to spare any expense in preparing their daughters for the journey. Lafargue had offered to pay, but Marx would not countenance such generosity—he had to appear to be a man of sufficient means to take care of his own family. He used money he had set aside for the rent to buy his daughters' steamer tickets and then turned to Engels for a resupply of funds to save him from a disastrous eviction.[25]

Jenny and Karl were aware that Lafargue's father was engaged in the wine trade (they believed on a large scale) and that he owned land and houses in Cuba, New Orleans, and France. The elder Lafargue's promise to give his son 100,000 francs[26]—or about £4,000—as a wedding gift was seen by Jenny as merely a down payment on a life of ease and wealth for her second daughter, and one that might also help her other daughters find comparable matches. There was apparently no thought that the Marx daughters, despite their obvious brilliance, might earn their own way in the world without the help of husbands. Jenny and Marx were too conventional in their thinking when it came to their daughters to make that sort of leap.

Dressed in their finest clothes the three young women departed for France under Paul's escort, but it became clear almost immediately that they would have been better off in the comfortable outfits they wore at home. Multiple train changes and carriage rides in inclement weather, not to mention cumbersome baggage, meant a long and difficult journey. By the end of their voyage their bourgeois garb was wrinkled, their styled hair limp, their scrubbed faces soiled. The boat trip, however, was wonderful. Jennychen said they were all in high spirits and found Lafargue's parents to be "grand and noble characters." In a letter to her mother, Jennychen said she had won them over by countering Paul's avowal of atheism with the comment that she thought it absurd to make a cult of any ism. She was struck, however, by the Lafargues' aversion to being described as mixed race. In a rare reference to Marx's Jewish roots, Jennychen wrote, "The chosen people ashamed of our origin can sympathize with them on that point."

The Marx women stayed in Bordeaux for a time and then accompanied the Lafargues for a long visit to the sun-dappled French coast on the Bay of Biscay. Jennychen was twenty-three, Laura not yet twenty-two, and Tussy twelve. It was the first time the three of them had been together outside England. Jennychen, who was the least vain of the daughters and therefore most believable on this point, said their dresses and toilettes created a "sensation" in France. Together they were a powerful presence—physically and intellectually—and mischievous as well. Paul fell in easily with their pranks, and soon Jennychen and Tussy accepted him as a brother.[27]

The Marx daughters were away at the beach for the entire month of August and did not return to London until September 10. Though their French adventure had seemed a lifetime away from their usual cares, throughout their journey they had followed the progress of their father's book, which both Marx and Jenny described optimistically. On the eve of their return home, Jennychen wrote, "At last those German blockheads are going to do our Mohr some little justice—they can never repay him for all that he has done for them."[28]

Proof sheets flew back and forth between London and Manchester. The postman's double knock that August almost always heralded a letter from Engels critiquing *Capital,* and the man in the red frock coat and top hat was nearly always sent away with more material bound for Manchester. Marx frequently talked to his letters from Engels, literally addressing the pages. (Tussy recalled hearing him in his study as if Engels were there, saying, "No, that's not the way it is," or "You're right there," or roaring with laughter at his friend's acerbic wit.)[29] Having the girls and Lafargue out of the house for the month seemed to help Marx race through his work. On August 14 he corrected his forty-eighth proof sheet and predicted he would complete the "whole vile business" that week.[30] For once he was actually early: two days later, at two in the morning, Marx finished the forty-ninth and last proof sheet of *Capital, Volume I.*

Exhausted, relieved, profoundly grateful, he wrote Engels a brief note. "So, *this volume is finished.* I owe it to **you** alone that it was possible! Without your self-sacrifice for me I could not possibly have managed the immense labor demanded by the three volumes. I EMBRACE YOU, FULL OF THANKS!... *Salut,* my dear, valued friend." Marx dedicated *Capital* to another companion who had been loyal and generous to the end: Lupus.[31]

Overall Engels was amazed that Marx had been able to explain complicated economic theory with ease and in such simple language. He said that for the first time, the relationship between labor and capital was laid out completely and in its full context.[32] "Marx found that capitalists, like the feudal system and the slave owner, advanced by exploiting a huge majority of the people," Engels would later explain.[33] But Engels was not uncritical, and his criticism foreshadowed the problems the book would encounter when it reached the hands of general readers:

> But how could you leave the *outward* structure of the book in its present form! The fourth chapter is almost two hundred pages long and only has four subsections....Furthermore, the train of thought is constantly interrupted by illustrations, and the point to be illustrated is *never* summarized after the illustration, so that one is forever plunging straight from the illustration of *one* point into the exposition of another point. It is dreadfully tiring, and confusing, too, if one is not all attention.[34]

By the time Engels made those comments, however, it was too late for the first German edition—the proofs were already with Meissner and the printers were setting the type. Marx and Lafargue had visited Engels briefly in mid-September so Engels could meet the young man, and when they returned to London, *Capital* was awaiting them: one thousand copies had been printed.[35]

The Marx circle deliberately kept the celebration brief. From bitter experience Marx, Jenny, and Engels knew that if the book did not receive press attention quickly, it would fail. They set to work to make sure this did not happen again. Laura and Lafargue began translating *Capital*'s preface into French for publication in a French newspaper.[36] Marx, Jenny, and

Jennychen wrote all their acquaintances in Germany, Switzerland, Belgium, and America to announce *Capital*'s release and to solicit sales and reviews. Engels produced at least seven anonymous reviews of the book for German and English publications in Europe and America, writing from various points of view—some favorable, some critical, some looking at economics, some examining the book's social points—and assuming different styles and characters.[37] (As a strictly dramatic feat, Jennychen applauded his ability to assume so many "viewpoints and in different disguises.")[38]

Engels prodded colleagues to do likewise to ensure *Capital*'s success. He told Kugelmann that both long and short press notices were needed, and that they must come "thick and fast. We must make it impossible for these gentlemen to pursue their policy of total silence, which they would dearly love to try." Engels suggested that the best thing would be to get *Capital* denounced: "The main thing is that the book should be discussed over and over again....And as Marx is not a free agent in the matter, and is furthermore as bashful as a young girl, it is up to the rest of us to see to it....In the words of our old friend Jesus Christ, we must be innocent as doves and wise as serpents."[39]

Marx, meanwhile, was wretched. Some colleagues who had received *Capital* were perplexed by the book. He told Kugelmann's wife, Gertruda, who admitted she did not know what to make of it, that he would send her a "recipe" for reading it.[40] Later he suggested several chapters as more readable than others and told Kugelmann to explain complicated terminology to his wife.[41] Peter Fox, the English delegate to the International who had pinioned Laura with his rambling conversation, said after receiving a copy that he "felt like a man who had been given an elephant and didn't know what to do with it."[42] One young German manufacturer who read the book thought that surely Marx had once been in the sewing-machine business.[43]

About a month after *Capital*'s publication, Marx could not sleep and was suffering from a fresh batch of carbuncles, some of which erupted in such a way that he was able to lie only on his side. He said he could not work on *Volume II* partly because of his health and partly because he was beset by financial worries now that Lafargue was practically living with them.[44] Of course the real reason for his creative paralysis was unquestionably anxiety while he waited for reaction to *Volume I*. Looking for a place to hide during this agonizing period, Marx found refuge in sixteenth-century French pornographic poetry, which he dutifully copied out and sent to Engels.[45]

By November no notice had been taken of *Capital*. Far from a bomb exploding over the heads of the bourgeoisie, it had made no impression whatsoever. "The silence about my book makes me FIDGETY," Marx told

Das Kapital.

Kritik der politischen Oekonomie.

Von

Karl Marx.

Erster Band.
Buch I: Der Produktionsprocess des Kapitals.

Das Recht der Uebersetzung wird vorbehalten.

Hamburg
Verlag von Otto Meissner.
1867.
New-York: L. W. Schmidt. 24 Barclay-Street.

Titelblatt der Erstausgabe

After at least sixteen years of work and sacrifice by his family, Marx's great book *Capital* was published in Hamburg in 1867 to no acclaim. (IISG, Amsterdam)

Engels. "Meanwhile, we must do as the Russians do—wait. Patience is the core of Russian diplomacy and of their successes. But the likes of us, who only live once, may well never live to see the day."[46] Through November into December, and silence still. Marx described himself as laid low. In his New Year's greeting to Engels he said he had "only been 'sitting up' again for three days, after lying all bent for so long. It was a nasty attack. You can judge this by the fact that for three weeks—no smoking! My head is still shaky."[47]

While Marx spoke of Russian patience, he was not a patient man, and he was notoriously wrong when it came to predicting people's readiness for change—whether that be their ability to accept new ideas or to rise up in revolt. He repeatedly stated that it would take years, if not decades, to educate and prepare the workingman to assume the reins of power, and yet he expected that same workingman not only to absorb and understand *Capital,* but to do so quickly. Yet the sheer physical weight of the book, not to mention its mathematical formulas, multiple languages, erudite literary and philosophical references, and abstract theorizing, made it nearly unapproachable. The concepts Marx presented appeared clear as day to him and to Engels because they had discussed them since 1844. The two friends seemed to have forgotten that Marx's ideas (though not all new or original[48]) combined to create a theoretical earthquake—a revolution in thought that shook the foundation of the young capitalist society, which in 1867 had reached its highest point to date.[49] In his book Marx held up a mirror to that society, daring exploiters and exploited alike to gaze on the awful truths of their relations as he saw them.

There was also a sense that *Capital* was actually two books. Marx's extensive use of footnotes—some taking up nearly an entire page—made the reader feel he was being asked to absorb a text and a running commentary in tandem. One has the sense of a pianist playing two sets of keys simultaneously, which made it difficult for the listener to give full attention to either. In a way the style was a return to the Marx family's deep rabbinical roots; it was not unlike the Jewish homiletic tradition Aggadah, which explained truths from classic texts using a two-tiered approach, overt and covert, shouts and whispers.

Marx's book was difficult to digest even for intellectuals, who may have been able to grasp its substance and who may not have been distracted by its form. Some regarded it as an eight-hundred-page act of aggression. British socialist Henry Hyndman described the initial reaction to *Capital* among his nineteenth-century contemporaries: "Accustomed as we are nowadays, especially in England, to fence always with big soft buttons on the point of our rapiers, Marx's terrible onslaught with naked steel upon his adversaries appeared so improper that it was impossible for our gentlemanly sham-fighters and mental gymnasium men to believe that this unsparing controversialist and furious assailant of capital and capitalism was really the deepest thinker of our times."[50]

In his book Marx set out to describe the origin, operation, and ultimate overthrow of the capitalist system. Readers acquainted with the *Communist Manifesto* may have come to *Capital* looking for yet another swift and stirring call to revolt. But *Capital* was often plodding—the work of a teacher, not a fighter. The revolution Marx described was the result of a long, slow process. It was at once as modest as the winning of a shorter workday and as bold as the obliteration of an economic and social system born in the sixteenth century that had grown into an industrial and military monster, devouring men and the environment to satisfy an insatiable hunger for profit.

> The discovery of gold and silver in America, the extirpation, enslavement and entombment in mines of the aboriginal population, the beginning of the conquest and looting of the East Indies, the turning of Africa into a warren for the commercial hunting of black-skins, signaled the rosy dawn of the era of capitalist production.[51]...Capital comes dripping from head to foot, from every pore, with blood and dirt.[52]

To get to revolution, Marx first took readers through the inner workings of the capitalist system, which is part of what may have confused and disappointed his immediate audience. In *Capital*'s first 250-odd pages he broke down economic, and consequently social, relations to the cellular level. He began the book with such a close examination of commodities, for example, that it was difficult for the reader to see the larger, dramatic picture.

> Let us take two commodities, e.g., corn and iron. The proportions in which they are exchangeable, whatever those proportions may be, can always be represented by an equation in which a given quantity of corn is equated to some quantity of iron: e.g., 1 quarter corn = x cwt. iron. What does this equation tell us? It tells us that in two different things—in 1 quarter of corn and x cwt. of iron, there exists in equal quantities something common to both. The two things must therefore be equal to a third, which in itself is neither the one nor the other.[53]

But as soon as Marx explained that the "something common to both" was in fact the commodity human labor, *Capital* became compelling.

Marx, the dialectical materialist, reiterated from his earlier works that economics did not exist in the dead realm of formulas comprehensible only to a select few who understood its laws. To believe otherwise would be to shroud the marketplace in mystery, obscure its operations, and condemn the masses to slavishly follow those shamans of finance who claimed to hold the keys to its secrets. Mankind would be left quaking in awe at such wonders, and lose the power to extricate itself from such chains. Marx was prepared to show that there *was* no mystery, though capitalists (like kings before them) hoped the proletariat would not discover that their power was less than divine.

Using as his model the industrial workplace of nineteenth-century Britain, Marx described a system in which man continued to be bought, though not in slavery. This workingman was the owner of a commodity—himself. He sold his labor to a buyer or employer for a certain period of time. In exchange, the employer gave him the use of equipment (the means of production) and a wage[54] (what Marx later called the "irrational outward form of a hidden relationship"[55]). But the question arose: how was that wage determined? In the marketplace that Marx described, the value of labor was determined by a so-called minimum wage, which was simply the amount of money needed to keep the laborer alive and able to work. Marx then added another element to that wage calculation. He coldly assessed man as machine—just as the new capitalist employer viewed him—and determined that the laborer could not work forever. Like equipment, he was subject to wear and tear, and would ultimately die. He must therefore be paid sufficient wages not only to eat and find shelter, but to reproduce—to have children who would become the next generation of labor, the new machines.

Marx posited that there were two particular characteristics of the labor relationship in the capitalist system. First, the laborer worked under the control of the capitalist, who purchased his labor for an agreed period of time, and second, the product of the laborer was the property of the employer. The product would then be sold, with the proceeds going to the employer.[56]

Suppose a capitalist pays for a day's labor power at its value; then the right to use that power for a day belongs to him, just as much as the right to use any other commodity, such as a horse that he has hired for the day.... The labor process is a process between things that the capitalist has purchased, things that have become his property. The product of this process belongs, therefore, to him, just as much as does the wine which is the product of a process of fermentation completed in his cellar.[57]

To make a profit, however, the employer had to find a way to squeeze more value out of the commodities he used. And the easiest place to find that extra value, Marx explained, was in the fluid commodity called labor. It was at that point that Marx introduced what he called the "general groundwork of the capitalist system"[58]—surplus labor and surplus value.

In hiring a worker, an employer agreed to a wage determined by the cost of keeping that person alive and the level of his skill. In return, the laborer agreed to work a set number of hours each day or week. But if, in the course of a twelve-hour workday, for example, the laborer produced enough in the first six hours to compensate his employer for his salary, he did not and must not stop; he was obliged to continue working for another six hours. The value of his production during that period did not go into his pocket, it went entirely to the employer or capitalist. The laborer thus worked six hours without pay, that excess becoming the capitalist's earnings or profit when he ultimately sold his product. The capitalist could further increase that profit by lengthening the workday or -week, reducing staff, employing women or children who earned less, or by introducing machinery that sped up production, which meant that a worker might pay back his wage in four hours, thus allowing the employer to collect eight hours of free labor: "The action of labor power, therefore, not only reproduces its own value, but produces value over and above it. This surplus value is the difference between the value of the product and the value of the elements consumed in the formation of that product, in other words, of the means of production and the labor power."[59] According to Marx, the secret ingredient to capitalist success was the ability to exploit not just labor, but *unpaid* labor.

In the precapitalist system, the artisan, small-factory owner, or agriculturalist had sold his commodities for money in order to buy other commodities (what Marx described as C-M-C), but Marx said capitalists began buying commodities in order to sell them to make money (M-C-M).[60]

The simple circulation of commodities—selling in order to buy—is a means of carrying out a purpose unconnected with circulation, namely, the appropriation of use values, the satisfaction of wants. The circulation of money as capital is, on the contrary, an end in itself, for the expansion of value takes place only within this constantly renewed movement. The circulation of capital has therefore no limits.

As the conscious representative of this movement, the possessor of money becomes a capitalist. His person, or rather his pocket, is the point from which the money starts and to which it returns...it is only in so far as the appropriation of ever more and more wealth in the abstract becomes the sole motive of his operations, that he functions as a capitalist.... The restless never-ending process of profit-making alone is what he aims at.[61]

With each transaction, the capitalist's money moved farther away from its source, the worker, but that distance, said Marx, did not weaken the link. Whether the surplus value appropriated by the capitalist was used to surround himself with luxury, or was turned into investments like property or stocks, or was shared among capitalists (effectively *only* among capitalists; Marx said it rarely trickled down) in the form of financial mechanisms such as credit and interest, all that paper and all those things were essentially "the materialization of unpaid labor."[62]

On the one hand, the process of production incessantly converts material wealth into capital, into means of creating more wealth and means of enjoyment for the capitalist. On the other hand, the laborer, on quitting the process, is what he was on entering, a source of wealth, but devoid of all means of making that wealth his own.... The laborer therefore constantly produces material, objective wealth, but in the form of capital, of an alien power that dominates and exploits him.[63]

As Marx further described it, "In capitalist society spare time is acquired for one class by converting the whole lifetime of the masses into labor time."[64]

Marx recognized the employer's claim to compensation—he had provided the factory and equipment where and with which the worker was able to produce. In *Capital*, Marx's fictional factory owner cried, "And as the greater part of society consists of such ne'er-do-wells, have I not rendered society incalculable service by my instruments of production, my cotton and my spindle.... Am I to be allowed nothing in return for all this service?"[65] Marx did not begrudge a man compensation for work or financial outlays, or perhaps even anxiety about an enterprise's success, but he held that it must not come at the expense of another. And yet that very injustice, as he saw it, was intrinsic to the capitalist system, based as it was on private property and driven by greed. The prize profit was not shared with the laborer who produced it; quite the contrary, the capitalist continually looked to cut costs in order to make even more money—and the cuts that produced the greatest rewards could be made in the workforce.

Under capitalism, technical innovations, or fluctuating markets that thrived one day and crashed the next, or the competition among capitalists that caused small businesses to be consumed by larger ones, all produced one common result—they threw people out of work—and two common benefits—those capitalists left standing saw profits rise and had at their disposal a new and larger army of unemployed. And those people, whom Marx called the "industrial reserve army," stood ready as a promise and a threat. The promise was that employers would have a steady supply of manpower to take the place of laborers worked to death or to fill the ranks during economic upswings. The threat was unspoken but well recognized by workingmen and -women who feared that these unemployed would replace them because, in their desperation they would accept lower wages. In sum, the industrial reserve army was used by employers to restrain labor costs.[66]

Isaiah Berlin stated that if the workers who read *Capital* understood nothing else, they would have understood Marx's message that "there is only one social class, their own, which produces more wealth than it consumes, and that this residue is appropriated by other men simply by virtue of their strategic position as the sole possessors of the means of production, that is, natural resources, machinery, means of transport, financial credit, and so forth, without which the workers cannot create, while control over them gives those who have it the power of starving the rest of mankind into capitulation on their own terms."[67]

Marx illustrated his economic treatise with brutally clear examples of exploitation in the British factory system, describing not only the mistreatment of adult workers but of tens of thousands of children, some as young as two. He also freely used literary references to drive home his points: He depicted Robinson Crusoe, though alone and stranded, as behaving "like a true-born Briton" by using a watch, ledger, and pen to manage his island wealth. With a Dickensian flourish, Marx called the capitalist everyman he created "Moneybags."[68] And the book was rich in Gothic literary references. "Capital," he wrote, "is dead labor, that, vampire-like, only lives by sucking living labor, and lives the more, the more labor it sucks."[69]

> In its blind unrestrainable passion, its were-wolf hunger for surplus labor, capital oversteps not only the moral, but even the merely physical maximum bounds of the working day. It usurps time for growth, development, and healthy maintenance of the body. It steals the time required for the consumption of fresh air and sunlight.... It reduces the sound sleep needed for the restoration, reparation, refreshment of the bodily powers to just so many hours of torpor as the revival of an organism, absolutely exhausted, renders essential.[70]

Marx's *Capital*—which was in every way an epic of conquerors and the conquered—explained that while the laborer might be abused and exhausted, he was not without power. The very nature of capitalist production, in which workers were thrown together to form one heaving communal body, created a breeding ground for resistance; workers would recognize their own collective power and their antagonistic relationship with capital.[71] At a certain point these laborers would make demands—a shorter working day and compensation that reflected the true value of their work: "In place of the pompous catalog of the 'inalienable rights of man' comes the modest Magna Carta of a legally limited working day, which shall make clear 'when the time which the worker sells is ended and when his own begins.'"[72] The workers would, of course, make that demand as sellers to buyers who had no interest in their humanity, but that confrontation would then inevitably ignite a massive struggle between the capitalist class and the working class.

Marx also foresaw antagonisms among capitalists, who would destroy one another in their pursuit of wealth by hungrily absorbing their competition to create monopolies and business empires stretching across countries and continents. But that, too, according to Marx, would ultimately help the worker: fewer magnates at the top of the money pyramid expanded the base, and in that larger base would reside more misery and, at the same time, a heightened coalescence among those degraded unfortunates. They would form their own society, one that truly understood the means of production because they *were* the means of production. That class would in turn become too powerful for the capitalist yoke.[73] The result would be cooperative enterprises and common ownership of natural resources as well as the facilities and equipment needed to keep the wheels of commerce turning. Marx predicted that this social and economic revolution would occur with infinitely less bloodshed than had the birth of capitalism.

The transformation of scattered private property, arising from individual labor, into capitalist private property is, naturally, a process, incomparably more protracted, violent and difficult, than the transformation of capitalist private property, already practically resting on socialized production, into socialized property. In the former case, we had the expropriation of the mass of the people by a few usurpers; in the latter, we have the expropriation of a few usurpers by the mass of the people.[74]

In this singular work, Marx incorporated lifetimes of labor and thought—his own and that of the economists and philosophers who came before him. It was written on the one hand in a highly technical, academic style, and on the other—sometimes in the next paragraph—in the free-flowing, mocking style of his most eccentric polemics. If Engels detected in it a trace of Marx's carbuncles, equally apparent were the trials his family had suffered and the misery he had seen in London and Manchester. The man who wrote *Capital* was an extraordinary philosopher, economist, classicist, social scientist, and writer, but he was also someone intimately acquainted with the slow death of the spirit suffered by those condemned to poverty while surrounded by a world of wealth.

While the Marx household waited for someone to notice Karl's work, on December 23 Kugelmann produced a bizarre tribute to the man he idolized. Jenny described the scene:

> Yesterday evening we were all at home together sitting downstairs, which in English houses is the kitchen area from which all "CREATURE COMFORTS" make their way up to the higher regions, and were busy preparing the CHRISTMAS PUDDING with all due thoroughness. We were seeding raisins (a most disagreeable and sticky task), chopping up almonds and orange and lemon peel, minutely shredding suet, and with eggs and flour kneading together the oddest potpourri from the whole mishmash; when all at once there was a ring at the door, a carriage was stopped outside, mysterious footsteps were going up and down, whispering and rustling filled the house; at length a voice sounded from above: "A great statue has arrived."

Such was his Olympian regard for the author of *Capital* that Kugelmann had sent Marx a massive bust of Zeus.

Jenny thanked him for his efforts in trying to get reviews and excerpts published in German papers: "It would seem that the Germans' preferred form of applause is utter and complete silence.…Dear Mr. Kugelmann, you can believe me when I tell you there can be few books that have been written in more difficult circumstances, and I am sure I could write a secret history of it which would tell many, extremely many unspoken troubles and anxieties and torments. If the workers had an inkling of the sacrifices that were necessary for this work, which was written only for them and for their sakes to be completed they would perhaps show a little more interest." She ended her long missive by saying she also had a bone to pick with Kugelmann. "Why do you address me so formally, even using the title 'gracious,' for me, who am such an old campaigner, such a hoary head in the movement, such an honest fellow-traveler and fellow tramp?"

She signed her letter "Yours, Jenny Marx, not gracious and not by the grace of God."[75]

33

<hr style="width:10%" />

London, 1868

Capital will not even pay for the cigars I smoked writing it.
—Karl Marx[1]

"I AM WRITING to you naked with alcohol compresses. I went out again for the first time the *day before yesterday,* to the British Museum, of course, because I cannot write yet. Then yesterday there was a new outbreak under my left breast."[2] So Marx wrote to Engels in one of his first letters of 1868. He had been sick for four months, since about the time he received the published version of *Capital.* He reported carbuncles blossoming on his loins, "withered buds" under his arm,[3] and a "monster" on his left shoulder blade: "It appears this shit will never end."[4] To these boils Marx added two new complaints—a raging headache and "a stinging prickle in my body, that is my blood." His conclusion was that in order to be healthy one had to have money, "instead of being a poor devil like me, poverty-stricken as a church-mouse."[5] Later he observed, "How right my mother was: 'If only *Karell* had made capital instead of etc.' "[6]

If Marx's body was in a state of rebellion over the public's lack of interest in his book, Jenny seemed utterly defeated. She had lived for the promise of *Capital,* perhaps even believing that it would produce the desired effect—that it would change Germany, change the world, change their lives for the better. Now that it had been published and had gone virtually unnoticed, she must have looked at her life and asked whether the sacrifices had been worth the cost: Losing Musch? Years of miserable poverty and illness? The prospect that her daughters' futures were jeopardized by

359

their parents' past? Nothing in her writing indicates that Jenny ever abandoned the ideas swirling around in her husband's head, but as the silence that greeted *Capital* persisted, she admitted to Kugelmann, "of late I have lost much of my 'faith,' my courage in facing up to life."[7] She would turn fifty-four on her next birthday. After living half her life as Marx's wife, she was weary. Jenny even compared Ernestine Liebknecht's situation favorably with her own when she learned that her husband Wilhelm had been arrested in Prussia. "To be frank, there are a lot more harrowing struggles and suffering in daily life than even those of such striking nature," Jenny wrote Ernestine. "Moreover, I myself have experiences that in such extreme crises friends and party comrades come to someone's aid and help the wife and children more than if the husband is active."[8]

Her mood dismal and often black, Jenny was ill tempered with her daughters and her husband. She continued to play the role of hostess for Marx's friends in the International, but she had become more independent, traveling on her own, associating with "philistine" friends more freely. Jenny loved her husband and, as she told Kugelmann, considered herself an old campaigner for the party, but she finally appeared to be looking for the freedom to develop outside her husband's burdensome shadow.

As agreed with Meissner, Marx was supposed to be hard at work on *Volume II* of *Capital,* but between his illnesses and anxiety over *Volume I,* he was incapable of making progress. Instead, he scrutinized the world press for mention of his book and was heartened in mid-January to see a small piece in London's *Saturday Review* that noted, "The author's views may be as pernicious as we conceive them to be, but there can be no question as to the plausibility of his logic, the vigor of his rhetoric, and the charm with which he invests the driest problems of political economy."[9] Still, is was not nearly enough to compensate for the utter lack of interest in *Capital.* Luckily for Marx and his family, personal and political events conspired to divert their attention away from their disappointment over what they called *"das buch."*[10] One of these was the Irish question, and it would absorb the Marx household, especially the daughters, for years.

The tragedy of Ireland was centuries old, but one of its darkest moments occurred in 1801, when Ireland, defeated in a war of rebellion inspired by the revolutions in America and France, was forced into a union with the victor, England. The five-hundred-year-old Irish parliament was abolished and a reduced number of members were absorbed into the parliament at Westminster. Even the Church of Ireland was absorbed into the Church of England; from the moment of political union there was to be religious union as well. The next watershed moment came during the potato famine in the 1840s, when millions of Irish died or emigrated. That crisis was blamed in part on agrarian reforms instituted by English landowners that forced peasants onto small plots whose sole food crop was potatoes, and partly on the policies of the English government. Once the famine had commenced, these policies left the fate of starving peasants largely in the hands of landowners, who, ignoring those dying around them, busily exported meat and grain from Irish farms to lucrative foreign markets. This crime was branded into the memories of the Irish, who were bitterly aware that many British parliamentarians with economic interests in Ireland had benefited from their misfortune.

The famine left Ireland forever changed. Medium-sized estates appeared not far from villages of peasants who seemed to live on grass and in mud. But many of the vibrant communities were gone, and in the countryside vast swathes of rich land were left fallow. The English government, noting those green pastures and in need of land for livestock to feed its swelling population, passed an act in 1849 that allowed estates to be taken over and consolidated if the owners were bankrupt and no longer able to maintain them. That forced more Irish off their land and others out of work as fields that had once been tilled were given over to grazing.[11] Marx observed that between 1855 and 1866 more than a million Irish were displaced by more than ten million cattle, pigs, and sheep. He believed England's goal was to clear Ireland of the Irish and transform it into an English agricultural district.[12]

In the 1850s Irish immigrants in America had formed a group called the Irish Republican Brotherhood, better known as the Fenians, which plotted an armed uprising to exorcise the English from Ireland. Many of these men became experienced soldiers in the 1860s, while fighting in the U.S. Civil War. As they filtered back to Ireland, they had a relatively easy time radicalizing the local citizenry, who needed only weapons and organization to turn themselves into an insurgent army; within a few years the Fenians had an estimated hundred thousand sworn followers in Ireland.[13] In and around Manchester, with its large Irish population, it was estimated that one in six people were either Fenians or Fenian sympathizers.[14]

In September 1867 two Irish veterans of the U.S. Civil War were arrested in Manchester for loitering. Just as the seemingly insignificant pair was about to be released, police discovered that they were important Fenians. One was Colonel Thomas Kelly, a leader of a failed Irish uprising earlier that year, who was poised to take control of the Fenians in England. The other was his aide-de-camp, Captain Michael Deasy. Their arrests caused a sensation among English security forces, who were well pleased with the capture of the notorious pair. It also caused a sensation among the Irish in Manchester, who immediately began devising plans to free them.[15]

Engels's "wife" Lizzy was involved in the plot[16] that culminated on September 18, when a police van carrying Kelly and Deasy was attacked as it drove under a Manchester railway arch. Seven policemen faced off that morning against thirty to forty Irishmen, most of the latter wielding tools for weapons but some armed with revolvers. A shot from the mob felled a horse pulling the van, and the Irish rushed the disabled vehicle to try to free the prisoners inside. In the frenzy more shots were fired, and one constable and a bystander were killed. Police reinforcements swarmed the area and more than two dozen Irishmen at the scene were quickly arrested, but Deasy and Kelly escaped with the help of an underground web of supporters.[17] Lizzy Burns, who had extended hospitality to many Fenians on the run, was said to have sheltered them at the home she kept with Engels.[18] Leaving social chaos in their wake, the fugitives eventually made it to America.[19]

Marx and Engels rejected the Fenian use of violence and conspiracy, but they were firmly in favor of the Irish in their fight against England.[20] Perhaps concerned that Lizzy's involvement might be discovered if Marx produced a statement in support of the Irish at that moment, Engels warned him that under no circumstances should they be seen as making themselves responsible for acts committed by Fenians, who he said were led by "jackasses" and "exploiters."[21] But privately Engels praised the rescue and even took Lafargue to the railway arch four days after the melee.[22] Engels boldly wrote Kugelmann, "You will have heard about our little Fenian surprise attack here. The affair was splendidly organized and executed; but the ringleaders were caught unfortunately."[23]

Marx's friend Ernest Jones, meanwhile, acted as defense lawyer for those on trial in the van attack. Of twenty-six defendants, five were considered principals and charged with murder. The outcome of their case surprised no one: five guilty verdicts and five sentences of death, each one met with a cry from the defendants' box, "The Lord have mercy on your souls" and "God Save Ireland."[24] Soon, however, one of the five was pardoned over false evidence, and the case of the remaining four—who, the argument went, were victims of the same shoddy investigation—became a cause célèbre among the Irish, opposition groups, and even parts of the mainstream press.[25] Marx tried to incite English International members to join the protest in favor of the Fenians, saying, "Quite apart from international justice it is a *precondition to the emancipation of the English working class* to transform the present *forced Union*, i.e. the enslavement of Ireland—into *equal and free confederation* if possible, into *complete separation* if need be."[26]

Twenty-five thousand people gathered in London on November 21 to petition the queen for clemency. But two days later three of the Fenians were hanged.[27] That outcome, too, surprised no one. At the hour of their execution, the streets of Manchester's Irish districts were empty but the churches were full: the Irish Catholic parishes were holding funerals for the men on the gallows.[28]

Charles Stewart Parnell, a member of the British Parliament representing Ireland's County Wicklow, caused an uproar in the House of Commons when he declared he would never believe the executed men were killers. To English MPs his claim was heresy, but cheers rang out among the Irish from Soho Square to Boston for his boldness in the house of the enemy.[29] Engels claimed the English had given the Irish the only thing they lacked to fire their fury—martyrs—and that the Manchester events "will now be sung at the cradle of every Irish child in Ireland, England and America. The Irish women will see to that."[30] That song would be both lament and war cry.

In December the Fenian violence came to London, when another attempt to free Irish prisoners was made, this time with explosives placed along a wall outside the Clerkenwell House of Detention. The explosion did not damage the jail but it destroyed nearby houses, killing twelve people and injuring more than one hundred. The attack sent London into a panic, and more than 150,000 people volunteered as citizen constables to protect the city. Any English sympathy won for the Irish in Manchester was now lost in the capital.[31] Engels denounced the bombing as the work of a few fanatics who believed they would be able to free Ireland by setting fire to London shops.[32]

Jennychen, however, was committed to the cause *and* the methods. She wore black in honor of the Manchester Martyrs and hung a Polish cross she had won in a lottery the year before on a green ribbon around her neck.[33] She applauded the use of violence, saying, "Greek fire and a few shots are very useful when applied at the right moment!"[34] Jennychen's immersion in the Irish cause was complete, and she began to focus on freeing Irishmen jailed by the English. Though political prisoners, they were said by critics to have fewer rights than murderers and thieves. Engels sent Jennychen an article about the trial of a young woman sentenced to five years' penal servitude for shooting at a policeman guarding a witness in the Fenian trial.[35] It was unclear whether he sent the clip because he knew she would be interested or because he was afraid of what she might do.

Amid all the political activity and literary inactivity in the Marx household, Laura and Lafargue decided to set a date for their wedding. There seemed to be no reason to wait the two years Marx had originally prescribed for their courtship: Lafargue was already considered part of the family and privy to all its secrets—except, of course, its finances. The couple, therefore, determined to marry in April 1868, and while the decision for them was easy, it presented a host of problems for Marx and Jenny. Marx turned to Ernest Jones, fresh off his defense of the Fenians, to ask advice about how Laura and Lafargue could obtain a civil marriage in London. The wedding was to have taken place in Paris, but Marx explained he would have to prove his identity there and "in so doing, might strike the police as being a little too familiar." (His last expulsion order from France had never been rescinded, and the French government had begun to crack down on members of the International, in part for their support of the Fenians.) For her part, Jenny wanted to ensure that any marriage in London would be a quiet affair because she did not want her English friends gossiping over why it was not held in a church.[36]

Jones may have been relieved to be asked such a delightfully mundane question, and within two days Marx had his answer: the marriage could occur in a district registrar's office with two or more witnesses, and a public announcement, known as banns, should be posted fourteen days in advance. As for Jenny's concern, Engels suggested that she "tell her philistine neighbors that this way was chosen because Laura is protestant and Paul catholic."[37]

In France Paul's father, François, took the necessary steps to post banns announcing that the marriage would occur on April 1. The plan, as Lafargue's father understood it, was that the couple would honeymoon in Paris; return to London, where his son would take his final medical exam; go to France for his French examinations; and then the young pair would move to the Lafargue home in New Orleans.[38] But Marx and Jenny refrained from making a formal announcement. It was—as was so often the case—a question of money: they did not have enough to prepare a trousseau for Laura, which generally cost about twenty pounds,[39] or to pay the fees attendant on the wedding ceremony. Marx told Engels, "She cannot be sent out into the world like a beggar."[40] Desperate, he wrote his family in Holland for help, but his uncle had died and his cousins were not as willing to extend funds as their father had been; they greeted Marx's request with silence.[41]

His pockets empty, Marx convinced Laura and Lafargue to postpone their marriage until April 8, while he scrambled to get the money to pay for it. He told Kugelmann that in the previous four months he had spent so much on doctors, government documents, and reports from the United States in researching *Volume II* that he had no money left for Laura. Kugelmann heard

Marx's not too subtle plea and sent him fifteen pounds.[42] Engels provided another forty, which meant that Marx now had enough to launch his daughter properly into her new role as wife. But there was a fresh wrinkle: Engels said he could not attend if the wedding was held on April 8, a workday.[43] His absence was unacceptable to everyone involved. Lafargue had wanted Engels, along with Marx, to be a witness. "To give this act all its social value, it seems indispensable, I don't know why, that two witnesses be present," Lafargue wrote Engels, making light of the union he was about to enter. "Although you are far from having all the moral qualities requisite to the fulfilling of this respectable bourgeois function in a respectable way, there is no man whom I should like better than yourself to stand by me during so formidable a ceremony."[44] Laura, too, begged him to come, saying she would be on "pins and needles."[45] Finally, Marx insisted the day be changed to accommodate Engels. Laura would marry Lafargue on April 2.

Whether it was the approach of the wedding (Marx once said he was partly jealous Lafargue was making off with his daughter[46]), the pressure to produce *Capital, Volume II,* or his finances—or likely all three—Marx was stricken by multiple illnesses in late March: bleeding shingles, carbuncles on his thigh that resulted in a "difficult gait," and on one occasion "something like a black veil before my eyes...a frightful headache and chest constriction."[47] Nevertheless, on the appointed day Marx dressed his carbuncles, took a dose of arsenic, and worked his racked body into a formal black frock coat. Accompanied by Engels, he went to the St. Pancras Registry Office to witness the marriage of his daughter Laura to Paul Lafargue.[48] He was gripped by pain throughout, but Engels was in his best form participating in this rite called wedlock that he had never deigned to undertake. (His jokes and teasing during the postceremony lunch at Modena Villas proved a bit too acerbic for the young bride, who burst into tears and left the table.)[49]

During the newlyweds' honeymoon in Paris, Laura absorbed all the wonders of that city, which she had visited only briefly as a young girl. Despite her surroundings she pined for her family, and sent multiple letters each day to London,[50] where the family missed her terribly, too. Jenny-chen admitted that the day Laura and Paul left for France

> was one of the longest and dreariest days I have ever passed....Papa suggested a walk on the Heath, for the purpose of taking tea in the valleys. His advice was followed—but the tea had little flavor in it—there was no one to eat the bread and butter and to enjoy eating it....On our return from the Heath we settled down in the drawing room and after manifold attempts at gaiety, as dismal and unnatural as those of the clown in the pantomime, Mama and Helen broke

down and finally snoozed away to their hearts' content. Papa and Engels took a few hours for themselves and I kept up the show of a conversation by asking Lina [Schöler] endless questions to which I did not wait for answers.[51]

On April 11, less than a week after the couple had arrived in Paris, Marx showed how much he missed his chief researcher by interrupting Laura's honeymoon to ask that she visit at least five people or libraries around Paris to collect catalogs for him or discuss *Capital.* By way of apology he said, "You'll certainly fancy, my dear child, that I am very fond of books, because I trouble you with them at so unseasonable a time. But you would be quite mistaken, I am a machine, condemned to devour them and, then, throw them, in a changed form, on the dunghill of history."[52]

Laura and Paul returned to London in late April "love-SICK"—according to Marx—and settled into an apartment on Primrose Hill, within walking distance of Modena Villas.[53] They arrived in time to join the festivities surrounding Marx's fiftieth birthday, on May 5. Engels, who remained in Manchester, sent his friend a distant toast. "I congratulate ANYHOW on the half century, from which, incidentally, I am also only a short span away. Indeed, what juvenile enthusiasts we were twenty-five years ago when we boasted that by this time we would long have been beheaded."[54]

Laura's wedding was behind them, as was Marx's important milestone, but he was still too agitated to sit down to work on *Volume II,* and so at the end of May he set off for Manchester with his thirteen-year-old daughter in search of distraction. Tussy's exuberant company would have been a perfect tonic for the intellectually stymied genius beside her. From the time she was a small girl Tussy had been remarkably quick-witted. Her areas of expertise—and they could truly be called that despite her age—ranged from literature to theater to politics. Her school notebook bore the handwritten title "Tutti Frutti," but taped inside were newspaper clippings on agricultural labor and village sewage, notes on French history—and drawings of women in bridal gowns.[55] When she was eight, she considered herself a friend of the radical Blanqui, who made the French government shudder, and felt firmly on the side of the Poles in their 1863 fight against Russia. She had written her father's uncle Lion Philips, "How do you think Poland is getting on? I always hold up a finger for the Poles, those brave little fellows."[56]

Though immersed in the family fight for the downtrodden, Tussy also enjoyed a rich imaginary life. In the Marx home there was a fantasy empire, in which Jennychen was the emperor of China and Tussy her successor, which required her to invent a language she used in writing letters (though the recipient would be in the dark as to their meaning). Another persona she often assumed was "Alberich," a sometimes strong, sometimes grim dwarf.[57] Indeed, it seems that the family actively encouraged her role-playing: As often as the family referred to Tussy as "her" they teasingly referred to Tussy as "him," partly because of the male parts she inevitably chose when performing in the family's theatricals, and partly because of her audacious character.[58] Her parents could not have helped but see Musch's extravagant personality in this daughter born just a few months before his death—the appellation "him" for Tussy may have represented a forlorn slip and a yearning. But the lovely girl with waist-length black curls was not a "him": she was a rapscallion, a rogue in a petticoat.

Traveling to see Engels with her father was something akin to a rite of passage for Tussy. They stayed with Engels and Lizzy and Lizzy's seven-year-old niece, Mary Ellen, and Tussy immediately became a devotee of Manchester and a self-proclaimed Fenian sister. Irish passions were once again stirred that month when an Irishman named Michael Barrett was hanged outside Newgate Prison in London for the Clerkenwell bombing. (Barrett would be the last man publicly hanged in England.)[59] The Irish were outraged over his execution, and Tussy rewrote "God Bless the Queen": "God save our flag of green / soon may it bright be seen / God save the green / Send it victorious, peaceful and glorious / God save our flag of green / God save the green." She also began reading the *Irishman* newspaper; the sales agent blessed her, proclaiming Tussy *"thrue to the ould counthrey."*[60] Bursting with pride, Tussy reported her activities to Jennychen, who playfully scolded her about visiting the site of the van attack and lurking around Fenian pubs: "You little rebel. The police will pick you up one of these days and favor Engels with a visit."[61]

Marx and Tussy spent two weeks in Manchester, and when they returned, Marx told Engels, "Tussychen generated something approaching bad blood here in the house with her dithyrambic praise of the Manchester HOME and her openly declared wish to return there as soon as possible."[62] When Jennychen accused her of going over to the Irish and no longer paying proper respect to her as Chinese emperor, young Tussy replied, "FORMERLY I CLUNG TO A MAN, NOW I CLING TO A NATION."[63] But it wasn't just the Irish that drew Tussy north. She deeply loved Engels, connecting with him intellectually and personally, the way her father had so many years before. Engels had sent Tussy six letters, and Marx told him she knew them all by heart.[64]

Tussy's childish desire to depart Modena Villas had a poignancy for Marx and Jenny that she probably did not understand. The children were leaving the fold. Paul had just passed his medical exams and was now a member of the Royal College of Surgeons (which Marx called a "patent for THE KILL-ING OF MEN AND BEASTS"[65]), and he and Laura would be moving to Paris. Jennychen, too, had announced that she was leaving. Unbeknown to her parents, though Jennychen had confided in Laura and Lenchen, she had accepted a governess job with a Scottish family in London.[66] Jennychen must have felt she could no longer live as a dependent daughter at home after Laura's marriage—her sister's absence would have been a constant reminder that she had accomplished nothing, despite ambitions to do *everything.* Marx had introduced his daughters to the worlds of literature, politics, history, and science, and yet seemingly expected them to sit quietly and contentedly in his home while waiting for a husband to remove them to another, for more of the same. Remarkably, he simply did not, perhaps could not, recognize their yearnings to make something of themselves.

In Jennychen's case he blamed her decision to get a job on his wife's indisposition and did his best to limit the damage by making sure the contract was not binding. Exhibiting the hurt pride of a bourgeois dismayed by his daughter's decision to soil her hands with labor, he wrote Engels, "Though the matter was extremely embarrassing to me (the child would have to teach small children almost all day long)—I do not need to emphasize this—I consented on this condition, since I found it favorable that Jennychen would be diverted by some sort of occupation and, in particular, get out of these four walls. For years now my wife has quite lost her temper—understandable under the circumstances, but not thereby made pleasanter—and tortures the children mortally with her complaints and irritability and BAD HUMOR, though no children could bear it all IN A MORE JOLLY WAY. But *there are, after all, certain limits.*"[67]

Jennychen left in January. The loss of this, his favorite daughter, so soon after Laura's departure was a severe blow to Marx. He could still find Tussy and her menagerie of pets roaming the halls of their sprawling home, a dog or cat seemingly always underfoot, but the bustle was greatly reduced without the two women he still considered his little girls. He had embraced his daughters as trusted comrades as they fled with him from one country to another. Having them along increased the adventure. Surrounded by children, Marx was as playful as a child (he often said they were his preferred companions), and in their absence he was gloomy. The weather seemed to reflect his mood: London was engulfed in dense fog, and Marx was bottled up in the house, succumbing to the flu and his memories.[68] What a wonderful surprise, then, when Lafargue wrote Marx from Paris on January 1 to report that Laura had had a son. Marx dashed off a note to Engels: "Happy New Year! From the enclosed letter from Lafargue you will see that I have received a special NEW YEAR'S GIFT — THE DIGNITY OF GRANDFATHER."[69]

The entire Marx household was in an uproar over the little boy with the grand name: Charles Etienne Lafargue. Tussy dressed her cat and carried it around, pretending she was holding the "little man," as she put aside her Fenian plotting to focus on machinations to pry the child away from his parents. Jennychen jokingly alerted Laura to Tussy's plan, quoting her younger sister as saying, "If I could only get Master Lafargue away from the old ones [Paul and Laura] and have him all to myself..."[70] Jenny was rather piqued at not having been summoned to Paris to attend to her first grandchild, even more so when friends persistently asked why she was not yet there (not to mention questions about the child's baptism).[71]

The exultant parents had nicknamed the baby Fouchtra (which, in the dialect of France's Auvergne region, could mean either a silly boy or a less-than-polite exclamation of frustration). Laura said he looked like Marx, but it was unclear whether his thoughts would make him a "Fichte, Kant or Hegel." Regardless, Marx was beside himself with joy over the latest member of the family, all the more so because it was a boy.

It was true, the house was far emptier in January 1869 than it had ever been. But Fouchtra's birth was the latest sign that the new year portended well for the family. The previous fall Marx had received a letter saying, "The significance of your latest work — *Capital. Critique of Political Economy* — has prompted one of [the] local publishers (N. Polyakov) to undertake its translation into Russian." The book had made its way to St. Petersburg, where an economist and writer named Nikolai Danielson, along with two associates, wanted to translate it.[72] "It is an irony of fate that the Russians, against whom I have been fighting incessantly for twenty-five years, not only in German, but also in French and English, have always been my 'patrons,'" Marx wrote Kugelmann. "In 1843–1844 in Paris, the Russian aristocrats there waited on me hand and foot. My book against Proudhon (1847), ditto that published by Duncker (1859), have nowhere had such good sales as in Russia. And the first foreign nation to translate *Capital* is Russia." He added, "Yet not too much should be made of all this. The Russian aristocracy are educated, in their youth, at German universities and in Paris. They always yearn for the most extreme the West has to offer.... It does not hinder the very same Russians from becoming scoundrels as soon as they enter government service."[73]

Along with that good news came a bombshell from Engels. He fully expected his partner, Gottfried Ermen, to buy him out of the business in

1869, and Engels wanted to be sure he would realize sufficient money from the deal to support himself and Marx for as long as possible. Without forewarning he wrote Marx in November 1868: "Dear Mohr, Consider *very precisely* the answers to the enclosed questions, and answer them for me by return, so that I may have your reply on Tuesday morning. 1. How much money do you need to pay *all* your debts, SO AS TO HAVE A CLEAR START? 2. Can you manage with 350 pounds for your *usual* regular needs for a year (from this I exclude extra expenses caused by sickness and unforeseen events)....If not, tell me the sum required for it." Engels explained he was trying to calculate how much Marx would need to live on, because he believed he could negotiate a sum with Ermen that would allow him to provide all the Marx family required for five or six years. "What will happen after the five–six years mentioned above is not clear to me either....Yet much may change by then, and your literary work will be capable of bringing something in for you."[74] (Though a year and a half after *Capital*'s release it had still not sold enough to cover its production expenses.)[75]

In 1867 an annual income of £350 a year was considered the low end of the scale for a middle-class English family,[76] but Marx took the offer for what it was, fantastically generous—indeed, he said he was "KNOCKED DOWN" by it. He and Jenny calculated their debt and discovered that it had reached £210, excluding doctor bills. As for their annual needs, Marx said, "During the past few years we have used more than 350 pounds, but the sum is absolutely sufficient, since 1. during the past few years Lafargue was living with us, and expenses were much increased by his presence in the house; and 2., owing to the debt system, everything cost much too much. With a complete CLEARANCE of the debts, I would be able for the first time to enforce a STRICT ADMINISTRATION."[77] It is likely that Engels viewed a promise of strict financial administration from his profligate friend, who recognized economy only when he wrote about it, as laughable. But it represented a commitment from Marx that he would try.

34

London, 1869

*Men are small, parties are blind, their methods are violent or
inept, but beneath these miseries the political revolution, the
social revolution follows its inevitable advancement.*

—Charles Prolès[1]

IN 1869 the International was more than four years old, and since its
inception it had grown remarkably in strength and membership. It had
branches in nine countries, numerous newspapers at its disposal, and had
held four annual congresses. But the IWMA General Council in London
had been beset by conflict from the start. Each delegation to the council
was embroiled in its own internal disputes, while accusations based on
national prejudices flew among the various international members—the
Germans had too much power, the Italians were scheming to take control
of the group, the French appeared bent on fratricide and were addicted to
drama, the English seemed ready to sacrifice the worker in favor of mainstream politics and electoral victories. Marx was officially listed only as
correspondence secretary for Germany, but he was acknowledged as the
IWMA's brains, heart, and guiding spirit. He adjudicated all the petty
squabbles, working behind the scenes to settle them when possible or
launching a public tirade when quiet diplomacy would not do. His intention was always to resolve party conflict in such a way that the International's integrity was preserved and the organization survived—even if
individuals had to be sacrificed along the way.

Marx's dominance of the IWMA was called a dictatorship by his critics,
and some formed rival organizations. Prominent democrats, among them
Victor Hugo, Louis Blanc, John Stuart Mill, and Giuseppe Garibaldi,

formed the League of Peace and Freedom in 1867. It was a bourgeois, pacifist organization of high-minded notables who hoped to attract the proletariat but offered no real workers' program.[2] On the periphery of the group was Bakunin. He addressed its opening session, and though his speech made little sense and had even less substance, he so thrilled the crowd that one observer reported, "If he had asked his hearers to cut each other's throats they would have cheerfully obeyed."[3] But Bakunin found the league too tame, so he joined the IWMA in Geneva with the aim of taking over the organization.[4] Like Marx, he did not seem capable of being a mere member of a group; he had to be its leader, even while insisting that he did not want the job. Bakunin thus pretended to be loyal to the IWMA while at the same time setting up a clandestine group to work toward his real goal of seizing control from Marx.

It was a prize to be sought. Membership had grown thanks to several successful IWMA strike interventions. Those walkouts had followed an economic crisis in 1866 that hit railways, manufacturing, and mining—operations at the very heart of industrial Europe. Wages had been cut, factory output reduced, and hours lost, leaving men and women without support and unable to help themselves.[5] In response, the International solicited money for strike funds, engaged in propaganda, and, perhaps most important, organized workers to ensure that management did not resort to the old method of employing men from one nation as scab labor to break the back of a strike in another. In reality the IWMA's funds were limited (in 1869 its income was about fifty pounds[6]) and the number of people responsible for coordination few. But Marx boasted, not without evidence, that the merest hint that the IWMA was mobilizing to intervene in a strike was enough to bring management to the negotiating table.[7]

Governments in Europe had reluctantly tolerated the International as an adversarial labor organization until it displayed its political colors by condemning the execution of the Manchester Fenians and mounting rallies in support of the Irish cause—moves that, unsurprisingly, earned the condemnation of the British government.[8] When Paris IWMA members rallied in support of the Fenians, French security forces raided their homes and offices, finding enough so-called evidence to convict two dozen men of belonging to an illicit society.[9] Marx implied in a letter to Engels that Napoleon had little real concern about IWMA support for the Irish, but was trying to gain favor with England (or as he more colorfully put it, "creeping dolefully up the arse of the British government"[10]). French concern, however, rose in the summer of 1868, when a French IWMA branch in Brussels, which Marx described as comprised of "pimps" and "rabble," sentenced Napoleon to death in a mock trial. On behalf of the London council, Marx publicly denounced the branch's actions, but the affront was not forgotten, and suspicion of the IWMA grew.[11]

This of course was the France to which Laura and Paul had relocated. In the fall of 1868 they had moved into an apartment in a narrow building on a crowded back street in Saint-Germain, about a block from the medical school. Lafargue was ostensibly in Paris to arrange his French medical exams, but he seemed more interested in politics than in study: he immediately joined the local IWMA and resumed contact with the Blanquists he had known two years before. From the moment of his return to Paris he was under police surveillance. (A police agent described him as looking four or five years older than his twenty-six years, taller than average, with a dark complexion and light brown hair. The agent also noted that Lafargue possessed an air of elegance.)[12]

French academic officials, perhaps for political reasons, did not recognize Lafargue's English medical degree and required him to take five examinations, rather than the two or three he expected, in order to practice medicine in France.[13] Since he wanted to take these exams in Paris, he needed permission from the education minister as well as the state's academic council because of his previous expulsion from the University of Paris. That body, however, would not meet until December,[14] which gave Lafargue plenty of time to lose interest in medicine altogether and immerse himself in International affairs. In November, Longuet was released from prison and was back in his Latin Quarter haunts, smoking and playing dominoes, according to Laura.[15] Laura and Lafargue were also visited by Marx's 1848 and IWMA friends, who made the steep ascent to their fifth-floor furnished apartment, complaining bitterly all the while about the climb.[16]

At the end of December, as if signaling Paul's complete disinterest in his exams, he and Laura moved away from the medical school to a new Left Bank flat on the rue du Cherche-Midi. The street pulsed with noisy Parisian life (shops overflowing with bread, vegetables, and cheese; a laundry reeking of bleach and filled with chattering women; a smoky café redolent with the aroma of strong coffee), and the small apartment was in no way luxurious, but Laura said it was of a bohemian style she favored, and she prepared to settle into a happy domestic routine there.[17] In the midst of their move, however, the Lafargues had made the disconcerting discovery that they were being watched. Until they could ascertain the extent of the police interest, Laura told Jennychen to address her letters to Madame Santi, a relative of Paul's who helped Laura, and she would in turn mail all letters to Jennychen under Lenchen's name.[18] Their concern was soon justified.

Marx had been corresponding with International members who reported having been at the Lafargues' but had not seen Laura. Suspicious that she was unwell, he decided to go to Paris himself.[19] (What he did not know was that Laura had taken a fall in the weeks before she gave birth and was still bedridden.)[20] Marx was concerned that he might be even less welcome in France than usual because his *Eighteenth Brumaire of Louis Bonaparte*—the story of Napoleon III's coup—had been published in a second edition, so he instructed the Lafargues, "Do not, in your letters, drop any hint as to my secret plan."[21] Within a week, however, a stranger appeared at their apartment asking if Monsieur Marx had arrived yet, because he had something to tell him. Marx and the Lafargues assumed the man was a police agent and that their mail had indeed been intercepted and read.[22] Marx canceled his trip, but his worry about Laura persisted, and he began devising plans to send Jennychen and Tussy to Paris in his stead.[23]

By February 1869 Lafargue had been back in Paris for four months but had made no effort to complete his medical examinations. In a generous mood, French academic officials had agreed to require him to take only two exams to get his medical license, though they stipulated they must be taken in Strasbourg.[24] Paul had shown almost no interest in sitting for his exams in Paris, and now that he would have to travel nearly to Germany to do so, his rejection of the process became inevitable. Besides, he was now involved in another venture that made leaving Paris impossible. He and some Blanquist friends announced that they would begin publishing a newspaper that month called *La Renaissance*. They did not, however, have the £250 "guarantee money" required by the government to publish, and they lacked operating funds. All they had, in fact, was their enthusiasm and support from Blanqui himself.[25] Lafargue tried to convince Marx to contribute articles or appear on the masthead as a coeditor,[26] but his father-in-law pleaded that he had no time, and in any case he and Engels were united in the opinion that Lafargue should put aside politics until he established himself as a doctor.

Marx was thinking about Laura's future and Paul's safety, but also about Lafargue's father, who he strongly felt should not be alienated from his son. Marx wrote Paul,

> The intended paper will probably involve you and your friends in judicial conflicts with the government, and your father, becoming sooner or later aware of my name figuring among the editors of that paper, would be likely to draw the conclusion that I had pushed you to premature political action, and

prevented you from taking the steps necessary (and which I am continuously urging you to take) to pass your medical examinations and establish yourself professionally.[27]

Separately to Jennychen, Marx wrote that he would like to oblige Blanqui by helping with the newspaper, but out of regard for François Lafargue's feelings he could not: "As it is, he has not much reason to delight in his connection with the Marx family."[28]

Over the next months Marx became increasingly concerned about Paul's dangerous and naive game. Blanqui was back in Paris but in hiding, never sleeping in the same place twice. He began setting up cells of ten people, who did not know members of the other cells, in order to foil police infiltrators. Paul was among those who met every week at a house frequented by Blanqui on the Ile St.-Louis, on a street called La Femme sans Tête (The Headless Woman).[29] Blanqui had spent half his life in jail, and anyone closely associated with him could eventually expect to find their way there, too. Marx wanted to go to Paris to counsel his son-in-law as well as survey the situation firsthand. He told Engels he would try to have himself naturalized as an Englishman in order to travel legitimately to France. In the meantime, Jennychen and Tussy would go.[30] The sisters were eager to do so, though they were less concerned about Lafargue's politicking than about Laura's well-being; her letters to Jennychen had evinced an undeniable air of melancholy.

Laura had been in bed for three months, alone except for Madame Santi, while her husband was engaged in long nights at cafés and closeted in crowded rooms, hatching plots against the emperor.[31] Unlike those in 1848, the new insurgents included women like Louise Michel, who hid a dagger in her clothes and, when the situation required, dressed as a man,[32] and Paule Mincke, a journalist who visited Laura and Paul, and whom Paul visited in return.[33] Laura told Jennychen, "Formerly, you know, Tooley would hear nothing of women out of the kitchen and the ballroom: at present he prefers seeing them in the readingroom."[34] These Frenchwomen earned their own money, made their own way in society, and considered themselves equal to the men around them. As one put it, "The inferiority of women is not a fact of nature; it is a human invention and a social fiction."[35] These were the women Jennychen strove to emulate. But Laura, having opted for the traditional role of wife and mother, found herself caught between eras. She was also awakening to the differences between life in England in the family fold and life in France with a largely absent spouse. In a letter to Jennychen she observed that Frenchwomen did not believe that their husbands had an exclusive right to pay them attention: "On the contrary, their husbands are sometimes the only men in the world who pay them none. A Frenchman is often enough ashamed of confessing that he loves his wife, a Frenchwoman is never afraid of confessing that she is loved by a host of men, excepting indeed her husband."[36]

Jennychen and Tussy took a steamer to Paris on March 23. Once there, the Marx women found their nephew beautiful and blessed with an immense forehead like his grandfather, Laura's apartment small but nice, and Madame Santi amiable though "rather cracked."[37] Jennychen, on leave from her governess duties, stayed only until April 14,[38] but Tussy remained in Paris for two months. She could not tear herself away from the baby, who had earned a new nickname—Schnapps—because he drank so much (also like his grandfather).[39]

The climate in the Marx household in London had changed considerably. Engels had begun supplying Marx with quarterly installments of funds in anticipation of his retirement from Ermen & Engels. And Marx's literary attention was fixed primarily on translations or second editions of earlier works, from a French *Communist Manifesto* to a Russian *Capital*. After the muted reception for *Volume I* (an English review in June 1868 concluded, "We do not suspect that Karl Marx has much to teach us"[40]), near silence emanated from Modena Villas with regard to *Volume II* (this though Marx had been expected to submit *Volumes II* and *III* to the publisher the year before). Nor did the family feel inclined to push him toward its completion. Jennychen told Kugelmann, "Our exile, our years of isolation, etc etc were sacrifices to the noble cause of the proletariat and I don't regret them. But I admit nonetheless a certain human frailty and that the health of my father is more precious to me than the completion of the second volume of *Capital,* and I say in passing that the grand German nation hasn't deigned to read the first volume."[41] Marx essentially halted Engels's inquiries on the subject when he announced he had to teach himself Russian in order to read new books on social relations and economics in that country, which he wanted to include in his next volume.[42]

Though Marx was still fully engaged in the work of revolution through his writing and the IWMA, the ambience at Modena Villas was one of almost bourgeois normalcy. The painful dramas that had plagued the family from the moment they arrived in London had dissipated; the Marx household was what had once seemed impossible—dull and comfortable. In a letter to Lafargue that spring Jennychen related that their most rebellious activity that day had been Marx's proposal that they have a fresh leg of mutton for dinner.[43] Indeed, a letter Marx wrote Tussy in Paris is a good example of just how sedate and domesticated he had become. After giving a detailed report on her pets, he described a special musical bond he had developed with her bird, Dicky.[44] In early May Jenny abandoned Marx to the animals and traveled to Paris to see her grandson and collect Tussy. Engels invited Marx to visit him in Manchester, but Marx declined, saying he was already engaged: "Jennychen was looking forward to my wife's short absence in Paris, to have me entirely at her disposition and be able to let herself go."[45]

That spring Dr. Karl Marx and his eldest daughter appeared on London's social circuit together. They attended IWMA General Council meetings, where she heard him loudly praised at one for a vitriolic address protesting the massacre that April of unarmed strikers at the Cockerill Ironworks in Belgium.[46] The father and daughter team next appeared among society's "upper ten-thousand" in evening dress at the annual Royal Society of Arts and Trades soirée at the Kensington Museum. In recognition of his scholarship and writings, Marx had been elected a member. (He told Engels he wanted to use the society's library.) The result was a much-sought-after invitation to a society conversazione to be attended by "royal and other distinguished persons."[47] Marx and Jennychen chuckled mightily over the invitation, which instructed attendees to "assist in preventing the mobbing and following" of distinguished guests.[48] The actual event, according to Jennychen, was a bore: "Fancy crowd of some seven-thousand mutes in full evening dress, wedged in so closely as to be unable either to move about or to sit down, for the chairs, and they were few and far between, a few imperturbable dowagers had taken by storm."[49]

Later in the year Marx and Jennychen traveled to Germany to see old friends and meet new comrades among the growing workers' political movement there.[50] But well before Marx embarked, he delivered his youngest daughter to Engels. Fresh from her Paris sojourn, Tussy was to stay in Manchester for four months. She would come of age that summer. A girl of fourteen traveled north by train with her father. A young woman would return home in the fall.

Under Lizzy Burns's tutelage Tussy received an advanced course in English injustice—not through books, because Lizzy was illiterate, but through the colorful stories she told as they roamed the city's streets. Lizzy took Tussy to see the places in Manchester that had become points of pilgrimage for the Irish: the railway arch (now known locally as Fenian Arch), the market where the now fugitive Thomas Kelly had once sold pots, the house where he had lived, the places where Lizzy had met up with the other escapee, Michael Deasy. Tussy wrote Jennychen, "It was really very amusing and Mrs. B. has been telling me a great many amusing things about 'Kelly and *Daisy*,' whom Mrs. B. knew quite well, having been to their house and seen them three or four times a week."[51] Engels introduced Tussy to German literature. In June he had her reading Goethe, epics, and folktales, all in the original German and all on her own. Together they tore through tales in Danish.[52]

But the lesson from her Manchester visit that Tussy remembered most vividly was Engels's joy on the day he escaped what Marx called "Egyptian bondage."[53] On July 1, 1869, Engels ended his business career. Years later, Tussy wrote, "I shall never forget the triumphant 'for the last time!' which he shouted as he drew on his top boots in the morning to make his last journey to business. Some hours later when we were standing at the door waiting for him, we saw him coming over the little field opposite the house where he lived. He was swinging a stick in the air and singing, his face beaming. Then we set the table for a celebration and drank champagne and were happy."[54] Engels wrote Marx, "Hurrah! Today sweet business is at an end, and I am a free man.... Tussy and I celebrated my first free day this morning with a long walk in the fields."[55]

Engels left Ermen & Engels with about £12,500 in his pocket (in today's money about $2 million).[56] He told his mother he was a new man:

This morning, instead of going into the gloomy city, I walked in this wonderful weather for a few hours in the fields; and at my desk, in a comfortably furnished room in which you can open the windows without the smoke making black stains everywhere, with flowers on the windowsills and trees in front of the house, one can work quite differently than in my gloomy room in the WAREHOUSE, looking out onto the courtyard of an alehouse.[57]

The celebration lasted for weeks. Engels was the only one in his household who had had a job, and yet everyone in his small circle acted as though they, too, had been liberated. He treated the women in his house — Lizzy, Tussy, Lizzy's niece Mary Ellen, and his dog, Dido — to a six-mile walk that ended in a pub, where Lizzy and Tussy imbibed enough beer that they all had to return home by train.[58] Tussy described Engels during another night out as being "drunk as jelly" after celebrating with some friends from the warehouse. Weeks after Engels's retirement they were still at it. On a particularly hot July day, Tussy reported, while Engels attended a society picnic with "Periodical ladies" and "Lords of the Creation," she, Lizzy, and their maid, Sarah, spent the afternoon and evening drinking beer and claret. Engels came home to find them "all lying our full length on the floor, with no stays, no boots, and one petticoat and a cotton dress on, and that was all." The next day they witnessed the Prince and Princess of Wales traveling through Manchester. Tussy told Jenny-chen beforehand, "What fun if a lot of children sing 'The Prince of Wales in Belle Vue jail / For robbing a man of a pint of ale.' "[59] Such was the edu-cation of Eleanor Marx that summer.

The instruction, however, did not end in Manchester. In the fall Engels hit on the idea of taking Lizzy and Tussy to Ireland. Tussy was a devotee of all things Irish—she read the novels, she knew the songs, she could recite the verse—and now she saw the depopulated hills, the abandoned villages, the mounds of mud with smoke rising from the top that indicated a home with people inside, the grimy children barefoot and without coats in the howling wind of wet and raw Dublin, Killarney, and Cork. She saw, too, the soldiers pounding down the streets on horseback, dressed in crisp uniforms and high boots, weapons at the ready. Engels described Ireland as in a "state of war": "The ROYAL IRISH rush about everywhere in squads, with sheath-knives and sometimes revolvers at their belts, and unsheathed police batons in their hands; in Dublin a horse-drawn battery drove right through the center of town, something I have never seen in England." The English-allied ruling class in Ireland was terrified of the populace, who though unschooled and disorganized vastly outnumbered the landlords they despised.

Back in Manchester, Engels joked that Tussy had returned more Irish than ever,[60] but the trip did indeed leave an indelible mark on her, much as Marx's visit to Manchester with Engels twenty-four years earlier had left on him. Tussy had been raised on stories of such misery. In her world it was a given that governments were oppressive and people were denied their rights. Still, after coming face-to-face with the eyes of starvation and the awful power of a man armed with a weapon and authorized by the state to kill, she was transformed. She was still guileless and gay, but her schoolgirl commitment to political causes had matured. Her letters were more reflective. There were glimpses in her words of the woman she would become, the one who would spend her life working past the point of exhaustion on behalf of the poor. Marx had once said of his daughters that Jennychen was most like him. But he finished that quote by declaring that Eleanor *was* him.

The reason for the heightened security in Ireland during Tussy's trip was mounting anger over the treatment of Irish political prisoners by English jailers. The arrests dated back to 1865 and a crackdown on the press that netted the staff of *The Irish People* in Dublin, including its manager,

Jeremiah O'Donovan Rossa. The prosecution charged that the paper promoted redistribution of property to the poor and the assassination of the
ruling class, including Catholic clergy. Thirty people had been arrested
in that case,[61] with some condemned to twenty years' hard labor for crimes
that normally received sentences of no more than six months in jail.[62] In
the following years more Irish were arrested for so-called political crimes
and given similarly harsh sentences.

On October 24, 1869, a demonstration in support of amnesty for Irish
prisoners was held in Hyde Park. At Tussy's insistence Marx, Jenny, and
Jennychen attended.[63] The vast park near the heart of London had been
blackened by the mourning clothes of the tens of thousands gathered
there. The sky above, however, fluttered with color. Handmade flags of
green, white, and red, and banners proclaiming "Disobedience to tyrants
is a duty to God" and "Keep your powder dry!" moved from one end of
the park to the other, while red Jacobin hats bobbed overhead on sticks.
The grounds were full, as were the trees, with children perched in the
branches to get a better look at their elders singing Irish ballads and the
"Marseillaise" in a boisterous show of defiance of the crown.[64] Newspapers, notorious for downplaying attendance at such demonstrations, put
the crowd at seventy thousand and called the event a "shabby failure."[65]
Marx called it a ringing success.[66]

To calm tensions Prime Minister William Gladstone had in the previous months taken steps to appease Ireland, but his gestures were seen as
woefully inadequate by those who wanted not just justice but independence.[67] Less than a month after the Hyde Park rally, Irish voters used
English elections to make a mockery of the country's political and judicial
systems, electing O'Donovan Rossa to represent Tipperary in the British
House of Commons.[68] At the time he was languishing in an English jail.
Marx and Engels cheered his election, Engels proclaiming it a sign that
the Fenians were abandoning conspiracies in favor of a far more effective
and revolutionary method — the vote — which had the added advantage
of being legal.[69] Jennychen told Kugelmann, "On the day we received
the news of Donovan's election we all danced with joy — Tussy was quite
wild." She added that England at that moment was a "country of horrors.
In the East End of London famine fever has broken out."[70]

Marx and Engels were convinced the path to emancipation of the
working class began in Ireland. Marx wrote, "To accelerate the social
development in Europe, you must push on the catastrophe of official England. To do so, you must attack her in Ireland. That's her weakest point.
Ireland lost, the British 'Empire' is gone, and the class war in England, till
now somnolent and chronic, will assume acute forms." If the workers in

the most industrialized nation in the world were freed, Marx was certain the rest of Europe would soon follow.[71]

At the very time Marx and Engels were focused on Ireland, however, rumblings were being felt on the Continent that would affect the workingman into the next century. The country that had given rise to every major European revolt since 1789 was about to explode again, and its epicenter, as always, would be Paris.

On January 10, 1870, Napoleon III's cousin Prince Pierre Napoleon Bonaparte shot dead a journalist for the popular republican newspaper *La Marseillaise* who was at Bonaparte's home to act as a second for a Blanquist challenging the prince to a duel. The bullet that struck Victor Noir was widely seen as a shot to the heart of increasingly powerful French leftists.[72] In an election the previous May, the opposition had won 45 percent of votes cast, and thirty "red" candidates were elected to the Corps Législatif. The shift had forced Napoleon to make liberal reforms that raised concerns among his most ardent followers, those who had remained loyal through his improbably long rule of nearly two decades but who now wondered whether the aging sovereign was capable of facing a new menace from the left and its army of workers.[73]

From his apartments at the Tuileries, Napoleon could still comfort himself with the cries of *"Vive l'Empereur"* from the courtiers and other sycophants dependent on his beneficence, and he enjoyed the support of the new power in France—the capitalists—who had been allowed to build empires of their own in exchange for financing his throne. Paris was inarguably magnificent as a result of policies instituted during Napoleon III's rule and France considerably richer. But the social problems that existed before his reign persisted and in some cases had grown much worse. Outside the emperor's pampered inner circle discontent was growing.[74] During the Second Empire wages had risen as much as 30 percent, but the cost of living had soared 50 percent.[75] Organized and emboldened workers walked off the job over pay that did not meet a family's most basic needs and long hours that robbed men, women, and even children of their health, if not their lives. The strikes were not confined to Paris, but the capital's population was greatest and so it was, once again, the center of revolt. In 1869 spontaneous protests (*attroupements*) had begun throughout the city. Men and women would mingle until there were enough of them to block a square or boulevard. Police would then sweep in and make arrests, but the next night more men and women would appear to engage in a fresh show of resistance.[76]

Victor Noir's January 12 funeral provided an opportunity for a less spontaneous and more massive demonstration against the government. An estimated two hundred thousand people gathered on the Champs Elysées to mourn Noir but also to throw down the gauntlet to Napoleon.[77] Louise Michel, the revolutionary who had befriended Lafargue on his return to Paris, noted, "Almost everyone who turned up at the funeral expected to go home again as members of a republic, or not to go home at all." The government expected trouble, too: sixty thousand soldiers were on hand to control the mob.[78] Yet as much as the crowd may have wanted one, there was no revolt. Cooler heads knew that the result would be a slaughter. The new generation of radicals in France had learned the lessons of 1848.

It is not clear whether Lafargue attended Noir's funeral; he was focused on personal matters. On January 1, Laura had given birth prematurely to a daughter named Jenny. Lenchen was so worried about the baby after reading Laura's letters that she sent the Lafargues money for medical care, but Paul was convinced the infant was healthy and refused the services of a wet nurse, explaining that if little Jenny did not respond to cow's milk (which was being touted as an alternative to breast milk), he would hire a nurse from London.[79]

Marx may have been relieved that Lafargue's familial duties might distract him from politics at that moment. The previous summer Marx had slipped incognito into Paris for several days after receiving an alarming letter from Lafargue's father, who feared his son had abandoned his studies. Paul assured Marx that it was not politics that kept him from his exams but Laura's health, and he promised to take his tests that fall.[80] By February he still had not, but he could continue to blame the delay on concern for Laura. There is no doubt that Lafargue was concerned about Laura, but also little question, despite what he told Marx, that politics had become his mistress.

Several weeks after Noir's funeral, Henri de Rochefort, editor of *La Marseillaise,* was arrested in Paris after calling for an uprising against the empire in an article about the journalist's murder.[81] One of Rochefort's defenders was a well-known republican named Gustave Flourens. Flourens was a passionate—some would say reckless—advocate of those he believed wronged, and he responded immediately to the arrest by declaring a revolution. He had been meeting with Rochefort when the editor was seized, and in response had promptly detained the police commissioner who was present and assembled a group of sixty people to act as an impromptu militia. They headed to the working-class district and hotbed of Parisian radicalism, Belleville, where he planned to confiscate government weapons and organize his revolt. The insurrection, however, was a dismal failure: by morning, Flourens's call to arms found only one eager but unknown young man at his side.[82] Flourens eluded capture in Paris for more than a month and eventually fled to Holland and then on to London. Once there, in March, he joined the IWMA and made his way to the Marx home.[83] (A Tours jury, meanwhile, had acquitted Bonaparte of Noir's death.)

Rochefort was a friend of Longuet's, the two having met several years before at Sainte-Pélagie prison, where a wing was devoted to political detainees, and Longuet had also written for *La Marseillaise*. Lafargue, on the other hand, had no personal or professional relationship with the now imprisoned editor. Nonetheless, he decided to try to take over the newspaper while Rochefort was locked up. Lafargue was not unlike the young Marx in believing that all he needed was a newspaper to launch his views. But Paul's attempts must have seemed ludicrous to the staff; he was, for starters, not even a practicing journalist, and while his overtures were received politely, he was generally ignored. In the end he could not even publish a single article in *La Marseillaise*.[84] Another family member, however, had more luck in that regard.

By late February, Marx had decided that English newspapers were incapable of reporting fairly on the Irish political prisoners held in British jails, so he wrote a young International colleague in Brussels, César De Paepe, suggesting points for an article his newspaper should publish on the detainees.[85] De Paepe published Marx's letter verbatim in two installments.[86] In them Marx charged the "land of bourgeois freedom" with torture. Perhaps because he had not expected his letter to be published, he wrote in a clipped style, with none of his usual literary arabesques. This made his words all the more effective. He detailed the ongoing abuse of Irish prisoners: Dennis Dowling Mulcahy, physician and subeditor of *The Irish People* newspaper, "harnessed to a cart loaded with stones with an iron collar around his neck"; O'Donovan Rossa, owner of *The Irish People,* "shut up for 35 days in a pitch-black dungeon with his hands chained behind his back day and night"; Charles Kickham, editor of *The Irish People,* unable to use his right arm because of an abscess, forced to break stones and brick with his left hand and given but six ounces of bread and hot water for a meal; O'Leary, a sixty- or seventy-year-old man whose real name was Murphy (but whose first name was unknown), placed on bread and water for three weeks because, as a declared atheist, he would not, even under threat of force, adopt a religion. The litany of abuse was long and included the death by torture of one Irish inmate. Marx further noted that there had been inquiries into prisoner treatment, but requests to visit their jails as part of the probes were denied.[87]

In such written appeal he was to be joined by another Marx: Jennychen was incensed when *La Marseillaise* supported an English newspaper that cautioned against viewing the Irish prisoners as political martyrs, and she fired off a response (signed "J. Williams") on February 27 that made its way into the French newspaper on March 1.[88] In return she received an invitation from *La Marseillaise* to write more.[89] Thus began Jennychen's double life as governess by day and defender of Irish inmates by night. She was ecstatic over the prospect not only of having her articles published but of using her pen to expose injustice. Her life had been spent anticipating the effect of her father's words, and now she had a chance to test the power of her own.

Jennychen's first piece had ended with the provocative phrase "*Twenty Fenians have died or gone mad* in the prisons of humanitarian England,"[90] and her next article was bolder still. In it she accused Prime Minister Gladstone of lying to hide his government's crimes, and as evidence she used a letter by O'Donovan Rossa written on toilet paper with pencil fragments and smuggled out of prison.[91] (Flourens, now a regular at the Marx home, translated the letter into French, and Jennychen used it in its entirety in her piece.)[92] The Irishman described being forced to eat his meals like an animal, on his knees and elbows, and being harnessed to a cart by a rope tied around his neck. Beaten and deprived of food, he recounted watching fellow inmates die as a result of the conditions in which they were held: "I am not complaining of the penalties which my masters inflict on me—it is my job to suffer—but I insist that I have the right to inform the world of the treatment to which I am subjected....If I am to die in prison I entreat my family and my friends not to believe a word of what these people say." The letter was signed "O'Donovan Rossa, Political prisoner sentenced to hard labor."[93]

The letter caused a sensation. It was almost Shakespearean, as if O'Donovan Rossa had spoken from the grave to denounce his murderers. *La Marseillaise* rushed out a special edition featuring only articles by political prisoners, and Jennychen's report spread like fire through Brussels, Berlin, Dublin, and all the way to America. Within days English newspapers from Manchester to London—the *Times,* the *Daily Telegraph,* the *Standard*—reprinted the piece.[94] On March 16 London's *Daily News* published a response from the British home secretary denying O'Donovan Rossa's claims but admitting that he had been put in irons.[95] That gave "J. Williams" fodder for another article for *La Marseillaise,* which Jennychen and Marx wrote together.[96]

Marx was beside himself with pride over his daughter's achievements. Her articles had prompted a call in Parliament for a full public inquiry into the treatment of Irish detainees, which Gladstone was forced to accept. Not only was Jennychen working toward ultimately winning the inmates' freedom, she was trying to improve their conditions in the meantime by keeping the issue alive in a stream of articles. Marx also believed she had helped destroy the illusion that liberal governments were more concerned about rights than reactionary regimes.[97] He mentioned Jennychen's articles in every letter he wrote during this period, no matter how disinterested his correspondent. Engels, too, was elated. "Jenny can shout: *victory along the line!*" he wrote Marx. "If it were not for her, the honorable Gladstone would never have granted the new inquest."[98]

Jennychen's world expanded brilliantly that spring. Although her articles were printed anonymously, it was generally known in her father's circle that she was the author (O'Donovan Rossa's wife, Mary, however, thought J. Williams was a man; she was friendly until she discovered that J. was Jenny, at which point jealousy proved a stronger emotion than gratitude[99]). Jennychen began to receive invitations not as Karl Marx's daughter but as Jenny Marx the writer. An Italian merchant's wife invited her in late March to a London soirée full of English notables, where Jennychen gave a recitation from Shakespeare and was a "furious success," according to her entirely biased father. She had even started taking singing lessons again, with an eye once more turning toward the stage.[100]

Jennychen also had the attention of Flourens. Broad-shouldered, blond, bearded, and with clear blue eyes, at thirty-two he was in many ways a throwback to the men of 1848—an impetuous romantic, a ruling-class renegade. The son of a French aristocrat and member of the Paris Academy of Sciences, Flourens had also been trained in science and had written a book on ethnography, but—drawn to greater adventure—became a freelance soldier, offering his considerable abilities to whatever country or whatever cause he thought worthy. He exuded physical power, though in the Marx drawing room he was gentle, meticulous in his manners, and—well, fun.[101] The Marx women, one by one, fell madly in love with him. Jennychen was especially smitten, calling Flourens "a most extraordinary mixture of a scholar and a man of action."[102] The two worked together on behalf of Irish inmates while also keeping an eye on France, where Napoleon's efforts to regain his authority seemed increasingly likely to produce the opposite result.

A plebiscite had been scheduled for May 8, 1870, in which French voters would be asked to approve constitutional amendments allowing Napoleon III to bypass the legislature and go directly to the people to change the law. From Napoleon's standpoint the language of the plebiscite was written brilliantly—the wording was so vague that whichever way the vote went, he could claim victory. But what Napoleon considered a clever move was viewed by his critics as an act of desperation by a leader whose power had so eroded that he had to trick his people in order to ensure their support.[103] International members exposed the emperor's maneuver in a meeting in late April attended by twelve hundred people, and urged voters to abstain from the sham plebiscite. In response, security forces raided IWMA offices in Paris, Lyons, Rouen, Marseilles, and Brest.[104] They claimed the International was an illegal, secret organization and that its members were plotting to kill Napoleon. In fact such a plot was in the air, but it was not the work of the IWMA: police had hatched a false conspiracy against the emperor in order to justify a crackdown on the opposition.[105]

Amid all this drama, Lafargue and Laura, who normally reported regularly to Marx on events in France, had been silent. In late February their daughter Jenny, whom Lafargue had insisted was healthy, had died.[106] Laura described herself as too "knocked up" with grief to think about writing.[107] When Marx finally learned what had happened, he sought to console her, but acknowledged his words were meaningless under the circumstances: "I have suffered myself too much from such losses to not profoundly sympathize with you. Still from the same personal experience I know that all wise commonplaces and consolatory trash uttered on such occasion irritate real grief instead of soothing it."[108]

Laura's loss came at the very time the family was celebrating Jenny-chen's success, which was undoubtedly doubly painful for the Lafargues because her articles appeared in the same newspaper that would not offer Paul the courtesy of an opening. On the surface Lafargue appeared unconcerned and began work on a series of articles attacking Victor Hugo, whom he and Marx had come to consider a utopian democrat and publicity-hungry bourgeois.[109] By now Marx understood that Lafargue had no intention of finishing his medical studies, for reasons that had nothing to do with Laura's health. He gently confronted his son-in-law by letter, and while not passing judgment insisted that Paul owed his father an explanation.[110] Lafargue, shrinking from an exchange he knew would be explosive, said he thought it better if the disclosure came from Marx.[111]

There could not have been much jubilation at Modena Villas over Paul's decision to give up medicine. A large part of his attraction for Jenny and Marx when they consented to the marriage was that Lafargue would be financially independent, with a good and noble career. Now it appeared he had thrown this over in order to play politician and writer, having exhibited no aptitude for either occupation. Laura, too, likely felt the weight of their situation. She knew what it meant to be the wife of a brilliant revolutionary thinker—she had watched her mother's suffering—and could not have failed to fear a future tied to a well-meaning but much lesser light. In a letter to Jennychen she confessed that she was "shut up in a new prison."[112]

Jennychen celebrated her twenty-sixth birthday on May 1, capping off the most successful and rewarding year of her life with a party. Among those invited was Flourens. Having easily won over the Marx women, by that time he had also gained the confidence of the head of the household: "Full of illusions and revolutionary impatience, BUT A VERY JOLLY FELLOW WITH ALL THAT, not one of those 'damned serious' school of men," Marx explained to Engels. Flourens's most dominant characteristic, as Marx saw it, was audacity, but he was also very well educated, had lectured at the University of Paris, and had traveled to the far corners of the world. Marx proposed that Flourens join the International General Council and said he hoped he would remain in London a little longer,[113] perhaps thinking not just of politics but also of Jennychen.

It was while attending her party that Flourens received word that he had been charged in the so-called plot against Napoleon. There were fears the French would demand his extradition, and the atmosphere at the party changed in an instant from joy to apprehension. Jennychen wrote that though there was no evidence against him, "we did not know at the time but what M. Flourens might not be at once arrested." In words that echoed her mother's in 1848, when she had expressed shock that the Belgian government was concerned about Marx buying weapons to arm workers, Jennychen said that although it was true that Flourens had "sent money to Paris for the purpose of arming the people with bombs...that does not imply that he had anything to do with the intended assassination of the Emperor." Her birthday all but forgotten, Jennychen, Flourens, and others at the party left Marx's house for a walk on the windy Heath to discuss the dramatic turn of events.[114]

As word of the charges spread, rumors began flying in IWMA circles in England that Flourens would be detained and International members arrested during an upcoming meeting. Marx dug through previous legal cases involving foreigners wanted for crimes allegedly committed abroad and determined Flourens had nothing to fear from English authorities under normal circumstances. But the times were not normal, and the English government was still smarting from the abuse it suffered in the French opposition press over its treatment of Irish prisoners. It may have been tempted to send one of the republican scoundrels back to Paris to face justice. So widespread were the rumors of arrest that members of the press showed up to document the police raid of the IWMA meeting. They left disappointed when the raid did not occur.[115]

It was against Flourens's nature to shrink from a challenge, so three days after he was officially named a suspect in the plot, he returned to Paris and disappeared into the opposition underground.[116] Perhaps not surprisingly, Jennychen quickly abandoned her all-consuming devotion to Ireland. Her mother described her from that moment on as "totally 'FRENCH.' "[117]

With the influx of young blood into the movement (including his daughters), Marx and Engels began to speak to each other in the language of party elders. Marx had even begun calling himself "Old Nick," because his black beard had turned white. Their generation was dying, the list of deceased comrades growing—Weerth, Weydemeyer, Lassalle, Lupus. Most recently it had been Schapper, he of the Communist League days, who had broken with Marx over the issue of immediate revolution (which he favored and Marx did not). When Marx visited his sickbed, they exchanged tales about the many characters they had known and the many nooses they'd slipped—the last one, however, being inescapable. Schapper told Marx in French, so as not to upset his wife, "I shall soon pull my last face." He died the next day.[118]

Marx and Engels had been the closest of friends since 1844, but after 1850 their relations had been primarily epistolary. In 1870 Engels announced that he would be moving back to London.[119] Marx was not the only one to rejoice at the news: through the years Jenny had often told Engels how much she regretted that he lived so far away, because she could not control Marx on her own. She also seemed to have adopted a new attitude toward "Mrs. Engels." Jenny had never mentioned Mary Burns in her letters to Engels (at least none that still exist), but she seemed to take a different attitude altogether toward Lizzy. In July, Jenny reported that she had found them a home at 122 Regent's Park Road, about ten minutes from Modena Villas. She added, "You know we shall be very happy to have her with us."[120]

35

Paris, Fall 1870

History is made in such a way that the ultimate result is invari-
ably produced by the clash of many individual wills. . . . For
what each individual wants is obstructed by every other individ-
ual and the outcome is something that no one wanted.
— Friedrich Engels[1]

TENSIONS BETWEEN FRANCE and Prussia had been building inexorably since 1815 and accelerated in the 1860s as each sought alliances to strengthen its position in case war broke out again in Europe. By the time the two armies met in July 1870 there appeared to be no alternative to battle. Napoleon III, ill and weakened domestically, needed to prove his might with a great military victory, while Bismarck saw within his grasp two long-sought goals: Prussian ascendancy on the Continent and a united Germany whose center of power was Berlin.

Strangely, the dispute that led to war began in Spain. In 1868 Queen Isabella II was overthrown by the army and fled to France, leaving a royal vacuum. The new pro-Prussian military chiefs in Madrid wrote Bismarck to say they wanted a member of the Hohenzollern line of King Wilhelm on the throne in Spain. Appalled at a prospect that would essentially sandwich it between Prussian powers, France declared war.

It was a risky decision for Napoleon, who would need his people to fight, people he could not even count on to vote as he wished. But in this case he gambled well: the French rallied behind their emperor. Crowds surged along gaslit Parisian boulevards shouting, "To Berlin in eight days," and singing the "Marseillaise."[2] There was also jubilation in Napoleon's court. The palace had grown dull after more than a decade of relative peace, and its courtiers thought a war was just the thing to quicken the blood.[3] It did just that for the sixty-two-year-old emperor. Taking command of the army, Napoleon proclaimed: "Frenchmen! There are in the lives of people solemn moments, where national honor, violently excited, imposes itself as an irresistible force, dominates all interests, and takes in hand the direction of the destinies of the country. One of these decisive hours has just sounded for France." With that, Napoleon III left his palace at St. Cloud and, surrounded by a vast entourage (almost a mobile village), rode east into battle against Prussia.[4]

The Marx household was dumbfounded by the turn of events. "It is not easy to reconcile oneself to the thought that instead of fighting for the destruction of the empire, the French people are sacrificing themselves for its aggrandizement, that instead of hanging Bonaparte they are prepared to enroll themselves under his banner," Jennychen wrote Kugelmann. "Who could have dreamt such a thing a few months ago when the revolution in Paris seemed a fact?"[5]

At the outbreak of war the French opposition was in disarray; there were too many factions, with too many diverse agendas. Worse still, each group was headed by an ego-driven leader who declared himself willing to give all for the greater good but who was actually willing to give only enough to satisfy his ambition to lead a new republic should Napoleon falter. The left, from the liberals to the IWMA, had also been weakened by government harassment. That summer the men accused of trying to kill Napoleon were tried. Of the seventy-two defendants in the sham case based on a fictitious plot, most were sentenced to penal servitude of five to twenty years or exile. Among them was Flourens.[6]

From London, Marx looked at the continental workers' movement in light of the Franco-Prussian conflict and concluded a Prussian victory would be beneficial. There were two main workers' parties in Germany—the Lassallean General Union of German Workers and the Social-Democratic Workers' Party. The latter, whose leaders were August Bebel and Marx's friend Wilhelm Liebknecht, represented 150,000 members and had adopted the IWMA's rules as its own.[7] Marx wrote: "You need only to compare developments in the two countries from 1866 to the present day to realize that the German working class is superior to the French both in theory and organization."[8] Yet this was not simply a political assessment. Marx expected a Prussian victory would result in the predominance of his version of socialism over the Proudhonism still prevalent in France.

In the meantime, no matter what outcome he privately favored, Marx and the International insisted that its members refrain from enlisting on either side. It was a basic tenet of the IWMA that workers should not fight their kings' battles. French workers extended the first hand of peace. On July 12, when war appeared inevitable, they wrote in the republican weekly newspaper *Le Réveil,* "War for a question of preponderance or a dynasty, can, in the eyes of workmen, be nothing but a criminal absurdity.... Brothers of Germany! Our division would only result in the complete triumph of despotism on both sides of the Rhine.... We, the members of the International Working Men's Association, who know of no frontiers, we send you as a pledge of indissoluble solidarity the good wishes and the salutations of the workmen of France."[9] German workers quickly responded with three published messages to the French — one in a German newspaper and two in French opposition papers. Wrote the Berlin IWMA, "Solemnly we promise that neither the sound of the trumpet, nor the roar of the cannon, neither victory nor defeat shall divert us from our common work for the union of the children of toil of all countries."[10]

On the day fighting erupted, Marx penned on behalf of the London IWMA his "First Address on the Franco-Prussian War," declaring that the "alliance of the working classes of all countries will ultimately kill war."[11] Published by the International as a leaflet, it was reprinted in the British press and won plaudits for its pacifist position from English philosopher and economist John Stuart Mill and the London-based Quaker Peace Society, which donated money to have the leaflet distributed more widely. Those funds paid for thirty thousand copies printed in French and German,[12] making this antiwar proclamation Marx's most widely distributed work to date.

Engels, meanwhile, was thoroughly enjoying the conflict — from the comfort of his desk and a purely analytical perspective. He had begun a series of articles on the course of the military campaign for London's widely read *Pall Mall Gazette* newspaper. His initial agreement had been for two pieces a week, but his "Notes on War" were so informed and his predictions were so prescient that the editor told him to send in as many articles as he liked. Engels would write fifty-nine total, the first three bylined "Z" and the remainder unsigned.[13] He protested (not without pride) that his articles were plagiarized by all the other newspapers in England.[14]

Engels was at heart and by experience an artilleryman, but his success at the *Gazette* led Jennychen to elevate him by several ranks. She began calling him the General, and from that moment on, the Marx family and the circle around them knew Engels by no other name.[15]

The French army shed first blood on August 2, during a skirmish at the German border town of Saarbrücken, east of Paris. Two days later, in the

Alsace town of Wissembourg (Weissenburg in German), France suffered a serious defeat and lost one of its best generals.[16] Cynically, however, false reports were sent back to Paris that the French had been victorious and a Prussian prince captured. Stocks soared 4 percent as many investors made money off the fiction. But by August 9 there had been three French defeats in six days, and the French people had begun to seriously consider the country's political future if the emperor went down to defeat.[17]

Marx feared the opposition would see the moment as opportune for declaring a revolution. At the best of times such a move would be danger-ous, but without a unified opposition and in the midst of war, it would be disastrous.[18] In fact there was a gathering at the Place de la Concorde on August 9, the crowd waiting excitedly for a republic to be declared, but such was the disunity among the left that it did not occur. The people went home to the prospect that Paris might be overrun by Prussian troops with no government in place to defend them.[19]

On August 11 a state of siege was declared in the capital: Prussians were massing on French soil.[20] In June, Laura and Lafargue had moved to the town of Levallois-Perret, on the outskirts of Paris. They had been there only a few weeks when they were told they would have to leave: their home was near military fortifications and would be torn down to increase the army's defensive capabilities. They had promised the family in Lon-don that they would soon leave to stay with Paul's parents in Bordeaux, far from the fighting, but by late August they still had not relocated. Lafargue was actually considering returning to Paris.[21] Frequent trips into the city had shown him the chaotic situation, yet he was prepared to hold out there with Laura and Schnapps as long as possible. Marx was furious at the Lafargues' indecision, positively growling in a letter to Engels, "The fools' dawdling over their retreat to Bordeaux is unforgivable."[22] Finally, how-ever, on September 2 they left Levallois to join a growing migration head-ing south, away from the front and Paris. They did not yet know how lucky they were to have fled when they did. That same day the French army was defeated. More than one hundred thousand French troops were taken prisoner, the emperor among them. Napoleon had surrendered.[23]

The news did not reach Paris until just before midnight on September 3. As word spread, people spilled out onto the streets and thronged the boulevards, shouting in fear and despair.[24] The next day, Sunday, political leaders gathered to decide whether to formally end Napoleon III's rule, carry on the war against Prussia, and declare a provisional Government of National Defense. The crucial question was whether the military would support such a move. The answer came quickly and with great symbolism. Armed national guardsmen and Guard Mobile marched in formation to

the Palais Bourbon, on the left bank of the Seine near the Pont de la Concorde, where the legislature met. As the troops neared the building, people could see that the butt ends of their rifles were turned up and some had
placed sprigs of greenery in their muskets: they would not oppose a new
government. In a cry that seemed to echo the exultations of 1848, someone inside the hall called out, "To the Hôtel de Ville!"[25] The crowd
rushed to the city hall, where veteran agitator Léon Gambetta climbed
onto a window ledge and declared a French republic. An estimated three
hundred thousand people gathered below roared their approval. Next stop
was Napoleon's base at the Tuileries, where sixty thousand marched on
the palace to lower the imperial flag.[26] The Empress Eugénie had already
escaped and was on a yacht on her way to England.[27] Tens of thousands of
Germans living in Paris had also fled or were trying to do so; the Gare du
Nord was packed with people anxious to catch a train before they were
branded as hostiles.[28]

But, despite the well-grounded fears, there was no violence in Paris.
Three hundred thousand French soldiers were in the city, but they were
mainly availing themselves of the cafés and the attentions of women;
instead of aiming their rifles, the uniformed men could be seen lounging
on the boulevards, drinking wine and smoking cigarettes.[29] U.S ambassador to France E. B. Washburne said, "In a few brief hours of a Sabbath day
I had seen a dynasty fall and a republic proclaimed, and all without the
shedding of one drop of blood."[30]

On Sunday the *Journal Officiel de l'Empire Française* was published as
usual. On Monday it reappeared as the *Journal Officiel de la République Française.*[31] That was perhaps the last moment of orderly transition. There was
a calm, and then there was a storm.

Marx learned of the French Republic at four in the morning on September
5, when he received a telegram from Longuet: *"The Republic has been proclaimed. Advise the republican movement in Germany."*[32] Marx did so and began
organizing English members of the International to press Britain to recognize the republic. By September 6, French IWMA members in London
were on their way to Paris, intent on undermining the newly installed
Government of National Defense by trying to place their own people in
leadership positions. Marx called such action pure folly and expressed relief
that Lafargue was in Bordeaux, otherwise he surely would have been in the
middle of it.[33] Lafargue was in fact dying to get back to Paris. All his friends
were there, and he desperately wanted to throw himself into the action.
But two factors held him back: one, Laura was pregnant, and he did not
want to leave her alone; and two, his father was by now apoplectic with

rage over his son's decision to abandon medicine for a life of radical politics and journalism. Laura informed Jennychen that their situation was extremely disagreeable: "Paul is bullied by his father at every attempt he makes at being of some service to the International; while his Parisian friends are doubtless at the same time blaming him for his absence from Paris." Paul tried to begin a newspaper, *La Défense Nationale,* in Bordeaux, but it failed. "I was a good deal annoyed at his engaging himself in it," Laura said, "as nothing beyond the anger of his father was to be expected from that enterprise." And yet, she told her sister, "you will admit that he cannot remain with his arms crossed at a moment like this."[34]

Though Napoleon III had surrendered, his former subjects had not. September 19, 1870, marked the first battle between French republican forces and Prussian troops at the walls of Paris. It ended badly for the French, their soldiers falling back and fleeing into the city. With no reason to tempt fate, the locals quickly closed the city gates behind them, sealing off the entry points that the Prussians might have easily penetrated had they been ordered by their commanders to do so.

There was a strange quiet in Paris that came from the realization that the capital was surrounded by foreign troops and cut off from the rest of France. Two million civilians and thousands of soldiers were inside its walls, but the feeling was one of isolation. "Every carriage of leisure has disappeared, the streets are no longer sprinkled or cleaned, and before the recent rain the dust on the Champs Elysées was so great that you could hardly see a rod before you," noted Ambassador Washburne. "The city is one vast camp.... There are soldiers everywhere, of all arms, uniforms, shades and colors.... The garden of the Tuileries is filled with artillery."[35] Washburne said no one expected the siege to last long: "That man would have been deemed insane who would have predicted that the gates of the besieged city would not be open until the last day of February."[36]

The declaration of a republic meant that those opposition leaders imprisoned by Napoleon were now freed. Flourens—or as Jenny Marx called him, "*cher* Gustave"[37]—was among them. He quickly established a home guard unit to fight the Prussians should they breach the city walls. In fact throughout the city's twenty arrondissements, everyone readied arms—some to fight the Prussians, while others stockpiled munitions for a possible battle against the provisional government. Leftists and workers mistrusted this government, which was headed by General Louis Jules Trochu, the Napoleon-appointed former military governor of Paris.[38]

On October 31 crushing news telegraphed from house to house throughout Paris and into France's distant provinces: the last of the country's intact army units had been defeated near the border at Metz, the French defending the city of Le Bourget, outside Paris, were routed, and—most shocking of all—the Government of National Defense was trying to negotiate an armistice with Prussia.[39] From Paris to Marseilles, outrage over the prospect of surrender was palpable.[40] Crowds in the capital, drenched by a relentless rainstorm, swarmed the Hôtel de Ville, crying, "No Armistice!," then penetrated its Hall of the Municipality, which was lit by only two oil lamps, demanding that Trochu be ousted and a Paris commune declared. They instructed Louis Blanc, Ledru-Rollin, Victor Hugo, Blanqui, and François Raspail, among others, to organize elections to be held within forty-eight hours.[41]

Hardly a moment passed before Flourens and a coterie of armed men burst into the dingy room. Flourens stood on a table, called for a committee of public safety to be formed, and ordered that the members of the provisional government be detained. He pledged to keep them safe despite calls from the furious crowd, who wanted them shot. Soon the city hall was a scene of utter chaos, filled with diverse bands making demands.[42] But that burst of civilian passion in the face of military defeat did not last. Government troops used a secret tunnel to enter the building and arrest Flourens's men (though Flourens escaped). Trochu's government was restored.[43]

In truth, the boisterous men who tried to overthrow the government at the Hôtel de Ville were the least of Trochu's problems. The real threat came from the streets, where angry citizens fed on despair. With no supplies coming into Paris, meat had become scarce. Horse flesh was a mainstay; then people began to settle for mule. Shortages of food were matched by shortages of wood—Parisian streets were systematically stripped of trees.[44] The changes were incremental but alarming and, like a terminal illness, sure to become more severe with time. By the end of October foreign governments had recognized the dire situation in the French capital and reached a deal with Bismarck to provide a corridor for their citizens to leave. Hopeless Parisians watched in gloomy silence as twenty-six carriages under military escort bore these lucky few to safety.[45]

The Marx household in London had effectively become a refugee center for people fleeing France. In November the doors at Modena Villas opened to a trickle of exiles, escapees sent via International connections to the father of the organization. Soon the trickle became a flood. Tussy said the house often felt more like a hotel than a private home.[46] The first exiles were Prussian, but soon afterward came Russians who had fled to France to escape a crackdown in their own country before being uprooted again and making their way to England.[47] Marx, who believed language was a "weapon in the battle of life,"[48] had been studying Russian in order to read it and was now confident enough to also speak. He told a friend the effort was worth it, even for a man of nearly fifty-two: "The intellectual movement now taking place in Russia testifies to the fact that things are seething below the surface. Minds are always connected by invisible threads with the BODY of the people."[49]

The flood of mail and publications coming into and going out of the Marx home was massive; Jennychen said at one point she was scouring one hundred newspapers — English, French, German, Swiss, American — to keep her father up-to-date on the news and on how events in France were being interpreted abroad.[50] Marx claimed he never went to sleep before three in the morning, and though his health had been abominable, he could not give a "thought to such trivia at a time of such momentous historical events!"[51] International members who remained in London made their way to Marx's study for near constant conferences on the upheaval in France. The shared fear was that the extreme radicals would be as hungry for revolution as Napoleon's courtiers had been eager for war. These men had been sitting on the sidelines of history since 1849, and it was unlikely that they could long resist the chance to be at the center of it once again.

Engels had moved to London just in time to be part of the activity. He visited Marx every afternoon for a walk either in Marx's study — where the two men, anxiously strolling from corner to corner, wore an X-shaped path into the carpet — or out on the Heath. In the evenings he and Lizzy both went to the Marx home.[52] With Engels on hand, Jennychen said, Marx was in better health than he had been in years, and the mood at Modena Villas was often festive. "The other evening," she wrote Kugelmann, "a grand patriotic performance took place at our house." The entertainments featured a duet sung by Marx and Engels.[53]

By contrast, Laura found herself isolated and depressed in Bordeaux. Paul's father had been ill for months, torturing one and all with bursts of anger from the confines of his room. His death on November 18, however, did not bring peace.[54] Madame Lafargue blamed Paul and Laura for the loss of her husband, and she launched a vindictive campaign against them. Laura told Jennychen that some of the details were too painful to recount in writing, but she summarized by saying, "Never in my life have I been so abused as here by my venerable mother-in-law — since M. Lafargue's death." She confided that the one time she tried to defend Paul against his mother's attacks, Madame Lafargue told her "in not the politest manner" to hold her tongue. From that point the situation worsened.

Laura was caught in the middle of a battle of wills between her husband and his mother.

This was more than a mere war of words. Despite the winter cold, Madame Lafargue would not allow Laura, who was now seven months pregnant, or her son Schnapps to have a fire in the rooms where they sat or slept. Paul's mother also would not allow her servant to ready Laura and Schnapps's bed so they could retire, and Paul obstinately refused to allow Laura to do it, so she and her son sat in the cold until the servant finally slipped into their room and did the job. Laura said her mother-in-law came to begrudge them the food they ate, the wine they drank, the oil they burned. Finally Madame Lafargue moved out of the house in December, taking with her nearly every stick of furniture, all the linens, and all the kitchen utensils. Laura was left with an empty house—but at least, she said, they had peace of mind.[55] Paul must have especially appreciated this new freedom; he would no longer have to hide his politicking from his seething parents. From his point of view the timing could not have been better.

Because of the siege in the capital, the French provisional government had moved its operations from Paris to Tours and eventually to Bordeaux. Lafargue was now in regular contact with republicans in the government like Gambetta, who had dramatically flown out of Paris in a hot-air balloon to join his colleagues and report on conditions in the capital.[56] Lafargue spent his time scurrying from one meeting to another, seeking potential backers for the newspaper he dreamed of editing or conferring with International members and government officials. According to Laura, he was optimistic that France could still defeat the Prussians and save Paris.[57]

Only Lafargue, who perhaps to his credit was optimistic even when staring into the jaws of defeat, could have been so certain of victory. The ice in Paris was half an inch thick, and cannon fire could be heard all day and night outside its gates. Rumors spread that bread would soon be rationed. Omnibuses had stopped running because the horses that pulled them had been slaughtered for food, and fuel was running short. Many of the troops camped inside the city had frozen to death. At Paris's normally bountiful markets signs advertised "a common cat, eight francs...a common rat two francs, long-tailed rat, two francs and a half." There was no shortage of takers.[58]

News from outside the city gates was grim as well. The army was falling quickly. In early December word reached Paris that twenty-three thousand men had been killed in one battle alone.[59] Ambassador Washburne provided a sober counter to Lafargue's rosy forecast: "Without food, without carriages, without lighted streets, there is anything but a pleasant prospect ahead." He wrote those words on December 23, the ninety-sixth day of the siege of Paris.[60]

In France and Germany, International members and workers had come under greater scrutiny, in part because of their widely published declarations of solidarity. In some cases the vow not to fight their French or German counterparts was viewed as treason. Indeed, Marx said after the October 31 melee at the Hôtel de Ville the provisional government in France was more intent on going after "reds" than after Prussians.[61] Once again, among those arrested in Paris was Flourens.[62] In Germany, meanwhile, Liebknecht and Bebel had been seized. They had very publicly abstained in July from a Reichstag vote to fund Bismarck's war against France. When the issue of continued funding arose in November, they again spoke out against it and in favor of peace. In mid-December, when the Reichstag session ended for the season, they were arrested. The charge was high treason.[63]

Marx wrote Liebknecht's wife to assure her the party would take care of her financially and indeed all the "persecuted" German patriots.[64] Engels also offered her words of support, adding that the news of their comrades' arrests was particularly poignant, coming when it did. That very day, the Engels and Marx households had been celebrating: they had learned that after eight months of hearings and deliberations, the parliamentary inquiry into the treatment of Irish inmates convened as a result of Jennychen's articles had resulted in their amnesty.[65] Gladstone announced the Irishmen could leave prison as long as they never returned to England. O'Donovan Rossa was among the released.[66]

Jennychen's efforts had succeeded beyond her wildest dreams. Her words had freed men. Unfortunately, O'Donovan Rossa did not credit Jennychen for her advocacy, and her contribution has largely been lost in historical accounts of the Irish prisoners' struggle. In his autobiography O'Donovan Rossa wrote, "While I was in prison in England, publicity of my treatment was the only protection I had for my life. There was a French exile in London named Gustave Flourens. He became interested in my case...more interested than any Irishman....He translated an account of my treatment into French and German and had it published in the continental newspapers. This vexed England...and she conceded a commission of inquiry."[67] If Jennychen had to relinquish writing credit to anyone other than her father, no doubt it would have been to Flourens. Now it was he who was the prisoner, and no newspaper campaign would free him. Indeed, no one would have taken note of one man's plight in Paris at that moment. The entire city was under attack.

398

★   ★   ★

On January 5, 1871, Prussian shells hit the Latin Quarter.[68] By January 7 as many as four hundred were falling inside Paris each day.[69] A placard appeared on the walls of the snowy capital proclaiming, "Make way for the people. Make way for the Commune." Trochu countered with his own declaration: "The government of Paris will never capitulate."[70]

Yet despite Trochu's assurances, capitulation was exactly what French officials had in mind. The Government of National Defense saw clearly that weak and weary France could no longer hold out against Prussia, much less hope for victory. On January 18 two dramatic events occurred that the provisional leaders of France believed would make surrender easier to sell to the people. In the Hall of Mirrors at Versailles, Prussia's King Wilhelm was proclaimed emperor of Germany (with Bismarck soon named chancellor of the Second Reich).[71] No Frenchman could possibly mistake the significance of this ceremony. Germany had already defeated France.

The other event on that fateful day occurred on a field outside Paris. Trochu had been under pressure to move aggressively against the Prussian troops encircling the city, in part to quell growing anger among the starving population stranded inside. Needing to be seen doing something to end the siege, he led a national guard assault on an area near Versailles called Buzenval that was heavily fortified by hardened Prussian soldiers.[72] Old men, young boys, and women carrying satchels or rifles for their men joined the march toward the Prussian line, making up in enthusiasm and numbers what they lacked in experience. The French took massive casualties—perhaps as many as ten thousand dead—but, surprisingly, managed to push the Prussians back and gain ground. They were exhilarated by this small victory after weeks of waiting impotently for a chance to defend themselves. But the next day Trochu ordered a retreat, forcing the guard to give up their gains for no apparent reason.[73]

Journalist Prosper Lissagaray (a generally unbiased witness who disdained all the leaders equally) reported the French battalions returned to Paris weeping with rage. Rumors spread that the government had wanted a slaughter, to be able to declare total defeat and then surrender. This suspicion was soon confirmed, when Trochu proclaimed all was lost.[74] "Thus when the fatal words were uttered, the city seemed at first wonderstruck, as at the sight of some monstrous crime, unnatural," Lissagaray wrote. "The wounds of four months opened again, crying for vengeance. Cold, starvation, bombardment, the long nights in the trenches, the little children dying by the thousands, death scattered abroad in the sorties, and all to end in shame."[75]

Crowds gathered at the Hôtel de Ville demanding to govern themselves—they wanted a commune. The people blamed Trochu for the debacle at Buzenval and for waiting too long to defend Paris, but Trochu had already been replaced at the head of the provisional government by a hard-liner named General Joseph Vinoy. Opposition leaders in Paris huddled to discuss the next step. Events, however, were already beyond their control.[76] The Belleville battalion, which had been commanded by Flourens, was on the march, and the mob grew as they traveled into the heart of the city. On January 23, at three in the morning, the crowd attacked the Mazas prison and freed Flourens and other republican and radical leaders held there.[77] Vinoy's response was swift: the government ordered all opposition clubs closed, suppressed opposition newspapers, and issued new arrest warrants.[78] When hungry Parisians gathered outside the Hôtel de Ville on that 127th day of the siege and cried, "Give us bread," Vinoy's forces opened fire from every window overlooking the plaza. Five people were killed and eighteen wounded.[79]

That same day Foreign Minister Jules Favre began armistice talks with Prussia to end the costly war and try to contain the mushrooming social crisis. Four days of talks led to an agreement, and on January 27 the Prussian cannons stopped firing. The siege of Paris was over. Favre and Bismarck had reached a preliminary armistice, which the provisional government wanted a soon-to-be-elected French national government to ratify.[80] The silence in Paris in response to the deal was deafening. Armistice did not mean peace, it meant surrender. If anyone doubted this, they needed only to look at the city's forts. The German flag flew above them.[81]

National elections were held on February 8, and the split between the Parisians and the rest of France was soon clear. The countryside had not been under siege, and what it wanted more than anything was stability—a choice it had made at the polls countless times before. Out of 750 National Assembly members elected, 450 were monarchists and about 150 republicans. Those members considered on the far left—there were about twenty—were mostly from Paris. "Paris became a country unto itself," Lissagaray said, "separated from hostile provinces and a hostile government."[82]

The new National Assembly overwhelming approved the odious terms of armistice: the regions of Alsace and most of Lorraine were annexed by Germany, and France was required to pay Germany five billion francs—about a billion dollars—within four years. Until the indemnity was paid, Germany's army would remain in France's eastern provinces. Their war sorted, the governments of France and Germany next set to work to pacify Paris.

36

⤳

Paris, 1871

The soldier of the present revolution is of the people. Just
yesterday, he was in his little shop, his chest bent down to his
knees, plying his awl or his needle, or hammering iron. How
many people passed by without knowing, without believing,
that a man was there.

—André Léo[1]

PRUSSIAN FORCES MARCHED into Paris along the Champs Elysées on March
1 and found that the City of Light was dark. Black flags were draped on
the front of buildings, the shops were closed, gaslights extinguished, and
prostitutes hoping to earn a few sous servicing the Prussians were publicly
whipped if discovered. Cafés that dared feed the invaders were ransacked.
Provincial papers described rampant crime and arson throughout the capital, but in truth there was no crime. There was no visible life. Paris had
gone underground, preparing for a fight.[2] National guard units, still seething over the Buzenval massacre in January, had stealthily gathered up all
the weapons they could find, including some 250 cannons that they positioned around the city.[3] Citizens armed themselves, too, making ammunition and constructing barricades as tall as buildings. Men, women, and
children worked quickly and quietly, preparing their defense.[4]

The government had remained in Bordeaux, southwest of Paris, because
it was too dangerous to return, and from that distance it issued a series of
decrees that were perhaps more inflammatory than even the truce that had
allowed Prussian troops into the capital. On March 13 the government
declared that all debts due since November, whose collection had been
deferred by events, were now to be paid. This meant that Parisians who

had been unable to work because of the siege, who had spent their last coins on cat or rat meat, had to come up with money for months of back rent, taxes, and countless other bills. There was also a rumor that the national guard was to have its salary revoked.[5] On the same day the debt decree was issued, the government ordered the closure of six more newspapers and condemned to death the men involved in the October takeover of the Hôtel de Ville, including Flourens and Blanqui.[6]

In defiant response, Paris erupted in color. Denied newspapers, people pasted placards of every hue on the city's walls to be eagerly read by its citizens, who crowded around as each new report appeared.[7] Among them was one from Flourens responding to his death sentence:

> In the presence of the judgment against me, it is my right to protest in the most energetic fashion the violation of all rights inscribed in the constitution.... On the other hand, I have long understood that liberty is strengthened by the blood of martyrs... if mine can serve to wash this stain from France and cement the union of the people and of liberty, I offer myself voluntarily to the assassins of the country and the murderers of January.[8]

Paris was full of such willing men—up to 300,000 of them in its militias and many more who comprised its 250 national guard battalions.[9] And then there were the citizens armed with knives, stakes, and clubs, who waited in doorways as vigilant as sentinels guarding a palace. They would be instrumental when the defense of Paris was put to the test.

On March 18, at three in the morning, the French government sent 25,000 troops into Paris. All around the city, while its residents slept, the soldiers seized the national guard's heavy artillery. By six the government had control of the rebels' cannons, but as luck or fate or incompetence would have it, the soldiers had not brought along horses to pull the weapons to safety. While they waited for the horses to arrive, the women of Paris awoke. Word spread from house to house via the milkmaids, who supplied the city each morning, that the soldiers were trying to make off with the cannons. Soon drums sounded the alarm across the rooftops.[10]

In Montmartre, General Claude Lecomte was assailed by women and children haranguing him for what his men were trying to do. In a display of contempt for those assembled, he ordered his troops to fire on the crowd,[11] but the women challenged the young men with the guns, shouting, "Will you fire on us?" They would not. These soldiers had no heart for a fight against fellow Frenchmen, let alone Frenchwomen. Some had been at war since the previous July. Some were as disgusted with the government as the Parisians were. The general lost control of his soldiers, who began fraternizing with the women. Lecomte was then taken captive by the national guard and forced to sign an order telling his men to evacuate and leave the cannons behind.[12]

By noon all but ten cannons were back under the control of the Parisians.[13] Tragically, the crowd that had been controlled to that point turned savage. Lecomte and another general, Clément Thomas, were executed at the behest of the mob.[14] That was a serious mistake: the killings were all the government needed to justify an attack with full force and without mercy.

In the pause before that inevitable retaliation, on March 26, Parisians voted to elect their own government. An estimated two hundred thousand people gathered at the Hôtel de Ville the next day to greet their new leaders. The excited crowd grew silent while the elected walked onto a platform, red scarves draped dramatically over their shoulders, as their names were solemnly read. Finally, when the Parisian government was assembled, one member shouted, "In the name of the people the Commune is proclaimed!" and the massive, jubilant audience replied as one, *"Vive la Commune!"* Caps flew skyward. Cannons fired, flags fluttered from windows and roofs, thousands of hands waved handkerchiefs.[15]

Meanwhile, the French national government, whose leaders had now moved closer to the capital and were at Versailles, had decided to take back the city by force on April 1. Government commanders tried to prepare reluctant troops by painting the Paris resistance as the work of foreign agitators. The troops would not be fighting fellow Frenchmen, they explained, they would be fighting foreign infiltrators.[16] And there was one foreigner identified as a ringleader: beginning in March reports had appeared in the French, English, and German press accusing Marx of directing the International's activities in Paris and by extension the Paris streets. One such article, headlined *"Le Grand Chef de l'Internationale,"* read, "He is, as everyone knows, a German, what is even worse, a Prussian." The article (which had Marx living in Berlin) reported that police had intercepted a letter from Marx to an IWMA member on how to proceed in Paris.[17]

Marx was not particularly bothered by the reports as long as they did not worsen the situation in Paris or divide French and German workers, who had so far maintained their solidarity. With those concerns in mind, he publicly declared that the letter attributed to him had been forged by police with the clear intention of implicating the International in any violence.[18] Despite his rebuttal, similar pieces continued to find their way into the press. In April, Laura sent her father a copy of a breathless article from a French newspaper that read: "A piece of news just arrived from Germany is causing a great sensation here. Authentic proof is now to hand to show that Karl Marx, one of the most influential leaders of the *International*, was *the private secretary of Count Bismarck* in 1857, and has never ceased to remain in contact with his former *patron*."[19] Thus Marx was at once both the chief communist and a confidant of the most powerful reactionary in Western Europe—in other words, a threat no matter which side one was on.

At one in the morning on April 2, French government forces opened fire on Paris, rousing the slumbering with the sound of cannon. Defensive militias, the so-called *fédérés*, scrambled into position, civilians rushed to the barricades, and drums beat a call to arms. By eight a.m. 20,000 men on the Right Bank and 17,000 on the Left were ready to counter the attack and march against French national troops. The resistance was armed and mobilized but without direction; the Parisian officers who had been expected to devise a war plan had none.[20]

Undeterred, Flourens led a group of about 1,000 men in an April 3 advance on government forces, but they were easily repulsed; as soon as the *fédérés* were attacked, they broke formation and fled. Flourens was exhausted by the battle and depressed by the cowardice of his soldiers.[21] His aide-de-camp convinced him to stop at a hotel to rest, but the hotelier betrayed them by alerting the government that a rebel leader was inside. Police and government soldiers burst into the hotel, killing the aide-de-camp outright. They then took Flourens into custody, discovering his identity after finding a letter from his mother in his pocket. "It's Flourens!" cried a policeman, according to an English tourist who witnessed the incident. "Take him this time, he won't escape." Indeed, Flourens didn't make it past the hotel yard. The witness said his apparent calm in the face of twenty armed men so enraged the officer interrogating him that the policeman raised his saber and brought it down on his head. While his body lay in the dirt, another officer put the muzzle of his gun to Flourens's eye and pulled the trigger.[22]

Flourens's death was an early prize in the French government's fight against Paris. Along with the corpse of his aide-de-camp, his body was loaded into a cart and wheeled to Versailles, where fine ladies and gentlemen—now courtiers of the government as they had once been courtiers of the emperor—cheered when they saw the bodies on display.[23] In Paris, placards did not announce his death; they merely said Flourens had reached Versailles. Everyone thought that this meant victory, and three hundred joyous women marched up the Champs Elysées vowing that they, too, would go to Versailles. The next day the true nature of the so-called victory was revealed. Flourens was dead, and nine other soldiers had been captured and executed.[24]

Lissagaray concluded that the fight for Paris changed after April 3. Parisians, no longer expecting their generals to lead the charge, took their defense into their own hands.[25] A placard appeared on April 5 that read: "If you are tired of vegetating in ignorance and wallowing in misery, if you want your children to be men, enjoy the benefit of their labor, and not mere animals trained for the workshop and the battlefield, if you do not want your daughters, whom you are unable to educate and look after as you yearn to do, to become instruments of pleasure in the arms of the aristocracy of money, if you at last want the reign of justice, workingmen, be intelligent, rise!"[26]

A funeral was held the next day, as if to bury not just those killed in battle but the Parisians' crushed hopes. Lissagaray described the three funeral biers, adorned with red flags and carrying thirty-five coffins each, as they made their way to Père-Lachaise cemetery: "Widows of today supported by the widows of tomorrow" walked side by side toward the mass grave prepared for the fallen. "On the great boulevards we numbered two hundred thousand and one hundred thousand pale faces looked down on us from the windows."[27]

Flourens was buried at Père-Lachaise the next day.[28]

News of Flourens's death had reached London on April 5. The *Daily Telegraph* reported, "The successes of Monday were crowned by the death, so it is said, of M. Flourens, one of the most uncompromising and reckless of the insurgent chiefs. The body of M. Flourens is at Versailles."[29] The grief in the Marx home was palpable, especially among the women, who called him the "bravest of the brave."[30] Jennychen raged that such a man could be betrayed by a petit bourgeois hotelier and butchered by his own countrymen.[31]

The following day Marx told Liebknecht that Tussy and Jennychen had decided to go to France.[32] Word of Flourens's death, coming after weeks of reports on the deteriorating situation in Paris, no doubt stirred them to action. Like Karl and Jenny in their youth, the Marx daughters were unable to sit on the sidelines of a revolt; even if they did not join the fight, they needed to be close to it. They also had an urgent personal motive: Laura had had another son, and he was unwell. Paul cheerfully wrote that Laura was trying to nurse the child,[33] but the family received that news with dread. They knew Laura was ill, and Jenny especially could not have helped but remember her futile attempts to nurse Fawksy back to health.

After François Lafargue's death, Paul had indeed inherited the hundred thousand francs he was to have received on his marriage, but most of it was tied up in property, stocks, or bonds.[34] As a result the family worried Laura had neither the material nor personal support she needed to get through this latest crisis. Paul's letters were full of political comment and proclamation, and it was obvious he was anxious to leave Bordeaux now that the government had moved to Versailles and a commune had been installed in Paris. Laura had said plainly, "I am used to being alone. Paul since many months is hardly ever at home and I have hardly stirred out of the house for the last six or eight months."[35]

If there was any hesitation on Jenny and Marx's part concerning Jenny-chen and Tussy's proposed trip, it evaporated after Jennychen received news that Paul was in Paris. He had decided to go back just at the moment when Bismarck freed sixty thousand French prisoners to help pacify the capital. Laura wrote in early April that she had not heard from him since he left, and

> to make matters worse my poor baby has been so ill that during eight or ten days I expected every moment to see him die. He is much better since a day or two and I think will continue to improve. For the last week, I carry him up and down the room nearly all day and rock him in the night....As to Paul, I don't know what to think. He certainly did not set off with the intention of remaining so long. But perhaps he cannot get back even did he wish to, or perhaps the sight of the barricades have tempted him to go in for fighting. I should not wonder, and I should not mind if I were with him, for I should have fought too.[36]

Jennychen decided to leave for France immediately, confessing to Kugelmann that if her parents had not agreed, she would have stolen off on the sly.[37]

In trying to arrange their departure, Jennychen and Tussy encountered frustration on all sides. The London steamer was overloaded with goods bound for France, and the captain refused to take passengers. Their only option was a boat from Liverpool on April 29, which under the circumstances Jennychen considered an agonizingly long wait. She next discovered there would be problems in France: train lines from the port were either cut or monopolized by troops. Furthermore, she and Tussy would need passports, as nobody was allowed into France without one.[38] But they did not dare travel as Jenny and Eleanor Marx; they would need false documents if they hoped to rescue Laura from her frightful solitude.

It is not clear why Lafargue went to Paris. Some said he wanted to research a book, others that he sought approval from the communards (as they came to be known) for an insurrection in Bordeaux.[39] Whatever the reason, he was back in Bordeaux around April 18, when, coincidentally, a number of disturbances were reported: police agents were detained, infantry barracks pelted with stones, and cries of *"Vive Paris!"* were heard.[40] Was this Paul's insurrection? It seemed that local police thought so, blaming the agitation on International agents. Making no attempt to conceal his political activities, Lafargue posted placards in support of the Commune and even ran in (and lost) municipal elections as a member of the IWMA. Perhaps not surprisingly, the police opened an investigation into whether this man they considered a fanatic should be arrested immediately. Among those giving information against him was a source who said Lafargue was a recruiter for the International and attended its meetings every night. Uncertain whether those were grounds for arrest, Bordeaux police consulted Emile de Kératry, a superior from a neighboring region, about the case.[41]

Against that backdrop Jennychen and Tussy, traveling under the surname Williams, arrived in Bordeaux on May 1, 1871, after a four-day journey on rough seas. Jennychen was ill through most of the transit but Tussy, now sixteen, reveled in the adventure and the fact that she was traveling incognito. Jennychen told her parents Tussy spent from morning to night on deck, talking to the sailors and smoking cigarettes with the captain. Engels had suggested that on the ship they act the part of bourgeois English girls, which they did to great effect. "We were treated like princesses on the boat," Jennychen chuckled. "Mates and stewards rushed about to get us rugs, stools and cushions, the captain brought us his glasses whenever anything was to be seen, and actually had his huge armchair transported on to the quarter deck for me." Once in France, they were taken for Parisians and did not have to display their passports or bourgeois facades.[42]

The Bordeaux they arrived in was at once unremarkable for its calm— cafés were full, domino and billiards games continued uninterrupted, restaurant meals were eaten with gusto—and at the same time terrifying. As in all the provinces where agitators were active, those of rebellious inclinations were being watched, their names added to suspect rolls.[43] The provincial administrations were following the lead of Versailles, which was busily identifying leaders of the rebellion for arrest or execution after a final assault to crush the uprising.

At the beginning of the Paris siege, Marx and Engels had warned against revolt, which they said would be utterly futile. By April, however, they saw in the Commune true heroism, and cheered on the Parisians even as they predicted they would lose. "What resilience, what historical initiative, what a capacity for sacrifice in these Parisians!" Marx declared. "After six months of hunger and ruin, caused rather by internal treachery than by the external enemy, they rise, beneath Prussian bayonets, as if there had never been a war between France and Germany and the enemy were not still at the gates of Paris! History has no example of a like greatness."[44]

In early May the Paris weather was so fine that it contributed to a carnival atmosphere. The sound of cannons and the thud of shells were a constant reminder the city was under attack, yet a gingerbread festival at the Place de la Bastille was such a success it was extended for a week. Laughing children soared through the air on swings, men and women momentarily forgot their uncertain futures and spun the wheels of fortune, and merchants did a brisk business selling cheap domestic wares to housewives who had donated their pots to be smelted for bullets and shot.[45] On May 16 the artist Gustave Courbet, who was part of the Commune's department of cultural affairs, arranged for another joyful distraction at the Place Vendôme, north of the Tuileries on the Right Bank: bands played and the crowd pressed in as men spent hours sawing through the massive shaft of the column erected there by the first Napoleon in honor of the 1805 French victory at Austerlitz. Finally it fell, Bonaparte's head rolling on the ground as surely as if it had fallen to the guillotine. The delighted crowd roared its approval.[46]

Finally, on Sunday, May 21, a huge afternoon concert was held in the gardens of the Tuileries. Women were dazzling in their spring dresses—Lissagaray said they positively lit up the green alleyways of the palace gardens while, nearby, at the Place de la Concorde, bursting government shells provided unexpected (and unwanted) percussion. Still, the crowd, numbering in the thousands, did not scatter.[47] The Parisians may have sensed that this was the last fest they would attend for some time. Indeed, unbeknown to concertgoers, Versailles troops were pushing into Paris in a major assault. By three o'clock on that sunny afternoon they had come in through five gates; seventy thousand government troops began swarming through the city, and gunboats with heavy weapons arrived on the Seine, positioned to fire.[48]

Paul Verlaine worked in the Commune press office and said he learned the news first from his wife, who dreamed that the troops were inside Paris. (Verlaine was, after all, a poet.)[49] As word spread more conventionally, men, women, and children rushed to the barricades, the cannons, and gun positions to await the approach of the Versailles forces along

Haussmann's grand boulevards. Thus began what would become known as *La Semaine Sanglot*—the Bloody Week.

For five days there was no business in Paris except war. There was no front, no rear; the battle was everywhere. Stripped to the waist, streaming perspiration, and blackened by powder, men held matches in both hands while their fellow fighters loaded the weapon they would ignite.[50] At one spot fifteen hundred women gathered to sew sandbags to reinforce breaches; others, with powder-blackened hands and shoulders bruised from their rifles, mounted the barricades. Boys took up their fathers' guns when they were killed, and kept firing.[51] No one was exempt from service, no one could avoid the fight.

At Montmartre, Versailles troops executed forty-two men, three women, and four children in retribution for the March killings of Generals Lecomte and Thomas, the spot on the rue des Rosiers becoming a favorite for state-sanctioned murder. Day after day captured communards were led to the butte overlooking Paris, placed before the bullet-pocked wall, shot, and then tossed down the slope overlooking the rue St.-Denis.[52] Atrocities were committed by the communards as well. On May 25 the archbishop of Paris and five priests were executed by national guard units who were so inept they failed to kill the archbishop with five rounds of gunfire. Finally they tore his body apart with bayonets.[53] (The IWMA was accused of ordering the murders from London.)[54]

By midweek Paris was on fire: the Tuileries, the Palais Royal, the Palais de Justice, part of the Louvre. The city had no gaslights, but the night was bright as day, ghastly in its orange-red glow as Haussmann's grand plan went up in flames.[55] (There were rumors that eight thousand women had used everything from explosive bottles to gasoline-filled eggs to start the fires. The fable of the women incendiaries was just one of hundreds passed from ear to ear throughout the frantic city.)[56] The fires had been abetted by a weeks-long drought, but then, on the fifth day of battle, the sky burst open and the rain began. Just as quickly, the fighting stopped. It was over. Too many people died, too much of Paris was destroyed.[57] The head of the Versailles troops, Commander in Chief Marshal MacMahon, announced on May 28, "Inhabitants of Paris, Paris is delivered."[58]

All the while, Marx had been drowning in Commune-related work. Kugelmann wrote Engels to say he feared for Marx's health, but Engels assured him, "Marx's way of life is by no means as crazy as people imagine. While the excitement that started with the war still persists, he has given up work on heavy theoretical matters and is living fairly rationally."[59] In fact Engels's proximity meant that Marx finally had someone to share his load. They both corresponded with IWMA members throughout Europe and America and were now both consulted on International matters in London. What had been a Marx-dominated group now became a Marx and Engels enterprise.

The two men kept up with events in Paris through a German merchant who traveled frequently between London and France,[60] as well as a glamorous young Russian named Elizabeth Dmitrieff Tomanovskaya, whom Marx had sent to Paris on numerous missions but who finally remained there to join the fight.[61] Marx also had a source close to Bismarck, an old Communist League associate who kept him informed on moves by the German side.[62] And Jennychen was able to send mail from Bordeaux to London, addressed to A. Williams from his daughter J. Williams. (Marx described A. Williams to one correspondent as a friend who lived at his house.)[63] Jennychen told her father she was anxious to leave Bordeaux and fearful that if they stayed, Paul might be arrested. A neighbor had reported suspicious people were asking questions about him: "Were it known that he was the son-in-law of Marx he would long ago have been placed under lock and key. You, my dear Mohr, act upon the bourgeoisie of France as a bogey man!"[64]

Though Marx—and things done in Marx's name—would be linked to revolutionary jolts and violent spasms, he remained consistent in the belief that such actions were foolish and self-defeating. Jennychen knew as much, writing him, "You must be suffering so much. To have witnessed the days of June [1848] and then after more than twenty years....Do you not think that this massacre will crush the life out of the revolutionists for years and years to come?"[65] When Jennychen wrote her father she spoke as if the worst were over. Actually, it had just begun.

The May 28 declaration by MacMahon announcing the end of the Commune by no means halted the killing. On that very day the body of the murdered archbishop was discovered in Père-Lachaise cemetery. Versailles's response was swift and brutal: more than five thousand prisoners were taken from the neighborhoods around Père-Lachaise and divided into those who would die and those who might live. From Sunday to Monday thousands of detainees were killed at La Roquette prison, L'Ecole Militaire, and other spots around Paris: witnesses described the sound of a seemingly uninterrupted fusillade.[66] Jean-Baptiste Millière, who had been arrested in the October Hôtel de Ville revolt, was finally taken to the Panthéon to be executed. When the squad was in position to fire, he cried, "Long Live the People! Long Live Humanity!" The soldier on duty replied, "Go fuck your humanity!" Millière fell in a hail of bullets.[67]

Driven mad by war and fear, many Parisians chose suicide rather than arrest. Young women in silk dresses fired their revolvers randomly in the street, shouting to the soldiers who would be their executioners, "Shoot me at once!"[68] A reporter for the Evening Standard in London said, "The sun of the Commune has set literally in a sea of blood. What is the actual number of victims we know not and probably never will know. Suffice it to say that it is appalling."[69] The newspaper quoted an official with knowledge of government forces as saying two courts-martial alone were executing five hundred people a day; open vans collected the corpses and dumped them into neighborhood squares to remind residents of the extent of their defeat.[70] Lissagaray wrote, "At last the smell of the carnage began to choke even the most fanatic.... Myriads of flesh flies flew up from the putrefied corpses.... They were seen to be in heaps everywhere, half white with chloride of lime. At the Polytechnic school they occupied a space of one hundred yards long and three deep.... Arms and hands poked out from shallow mass graves at the Trocadéro."[71] Finally, even newspapers that were soundly against the communards expressed disgust at the government's excesses. The Standard in London, which had spent weeks lambasting the rebels, carried a report from its Paris correspondent on June 2:

With stray shots still ringing in the distance, and untended wounded wretches dying amid the tombstones of Père Lachaise—with six thousand terror-stricken insurgents wandering in agony of despair in the labyrinth of the catacombs, and wretches hurried through the streets to be shot down in scores by the mitrailleuse—it is revolting to see the cafés filled with the votaries of absinthe, billiards, and dominoes; the abandoned women perambulating the Boulevards; and the sound of revelry disturbing the night from the cabinets particulaire of fashionable eating-houses. Anyone... would fancy that Paris was rejoicing over some auspicious event, and would hardly realize that the destruction of most public buildings, fully two thousand private houses, and more than twenty thousand French lives, was deemed consistent with this indecorous manifestation of public joy.[72]

As many as 40,000 people out of a population of two million were taken prisoner during the Bloody Week and the terrible days that followed: men, women, old, young, provincial, Parisian, foreign, all were swept up, placed in chains, and forced to walk in convoys to prisons or to the ports for deportation. Furious crowds of bourgeoisie, or those who considered the communards responsible for the misery inflicted on Paris over the previous nine months, shouted abuse and demanded that the prisoners be shot on the spot and the women branded as whores.[73] (A French paper described elegant women poking at the chained women with their parasols.)[74] The death estimates varied, but it was generally agreed among chroniclers at the time (and is still held by modern historians) that around 25,000 men, women, and children were killed in Paris during that brief period. Three thousand more died in prison, nearly 14,000 were jailed for life, and 70,000 children or elderly were left to fend for themselves because their families or protectors were dead or imprisoned.[75]

The hunt for communards and their sympathizers was not confined to Paris. Officials fanned out around France and even beyond its borders searching for those responsible for the violence. Increasingly, the finger of blame pointed at the International and Marx. In an irony that would long outlive Marx, credit for what he *had* done was thoroughly obscured by amplified accounts of what he had not. In this instance he was portrayed as a demonic puppetmaster directing the Paris revolt.

Attention came Marx's way in large part because of an address he gave that was then published as a thirty-five-page pamphlet titled *The Civil War in France*. Like all of Marx's writing, it was late: he had hoped to finish it by the end of April but handed it to the International General Council in London on May 30, after the Commune was officially declared over.[76] The delay, however, had no impact on the pamphlet's power or the reaction it provoked. In it Marx lavishly praised the Parisians for their efforts, even if he disparaged their methods: "When the plain working men for the first time dared to infringe upon the governmental privilege of their 'natural superiors'...the old world writhed in convulsions of rage at the sight of the Red Flag, the symbol of the republic, floating over the Hôtel de Ville."[77] As for the International, he wrote:

> Wherever, in whatever shape, and under whatever conditions the class struggle obtains any consistency, it is but natural that members of our association should stand in the foreground. The soil out of which it grows is modern society itself. It cannot be stamped out by any amount of carnage. To stamp it out, the Governments would have to stamp out the despotism of capital over labor—the condition of their own parasitical existence.
>
> Working men's Paris, with its Commune, will be forever celebrated as the glorious harbinger of a new society. Its martyrs are enshrined in the great heart of the working class. Its exterminators history has already nailed to that eternal pillory from which all the prayers of their priests will not avail to redeem them.[78]

The Civil War in France sold thousands of copies, went through three editions in two months, and was translated into every European language.[79] It was Marx's most successful writing to date, topping his address on the Franco-Prussian War. An early Marx biographer observed that prior to the Commune, not even one in one hundred members of the International in France, let alone the general public, knew Marx's name. In London he was nearly a complete unknown.[80] But after the Commune, his years of obscurity were over. Karl Marx was known to the world: he was the evil architect of the Commune, the father of revolution. Marx's pamphlet earned him death threats by post and denunciations in papers as far away as Chicago:

The *Pall Mall Gazette,* London, May 1871: "I have before me an elaborate account of this society from which it would appear that although only nine years have elapsed since its foundation, it counts upwards of two million five hundred thousand members.... The Central committee of this association...is in London and its presiding spirit is a German."[81]

The *New York World,* June 3: "It has been discovered that the real leaders of the Commune are Karl Marx.... Papers have been seized which show that these men are in London, and are now planning new schemes designing to make Lyons, Marseilles, Madrid, Turin, Rome, Naples, Vienna, Moscow, and Berlin scenes of conflagrations."[82]

The *Chicago Tribune,* June 5: "Another notable insurgent boasts that the burning of Paris will be considered insignificant when the London docks, with all their wealth, are consumed as a great lesson to the middle classes of Europe.... Papers have been discovered which show that the operations of the communists were directed from London."[83]

The *Evening Standard,* London, June 23: "Unfortunately for Europe a new revolutionary party more terrible than any previously existing has come into existence.... Deplorable circumstances has led it to take Paris as its first battlefield, but it is likely that in any other of our world capitals it could easily bring forward force equally formidable."[84]

And just in case there were any doubts, Louis Blanc offered his opinion as an opposition insider: the Commune was comprised of agents of the International; the IWMA General Council dispensed the cannons and the munitions, and controlled all the material forces of the revolution.[85]

In reality there were few International members in the Commune leadership—of the ninety-two Commune council members, only seventeen were in the IWMA.[86] But in trying to repair the badly damaged French society, it was convenient to blame outsiders for the unrest. On June 6 the French foreign minister asked all European governments to work together to destroy the IWMA and hunt down its members, declaring the group the "enemy of family, religion, order and property."[87] From his study Marx relished the official frenzy, joking in a letter to Kugelmann, "I have the honor to be AT THIS MOMENT THE BEST CALUMNIATED AND THE MOST MENACED MAN OF LONDON. That really does one good after a tedious twenty years' idyll in the backwoods."[88]

With the persecution of "reds" rampant, it became imperative that Marx's daughters, his son-in-law, and his grandchildren leave Bordeaux. Paul applied for a Spanish passport (to which he was entitled because he had been born in Cuba), and when he received it, the group headed south-west, eventually reaching Bagnères-de-Luchon, a resort in the French Pyrenees known for its mineral baths. They used false names—"Mora" for the Lafargues and "Williams" for Jennychen and Tussy—and they did not socialize. They allowed no one into their home except the maid, the landlady, and the doctor. Laura's youngest child, Marc-Laurent, was now four months old, and still gravely ill.[89]

Despite these precautions, Marx learned in June that Paul had been detected and was about to be arrested. In coded language he told his daughters the group had to flee Luchon.

> Now, generally speaking, after consultation with doctors of notorious sagacity, and in *possession of full information,* I think all of you ought to leave the French for the Spanish side of the Pyrénées. The climate is much better, the change you all stand in need of much more marked. As to Toole, in par-ticular, his health will deteriorate and may even incur great danger, if he any longer hesitates to follow the advice of medical men who know everything about his constitution and have besides consulted his former doctors in Bordeaux.[90]

Jennychen, however, wrote Engels that they would not be leaving any-time soon. Using Marx's coded language she said, "In consequence of which discreet conduct Toole's health is so good that there is no need whatever for change of air." In any case, little Marc-Laurent was too ill to travel, and they would remain where they were as long as necessary for his improvement.[91] But he did not improve: on July 26 the child died, the second Laura had lost in two years.[92] His burial in Luchon was particularly sad, because they knew he would lie alone in that strange place forever.

*   *   *

Lafargue may have thought he was being discreet, but on August 4 a man knocked on the door and said, according to Engels, "I am a police officer but a Republican; an order for your arrest has been received; it is known that you were in charge of the communications between Bordeaux and the Paris Commune. You have one hour to cross the border."[93] Lafargue heeded the officer's advice and set out on a mule path from Luchon to the Spanish town of Bosost, about twenty-five miles away.[94] Hours after he left, police arrived at the cottage where Laura, her three-year-old son, Schnapps, Jennychen, and Tussy were staying. Authorities searched the place and found documents and letters about IWMA recruitment that they linked to Lafargue. There was nothing to immediately implicate the women, but their cottage was placed under surveillance.[95] Soon they would be under house arrest.

37

Bagnères-de-Luchon, France, Summer 1871

One could afford to treat with silent contempt a government run mad, and to laugh at the farces in which the pottering pantaloons employed by that government play their muddling and meddling parts, did not these farces turn out to be tragedies for thousands of men, women and children.

—Jennychen Marx[1]

TWO DAYS AFTER Lafargue fled Luchon, the Marx women and Schnapps set off by carriage to visit him and make sure he had arrived safely in Spain. Laura was anxious about her husband, shattered by the death of her child, and full of dread about her surviving son, who was now also showing signs of illness.[2] Jennychen, however, was lost in what she described as "scenes of matchless beauty.... We saw snow-white mountains and mountains black as night, bright-green meadows and gloomy forests, busy rapids and lazy little rivers. As we approached Spain the mountains grew wilder, more rugged and uncultivated." They arrived dirty and parched in Bosost, a poor peasant town in the Spanish Pyrenees, and found its square filled with children playing with pigs. A fair was under way.[3] Those scenes of innocent revelry and the discovery that Paul was indeed comfortable and safe revived even Laura's low spirits.

By the end of the day, however, Schnapps was indisputably ill with what would turn out to be dysentery. Not wanting to take a chance with the life of another child, Laura decided to stay with Paul in Spain while Jennychen and Tussy headed back to France.[4] They found a sympathetic

416

coachman who gingerly drove their carriage along the narrow mountain roads to the town of Fos, across the French border, where they presented themselves at the customs house. The two women, carrying nothing, wearing cloaks suitable for a day trip, passed a visual inspection, and the coachman was ordered to drive on. But before he could, a public prosecutor appeared and commanded, "In the name of the Republic, follow me." The pair got out of the carriage and walked into a small room, where a woman stood waiting to search them. Neither Jennychen nor Tussy wanted to submit to the rough-looking creature and offered to undress themselves. The woman said no, and left the room to get the prosecutor.[5] During that time Jennychen pulled from her pocket an old letter she was carrying from Flourens and hid it in a dusty account book in the office. Engels later remarked, "Had the letter been discovered, a journey to [the French penal colonies in the Pacific at] New Caledonia was sure to follow for the two sisters."[6]

The customs woman returned with the prosecutor, who said to Tussy, "If you will not allow this woman to search you, I shall do so." He may have thought he could frighten a young girl into cooperating, but Tussy shot back, "You have no right to come near a British subject. I have an English passport." Unimpressed, the prosecutor appeared ready to make good on his threat, so they reluctantly allowed the woman to inspect them. The search was extensive — they were forced to strip to their stockings, the seams of their dresses were inspected, the hair on their head spread. Nothing was found except a newspaper on Jennychen and a torn letter on Tussy (which she had tried without success to swallow). The prosecutor was still not satisfied. He dismissed the Marx daughters' coachman and placed them in an official vehicle with two officers seated on either side. They then proceeded to Luchon, through villages where crowds gathered to gawk, believing the sisters to be notorious thieves or smugglers. The group finally reached Luchon at eight that night, and the carriage stopped in front of the home of Emile de Kératry, the very official who had been alerted to Lafargue's suspicious behavior months before in Bordeaux. He was attending a Sunday concert and had given instructions not to be disturbed, so Jennychen and Tussy were taken to their own cottage to await his arrival.

Aside from the concert, Jennychen said, she and Tussy appeared to be the town's main attraction that evening. Their rooms were filled with spies and police wanting to catch a glimpse of the dangerous pair. The house was also searched, in case they were incendiaries responsible for burning down Paris. Even the night lamp used to warm the baby's milk was examined, Jennychen said, "as if it were some diabolical machine."

The men made themselves at home in the chairs and on the sofa and tried to engage Jennychen and Tussy in conversation, but the women remained mute. In return the local authorities stared at them menacingly until 10:30, when Kératry, the prosecutor general, two judges, and the police superintendents of Toulouse and Luchon appeared.

Tussy was escorted into a separate room while Jennychen was left in the parlor surrounded by a panel of inquisitors. For more than two hours Kératry questioned her about Lafargue, her friends, her family, and her reasons for being in Luchon. She refused to answer, except to say she was there to take the waters because she suffered from pleurisy. Kératry warned that if she persisted in refusing to respond, she would be deemed an accomplice. "Tomorrow," he announced, "the law will compel you to give your deposition on oath, for, let me tell you, Monsieur Lafargue and his wife have been arrested."

Tussy was brought back into the room and Jennychen was told to turn away from her sister in order not to influence her replies. An officer was placed in front of her to make sure she did not attempt any hand signals. Tussy was told to respond yes or no to statements on a piece of paper that police claimed was Jennychen's declaration, though in fact it was merely a list of allegations they were trying to substantiate. Not wanting to contradict Jennychen, Tussy said yes to some of the statements.[7] Later Tussy said of her interrogation, "It was a dirty trick wasn't it. However he heard precious little with all that."[8] But Jennychen was outraged as she described their travails in an American newspaper: "A young girl of sixteen, who had been up since five a.m., had traveled nine hours on an intensely hot day in August, and only taken food quite early at Bosost, cross-examined until half-past two in the morning!" The grilling ended for the night, but the Toulouse superintendent and several police remained in the house.

Despite their exhaustion, the sisters did not sleep. They tried to devise a plan to get a message to Lafargue in case he had not in fact been arrested. Recalled Jennychen, "We looked out the window. Gendarmes were walking about in the garden. It was impossible to get out of the house. We were close prisoners—not even allowed to see the maid and the landlady."

The next day the questions resumed under oath, which meant that if they were caught lying, they could be prosecuted. But Jennychen's anger had only deepened overnight, and she refused to respond. Tussy, too, refused to take the oath or respond to questioning,[9] and Kératry left in a rage, Engels said, over "the energy that seems peculiar to the women of this family."[10] Jennychen and Tussy feared their parents might hear of their arrest, so they asked permission to write a letter in French, which the police could read, to reassure them that they were all right. The police refused, saying the women might use a secret code to pass along dangerous messages. Among Paul's possessions they had discovered papers with references to sheep and oxen, and they were sure the sheep were communists and oxen, IWMA members.

All day Monday the women remained under house arrest. On Tuesday they had another visit from Kératry, who told them the police had been mistaken and there was no foundation for the charge against Lafargue, who was free to return to France. But, he said, "as for your sister and yourself, there is much more against you than against Monsieur Lafargue." He was Marx's son-in-law—but they were his daughters! "In all likelihood," he explained, "you will be expelled from France. However, an order from the government for your liberation will come in the course of the day." Jennychen and Tussy viewed this strange turn of events and the contradictory information with suspicion. Through a friend they sent Paul a note containing money and the advice that he travel deeper into Spain.

All day the sisters waited for their "liberation," but at eleven at night the prosecutor flanked by several police arrived at their home, and they were told to pack a trunk and follow him to jail. Jennychen later described the scene: "We got into a carriage occupied by two gendarmes in the dead of night, in a strange country, to be taken whither we knew not. The gendarmerie barracks proved to be our destination; a bedroom having been shown us, our door having been duly barricaded outside, we were left alone." Again they waited all day. Finally, at five in the evening, Jennychen demanded to talk to Kératry and asked why they were sitting in the police station when he had promised they would be freed. "Thanks to my intercession," he explained, "you have been allowed to spend the night at the gendarmerie. The government would have sent you to the prison of St. Godins, near Toulouse." He handed Jennychen an envelope containing two thousand francs that Lafargue's banker had sent him from Bordeaux. Police had intercepted it, and now Kératry turned over the money to Jennychen and told her she and Tussy were free to go. But he did not return their passports. "We were still prisoners," she reported. "Without a passport there was no getting out of France, in which country we were evidently to be kept, until some event or other should afford a pretext for again arresting us." Days of jousting with police, and the strain of their incarceration, made the Marx women reckless. They wrote Laura a letter explaining all that had happened, including what was said about Paul. They did not know whether it would reach her or what had befallen the Lafargues.[11]

*   *   *

After Jennychen and Tussy's coachman was dismissed by French police in Fos, he was asked to go to Bosost and retrieve Lafargue. The police made the request casually, but the coachman was suspicious and refused. The prosecutor and several police then set out on their own. On reaching Bosost they had no difficulty learning where the Lafargues were staying, because the village had only two inns. Rather than proceed surreptitiously with their arrest, the French made a noisy show of their arrival in Bosost's small square, as if the commotion would lend authority to their mission. This gave the locals time to alert Paul to his imminent arrest and lead him out the back of his inn to a path known only to "guides, goats and English tourists."

French police finally moved to capture Lafargue at three in the morning, bursting into his room and, accompanied by four of their Spanish counterparts, pointing their carbines at the bed, where they found not the man but his wife and son, asleep. Schnapps began to scream, as did an indignant Laura, alerting the entire inn to the police raid. When the police discovered Paul had fled, they prepared to arrest Laura. The innkeeper intervened, insisting that Spanish law would not permit it. Perhaps intimidated by the hostile crowd gathered in the doorways and hall, the police retreated—but not too far. Establishing a headquarters in the hotel, they kept Laura under constant surveillance. The peasants—no friends of their own police— resented the presence of French authorities on their soil. Consequently they acted as go-betweens and informants, alerting Laura that Kératry himself was coming to Bosost to question her and helping her escape before he arrived. The peasants also traveled the remote paths through the Pyrenees to take word of events in Bosost to the Marx daughters in Luchon.

Such was how Jennychen and Tussy finally learned that Laura was safe, and how they discovered Paul had indeed been detained. He had traveled through the mountains for three days after he fled Bosost before being arrested farther inland, in the Aragon region of the Pyrenees at Huesca.[12] The Spanish government—the only European administration to consent to France's request to extradite International members—at once agreed to turn him over to the French.[13]

On the very day Spain acceded to the French request, Jennychen and Tussy's British passports were returned. Their first impulse was to go to Huesca to assess Paul's situation, and then to find and rescue Laura. They journeyed as far as the Spanish coastal town of San Sebastián, and discovered Laura was already there and that Lafargue, true to his incredible luck and indomitable spirit, had been freed.[14] He said he had been transported on muleback by two civil guards carrying loaded rifles walking on either side of him. As they traveled through villages, Lafargue was taken for an important man being protected by police.[15] For their part, Lafargue said, "police were happy with such a prisoner.... Everything was primitive in the Spanish Pyrenees. Wine, food were abundant, and at twenty-five sous a person I had gargantuan meals." Received by the governor of the province with wine and cigars, he soon determined that the governor was politically sympathetic. No doubt much to Kératry's consternation, Paul was freed because local Spanish officials decided the charges against him were unsubstantiated. He went to San Sebastián, and, reunited, the Lafargues decided to remain in Spain.[16] The Marx daughters, however, had had enough of the Continent. They returned immediately to England.

Jennychen and Tussy were far from alone in heading north. Once again, England had become the destination for exiled and hunted kings and revolutionaries. Napoleon III had spent from September 1870 to March 1871 in Prussian captivity and when freed went to southeast England to settle in Chislehurst, Kent, where his wife and son awaited him.[17] But most of the exiles arriving in Britain headed for London. Marx described them as "cousins from the country.... You recognize them at once by their bewildered airs, their astonishment at everything they see and their feverish anxiety at the convolution of horses, cabs, omnibuses, people, babies, and dogs."[18] Most arrivals spoke no English and had no local friends or acquaintances. As they had in 1848, many of these newcomers gathered in Soho, without money, without food, without hope.

In the past the English had been indifferent to immigrants, but they suspected that those exiled from the Commune were dangerous and wondered whether they should be allowed entry. The newspapers were full of frightening tales of the International's plans to reduce London to a charred ruin.[19] In fact the exiles arriving in London (perhaps excepting a fringe few) were not interested in burning down the city, though many *were* the men and women the French government wanted extradited as communards. Had England cared to look for them, they could be easily found: they met nearly every night at the place radicals now considered both a headquarters and a place of pilgrimage — Marx's home in Modena Villas.

Part VI

The Red Terrorist Doctor

38

⌒

London, 1871

*The thunder of the cannon in Paris awakened the most
backward sections of the proletariat from their deep slumber,
and everywhere gave impetus to the growth of revolutionary
socialist propaganda.*

—Vladimir Lenin[1]

THE MARX AND Engels households worked furiously during the summer
of 1871 soliciting money and arranging shelter, schools, and jobs for Commune refugees. For those still stranded in France, Marx used a network of
people in England and on the Continent to secure passports to get them
safely out of the country. Time was of the essence—French officials had
rewritten the history of the previous six months and turned the Commune into a criminal uprising and the communards into thieves and thugs
who, if left at large, threatened every village in France and beyond. It was
a tale the French people seemed eager to believe. The most popular performances in France that season were courts-martial of the communards;
two thousand people attended the opening proceeding in August,
equipped with fans, lorgnettes, and opera glasses. Such legal spectacles
would continue for three more years, as men and women by the thousands
were condemned to death or deportation for their alleged role, however
tenuous, in the 1871 uprising in Paris.[2]

Lissagaray made his way to England after witnessing the mass execution of
communards at Père-Lachaise on May 28. By mid-August Longuet had also
arrived, tremendously fortunate to have escaped.[3] Not only had he commanded a regiment of *fédérés,* but he was a member of the Commune Central
Committee as well as the International. Moreover he had introduced the

first real communist note into the uprising by coauthoring a March 21 piece challenging workingmen and -women to free themselves from bourgeois rule.[4] With the help of a military doctor who at great personal risk hid him in his home, Longuet managed to cross the border to Belgium and then travel on to England.[5]

Like so many others, Lissagaray and Longuet had immediately found their way to Modena Villas. Liebknecht recalled that after the Commune, the Marxes always housed at least one if not several French emigrants,[6] and nearly all the letters from the Marx and Engels homes at this time described the rap at the door and the friendless refugee standing outside. Jennychen and Tussy had still not returned from France, so it was left to Jenny and Lenchen in the Marx home and Lizzy Burns at Engels's place to open the door to these desperate arrivals. Jenny likely saw in the eyes of the beleaguered families gathered on her doorstep, staring through gleaming windows at the sumptuous furnishings inside, the same trepidation she and her children had experienced when they arrived at Leicester Square in 1849. And, no doubt, she would have appeared as if out of a dream to these refugees, an angel of wealth and comfort extending a hand of friendship. There was nothing haughty or condescending about this mercy. Lafargue remarked that for Jenny, social distinctions did not exist; she entertained working people in her home and at her table as if they were earls or princes. "I am convinced not one of the workers ever suspected the woman who received them so cordially was descended from the Duke of Argyll," he noted, "and that her brother was a minister of the king of Prussia."[7]

Lenchen was not quite as uncritical. She had made it her duty to protect Marx from unwanted visitors, and now there were many. Since Marx had been identified as the brains behind the Commune and the International, members of the press from as far away as New York set out to interview "revolution incarnate."[8] *Vanity Fair* in London wanted to run his photograph.[9] One suspects that most reporters came away from their encounters disappointed that the gray-haired gentleman in the bourgeois home did not have horns. A correspondent for the *New York World* thought Marx's study, decorated with a vase of roses and a tabletop book of Rhineland landscapes, could have belonged to a stockbroker.[10] Another described Marx as open and amiable in his conversation, an obviously educated and intelligent man, but one given to utopian ideas.[11] Yet another seemed more frightened of Lenchen than of Marx.[12]

All those guests, all that chatter, soon became tiresome, and Marx began to resent the intrusions. He snapped at one reporter who asked him to clear up the mystery of the International: "There is no mystery to clear up, dear sir...except perhaps the mystery of human stupidity in those who perpetually ignore the fact that our association is a public one and that the fullest reports of its proceedings are published for all who care to read them."[13] Nevertheless, with or without Marx's cooperation, the press coverage continued. Articles claimed that Marx had been arrested in Belgium, others that he had died.[14] There had even been a story in the French press about Jennychen and Tussy's arrests, bizarrely describing the two as Marx's brothers.[15] Finally, the *National-Zeitung* in Berlin resurrected the old accusations that Marx lived off the workingman and that the IWMA shamefully abused the workers: "Out of their hard savings the infatuated workmen furnish the members of the council with the means of living agreeably in London."[16] The report was widely reprinted, which forced Marx and Engels to mount an aggressive defense at the same time they were coping with the refugee invasion. Marx wrote Kugelmann,

If the day had forty-eight hours, I would still not have finished my day's work for months now. The work for the International is immense, and in addition London is overrun with REFUGEES, whom we have to look after. Moreover, I am overrun by other people—newspaper men and others of every description—who want to see the "MONSTER" with their own eyes. Up till now it has been thought that the emergence of the Christian myths during the Roman Empire was possible only because printing had not yet been invented. Precisely the contrary. The daily press and the telegraph, which in a moment spreads its inventions over the whole earth, fabricate more myths in one day (and the bourgeois cattle believe and propagate them still further), than could have previously been produced in a century.[17]

In mid-August Marx escaped to the coast at Brighton in search of rest, but even there he was pursued. "The second day after my arrival here, I met a chap in a waiting posture at the corner of my street," he told Jenny, describing him as the same man who had several times followed Engels and Marx on their way home. "As you know, GENERALLY SPEAKING I am not good at detecting spies. But this fellow has obviously and undeniably dogged my every step down here. Yesterday, I became fed up with it, so I stopped, turned round and stared at him with my notorious EYEGLASS. WHAT DID HE DO? He doffed his hat very humbly and today he no longer honored me with the pleasure of his company."[18]

From the time Marx and Jenny left Soho, they had largely been isolated from the outside world and each other. They shared many miseries but only sporadic joy. They lived side by side, but theirs had become more a working relationship than a passionately loving one. They seemed happiest when they were away from London—separately. Indeed, it would have been remarkable if their troubled existence had not affected their marriage. But beginning in 1871 their relationship began to change again. There was a tender new regard, a fresh joy in each other's company. It may have been that Engels had relieved them of their soul-destroying financial worries. It may have been Engels's presence in London, and the fact that they were once again at the center of a huge social network. Or it may have been that Marx had finally rid himself of the burden of *Capital* by producing *Volume I*. Whatever the reason, that year Jenny and Marx seemed to begin their love affair all over again. Marx wrote Jenny from Brighton, "Throughout the whole period I have regretted nothing so much as the fact that you were not here."[19]

In early September Jennychen and Tussy returned from their long ordeal in France, arriving just in time to help their father prepare for a private IWMA congress in London. (The annual congress had been scheduled for Paris, but under the circumstances that was impossible. It was also felt that due to the overwhelmingly negative attention the International had received, a public congress would attract too much notice.) The group would not only decide a future course in the post-Commune environment, but Marx and Engels wanted to plot a response to Bakunin's latest attempts to take over the organization.

Since his last visit to Marx's home in 1864, Bakunin had been busily conspiring to relieve the IWMA of Marx's dominance. He had founded an anarchist group in 1868 that wanted to ally itself with the International, but it was rejected. To comply with IWMA rules, Bakunin claimed to have dissolved the group, but in fact he kept it alive as a clandestine organization.[20] Then action beckoned. Looking in part to broaden his anarchist circle, though mostly because he could not resist a fight, in 1870 Bakunin flung himself into the turmoil in France. The huge, shaggy, toothless Russian's call to arms was met however with alarm and suspicion. He was arrested and thrown into a Lyons dungeon before escaping to Marseilles, where he sold his last possession—his revolver—shaved his head and beard, and fled back to Switzerland.[21]

It would have been easy to dismiss Bakunin as an impulsive buffoon, but his legend was potent and somehow withstood the failures of the man. Marx knew his rival's appeal was such that he posed a real threat to the IWMA and to his leadership. Bakunin, who had exchanged his trademark cap for a broad-brimmed straw hat with a red ribbon,[22] was particularly successful in Italy and Spain, and had a core of followers in Switzerland. The London conference was critically important to check his advance as well as settle disputes among English delegates over Marx's embrace of the Commune. Just when the world viewed the International as at the height of its treacherous power, it was at the greatest risk of splitting apart.[23]

Delegates arriving in London for the congress made their way first to Marx's home. Many had never actually met Marx—he existed as a name on documents or in newspapers. That had been Spaniard Anselmo Lorenzo's experience until their memorable first meeting.

> We stopped before a house, framed in the doorway appeared an old man with a venerable patriarch appearance. I approached him with shy respect and introduced myself as a delegate of the Spanish Federation of the International. He took me in his arms, kissed me on the forehead and showed me into the house with words of affection in Spanish. He was Karl Marx. The family had already retired and he himself served me an appetizing refreshment with exquisite amiability.

Lorenzo spent the night at the Marx home and was just as delighted the next day by his encounters with Jennychen and Tussy. He described Jennychen as "a girl of ideal beauty, different from all the types of feminine beauty I had so far met. She asked me to read something for her so she could hear the correct pronunciation." Next he met sixteen-year-old Tussy, who was enlisted to help Lorenzo send a telegram to Spain. "I was most surprised and touched by the alacrity with which the young woman helped a foreigner whom she did not know, this being contrary to the customs of the Spanish bourgeoisie. This young lady, or rather girl, is beautiful, merry and smiling as the very personification of youth and happiness." Tussy, unlike her father and eldest sister, did not speak Spanish, so they struggled to communicate: "Every time one of us made a blunder we both laughed as heartily as if we had been friends all our lives."[24]

The International met for five days. Friedrich Lessner recalled a chaos of languages, profound differences in temperament, and a variety of views. The atmosphere was so charged, he said, that everyone was at loggerheads, and the meetings were stormy and frustrating.[25] But by its end the conference had produced seventeen resolutions, including a response to Bakunin's threat and an important statement on the next step for International members.[26] Despite alarmist reports that the IWMA wanted to destroy the world's capitals, the group's first post-Commune congress called instead for a far more legal method of revolt: "The working class cannot act, as a class, except by constituting itself into a political party," a move described as "indispensable in order to insure the triumph of the social Revolution and its ultimate end—the abolition of classes."[27]

On September 24, the day after the conference closed, the IWMA held a grand dinner to celebrate its seventh anniversary.[28] (Engels attributed the organization's unlikely longevity entirely to Marx: the very characteristics that had earned him criticism—his "corrosive *domination* and his jealous nature"—were the secret behind the International's cohesion. Marx simply would not let it be steered off course or fail.)[29] Banquet tables were loaded with food, wine, and beer, and speeches were made throughout the night. Marx finally delivered his. He equated the persecution of the IWMA with the persecution of the early Christians, noting that those assaults had not saved Rome, and neither would the modern onslaught against the workers' movement save the capitalist state. The International's Resolution IX had called for the establishment of workers' political parties, and Marx sounded a warning to governments that might try to impede the participation of workingmen, declaring, "We must answer them with all the means that are at our disposal...we must declare to the governments: we will proceed against you peaceably where it is possible and by force of arms when it may be necessary."[30]

Engels and Marx described the congress as more successful than all previous such gatherings because it had been kept private and small, and therefore delegates had less inclination to grandstand.[31] With that work behind them, the two men did what they had never done before—they went to the seaside to spend five days alone with their wives,[32] who had gone ahead to Ramsgate while the men did their politicking.[33] Jenny had not had a female friend in the movement since Ernestine Liebknecht left London for Berlin in 1862, and though they had corresponded by letter, that too had ended when Ernestine died in 1867. But Jenny and Lizzy had become fast friends. At forty-four, Lizzy was considerably younger than Jenny (now fifty-seven), yet she seemed older, likely because, as a working girl, her adulthood had begun prematurely. For her part, Jenny had been deprived of so much for so long that now that she had a chance to enjoy life, she'd gained a vitality that belied her age.

Fresh from their revolutionary activities, during which government informants no doubt claimed they had hatched new and even more heinous plots, Marx and Engels played tourist with Jenny and Lizzy. They walked the cliffs, bathed in the sea, sat by the beach, watched fire-eaters and Punch-and-Judy shows, and indulged themselves with large meals and heavy drinking. Engels said he slept ten hours a day.[34] Jenny told her daughters Marx was positively rejuvenated by the excursion.[35]

If those four felt like family, however, other relations—and relations with those relations—were less amiable. Engels had translated Marx's *Civil*

War in France into German, and when it was excerpted in the German press[36] his seventy-four-year-old mother was alarmed to see her son not only still involved in radical politics but still involved with Marx. She demanded answers. Engels had not been close to his father, but he loved his mother and thought her capable of understanding him. He told her not to believe the reports on events in Paris, and as for himself:

> You knew that I had not modified my opinions, opinions which I shall soon have held for thirty years, and it could not come as a surprise to you that, as soon as events compelled me to do so, I should not only speak up for them but would do my duty in other respects too.... If Marx were not here, or did not even exist, it would make absolutely no difference at all. It is therefore quite wrong to put the blame on him. Incidentally, I can also remember the time when Marx's relations maintained that *I* had been the ruin of him.[37]

Marx's siblings were aghast that their brother had chosen such a reckless path. During a visit to London, his sister from Cape Town scolded him at the dinner table, saying she could not countenance her brother being the leader of the socialists because he came from a respected family and their father had been a popular lawyer. Accustomed to much harsher criticism, Marx listened to her politely and then exploded with a high-pitched peal of laughter.[38] Neither he nor Engels was ready to repent—in fact, they were just getting their second wind. There was even good news on *Capital, Volume I.* After four years the first thousand German copies had finally sold, and the publisher was printing a second edition.[39]

Jennychen was out of work. The family that had employed her as a governess for three years had dismissed her "because they have made the terrible discovery that I am the daughter of the *incendiary* chief, who defended the iniquitous Communal movement."[40] It is unlikely that she would have fit neatly into the role of governess again in any case—she could not ignore the destitute refugees or the reams of letters demanding attention from Marx's inner circle. Indeed, mail from Italy, Sweden, France, Russia, and Hong Kong was piling up, and though it had been many months since the Commune had failed, the flood of refugees was undiminished. If anything, those arriving in the fall were needier still, because had they possessed any money at all, they would long before have bought their way out of France. Jennychen spent her days rushing from one end of London to the other on their behalf and her nights—well into the early hours of the morning—writing letters soliciting funds to pay for the exiles' limitless needs. It was exhausting work, and over the previous two years Marx's twenty-seven-year-old daughter had been anything but well. The doctor had diagnosed her respiratory problem as pleurisy, and while she had acute phases and merely annoying phases, overall she never breathed easily. Yet Jennychen threw herself into her work, in defiance of what her body required most—rest. In a letter to the Kugelmanns in December 1871, she admitted that despite her efforts, she had not been successful in finding support for the refugees: "The employers will have nothing to do with them. The men who had succeeded in obtaining engagements under borrowed names, are dismissed as soon as it is found out who they are.... Their sufferings are beyond description—they are literally starving in the streets of this great city—the city that has carried every-man-for-himself to its greatest perfection."[41]

The most desperate of the refugees—460 of them—had arrived in November after being held on prison pontoons off the northern coast of France for five months, until the French government determined they could not be prosecuted. They were deposited on the English coast without food, money, or warm clothes, in a hard rain and cutting wind, and told to apply to their respective consuls for help.[42] The penniless hundreds then set out on foot for London. Some found their way to the International, whose funds were quickly depleted by the sheer volume of their needs.[43]

For all Jennychen's difficult and oftentimes disappointing work, however, she was singing again. In a letter to Lafargue, Engels called her voice stronger and clearer than ever before. He attributed this to improving health;[44] actually, it was a sign that Jennychen was in love.

After returning to London, Charles Longuet had immediately rejoined the International's General Council and resumed his association with Marx. During earlier encounters with the Marx family he had been attracted to Jennychen but did not express his interest. Now he made his feelings clear, and she did not resist his blandishments. It is easy to see why. First, Longuet needed rescuing: he was raw from the recent conflict, bearing the emotional scars of those horrible weeks in Paris and the terror of his escape. Second, he was not Flourens, but he was noble in his own way. In fact, he was more like her father than her previous amour had been. Now thirty-two, Longuet was a man of action only when circumstances required it; he was much more comfortable as a writer and a thinker. His history even recalled Marx's. He came from a bourgeois family in Normandy, studied law, rebelled against his caste, edited the most popular socialist newspaper in France, was a ferocious debater, and had been expelled from country after country for his political views. Perhaps most important, from Jennychen's perspective, however, Longuet revered her father. No man could replace Marx in her heart and mind. A spouse would have to understand that, and understand why. Longuet did both.

The Marx family was unaware that the pair's relations had become intimate until, at the beginning of 1872, Jennychen let slip an innocuous but revelatory remark. Marx had announced that he planned to go to Longuet's apartment to discuss a newspaper article with him. Jennychen blurted, "I must needs say, you will not find him at home, he has gone to Jung's on business." Her father, mother, and Engels stopped in their tracks, she told Longuet, and looked at her "not a little surprised to hear I was so well informed as to your whereabouts."[45] Unable to hide their feelings any longer, the couple decided Longuet should have a "conference" with Marx on February 19 to ask his permission to marry Jennychen. When she suggested they not see each other beforehand, Longuet could not wait—"two days can be a century." He suggested that she appear as if by accident at Engels's home on that Sunday night, when he would be there. Jennychen had an engagement to sing that weekend, but Longuet claimed precedence. "I know very well—my adored one—that you want to sing me things you have never said, but that I have read in your eyes and that, without words, my lips have gathered from your lips." He did not see the risk in their supposedly chance encounter, because he could not imagine anyone, least of all her father, being sensitive enough to recognize their feelings unless they were announced outright: "To guess that I love you the way I love you, it would require one to be capable oneself of loving like that—and that, I feel, is impossible," he wrote, paraphrasing Goethe. "In any case, I will dream of you.... I want your kisses all my life."[46]

Jennychen's terror over Longuet's meeting with her father, and a nagging awareness that by marrying she was abandoning her independent life as an activist and writer, were evident in her businesslike response to her lover's passion: "At the conference on Monday I am very anxious that you should appear in a black cravat, or at least a dark-colored one instead of the red ones you usually wear, and which are not harmonious and do not suit your face." Jennychen confessed that as she wrote those words, she blushed to think what her Russian revolutionary friend Elizabeth Dmitrieff would say if she read them. "How disgusted, how disappointed she would be! She who had set her heart upon making of me a heroine, a second Madame Roland.... Do not forget that it is you who have deprived the world of a heroine."[47]

Unfortunately we have no description of the Marx-Longuet meeting, but the result was what had been hoped for: Marx granted his permission for the marriage. Yet Madame Marx was not thrilled at the prospect. She wrote Liebknecht,

Longuet is a very talented and very good, honest and respectable man, and the agreement of views and convictions between the young couple is surely an assurance of their future happiness. On the other hand, I cannot anticipate this bond without anxious worries, I would have really wished that Jenny had chosen (for a change) an Englishman, or a German, instead of a Frenchman, who of course besides displaying all the amiable traits of his nation, also isn't without its weaknesses and deficiencies. . . . I cannot help but dread that Jenny's lot as a political woman will expose her to all the worries and agonies which are inseparable from it.[48]

The decision would not have been easy for Marx either, both for the reasons that troubled his wife and also because he did not want to part with his favorite daughter. Longuet's suit, however, was much aided by a piece of business he had transacted for Marx in Paris. In December, Lafargue, who was still in Spain, had found a French publisher for *Capital* and had offered to pay the two thousand francs the publisher, Maurice Lachâtre, required to set the process in motion.[49] In January, Longuet found a man in Paris to translate the work. Joseph Roy was an experienced hand at difficult German material—he had previously translated Feuerbach.[50] (Conveniently, Roy had been on the point of asking Marx's permission to translate and publish a portion of *Capital*.) He promised to devote six or seven hours a day to the new project,[51] a bit of good news that Longuet shrewdly sent Marx just before their private conference.

However tepid the Marxes' initial response to the prospect of the Longuet union, by March, when the engagement became official, they were rejoicing. Engels assured Laura that he was teasing Jennychen as unmercifully as he had once teased her. Lenchen even allowed Longuet into the kitchen to perform feats of not entirely successful French culinary magic.[52]

Meanwhile, unnoticed amid Jennychen's blooming romance, Tussy, too, had fallen in love.

Eleanor Marx had grown into a beautiful young lady. Her black hair hung nearly to her waist in long locks that Kugelmann's daughter Franzisca said were "indeed very fetching but also rather flashy."[53] Tussy's complexion was as dusky as her father's and her face defined by thick dark eyebrows. But where Marx's face could appear stern, Tussy's looked sensual. One Russian described her as slim and seductive, a kind of German Romantic heroine.[54] Yet her beauty was not classical. Like her personality, it was elemental, clarified and fundamental. She was completely bold and alive, her eyes sparkling in anticipation of the next amazing occurrence or witty exchange. She could traverse the distance from a smile to a storm and back again in a matter of minutes, but it was her laughter that best character-ized her.

Since her return from France, Tussy had worked as a correspondent for her father, sending "business" letters to radicals from St. Petersburg to Paris and becoming in the process "political top to bottom," according to her mother.[55] Her correspondence exhibited fluency with language (French, German, and English) and social conflict. It also displayed a pre-cocious maturity mixed with charming impetuousness; what Marx dubbed her "ferocious" personality[56] leapt off every page. Part of her appeal was that she did not pretend to be other than what she was, a sixteen-year-old emissary of her father, alternately learned and amusing, a committed socialist and a silly girl. In the reactionary European environ-ment of that time, a letter from Karl Marx invited at least government scrutiny and at worst arrest.[57] Tussy's letters made the enterprise of revolu-tion seem much less dangerous or sinister. It was a family affair.

She was adept at excuses. To *Capital*'s Russian translator she wrote: "Dear Sir, Papa is so very much overworked. . . . He says I am to tell you . . . he is up the greater part of the night writing, and all day he does not leave his room."[58] And she was reassuringly warm. Addressing Liebknecht as "My dear old Library," she wrote of the refugees' struggles (adding sarcas-tically, "I wish they'd taken some of the millions they're accused of having stolen") and of herself: "You I should know anywhere, though I'm sure you'd never recognize *me*. People that saw me only two or three years ago hardly know me again. . . . Kiss all at home for me. . . . I must apologize for my dreadful writing, but I've such a wretched pen and almost no ink."[59] Tussy wrote to the revolutionaries of Europe as if they were the most nor-mal correspondents for a teenage girl.

Her closest friend was one of the world's most brilliant minds—her father.[60] She would, therefore, hardly be satisfied with just any man. She had attracted innumerable suitors among the refugees,[61] and though flat-tered by the attentions of these desperate communards, she did not fall in love with them. Yet one within the circle stood out: Hyppolite-Prosper-Olivier Lissagaray.

Lissagaray was certainly man enough for Tussy, he seemed cut from the pages of a Sir Walter Scott novel. He had been born a count into an old French Basque family that cast him out because of his radical social ideas. He then launched a varied career as a lecturer at an alternative university established by professors denied posts for political reasons, a journalist who spent his writing career in and out of prison because of the radical content of his newspapers, and finally a soldier in Gambetta's army in

1870, when it was left to the new French Republic to fight Prussia. After the armistice—which he viewed as a defeat—he went to Paris to publish a newspaper, and when that was no longer possible, he exchanged his pen for a gun and mounted the barricades at Belleville.[62] A dead shot and an expert with a saber, he did not shrink from duels, and came away seriously wounded from two.[63] In London he lived with an arrest warrant hanging over his head, aware that the French were pressuring England to extradite him.

Lissagaray visited Modena Villas frequently and was well regarded by the entire Marx family. Jennychen reflected her father's view when she told Kugelmann that a short work published by Lissagaray that past fall, *Eight Days of May Behind the Barricades,* was the only book on the Commune worth reading.[64] But the family had apparently failed to detect the attraction between this exiled nobleman and its youngest daughter. In March 1872, Lissagaray and Tussy became secretly engaged. He was thirty-four and she just seventeen.

Engels, who knew Tussy very well, may have noticed the more than casual friendship between them. (He told Laura how happy Tussy was for Jennychen "and really gives the impression that she **should not mind to follow suit.**")[65] But Marx and Jenny would not countenance such a step. The last thing they wanted was another French exile as a son-in-law or to see their gregarious child bound to a man twice her age. In any case it was too much to think about at that moment. The entire family was worried about Laura.

Laura and Lafargue had been living quietly in the Spanish port town of San Sebastián when, in September 1871, local officials announced that Paul had six hours to leave or be arrested.[66] The political temperature in Spain had changed yet again. Lafargue fled, but Laura and Schnapps could not accompany him.[67] The child had never recovered from his illness of the previous summer and now appeared to have a form of cholera. All of Marx's children were gifted linguists, but it was not clear how much Spanish Laura spoke or whether she had a network of local friends for support. She would have needed both: she spent nine months at Schnapps's bedside, trying to nurse her only living child back to health. By December he was still unwell but fit enough for travel, so Laura and her fragile charge headed south to meet Lafargue in Madrid.[68]

Marx and Engels were happy to have Lafargue in the Spanish capital to counter Bakunin's influence there, but Jenny was fearful for her grandson and grew increasingly annoyed that Paul's letters, full of optimistic reports about the International's great successes in Spain, contained very little news about Schnapps. In February, Marx prodded Paul, saying he provided interesting details on the movement "but a mere blank in regard to that dear little sufferer."[69] Anxiously, in March Marx asked again for news of his grandson.[70] By May he had it: Schnapps was ill and getting weaker.[71]

Jennychen and Longuet had set a wedding date for mid-July. The Parisian press (or the police press of Paris, as Jennychen called it), which considered her the notorious offspring of the International rebel-in-chief, filled gossip columns with stories on her personal life without regard to the actual details. The rightist journal *La Gaulois,* she said, had her married off twenty times. "When I am married for real, I suppose these stupid scribblers will leave me in peace," she told the Kugelmanns in June.[72] But Jennychen's wedding did not occur that July. She and Longuet postponed it out of respect for Laura and Paul.[73] On July 1, 1872, Lafargue wrote Engels, "Our poor little Schnapps, after eleven months of physical and mental suffering, is dying of exhaustion."[74] By the end of July the boy was dead. Four-year-old Schnapps was the third child Laura had lost in as many years.

Laura had always been somewhat remote, and that trait was tragically exacerbated by the deaths of her children. A photograph from the period told the story eloquently—the formerly voluptuous young woman appeared hollow, her eyes lifeless, her face drawn and stern. She and her husband had strayed into Spain because of Lafargue's politicking and remained there at the behest of the "party" (Engels and her father) so Lafargue could build the Spanish IWMA. It is not hard to imagine that she blamed all three of the men in her life for her sorrow. Their devotion to politics, to the worker, had cost the Marx family yet another young life. She was not a widow; it was worse. She had traveled to the Pyrenees a year before as mother of two children, and now she was the mother of none. What made her pain even more intense was that her losses seemed to be for naught.

Despite Lafargue's rosy reports on political progress in Spain, the socialists there were hopelessly split, and Bakunin's influence was as great as ever. (Bakunin dismissed Lafargue as a "mound of refuse.")[75] Based on Lafargue's information, Engels had boasted to colleagues that the IWMA was *the* party of the Spanish workingman,[76] but in fact Lafargue had not managed to make any significant inroads with the workers. This was not necessarily Paul's failure as much as a matter of culture. Spanish socialists were suspicious of Marx's emphasis on organization, his Prussian "authoritarianism," and preferred Bakunin's anarchism instead.[77]

Politically defeated and personally bereft, the Lafargues left Spain shortly after burying Schnapps and headed to Portugal, their first step along a path that would take them back to London. Paul described the trip as "a trifle long, a trifle hot, and a trifle arduous: thirty hours on the train in heat that would have hatched out lice on a pane of glass. Fortunately we had an enormous sandia [watermelon] weight eighteen pounds which slaked our thirst in the La Mancha desert."[78]

The indomitable Lafargue would bounce back quickly from his misfortunes, but Laura never fully recovered. At twenty-six she was still young enough to have more children but did not. It was as if she had buried herself, bit by bit, in the three small graves she left behind in Paris, Luchon, and Madrid. And it was not just love that was lost, but faith. Of all the Marx women, Laura was perhaps the only one to fundamentally question the future her father promised, because of the high price the family had been forced to pay to achieve it. In the coming years she would continue working to further Marx's goals, but unlike her sisters and mother, she would not do so out of devotion to the cause. Robbed of her children, her happiness, her life, she had lost her religion. What remained was simply the family business.

39

The Hague, Fall 1872

*No, I am not withdrawing from the International, and the rest
of my life will be devoted, like my efforts in the past, to the
triumph of the social ideas which one day, be sure of it, will
bring about the universal rule of the proletariat.*

—Karl Marx[1]

IN MAY, Marx began hinting that he would quit his leadership position in
the IWMA that fall, after the annual congress.[2] He had stuck with the
organization for eight years—a remarkably long time, given the warring
parties within its ranks. Many International members left the group
because they could not agree with Marx. He especially annoyed the English with his support for the Irish, and alienated even more when he was
perceived as wholeheartedly embracing the treacherous radicals of the
Commune. Others agreed with him philosophically and politically but
resented his autocratic style, suspecting his real goal was simply self-
aggrandizement.

Marx had fought with IWMA members, against governments, and for
workers to nurture an organization he believed gave the proletariat a sense
of its own power and a foundation from which to mount a political challenge to the capitalist ruling class. But he was ready to pass the torch to a
new leader—or rather, many leaders. In the months after the Commune,
despite ominous warnings from governments about this malevolent organization, new IWMA branches had sprouted in Denmark, New Zealand,
Portugal, Hungary, Ireland, Holland, Austria, and America.[3] The association had a life of its own, and its figurehead hoped that he might be able to
quietly withdraw to the sidelines to watch it flourish. Marx told a Belgian

delegate, "I can hardly wait for the next Congress. It will be the end of my slavery. After that I shall become a free man again; I shall accept no administrative functions anymore."[4]

Though he was undeniably exhausted, Marx's desire to get out of active politics resulted from more than mere fatigue. The Commune had introduced Marx to the world as a revolutionary strategist and, importantly, as a theoretician. His writings were suddenly in relative demand—that is to say, they went from being completely ignored to attracting a modicum of attention. Meissner wanted to publish a second edition of *Capital, Volume I,* but Marx insisted he be allowed to rework some of the text, which took him more than a year.[5] In Paris, Roy was translating the first volume into French, and while Marx was initially pleased with his work, he soon found it required laborious rewriting.[6] Marx and Engels also produced a circular on splits within the International, which they blamed on Bakunin. And there were requests to publish the *Communist Manifesto* with a new preface in Germany and to translate it into French and English.[7] In addition Marx oversaw as much as he could the Russian translation of *Capital.*

Marx had often dismissed his Russian peers' commitment to socialism because most were aristocrats or from the country's social elite. But the new generation who wrote him from St. Petersburg or from exile in Geneva, or who appeared at his door were, according to Engels, "of the *people....* They have a stoicism, a strength of character and at the same time a grasp of theory which are truly admirable."[8] Marx's friend Pyotr Lavrov, an IWMA colleague and math professor who lived in Paris after being driven out of St. Petersburg, had written a series of published letters in which he declared that Russia's intelligentsia owed an enormous debt to the toiling masses for the privileged conditions that allowed them the freedom to think and develop.[9] Many of these intellectuals recognized that debt, aligned themselves with the peasants newly freed from serfdom, and began propagandizing in factories and villages throughout Russia in an effort they called "going to the people."[10] These young educated Russians wanted a country that would provide the benefits of Western society to all its citizens without having to adopt a capitalist system. Socialism, they argued, was the natural choice because it reflected Russia's communal traditions. But even where there was accord on what this society might ultimately look like, disputes emerged over how to get there.[11] Followers of Bakunin—anarchists and nihilists—promoted violence. Others, including those receptive to Marx, advocated political education as an essential step toward changing Russia.[12]

Marx's *Capital* made it past Russian censors, who said it was so difficult to understand—if there was anything *to* understand—that no one would buy it, and in any case it would be impossible to prosecute in court because it was too mathematical and scientific.[13] The only thing the censors would not allow was a picture of Marx in the book. (Marx biographer David McLellan said authorities felt that to do so "would imply too much respect for Marx's personality.")[14] That minor point agreed, a print run of three thousand copies rolled off the press at the end of March 1872.[15] It sold out remarkably quickly — in less than two months — and earned a readership much greater than its sales figures implied.[16] *Capital* was often passed from one Russian reader to another, sometimes concealed inside the covers of the New Testament.[17] Unlike the French translation, this version thrilled Marx; he called it *"masterly."* He received a bound copy in May and asked Nikolai Danielson to send a second. He wanted to donate it to the British Museum.[18]

Surprisingly, despite so much work and so many deadlines, Marx was not particularly ill. Jenny, on the other hand, seemed to have absorbed all his worries. Now that her husband was to a certain extent in the limelight — a position she had long hoped he would attain and which she believed he deserved — she actually pined for the days when he worked as an obscure scholar. She told Liebknecht that as long as Karl claimed no credit for himself and was a relative unknown outside the International, "the riffraff was silent. But now that his enemies have dragged him into the light, have brought his name to the foreground, now the mob is conspiring and policemen and democrats are whining the same chorus of 'despotism, addiction to authority, ambition!' How much better would he be, had he worked on quietly and developed the theory of struggle for those in the fight."

Liebknecht was awaiting sentencing in Germany on charges of high treason, and Jenny wrote him that his new wife, Natalie, was often in her thoughts:

> In all these struggles we women have the harder part to bear, because it is the lesser one. A man draws strength from his struggle with the world outside, and is invigorated by the sight of the enemy, be their number legion. We remain sitting at home, darning socks. This does not banish the worries and the daily small miseries gnaw slowly but steadily on one's courage to face life. I speak out of thirty years' experience, and I can probably say that I didn't lose heart easily. Now I have become too old to hope for much and the last unfortunate events [the Commune] have completely shaken me. I fear that we...won't experience much good anymore and my only hope is that our children will have an easier time of it.[19]

Much of Marx's work that spring (and a source of the aggravation Jenny described) involved preparation for a titanic battle for the future of the working-class movement between himself and Bakunin. Bakunin had been an effective agitator during his years in Italy and Switzerland, associating with notable revolutionaries, generating pamphlets, and spawning surrogates who in turn spread the myth of the mighty Russian fighter able to lead their charge. In 1869 he had encountered a twenty-two-year-old Russian nihilist in Geneva named Sergei Nechayev, who if not an outright psychopath was dangerously unstable. Nechayev had invented revolutionary credentials, including a purported escape from the Peter and Paul Fortress where Bakunin had also been imprisoned. He claimed to be the head of an underground group in Russia with thousands of members.[20] Whether Bakunin believed him is questionable, but he fell under the sway of this young man who stirred his love of conspiracy and made him feel reconnected to the Russia to which he could never return.

During his association with Nechayev, Bakunin wrote his *Revolutionary Catechism,* which promoted two basic principles: "the end justifies the means" and "the worse, the better." As one historian has noted, Bakunin believed everything "that promoted the revolution was permissible and everything that hindered it was a crime." But it was more than that. In Bakunin's thinking, it was not enough to light the night with gas lamps—the whole metropolis must be ablaze. "There is only one science for the revolutionary," he wrote, "the science of destruction."[21]

Bakunin may have been the least likely translator to tackle his nemesis Marx's work, but in 1869 he had received an advance from a publisher (worth more than Marx had ever made on his book) to help with the Russian version of *Capital.* He managed to get through only thirty-two pages before Nechayev convinced him he had better things to do.[22] A young Russian named Nikolai Lyubavin, who worked with Danielson on the project, had arranged Bakunin's translation deal, and it was to Lyubavin that Nechayev directed a campaign aimed at freeing his older friend from his obligation. Nechayev sent Lyubavin a letter, supposedly on behalf of his vast nihilist organization, accusing the student of exploiting Bakunin and threatening to use "less civilized measures" than a letter if he did not release Bakunin from his contract.[23] The threat of violence was not empty: Nechayev had beaten, strangled, and shot a student to death in Moscow merely for questioning the existence of his underground group.[24]

Marx knew these details and informed the General Council of the sordid story. To prepare for the September 2, 1872, showdown at the International's annual congress at The Hague, Marx began collecting evidence on Bakunin's relations with Nechayev and corroboration that Bakunin had continued to run his anarchist group contrary to IWMA rules. He hoped to use those points to have Bakunin and his followers expelled from the International. In fact, these were moral trifles to Marx—he wanted Bakunin out because of their fundamental ideological differences.[25] The Russian did not think the workingman should engage in a *political* fight or that there should be a workingmen's party. On the contrary, he believed the worker should show his power by using force to win his rights.[26] Marx had fought that sort of thinking since 1849, but now, because ideas spread more swiftly and broadly, it was more dangerous. Marx believed revolution always resulted in bloodshed but violence should not be the path of first resort; he emphatically did not want to see the International turned into an insurgent army.

Marx had never attended an International Congress outside London, but such was the importance of the 1872 event that he and his entire family— including the two Frenchmen who hoped to become family, Longuet and Lissagaray—traveled to Holland. So, of course, did Engels. The meeting would be the International's first public gathering since the Commune, and rumors flew through the press that members would be deciding their next acts of terror. Journalists from around the world descended on The Hague to report on the coven of violent radicals. Marx was mobbed by reporters. Some simply wanted to see him; others wanted to scoop the competition by being the first to reveal his dastardly plans.[27] The hysteria was pervasive. A local paper warned citizens not to allow their wives and daughters on the street while the International was in town, and jewelers were told to shutter their shops.[28] But the press and the police were disappointed: the delegates were as orderly as commercial conventioneers, down to the blue bands they wore to be easily recognizable.[29]

About sixty-five delegates from fifteen countries arrived to participate, and for the first three days discussions focused on who would be awarded credentials to attend.[30] Finally, on September 5, the Fifth Annual Congress of the First International Working Men's Association got under way in a dance hall next to a prison in a working-class district of The Hague. The tables were arranged in a horseshoe pattern, and the hall featured a balcony from which spectators could watch the bureaucracy of revolution in action.[31] The Marx women joined those viewing from above.

After her traumas in France and Spain, Laura had arrived at The Hague thin and ill; the family was aghast at the change in her. Despite her weakened state, she took pains with her appearance so that the world might not see her sorrow—Laura, inheritor of her father's pride, would not give the "philistines" the satisfaction of seeing her suffer.[32] Kugelmann, who had never met her, found her beautiful, elegant, and amiable. He also encountered Jenny for the first time. After corresponding with her for years and hearing of the family's hardships, he might have expected a matronly woman with a face lined with cares. Instead, Jenny was slim and seemingly much younger than her fifty-eight years. So absorbed was she in the proceedings that Kugelmann came away believing it was Jenny who had lured Marx into radical politics in the first place.[33]

Tussy, there with "Lissa," looked very much the young woman.[34] She now wore her hair piled high, with a few stray curls escaping down her forehead. Around her neck she wore a velvet ribbon, and her neckline had plunged by several degrees. The style was in no way revealing, but it was a greater exhibition of flesh than the Marx women had been known to indulge in. Finally, Jennychen: of all her siblings she had changed the least, except that her quiet inner happiness had become uncharacteristically public due to her engagement to Longuet.

Down below at the tables, Marx sat behind Engels. But if he was trying to remain in the shadows, he failed utterly: all eyes in the spectators' gallery were fixed on him, a brooding giant with a shock of gray hair and beard, smoking and writing furiously on a notepad, the very embodiment of their rebellion.[35] Though the number of delegates in attendance was rather small, those watching were many—one newspaper said there were ten times more people than the room could accommodate[36]—and it seemed that almost everyone had something to say. The din was atrocious. Calls to order were ignored, shouts turned to arguments, and arguments nearly became fistfights.

From the beginning Marx's allies had the advantage. Numerically they were far superior to Bakunin's supporters, and Bakunin had chosen not to attend. The first vote was a proposal to allow the General Council to remain as the brains of the organization rather than reduce its power, as Bakunin's followers wanted, to a mere postal address and correspondence center. The Marx faction won, and the council retained its power. Next on the agenda was an item that one delegate called nothing less than a "coup d'état." Marx and Engels had orchestrated the move in advance. Engels stood, cigar in hand, and in his usual conversational tone, occasionally replacing a stray lock of hair that had tumbled across his forehead, he proposed that the General Council be moved from London to New York. What he didn't say was that such relocation would help Marx ease his way out of the International leadership and ensure that Bakunin did not get hold of the group. Though there were anarchists in the United States, their numbers were minuscule, and the American horror of political violence would be a bulwark against their making significant gains. When Engels finished speaking, the room erupted. Critics protested that the council might as well be transferred to the moon. Like any good politician, Marx had calculated the votes in advance of Engels's move, to make sure it would pass—which it did, with help from Bakunin's followers, oddly enough, who believed moving the IWMA to New York was tantamount to stripping it of all authority, which was what they wanted anyway.[37]

On the final day of the congress it was Marx's turn to drop a bomb in his long battle against Bakunin. Since arriving at The Hague he had been so nervous he'd barely slept. In that enervated condition, after days of largely sitting quietly while everyone else in the hall stood, Marx pushed back his chair. The room went quiet. It fell to him to describe how Bakunin and a group of his followers had secretly worked to undermine the International and how a "personal affair" (the Nechayev threat and murder) that had been discussed in an investigating committee but would not be aired publicly proved the reckless nature of Bakunin's anarchists. In fact Marx did not have to disclose the Nechayev story—it had already raced through the hall. Everyone knew what he meant.[38]

Marx was a forceful speaker in front of a small group, but faced with a larger audience, his strength of voice and manner were diminished. As he'd aged, he increasingly resembled an erudite and somewhat eccentric professor; the monocle in his right eye fell out periodically during his address, and he would stop his speech to replace it.[39] Yet even without a dramatic delivery, the room listened intently to his every word. Most important, the audience agreed with him: Bakunin and a colleague were expelled.[40] After the vote was read, a Spanish Bakunist with a red flag tied around his waist pulled out a gun and, turning to the delegate who announced the result, shouted, "A man like that ought to be shot!"[41] He was quickly seized and disarmed. Marx could not have asked for a better illustration of his argument against Bakunin.

With that, Marx's work in the International officially ended. That night he took his family and a few friends to the Grand Hotel at nearby Scheveningen. The elegant hostelry was just the sort of place Marx and Jenny would have known in Trier. As its gaslights reflected off the North Sea waters, music from a string orchestra filled the air. Now, with his "enslavement" to the IWMA ended, Marx could return to private life as a husband, father, and theoretician. That night he began the transition, surrounded by his daughters and closest friends. The party dined, danced, and went for a swim. Still, because this was a Marx gathering, it was not without drama: one member of the group swam out too far, and Engels, the good soldier, dove to the man's rescue.[42]

The next day, September 8, 1872, Marx gave his last public speech, an address arguably much more important than anything he had said at the congress just ended. It helped fuel debate among his followers into the next century as ruptures formed between those who believed Marx to be a pacifist at heart and those who believed him to be an advocate of violent revolution. In fact, his speech to the IWMA local in Amsterdam showed him to be both. Marx emphasized that historical precedents would dictate how revolution would be achieved in each country and that the answer would not be the same for all.

> One day the worker will have to seize political supremacy to establish the new organization of labor; he will have to overthrow the old policy which supports the old institutions if he wants to escape the fate of the early Christians who, neglecting and despising politics, never saw their kingdom on earth.
>
> But we by no means claimed that the means for achieving this goal were identical everywhere. We know that the institutions, customs and traditions in the different countries must be taken into account; and we do not deny the existence of countries like America, England, and if I knew your institutions better I might add Holland, where the workers may achieve their aims by peaceful means. That being true we must also admit that in most countries on the Continent it is force which must be the lever of our revolution; it is force which will have to be resorted to for a time in order to establish the rule of the workers.

Marx pledged his fidelity to the struggle even as his day-to-day involvement diminished. "I am not withdrawing from the International," two press reports quoted him as saying, "and the rest of my life will be devoted, like my efforts in the past, to the triumph of the social ideas which one day, be sure of it, will bring about the universal rule of the proletariat."[43]

Marx's path out of the International and his battle with Bakunin had both, in the end, been relatively easy. Marx had prepared his case well and made sure that the delegate count was in his favor. But he was also aided by the fact that Bakunin was not there. The Russian claimed that he hadn't attended the Hague meeting because of a lack of money,[44] but he may have known from experience that it wasn't worth exerting himself because his rival could not lose—the International was, after all, Marx's offspring. In any case, Bakunin had had nothing but bad luck that year and seemed to have no energy for a fight.[45] His friend Nechayev had been arrested in Switzerland and would eventually be sent to the Fortress of Peter and Paul.[46] Bakunin's young wife, Antonia, had taken an Italian lover and had two children with him, a union ultimately sanctioned by Bakunin because he did not, perhaps could not, give her the attention she required or deserved.[47] Finally, the already enormous Russian had become even heavier. (Friends described him as elephantine.) He panted at the slightest movement, and when he tried to put on his boots, his face turned blue.[48] Two years after the congress Bakunin would announce his withdrawal from public life, declaring, "Henceforth I shall trouble no man's repose, and I ask in my turn, to be left in peace."[49] He refurbished his wardrobe and fitted himself up as a proper Swiss bourgeois. He called himself the "last of the Mohicans"[50] and said if there were three people in the world, two of them would want to repress the third.[51] Like his German rival, Bakunin had realized that it was his time to step aside.

On October 9, 1872, a month after the meeting, Jennychen and Longuet finally married at the St. Pancras Registry office where Lafargue and Laura had been wed more than four years earlier.[52] It was an altogether more businesslike affair than the Lafargue marriage, partly because Jennychen and Longuet were now twenty-eight and thirty-three respectively, and partly because their original plan to marry had been postponed. Everyone in the Marx family already considered them husband and wife by the time the law recognized their union as official.

The Longuets left London immediately for Oxford, where Charles was employed giving French lessons, but the start of their married life was not auspicious. Longuet's name had been listed among the IWMA members attending the Hague gathering, and one by one his pupils offered apologies and declined further instruction.[53] He and Jennychen had no time to settle into a pleasant routine before they were plunged into an all-too-familiar struggle for survival. Jennychen did not mention their situation to her family; she was much too independent to throw herself on the mercy of her parents. But there was an undercurrent of anxiety in her letters to Marx that one might not expect from a new bride. On October 30 she wrote: "My dear Nicky—you cannot imagine how I long to see you again. I feel as if I had been away from you all for centuries. This morning when I saw your handwriting again I could not help having a good cry."[54] In another letter she confessed, "I had a great longing to come over to Hampstead last Sunday. The devil bade me go by all means—but conscience that makes cowards of us all advised me to be prudent and reminded me that the journey to Hampstead costs twenty shillings—to remain where I was."[55] Perhaps Marx recognized all was not well, because in November he went to Oxford. Longuet was reviewing the French translation of *Capital,* so Marx's visit would not have raised suspicions that he was on a mission to discover how married life was treating his daughter.[56] Yet soon afterward, whether at Marx's instigation or prompted by the realization that they simply could not afford to remain in Oxford without work, Longuet and Jennychen decided to move back to London.

The Lafargues had been in the city since late October, having stayed in Holland for a holiday after the congress before making their way to Modena Villas. Her parents both remarked that Laura looked much better than when she had arrived at The Hague, but she was far from well. The Lafargues moved back into the Marx home, where Lenchen and Jenny, singularly well suited to care for a young woman who had lost her children, worked to bring Laura back to life. By mid-November she was restored enough that she and Paul decided to move into a flat nearby. As the Marxes' revolving door swung open for their departure, it admitted the Longuets.

Jennychen was disappointed that their Oxford experience had been a failure but soon admitted that she could not be happy away from London. She told Kugelmann, "London contains Modena Villas and in the front room first floor of Modena V. I can always find my dear Mohr. I cannot express to you how lonely I feel when separated from him—and he tells me that he also missed me very much and that during my absences he buried himself altogether in his den."[57]

On December 7 a delighted Engels announced in a letter to a colleague in New York that for the first time in four years Marx *père* was once again surrounded by his entire family.[58] As a statement this was true, but any implication of domestic harmony would have been less than accurate. Before Jennychen returned from Oxford, Tussy had written her an angry letter describing a scene involving Lafargue and Laura upon meeting Lissagaray at the Marx home. He was there with a friend, with whom the Lafargues shook hands, but when they turned to Lissagaray, Lafargue and Laura merely bowed. That same coldness was displayed the next night. Astounded by their rudeness, Tussy wrote her eldest sister, "Either Lissagaray is the perfect gentleman Paul's letter and his own behavior proclaim him to be, and then he should be treated as such, or else he is no gentleman, and then he ought not to be received by us—one or the other—but this really unladylike behavior on Laura's part is very disagreeable."[59]

The episode would hardly be worth mentioning except that the Lafargues' decision to shun Lissagaray colored Tussy and Laura's relationship for years. In fact, it never fully recovered its warmth. It was not clear why the Lafargues behaved the way they did; no explanation was passed down in family lore, and there are no letters to provide a hint. It may simply have been that the two men's paths had crossed in journalistic circles in France and somehow Lissagaray had offended Paul, who could not abandon the grudge. Or perhaps it was Laura who objected to his presence. In her fragile state she may have been unable to countenance another Frenchman (with nothing more than revolutionary credentials to recommend him) seducing another Marx daughter. As she looked at her own and Jennychen's lives, she could not have helped but see that far from escaping their mother's lot they had run headlong into it. (Jennychen even told Longuet she had dreamed she had smallpox like her mother and was so hideous he refused to see her.)[60]

Both young married couples were beset by financial woes. In Spain, Lafargue had spent nearly his entire inheritance from his father.[61] He had his English medical license but refused to practice, explaining that he could not enter a field that had failed to save his three children. That left him and Laura scrambling for work. Marx tried to help by soliciting writing jobs for Lafargue from as far away as Russia, but such work was hard to get and notoriously low paying.[62] In February, Lafargue turned his hand to business, going in with Marx's friend from 1848 Eugène Dupont on a workshop that used Dupont's patent to make brass musical instruments. They lacked the capital needed to thrive, and the business soon failed.[63] So, too, did another opportunity involving an engraving patent that partnered Lafargue with socialists George Moore and Benjamin Le Moussu.[64] In that case Marx briefly stepped in to take Lafargue's place and assume his financial responsibility, but by the end of the year Marx had withdrawn and Engels was forced to pay debts amounting to about £150.[65] Lafargue might have realized he had no talent for business, but, ever the optimist, he tried again, this time setting up a photolithographic and etching workshop in his kitchen with the goal of becoming financially independent.[66] Meanwhile, as her husband bet on doomed ventures, Laura helped pay the bills by giving private language lessons.[67]

Longuet could not find work either. He had not had steady employment in the two years since the end of the Commune, and London was crawling with French refugees vying for teaching and writing jobs.[68] Like Laura, Jennychen made up for his lack of income by tutoring. She posted placards in nearly every shopwindow in the vicinity and scoured the city offering her services as a teacher of language or music, an endeavor she mockingly called "the delightful battle known as the struggle for life." Blaming herself in part for Longuet's inability to find a job, Jennychen worked doubly hard. She told Kugelmann they would have had more luck in a small town, but "despite my marriage, my heart is bound to the place where my father is found and life elsewhere would not be life for me. If all fails however I suppose I must leave him.... But sufficient for the day is the evil thereof—I will not think of it beforehand."[69]

Madame Marx, however, equated Longuet's joblessness with a lack of industriousness. In a long lament to Liebknecht she wrote, "We are now atoning, in all respects for our youthful enthusiasm for the Paris Commune and its refugees (political loafers par excellence). I cannot go into details here as they are not fit for letters."[70] She may have also had Lissagaray in mind.

In March, Marx and Tussy went to Brighton. Marx was exhausted from his work on the French translation of *Capital* and the second edition of *Capital, Volume I* for Meissner. The French version was to appear in forty-four installments, which dragged out the already difficult translation process over three years. The second German edition would also appear in installments—in that case only nine, between July 1872 and April 1873—after which it would be published again as a book.[71] For Marx the intensity of the project was no less than if he were writing *Capital* for the first time. He was a phantom in his own household. Rising every day at seven for several cups of black coffee, he then retreated into his study until the early afternoon, when the General arrived[72] for what Jennychen called forced marches on the Heath.[73] Next came dinner at five (Marx usually had to be called three times for meals), and then after the last mouthful he returned to his study, where he remained until two or three in the morning.[74]

Tussy also needed a break; she was not overworked, but overwrought. She was now eighteen and passionately involved in a forbidden affair. Her family knew about Lissagaray, but her father had employed his rarely used veto to block her putative happiness. Perhaps Marx thought that away from London, he could gently persuade Tussy that the marriage would never work. The Marx powers of persuasion failed on this occasion, however, and an affronted Tussy announced to her father that she intended to stay in Brighton and find tutoring jobs there. Marx may have been stunned by the turn of events but, perhaps believing that in relocating, Tussy might more easily discard Lissa, he agreed. Jenny, however, saw her youngest daughter's decision as rash and potentially dangerous. In May and June she sent Tussy numerous letters full of the pettiest concerns.[75] She tried to reassure Tussy she understood "how much you yearn for work and independence, the only two things that will help to overcome the suffering and worries of the current situation."[76] And again, remembering her own forbidden love for Marx when she was a girl, Jenny wrote, "Be *brave,* be *courageous.* Do not let this fearful crisis overwhelm you. Believe me, despite appearances to the contrary, nobody understands your position, your conflict, your embitterment better than I do."[77] Jenny left much unsaid, but the urgency and frequency of her letters underscored her comprehension of Tussy's turmoil and her awareness of the impact that stress—or worse, depression—could have on her daughter's health (Jenny's own depression, not to mention Marx's creative turmoil, had often manifested itself as a physical ailment). She was also sensitive to the imprudent actions Tussy might take if she felt unloved or misunderstood.

In May, Tussy began teaching German and French part time at a seminary for young women.[78] After less than a month, however, she began coughing up blood, and Jenny rushed to Brighton to be with her. She discovered her daughter was indeed ill but refused her entreaties to return to London.[79] Jenny also learned from the women who ran the school that a man they referred to as "Tussy's fiancé" had visited her there several times and was allowed to do so because they were engaged. To save her daughter from embarrassment Jenny did not clarify the relationship, nor did she tell Marx what she had learned. She knew that Marx planned to write Tussy about Lissagaray, and the new information would only inflame the situation.[80]

Marx, in fact, wrote two letters, one to Tussy and one to Lissagaray, but because neither is known to exist, there is no way of knowing what they contained.[81] The only hint comes days later when Marx, writing to Engels, described Tussy's reply. Tussy reproached Marx for being unfair, but he told her, "I asked nothing of [Lissagaray] but that he should provide proof instead of words that he was better than his reputation and that there was some good reason to rely on him." He told Engels, "The damned nuisance is that I must be very circumspect and indulgent because of the child. I shall not answer until I have consulted you on my return. Keep the letter by you."[82]

Jenny, meanwhile, tried to lure Tussy away from Brighton, away from Marx and Engels, and away from Lissagaray, by suggesting that she accompany Lenchen to Germany in June. Tussy seemed receptive to the idea, aside from the impediment of her teaching job.[83] Indeed the headmistresses were outraged that she would want a holiday halfway through the school term, and drafted a haughty letter to Jenny declaring that they were "much surprised and annoyed" by the news. Jenny, who had no concern for and very little experience with such conventions as schedules, shot back, "I am much annoyed to hear you cannot spare my daughter."[84]

In the end Tussy did not join Lenchen on the trip. Instead, deflated at her failed first attempt at independence, she returned home, where the press reported that her father was very ill—and where her sister Jennychen tried in vain to conceal the fact that she was pregnant.

Since 1844 no Marx child had been born into wealth or comfort, and Charles Félicien Marx Longuet was no exception when he entered the world on September 3, 1873. After living at Modena Villas for eight months, Longuet still had not found work, "neither lessons nor literature courses, neither translation nor correspondence," Madame Marx wrote Liebknecht with unconcealed displeasure. "Jenny on the contrary has due to her utter energy, restless activity and constant walking through rain, wind and snow for hours found some lessons which however are not very profitable.... This distinguished being deserves better. Mohr overlooks a lot because of his fantastical love. Unfortunately, I cannot be that diplomatic, so I will probably get the reputation for being the evil mother-in-law."[85] Jenny's concern for her daughter was understandable, though she was not entirely fair to Longuet. He did try to find work, as far afield as Manchester, but was just one more destitute Frenchman, with the added burden of being a communard and a member of Marx's International.[86]

As to Marx's health, a British newspaper report in June 1873 claimed that Marx was gravely ill. The story came from an English member of the General Council, and it soon spread to newspapers throughout Europe. Used to announcements of his death or arrest, Marx's friends and family barely noticed such revelations. But perhaps because he had so abruptly quit the IWMA the previous year without clearly stating his reasons, this story of illness rang true, and letters poured in from anxious friends; curious others appeared at the Marx door to personally investigate.[87] Jenny joked about it with Liebknecht, who'd read the report in a German paper. "I hope that the newspapers have exaggerated and that the condition of my dear husband is not actually dangerous."[88] Yet the levity masked real concern: the Marxes did not want the world to know that Karl was indeed ill, and that his condition was more serious than his usual worry-induced maladies. For months he had suffered from insomnia and intense headaches. He tried sleeping potions but they had no effect. Through it all he refused to stop working on the translations of *Capital,* and behind his professional worries lurked his concerns over the turn his daughters' lives had taken[89] (what Jenny called "major, heavy, unutterable family issues"[90]). Finally, after Marx's blood pressure rose dangerously high, Engels persuaded him to go to Manchester to see the only doctor they both trusted, an eighty-year-old German named Eduard Gumpert. Gumpert ordered Marx to overhaul his lifestyle—limit his work, change his diet, drink soda water with wine. The most important recommendation was to stop late-night writing. That, if continued, could kill him.

Marx returned from Manchester much improved, and Jenny, Lenchen, and Engels made sure he stuck to Gumpert's prescription. They also agreed that the only way to ensure Marx would not slip into his old habits was for him to leave London for a long spa stay.[91] That fall he took Tussy with him on the first of what would be many trips in pursuit of restored health, on this occasion to the English town of Harrogate.[92] They arrived after the "season" and had the hotel to themselves, except for a world-weary Church of England parson who Marx—from a place of ideological consistency or mere observation—claimed cared for nothing except his belly.[93]

In his later years Marx would remark on the importance of the micro-scopic world versus the macroscopic—the microscopic being the family and the macroscopic everything else, but mostly things political. After the Hague conference he began to retreat into that small world of the people around him, but he did not stop working. And though he had formally disassociated himself from the IWMA, he was still an object of pilgrimage for visitors from around the world who revered him as its founder. The demands of such intrusions, however, gradually became nothing more than pleasurable social diversions; they did not consume him as they once had. Even pesky journalists, who periodically sought him out for an interview when they remembered a "terrorist" lived in London, were treated by Marx more as a bit of fun than antagonistic or challenging encounters. He was a large-pawed cat who gently batted around these small mice, knowing he could crush them but delighting in the game instead. He told Kugelmann he didn't "give a farthing for the public." Much more important now were the people within his reach.[94]

Secondary to that was his health. Gumpert had been suggesting for years that Marx go to Karlsbad to take a water cure, and for years Marx had resisted (he said the Austrian spa would be boring and expensive[95]). After a pleasant stay in Harrogate, however, he had finally come around to considering it. Though enjoyable, Harrogate had produced only tempo-rary relief. Gumpert assured him Karlsbad would result in a cure. Marx began contemplating the trip in May, but a few obstacles had to be cleared up before he traveled, one of which was the old matter of a passport. The year Laura had moved to Paris as a new bride, he had considered applying for some form of British citizenship yet had never followed through. To make a journey to Austria that year, he would need to.

European governments still saw the International as a driving force behind social violence. In 1872 and 1873 the Three Emperors' League—Austria-Hungary, Russia, and Germany—met to chart a defense strategy and devise a united front against the IWMA and its offspring.[96] A crack-down began almost immediately.[97] However, an economic crash in 1873 proved more terrifying than the threat of government reprisal, and once again men and women flocked to join workers' organizations seeking pro-tection from the vicissitudes of the capitalist marketplace.[98] In the wake of this upheaval, working-class parties in Germany made marked election gains. Meanwhile, Russia saw student riots in 1873 and 1874, and the simultaneous widespread persecution of socialists, liberals, and democrats. In one multicity sweep in 1874 alone, sixteen hundred Russian socialists propagandizing among the workers were arrested and held for trial; one of the texts they had used to educate the workers was *Capital*.[99] Finally, just as Marx was considering going to Karlsbad, a trial of socialist activists began in nearby Vienna. One man was indicted merely for mailing a picture of the "Social Communist K.M."[100] In such an environment Marx needed the protection of the British crown, so on the first of August, he applied to become a naturalized British citizen. Perhaps predictably, he was rejected. A Scotland Yard report noted, "With reference to the above I beg to report that he is the notorious German agitator, the head of the International Society, and an advocate of Communistic principles. This man has not been loyal to his own King and Country."[101]

By 1874 Lafargue was so broke he wanted to sell the only portion of his inheritance he still possessed—a home in New Orleans. He needed money immediately, so Engels loaned him six hundred pounds against the sale of the property.[102] Longuet, however, had no such reserve and still had not found work. His mother provided some money, and Jennychen worked as a governess and gave lessons, but they were extremely pressed for cash. Still, in April they moved out of the Marx home into an apartment nearby. Jenny later indicated that she and Karl had encouraged the move, but they clearly lived to regret it. Jennychen's health was poor— her breathing was labored and she could not sleep—and by summer the baby, nicknamed Caro, was ill.

At about this time Marx and Jenny took a rare trip together. Husband and wife, now fifty-six and sixty respectively, traveled to the Isle of Wight, five miles off England's south coast, and rented rooms at a sun-splashed house with huge windows on a hill in the town of Ryde, overlooking the sea. The climate was almost Italian. Marx wrote Engels, "This ISLAND is a little paradise." Usually Marx apologized for not corresponding because he was so busy. In this case he told Engels he could not write because he was so thoroughly idle. He and Jenny toured the island by boat and roamed its hills on foot, enjoying each other's company in a way they had not been able to do for years, perhaps decades. They laughed over a local election poster that baldly stated "Vote for Stanley, *the Rich Man*" and an excursion boat of temperance advocates, half of whom were drunk. (Marx told Engels, "Neither have I ever actually experienced such a mob of stunted, loutish and smutty-minded idiots all at once, the women as ugly

Jenny Marx in Brighton, England, in 1864, where she celebrated her family's new life of ease after receiving inheritances that provided them with more money than they had ever possessed. (IISG, Amsterdam)

Eleanor Marx at about fifteen, when her attention and that of her family turned to France's war with Prussia in 1870 and the 1871 Paris Commune. (IISG, Amsterdam)

Marx's daughters Jenny (standing) and Laura, circa 1865, when their father and the International Working Men's Association began to draw a younger generation of followers to their home. (IISG, Amsterdam)

French journalist Charles Longuet, circa 1871, the year he arrived in London after escaping prosecution in France for participating in the Paris Commune. (IISG, Amsterdam)

Paul Lafargue, circa 1866, when he arrived in London to become a member of the International Working Men's Association and met Marx's daughter Laura. (IISG, Amsterdam)

Hyppolite-Prosper-Olivier Lissagaray (undated). A French journalist and count whose family cast him out because of his radical politics, he was secretly engaged to Eleanor Marx when she was just seventeen and he thirty-four. (David King Collection, London)

Gustave Flourens (undated) arrived at the Marx home after having escaped Paris in 1870. He was a soldier and a scholar, and as such a favorite among the Marx women, especially Marx's eldest daughter, Jenny. (IISG, Amsterdam)

Friedrich Engels, now retired, moved back to London in 1870 to join Marx in running the International Working Men's Association and help handle the flood of refugees following the Paris Commune. (David King Collection, London)

Lizzy Burns lived with Engels from the time she was a fifteen year old working in a factory in Manchester. She was a radical Irish nationalist and a Fenian. She and Engels finally married on the eve of her death in 1878. (IISG, Amsterdam)

This photograph has been mistakenly identified in numerous books as a portrait of Helene Demuth. A Russian researcher discovered it was Lizzy Burns's niece, Mary Ellen Burns, taken in 1875 in Heidelberg. It could not have been Helene because, among other things, the year it was taken she was forty-five, and the picture clearly portrays a young woman. (IISG, Amsterdam)

Charles and Jenny Marx Longuet in Ramsgate in 1880, after an amnesty for former Communards was granted by the new French government and Charles prepared to return to France to resume his life there. (David King Collection, London)

The last picture of Jenny Marx, taken sometime in the year before her death from cancer in 1881. (IISG, Amsterdam)

Marx, circa 1881, when health and family troubles dominated his life. (IISG, Amsterdam)

The last photograph of Marx, taken in Algiers in 1882, during a year he spent traveling to recover his health and ease the pain caused by the death of his wife, Jenny. (IISG, Amsterdam)

Wilhelm Liebknecht (standing left), Edward Aveling, and Eleanor Marx-Aveling during their U.S. speaking tour in 1886. The tour ended in scandal when Aveling was accused of expecting workingmen to pay for his lavish spending. (IISG, Amsterdam)

From 1882 until her death in 1911, Laura Lafargue lived quietly with her husband in France, translating her father's and Engels's work, and haunted by the deaths of her three children. (David King Collection, London)

Marx; his wife, Jenny; their grandson Harry; and Helene Demuth were all buried under the family headstone at Highgate Cemetery in London. The family thought the simple stone (fourth grave from front, with urn and flowers) was all that was necessary to commemorate Marx. (IISG, Amsterdam)

In 1956 the Communist Party unveiled a monument to Marx that stands in Highgate Cemetery in London today and contains the remains of Marx; his wife, Jenny; their daughter Eleanor and grandson Harry; and Helene Demuth. (IISG, Amsterdam)

as sin.") Through it all, Marx declared his health improved, "above all no pills required."[103]

It was during this decade that family and friends often remarked on the deep love Marx and Jenny felt for each other. It may not always have been so. There were periods during the 1860s when Jenny seemed to have positively frozen her heart to him—when he was being entertained at the opera in Berlin with Lassalle and the countess while she struggled to buy coal; or later, when she and the girls celebrated Christmas like paupers, without even a letter from Marx, while he was pampered by his uncle Lion and cousin Nanette in Holland. But in their later years, the Marxes were again true partners in every sense. Tussy said they were like children: "Again and again, especially if the circumstances were demanding decorum and sedateness, have I seen them laugh till tears ran down their cheeks, and even those inclined to be shocked at such awful levity could not choose but laugh with them. And how often have I seen them not daring to look at one another, each knowing that once a glance was exchanged uncontrollable laughter would result."[104] A Russian friend, Maxim Kovalevsky, said, "Marx more than anybody else I have ever met, not excluding Turgenev, had the right to say of himself that he was a man of one love."[105]

They might have suspected that their precious time alone together would not last, and it did not: Marx and Jenny were called back to London in late July. Jennychen's eleven-month-old baby had died of what Marx called a "sudden and terrible attack of gastroenteritis."[106] Once again sorrow pervaded the Marx home. Four children had been born to the Marx daughters, and four children had died. Marx told Engels he slept badly: "I had taken the little chap to my heart."[107] But he was no doubt more troubled by Jennychen, who was devastated by her loss. Engels insisted that she leave London immediately to stay with him and Lizzy in Ramsgate. She agreed.[108]

Marx arrived back in London in time to accompany his grieving daughter to the coast on August 6. They traveled quietly together by train through the Kent countryside, a land as lush and fertile as the travelers were joyless and empty.[109] As if the trip had been designed to make her pain even worse, Jennychen was tormented by the presence in their car of a young mother and her bouncing nine-month-old infant.[110]

Marx was haunted by his grandson's death and his daughter's agony. Though it was high summer in London, even at noon the sky was fittingly gray and somber. He wrote Jennychen after returning to Modena Villas, "My darling child...the house is as silent as the grave, now that our little angel is not there to animate it. I miss him at every turn. My heart bleeds when I think of him, and how can one get such a sweet, lovable little chap out of one's mind! But I hope, my child, that you will be brave for your old man's sake."[111] He considered delaying his trip to Karlsbad, but may have felt reassured that Jennychen was being taken care of by Engels, who had decided to travel on from Ramsgate to Jersey with Jennychen and Lizzy. In any case, Tussy, too, represented something of an emergency. She had been ill for months, refused to eat, and was again spitting up blood. She was also moody and glum—in short, the mirror opposite of the buoyant young woman who had once charmed everyone she met. The source of her emotional anguish was her father's edict against her relationship with Lissagaray. In March Tussy had written Marx a pleading letter begging him to allow her to see her lover.

> My dearest Mohr,
> I am going to ask you something, but first I want you to promise me that you will not be angry. I want to know, dear Mohr, when I may see L. again. It is so very hard never to see him. I have been doing my best to be patient, but it is so difficult and I don't feel as if I could be much longer.... Could I not, now and then, go for a little walk with him?... No one moreover will be astonished to see us together, as everybody knows we are engaged.

She told her father that when she was ill in Brighton, Lissagaray left her stronger and happier with each visit. "It is so long since I saw him and I am beginning to feel so very miserable notwithstanding all my efforts to keep up, for I have tried hard to be merry and cheerful. I cannot much longer.... My dearest Mohr, please don't be angry with me for writing this, but forgive me for being selfish enough to worry you again.... This is quite between us."[112]

Perhaps the family had enough troubles after Caro's death without creating new problems, so the ban was lifted.[113] By mid-August, Marx told Engels, "Tussy is feeling much better; her appetite is growing in geometric PROPORTION, but it is the characteristic feature of these women's ailments in which hysteria plays a part; you have to pretend not to notice that the invalid is again living on earthly sustenance. This too becomes unnecessary once recovery is complete."[114] To make sure, however, Marx decided to take Tussy to Karlsbad. He would travel without a passport, and if he encountered trouble, retreat to less reactionary Hamburg. He told Jennychen he was vexed by all the political intrigue at just that moment: "After a long period in which neither the 'International' nor myself had attracted any attention, it is very curious that my name should have figured again JUST NOW in trials in Petersburg and Vienna, and that ridiculous RIOTS in Italy should be connected not only with the 'International' but...directly with me."[115]

Karlsbad was a bourgeois retreat with a legendary guest list—Bach, Goethe, Schiller, Beethoven, and Chopin.[116] One of Marx's neighbors at the Haus Germania was the Russian novelist Ivan Turgenev. Neither man mentioned the other in his correspondence,[117] but it was a near certainty that they at least knew of the other even if they were not in fact acquainted, since Turgenev was a lightning rod for both radicals and conservatives in Russia, and he had been one of Bakunin's closest friends in Berlin.

Kugelmann had made the arrangements for Marx and Tussy's stay. He and his wife and daughter were also there, on what seemed from his letters to be almost an annual visit to the spa in what is today the Czech Republic. To deflect suspicion, Marx took pains when he registered to appear to be a man of independent means. He signed in as Herr Charles Marx, private gentleman, and looked every bit the part.[118] At the time of Marx's stay a Polish aristocrat named Count Plater was also in residence at Karlsbad. So impeccable was Marx's dress that another guest said if one were asked which of the two was the count, the answer would be Marx.[119] Before long Marx and the count were friends, a relationship that fired the imagination of a local reporter, who with the usual flair for fiction wrote that Count Plater was the "chief of the nihilists" (Tussy noted, "You may suppose how horrified the old fellow was"[120]) and that he was consorting with Marx, "the chief of the International."[121] Police did, in fact, have Marx under surveillance, but left him unmolested, since he did not appear to be plotting anything more than a speedy recovery from liver trouble. Doctors described him as a model guest.

Franzisca Kugelmann was several years younger than Tussy, and neither she nor her mother, Gertruda, seemed to have entirely approved of Tussy's behavior or her father's permissiveness. Franzisca described Tussy's dress as elegant but too showy (Marx, she said, defended his daughter by saying, "Young women must smarten themselves up"). The Kugelmann women found her too direct ("She would say straight out to anyone what she thought—even when it was something she disliked about the person"). And they were appalled by her manners ("She sat in restaurants smoking cigarettes and buried in newspapers"). Tussy also set tongues wagging by showing Gertruda a letter from Lissagaray addressed to Tussy as "my little wife."[122]

The Kugelmann women's simmering resentment over Tussy's independence may have had something to do with Gertruda's own sense of imprisonment. In fact, during his stay Marx grew to absolutely despise Kugelmann for his treatment of his wife. Marx's room was adjacent to the Kugelmanns' suite, and he was forced to listen to what Tussy called an "abominable scene" between husband and wife over Kugelmann's long-standing complaint that Gertruda was ungrateful for his material kindness. The event that had ignited the fight was Gertruda's failure to lift up her dress on a dusty day to protect the hem. Marx moved to a higher floor and severed all ties with this loyalist and sometime benefactor.[123]

After leaving Karlsbad and its bitter taste of Kugelmann, Marx took Tussy on a tour of, among other places, the spot where he and Jenny had spent their honeymoon. He also wanted to see old friends and meet new party members.[124] Stopping in Leipzig to see Liebknecht, Marx was informed that a twenty-five-year-old social democrat named Wilhelm Blos was about to be released from prison, where he had served time for his political views. Blos strode through the prison door a free man to find Liebknecht, his son, and, to his amazement, a beautiful young woman nearby on the arm of a white-haired gentleman: "I recognized him immediately from his picture: it was Karl Marx."[125]

Father and daughter had two more stops to make. One was to see the publisher Meissner in Hamburg and the other to see Edgar von Westphalen in Berlin. After leaving Modena Villas, where he'd stayed for six months recovering from his Civil War experience, Edgar had settled among his family in Germany, still Marx's devoted follower but dependent on the charity of the reactionary side of the family. Managing to evade security, Tussy and Marx remained in Berlin for three days, visiting Edgar and touring Marx's old haunts. Edgar later told them that the police had arrived looking for Marx an hour after he and Tussy had checked out of their hotel.[126]

The pair returned to London more serene in every way than when they had left. Karlsbad may not have resulted in a cure for their ailing bodies, but it provided enough of a temporary balm that they both looked forward to getting back to work. And, more important, they were reconciled after their breach over Lissagaray. Marx seemed to have accepted the fact (at least temporarily) that his eighteen-year-old daughter had accomplished what political foes and rival revolutionaries alike had failed to do—best him in a contest of wills. He continued to object to her engagement, but his only recourse was to let things take their course and hope that Tussy had the wisdom to end the relationship. Given the misery of his other daughters, Marx may have wished they'd had such wisdom, too.

40

London, 1875

I am in this respect less stoical than in others and family afflictions always hit me hard. The more one lives, as I do, almost cut off from the outside world, the more one is entangled in the emotional life of one's own circle.

—Karl Marx[1]

JENNYCHEN'S GRIEF OVER the death of her first child was profound. The baby was buried at Highgate Cemetery, which she could see from her bedroom window. Caro's resting place was therefore close enough to comfort her with the thought that her son was still near, but too close to provide any relief from her guilt and sadness. She told Longuet she imagined their "sweet birdie in the damp cold earth" and wished "we were both of us there with him."[2] The streets and shops were haunted by images of him, every child's cry or giggle, every brown-haired boy, reminding Jennychen of what her Caro might have become. Physically she grew stronger, but that only made her feel worse.[3] Like her father, she found that physical pain helped numb her emotional anguish; it made her heartache almost bearable.

Engels and Lizzy had done their best in the weeks after Caro's death to distract her. Engels was aware that she spent sleepless nights brooding over the child, yet in his robust fashion he assured Marx that with rest, she would recover.[4] But Jennychen told Longuet she did her best to hide her true feelings: "I wear my usual mask and so I trust do not spoil the stay of my friends by showing them my hopeless face." She counted the moments when she could return to London. The days felt like weeks, the weeks, months.[5] From Jersey she wrote her husband,

It is strange, the calm and smiling beauty of this summer island only makes me feel more and more restless and hopelessly sad. Yesterday we drove through the most lovely country, through gigantic trees of oak with their boughs spread out like huge tents, through bright lanes of splendid chestnut and elm trees, by hedges of the most luxuriant evergreens I have ever seen....And yet, my dear Charles, all this beauty of form and color gives me no pleasure....Many and many a time I shut my eyes and they rested on the quiet fields of Highgate.[6]

She added, "All my hope and joy lies in the cold cemetery."[7] Weeks later, more despairing still, she confessed: "Every day, every hour, I feel more and more how inexpressibly unhappy we are."[8]

Longuet's widowed mother, Félicitas, had come to London for Caro's birth and in the subsequent months corresponded regularly with Charles, Jennychen, and Jenny. She did what she could to help the couple financially and after Caro's death wrote Jenny an angry letter implying that she and Marx had not done likewise. Jenny responded with candor: "You believe that our daughter should not have left our house and that we could have lived more economically together than separated. Regarding the financial question I completely agree with you, and it is clear as daylight that the two families spend less money living under the same roof." But, she said, there were considerations beyond the "monetary question."

> Honestly, my husband and I (after having spent a very turbulent life full of worries and disappointments) need—and as I dare to say—deserve some repose and tranquility, especially my husband who has been suffering for years. We would like to live with fewer restrictions and without constraints. We appreciate home comforts, the small details of life, the meal times, the bed times etc., according to our old habits. And what I claim for the old people holds for the young as well. Everyone wants to live in his own way.
>
> Apart from that there are people who never make use of their capacities, their talents and their energy, if they are not limited to their own resources. That is why I prefer the English system to the one in Germany and France. In England, parents give their sons an education according to their means and their position. From the age of sixteen to twenty on, the young people are generally forced to earn some money. In many cases, parents (and even rich people) abandon them to their own resources. This is how the sense of independence is impressed upon the young spirits and very strongly developed.

And then, Jenny said, there were her other daughters to consider. She told Madame Longuet that familial justice required that all three girls be treated equally; sacrifices made for one must be made for them all. "My daughters, I am sure, have never thought of this, but Tussy is now engaged with Mr. Lissagaray, and we have to do the same for her which we did for Jenny—receive them at our home and come to their aid. Unfortunately, Mr. Lafargue has also lost some money with unhappy speculations. He had too much confidence in a few friends and he was too generous. He was betrayed, stolen from and made a villain of."[9] (Another reason Jenny and Marx encouraged the Longuets to move was left unsaid by Jenny in her letter: Marx by now found Charles so argumentative that he did not want to eat if Longuet was at the table at the same time.)[10]

Earlier that year, in relating family news to Liebknecht, Jenny had said that after thirty years of being a political wife and mother, she had by necessity developed thick skin.[11] Having lost four children herself, she did not minimize Jennychen's sorrow or Madame Longuet's frustration over the death of her grandson. But she knew that life went on, and no matter how much one thought it was impossible to continue, it was possible and it was necessary. There were sorrows to come, but also happiness. As they were growing, Jenny had not been able to give her daughters any of the gifts or advantages in life she would have liked. But now she could give them her strength and wisdom.

> I know only too well how difficult it is and how long it takes to regain one's own balance after losses of this sort; it is then that life comes to our aid, with its little joys and big worries, with all its little, day-to-day drudgeries and petty vexations, and the greater sorrow is deadened by lesser, hourly ills and, without our noticing it, the violence of the pain abates; not that the wound has ever healed, and this is especially so of the mother's heart, but little by little there awakens in one's breast a fresh sensibility, a fresh sensitivity even, to new sorrows and new joys, and thus one goes on and on living, with a sore if ever hopeful heart, until at last it ceases to beat and gives way to eternal peace.[12]

By December 1874 Jennychen and Longuet's life did indeed brighten on one front: Longuet was named a professor of French at King's College in London, making £180 a year. He had been working at the college on a temporary basis, and when the permanent post came open, he threw himself into the application process.[13] Victor Hugo and the French National Assembly member and historian Edgar Quinet wrote him recommendations; out of 150 candidates, Longuet came out on top.[14] Jennychen also found a job, at the Clement Danes School for girls near the Strand.[15] With those positions, and £100 from Engels, they were able to move out of the apartment where Caro had died and into a small house, which they spent the early months of 1875 furnishing from items acquired at auctions.[16] (Longuet filled their home with French furniture, which Marx called rubbish.)[17]

Marx and Jenny moved, too. Now that the children, except for Tussy, were established, they no longer needed a residence the size of Modena Villas. In early 1875 they moved to a house at nearby Maitland Park Crescent.[18] Still grand by comparison with Grafton Terrace, it was attached on either side to other homes. The change was merely superficial, however— the industry inside the new residence was the same. The first floor still housed Marx's study, and the deluge of words emanating from within those novel walls would still fill volumes.

Meanwhile, Lissagaray had begun his great work, *The History of the Commune of 1871,* and he and Tussy were busy with a journal he had founded titled *Rouge et Noir.* Tussy described it as a weekly review of politics from a revolutionary perspective, and they counted on articles from throughout Europe and America.[19] Tussy now did for Lissagaray what Jenny Marx had done for her husband so long ago in Brussels, when he set up his correspondence society: she wrote to socialists and communists everywhere, soliciting pieces for Lissa's publication. Alas, though *Rouge et Noir* began with a flourish in the fall of 1874, by January 1875 it was dead.[20] The international movement of socialists had once again turned inward. Men—and significantly women—were working within their own countries to try to form local political parties and had less interest (for the moment) in communicating across borders.[21]

By 1875, after a politically turbulent post-Commune period, France had a new constitution that stipulated a chamber of deputies and a senate, which together would elect the president of the Republic. (The first president was MacMahon, the man whose troops had put down the Paris revolt.) This new structure meant that the door had opened ever so slightly for workingmen's concerns to be heard in the halls of a more broadly elected government.[22] Yet as welcome as the changes in France may have been, the most dramatic events occurred in Germany.

In March a draft program was published there for the merger of the two parties representing the workingman—the General Union of German Workers and the Social-Democratic Workers' Party. The two parties had previously split the support of the working class, which diminished the power and effectiveness of both. Now their leadership, having found sufficient areas of accord, proposed a new party, the Socialist Workers' Party of Germany (SAPD). A surprised Engels and Marx had known nothing of the unity efforts, and while not against the idea, they feared that Liebknecht (who along with Bebel led the Social-Democratic Workers' Party) had given up too much ground to the other party's doctrine (shaped by Marx's deceased rival Lassalle). That doctrine, according to Marx and Engels, inaccurately interpreted history, did not sufficiently emphasize the importance of international solidarity among workers, was based on outmoded economic theory, and included only one social demand—state aid.[23] Worst, the program made absolutely no mention of trade unions. Engels told Bebel, "That is a point of utmost importance, this being the proletariat's true class organization in which it fights its daily battles with capital, in which it trains itself and which nowadays can no longer simply be smashed, even with reaction at its worst."[24] Despite the reservations in London, however, a Unity Congress held in May at Gotha, in central Germany, approved the merger to form a new workers' party (which in 1890 became the still-extant Social Democratic Party of Germany).

Marx and Engels had planned to remain quiet and distance themselves from the new party's program,[25] but in the end Marx decided he had to respond. He produced a pamphlet entitled *Marginal Notes on the Program of the German Workers' Party* in which he ruthlessly picked apart the party document nearly word by word.[26] "It is altogether self-evident that, to be able to fight at all, the working class must organize itself at home *as a class* and that its own country is the immediate arena of its struggle," Marx wrote in response to the new party's contention that emancipation was primarily a national battle. However, he argued, it was naive to assert that in an age of global transactions a country could isolate its economy and that international unity of the working class was a secondary concern.[27]

He famously countered the Gotha doctrine's vague call for a fair distribution of labor, which failed to explain how that might be achieved, by using (for the first time in writing) the slogan "From each according to his abilities, to each according to his needs!"[28] He also dismissed Gotha's view of man's relation to the state, saying, "Freedom consists in converting the state from an organ superimposed upon society into one completely subordinate to it."[29]

Finally, Marx described the long path ahead toward a classless society: "Between capitalist and communist society lies the period of the revolutionary transformation of the one into the other. Corresponding to this is also a political transition period in which the state can be nothing but *the revolutionary dictatorship of the proletariat*."[30] By way of punctuation, Marx ended his eighteen-page rebuttal with a quote from Ezekiel: "I have spoken and saved my soul."[31]

One has the sense that in writing his *Marginal Notes,* Marx enjoyed a return to the freedom of a good, clean polemic. He had been buried in rewriting and translating his own works for more than five years, and in 1875 had finally sent to the French publisher the last proofs of the translated and rewritten manuscript for *Capital, Volume I.* (He dedicated it to Jennychen.) The edition's ten thousand copies sold quickly, attracting a new audience in France and also in England.[32] In March a short article appeared in London's *Fortnightly Review* titled "Karl Marx and German Socialism," which critiqued *Capital* as a diatribe against authority written in the ill-mannered language of the street. The author appeared less offended by what Marx had to say than by the vehemence with which he said it. If the piece had been published when *Capital* first appeared eight years earlier, Marx and Engels would have been thrilled at the mention. As it was, it was merely an amusing confirmation that Marx's book was at least still remarkable enough to inspire ridicule. Yet one line from the review would turn out to be prophetic: "People may do him the honor of abusing him; read him they do not."[33]

That summer the Marx family dispersed from London. Marx decided to go again to Karlsbad, this time alone. Jenny used his time away to make a journey of her own, to Geneva, where she socialized with party (in the political sense) friends, and then on to Cologne to see personal acquaintances.[34] Jennychen and Longuet spent part of August in Germany, perhaps trying to distract themselves from the painful first anniversary of their son's death. Aside from the discomfort of travel in the summer heat (which required Jennychen to remove one of her three flannel petticoats[35]) and numerous missed encounters with friends, the Marx women's visits were remarkable only for their lack of any drama. Marx's trip, too, passed without incident. On the ship to the Continent, his traveling companions included a corpse en route to Mainz and a Catholic priest who showed him an empty bottle and told Marx he was both hungry and thirsty. Marx offered him his own bottle of brandy, from which the priest took several swigs before launching into a round of bad jokes at the expense of the other passengers.[36] In Karlsbad, Marx found the residents the same as the year before — either "round as a barrel" or "thin as a rake." He did not bother to register as a man of means this time; now he signed in as "Charles Marx, Doctor of Philosophy, London," and thereby paid a lower tax.[37]

A police captain in Karlsbad, who was told to keep an eye on Marx, reported that his subject "has kept calm, has little dealings with other spa visitors and often goes on long walks alone."[38] That assessment contrasted with one in a Viennese paper, whose gossip column was full of praise for this fascinating man "of exceptional learning, which is as deep as it is broad...he always has to hand the right word, the striking smile, the suddenly illuminating joke." When addressing a woman or child, he became a "riveting raconteur.... He is indubitably more of a philosopher than a man of action and has in him more of the historian or perhaps strategist of a movement than of the experienced fighter." The author of that glowing report may have been Marx's doctor, Ferdinand Fleckles,[39] but whoever wrote it, the point is that the paper was willing to run such a piece about a man identified only the previous year as a menace.

Certainly, at fifty-seven Marx no longer appeared the fearsome revolutionary. He was heavyset, with a shock of soft white hair and beard, and the smiling face and playful eyes of a man who enjoyed a good life. Maxim Kovalevsky, who met Marx in Karlsbad and then resumed his friendship with him in London, observed, "People still think of Marx as a gloomy and arrogant rebel against bourgeois science and bourgeois culture. But in reality Marx was a highly cultivated gentleman of the Anglo-German pattern. Thanks to the fact that the conditions of his personal life were now as favorable as possible he was a happy man."[40]

Jenny was also a happy woman. That fall a German newspaper published a tribute she had written about an English actor. The *Frankfurter Zeitung und Handelsblatt* so liked the piece that she was asked to write a series on English theater and cultural life. The assignment not only allowed her to spend more time at the theater, a diversion both she and Marx loved, but it was a recognition of her talent. She was published not because she was Karl Marx's wife but for her style and wit. Though flushed with excitement, in keeping with a lifetime spent in her husband's shadow, Jenny asked that her articles be published anonymously.[41]

On December 31, 1875, Marx held his wife by one hand and Lizzy Burns by the other and led them in a "solemn march"[42] onto the makeshift dance floor at Maitland Park Crescent as the household, dressed in holiday finery, dipped and twirled its way toward midnight and the new year. Marx and Engels and their wives, Lenchen, the Marx children, and various spouses had much to celebrate: Jennychen was pregnant again,[43] and this time the child would not be born into want. The baby was due in May, and Jennychen agreed to stop teaching by March, because her small family could now live off Longuet's earnings. She would even employ a wet nurse (recalling that one had saved Tussy's life when she—the last Marx offspring to have survived childhood—was born in 1855).[44] The Longuets planned to take every precaution to protect this baby. They could not— the family could not—bear to lose another.

Marx was exuberant. Even Engels remarked that after his return from Karlsbad, he seemed a different man, "strong, invigorated, cheerful and healthy."[45] At the spa Marx had discovered filters for cigars and ordered two hundred of them.[46] For years his doctor had advised him to stop smoking, but his stock of filters gave him an excuse to continue. Nor did he or Engels cut back on drinking, though Marx suffered the effects of excessive alcohol intake. On Sundays extended family and friends would regularly meet at Engels's for dinner, which was announced for three but did not begin before seven. In the meantime guests imbibed beer, claret, and champagne, and they continued to do so through dinner and into the early hours of Monday. (Jennychen worried that one emaciated Russian who had just escaped from Siberia would literally drown in Engels's generosity.)[47] None enjoyed the evenings as much as their host, except perhaps for his friend Karl.

In the weeks before Jennychen was to give birth, Longuet went to the Isle of Wight with his mother, and Jenny and Lenchen descended on the Longuet house to disinfect every corner in preparation for the new child. Jennychen was confined to a single room while they cleaned walls, floors, furniture, and curtains. When they were finished with that, they busily sewed baby clothes. Jennychen told Longuet she took no interest in the activity but indulged the older women who hovered around her as protecting angels.[48] That activity continued until May 10, when Jennychen gave birth to a second son, Jean Laurent Frédéric Longuet. The family called him Johnny. Marx reported to Engels the child was named Jean after Longuet's father, Laurent after Laura, and Frédéric after the General himself.[49]

Tussy had celebrated her twenty-first birthday that January. She was now of age and could, if she chose, decide her own fate concerning Lissagaray—if she wanted to risk alienating her father. For a Marx daughter, however, that was impossible. No suitor, no matter how adored, could ever cause them to abandon their Mohr. Nonetheless, storm clouds once again began forming over her head. Apparently Marx's decree had been that until Lissagaray had a secure position, he and Tussy could not marry. And because Lissagaray lacked such employment, Tussy's young life was on hold. Each day she dragged herself off to work as a governess, hoping her situation would change.[50] But not only had Lissagaray not found work, he seemed disinclined to stay in England. (After five years he still did not speak English.)[51] He occupied himself with his book on the Commune and in lobbying the new French government to grant an amnesty that would allow exiled communards to return home. Speaking of Tussy, Jenny told a friend, "The poor child will still have to experience some disappointments in her life, just as us all."[52]

Tussy's body was a barometer of her state of mind, and by the summer neither was healthy. London was in the midst of a heat wave that no one in the Engels or Marx households could tolerate; everyone rushed to leave town. In August, Tussy accompanied her father to Karlsbad in search of relief, but from the start the trip was a disaster. They could not find a hotel to stay in en route and spent the night in a train station, and when they arrived in Karlsbad the heat had been so severe there was a water short-age.[53] The only thing Marx had for entertainment was a book on the functions of the state in the future, and even he—for whom such tomes were nearly the equivalent of leisure reading—was so deflated by the temperature that he surrendered and spent his time listening to gossip about Wagner's private life, the favorite topic of the idle rich around him.[54]

Marx and Tussy stayed at Karlsbad until mid-September, and when they returned to London, Marx set to work trying to find a German pub-lisher for Lissagaray's *Commune,* which a Belgian firm had agreed to pub-lish in French. Marx called it the first authentic history of the 1871 conflict, and in making his appeal on Lissagaray's behalf described the author as a refugee in London whose life "isn't exactly in a bed of roses."[55] Such was Marx's interest that he acted as editor in reviewing proofs; such was Lissagaray's trust in Marx that he gave him full power to negotiate in his name. Once again a Marx woman had pinned her future on the suc-cess of a book. Tussy may have believed the work would earn Lissa enough money that they could marry. But just as that became a possibility, she appeared to have second thoughts.

By 1876 Tussy had been linked to Lissagaray for more than four years. Her initial girlish enthusiasm for him in the aftermath of the Commune, when every Frenchman arriving in London was viewed by the Marx fam-ily as a romantic hero, had matured. Perhaps Marx and Jenny knew this would be so, and for that reason had stubbornly tried to delay a marriage between their youngest daughter and this much older man. Now Tussy's interests began to shift away from those of the seventeen-year-old who staked her future on a rebellious count. She kept one foot in politics, involving herself in local school board elections by supporting a woman candidate,[56] and she began translating Lissagaray's *Commune* into English, but Tussy planted the other foot firmly in the theater—a pursuit quite apart from any of Lissagaray's interests.

Tussy had joined the New Shakespeare Society, run by Frederick James Furnivall, a Christian socialist and ardent feminist. He was also secretary of the London-based Philological Society, founder of the Browning and Chaucer societies, and initiated the collection of material that grew into the *Oxford English Dictionary.* Furnivall mingled with the British elite, but had few class prejudices (his wife had been a lady's maid).[57] He understood Tussy's longing for things intellectual; he encouraged her interest in Shakespeare, and shortly after joining his group she translated, and the society published, a German article on the Bard.[58] (The author of the original sent her a letter of congratulations, which Jenny hoped would help her daughter gain access to literary magazines where she might find paid work.)[59] Shakespeare Society meetings were held every two weeks at members' homes, but Marx so loved the get-togethers that they were held most often at Maitland Park. Tussy's circle of acquaintances grew, and, significantly, she began to socialize with men and women her own age, most of whom were English. No matter that she had grown up in a German household, Tussy was by every measure a young Englishwoman, and through her beloved Shakespeare she soon found a comfortable niche among like-minded company.

In 1876, thirty years after Marx's vituperative campaign in Brussels against utopian socialists, he and Engels found themselves fighting the old fight against a new generation of such dreamers. Eugen Dühring, a blind German socialist, philosopher, and university lecturer, had published a leftist critique of Marx's thinking (he dismissed Marx respectfully as an "old Young Hegelian"[60]) and had gained important followers among the leadership of the German workers' party formed at Gotha. Engels and Marx thought it imperative that they respond, because in the wake of the Commune and in the midst of a burgeoning working-class political movement in Europe they could not risk a return of the utopianism that they believed was at the root of Dühring's philosophy.[61] Engels took up the charge (he described it as breaking "a lance with the tedious Dühring") with a polemic called *Anti-Dühring*. The book was more than mere invective; in it Engels did remarkable service to those trying to comprehend Marx's thinking—and, in particular, *Capital*. In his clear, fluent style, Engels described Marx's theories and his creation of scientific socialism through two great discoveries, "the materialist conception of history and the revelation of the source of capitalistic production through surplus value."[62] *Anti-Dühring* became a crucial primer in the study of Marx and a classic in Marxist literature. It was not simply a compendium of Marx's thoughts; it also reflected Engels's particular areas of expertise. Where Marx talked of money, property, and a monopoly on ideas as capitalist tools to oppress the masses, Engels described the role of military might in that system.

Through the years Marx and Engels had stressed that the right to vote must be backed up—insured—by the right to bear arms. As long as weapons and the army remained under the control of the ruling class, the masses would be their subjects whether the society was called a monarchy or a democracy.[63] In *Anti-Dühring* Engels described the issue of arms in economic terms, arguing that once man was no longer able to fashion his own weapons out of stone or metal or wood, he became the subject of whoever controlled the means to produce more sophisticated arms. In other words, whatever class represented a society's economic power would by necessity also be its military power. By the midnineteenth century, Engels posited, an individual's ability to wage anything but a guerrilla war was out of the question, because the production of advanced weaponry was not only controlled by the ruling class but "devilishly expensive."[64]

Marx read through proofs and drafts of *Anti-Dühring* and provided a chapter for what would be the last major collaboration for the two men. Over the following years both would be preoccupied with personal matters. Marx, Engels, and Jenny all had the sense that their youth was well and gone forever. Jenny described the feeling to a friend in Geneva: "The older one gets and the worse the times become, the quicker they pass and the faster the hours fly by...it's utterly wretched and miserable to be no longer young and lively and 'sound.' "[65] There was still work to be done, but this trio knew they had begun the final act of their great drama.

41

London, 1880

*It is not for those days that compatibility of character is a prime
necessity, it is for the stage of life wherein each seeks in the
other's heart oblivion to time that pursues us, and to men
who abandon us.*

—Madame de Staël[1]

LIZZY BURNS HAD been known as Engels's wife for fifteen years, since the
death of her sister Mary, and for more than half of that time her niece, Mary
Ellen (or "Pumps," as she was called), was considered their "little one."
Engels in fact viewed himself a married man and father, and by the time he
and Lizzy moved to London they had acquired all the trappings of a prosperous bourgeois family. (Lizzy even had a pet poodle.)[2] Engels and Lizzy
were an odd-looking couple. He was about six feet tall, slim, soldierly in
bearing, and reserved when meeting strangers. Lizzy was short, round as a
dumpling, and embraced any passerby with all the warmth of her Irish
nature. Engels was bookish and quiet; Lizzy could not read and never
stopped talking. Yet despite their differences Engels loved her and proudly
wrote of her as his Irish revolutionary wife. She and Jenny Marx were also
perhaps unlikely companions but had become the closest of friends.

In the mid-1870s Lizzy became ill frequently. No one expressed undue
concern, because everyone in their circle oscillated between good health
and bad. In the summer of 1877, however, she did not recover quickly or
completely. Engels wrote Marx from Ramsgate in July, "Since yesterday,
for no apparent reason, Lizzie has been extremely unwell; the magic powers of sea-bathing have failed her for the first time and I'm beginning to
get seriously alarmed."[3] Apparently Engels believed the only way to help

her recover was to keep her out of London, so as soon as they arrived at home in September, they left again for Scotland.[4]

Marx, Jenny, Lenchen, and Tussy were also ill and considered going to Karlsbad, but the cost was too dear even for Engels, who paid the Marxes' medical bills on top of a living stipend. Marx's doctor suggested a less expensive spa at Bad Neuenahr, in western Germany.[5] Marx delivered Lenchen to her family nearby and then he and Jenny and Tussy proceeded to the resort in the Ahr Valley and later, farther into the Black Forest.[6] The family was gone from London for a full two months, but Jenny and Marx returned in not much better health than when they had left. Karl had a chronic cough so deep that one friend said it seemed as if his powerful chest would burst.[7] Jenny was even worse off. She had headaches for months on end, but her most serious pain was located in her stomach. In November she went to Manchester to be treated by Gumpert, who gave her turpentine and belladonna pills.[8]

Throughout that difficult period Johnny Longuet was a constant joy to his grandparents. Marx called him the "apple of my eye,"[9] and Jenny said when he arrived in his pram "everyone rushes out joyously to meet him in the hope of being the first to pick him up, OLD GRANNY at their head."[10] This child who could barely walk represented a fresh and innocent new world to them, and in July 1878 Jennychen made Marx and Jenny happier still: she had another boy she named Henry—forever known as Harry. Marx's study was still a prime destination for (ever younger) radicals from around Europe, as well as his oldest friends whenever they were in town. But now, in addition to refugees and rebels, they found a toddler crawling around, along with three dogs—Whiskey, Toddy, and a third whose name is unknown (but was alcoholic in nature, according to one visitor)[11]—and heard the sharp cries and giggles of an infant. In the midst of it all the giddy master of the house, the scourge of Europe, was delighting in the role of grandfather.

Shortly after Harry's birth, Marx and Jenny planned, despite the cost, to go to Karlsbad for their annual treatment, but the trip turned out to be impossible. There had been two assassination attempts on Emperor Wilhelm that year, one by an unemployed tinner and the other by an anarchist. Bismarck had used the attacks to justify laws that would make the Socialist Workers' Party of Germany illegal, along with all unions and any meetings, publications, or speeches by socialists or communists. The assassination attempts thus gave Bismarck the ammunition he sought to counter the increasingly powerful workers' movement.[12] Elections in early 1877 had moved the Reichstag to the left, with the Socialist Workers'

Party polling 20 percent of the vote and winning twelve seats.[13] Marx could not risk going to Karlsbad in this climate. He considered sending Jenny there alone, reasoning, "It seems unlikely that her ex-ladyship, the ex-Baroness von Westphalen, will be regarded as contraband."[14] However, she was not up to the journey and went instead to a noted English spa at Malvern, where Jennychen and Johnny joined her.[15] Longuet and Lissagaray were in Jersey meeting other French refugees lobbying to return home.[16] Jenny may have sensed that Longuet was growing tired of England, telling a friend her already "excitable, vociferous and argumentative" son-in-law had grown even more edgy and irritable.[17]

Marx looked forward to his annual spa sojourn and joined his wife, daughter, and grandson at Malvern in early September. But almost as soon as he arrived, Engels summoned him back to London. Lizzy had died at half past one in the morning of September 12.[18] The evening before her death Engels, now fifty-seven, and Lizzy, fifty-one, were legally married by a Church of England vicar who came to their home. She could thus be buried in a Roman Catholic cemetery, under a Celtic cross.[19] Tussy and Marx, the Lafargues, and a small group of family and political friends attended the funeral in London, and then Engels left with Pumps and a friend for the coast at Southampton.[20] He was inconsolable. On receiving a letter from him, Jennychen told Longuet, "He seems to be in utter despair and thinks he will never be happy again."[21]

In the past Engels had rarely turned his back on party work, but after Lizzy's death he may have realized he could no longer put off his own projects in order to answer his seemingly limitless correspondence or satisfy the vast number of requests to write articles that he received. Finally back at home, he rejected the entreaties of a young Zurich editor named Eduard Bernstein, explaining, "During the nine years I have spent here in London, I have learnt that it's no good trying to complete more substantial works while simultaneously engaging in practical agitation. I grow no younger with the passage of time and must at long last restrict myself to definite tasks if I am to get anything done at all."[22]

And what of Marx's writing? Even with countless family dramas and continued illness, Marx *was* working. As always, his investigations took him deep into obscure fields and required familiarity with many languages. (One friend recalled him reading a Romanian newspaper.)[23] This man who had spent a lifetime in study was still as intrigued by the world in his later years as he had been as a young journalist in Cologne discovering the economic basis of social relations through the story of fallen timber. For Marx every development—whether economic, social, or political—in whatever corner of the globe was connected and therefore critically important if he hoped to do his duty to humanity (the constituency he had chosen for himself as a boy in Trier), which in effect was to pass along a deep understanding of the world in his books. Knowledge, he believed, was the most revolutionary weapon of all.

In the fall of 1878 Marx told Nikolai Danielson he did not expect the second volume of *Capital* to go into print in Germany before the end of 1879, ten years after he had promised it to Meissner in Hamburg.[24] Then, in the spring of 1879, Marx wrote Danielson confidentially that he had been informed the second volume could not be published while the German government's antisocialism law was in place. Marx said that suited him, because he could not possibly have finished it before he knew how an industrial crisis then under way in England would be resolved, and he was happy to have a "pretext" for further study of materials he had received from the United States and Russia. His health, in any case, would not allow prolonged work.[25]

When not in London, Marx was on a dead run from one resort to another, trying to strengthen his constitution. His efforts were nearly always disrupted by crisis. In August 1879 he and Tussy took a long-planned trip to Jersey but while there received word that Jennychen had given birth prematurely on August 18, while she and Longuet were at Ramsgate.[26] The baby was another boy: Edgar, named after Musch. Marx rushed her a note: "My dear beloved Jennychen, Long live the little citizen of the world!"[27] Jenny had already arrived at Ramsgate, but Marx insisted he must be there, too, to comfort his daughter as well as ease his own worries. Marx arrived during a spectacular lightning storm. He reported to Engels that Jennychen was fine but that he was rattled and unwell, his mind racing and his thoughts jumbled. (He had tested his mental acuity by looking at some mathematical notebooks and found he could not decipher them.)[28] Laura and Lafargue were staying with Engels at the nearby resort of Eastbourne when Marx wrote.[29] Recognizing her father's anxiety, Laura headed to Ramsgate to try to distract him while her mother attended to her sister. Under Laura's care Marx was soon much better, and Jennychen improved, too. So on September 15 she, her husband, three children, their two grandparents, and their aunt set out by train for London, one more extended family trundling home after a seaside holiday.[30]

Marx liked to regard himself as a mere paterfamilias, but to European governments he remained a source of concern at the highest level. Queen Victoria's daughter, Crown Princess Victoria, was the wife of the future German emperor, and she asked a British member of Parliament what he knew about Marx.[31] Sir Mountstuart Elphinstone Grant Duff knew nothing of him but made it his duty to find out what he could in the most genteel manner possible; he asked Marx to join him at his club. Marx accepted, and the two men talked for three hours over lunch at the Devonshire. Duff happily reported to the princess that Marx did not appear to be a "gentleman who is in the habit of eating babies in their cradles—which is I daresay the view which the Police takes of him." He was impressed by Marx's command of the past and the present but much less sure of his projections for the future, noting, for example, that Marx looked to a great crash in Russia, followed by revolution in Germany. When Duff asked how Marx could expect the German military to rise up against its government, he pointed to a high suicide rate in the army and said the step from shooting oneself to shooting one's officer was not long. When Duff suggested that European governments might one day jointly agree to reduce their arsenals and thereby lessen the threat of war, Marx deemed this impossible: competition and scientific advances in the art of destruction would make the situation even worse. Each year more money and material would be devoted to the engines of war, a vicious and inescapable cycle.

Duff reassured the princess that in general Marx's ideas were too "dreamy to be dangerous.... Altogether my impression of Marx, allowing for his being at the opposite pole of opinion from oneself, was not at all unfavorable and I would gladly meet him again. It will not be he who, whether he wishes it or not, will turn the world upside down."[32]

Yet in some ways he already had.

In 1879 republicans in France were finally firmly in control of the government, both national and local. MacMahon, the scourge of the 1871 Commune, resigned his presidency and the position went to a seventy-one-year-old republican named Jules Grévy. Each development, each shift of the political sand, was scrutinized by the French refugees in London, who awaited an announcement of a general amnesty that would allow those who had fled or were forced into exile to return home. The three Frenchmen most closely associated with the Marx family—Lafargue, Longuet, and Lissagaray—were among the attentive.

Marx and Jenny were both ill, but their physical pain was matched by their anxiety over the possibility that Longuet would return to France and take his family with him. Jennychen's boys were the light in the Marx household and the only thing that brought Jenny true joy. It was the same for Marx. His love for children in general was often remarked on by friends and family. Liebknecht recalled that during the Soho years, when his own family had nothing, Marx would often trail off in midsentence if he saw a neglected child on the street. As broke as he was, if he had a penny or ha'penny he would slip it into the child's hand. If his pocket was empty, he would offer comfort by speaking gently to the youngster and stroking his or her head. In later years he could often be seen on the Heath, trailed by a gaggle of children who apparently saw in this stern revolutionary an apparition of Father Christmas.[33]

Still, for all his regard for children, Marx had not done all he could for his own daughters, not to mention the four children who died young. And then there was Lenchen's son, Freddy, now twenty-nine and married. Unmentioned in any existing family correspondence between his birth and 1880, he resurfaced that year in a letter Jennychen wrote to Longuet. Freddy had apparently always been at the periphery of the family and in contact with his mother; in fact, Jennychen knew him well enough to consider him and Lenchen her "usual bankers" when she needed to borrow money (she told Longuet she drained them as "dry as Engels's throat on a summer's day"), and she was familiar enough with Freddy's wife to borrow a hat for a special event.[34] One wonders whether Marx ever thought about the son, now a man, he had abandoned to strangers. Even when considering his immediate family, it is difficult to reconcile Marx's love for children with the many decisions he made through the years that had so devastating an impact on his own. Some would accuse him of selfishness. He would have called it selflessness. In his painstaking efforts to lay a foundation for change and his fear of sudden revolution, Marx had consistently agitated less for his generation, or even his children's generation, than for those in the future. To Marx his family's sacrifices had been politically necessary, but such sacrifices were no longer required. The movement he had helped spawn had a life of its own, and now so could he. He and Jenny had the time and money to devote to their grandchildren as they had not been able to do with their own children. It is the way in many families, and so it was for the Marxes.

Thus the prospect of amnesty hung like a sword over the grandparents' heads, though the wait was made somewhat easier by the bustle of activity in the Marx home that year. Tussy's circle had grown to include political activists, actors, and undiscovered writers. She had received a pass for the British Museum Reading Room,[35] and like Marx and Laura before her, began going there nearly every day. Smoking was forbidden, so those who indulged in that habit—Tussy among them—gathered for breaks in a special alcove. The elderly men seated there with their pipes and cigars watched with proprietary disdain as the space filled with young bohemians whose chatter ran from theater to politics to religion, all of it alarmingly left if not socialist.

Tussy's friends followed her back to Maitland Park, where Marx allowed her to convene meetings of a Shakespeare reading group known as the Dogberry Club in the drawing room off his study. Engels and Marx considered themselves honorary (if sometimes disruptive) members. One of Tussy's friends, Marian Skinner, recalled being asked to read the moving part of a young Prince Arthur in *King John,* but she could not concentrate on her lines because her attention was fixed on Marx and Jenny. She described Marx as forceful and dominating though somewhat shaggy, while seated next to him was his wife, whom Skinner characterized as charming, albeit a shadow of her former self. Neither Skinner nor anyone else could fail to see that Jenny was ill. Her skin was waxen, and there were purplish rings below her eyes, "yet there was still an air of breeding about her and a certain distinction of manner." Also evident was the love between husband and wife; even after decades of marriage Jenny was obviously devoted to Marx.

The Dogberry nights concluded with games and charades, mainly, Skinner thought, for Marx's pleasure. Engels, who often joined the fun, went so far as to incorporate Tussy's friends into his own circle. (He invited Marx to a party he threw for Pumps that featured the Dogberry women, but Marx would not attend because he claimed not to like company older than his grandsons.)[36]

Another frequent visitor at this time was one of Marx's earliest English supporters, Henry Hyndman.[37] Although the epitome of an upper-class gent, from his silk top hat to his silver-topped cane, Hyndman considered himself a worthy candidate to lead the workingman: he called working-class acquaintances "comrade"[38] and Marx the Aristotle of the nineteenth century.[39] Nevertheless, Hyndman had read *Capital,* and that may have been enough to gain him entrée to Marx's study. Hyndman flattered himself that his friendship with Marx made Engels jealous, a notion that would have been hilarious to Marx and Engels had Hyndman been rash enough to voice it. In any case, within a year the relationship had soured. Hyndman published a book, *England for All,* in which he borrowed liberally from *Capital*—sometimes verbatim—without attribution or even mention of Marx. This was particularly annoying because Marx's work had not yet appeared in English, which meant that this audience's introduction to his thinking was issued under another man's name.[40] What undoubtedly irritated Marx even more was that his ideas were mixed in with what Engels called Hyndman's "internationalist phraseology and jingo aspirations."[41]

But all this was mere distraction while the family anxiously awaited the decision from Paris. It came in July 1880: amnesty was granted; France's doors were opened to her exiles.

★ ★ ★

Lissagaray left London immediately to plunge back into journalism in France. One can imagine the relief Jenny and Marx felt, but also the fear. Tussy's marriage plans were inconclusive at best. She had been engaged to Lissagaray for eight years, yet neither of them seemed inclined to take the next step. Even Jenny had expressed surprise the previous year in a letter to her daughter. After extolling the joys of motherhood she asked, "Haven't you two made up your minds yet?"[42] To push Tussy on the point too aggressively, however, risked making her ill or creating a scene. Jenny-chen declared Tussy unapproachable on the subject.[43]

For his part, Lafargue did not seem in a rush to return home. Indeed, his financial situation was such that he could not afford to. He and Laura had lived off earnings from her lessons and the paltry returns from his photolithography business, but mostly on the proceeds of the house he had sold in New Orleans. When that money ran out, he was virtually bankrupt.[44] The Lafargues' survival was likely due to Engels. Lafargue had shown no compunction about asking him for money while he waited for his numerous ships to come in. He still expected great things from his business and decided that, for him to return to France and give that up, he needed a permanent job. He consulted Engels about a possible Paris enterprise built around publishing guidebooks, but Engels saw immediately Lafargue had no protection for his investment and that the deal offered no guarantee of returns. Frustrated at Lafargue's childish faith in his potential partners, Engels said, "One would think you were begging to be robbed."[45] Lafargue soon abandoned the plan.

It was Longuet's decision, however, that everyone awaited, and it came soon after the amnesty was announced. His old friend the radical leader Georges Clemenceau invited him to come back to Paris and edit the foreign political section of his newspaper, *Justice*. Longuet was at heart a journalist, not a language professor, and in any case he would not have been able to resist the draw of a republican France in which radicals, socialists, and workingmen alike could secure their gains if their numbers were great enough. Agreeing to the job, he left immediately to meet with Clemenceau but pledged to return to London in mid-August to join the family at the seaside.[46] That summer Marx and Jenny did not take their usual spa holiday. They rented a cottage in Ramsgate and gathered their children around them. Engels was there, too. A feeling of finality hung over the gathering. There were no immediate plans for Jennychen to go to France with the children, but it was just a matter of time before she would. And there was Jenny's health: that year Marx had begun to use the word "incurable" in reference to her illness, which although still not properly diagnosed increasingly looked like cancer.[47]

477

Tussy was the only member of the family not at Ramsgate that August. Strained relations between her and the Lafargues had only worsened after Lissagaray's return to France, so much so that Engels could not have the two sisters in his home at the same time.[48] It may have been that Tussy feared seeing Laura's satisfaction over Tussy's apparent abandonment by the man she had so ferociously defended. The family acknowledged the sisters' estrangement but did not discuss it openly. Tussy had sprained her ankle that month, and that was a plausible enough excuse for her absence to avoid any more contrived explanations.[49]

Surprisingly, Marx invited a New York journalist to visit him during the family holiday. John Swinton, a liberal reformer, made the journey south to meet the man he said stood behind more political earthquakes in Europe than any other. He found Marx in a most improbable setting of brightly painted wooden homes perched high on the cliffs and the honky-tonk merriment of a seaside resort at high season. After a private conversation in which Marx took Swinton on a tour of the world from his perspective, Swinton declared him a Socrates. He then asked Marx, "Why are you doing nothing now?" Not replying directly, Marx proposed a walk to the beach. There on the sand the two came upon the Marx family: Jenny, Jennychen, Laura, and the children, and Marx's two sons-in-law, one of whom Swinton described as a professor at King's College and the other as a man of letters.[50] (Lafargue had just completed a short book he entitled, seemingly without irony, *The Right to Be Lazy*. When it was published the next year, he was accused of plagiarism.)[51] Swinton reported, "It was a delightful party—about ten in all—the father of the two young wives, who were happy with their children, and the grandmother of the children, rich in the joysomeness and serenity of her wifely nature." Marx, Swinton, and the two younger men then left the women for a chat and a drink. Swinton said he had been waiting all afternoon to pose a question to Marx about what Swinton called the "final law of being." Finally he had the chance, and asked, *"What is?"* Marx looked at the roaring sea and the restless crowds on the beach and replied: *"Struggle!"*[52]

In mid-August, Longuet left Jennychen and the children in Ramsgate and settled in Paris. There was no doubt he wanted to depart England for France, but he did not leave his family lightly. On arriving in Paris, on August 24 he wrote Jennychen, "I do not believe that I can be optimistic or happy. My voyage was too sad. First I cried with rage and then sorrow....I went back to find you but at that moment the signal sounded. This mix-up made my crossing much sadder. It seemed to me I did not kiss you enough and that you would accuse me of a lack of feeling. And then I could not forget the poor little one [Jean] and good Harry. . . . I am so unhappy to be away from you. I am so little used to it."[53]

Jennychen, with three children to care for and only the help of a wet nurse for Edgar, was forced to return to her teaching in September. But as difficult as that was for her, the prospect of life in France was more so. As a journalist Longuet would not earn nearly what he had at King's College or enjoy comparable job security, given the notorious unreliability of newspaper work. There had even been talk that Longuet might return to King's College, but after a brief visit to England in mid-September he left again, resolved on his course with Clemenceau. Given his preference for Paris over the security of the life they had in England, Jennychen began to question her husband's feelings. After seeing Longuet off, she wrote with cold sadness:

> When I left you on the platform I felt wretchedly lonely, more lonely I think than I have ever felt in my life and all the long dreary way home in the omnibus I had to pretend something had got into my eye. It seemed to me that the parting for so many months caused you but very little regret, for the most trivial matters you had spent the whole day in town alone. . . . What a contrast with your first departure from London and that from Ramsgate. Paris has got hold of you once more and made you quite its own again to the exclusion of all else! And perhaps it is well it has—for your [attitude] has in the end had a good effect upon me . . . pray do not flatter yourself that I am eating out my heart in solitude. I shall take the good things of the world as they come.[54]

Liebknecht, as usual between prison terms, was in London on a rare visit, and Jennychen took the boys to Maitland Park to see him. Johnny—Marx's favorite—jumped into his grandfather's arms and demanded a ride on his shoulders. Quickly roles were assigned: Marx was to be the omnibus, and Liebknecht and Engels were to be the horses pulling him along. The three old radicals who had made governments quake ran briskly around the garden as the child on Marx's shoulders shouted "Go on! *Plus vite!*" Liebknecht recalled Marx dripping sweat. He and Engels were hoping to slow down, but Johnny cracked an imaginary whip and cried, "You naughty horse!" and off they went again, until Marx, at once exhausted and exhilarated, could perform his duties no longer.[55]

Marx's children were Engels's children, too. He appeared at the Marx house every afternoon to discuss political matters, disputes within their vast network, and family concerns (he was, after all, the prime breadwinner). By 1880 Marx and Engels's lives had become so intertwined—and so patterned—that each had his particular portion of carpet in Marx's study on which to walk. That diagonal cross had become unconscious choreography. Engels was consulted on every decision involving the children, and the sicker Jenny became, the more Marx kept family problems from her, discussing them only with Engels. Interestingly, the only existing family photo features not Marx, Jenny, and their three daughters, but Marx, Engels, and the girls.

The two men were also viewed by the new generation of socialists and communists as the "spiritual fathers" of the movement.[56] (One young follower said they were considered a "court of ultimate appeal.")[57] Men and women, most the age of Marx's daughters, came to seek protection, advice, or their blessing for a new political party or newspaper. One was Leo Hartmann. He had escaped Russia in 1879 after trying to assassinate Czar Alexander II. (He and Sofia Perovskaya posed as husband and wife, and rented a flat from which a tunnel was dug under a railbed in a plot to blow up the train carrying the czar. The plan was aborted at the last minute.)[58] Hartmann presented himself at Marx's door the day he arrived in London, and Marx immediately took him in.[59]

Also appearing that November were two men who would be critical to the future of the movement that Marx and Engels had begun: Eduard Bernstein, known as Ede, a Zurich newspaper editor, and August Bebel, Liebknecht's close colleague in the Socialist Workers' Party of Germany. By now many men and a smattering of women were involved in socialist journalism and politics, but Marx and Engels thought these two among the most able.

Their first meeting was with Engels, who shouted, "Drink, young man!" and filled glass after glass with Bordeaux, all the while engaging the new arrivals in a violent political dispute. After an hour he suddenly declared, "Now it's time to go to Marx," and strode off so quickly that Bernstein and Bebel had difficulty keeping up with him. By now Bernstein was rather terrified of Engels, and he anticipated worse from Marx. "I had expected to make the acquaintance of a fairly morose and very irritable old man, and now I found myself in the presence of a very white haired man whose dark eye held a fire and smile, and whose speech was full of charity."[60]

If Marx was gentle with Bernstein and Bebel during their first encounter, it was because he viewed them as his political offspring, mere adolescents in the movement, which at that moment was being pulled in a multitude of directions as new political freedoms increased the flow of ideas in government and on the street. Marx wanted to be able to steer this younger generation onto a correct course, preferably during the time he had left. It was increasingly clear to him that they, not he, would be left with the task of making his vision of a classless society a reality.

42

London, 1881

So I hold tight to every straw. I would like to live a little longer,
good, dear doctor. It's peculiar, the closer the story comes to an
end, the more you cling to this earthly vale of tears.

—Jenny Marx[1]

By NOVEMBER 1880 Jennychen and Longuet had decided she and the boys would move to Paris at the start of the new year. But at that very moment the tone of Jennychen's letters changed from expressions of longing for her husband to lists of irritations, personal and political. She told him she was shocked that his writing in *Justice* exhibited such careful regard for bourgeois sensibilities. She said that after reading his last article, "I felt more disappointed, more desolate than I have ever felt in my life."[2] She feared the man she knew and loved in London had changed now that he was back among his friends in Paris, and she bluntly told Longuet,

> When I speak to you it is like talking to the wind—I have absolutely no influence with you. It is even so when we are together—you would act just as you act now, were I at Paris, so much I have learned from experience.... You ask me how I manage to get on without you. Feeling that at Paris I should not see much more of you than I do here, that our home would be no home under such circumstances, I take things philosophically, and enjoy the perfect rest and peace of my present existence.[3]

Jennychen was full of dread about their move, apprehensive of the dominance of Longuet's mother, who had chosen a house for them in Argenteuil, twenty minutes by train from Paris, despite Jennychen's express wishes that they be nearer the city so Longuet could be close to his family.[4] She was further annoyed that her mother-in-law had cut off support money as soon as Longuet returned to France, even though Jennychen needed it more than ever. "It is sad enough for me to leave my poor fond sick mother," she explained impatiently, "to enter a new family which receives me thus." And Jennychen accused Longuet of being blind to the amount of work she had to do to prepare for their move: "You look at everything from a fantastic point of view, you call it optimist. Did you not even defy the weather and assert that there would be no winter, when I suggested the snow would still come?"[5] These outbursts may have appeared aberrational, but Jennychen was mentally and physically drained. She was worried about her parents: her mother was weakening by the day, and Marx was coughing up blood. She was also concerned about her own health. At thirty-six she was expecting again, her fourth pregnancy in five years.[6]

Longuet had planned to return to London for Christmas. From the moment he left in August the family had looked forward to being together at the holiday, but in early December he told Jennychen he would not be back. He wanted to run for municipal office, and after consulting Lissagaray he concluded he had no hope of winning unless he remained in Paris to campaign.[7] Jennychen was incensed that he had chosen Lissagaray and not her as his adviser on such an important decision. She waited several days to calm down and talk with her father before responding.

In fact Marx responded first. Without trying to influence his decision, Marx told Longuet the choice was as simple as it was grave—his children or political office. But Jennychen did not force him to choose. She acted as her mother would have, writing,

It is evident that if you are willing to go in for the municipal fight, you cannot leave the battlefield at the decisive moment—now is the time for action, and it is better we should put off our jollities until after the elections, than that you should fail because of such childish reasons. I should never forgive myself, if for personal pleasure, I had induced you to ruin your political prospects....I hope I shall always be able, without grumbling, to bow my head to the inevitable, to make the best of it and above all, never stand between you and your public duties.[8]

Longuet remained in Paris and lost the election.

Come February, 1881, Maitland Park was in an uproar. Jennychen and the children had moved in with Marx and Jenny after the Longuets' belongings were sent to France. Now that it was time for mother and sons to follow, nothing seemed ready, least of all themselves. Jenny had spent the weeks furiously sewing new clothes for her grandchildren, working like a woman in full health, making them everything from coats to underwear. Jennychen told Longuet her mother was so absorbed in her love for the boys that her spirits seemed undiminished by her disease, which the doctor had now positively identified as cancer.[9] But seeing her so active only made those around her more fearful for the days when the boys were no longer in London. Marx said the separation would be very painful. He told Nikolai Danielson, "For her and myself our grandchildren, three little boys, were inexhaustible sources of enjoyment, of life."[10]

Jenny was also worried about the journey her daughter was about to undertake. Jennychen's trip to Paris was reminiscent of the one she had made in 1849. She, too, had been in her midthirties, seven months pregnant and traveling by sea with three small children to meet her husband. The voyage had been terribly difficult, even with Lenchen's help. Given all of this, Marx and Jenny tried to convince their daughter to leave Harry behind. They believed the boy would be an extra burden because he was slow-witted and sickly, and needed as much attention as the baby.[11] Longuet, however, would not agree, and so when Jennychen set out in mid–March for Paris, she did so with her full personal load.[12] While her parents worried, she did not. By then she was resigned to her fate and even allowed herself to be cautiously optimistic that she and her children might be happy in France and that her husband would be ready to return to family life.[13]

Indeed, Longuet was eager to see his family. In the weeks before her arrival he'd assured Jennychen that there would be friends for the boys at the home of Gustave Dourlen, the doctor who had helped him escape the Commune and who lived nearby, and that she needn't worry about his mother's interference.[14] But when she arrived at Argenteuil she found the house not only shut up but unfurnished and nearly uninhabitable because repairs were still under way. And, within her first week there, her fears about Longuet's activities in Paris were justified. He had gone to work one day and missed his train home, not arriving back at Argenteuil until the next morning.[15] That pattern would continue, leaving Jennychen alone in a country she did not know, isolated in a drafty, barren house with her young sons.

After two weeks she said she felt she had been in France a century, the days distinguished only by extra doses of misery. She told Laura she was "wretchedly hopelessly nervous—ill at ease mentally and physically." One of the children invariably kept her up at night, and at least one was always sick: "The free independent active though monotonous existence I lived for some months in London have spoiled me and made me unfit for fights with servants and babies and all that sort of thing. It is all so unbearable to me now that I feel as if some years, nay months, of this existence in a strange country, among strange people, would make an incurable idiot of me." She added, "I cannot send you Charles' regards, because he is not here."[16]

If Jennychen was lonely, Maitland Park was lonelier still. Sometimes when Marx heard children's voices outside on the street, he hurried to the window thinking they were his grandsons, until he remembered that this was impossible because they were on the other side of the English Channel. He told Jennychen the house was utterly boring since they had left. The only activity had been the arrival of a new doctor for Jenny, who, he said, given the hopelessness of her condition, was no better than the first but did seem to cheer her up with the possibility of change.[17] Marx had also been visited by a twenty-six-year-old named Karl Kautsky, whom Engels liked because of his considerable drinking ability. Marx, however, thought him a "mediocrity, narrow in outlook," who made little sense and was a philistine; "for the rest, a decent fellow in his own way." Marx "unloaded" him onto Engels as much as he could.[18] At the time Kautsky was merely an up-and-coming socialist journalist and economist, but one day he would be the leading German Marxist theoretician and edit the "fourth volume" of *Capital*.[19] With his neatly trimmed beard and wire-rimmed glasses Kautsky gave an impression of precision. He looked more accountant than socialist agitator as he approached Marx in his study, his heart, he recalled, pounding in fear. But instead of grilling him on theory, Marx asked him about his mother.

Kautsky was amazed by Marx's warmth but found no levity in the house, which was pervaded by the gloom of illness. He recalled the only laughter coming from the least likely source — Jenny.[20] Despite her weakness, Jennychen said, her mother always made it a point to greet young party members, drawing from a reserve of strength to show the same "fiery public-spiritedness, the same keen sensitiveness for the sufferings of humanity . . . that have ever distinguished her."[21]

In an effort to restore some of the life that had left the Marx home with the children's departure, Tussy's Dogberry friends literally brought the theater into their living room, which cheered Jenny immensely. She was less interested in their amateur readings than in the romances flourishing among the group, and may have even had her eye on a young British lawyer named Ernest Radford for Tussy — if Tussy ever decided, that is, to end her relationship with Lissagaray.[22] But none of the guests, no matter how amusing, could act as balm for the lonely grandparents. Marx told his eldest daughter, "It is a strange thing that one cannot well live altogether without company, and that when you get it, you try hard to rid yourself of it." In his long letter listing disappointments and complaints, the one bright spot for Marx was the assassination in March of Czar Alexander II. The trial of his assassins, who included Hartmann's former partner Sofia Perovskaya, ended with the execution of all but one of the six accused. Perovskaya was among those sent to the gallows. Marx called the defendants "sterling chaps through and through, without melodramatic posturing, simple, matter-of-fact, heroic."[23]

In late April Jennychen bore another son. Marx congratulated her on the delivery of young Marcel, saying, "My 'womankind' expected the 'newcomer' to increase 'the better half' of the population; for my own part I prefer the 'manly' sex for children born at this turning point of history. They have before them the most revolutionary period men had ever to pass through. The bad thing now is to be 'old' so as to be only able to foresee instead of seeing."[24]

Engels immediately set in motion a plan to get Marx and Jenny to France to see their new grandson[25] (whom Marx called "the great unknown one"[26]). The doctor thought Jenny might be strong enough to make the trip, but her condition fluctuated. Sometimes she was confined to bed, other times she felt so well she went to the theater. By June, however, her health had deteriorated to the point that she had trouble dressing herself. The doctor suggested that Marx and Jenny go to the seaside to see how much travel she could tolerate. Laura accompanied them to Eastbourne as nurse for both parents, Marx's own ailments having been exacerbated by his worry over his wife.[27] Both Marx and Jenny held up surprisingly well, and the doctor was impressed enough by Jenny's recovery that he approved the trip to France.[28] Marx also received an all-clear from the French government: Clemenceau assured Longuet his father-in-law had nothing to fear from the police.[29]

Jennychen was overjoyed at the prospect of having the company of her parents and Lenchen. She waited fearfully for a telegram saying they would not be able to make the trip, but the news was good: they would be coming. She wrote by return post, "I do not know how I shall manage to live till Tuesday. . . . My hand trembles so I can scarcely hold the pen."[30]

In late July, Marx, Lenchen, and Jenny set off. Mother Nature, for the first time ever in their journeys to and from the Continent, cooperated; Marx said the sea was calm and the weather couldn't have been finer. But the train ride between Calais and Paris was grueling; Jenny was seized with cramps and diarrhea, and once in Paris the logistics became quite complicated. They were met by Longuet at one station but had to leave for Argenteuil from another, which involved transfers and long waits. The party did not arrive at Jennychen's home until ten at night.[31] The ever-generous Engels wrote as soon as they were settled to say Jenny "must not and shall not want for anything." His wallet was at their disposal.[32] Marx wanted to keep Jenny in Argenteuil as long as he could. Her bouts of stomach pain had been coming on more frequently in London but had subsided somewhat after a few days in France, perhaps for no other reason than the distraction of the children. Though Marx was sure his wife's condition had not improved, she believed it had, and that was critically important.[33]

It had been thirty-two years since Jenny and Marx had been forced to leave Paris, and the city had changed considerably from the one Jenny knew and loved. While Haussmann had destroyed that Paris, he had built something admittedly grand in its place. In early August, Jenny told Marx she wanted to see what he had done. She had been growing thinner seemingly by the day and was now occasionally bleeding from small cracks in her skin. Marx wanted to take her back to London immediately, but she tricked him by sending out their laundry, which would not be ready until the end of the week. Seeing that even in her incapacity she was too strong willed to be dissuaded, Marx relented.

A French doctor gave Jenny enough opium to kill her pain, and Marx and Jennychen took her to Paris for a tour of the great metropolis where she had once been so happy. They rode in an open carriage along boulevards that had not existed in 1849, past what Marx called a perpetual fair in all its colorful glory. Next to gray, gray London, Paris *was* a carnival. Jenny floated through it on her cloud of opiates and was so pleased to be back that she wanted to take a coffee at a café—and so they did, sitting outside at a small table, once again part of Paris street life.[34] For a moment, Marx and Jenny may have even imagined themselves young again, he the fiery black-haired philosopher turned revolutionary, she the belle of Trier, both eager to challenge the world. Now they were just two old people, indistinguishable from thousands of others, he stout and gray, she shrunken and frail. What had not changed was the passion of those two younger people. All those years ago they had said hello to each other and could not look away. Soon, both knew, they would have to say good-bye forever. But for now, just for now, it was as it had ever been.

Jenny became sick on the way back to the train station. The visit had been too much for her physically, but she so enjoyed the excursion that she asked Marx to take her to Paris again. That was not to be, however. In mid-August Marx received a letter from Tussy's friend Dolly Maitland saying his youngest daughter was gravely ill and refusing the help of a doctor.[35] Marx left France alone on August 17 to attend to her.[36]

* * *

While the rest of the family had been preoccupied with Jenny's and Marx's health and the Longuet family's return to France, Tussy had blossomed in her new circle of friends in London. Furnivall had given her paying research work on what would become the Oxford dictionary,[37] and she was also beginning her career as a rights campaigner. A group called the Land League had been pressing the British government to change laws in Ireland that favored big landowners; specifically it called for the end of capricious evictions of tenant farmers. The Land Leaguers' ultimate goal was independence for Ireland, but some argued for the interim step of Home Rule, in which Irishmen would govern themselves while remaining part of the British Empire. Irish MP Charles Stewart Parnell, who led the fight, had raised $200,000 for the campaign in the United States.[38] When Jennychen was in England, she had sent her husband articles about the Irish developments for his newspaper. The youngest Marx daughter, however, did not restrict herself to words. Tussy took to the street, joining a crowd outside a police court to support a jailed Fenian and Land League founder. But those gathered had been deceived—the Irish prisoner had already been secretly moved—and so Tussy, who was neither tall nor broad, angrily confronted a barrel-chested Irishman on the London police force, accusing him (to the delight of the mob) of doing the dirty work of the English.[39]

In the spring of 1881 Henry Hyndman had formed an organization called the Democratic Federation, which he envisioned as an umbrella of workers' organizations. Despite Marx's antipathy toward him, Tussy had joined.[40] If she was going to be an activist working on behalf of the downtrodden in England and Ireland, she needed to begin forming her own political associations. This was not out of character. Marx's two eldest daughters had always been content to work behind the scenes as part of their father's network, but Tussy wanted to be at the forefront of her own causes. The young people around her at the Reading Room, part of a new political awakening in England, differed from their socialist predecessors because they combined concern for social issues with art, literature, and music. (One of her friends was a newly arrived Irishman named George Bernard Shaw, who had read *Capital* in French and was on his way to becoming a convert.)[41] This milieu could not have suited Tussy better: she would not have to choose between the theater and politics—she could have it all.

In March she had given a performance at St. Pancras on the anniversary of the Commune. The hall was about two-thirds full of notable radicals, including her father, Engels, Leo Hartmann, and August Bebel. Tussy took the stage and recited "The Pied Piper of Hamelin." Ede Bernstein recalled her voice as musical and her personality as unusually vivacious: "As my English was still very weak, I could not follow the words at all adequately. I only noted that Eleanor's recitation was full of life and that she spoke with a great wealth of modulation and earned a great deal of applause."[42]

In July, when her parents were testing their health in Eastbourne for a possible trip to Argenteuil, Engels had again been in the audience to see Tussy perform, this time in two one-act plays at the Dilettante Club theater. He reported to Marx that she showed "a great deal of SELF POSSESSION and looked quite charming on the stage." His overall impression was that she acted very well,[43] though it was clear that Marx and Engels regarded Tussy's acting as a hobby. Tussy, however, most certainly did not. The month before, she had confided in Jennychen that she wanted to pursue the stage as a profession, and she turned to the same acting coach Jennychen had consulted so many years before. Tussy knew Marx would be opposed, partly for financial reasons (he had added debts at that time due to Jenny's health and Jennychen's move), but she told her sister that he had spent much less on her education than he might have, and she would do all she could to help defray the cost.[44] "I hope I shall be able to do it—it would be such a comfort. Well I'll try anyway—if I fail, I fail. You see dear, I've a goodly number of irons in the fire, but I feel I've wasted quite enough of my life, and that it is high time I did something."[45]

Unfortunately for Tussy, her needs had been the last thing on anyone's mind that summer. She was alone in London. Her parents and Lenchen were in France; even Engels was away, in Yorkshire. And she was still not speaking to Laura because of her slight to Lissagaray. Tussy sank into a depression that devolved into anorexia. By the time Dollie Maitland summoned Marx and he arrived in London in mid-August, Tussy was not sleeping and had eaten next to nothing for weeks. Her hands trembled and she had facial tics. She was in a "STATE OF UTTER NERVOUS DEJECTION," her father told Engels. The doctor found nothing wrong with her physically except for a "PERFECT DERANGEMENT OF ACTION OF STOMACH" resulting from lack of food and a "DANGEROUSLY OVERWROUGHT NERVOUS SYSTEM."[46]

Jenny and Lenchen were back in London two days later to find Marx and Tussy in the parlor, with Tussy propped up with cushions on the sofa. "Her crazy mode of life has left her in such a weak and feverish state that she can walk no better than I do," Jenny told Jennychen. As for leaving Argenteuil, she told her eldest daughter, "the memory of you and your love and kindness remains nevertheless as the richest treasure of my heart, on which I shall feed like a MISER."[47]

*　　*　　*

By October Tussy was well, but the household was on a deathwatch for Jenny. She rarely left her bed, and when she did, it was for a chair nearby. After months of worry about his wife, his daughters, his grandchildren, Marx's own maladies had intensified. His problems during that period were almost always respiratory, first bronchitis, then pleurisy. His lungs were without doubt weakened by a lifetime of smoking, especially in his early years, when he had smoked the most wretched of cigars because he couldn't afford any others. But everyone agreed Marx's physical ailments were worsened by anxiety, and such was certainly the case that fall. The friend of his youth, his comrade, his "unforgettable beloved partner," was dying, and he was confined to a small room adjoining hers, under doctor's orders not to leave his bed to see her.[48] Jennychen wanted to come home to try to restore her mother's spirits by bringing the boys, but Laura informed her that their mother was too far gone to appreciate them. Besides, she said, they were alive in her thoughts, and she clung to every letter from Jennychen.[49]

With her last bit of strength Jenny wrote Jennychen in October. The letter was entrusted to Tussy to mail, but for unknown reasons it never reached France. "I was more deeply grieved than I can say to hear that what was probably her last letter never reached you," Laura wrote Jennychen. "She would be inconsolable if she knew it. It had cost her such an effort to write and she had put so much into it to which she looked for an answer from you that the loss of the letter is irremediable." Laura hinted that Tussy may not have mailed it, as an act of extreme selfishness and peevishness by a spoiled child who resented the love between her mother and her eldest sister.[50] This insinuation may simply have been the result of the bad blood between Laura and Tussy; in a letter to Jennychen, Tussy described how painful it would be for her mother if she believed the letter was lost and suggested Jennychen pretend that she received it.[51]

In late October the doctor finally told Marx he could see his wife. Years later Tussy wrote, "Never shall I forget the morning when he felt strong enough to go into dear mother's room. They were young once more together—she a blooming girl and he an adoring youth...not an old man wrecked by sickness and a dying old woman."[52] Marx would say he had waited seven years to marry Jenny, but that they seemed like seven days because he loved her so much. Tussy wrote that during his whole life he did not love his wife, he was *in love* with her.[53]

That month the Social Democrats in Germany had won three more seats in the Reichstag. If Bismarck's antisocialist laws were meant to disable or kill the workers' movement, they failed; the movement simply went underground, and if anything grew stronger.[54] Though full of morphine, Jenny understood the significance of this and along with Marx and Engels cheered the results.[55] The old fighters were gathered at her bedside, marveling at how far they had come. It had taken nearly half a century, but the king had lost his divinity and the workers—those exploited masses who had once dumbly accepted their fate without recognizing their power—now formed part of government. Yet despite those truly remarkable strides, Jenny had not seen her husband take his place in the pantheon of great thinkers, as she had fully expected him to do when they were young. And she had not seen his masterwork, *Capital,* change the world as he had promised. She had sacrificed her own and her children's lives to the ideal that animated her husband, but it appeared now she would not live to see it become a reality.

In late November, however, posters appeared in London's West End advertising a monthly review called *Leaders of Modern Thought,* which included the first independent article in English praising Marx's work. On November 30 Marx sat at Jenny's bedside excitedly reading her the piece by a young man named Belfort Bax,[56] who wrote that *Capital* "embodies the working out of a doctrine in economy comparable in its revolutionary character and wide reaching importance to the Copernican system in astronomy, or the law of gravitation and mechanics."[57] Engels couldn't have said it better himself. Jenny was thrilled. Even if the philistines had failed to recognize it, she had known her husband was a genius. Marx described her eyes at this time as "larger, lovelier and more luminous than ever."[58]

Jenny died two days later, on December 2. She was sixty-seven.

Jenny Marx was buried at Highgate Cemetery in unconsecrated ground near her grandson Caro. Marx did not attend the funeral. No one in the family wanted him to venture out into the cold in his condition. Jenny had even told her nurse, in regard to the formalities of dying, "WE ARE NO SUCH *EXTERNAL* PEOPLE!"[59] Engels stood in for the husband and read a eulogy:

> The contribution made by this woman, with such a sharp critical intelligence, with such political tact, a character of such energy and passion, with such dedication to her comrades in the struggle—her contribution to the movement over almost forty years has not become public knowledge; it is not inscribed in the annals of the contemporary press. It is something one must have experienced at first hand. But of one thing I am sure: just as the wives of the Commune refugees will often remember her—so too, will the rest of us have occasion enough to miss her bold and wise advice, bold without ostenta-

tion, wise without ever compromising her honor to even the smallest degree. I need not speak of her personal qualities, her friends know them and will not forget them. If there ever was a woman whose greatest happiness was to make others happy it was this woman.[60]

Tributes from around the world poured in from friends and party members as news of Jenny's death spread. Sibylle Hess, who had not seen Jenny since their Brussels days, wrote: "In her, Nature has destroyed its own masterpiece, for never in my life have I met so witty and loving a woman."[61] But as Marx himself had once said, words of consolation, however welcome, do little to mitigate the pain of profound loss. Among themselves Marx's friends worried about his fate now that his wife was gone. Engels said it most plainly: "Mohr is dead too."[62]

43

London, 1882

Lear: Does anyone here know me? This is not Lear.
  Does Lear walk thus, speak thus? Where are his eyes?
  Either his notion weakens, his discernings
  Are lethargied — Ha! Waking? 'Tis not so!
  Who is it that can tell me who I am?
Fool: Lear's shadow.

—William Shakespeare[1]

OF COURSE MARX was not dead, not literally, but he was a ghost, a sad figure who roamed a large house without the comfort of the woman who had been at his side for thirty-eight years. Sometimes he would put on his heavy black coat and felt hat, and leave home to wander the park outside or up onto the Heath.[2] These were wanderings without destination; the map that Marx had long relied on was gone. He was now so nearsighted that on returning he could not always distinguish his own house from the neighbors'—it became clear to him only when his key did not fit the lock.[3] His daughters, along with Engels and Lenchen, all agreed they had to get him out of London. Maitland Park was as full of sadness as Dean Street after Musch's death. He would never recover his health there.

Yet far from being concerned about it, Marx took comfort in his weakened state. On doctor's orders he painted his body with iodine, which produced a painful inflammation of the skin. "The said operation...is therefore doing me sterling service just at this moment," he told Jennychen. "There is only one effective antidote for mental suffering, and that is physical pain. Set the end of the world on the one hand against a man with acute toothache on the other."[4] Anger also helped him bury his grief.

Marx may have been harboring ill feelings toward Longuet about taking Jennychen and the children to France, but that hostility erupted into fury when he read the obituary of his wife published in Longuet's newspaper. In it Longuet referred to prejudices Jenny and Marx had had to overcome in order to marry because he had been born Jewish. Marx accused Longuet of inventing history, insisting that there was no such prejudice. (Marx was likely guilty of rewriting history himself, because there was no doubt such bias.) Countless other small details also irritated him, because they would be picked up and repeated in the European press. He positively railed against his son-in-law for defiling Jenny's memory, telling Jennychen, "Longuet would greatly oblige me in never mentioning my name in *his* writings."[5]

Marx told Nikolai Danielson he hoped to get to work in earnest on the second volume of *Capital* because he wanted to dedicate it to Jenny.[6] At that very moment, however, Meissner revealed that he planned to publish a third edition of the first German volume, which would normally require an updated preface and other changes by Marx.[7] Marx was deflated by the news. He had no real interest in going back once again into *Volume I.* Uncharacteristically, he decided to make the fewest possible alterations and leave the rest to Meissner.[8] This, more than anything, was an indication to friends and family of just how much Marx was affected by Jenny's loss. In the past he had been incapable of allowing his work to be reissued without a virtual line-by-line review. Now he hardly seemed to care about it at all.

Marx's doctor wanted him to go south, as far as Algeria, to try to recover from his illnesses, but Marx was not ready for something so adventurous and settled instead on the Isle of Wight, which he had called a paradise when he had visited it with Jenny seven years before.[9] In Victorian families it was the custom for a daughter—usually the youngest—to remain at home to care for her elderly parents.[10] Marx, Lenchen, and Engels thought it natural, then, that Tussy should dedicate herself to her father. But that call to sacrifice came just when Tussy was intent on making something of herself. As much as she loved her father, the last thing she wanted was to play nursemaid. She believed her father was demanding that one more Marx woman surrender her life to him, and she refused. Tussy told Jennychen she felt selfish because she loved her father more than anything, and yet "we must each of us, after all, live our own life... hard as I have tried I could not crush out my desire to *try something.* The chance too of independence is very sweet."[11] Her rebellion would come at a significant cost.

Jennychen, whose own bid for independence had been sadly brief, understood Tussy's inclination better than anyone, and she tried to persuade her father that Lenchen, not Tussy, could best take care of him.[12] But Marx insisted that his youngest daughter accompany him, and so on December 29 they left London together to see in a new year both dreaded. The weather reflected their moods: gale-force winds lashed the island and howled through the night; the days were cold, the sky leaden, the rain torrential. Marx's cough grew worse rather than better. In a letter to Laura he described Tussy as eating practically nothing, suffering from nervous tics and insomnia. She spent all her time reading or writing and "seemingly endures staying with me simply out of a sense of duty, as a self-sacrificing martyr."[13]

Marx had no idea what his daughter was suffering, or why. Tussy wrote to Jennychen that she feared she was heading for a complete breakdown, explaining that in the previous two weeks she had not slept six hours. She confided the same fear in a letter to her friend Clementina Black, who spread the word to Dollie Maitland and Ernest Radford. Alerted to the possibility that Tussy might be on the verge of collapse, the Dogberry Club asked Lenchen to go to her, but she could not leave London, so it was Dollie who showed up at the Isle of Wight. Her arrival was the first indication Marx had that Tussy was ill, and he was angry that she had told her friends but not him. She said she had not done so because she feared he would either scold her for indulging in illness at the expense of family or obsess about her health, neither of which would do them any good.

> What neither Papa nor the doctors nor anyone will understand is that it is chiefly *mental worry* that affects me. Papa talks about my having "rest" and "getting strong" before I try anything and won't see that "rest" is the last thing I need—and that I should be more likely to "get strong" if I have some definite plan and work than to go on waiting and waiting. . . . It drives me half mad to sit here when perhaps my *last* chance of doing something is going.

Tussy still had it in mind to try her hand at acting, and she felt the clock ticking. That month she would turn twenty-seven: "I am not young enough to lose more time in waiting—and if I cannot do this *soon* it will be no use to try it at all."[14] She described herself as "not clever enough to live a purely intellectual life" but "not dull enough to sit down and do nothing."[15]

Tussy wanted Jennychen to rescue her, and Jennychen did. Now the matriarch of the family, from her distant perch surrounded by four boys clamoring for attention, she nonetheless found the strength and grace to patiently direct and advise her feuding family in England. First she wrote Laura a letter laying out Tussy's position. Laura and Tussy had appeared together at Jenny's deathbed in an effort to show their mother that they had reconciled.[16] The strain remained, however, and so from Argenteuil Jennychen had to act as mediator between sisters who lived barely ten minutes apart. She told Laura that she feared Tussy was very ill and blamed it in part on her long and still unreconciled engagement to Lissagaray: "In every way she has been more sinned against than sinning and is sincerely to be pitied. Though I think her health will be a great impediment to her, yet I feel convinced that, in order to rouse her and to console her, the best thing for her will be to try her luck in the dramatic line. Only work, hard work can give her back the rest and comfort of which her unfortunate attachment deprived her."[17]

Next she wrote her father. That letter no longer exists, but Marx immediately wrote a note to Engels that likely echoed what Jennychen told him. He said he wanted to relieve Tussy of her role as his companion. "She has an ardent desire to open up a career for herself, or so she imagines, as an independent, active artist and, once this has been conceded, she is undoubtedly right in saying that, at her age, there's no more time to be lost. Not for anything in the world would I have the girl think she is to be sacrificed as an old man's 'nurse' on the altar of family."[18] Tussy saw her sister's hand in her father's changed position and thanked her heartily for her intervention. She also announced that as part of her resolve to start her life anew, she had broken her nine-year commitment to Lissagaray: "For a long time I have tried to make up my mind to break off my engagement. I could not bring myself to do it — he has been very good, and gentle, and patient with me — but I have done it now. . . . At last I screwed my courage to the sticking place." She hinted that there were reasons for the move she could not explain in writing, which in Marx family code probably meant that she had met someone else. "But this is over: I mean to try hard by dint of hard work to make something more and better of my life. . . . Tomorrow is my birthday — if I keep but half my good resolutions for the coming years I shall do well."[19]

Tussy's crisis was Jennychen's first test as her mother's successor in handling delicate family affairs, and she passed it admirably. At the end of January she wrote her youngest sister,

I grieve over all the torments your engagement has cost you these many years, and congratulate you on the strength of mind you have now shown. . . . I can so well sympathize with you, because I am made of the same mettle. Inaction is death to me as to you. You will smile when I tell you that often I long for the daily drudgery of my school work, and the railway and the streets full of life and interest that carried me far from the killing tediousness of the household and its harassing round of duties.[20]

She said she rejoiced in Tussy's liberation, in her "prospect of living the only free life a woman can live—the artistic one." Finally, she advised her not to fear approaching veteran actors for help. "There is always something in a name and yours is Marx."[21]

Marx's doctors decided he could not tolerate a winter in London, but his southerly choices were limited. He could not go to Italy because he might be arrested. He could not go to Gibraltar by steamer without a passport. His doctor wanted him to go to Algeria, but the only way to reach that country would be by a long journey through France. Nevertheless, Marx finally chose that route, figuring that he could break up his trip by stopping to see Jennychen. Tussy would accompany him as far as Argenteuil and then return to London.[22] At Argenteuil, even with the distraction of his grandsons, Marx's health did not improve, so he set out immediately for the south of France. Incredibly, the black cloud that had hung over him on the Isle of Wight and never left him in London awaited him in Marseilles. He arrived there after two in the morning and had to shelter—a solitary old man wrapped in a greatcoat—in a cold and windy train station.[23] He told Engels, "To some extent I was MORE OR LESS FREEZING . . . the only antidote I found being 'alcohol' and I AGAIN AND AGAIN RESORTED TO IT." He stayed in Marseilles overnight and then sailed on to Algiers, where he was to be met by a friend of Longuet who had been deported to Algeria under Napoleon III and had risen to the position of appeals court judge.

Marx's greeting among compatriots there was warm, but once again diabolical weather pursued him. He had not slept for two nights on the steamer because of the noise of the engines and the wind, and he arrived in Algeria just in time for the cold rainy season. By then he was "frozen to the marrow." He described his dilemma to Engels: "No sleep, no appetite, a bad cough, somewhat perplexed, not without an occasional bout of *profunda melancolia,* like the great Don Quixote." He considered returning immediately to Europe but could not face another crossing. He also pondered going farther inland, to Biskra, but that would take seven or eight days. Finally the sun broke through and he found a hotel outside Algiers, on a hill overlooking the Mediterranean, and decided to stay. "At eight o'clock in the morning there is nothing more magical than the panorama, the air, the vegetation, a wonderful mix of Europe and Africa." This proved only a temporary balm: a nine-day tempest had begun. Marx replaced his huge London coat with a lighter version and hunkered down against the remorseless wind.[24]

A local doctor examined Marx and was alarmed by his condition. He forbade him to walk or talk, ordered that ointments be painted on his body each day, his blisters lanced, and that he lie still. Marx was prodded and poked and made entirely convalescent. In this state there was no place for him to go but his memories. He told Engels, "By the by, you know that few people [are] more averse to demonstrative pathos; still, it would be a lie [not] to confess that my thought to great part [is] absorbed by reminiscence of my wife, such a part of my best part of life!"[25]

Amid all the attention to his body, one of the world's greatest minds had begun to show signs of decline, and no one was more aware of its failing than Marx himself. Almost by way of footnote he remarked in a letter to Engels, "*Mon cher,* like other FAMILY MEMBERS, you, too, will have been struck by my mistakes in spelling and syntax, and bad grammar; I never recall these—my absent-mindedness being still very great—until after the event."[26]

By mid-April the wind still had not stopped, but the rain was replaced by dust and the sun was now blazing. Marx took the radical step of having his hair cut short and his beard shaved off, but lest the world forget him in his full ferocity, he had himself photographed before "offering up" his mane on the "altar of an Algerian barber."[27] That picture, Marx's last, showed a softer version of the once stern man. On the eve of his sixty-fourth birthday Karl Marx appeared to be in his dotage.

The heat and dust had caused Marx to start coughing again, and he was afraid he would be stranded for the duration of another storm if he stayed. He had had enough of Africa, and on May 2 returned to Europe, landing at Monte Carlo. It had not rained there for months, but on the day Marx arrived, it did. Still, he was quite happy, if for no other reason than that the casino had a reading room with a good selection of newspapers in German, French, and English.[28]

When not reading, Marx amused himself studying the hotel guests as they threw away their money at the gambling tables. But his amusement soon turned to disgust as he watched them pay experts to learn the "science" of conquering roulette. Those hordes intent on winning sat hunched, pencil in hand, scribbling out a system that they tried each day and that each day failed them. "It's like watching a bunch of lunatics," he said.[29] He had also met an Alsatian physician who thought the "doctor" in Marx's title meant that he, too, was a medical man. The Alsatian therefore spoke freely, advising Marx that his pleurisy had returned and that his bronchitis was chronic.[30]

Recognizing that there was no medical reason to stay in Monte Carlo (and in any case he had not found restorative weather anywhere he had traveled), Marx set off for Argenteuil. He implored Jennychen not to tell anyone he was coming; he wanted absolute quiet. "By 'quietness' I mean the 'family life,' 'the children's noise,' that 'microscopic world' more interesting than the 'macroscopic.' "³¹ Marx longed for an idyllic world that did not exist, most certainly not in Argenteuil.

Before Tussy left France for London, Lissagaray had asked to see her in Paris. Jennychen accompanied her sister to the Gare Saint-Lazare and reported to Marx that the two conducted themselves as old friends, without animosity or drama. Jennychen expressed extraordinary relief, because "Lissagaray's friendships and love affairs generally ended in a row or blue fire." She said she herself was more amiable to Lissagaray than usual, "for I could not but feel grateful to him for not having carried out his plan of becoming my sister's husband. French husbands are not worth much at the best of times—and at the worst, well the less said of it the better."³² Jennychen's observations hid her own tale of domestic hell. Because Longuet was rarely home, she brought a young girl over from England to help with the boys. But Emily, as she was called, became increasingly belligerent, hostile, and reckless the longer she stayed. She began loitering around the train yards, trying to seduce railwaymen, and when Jennychen tried to put a stop to it, she spread vile rumors about the Longuets to ensure that if she left their employment, no one else would work for them. Jennychen told Tussy that Emily was "clean out of her wits" and driving her mad as well.³³

Lacking assistance, Jennychen worked night and day on the house and caring for the four boys—and yet, she reported, Longuet did nothing but scream at her and grumble every minute he was home. Jennychen had moved to France so her husband could pursue a career that would make them both proud. At first Clemenceau's newspaper was full of Longuet's articles, but by early 1882 they appeared less frequently, and Jennychen said it was evident Clemenceau no longer needed, or perhaps appreciated, Longuet's work as he once had.³⁴ Money from the newspaper came in only sporadically and they were always in debt, a condition Longuet's mother blamed on Jennychen: she said her daughter-in-law was idle and should go to work. With Longuet seemingly in no rush to extricate them from their financial woes, Jennychen told Tussy her only option was to find local children to whom she could give lessons, or try to get children from London as boarders and students.³⁵ (Among those to whom Jennychen owed money were Lenchen and Freddy, which she said haunted her like a crime.)³⁶

In an undated letter to Longuet, written when he was recovering from an illness at the coast, she described her concerns.

> You know that to save you pain and trouble I would coin my heart's blood—but dishonor I could not brave even for you.... Your irregular life, which has

brought so much suffering to you, has not therefore been the means of securing you a good position at your paper! There is not even that consolation for me! It is time I tell you once more to look reality in the face and to consider whether it is possible for you to live the life of a journalist.... Were you with me now I should scarcely dare to speak to you thus, you are so violent, and most so when in the wrong.[37]

Feeling herself drowning in despair and frustration, Jennychen told Laura that she longed for "no matter what release" from her cares. Stuck in Argenteuil in a drafty old three-story house and increasingly estranged from her husband, she dreamed of life in London, of the Underground, Farringdon Street, running down the muddy Strand amid its garish advertisements for plays and musical extravaganzas.[38] "I feel more sick of life than I can say," she wrote Tussy, "and if it were not for the poor children, I should soon know how to change my most uncongenial existence."[39]

If this was not sufficient burden, Jennychen said she had the "unspeakable ill-luck" to be pregnant again. She also had begun to fear that she was seriously ill. "I have a strange inward pain since some time as if I had an abscess or a tumor—and have not yet made up my mind to consult a doctor." It was excruciating for her to lift the children or run up and down the stairs, so much so that she dropped to the ground after such exertions. "By the by, Papa knows nothing of this and is not to be told. It would only worry him."[40] Indeed, when Marx arrived in June he had no inkling of the state of affairs at Argenteuil. He went to bed early, slept late, and spent much of the day roaming nearby woods and vineyards with the boys.[41] Lafargue described him as in seventh heaven, trailed constantly by his young army.[42] But Marx soon began to suspect things were not well. The boys had grown wild since they returned to France, in part because Jennychen could not discipline them on her own. Longuet was often away in Paris all night, and when he returned in the morning, went straight to bed.[43] Baby Marcel had been nicknamed Par or Parnell, after the rabble-rousing Irish MP, because of his insistent cries.[44] Edgar was called Wolf, because at eighteen months he was caught eating a piece of raw liver he had mistaken for chocolate.[45] And Johnny was the ringleader, a bright boy who, Marx said, had grown naughty out of boredom.[46] Harry had still not shown signs of normal development.

In July, Tussy and Lenchen arrived in Argenteuil, a hearty cavalry summoned partly to attend to Marx and partly to help Jennychen. Tussy was thriving intellectually. That month she had given a recitation for the Robert Browning Society at University College that went off so well a society matron wanted to introduce her to Browning so she could recite his poems for him. Tussy had also been invited to an evening at Lady Wilde's. She told Jennychen, "She is the mother of that very limp and very nasty young man, Oscar Wilde, who has been making such a d.d. ass of himself in America."[47] Beset by troubles, Jennychen took delight in hearing of her little sister's activities: "I congratulate you with all my heart and rejoice to think that one of us at least will not pass her life in watching over a pot au feu."[48] Now a free woman, Tussy was also thriving physically. There were no more complaints of illness; her nervous system was calm. As happy as she had been when a child, she arrived in Argenteuil full of energy to assist her sister.

It was now clear even to Marx that Jennychen was pregnant again, and he became preoccupied with her troubles. He discovered that she was being harassed by the landlord for rent and he felt her health was not good. Marx wanted Tussy to take Johnny back to London to ease some of the burden, but Longuet did not want his son to miss his summer holiday at the seaside in Normandy. "Longuet doesn't care a damn whether it's a respite for Jennychen or good for Johnny," Marx told Engels. "Monsieur Longuet does 'nothing' for the child, but his 'love' consists in not letting him out of his sight during the brief intervals when he himself is visible, for in Argenteuil he usually spends the morning in bed and leaves for Paris again at five in the afternoon."[49]

Despite Longuet's objections, Marx prevailed. Lenchen and Tussy departed for London with Johnny in August.[50] Soon afterward Marx left, too, for a brief health excursion to Switzerland accompanied by Laura. She and Lafargue had moved back to Paris that year, after Paul secured a job at an insurance company. He was also involved in politics, basing his positions on a mélange of argument and analysis he and his close associate Jules Guesde called "Marxist." Marx, however, wanted no part of it, assuring Lafargue, "If anything is certain it is that I am not a Marxist."[51]

Lafargue had collected enemies as soon as he returned to France, both on political grounds and because of his perceived arrogance. Some of his critics had so little regard for his abilities that they spread rumors to the effect that Laura wrote his newspaper articles. Lafargue laughed off the criticism and continued to pontificate.[52] In his mind he was Marx's disciple (or as Marx jokingly called him, a "big oracle"[53]) and that alone was enough to earn him a place in the upper echelon of socialist circles. The problem was that although Marx was associated publicly with the Commune, his ideas were still barely known in France. Marxism per se did not exist, except in Lafargue's vocabulary.

Not surprisingly, Lafargue's business and political lives were incompatible. The month Marx and Laura set off for Switzerland, he lost his job.[54]

The formal reason was that his company had merged with another, but his employer was also unhappy with his performance. With no work and no money, Lafargue turned to Engels, as was the Marx family tradition. His letters to the General nearly always included a casual plea for cash, because he was "devilishly hard up."[55]

On September 5 Longuet left Argenteuil for Normandy with Wolf and Harry, leaving Jennychen alone with little Par. She felt relieved. With only one child in residence the house was finally quiet. Moreover, without Longuet there were no fights.[56] The calm lasted for eleven days. Then, on September 16, she gave birth to a baby girl. (Longuet's Commune protector Dourlen delivered the child.) The infant was named Jenny,[57] and she was all Marx, her skin dark, her hair black.

Marx and Laura were still in Switzerland when they received the news. They returned at once to Paris, where they found the Lafargue apartment in such disarray that, Laura wrote Engels, "words are quite powerless to describe the state of filth and disorder in which I find these rooms of mine.... We go to Argenteuil this morning. Paul is the lord knows where."[58] Lafargue, whom Marx now mockingly called Saint Paul,[59] was on a speaking tour with Guesde that had prompted a warrant for their arrest on charges of incitement to murder, pillage, and arson.[60] Marx and Laura did not know of the warrant and did not wait for Paul's return. Arriving in Argenteuil, they found Jennychen still alone. Longuet, the new father, would not return until October.

Marx seems to have had enough of both of his sons-in-law. He abhorred Longuet personally and thought Lafargue shameless politically. He especially fumed at Lafargue's penchant for quoting himself, as if his thoughts were worth repeating when, by all accounts, they were recycled from earlier thinkers. Marx fairly spat in a letter to Engels, saying, "Longuet as the last Proudhonist and Lafargue as the last Bakunist! *The devil take them!*"[61]

The first anniversary of Jenny's death found Marx back on the Isle of Wight, still searching for good health. He left Engels in charge not only of his family but of nearly all his correspondence as well. Engels had, in effect, taken over the business of revolution. Even with that onus lifted, Marx did not find peace, only more wind, more rain, and more gloom. By mid-December a local doctor had confined him to the house, and he received little news beyond what he heard from and about the family.[62] He was particularly pleased, then, to learn that even in his isolation, he remained an inspiration. A noted Russian economist had recently mentioned "socialists of the Marxian school" in a book.[63] Marx told Laura,

"Nowhere my success is to me more delightful; it gives me the satisfaction that I damage a power, which, besides England, is the true bulwark of the old society."[64]

Laura, meanwhile, wrote Engels that she was increasingly concerned about Jennychen's health.[65] She had what she described as an inflammation of the bladder, and though she downplayed its significance, Laura feared she did so for the family's benefit.[66] As to Jennychen's personal life, Laura said, "Jenny and I do nothing but rail against *La Belle France* when we meet."[67] Earlier that month Laura had been expecting Paul to bring home a salad for dinner, because she had spent the day cooking and was looking forward to a good meal. Instead, the salad was delivered by a young man who gave her the news that Paul had been arrested. "This is an awful place and an awful kind of existence, for one never knows what's coming next," she told Engels.[68]

By mid-November Jennychen had still not left her bed. She had decided to nurse the baby but confessed that it "makes life a hell to me."[69] Longuet now stayed home all day trying to help, but, she said, he only added to the confusion. He filled the house with stoves to warm the place and by late December employed three servants. All Jennychen could think of was the cost—additional stress that she did not need and, in her wilting state, could not withstand.[70]

Reports to Marx on her situation were invariably positive, tempered by concern about how worry might affect him. Engels, Tussy, Laura, and Lafargue each wrote to say she merely needed rest and medical attention to be fully restored. But Marx was not so addled that he failed to read between the lines. In early January he reported spasmodic coughing and a feeling of suffocation, which he attributed to worry over Jennychen,[71] telling Engels, "It is curious how, nowadays, any sort of nervous excitement immediately grips me by the throat."[72]

Finally the family admitted that she was going through a critical phase. Lafargue and Laura had gone to Argenteuil and were stunned by her condition. Jennychen could barely move or speak, and seemed to have sunk into a torpor. She was hemorrhaging, though her doctors did not know why.[73] Marx's first instinct was to go to France, but he was afraid he would only increase her burden.[74] In any case Laura was with Jennychen, and Marx quoted Lafargue as saying that "a turn for the better would seem to be assured." Though Marx had long since dismissed Lafargue as a medical crackpot, he told Engels he found this diagnosis reassuring, perhaps because he could not bear to think otherwise.[75] He mailed his letter to Engels on January 10, 1883. On January 11, Jennychen was dead.

44

London, 1883

*He who intends to dominate the times he lives in is entitled to
take all and risk all, for all that is belongs to him.*

—Honoré de Balzac[1]

THE TELEGRAM ANNOUNCING Jennychen's death had been sent to Maitland
Park. Still on the Isle of Wight, Marx as yet did not know the terrible
news, and the job of telling him fell to Tussy, who immediately left London for Ventnor, on the island's southern coast. During her frigid winter
journey by train and ferry, she endeavored to decide how best to break the
news: she felt she was bringing her father nothing less than his death sentence. But when she arrived she did not have to utter a word; Marx saw at
a glance why she was there. "Our Jennychen is dead," he said. He told
Tussy to go to France at once to see to the children. She argued it would
be best for her to stay with him, but he would not hear of it. Tussy stayed
in Ventnor no more than a half hour before she headed back to London
and on to Argenteuil.[2]

Marx did not attend Jennychen's funeral. He and Engels and Lenchen
mourned together in London, while in France his thirty-eight-year-old
daughter was laid in her grave. Engels could not have imagined that he
would be writing an obituary for another Jenny Marx so soon, but it fell
to him to eulogize this daughter who had grown up with their movement
from the time of her birth in Paris, and who had suffered alongside them
through their darkest days. He described her as retiring almost to the
point of shyness but noted that she "displayed when necessary a presence
of mind and energy which could be envied by many a man." He recalled

her work to free the Irishmen held by Britain and her arrest at Luchon, when she had the presence of mind to hide her letter from Flourens by stuffing it into a book. Engels wrote, "Perhaps the letter is still there.... The proletariat has lost a valiant fighter in her. But her mourning father has at least the consolation that hundreds of thousands of workers in Europe and America share his sorrow."[3]

Marx had been grateful for the tributes that came in after his wife's death, but he barely acknowledged those that arrived in the wake of his daughter's. That blow, on top of the still fresh wound of Jenny's loss, was too great. Letters came from friends around the world, but Engels told correspondents Marx was too ill to write and so hoarse he could barely talk. London was the worst place for him in winter, yet in his abject state London was where he had to remain. Engels and Lenchen hovered over him, though neither could persuade him to reengage with life.[4]

Engels told Laura her father was broken down intellectually by sleepless nights, reduced to reading catalogs and novels. And despite Lenchen's mastery of new dishes, he could not be enticed to eat. Marx's preferred meal was a pint of milk, sometimes with a bit of rum or brandy.[5] After Jennychen's death, Engels told a friend in America, Marx had developed an abscess on his lung that made his chronically troubled breathing even more difficult.[6]

March 14 was frosty as Engels walked to Marx's home in the early afternoon, a ritual he had followed every day for more than a decade. Since Jennychen's death he had hated to turn the corner, for fear he would see the curtains drawn in mourning.[7] They were not. Yet when Lenchen opened the door to admit him, she was in tears and told Engels that Marx was very weak. "Come with me," she said. "He's half asleep." Engels followed her up to Marx's bedroom and found him sleeping in his chair next to a fire, which for much of his life would have been an unspeakable luxury. But Marx was not sleeping, he was dead.[8]

"Mankind is poorer for the loss of this intellect—the most important intellect, indeed, which it could boast today," Engels wrote an old IWMA colleague in New Jersey. "The movement of the proletariat will continue on its course but it has lost its focal point.... Ultimate victory remains assured, but the digressions, the temporary and local aberrations...will now proliferate as never before. Well, we have got to see it through— what else are we here for?"[9]

Karl Marx was sixty-four.

Eleven people attended Marx's funeral at Highgate Cemetery on March 17, 1883, and saw him buried next to Jenny.[10] When he died the family had found three pictures in his breast pocket—his father, Jenny, and Jennychen. Engels laid the images in Marx's coffin.[11] Then, for the third time in less than two years, Engels had the sad task of eulogizing a member of the Marx family. In a draft of this speech he wrote, "Scarcely fifteen months ago most of us assembled round this grave, then about to become the last resting place of a grand and noble-hearted woman. Today we have it reopened, to receive what remains of her husband."[12] Marx's coffin bore two red wreaths,[13] and as the small group stood around it, Engels reminded them of his friend's long career and his place in world history.

"He was indeed what he called himself, a Revolutionist," he said. "The struggle for the emancipation of the class of wage-laborers from the fetters of the present capitalistic system of economic production, was his real element. And no more active combatant than he ever existed." The transcendent nature of his accomplishments was already evident: "The crowning effort of this part of his work was the creation of the International Working Men's Association, of which he was the acknowledged leader from 1864 to 1872. The Association has disappeared, as far as outward show goes; but the fraternal bond of union of the working men of all civilized countries of Europe and America is established once and forever."[14]

Marx was more than mere activist, Engels continued, he was a groundbreaking theoretician.

Just as Darwin discovered the law of development of organic nature, so Marx discovered the law of development of human history: the single fact, hitherto concealed by an overgrowth of ideology, that mankind must first of all eat, drink, have shelter and clothing before it can pursue politics, science, art, religion etc.; that therefore the production of the immediate material means of subsistence and consequently the degree of economic development attained by a given people or during a given epoch form the foundation upon which the state institutions, the legal conceptions, art, and even the ideas on religion, of the people concerned have been evolved....

But that is not all. Marx also discovered the special law of motion governing the present-day capitalist mode of production and the bourgeois society that this mode of production has created. The discovery of surplus value suddenly threw light on the problem, in trying to solve which all previous investigations of both bourgeois economists and socialist critics, had been groping in the dark.[15]

Engels described Marx as the "best-hated and most calumniated man of his time." Absolutist and republican governments alike had deported him. "Bourgeois, whether conservative or ultra-democratic, vied with one another in heaping slanders upon him. All this he brushed aside as though it were cobweb, ignoring it, answering only when extreme necessity compelled him." Yet, after so many years of marginality, he had "died beloved, revered and mourned by millions of revolutionary fellow-workers—from the mines of Siberia to California, in all parts of Europe and America—and I make bold to say that though he may have had many opponents he had hardly one personal enemy."[16] An overstatement, to be sure. Marx had made personal enemies aplenty, even if that animosity sprang from political differences. The scarce attendance at his funeral was, superficially at least, no confirmation of the "millions" of followers Engels described, but as the eulogy drew to a close, Marx's old friend, informed by sadness and faith, offered a prophetic declaration. "His name will endure through the ages and so also will his work!"[17]

Reuters carried the first news of Marx's death, but the initial report—like so many press reports about Marx—was incorrect, claiming that he had died in Argenteuil.[18] Even when it was determined that Marx had died in London, the British press picked up the information only after a *Times* correspondent read the news in a socialist paper in Paris.[19] Twelve years earlier Marx had been front-page news in the flurry of stories following the Commune, but in 1883 his passing barely warranted a mention.

It would be left to Engels and Marx's two daughters to ensure that though the man was dead, his ideas would not die along with him.

Part VII

After Marx

45

⌒

London, Spring 1883

Death is not a misfortune for him who dies
but for him who survives.

—Epicurus[1]

ON MARCH 25 Engels told Laura that Lenchen had found a five-hundred-page manuscript among Marx's papers. It was *Capital, Volume II.* "As we do not yet know in what state of preparation for the press it is, nor either what else we may find, it will be better to keep this piece of good news out of the press for the present."[2] Two weeks later a draft of *Volume III* was also discovered. No one had been sure while Marx was alive just how far along he was in his writing. Though he repeatedly claimed to be on the verge of completion, that verge was pushed back so often it seemed no more than a mirage. "He always refrained from telling us how far his work had progressed," Engels recalled, "for he was aware that, once people realized something was ready, he would be pestered until he consented to its publication."[3]

As Engels examined the material, he found it polished in substance but not in language or style. The *Volume II* manuscript, for example, was full of colloquialisms, coarse humor, and different languages running into each other: "Thoughts were jotted down in the form in which they developed in the brain of the author. . . . And finally there was the well-known handwriting which the author himself was sometimes unable to decipher."[4] Despite the difficulties, there was no question of leaving the manuscript to collect dust. It had to be published. Marx's death had created a vacuum at the top of the movement, but the posthumous publication of his writing, as well as Engels's own, would provide map and compass for budding socialist parties. Already younger followers were busily misinterpreting Marx's theories and rewriting the movement's history.

Among the reassessments was an account in which the "good" Marx was led astray by the "evil" Engels; in another, their roles were reversed.[5] Engels and the family howled with laughter when a German émigré in America wanted to delete from an article a reference to Marx's nickname, Mohr, because he thought mentioning it might hurt the party. (As if making the movement's leader human enough to have a pet name would rob him of the stature required of a socialist legend.) Engels said anyone who knew Marx knew him as Mohr, and had done so since his university days. "If I had addressed him in any other way he would have thought something was amiss."[6] As for himself, Engels politely but firmly corrected one petitioner who insisted on calling him Dr. Engels. "Allow me to say that I am no 'Dr' but a retired cotton-spinner."[7]

Outside his home, meanwhile, a London policeman had taken up a regular patrol route while Engels entertained friends in the days after Marx's funeral. Engels told Laura, "The imbeciles evidently think we are manufacturing dynamite, when in reality we are discussing whiskey."[8]

Engels and Tussy were designated joint executors of Marx's literary estate. As such, and with help from Lenchen, they found themselves up to their elbows digging through boxes of notes, notebooks, manuscripts, letters, newspapers, and books in which Marx had scribbled his thoughts in the margins.[9] Marx had left behind no money to speak of: his entire estate was worth £250.[10] But a lifetime of work was stacked in his study, and it required time and devotion to sort through. Tussy was determined to keep old family letters that might contain criticism of Engels or the Burns sisters out of Engels's hands. She wrote Laura, "I need not tell you that I have taken the utmost care to prevent our good General from seeing anything that is likely to give him pain. Indeed all the private letters I shall put aside. They are of interest only to us."[11] Marx was gone, but their lives were still dedicated to preserving and protecting him.

Tussy, however, had found another life requiring her devotion. It is not clear when she met Edward Aveling, who in March 1883 was a thirty-three-year-old doctor of zoology with artistic aspirations. The two could have crossed paths in any number of places—he was part of the British Museum Reading Room group, he had spoken on a platform in 1880 in support of the jailed Irish Land Leaguer whom Tussy had defended in the street, and he had run for the school board when Tussy was campaigning for a woman candidate. He had even taught at King's College during

Longuet's tenure, and he was part of London's fringe journalism world.[12] Aveling had a hand in every area that interested Tussy, from politics to Shakespeare to secularism. In addition, and perhaps most important, George Bernard Shaw observed that Aveling idolized Shelley, Darwin, and Marx.[13]

Aveling claimed he'd first met Tussy ten years earlier, when she'd attended one of his lectures with her father and mother.[14] But it was difficult to trust any version of history according to Edward Aveling—the one thing known of him for certain was that he was a habitual liar. He was also an accomplished seducer of women, which was a source of fascination for many of the men in their circle. Shaw said Aveling had the "eyes and face of a lizard."[15] He was described as "forbidding...ugly and even repulsive." One contemporary stated, "Nobody can be as bad as Aveling looks."[16] And yet it was also said that he needed but half an hour's start against the handsomest man in London to be able to successfully woo any woman he chose.[17] The future sexologist Havelock Ellis, who was one of Tussy's closest friends, said of Aveling, "There was about him an air of virile and intellectual energy, an outspoken spontaneity, which served at first to mask the more unpleasant features."[18] He had been the lover of the glamorous secularist Annie Besant and by 1883 had set his sights on Tussy. She, in turn, was enthralled by him, confiding to a friend that Aveling "brought out the feminine in me. I was irresistibly drawn to him."[19] She even chose to ignore an impediment that might have frightened off other women: Aveling was married. Seemingly without difficulty, this man who claimed to be both Irish *and* French (doubly victimized, for a woman like Tussy bent on rescue) quickly insinuated himself into the Marx inner circle.[20]

The search through Marx's papers had produced not one manuscript of *Volume II* but several texts and thousands of pages in various states of maturity. Far from being discouraged, Engels called the work a "labor of love," because he would be collaborating again with his old comrade. He told Johann Becker in Geneva, the only other remaining member of their 1848 crowd, "For the past few days I have been sorting letters from 1842–62. As I watched the old times pass before my eyes they really came to life again, as did all the fun we used to have at our adversaries' expense. Many of our early doings made me weep with laughter; they didn't after all ever succeed in banishing our sense of humor."[21]

As much as he enjoyed the project, however, Engels needed help. He had not only assumed responsibility for publishing Marx's theoretical work, but he was trying to cope with an avalanche of correspondence.

Letter after letter arrived requesting translations of published pieces, interpretations of past writings, and advice on the movement. A British publisher had even indicated interest in producing an English edition of *Capital, Volume I*—a triumph, no doubt, but also a burden. Day after day, night after night, Engels worked into the early hours deciphering Marx's minuscule script, and the effort was taking a toll on his eyes. Engels had Tussy on hand, but her time was divided between their work, her teaching, and two small newspapers she was editing with Aveling.[22] And, increasingly, the balance was tilting toward Aveling.

Sociologist and economist Beatrice Webb had met Tussy at the British Museum that spring and described her in her diary as "comely, dressed in a slovenly picturesque way, with curly black hair flying about in all directions. Fine eyes full of life and sympathy, otherwise ugly features and expression, and complexion showing the signs of an unhealthy excited life, kept up with stimulants and tempered by narcotics." Webb was no fan of Tussy's. She said it was useless to argue with her, especially about religion: Tussy took issue with Christ because, before his crucifixion, he had prayed that his cup might pass from him—in her eyes, he lacked heroism. Webb asked Tussy to explain socialism but Tussy declined, according to Webb, saying "I might as well ask her to give me a short formula of the whole theory of mechanics."[23] Tussy's uncharacteristic arrogance was for some dismaying evidence of Aveling's growing influence.

No longer able to rely on Tussy's help, Engels turned to Laura for assistance. He argued that she had plenty of time on her hands and reason to relocate temporarily to London: Paul had finally been imprisoned for a speech he had given the previous fall, when Marx and Laura were in Switzerland.[24]

Lafargue's path to jail had been filled with grand posturing. He and Guesde had ignored an order to appear in court in Montluçon, south of Paris, where the incendiary speech had been made. A warrant was duly issued for their arrest, but Lafargue said he would appear in court only if his train fare was paid and he was given a large hall in which to make a speech. He then published a letter to the magistrate in which he compared his own social satire to that of Jonathan Swift.[25] He was roundly ridiculed even by his then living father-in-law, Marx,[26] and in December was arrested and released pending trial. In March, while attending Marx's funeral in London, Lafargue was convicted.[27] He returned to France, an appeal failed, and by May 1883 he was on his way to the famed Sainte-Pélagie prison, east of Paris's Latin Quarter, to serve a six-month sentence.[28]

A trip to Sainte-Pélagie was almost compulsory for any self-respecting French revolutionary. Lafargue and Guesde were installed in the political wing—which Laura dubbed the Pavilion of Princes—and were allowed to bring their own furniture. Lafargue moved in a desk and armchair, and he requested that his wife join him every day for lunch, which she would either cook or they would have sent in from a nearby café.[29] Laura told Engels the inmates' appetites were "distressingly good.... I turn up every morning at about half past ten with a basketful of victuals cooked and uncooked—the raw material for lunch—and dinner." She smuggled in a bottle of brandy, and "benevolent party men" contributed wine, cigars, pipes, and tobacco.[30]

Engels interpreted this as evidence that Lafargue was in good hands and Laura could be put to much better use in London. But Laura jokingly retorted that she feared that if she left, the "two great men" would become very small.[31] Her concern for the two prisoners, however, may simply have been a mask to hide her real reason for not wanting to come to London. She was deeply annoyed that Engels had named Tussy coexecutor of Marx's literary works and further enraged by his revelation that Tussy was talking to an English publisher about a translation of *Capital* to be undertaken by Engels's barrister friend Sam Moore.[32] Laura suspected Tussy of attempting to claim sole right to their father's literary legacy, with Engels's apparent acquiescence.

It was not a matter of money for Laura, it was a matter of justice. Laura had dedicated her life—and sacrificed her children—to her father's work, and did not think it right that she should be cut off from his intellectual legacy. She wrote Engels a furious letter in which she said her father had told her in Switzerland that he wanted *her* to write a history of the International and to undertake an English translation of *Capital*. She and her father had planned to be together on the Isle of Wight after the new year to work on the project, but that plan was derailed by events: "When after Jenny's death I expressed a wish to see Papa I was told that my coming would alarm him. Tussy's letter asking me to come over reached me on the day after his death." As for the decision to make only one of Marx's two surviving daughters his literary executor, her outrage leapt off the page: "Papa in health would not have made his eldest and favorite daughter his sole literary executrix, to the exclusion of his other daughters, he had too great a love of equality for that...let alone the last of his daughters."[33]

Engels's response did nothing to calm Laura. He claimed it was Tussy who had told him of Marx's instructions concerning the handling of his works and that Lafargue had been in the room when it was discussed. He also cited English law as the reason Tussy was chosen as Marx's legal representative. He protested that he had no intention of causing another dispute between the sisters and suggested that instead of talking to him, they talk to each other. He, for his part, consulted Lenchen.[34] Thus, in addition to inheriting the full weight of Marx's political and theoretical work, Engels had also inherited the family's feuds. Overwhelmed in every way, this man who in over four decades had rarely succumbed to illness was ordered to bed for a month with a chronic ailment.

Throughout his life Marx was notoriously late for historic events. The *Communist Manifesto* was published too late to impact the 1848 revolts. His *Civil War in France,* meant to coincide with the Commune, appeared after its fall. Most famous of all was his 1851 prediction that he would finish researching *Capital* in five weeks and provide a riposte to the capitalist triumphalism of the First International Exhibition—a deadline he missed by sixteen years. Yet in another sense, Marx had been too early. The publication of the French translation of *Capital* and Bax's review of his work in 1881 were the start of what would become a surge of interest; by the end of 1884 three socialist organizations had taken hold in Britain, at least two of them rooted in Marx's ideas. Tussy was at the center of this new movement. She and many of its young followers gathered beside St. Paul's Cathedral on Paternoster Row in a cramped office that had been home to *Modern Thought,* the magazine that had printed Bax's article on Marx. In January 1884 it became a socialist journal called *To-Day.* Tussy wrote and solicited work for that publication as well as for *Progress,* edited by Aveling, which was also being transformed into a socialist magazine.[35] Hyndman began publishing his socialist newspaper *Justice* that same month.[36]

The birth of those publications was aided by a coincidental rise in popular dissatisfaction in Britain and a dramatic wave of bombings in London that began with a dynamite attack on Parliament three days after Marx's death (the attack and his passing were unrelated). Two more blasts followed later in 1883, both targeting the Underground system. The year 1884 also began with explosions: in January a device was found in a tunnel near Euston Station, and in February another went off in Victoria Station. The bombs were the suspected work of Irish radicals but also symptomatic of growing tensions throughout the capital—and indeed the country—due to economic distress.[37] Parliament had extended the vote to five million people, or two out of three men, but this franchise did nothing for the lower classes. Their lives had not materially improved no matter how many people could cast ballots, and they began to look beyond government for support. Many turned to trade unions, which were viewed with concern by capitalist interests in and out of government as the workingman's path to socialism.[38]

It is interesting that thirty years after Marx first launched his prolonged attack on capitalism, his ideas were still difficult to grasp even for the intellectuals in Tussy's circle. William Morris, a fifty-year-old architect, artist, poet, novelist, and social reformer, tried to tackle *Capital* in French but drowned in the economics.[39] Yet he said though he may not have understood surplus value, he knew a rotten system when he saw it: "It does not matter a rap, it seems to me, whether the robbery is accomplished by what is termed surplus value, or by means of serfage or open brigandage. The whole system is monstrous and intolerable. . . . It is enough political economy for me to know that the idle class is rich and the working class is poor, and that the rich are rich because they rob the poor. That I know because I see it with my eyes."[40] Morris joined Hyndman's group and was soon working with Tussy. So, too, was George Bernard Shaw, who had been won over to socialism by *Capital*. "Karl Marx," he said, "made me a man."[41] (Shaw's job on *To-day* was to fill empty pages with material from his novels, which no one would publish.)[42] Assessing Tussy's friends and the new British socialists, Engels called them a "motley society" but added, "Well, it's a beginning."[43]

At Maitland Park work on Marx's papers was still under way, but the house's two remaining residents were ready to move on. In September 1883 Tussy took an apartment in Bloomsbury, near the British Museum, and Lenchen moved in with Engels. Engels was thrilled to have her presiding over his house. Since Lizzy's death Pumps had served as his semi-official hostess, but she had since married, had two children, and moved out. Engels had no women in his house other than servants, and from his perspective there was no better person to help him make sense of the remnants of Marx's life than Lenchen, the only other person who knew it as well as he did.

For her part Tussy gained the independence she had long craved. Determined not to rely on Engels for money, she took jobs teaching, writing, researching—anything she could find to bring in a few pence. And in the fall of 1883, sixteen years after its publication, she and Laura received the first royalties from *Capital*. Engels handled the transaction and split the twelve pounds from Meissner three ways, among Tussy, Laura, and the Longuet children.[44] The sum was minuscule, but the recipients accepted it with relish—for both its symbolic and actual value. The Marx children were, in Lafargue's words, "hard up," especially he and Laura. Paul had no occupation other than writing for socialist newspapers and agitating on behalf of Marxist socialism, neither of which earned him a sou.

At least there was a growing audience for his leftist proclamations and protestations. The discontent among British workers was magnified several times in France, where even the agricultural sector was suffering. Improvements in trade and transport allowed grain and meat from Russia and the United States to flood French markets, pushing the price of local farm products down by as much as 25 percent.[45] Free trade also took its toll on manufacturing: German toys poured into France, as did furniture from Germany and Belgium. Even artificial flowers, a traditional Parisian industry, were being imported from Germany and England.[46]

At the same time a general industrial depression had hit France, costing many workers their jobs, and in March 1883, the month of Marx's death, masses of unemployed took to the streets in Paris. A series of strikes by an angry and energized working class followed. Their frustration involved not just low wages and long hours but the subhuman living conditions at the mines and factories where the poor flocked for jobs. The wooden dwellings erected for workers were shacks without water, without heat, without sanitation. They were fit for animals, perhaps, but not for families, generations of them squeezed into a single structure because they were unable to afford better. Adequate food was a luxury, medical attention unheard of. Businessmen feared socialist propaganda was filtering into these camps, and they wagered that allowing workers to form unions—the lesser of the two evils, in their view—would undercut the appeal of socialism. But they mandated that such unions were to address economics such as hours and wages exclusively, not social issues such as living conditions.[47]

Lafargue and Guesde resided at Sainte-Pélagie from May until October, while the tensions between French workers and capitalist employers were rising. Lafargue described his time behind bars as a lark. He got drunk on Cypriot wine, condescended to eat shell-less lobster (because it was more proletarian), and demanded game such as hare and quail from party comrades. But he was bored, telling Engels, "Walls have a strange nerve-racking effect."[48] Laura reported that Paul had begun to feel seedy, though she suspected it was due to too much fatty duck and fowl.[49]

Laura's life while Paul was in prison was much less amusing. They had moved into an apartment building near Montparnasse, on the Boulevard de Port Royal, that was full of what she came to suspect were at best practitioners of free love but more likely prostitutes. The Lafargues' apartment was separated from their neighbor's by only a thin partition—there was no privacy, no comfort, and very little quiet. There was also no money. Laura had begun playing the lottery in hopes of scoring a big win; for day-to-day funds she turned to Engels.[50] She accepted his money because she and Paul both worked for the party—and because she had no other option.

Solitary and estranged from her only living sister, Laura was cut off from the occupation that might have given her life meaning at that point: translating and editing her father's writings. She could not even take solace, as her mother had, in participating in her husband's work; Laura had little involvement in Lafargue's antic politicking, which on his release from prison sent him chasing audiences from one end of France to the other. And, of course, most painful of all were the memories of her lost children. Marking her birthday alone that fall, she wrote to Engels, "A few days back I was thirty-eight years old! Isn't it scandalous? I never thought that I should live so long, and nobody gives me credit for it. I am ashamed to say that I have stained this letter with very useless tears but that's your fault!"[51] Sixteen years before, she had married Lafargue, terrified but no doubt also excited by the adventure she had embarked on. Now, from her wretched flat among Parisian lowlifes, she must have marveled at how wrong it had all gone.

A commemoration was scheduled at Highgate Cemetery in March 1884 for the first anniversary of Marx's death. It was also to mark the thirteenth anniversary of the Commune. The previous year fewer than a dozen people had stood at Marx's graveside, but that spring as many as six thousand, nearly all wearing a splash of red, assembled at Tottenham Court Road in Soho to walk to his resting place. Though delegates had arrived from Germany and France, the crowd was overwhelmingly British. This was an amazing turn of events: Marx had never had more than a handful of English associates during his lifetime. When the procession arrived at the vast cemetery, having marched miles uphill through London's main streets and neighborhoods, the crowd found itself locked out. Tussy told Laura that five hundred police were positioned inside to make sure the massive gates were not breached. She approached an officer and asked if she and a few women could go inside to place wreaths on her father's grave but was told she could not. The crowd remained orderly and retreated to a nearby park, where their tribute continued unhindered but closely observed.[52]

This brilliant affirmation of Marx's influence on the new socialist movement in Britain was also a formal coming-out for Aveling, who addressed the crowd as if he were Marx's heir. A mere political shadow the year before, he had managed to maneuver himself into a position at the front of the "Marx party." Engels had even allowed Aveling to help Sam Moore translate *Capital* into English, despite the fact that he had no background in economics and his sample work, according to Engels, was "utterly useless."[53] He had agreed out of deference to Tussy, the first of many such concessions concerning Aveling that would have serious personal and political consequences. Some would later say that Engels's unquestioning embrace of Aveling inhibited the influence of Marx's ideas in Britain just when they were ripe to explode.

Several weeks after the Highgate event, the house at Maitland Park was finally emptied, its contents—books, furniture, papers—distributed by Lenchen and Engels among colleagues from Moscow to New York. Engels took the most valuable papers, which he would use to finish Marx's work, and some of his furniture, including the chair Marx had died in, which he placed in his own study.[54] Engels's home was now the official family residence and Engels de facto head of the Marx clan. Thus it was to him that Tussy went to get his blessing for her decision to "marry" Aveling.[55] She could not, of course, legally marry Aveling, because he already had a wife, so she proposed to violate social propriety by simply moving in with him. One can imagine the impossibility of Tussy approaching her father with that prospect; Marx would never have approved. But Engels, who had lived much of his life with two women who were only nominally his wife, had no problem with the arrangement.

Why was Aveling still married? Divorce had been legal in Britain since 1857, and while separation was still a risky proposition for a woman, because she would essentially be an outcast from society, a divorced man faced no such prejudice. Aveling offered several explanations for his circumstances. He had married Isabel Frank, the girl next door, after the death of her wealthy father.[56] (Aveling's brother contended that Edward had married Bell for her money, and when it was gone, so, effectively, was he.) Aveling told some that he and Bell had parted by mutual consent, or that she had left him to run away with a preacher. Still another version he circulated was that he had been entrapped by her. He described her as a spoiled rich girl who had spread nasty rumors about his involvement with his female students. She did not want to live with him, Aveling claimed, but also refused to grant him a divorce. In all these scenarios Aveling was either magnanimous or wronged, and thus merited Tussy's loyalty. The real reason Aveling chose not to divorce Bell was simple: the bulk of her portion of her father's £25,000 fortune was still untapped, and as long as she remained Mrs. Edward Aveling, under British law Mr. Edward Aveling—no matter how estranged—stood to receive some if not all of her inheritance at her death.[57] That part of the story was surely not disclosed or even suggested to Tussy.

In a spirit of honesty Tussy began a series of letters explaining her decision to move in with Aveling and asking for support. "You must have known for some time that I am very fond of Edward Aveling and he says he is fond of me," she wrote Laura. "So we are going to 'set up' together.

You know what his situation is and I would not say that this resolution has been an easy one for me to arrive at. But I think it is for the best. I should be very anxious to hear from you . . . do not misjudge me. He is very good and you must not think badly of either of us. . . . If you knew what his position is I know you would not."[58]

Tussy also notified the head of the school where she taught, mindful that her decision might jeopardize her job. (It did.)[59] Indeed, she was so scrupulous that she would not accept invitations without first describing her exact relation to the man with whom she would be arriving. To one such invitation she responded candidly,

> I should make my present position quite clear to you. I am here with Edward Aveling, hence forward we are going to be together as true husband and true wife. . . . He is, as you probably know, a married man. I have not come between him and his wife. For many years before I met Dr. Aveling he had been living alone. I may tell you also that my sister and my father's oldest friends fully approve of the step we have taken. I need not say it was not lightly taken or that I have overlooked the difficulties of the position. But on this question I have always felt very strongly and I would not now in act shrink from doing what I have always said . . . I distinctly feel to be right.

She signed the letter Eleanor Aveling.[60]

Engels and Lenchen were amused by Tussy's distress. Engels told Laura that Tussy and Aveling had pretended for months they were not lovers, "these poor innocents who thought all the time we had no eyes."[61] In fact Engels was relieved when they finally decided to make their romance public, because such secrets provided ammunition for their enemies. Engels was not certain that Tussy would escape criticism, and he tried to protect her, at least at the start, by cautioning Karl Kautsky of the risks of publicity about the union. "It will be time enough when, perhaps, some reactionary puts something in the papers about it. . . . My London is almost a Paris in miniature."[62] Kautsky had met Aveling at Engels's birthday party in November 1883 and found him repulsive.[63] It seemed only Engels and Lenchen approved of the match, and they may have been blinded to Aveling's failings because they were so happy to see Tussy in love.

In July, Engels gave Tussy and Aveling fifty pounds for a honeymoon in Derbyshire.[64] (The sum was extremely generous for such a stay, but Aveling had no trouble breezing through it.) Tussy's closest female friend at the time was a woman named Olive Schreiner, an ardent feminist and aspiring writer whose pen name was Ralph Iron. Olive was as unkempt as

519

Tussy—dark locks tumbled down her neck and over her forehead. She was small and sturdy, with lovely dark eyes. Tussy saw her almost daily, as Olive lived in an apartment near one Tussy had taken that summer with Aveling, on Great Russell Street—still in the vicinity of the British Museum. Tussy treated Olive like family, and when she and Aveling set off for Derbyshire, she suggested Olive take a cottage nearby.

Olive's closest male friend was Henry Havelock Ellis, who was every bit her physical opposite. Tall, blond, his hair swept back from a broad forehead, he was the picture of a young English gentleman. He was also eccentric to the core. His beard was neatly clipped on one side but a long and scraggly mess on the other. His area of expertise was psychology, his field of interest sex. Olive wrote him soon after learning that Tussy was to be called Mrs. Aveling: "I was glad to see her face. I love her. But she looks so miserable. Henry, what a great and solemn thing love is."[65] When Olive arrived in Derbyshire, she thought she understood why Tussy looked so glum. She wrote Ellis, "I am beginning to have such a horror of Dr. Aveling.... To say I dislike him doesn't express it at all. I have a fear, a horror of him when I am near.... He is so selfish, but that doesn't account for the feeling of dread."[66] Ellis wanted to see for himself. He had known Tussy before her association with Olive. Of their first encounter at Islington Hall, he said, "I still see her, with the radiant face and expansive figure, seated on the edge of my secretarial table, though I recall nothing that was said."[67]

In Derbyshire Ellis found Tussy "vigorous and radiant" and in "her full physical, mental and emotional maturity." And unlike Olive, he found Aveling amiable enough.[68] Only after he left did he learn that Aveling, whom he described as living freely at the hotel and drinking without stint, had left without paying. He had likewise cheated another landlord at a nearby hotel. Subsequently Ellis began to listen more intently to the rumors about Aveling that were circulating among members of Hyndman's Democratic Federation, which had been rebranded the Social Democratic Federation that summer, and of which Tussy and Aveling were members.[69] Ellis told Olive that an estranged colleague had accused Aveling of habitually borrowing money and failing to repay it, and the SDF board was considering ejecting him.[70] Tussy was aware of the rumors, but because they came from Aveling's enemies, she ignored them. She was a veteran of wars of personal invective; her father had spent a lifetime battling the lies of his critics. Still, the whispers did not stop, and soon socialists began to say they could not work with Aveling. Tussy welcomed the chance to defend the man she believed had been so wronged for so long. Years later, after the most tragic episode in her life, Liebknecht would observe, "The worse the reputation the brighter the merit, and it is not saying too much that just the badness of Dr. Aveling's reputation helped to gain him merit in Eleanor's sympathy."[71]

By December the acrimony in the Social Democratic Federation was such that the group ruptured. The rift was not over Aveling—though Hyndman blamed him and Tussy—but about tactics. The SDF was seen by some members as too autocratic, too nationalistic, and too willing to ally itself with existing political parties. In addition, Hyndman had set a date certain for revolution—1889—which would have been anathema to Marx, who argued that such a cataclysm could not be forced but had to evolve.[72] Some ex-SDF members joined an intellectual group of socialists in the Fabian Society, whose gradualist motto was derived from the Roman general who defeated Hannibal: "For the right moment you must wait, as Fabius did, most patiently."[73] Others, including Tussy, Aveling, Belfort Bax, and William Morris, left to form the Socialist League. Its declaration of principles identified its aim not as political adventure but as the teaching and preaching of socialism: "In England the one thing to be done at present is to educate and organize."[74]

Engels told Laura that Bax, Aveling, and Morris were probably the men least capable of running a political organization in all of England, but to their credit, he said, they were sincere.[75] In any case he had neither the time nor the patience to corral the warring socialist factions springing up in Britain, France, and Germany. He was much more pragmatic than his old friend in that regard. Marx had been willing to set aside his theoretical work to play party disciplinarian, but Engels believed the best way to direct the movement was to publish as much of their writing as possible, as quickly as he could. This man of action was now focused entirely on words.

46

London, 1885

*We play through our little dramas, and comedies and tragedies,
and farces, and then begin it all over again.*

—Eleanor Marx[1]

CAPITAL, VOLUME II went to press in January 1885, eighteen years after
Marx had promised it to his publisher. During the interim Marx had written two complete manuscripts and six partial texts. It took Engels a year
and a half to make sense of the tangled assortment.[2] Though drained by
the task, Engels feared that if he did not plunge immediately into *Volume
III* it would be lost forever, because no one else could decipher Marx's
writing or understand his meaning. At the very least, Engels said, he had
to get one full manuscript ready in clean script before he could happily
"kick the bucket."[3] Among Marx's papers he had found two complete
manuscripts and a notebook of calculations for *Volume III*[4] (parts of which
Engels said were so disordered they would "strike terror into a better man
than me"[5]), and about a thousand sheets of a very rough *Volume IV.* This
fourth volume was so far from finished that Engels said he would tackle it
only after he had completed all his other work—and that backlog was
enormous.[6]

Engels was now sixty-four, but his brain was seemingly as sharp as a
twenty-year-old's. In addition to preparing *Capital, Volume I* in English,
overseeing the publication of *Volume II,* and beginning his work on *Volume
III,* he was revising the French, Italian, Danish, and English translations of
his own and Marx's earlier works: *The Eighteenth Brumaire, The Origin of the
Family,* and *Communist Manifesto* (French); *Wage Labor and Capital* (Italian);

The Origin of the Family, Communist Manifesto, and *Socialism: Utopian and Scientific* (Danish); and *Socialism: Utopian and Scientific* (English).[7] Engels told one colleague he had turned into a "mere schoolmaster correcting exercise-books."[8]

His joy, though, was his work on Marx's unpublished writing. In March 1885 he told Laura *Volume III* was "getting grander and grander the deeper I get into it. . . . It is almost inconceivable how a man who had such tremendous discoveries, such an entire and complete scientific revolution in his head, could keep it there for twenty years." Writing on March 8, just before the anniversary of Marx's death, he proclaimed, "Two years already on Saturday! And yet I can truly say that while I work at this book, I am in living communion with him."[9]

Engels dated the preface to *Capital, Volume II* May 5, 1885. That would have been Marx's sixty-seventh birthday. As Marx had wished, the book was dedicated to Jenny. Engels noted that part of his problem in editing Marx's work was his friend's lack of experience with commercial arithmetic. Marx could study differential calculus but was not always good at interpreting balance sheets, and those very commercial transactions were at the heart of *Volume II,* which described the circulation of capital in business and society.[10] Throughout five hundred pages, Marx attempted to detail an ever-expanding system that created markets where none existed, merely to unload products on consumers who did not need or ask for them.

Among those marketplaces was a housing industry in which builders no longer built to order (funded by payments made by homeowners as the work progressed), but operated entirely on speculation. Such speculation involved not one house or four houses but hundreds. The magnitude of construction required the builder to greatly exceed his own financial resources and borrow capital on the premise that he could pay it back when he sold those homes that had been built for no one in particular. But that formula put housing, once a bedrock of social stability and development, into the same precarious position as other capital investments. Like the financial market, the building trade was now susceptible to crashes. If the builder could not repay the money lent him, Marx said, his entire enterprise collapsed: "At best, the houses remain unfinished until better times arrive; at the worst they are sold at auction for half their cost." Thus capitalist overproduction condemned one more industry to the system's cycle of boom and bust.[11]

Market excess, according to Marx, did not apply only to inanimate objects. He claimed that in the quest for quicker and greater profit in the agricultural sector, large-scale capitalist farmers even defied nature, by speeding the growth of animals—and thus shortening the amount of time before slaughter—through new breeding methods. That accelerated process upset the balance of agriculture and drew farmers away from traditional crops to focus on cows, sheep, and pigs, which commanded higher prices. This in turn resulted in gluts in some areas, shortages in others, and price increases for staple food items such as corn or oats that were either no longer grown in favor of more lucrative meat or sold as feed to fatten herds.[12]

In *Volume II* Marx described the impact that capitalist development and investment had had on society beyond the industrial areas he covered so microscopically in *Volume I.* The socially, politically, and commercially destructive system he described as operating in the factories of Victorian England was shown in *Volume II* to extend its reach into every household and onto the land itself.

Marx's friends in Russia had been anticipating *Volume II* since 1867. Engels was so anxious to finally deliver it to them that he sent Nikolai Danielson copies of proof sheets from the German edition before it had been published. Engels believed it was imperative that the book be distributed there quickly.[13] In 1883 exiled Russians in Switzerland had established a group called the Emancipation of Labor, whose goal was to spread Marx's writings in their homeland.[14] Momentum was building.

In February, Aveling, Tussy, and William Morris took their Socialist League message to Oxford's undergraduates. The meeting was disrupted by a stink bomb, but the three thoroughly enjoyed the evening and left behind a nascent Marx Club.[15] That outing among Britain's elite would have been a rare one for Tussy. She was increasingly involved in London's East End, where living conditions were even more abhorrent than they had been in Soho and St. Giles when her parents arrived in England. Aveling, on the other hand, had begun offering night courses on socialism in the West End, but when questions emerged in the Socialist League over the whereabouts of money collected at the door, he switched his subject to science and his location slightly north, to Tottenham Court Road. He could now pocket fees without complications.[16]

Aveling may have been a socialist—though that, too, was questioned by former associates who wondered at his sudden and full-throated conversion under Tussy's influence[17]—but it was more likely that he viewed the movement as an advantageous new stage. The socialists had attracted London's leftist intelligentsia, and without reaching too far Aveling could find connections to speed his entry into the theater as a playwright. Aveling had worked hard for socialism at times, but a contemporary said he did so in a mechanical way,[18] and after only two years in the movement he began to grow restless for his first love, the theater—and for the attentions of the pretty young actresses he saw on the streets around his lecture hall.

In April, Aveling developed what a doctor described as a likely kidney stone and went off to the Isle of Wight alone because he and Tussy could not both afford to travel.[19] The predicament sounded reassuringly familiar to Tussy; her father had, after all, spent the last decade of his life in search of health, and like him, Tussy blamed Aveling's illness on exhaustion. She told Laura, "Apart from the necessary work for getting a living—*however one can*—there is the constant worry from the 'Socialist League.' From childhood we have known what it is to devote oneself to the *'proletariat.'* It is superfluous to explain to you."[20] This was the first of many solo trips by Aveling, not all of them health related, which associates often hinted involved women other than his "wife" Eleanor. There is nothing to suggest Tussy suspected Aveling on this occasion, but she was unusually perturbed during this period. In June she wrote Shaw asking him to visit. She said she would be "quite especially thankful if you'd find it in your heart to look in and save me from a long day and evening of *tête à tête* with myself, the person of all others I am most heartily sick of." Tussy and her group had just discovered Henrik Ibsen and were consumed by his work. She was particularly drawn to the Norwegian's faith in the unmended. In her letter to Shaw she wrote that she thought it silly that people complained that Ibsen's plays did not end or have a solution: "As if in life things 'ended' off either comfortably or uncomfortably. We play through our little dramas and comedies, tragedies, farces then begin it all over again. If we could find the solutions to the problems of our lives things would be sane, in this weary world."[21]

Shaw noted in his journal that year that there was a rumor Tussy and Aveling had split,[22] and though there is no evidence they did, Tussy's letters were full of anxiety about relationships. She wrote Olive Schreiner, "Since my parents died I have had so little real—ie pure, unselfish love. If you had ever been in our home, if you had ever seen my father and mother, known what he was to me, you would understand better both my yearning for love, given and received, and my intense need of sympathy."[23]

There was also a question of guilt. Four years after her mother's death, Tussy was still filled with self-reproach for putting her own career and desires above those of her family during Jenny's final illness. A Marx daughter was not supposed to consider such bourgeois notions as joy derived from personal achievement; foremost were the needs of others— those immediately within reach and those millions she would never meet that her father claimed as his responsibility. Unlike her sisters she had tried to straddle both worlds, and she feared her mother had not understood. Perhaps her father had not either, but in her need to idealize everything related to him, Tussy convinced herself that he had. "Of my father," she added in her letter to Schreiner, "I was so sure! For long miserable years there was some shadow between us—I must tell you the whole story someday—yet our love was always the same, and despite everything, our faith and trust in each other." Not so with Jenny: "My mother and I loved each other passionately but she did not know me as father did. One of the bitterest in the many bitter sorrows of my life is that my mother died thinking, despite all our love, that I had been hard and cruel.... But father, our natures were so exactly alike."[24]

The Marx daughters had come of age in an exceptional household. Their parents certainly loved each other—almost fanatically so—and Jenny's dedication to Karl was a study in noble self-sacrifice. Each of their daughters looked for a model of that relationship in her own marriage, but found neither profound love nor misery equally shared. Jennychen, Laura, and Tussy had all been inveigled by men who waved the flag of revolution before orbiting away, red comets, leaving them to struggle on alone. "Edward is dining this evening with [an art critic] and went off in the highest spirits because several ladies were to be there," Tussy told Schreiner. "I am alone and while in some sense I am relieved to be alone, it is also terrible. How natures like Edward's (ie pure, Irish, French) are to be envied. Who in an hour can forget anything."[25]

Tussy's confusion at that time reflected her inner turmoil but also the discussions she had been having with friends who were questioning the relationship between the sexes. Theirs was not an exploration in the suffrage mold; it was an intimate examination of the lives and natures of men and women, public and private. It was clear to Tussy's group that women were made subordinate to men merely because of their sex—they exhibited no shortage of strength, talent, or intellect that ordained that they live their lives in a dependent state. Some argued that women were the last legally bound slaves. But that role was no longer a given. After long ignoring the issue, male socialists had finally begun to take a look at women's rights. In 1878 August Bebel had published a book called *Women and Socialism,* arguing that there could be no liberation of humanity without the social independence and equal rights of both sexes.[26] And a frank exploration of women's rights had begun to surface in the arts. Ibsen's influential play *A Doll's House,* published in 1879, was first performed in London in the early 1880s. Havelock Ellis's future wife, Edith Lees, said she, Schreiner, and Tussy, among others, had gathered outside the theater after the play, breathless with excitement. "We were restive and impetuous and almost savage in our arguments. What did it mean? Was it life or death for women? Was it joy or sorrow for men?"[27]

At about that time, a study conducted by Pall Mall Gazette editor W. T. Stead, the Salvation Army and other charitable organizations painted a graphic and disturbing picture of sexual commerce in London. Stead's group concluded that sex crimes could be more aggressively prosecuted and thus controlled by raising the age of consent for girls from thirteen to sixteen.[28] Tussy was outraged: the age of the woman was beside the point; as long as one class (or one sex) had the means to buy another, sexual exploitation in all its forms—whether in prostitution or marriage—would continue. Tussy and Aveling fired off a pamphlet on women's rights and the sex trade in response to Stead's study (Aveling's many critics might have seen him as something of an expert). Their conclusion was that women were "the creatures of an organized tyranny of men," that marriage and morality were mere business transactions. Yet their bold statement ended with a whimper in favor of monogamy—or, as they said, "the cleaving of one man to one woman."[29]

Tussy had been talking to Shaw about Ibsen for months, and he urged her to once again pursue her stage dreams. Perhaps as preparation, in January 1886 she held a reading of A Doll's House at her apartment. She played Nora, and Shaw was the blackmailer Krogstad. Tussy cast Aveling as the insensitive husband Helmer.[30] At the end of 1885 she was engaged to translate an even darker tale of female misery, Flaubert's Madame Bovary. Of Emma Bovary she wrote: "Her life is idle, useless, and this strong woman feels there must be some place for her in the world; there must be something to do."[31] It might have been a description of Tussy herself, as she assessed what her cherished independence had brought her and wondered whether what she had was what she had wanted.

Socialism was tested at the ballot box in Germany, England, and France in the fall of 1885. The mere appearance of socialist candidates was construed by their supporters as a victory, yet the mixed results were a sobering reminder of the long road ahead. Despite the antisocialist laws still in place in Germany, which had forced party leaders to adopt clandestine methods—collecting money under the guise of benign organizations, communicating via smuggled material, fielding candidates under the banner of fictitious groups—the Socialist Workers' Party increased its number of seats in the Reichstag to twenty-four, which gave its members the right to sit on committees and author legislation.[32] The timing of the victory was crucial for the German working-class movement: for the first time, more Germans were employed in industry than in agriculture, and German industry was run by cartels that concentrated power and money in the hands of an elite group.[33] Short of revolution, which the German proletariat was in no position to wage, the only way to counter that new force was from within the government.

Britain's elections that year were the first since voting rights had been extended to five million people, nearly twice as many as could previously cast ballots. Hyndman's Social Democratic Federation fielded three candidates but lost all three polls—a minor if disappointing setback on the socialists' first attempt on Britain's national electoral stage, except for the fact that it devolved into scandal when it was learned that Hyndman had accepted money from the Conservatives to run his candidates in areas where Liberals had expected to do well, thereby cutting into the latter's support. As a result, at its first outing the socialists were seen by many as dirty dealers.[34]

Soon they were also linked to violence. The winter of 1885/86 was one of the coldest ever in London, and in the East End, which had been hit by layoffs, families had no money to buy coal to warm their homes. Protests over joblessness and a lack of material goods—from food to fuel—were a nearly daily occurrence in one part of the city or another.[35] In February, East Enders took their grievances to the bourgeoisie, marching in a socialist and trade union–organized procession to Hyde Park from Trafalgar Square along Pall Mall, where they were jeered by members of private clubs. The huge, sparkling-clean windows that separated the desperate gray rabble from the upper-class club members nestled by their fires proved too great a temptation for the mob, which also included young toughs and outright criminals. They began smashing the imposing glass panes along Pall Mall and continued all the way to Oxford Street, shards littering the street.[36] Police were surprisingly scarce during the riot, intentionally so, Engels believed, in order to discredit socialists and workers by associating them with wanton destruction.[37] As news of the disorder spread, so did the panic. One paper reported that sixty thousand hooligans were preparing to march on London.[38]

But nowhere did the threat of violence have a greater impact than in France. The broad left had emerged victorious in the fall of 1885, yet within its ranks the splits were deep and the result was an all-consuming postelection power struggle—what Engels called the "parliamentary disease."[39] While deputies and ministers assailed each other month after month within their gilded assembly hall, they did not hear or feel the tremors shaking France. In factories and mines across the country, agitators—some socialist, some anarchist—were apprising workers of the fact that they had power enough in their numbers to cripple the capitalist system that exploited them. In 1885 Emile Zola had published his novel *Germinal*, which described not only the subhuman conditions miners and their families endured but also the murder of a mine manager at the hands of strikers driven to madness by want and maltreatment. In January 1886 a mob of striking miners in the Pyrenees town of Decazeville, whether consciously or not, mimicked that crime: they murdered a manager by throwing him out of his office window to a crowd below that proceeded to tear him apart with their coal-blackened hands.[40] That act of animal barbarism was enough to give pause to even the noisiest legislators in Paris and beyond. The fear it generated in representative assemblies and factory offices around Europe focused attention on workers' demands in a way that peaceful strikes had failed to do. Engels said it also signaled the death of utopian socialism in France;[41] pie-in-the-sky notions of a better life one day, however reassuring to intellectuals, were useless to workers robbed of everything, including their humanity.

Only three workingmen were members of France's newly elected Chamber of Deputies, but they used their influence to force attention onto labor issues, and in March 1886 the chamber passed an unprecedented resolution ordering that conditions at mines be improved. Engels's enthusiasm for the "revolution" in France positively jumped off the page in letters during that period. For the first time the French government had recognized the rights of labor.[42] Lafargue and Guesde's Workers' Party (established by Guesde in 1880 as the first French Marxist party) formed a National Federation of Unions to support its own and socialist candidates in local polls and to build on the gains that had sprung from the pits of Decazeville.[43] Engels did not see the English situation improving soon, because he considered British socialist leaders naive and without a proper plan. But he saw developments in Germany as positive and those in France and America as very important. In 1886 workers in eight U.S. cities protested in favor of an eight-hour workday (the average workweek was sixty hours). That action culminated on May 1 in demonstrations and strikes involving hundreds of thousands of people. Heartened by the efforts, Engels nevertheless feared the U.S. labor movement lacked solid theoretical footing.[44]

Marx's version of socialism (the term "communism" was now largely reserved for references to a future classless society), with its emphasis on empowering workers through education, unions, and political parties, with the goals common ownership of the means of production and ultimately the destruction of the capitalist system, had become more widely known, but it was still barely understood, especially in English-speaking countries. That, however, was about to change. Work on the English version of *Capital, Volume I* was proceeding quickly (though Aveling's contribution was unimpressive; in one chapter he missed fifty pages[45]), and Liebknecht, Tussy, and Aveling were setting out on a speaking tour of the United States to introduce "Marxian" socialism to that vast new audience.

Tussy and Aveling left Liverpool aboard the *City of Chicago* on August 31 and arrived in New York on September 10, 1886; Liebknecht traveled separately. The two men had been invited to America by the mostly German, New York–based Socialist Labor Party of North America. Tussy was not officially their guest, but the party took advantage of her presence, allowing her to speak at nearly every stop. Their timing was fortuitous. The socialist movement was young, and workers' issues were front-page news, in part because of the trial and expected execution of seven men blamed for a deadly blast during a workers' rally in Chicago that May, the so-called Haymarket bombing. Tussy was nervous about the trip and told Laura she expected a difficult time because of the Chicago case. Aveling, however, saw only gold awaiting him across the Atlantic, scribbling a note to Laura and Lafargue from Liverpool, "*If* we make millions of dollars we will spend some of the very first of them in a Cook's ticket" so the Lafargues could join them in the United States.[46]

From the moment of their arrival in New York, the Avelings were swarmed by the press. (Tussy said they descended like wolves.)[47] A reporter noted their disoriented appearance when they disembarked, describing Aveling as looking like a Quaker in his gray suit and broad black felt hat. Tussy, who leaned on his arm, wore a large white straw hat with a white bow, her skin tanned from her journey.[48] The trip had been difficult for her. One of the lower-deck passengers had died during the crossing, and as his grieving family stood watching his remains being consigned to the sea, a fellow passenger laughed and threw an orange peel after the coffin. Tussy was irate over the contempt the "higher class" showed for the poor, even in death. But she was not condemned to linger long among these shipmates.[49] At the docks men wearing red ribbons quickly rescued Tussy and Aveling. Among them was Theodor Cuno,[50] the man Engels had saved from drowning at Marx's dinner after the last International Congress at The Hague.

Tussy, Aveling, and Liebknecht's first lecture was to socialists in Bridgeport, Connecticut, after which they went on to New Haven to address students at Yale.[51] In all they traveled for twelve weeks, visiting thirty-five towns and cities where they met leftists, feminists, socialists, and labor union leaders, and spoke at nearly every stop, sometimes at four different events each. Tussy paid her way by writing newspaper articles. Aveling, meanwhile, attended ten theatrical performances: he was moonlighting during their socialist tour by writing theater reviews for London newspapers and magazines.[52]

In early November the group arrived in Chicago and made the front page of the *Chicago Tribune*.[53] Their arrival had been preceded by warnings that "Aveling and his vitriolic spouse" were coming to Illinois to stir up dangerous passions.[54] This seemed only to fuel interest in their visit. Thousands attended their lectures. In her standard address Tussy told American audiences to "throw three bombs amongst the masses: agitation, education and organization."[55] She spoke to them as a socialist activist, while Aveling lectured as a professor of socialist history and Liebknecht, who delivered his remarks in German, served as living witness to the movement's first half century. Their socialist road show, a grueling trip that took them by train and carriage as far west as Kansas City, was a success. Midway through the trip the group received word of an important workingman's victory in New York: Henry George, a candidate from the trade union–backed United Labor Party, had nearly been elected mayor, polling second in the contest and besting Republican contender Theodore Roosevelt.[56] Although the Marx "party" had had nothing to do with it (and weren't entirely keen on George), it was proof the political landscape was shifting. With this election as evidence, they could return to England triumphant over labor's—and socialism's—progress in America.

Their Socialist Labor Party hosts, however, gave them a tepid send-off. The SLP was annoyed by Aveling's unsolicited advice on the best way to take advantage of the growing power of the working class in U.S. politics. Aveling had suggested that the predominantly German SLP (which at one point claimed to have about three thousand members) align itself with larger, more powerful labor organizations, including those whose membership was comprised of manual laborers—both white and black—like the Knights of Labor. He pronounced this the only way for the movement to flourish in America. Engels said that though the Germans understood the movement's theory, in two decades of trying they had not made any inroads among Americans hungry for guidance.[57] Aveling's advice, no matter if it merely parroted Engels, was deeply resented, because of the messenger (the veteran German socialists viewed him as an English parvenu) and because of the implicit criticism of the SLP it contained. From that moment Aveling became an enemy. He had, in fact, made himself an easy target, but he and Tussy did not know that as yet, and they were caught unawares by the ferocity of the attack that awaited them.

★   ★   ★

In January Tussy returned to London and the good news that the English edition of *Capital, Volume I* was finally published and that sales of the German *Volumes I* and *II* were increasing.[58] They were by no means best sellers or even fair sellers; there was merely a respectable turnover that showed interest in Marx's work was finally on the rise. But any sense of pride Tussy may have felt over her American trip and her father's writing evaporated soon after she and Aveling reached home. Aveling was handed a copy of the *New York Herald,* which reported that American socialists were demanding answers about excessive expenses he had submitted for his tour of the States.[59] The newspaper gloated over the scandal, claiming Aveling, the "apostle of underpaid labor," had filed $1,600 worth of illegitimate expenses.[60] While the machinists, carpenters, and laborers he purported to champion earned no more than $2 a day, Aveling, the report said, spent $25 on flowers, $50 for cigarettes, $42 on wine at one hotel alone, and $100 on the theater.[61] The *Herald* story was picked up by London newspapers, among them the *Evening Standard,* which quipped, "The New York Socialists...have determined nevermore to import a professional agitation from the effete monarchies of Europe, the luxury is too expensive. It is a great thing of course to impress upon the people that a share of the wealth, which the rich squander so freely, is theirs; but the New York socialists do not want to import agitators to show how the squandering is done."[62]

The SLP might not have gone public with the charges, which could only hurt the party, had it not had a dispute with Aveling over organizational tactics prior to his departure from New York. But once aired, few besides Engels or Tussy doubted the merits of at least some of the accusations. The spending was quintessential Aveling, and some no doubt wondered whether all the flowers and wine were shared with Tussy. Many of their associates in London seemed to have experienced Aveling's loose handling of money—in all cases someone else's. Henry Salt, a socialist activist, said Aveling did not hesitate to borrow money from Salt's wife as soon as Tussy left the room.[63] H. W. Lee, who worked with Aveling on party matters, said he was "utterly unscrupulous about the way in which he satisfied his desires." Aveling wanted the best no matter the cost, and Lee gave one example: "One day he gave an order to a German tailor who belonged to the Communist Workers' Educational Association for a velvet jacket and waistcoat. The tailor, who could not get his money, was further grieved when he went to the Lyceum Theater and saw Aveling in the stalls attired in the unpaid for velvet jacket and...accompanied by a lady."[64]

Tussy and Aveling responded immediately to the SLP charges. Aveling explained that he did not expect the group to pay his bills; he merely submitted all his expenses so the party could decide which were appropriate, and he stood ready to cover his personal costs.[65] Engels joined in his defense. During his entire public career Marx had been accused of living in luxury off the back of the workingman, and Engels saw that same charge resurrected in this case. In response to a letter from the American translator of Engels's *Condition of the Working Class in England*, he railed against the accusations and the calls to have Aveling excluded from party activities or publications. He said he had known Aveling for four years and knew he sacrificed his social and financial position for the party. Moreover, Engels said, if Aveling was guilty of swindling the workers, he could not have done it without Tussy's knowledge. "And then it becomes utterly absurd, in my eyes at least. Her I have known from a child, and for the last seventeen years she has been constantly about me.... The daughter of Marx swindling the working class—too rich indeed!"[66]

Yet those who knew Engels understood that he was incapable of seeing flaws in men once he had accepted them as friends. Bax said, "No amount of evidence of Aveling's delinquencies in money matters or untrustworthiness and complete unreliability of his character generally as a man, would induce Friedrich Engels to cease placing his trust in him. What was worse he was continually trying to foist him as a leader upon the English socialist and labor movement."[67]

As for Tussy, her friends marveled at her inability—or unwillingness—to see Aveling's flaws. In his play *The Doctor's Dilemma,* Shaw based the characters of Dubedat and Mrs. Dubedat on Aveling and Tussy. He portrayed Dubedat as a selfish scoundrel weak in two areas: money and women. Out of respect and love his acquaintances kept information of his borrowing and philandering from Mrs. Dubedat. She believed Dubedat to be a genius who did not concern himself with pedestrian matters, and she chose to ignore his faults because she needed him to justify her very existence: she needed to save him to live.[68]

Tussy once wrote to Ellis, after she had been living with Aveling for a time, "There are some people one gets to know *at once,* and others that one is a stranger to after a lifetime passed together."[69] Did Mrs. Dubedat know her husband? Did Tussy?

47

⌒

London, 1887

I shall be glad to get any work I am capable of doing. I need much work and find it very difficult to get. "Respectable" people won't employ me.

—Eleanor Marx[1]

IN THE EARLY years of socialist agitation, when Marx and Engels began their work, protests, riots, and uprisings were rare. By the mid-1880s they were nearly constant. In any industrialized country in Europe, at any given time, one could find a strike, a protest, or mob violence directed against the capitalist system and its perceived government enablers. In the early years, when protests did arise, they were instigated by upper-class radicals and intellectuals who had adopted and led the cause of the worker (like Marx and Engels themselves), or artisans, the highest class of worker (such as members of the IWMA General Council). But by the mid-1880s the demonstrations were often spontaneous outbursts of frustration from the workers, by the workers, and for the workers. Strikes, too, were organized by labor leaders from within their ranks. These were men born in poverty, without formal education but with a natural gift for leadership and oratory that stirred their fellows to action unlike any intellectual agitator could. Initially governments tried to blame outsiders for industrial action by workers, just as French officials had tried to blame foreigners for the Commune. But it was clear to everyone from the factory floor to the elected assemblies that the discontent and those expressing it were homegrown.

Advances made as a result of the protests and strikes were usually limited and local, so in 1886 socialist leaders in France, Germany, and England

534

began discussing the creation of a Second International.[2] The First International had been disbanded in Philadelphia in 1876 after sputtering ineffectually for years in New York. Some believed it was time once again to try to gather all workers under the International umbrella, in part because capitalism had become a behemoth. Colonialism was in its glory: European countries were busily carving up the map of the world, gaining territories to rule, markets in which to sell, and natural resources—including people—to exploit.[3] In addition to the expanding world market, new technology and sources of energy, from oil turbines to the internal combustion engine, meant bigger and faster machines. Everything was accelerating and expanding, and the fortunes to be made were immense.[4]

In this environment a single trade union might earn higher pay or better work conditions from one employer, but such improvements would not extend to the next factory without a strike there, and there was no guarantee that any gains won would not be lost. The individual union was like a guerrilla unit with only light weapons trying to hold off a king's army. Some socialist leaders believed the only way to fight such an opponent was with one of comparable size and strength, and the only way to build such a power was through international solidarity.

French socialists hoped to convene the Second International in Paris in 1889, the hundredth anniversary of the French Revolution and the year France planned to host the World Industrial Exhibition, the capitalist festival that had begun in England in 1851.[5] Of course, it was easy to agree on the necessity of a meeting, but that was the only area of accord at the start of the planning. Each country's notion of what the new International should look like reflected its own particular concerns—the French were embroiled in a theoretical dispute; the Germans wanted to focus on politics, the English on economics. Now, however, there was no Marx to direct the discussions. Engels did his best to enforce cooperation by sending off vitriolic letters, but it remained a much less orderly process than the birth of the First International. Lafargue was deeply involved in organizing the event, and Longuet, too, had discussed it and the many intra-socialist squabbles in France with Engels. But Longuet was walking a political tightrope, aligning himself with moderates while feeding information to Engels that might be used against them. To protect Longuet's identity when discussing sensitive information, Engels referred to him simply as "Z."[6]

Longuet's relations with the Marx family had been strained following Jennychen's death in 1883. Lenchen and Tussy bore a grudge against him for his treatment of Jennychen and seemed convinced that because he had been a bad husband, he must also be a bad father. Tussy had returned to

London from Argenteuil after Jennychen's death with her nephew Harry, who was ill and in need of special attention. Tragically, the child died just three days after Marx had. (Harry was buried with his grandmother and grandfather at Highgate.) That spring Tussy also tried to convince Longuet to allow her to bring Johnny to London. She had written Charles insistent letters, demanding to know when Johnny would be placed in her charge. Longuet did not respond. When he finally did, it was only to say that he was thinking about it.[7]

From Longuet's point of view, he may not have been anxious to entrust his eldest son to London so soon after another child had died in his aunt's care. Yet that would have been as unfair to Tussy as was Tussy's view of him. For all Jennychen's complaints about Longuet, his letters indicated that he loved his children deeply, even if that love sometimes looked like neglect. In any case, the decision on the children's future was ultimately made by Longuet's mother. She did not want them to fall victim to the "cult" of their grandfather, and she did not like Tussy or Laura.[8] And so Longuet had turned the children over to his mother in Caen while he tried to sort out his life as a widower. But he had continued to correspond with Engels about politics, and in 1886, amid the International discussions, he finally took Johnny to London to stay with Tussy and Aveling.

There is no indication that Engels helped support the Longuets. The children were given one-third of the royalties from Marx's writings, but that money was put into a trust and was not accessible to their father, despite his chronic lack of cash. When Longuet arrived in London, Lenchen's son, Freddy, reminded the Frenchman again of the money he was still owed from Jennychen.[9] As this suggests, Freddy was now very much in the picture. After Lenchen moved into Engels's house, he visited her every week and would later say he spent evenings with Engels talking about Marx.[10] Freddy worked as a machinist and had a wife and son, just one more London laborer scraping by on his salary.[11] As a socialist, he looked to Marx and Engels as the two men who fought on his behalf, and his son reported that Freddy hung their photographs on the wall of his home.[12] But was that a tribute to their activism, or because one of these men held the key to his birth?

Both Tussy and Laura knew Freddy well, and one wonders whether they looked at his face, a face so much like their father's—the broad forehead, the arch of his eyebrows, the distinctive nose—or at his compact body and thick black hair, and saw Marx. Was there the slightest suspicion that he was their half brother? Tussy firmly believed that Freddy was Engels's son, but Laura may not have. Years later she seemed unperturbed by the disclosure of Freddy's parentage. It was, to her, apparently old news.

But that was Laura's response to just about any personal or political eruption. While the rest of her family—including her husband—indulged in high drama, she remained serene. After a lifetime of expecting miracles, she knew there were none to be had. In the spring of 1887 she greeted Paul's latest electoral defeat in that same manner. He had offered himself as a candidate in Paris's municipal elections and lost badly. Laura was under no illusion about her husband; she saw his faults so clearly that she was able to laugh about them. She told Engels after attending a campaign rally that the crowd around her considered Lafargue a "braggart," a "windbag," and a "ranter," when, she joked, his delivery had actually improved over earlier outings.[13]

For her part, Laura worked behind the scenes; she had not been barred, as she once feared, from the Marx literary business. She had translated the *Communist Manifesto* into French,[14] and was asked that spring by Edward Stanton, son of American women's rights advocate Elizabeth Cady Stanton, to write a piece on socialism in Paris.[15] Though penniless, Laura seemed to have accepted her fate as permanent and unalterable. When Engels sent her royalties from *Capital*—the first English edition had sold out in two months—she declared the money "more welcome than flowers in spring or a fire in December...it is one thing that is never out of season."[16]

The Marx contingent in London was not so tranquil. After their return from America, Aveling and Tussy lectured frequently on U.S. labor agitation. But even as they took the stage to cheering audiences eager for news from abroad, they were battling for Aveling's political life. In British socialist circles the accusations leveled against him in America were shorthanded into embezzlement.[17] And with each charge, further stories about his colorful past surfaced.

Engels went into full defensive mode on Aveling's behalf, dismissing the reports as the movement's usual tittle-tattle and mudslinging.[18] Frustrated associates again grumbled that Engels had always been a bad judge of character, and gradually people who had frequented his home began to stay away because of Aveling's presence. Yet there seemed no way of convincing Engels that Tussy's "husband" was a cad.[19] After months of defending him, however, he confided his frustration with Aveling to a longtime associate in New York: "The lad has brought all this down on his own head through his utter ignorance of the world, of men and of business, and his predilection for poetical dreaming." Charitably, Engels described Aveling as "a very talented and serviceable sort of chap and thoroughly honest, but gushing as a flapper, with a perpetual itch to do something silly. Well, I can still recall the time when I was much the same kind of idiot."[20]

Tussy and Aveling's lectures brought in some money but not enough.

Tussy's friends knew of her distress—personal and financial—and while they could do nothing about Aveling, they tried to help her find work. When Havelock Ellis asked her to assist him on a first English edition of Ibsen's plays, Tussy jumped at the chance and began teaching herself Norwegian.[21] In March 1887 they also discussed translating Zola into English. His stark portrayals of life under Napoleon III were controversial, and Ellis and Tussy were confident of finding English readers. Tussy was eager to take on that job, too, telling Ellis, "I shall be glad to get any work I am capable of doing. I need much work and find it very difficult to get. 'Respectable' people won't employ me."[22]

Tussy often remarked that no matter how dire their finances, nor how much opprobrium was directed his way, Aveling took no notice. She, however, absorbed it all. The battering was relentless and cruel, and Tussy felt she had no one to turn to, least of all Aveling. By this time he was showing signs not only that he was tiring of socialism but that he was tiring of her. In June he published an insipid poem, signed Lothario, that could be interpreted as a message to Tussy that he was not a one-woman sort of chap:

> *Pure love would consist, you contend,*
> *In devotion intense, without aim,*
> *Without hope, without bound, without end,*
> *But that wasn't the stake in our game. . . .*
> *These, Sweet, are my commonplace views,*
> *Though your eyes for a time overcame me—*
> *'Aut Caesar's the motto I choose,*
> *And I really don't think you can blame me!*[23]

The poem had many more verses, but the message was the same: Our love was fine while it lasted. No matter how tolerant Tussy was in her relations with Aveling, she could not have failed to be humiliated by such a public airing of his feelings, and in so adolescent a fashion. Distraught and depressed, Tussy tried to kill herself. "It was by deliberately taking an overdose of opium," Ellis wrote years later of the incident. "But by administer of much strong coffee and helping her walk up and down the room the effects of the poison were worked off. . . . Her friends were grieved, they were scarcely surprised."[24]

Perhaps trying to salvage their relationship, Tussy and Aveling rented a cottage in Stratford-upon-Avon that August. "Think of it, Laura, Shakespeare's home!" she wrote her sister. "We work two or three times a week at his 'birth place'...Edward is writing no end of things. Have you heard that a play of his, *Dregs* (a short one-act thing), has been accepted by a very popular and 'rising' actress Rose Norreys, and is to be produced shortly? And that he will probably have two other plays, one an adaptation of the *Scarlet Letter*, accepted also shortly?"[25]

Though Tussy painted an idyllic portrait, her letter was false in every respect. Its tone was meant to convey warmth and happiness, but it was painful to read; it was not joy that leaped off the page, it was loneliness, fear, and a desperate attempt to reconnect with her physically and emotionally distant sister (Laura rarely answered Tussy's letters). Her enthusiasm over Aveling's work was colored by foreboding: the further he moved along the theatrical path, the further apart they grew.

The year 1887 was a strange one in London all around. On the one hand it was Queen Victoria's Golden Jubilee (marred by what she described as a "horrid noise" called "booing" when she visited the East End[26]). It was also the year Buffalo Bill's Wild West Show opened in London (Engels and the Avelings attended, Engels declaring it "very nice"[27]). And it was the year of Bloody Sunday, when police seemingly declared war on unarmed civilians in Trafalgar Square because they were exercising their rights to free speech and assembly.

The reasons for the protest were many. Unemployment—a new term in the English lexicon for an old reality—drove many East Londoners to the West End, where men and women had been staging nearly daily rallies to draw attention to the plight of the working poor. With memories of the Pall Mall riot still fresh, the East Enders' presence in Trafalgar Square was seen as potentially dangerous, and the police chief banned trespassers (that is, demonstrators or anyone construed to be demonstrating) from the area. That ruling denying workers the right to assemble only triggered fresh calls for protests.[28] Finally, the perennial Irish question was also back on the activist agenda, following Parliament's passage of an Irish Coercion bill that gave police and judges in Ireland the right to outlaw whole groups and sentence civilians without a jury trial.[29]

Sunday, November 13, was chosen as the day to protest joblessness, support the Irish, and defend a Londoner's right to free assembly. An estimated 100,000 people gathered at various locations fanning out from Trafalgar Square—Clerkenwell, Holborn, Bermondsey, Deptford, Shaftsbury Avenue, the Haymarket—before marching en masse toward its center.[30] Alerted to the plan, authorities stationed some 2,500 police away from the square and about 1,500 more, as well as 400 soldiers, in the square itself.

Once past the first line of police, the protesters would be sandwiched between armed agents of the state.[31]

Tussy and Aveling marched in separate groups toward Trafalgar Square. As soon as the police attack strategy became clear, Aveling and his contingent ran away (or, as Engels said, did "a bunk at the outset"[32]) while Tussy's held together and proceeded against the police line. Caught in the heart of the melee, her coat and hat torn, she was hit on the arm by one police baton and knocked on the head by another. She would have been trampled to death, she said, if a stranger, bleeding from the face, had not helped her up off the ground. Her experience was relatively benign.[33] One witness reported: "I saw policemen not of their own accord but under the express orders of their superiors repeatedly strike women and children.... As I was being led out of the crowd a poor woman asked a police inspector or a sergeant if he had seen a child she had lost. His answer was to tell her she was a damned whore and to knock her down."[34] William Morris's daughter May recalled that on the tops of houses and hotels all around, crowds of well-dressed women and men clapped their hands and cheered the police action.[35]

Tussy eventually showed up in tatters on Engels's doorstep after having been arrested and released.[36] Thousands of people were in similar or worse condition that night: sixty had to be hospitalized with injuries, though, miraculously, no one died. Outraged and defiant, the protesters held another demonstration the following Sunday, and at that action one man was killed. The victim, a law clerk named Alfred Linnell, may not even have been part of the demonstration.[37] A funeral attended by 120,000 people was held for Linnell on December 18. Tussy, having tasted the wrong end of a police baton, had been completely radicalized. She had spoken with moderation, urging education and organization, just a year before in America; now she called for militant civil action against police. In Chicago four of the accused Haymarket bombers had been hanged that November despite evidence that an agent provocateur had been behind the blast, and now came the London brutality. According to a reporter who heard her, Tussy proclaimed in a speech, "You must make social war on the policeman. If you see a policeman go into a shop, do not go into it...don't enter the doors of a public house where a policeman goes." She called for civil disobedience on Christmas Day to ensure police had to work, explaining that she wanted to spoil the Christmas dinners of the "fat specials" and "murderous ruffians."[38]

As a result of their participation in the Bloody Sunday events and their continued agitation, Tussy and Aveling had earned a "blank warrant," which meant police could arrest them at any time, for any reason.[39] Tussy spoke of it almost with pride. Her commitment to the fight had grown immeasurably—but not so Aveling's. In November, under the name "Alec Nelson," a second piece of his was performed in London, an adaptation of a French play titled *By the Sea*. It was the story of a young woman's struggle between her loyalty to her older husband and her love for a young sailor.[40] Tussy played the main female character and Aveling, the husband. Engels, jolly as ever, went to the performance as part of his birthday evening. He declared Aveling and Tussy had acted their parts well and that the play was sure to succeed. A critic, however, was scathing in attacking Tussy, while praising Aveling to the hilt. The criticism of Tussy was so wounding, she may have wondered whether the reviewer had it in for her personally, and if so, why.[41] Tussy was crushed—she would never act publicly again. Aveling, meanwhile, was triumphant. He quit London that December to take his plays on the road, leaving Tussy on New Year's Eve to see in 1888 alone.[42] In January an actress named Frances Ivor played Tussy's role in *By the Sea*. This time the reviews were glowing, with "Alec Nelson" described in one as "a London journalist who is rising into repute as a dramatist."[43]

Engels embraced Aveling's changed focus, perhaps with a sense of relief. While he never said as much, he may finally have recognized that Aveling had become more of a liability to the movement than a player worthy of the stage Engels prepared for him. (He told a friend Aveling had "a capacity of neglecting facts, when they are contrary to his wishes, that is worthy of a more juvenile age.")[44] Engels and Tussy both spoke of being boycotted by English socialists,[45] and there is enough correspondence among their associates on the subject of Aveling to suggest he was the reason. Sidney Webb, a leader of the socialist Fabian Society, indicated that his group's quarrel was not with Marx's ideas but with the messenger: "When we run down Marxism, we mean Aveling."[46] Tussy and Engels declared that they didn't care about being cut off from the bickering English socialists, though Tussy was sorry that in the process she had also lost some of her friends. She wrote to George Bernard Shaw, who had joined Webb and Havelock Ellis in the Fabian camp, to ask where he had been: "You never come to see us now and I have sometimes wondered whether you are boycotting us too."[47] (Shaw had had a major falling-out with Aveling the previous spring, but Tussy either didn't know or pretended not to remember.)

In any case, Aveling's foray into theater drew him away from party business. In June his version of *The Scarlet Letter* was produced as a matinee in London. The reviews were mixed, but by the end of the month, after

Aveling's fifth play had been performed, Engels declared enthusiastically and prematurely, " 'He has struck oil,' as the Yankees say."[48] In July, Tussy and Aveling decided to return to America to try to peddle his dramatic works. Engels told Laura that Aveling had "to superintend the *mise en scene* of three of his pieces, to be played simultaneously in New York, Chicago and God knows where besides."[49] Such travel would have cost much more than Aveling and Tussy's purse could bear, and there was no socialist party to pick up the tab this time; Engels likely paid for the trip. Tussy was loath to accept money from Engels, but in this case she seems to have relented. Aveling probably sold the trip to her as critical to his career and to Engels as a good investment. Caught up in the excitement, Engels decided to accompany the couple to America, along with his old chemist friend Carl Schorlemmer (one of the founders of organic chemistry, known to the Marx family as Jollymeier[50]).

Engels wanted his trip to be a private matter, so he told almost no one, including the Lafargues. Laura would have been extremely vexed to be deemed unworthy of the General's confidence, but she was not Engels's concern: he was certain that Lafargue would insist on announcing that Engels had set out to conquer the New World.[51] In a letter from aboard the *City of Berlin,* Tussy apologized to Laura for the secrecy: "I should have told you this as soon as I knew it myself, but the General was so anxious to keep it dark I did not dare to. I thought if it leaked out we should get the blame."[52]

The small party sailed into New York primed with anticipation for Aveling's success. In an early letter Tussy mentioned Aveling overseeing rehearsals,[53] and Engels reported that Aveling had wrapped up his work by August 31,[54] but otherwise there was complete silence about his theatrical efforts. Engels, however, enjoyed the trip thoroughly, one of the high points being a visit to a New England prison. He was shocked to find that inmates could read novels, form clubs, talk without warders present, and eat meat and fish twice a day. They even had running water in their cells and pictures on the walls. "Chaps...look you straight in the eye with none of the hang-dog look of the usual criminal in jail—this is something you will see nowhere in Europe," Engels said, perhaps thinking less of the "Pavilion of Princes" at Sainte-Pélagie in Paris than of the fortresses in Germany and Russia. "I acquired a great respect for the Americans in that place."[55]

In New York City, by contrast he felt he had traveled to the beastly capital of capitalist production. Everything was manmade and, in his estimation, horrid.

We got into New York after dark and I thought I got into a chapter of Dante's *Inferno*...elevated railways thundering over your head, tram-cars by the hundred with rattling bells, awful noises on all sides, the most horrible of which are the unearthly fog horns which give the signals from all the steamers on the river...naked electric arc-lights over every ship, not to light you but to attract you as an advertisement, and consequently blinding you and confusing everything before you—in short a town worthy to be inhabited by the most vile-looking crowd in the world, they all look like discharged croupiers from Monte Carlo.

Still, Engels declared that Americans had the "makings of a very great nation in them, such as are only to be found in a people which never knew feudalism. They are long-suffering as to grievances of their own making...but when they do a thing they do it thoroughly."[56]

When the group returned to England Aveling seemed unperturbed by his lack of recognition in America, and he quickly lost himself in London's West End social life. Tussy, meanwhile, was consumed with the other side of town, the capital's own *Inferno*. In the second half of the nineteenth century a great wall of buildings rose that visually separated London's east side from the west. Office buildings were a Victorian phenomenon; the very notion that there were so many people pushing paper in need of space would have seemed absurd before the Great Exhibition in 1851. But as capitalism expanded, a new tier of society that would one day be known as white-collar workers formed. The grand structures in the City of London—the financial center where money moved from one business to another without anyone actually touching cash—heightened the barrier between London's haves and have-nots. The haves occupied the west (Belgravia and Mayfair were even gated off), their miserable counterparts the east.[57]

The East End had always been several degrees more wretched than even Soho, where there was at least a vibrancy because the poor mixed with the rich, and one found color and glamour and entertainment and life. It is safe to say that the poor of the East End never mixed with the rich unless they were employed by them. The district was mean and cramped. The houses were squat and seemed even more so because of the factory chimneys that towered over them, spewing filth and ash.[58] Did the sun rise? Did it set? It wasn't evident in Whitechapel, Bethnal Green, and Limehouse. In these hells the sky was two colors—brown from coal smoke, dirt, and dust, or dirty gray in the early morning, before the day's fires were stoked. An entire vocabulary existed to describe this opacity, terms that have since disappeared—"day darkness" for days when the fog was so dense it was impossible to see, and a slightly better "high fog," when the miasma hung higher but the sun still did not penetrate it.[59] It was this fog that made Jack the Ripper's work in the East End easy in 1888—that and the fact that no one cared about the human refuse who lived there.

During the previous decade the district had swelled with immigrants. Newly arrived Chinese built a Chinatown in Limehouse that thrived in part due to opium.[60] But the émigrés who changed the face of the East End were Jews from Russia, Prussia, Lithuania, and Poland. Some had fled poverty, others persecution. The assassins who killed Czar Alexander II had included one Jewish woman, and that was used as an excuse for pogroms: traditional anti–Semitism erupted throughout Russia and 5,000 Jews were killed. The able-bodied, and those with means and connections, escaped. By 1880 there were about 46,000 Jews in London, half of them working class or poorer.[61]

Tussy first visited the East End to lecture, but soon she was drawn down to the dark hovels to meet its residents. She wrote Laura in June 1888:

> I can't tell you the horrors I have seen. It is a nightmare to me I can't get rid of it. I see it by day and I dream of it o nights. Sometimes I am inclined to wonder how <u>can</u> one go on living with all this suffering around one. One room especially haunts me. Room! A cellar dark underground. In it a woman on some sacking and a little straw, her breast half eaten away with cancer. She is naked but for an old red handkerchief over her breast and a bit of old sail over her legs. By her side a baby of three and other children—four of them. The oldest nine years old. But that's only one case out of thousands and thousands.[62]

That year women at the Bryant & May match factory on the east side waged an unprecedented strike for better working conditions and won.[63] Tussy recognized in that victory the possibility of alleviating some of the misery she had seen, and she became more committed to direct labor agitation. She had realized, looking into the hollow eyes of the degraded people around her, that her father's brand of socialism, rooted though it was in material reality, was still too abstract for the starving; work and a living wage were dream enough for them. Tussy had long been looking for her own fight, and she found it in East London.

Tussy later told a friend that she also discovered her Jewishness among the East End immigrants and that she was the "only one of my family who felt drawn to the Jewish people."[64] She wore that reclaimed heritage with pride, declaring in a letter to Ede Bernstein, "I am a Jewess," and replying to an invitation to address Jewish socialists, "Dear Comrade, I shall be very glad to speak at the meeting of Novbr. 1St, the more glad, that my Father was a Jew."[65]

Increasingly, Tussy and Aveling lived in different universes. On December 31 she wrote to Laura, "Tomorrow Edward is going to Cornwall to stay with some friends of his who are also very anxious for me to go down. I cannot. I don't care for rich folks." She would instead go to Oxford to look at a copy of an Elizabethan play, *A Warning to Fair Women*. Ellis had asked her to prepare it for a series he was editing. She gladly did so, because it was concerned with a social question, and that, she said, was the only thing that mattered.[66]

48

⌒

London, 1889

Few save the poor feel for the poor, the rich know not how hard
it is to be of needful food and needful rest debarred.

—Keir Hardie[1]

DELVING INTO THE Marx family story inevitably leads one away from the larger picture and presents a distorted view of reality. While their universe was—bar the scantiest of exceptions—entirely socialist, the world at large was not. In 1889 there were no more than 2,000 socialists in all of Britain. There were about 750,000 trade union members, but socialists of the Hyndman stripe and the Fabians did not want to work with the unions, and the unions were equally skeptical of them.[2] Honoring Marx's belief that unions were the workers' best immediate tool to confront capitalism, Tussy and some of her colleagues enlisted to fight in union battles. One socialist said they were finally welcomed "not because of their socialism but in spite of it."[3]

The first major battle, in March 1889, was on behalf of gas workers, who formed Britain's first union of unskilled laborers.[4] Tussy and Aveling helped write its rules and constitution.[5] Within months membership in the National Union of Gas Workers and General Laborers of Great Britain and Ireland numbered in the tens of thousands. Within a year it had reached one hundred thousand, and members struck for and won an eight-hour day.[6] The leaders of that battle—Will Thorne, Tom Mann, and John Burns—were all workers (all would later be members of Parliament, and one a cabinet minister).[7] Thorne could not read or write, and Tussy set about teaching him.[8]

The East End was electrified by the gas workers' victory. And when, in the intense heat of summer, on August 13, a group of dockworkers decided they would continue their drudgery no longer, Thorne, Mann, Burns, and Ben Tillett, a twenty-seven-year-old self-described fanatic,[9] were called in to lead a strike.[10] They formed a dockworkers' union on August 19, and by August 20 the Port of London was closed for the first time in a century, its workers having walked off the job.[11]

The Thames formed one boundary of the East End, and from a distance the colorful flags fluttering high above the ships moored on the great river were signs of hope, hazy beckonings of new lands and bold opportunities.[12] But the activity on the docks below was such as made men animals. Thorne said quite simply, "I believe that nowhere in the world have white men had to endure such terrible conditions as those under which the dockers worked."[13]

Most were employed not by the day but for an hour or two, and forced to wait all day for what was known as a "call on," a chance to work. Explained Ben Tillett:

> Struggling, shouting, cursing, with a grinning brute selecting the chosen of the poor wretches. At the cage, so termed because of the stout iron bars made to protect the caller on, men ravenous for food fought like madmen for the ticket, a veritable talisman of life. Coats, flesh, even ears were torn off, men were crushed to death in the struggle...the strong literally threw themselves over the heads of their fellows and battled with kick and curse to the rails of the cage, which held them like mad human rats. Calls at any point of the day or night kept men for a week at a time hungry and expectant for the food and the work which never came.[14]

Sixty thousand dockers rejected that system and joined the strike. Their demands were modest: a minimum wage of sixpence an hour—a penny increase—topped the list.[15] But the shipping companies laughed at such nonsense. How could the most degraded workingmen in London hope to defeat a force as powerful as the men who controlled the trade of the seas? The companies did not reckon, however, on the strength of combined despair; the strikers were willing to die rather than return to work. They also arrogantly underestimated the new union leaders.

The strike was organized at the Wade's Arms pub on Ryden Street, just north of the docks. Tussy and John Burns's wife solicited funds, publicized the walkout, and organized the distribution of relief gathered from sympathetic citizens, philanthropic and political groups, and other unions.[16] Engels said Tussy was "head over ears in the strike" and working "like a

Trojan."[17] In early September she addressed a Hyde Park rally on behalf of the strikers. A correspondent for London's *Labour Elector* newspaper noted, "Curious to see Mrs. Aveling addressing the enormous crowds, curious to see the eyes of the women fixed upon her as she spoke of the miseries of the dockers' homes, pleasant to see her point the black-gloved finger at the oppressor, and pleasant to hear the hearty cheers with which her eloquent speech was greeted."[18]

The dockworkers had had nothing to begin with, and after two weeks without pay they were nearly starving. There were reports about the walkout in the press, and some university students had adopted the cause, but strike organizers believed they had to move their protest into the heart of London—they had to force the city to look at the men it so easily ignored—in order to pressure the shipping companies, win support, and attract the money needed to keep the dockers alive. The strikers' protest march through London was a procession of the nearly defeated. In their sorry state they lacked the energy for a rowdy demonstration, and for that reason Londoners looked on them with sympathy. "As soon as it became known that thousands of the strikers had marched through the city without a pocket being picked or a window being broken," one observer said, "the British citizen felt he could go back to his suburban villa and that he could afford to follow his natural inclinations and back the poor devils who were fighting...against overwhelming odds." But even that support was inadequate. Soon the strike relief fund was dry.[19]

Just when it seemed the men would have to choose between death and surrender, help came in the form of an impossibly large sum—thirty thousand pounds—all the way from Australia. Dockers there had taken up a collection that was supplemented by local philanthropic groups, and sent the proceeds to their colleagues in London.[20] The shipping firms viewed this show of solidarity as an ominous sign. Launched during their busiest season, the walkout was costing the companies dearly, and if strikers continued to receive aid they could keep the docks idle for months. There was also the possibility that the strike might not be confined to London. The balance in the dispute had tilted.[21] By September 16 the dockworkers had won nearly all their demands, returning to their jobs as victorious and full of pride as a triumphant army. Their victory was cheered in factories and farms around the globe. The most demeaned and powerless class of workers had succeeded because they were organized locally and supported internationally.[22]

Their victory was also a victory for socialists. Thorne said that after the strike, workers no longer saw socialism as utopian but as a system able to produce something tangible—a path out of poverty.[23] Engels declared: "It is the movement of the greatest promise we have had for years, and I am proud and glad to have lived to see it. If Marx had lived to witness this! If these poor downtrodden men, the dregs of the proletariat, these odds and ends of all trades, fighting every morning at the dock gates for an engagement, if *they* can combine, and terrify by their resolution the mighty Dock Companies, truly then we need not despair of any section of the working class."[24]

Engels said it was now critical to form a British labor party to represent those masses.[25]

For two years socialists had been planning a grand meeting in Paris for that summer, 1889, but in the final months schisms, nationalist quarrels, and ugly personal brawls threatened to derail what many hoped would be the timely birth of the Second International. The French socialist hosts were so divided they had decided to hold two separate congresses. In May, Engels wrote Lafargue to say that he and Tussy had labored to make theirs—the "so-called Marxists"—a success, but their work was repeatedly frustrated by diplomatic missteps by Paul (who alienated English socialists by inviting one faction rather than another) and Liebknecht[26] (who seemed not to be able to decide which French faction the Germans would support[27]). There was even a dispute about the date. As agreed in early discussions, the congress was to open in September, but Lafargue abruptly decided that July 14 would be better: it was the hundredth anniversary of the storming of the Bastille and the day the rival socialist meeting was to open.[28] Fuming, Engels told Lafargue to stick to the previous date and stop acting like a spoiled child.[29] Meanwhile, rival socialists tried to discredit Lafargue's congress as strictly a Marx family affair.[30]

In the end Lafargue won the argument, the congress opened on July 14, and delegates from as far west as the United States and as far east as Russia made their way to Paris. Lafargue was in charge of organizing rooms and the hall for the event, but he sloppily failed to reserve housing for the German delegation, which was difficult to find once they arrived in Paris because the city was swarming with visitors to the World Industrial Exhibition.[31] He had rented a hall he knew would be too small to hold all the delegates so the congress would appear to be a great success, a decision that did not go over well with attendees crushed together in the heat of a Paris summer.[32] He also opted to make the congress a private event because he feared press reaction if it was not a booming success. Engels was dismayed. The congress, he felt, was called precisely to get the world's attention and focus on "the eight-hour day, legislation on women's and children's labor, the abolition of standing armies." He wondered why on earth Lafargue would want to keep it a secret.[33]

Despite the missteps in the run-up to the event, the result was indeed historic. In Paris that July the Eiffel Tower was unveiled at the World Exhibition and the seeds for the Second International Working Men's Association were planted. The Marxist gathering opened at the Salle Pétrelle, on a back street in the district between the Gare du Nord and Pigalle. Engels chose not to attend—he had had aggravation enough in the planning—but Tussy and Aveling were among the English delegates on hand to witness the landmark congress. The hall was festooned in red flags and banners that recalled the glorious battles of 1848 and the Commune. As many as twenty countries were represented, and among the 391 delegates crammed into tight quarters was an international who's who of labor and socialist leaders: from Germany came Bebel, Liebknecht, Bernstein, and Clara Zetkin; Russia, Georgy Plekhanov; Belgium, César de Paepe; and Britain, Keir Hardie.[34] And while the rival socialist congress had six hundred attendees, five hundred of them were French. The numbers showed that the rivals were strong domestically but the Marxists were the international force.[35] The next day the Marxist gathering moved to a larger hall, aptly named the Salon des Fantaisies.[36]

Engels had had few hopes for the congress, but reports he received from the proceedings led him to proclaim after just three days that it was a brilliant success.[37] After six days of meetings, delegates passed resolutions supporting an eight-hour workday, the prohibition of child labor, and the regulation of work for women and adolescents. They also endorsed the need for political organizations for workers, the disbandment of regular armies, and their replacement with people's militias. Finally, the congress agreed to hold the first worldwide May Day demonstration the next year, 1890, in support of an eight-hour day and laws governing labor.[38]

The months Engels had spent mediating between warring socialists before the Paris congress robbed him of the time he needed to dedicate to *Capital, Volume III*.[39] He would turn seventy that year, and though Tussy declared him the youngest man she knew,[40] he was aware that he might not have time to finish all the projects he had set out for himself. In addition to overseeing the publication of all Marx's work, he had wanted to write a biography of his friend and a history of the International, and complete several of his own projects that had languished for decades. He came to the conclusion that he could not do it alone. The two younger men he most trusted in the movement were Ede Bernstein and Karl Kautsky. Engels made them a proposal: he wanted to teach them to read Marx's "hieroglyphics" so they could help with Marx's work and, when the time came, take his place as editor. Both men accepted.[41]

Engels had always been much more aware of timing than had Marx. In addition to the certainty that even generals do not live forever, he sensed that the movement was gathering steam and the need was greater than ever for Marx's writing to be disseminated in order to lay a strong theoretical foundation. Not only had the Second International been a triumph, but Engels believed that the dockworkers' strike represented an irreversible gain for unions and socialists. There had also been a significant political shift in Germany. "The 20th of February 1890 is the opening day of the German revolution," Engels declared.[42] Via the ballot box, socialists that day won more than 1.4 million votes, double their showing in elections three years before. After a second-round vote in March, thirty-five Reichstag seats were awarded to socialists. Engels said he was intoxicated by the results.[43]

Behind those German gains lay the deaths of two emperors. Wilhelm I had died and was succeeded in 1888 by his son Friedrich, husband of Queen Victoria's daughter. But Friedrich had cancer and had lived only ninety-nine days as emperor. He was succeeded by his twenty-nine-year-old son Wilhelm, who became Emperor Wilhelm II.[44] The young ruler was more liberal than his seventy-three-year-old chancellor, Bismarck, and was at least initially more sympathetic to the workers. Bismarck had warned a "red" uprising was imminent and argued that antisocialist laws should not only be made permanent but expanded to include expulsion for socialist activists.[45] His attempt to crack down on socialists was defeated in the Reichstag in January 1890, which only emboldened the Social Democratic Party he had hoped to destroy. In polls the next month voters had rushed to the left, producing the "revolutionary" results that Engels so roundly cheered.[46] On March 17 Wilhelm II demanded that Bismarck resign; he did so the next day.[47] The way was now clear for a cautious expansion of working-class agitation in Germany.

The Paris congress had set May 1, 1890, as the date for the first global demonstration on behalf of labor. Engels warned German colleagues to proceed carefully, because despite the emperor's apparent sympathy for workers, the military was under orders to halt any protest, and secret police wanted to provoke unrest in order to justify a crackdown.[48]

Elsewhere, however, May Day was celebrated with jubilation—just one more reminder, if Engels needed another, of the speed with which the working class was being politicized. The streets of Paris were filled with men and women in working attire strolling toward the Place de la Concorde, where a festival atmosphere prevailed. In 1870 these same crowds had gathered to learn whether France would become a republic and whether Prussian troops had breached the city gates. Fearing the streets of

Paris would again explode when overrun by workers, many bourgeois shuttered their shops and fled. They needn't have: workers no longer had to destroy to be acknowledged. The workingman still did not enjoy the same rights as France's upper classes, but at least he was now organized and represented in the government's halls of power. Lafargue and Laura attended the celebrations. Lafargue reported that a vast number of police were on guard, and every now and then they pushed at the crowd or rushed in on horseback. The workers gave way with good humor; it was more show than menace. Lafargue estimated the crowd at 100,000 men, women, and children; whatever the number, it was spectacularly impressive.[49] But London's May Day demonstration eclipsed it. Engels called it "overwhelming."[50]

The event was held on May 4, a Sunday, so more workers could attend. Fifteen platforms — most merely the backs of delivery vans — were set up at various spots around Hyde Park. From them speakers from all over Europe addressed the crowd not on political but on labor issues, specifically, winning workers everywhere an eight-hour day and overtime pay for any hours worked after that. According to Marxist theology workers would still be giving away their labor, but it was a step along the road toward redress.

People poured into the park from every direction, on foot and in carriages, in omnibuses and via the Underground. An estimated 300,000 attended. One reporter said he had never seen the park so full: "The washer woman, struggling along, following a small banner carried by a man; the little boy who hoped that we should get him the Eight Hours."[51] The speakers came from unions — Burns, Thorne, Hardie, Tillett — and all the English socialist organizations. Lafargue and Aveling delivered their remarks from one platform. Engels, who was also on the stage but merely as an onlooker, said Lafargue had spoken well and, despite his heavily accented English, elicited a storm of applause. Tussy and Ede Bernstein occupied another platform.[52] Since the dock strike she had become one of the most popular speakers on the labor circuit, and as a woman she attracted special interest.[53] To loud cheers she told the crowd that they had not come to do the work of political parties but to make the case for labor. She described herself as a trade unionist and a socialist, and she charted the growth of the movement, from the days when a handful of people turned up to demand shorter working hours, then a few hundred, and then hundreds of thousands. Finishing her speech with a quote from "The Mask of Anarchy," Shelley's ode to English workers massacred in 1819, Tussy cried out, "Rise like lions after slumber... Ye are many, they are few." The crowd positively roared in response.[54]

Wrote Engels later: "What wouldn't I give for Marx to have witnessed this awakening. . . . I carried my head a couple of inches higher as I climbed down from the old goods wagon."[55]

Engels was keenly aware that unless guided, this newly expanded base's first taste of power would surely be accompanied by recklessness. "Many of them have only the good will and good intentions with which the road to hell is notoriously paved," he told Liebknecht. "It would be a miracle if they were not burning with zeal like all neophytes."[56] He told a Dutch colleague the third volume of *Capital* weighed heavily on his conscience; he felt it was critically important to an understanding of Marx's theories, but it still required much work. "Certain parts are in such a state that they won't be fit for publication until they have been carefully revised and to some extent rearranged and, as you may imagine when so imposing a work is at stake, I shan't do anything of the kind without the most mature reflection." Working in Marx's name, he had to get it right.[57]

After the German elections of February and the excitement of May, Engels was able to concentrate on his work in part because of Lenchen. He would say, "If Marx was able to work in peace over a period of many years as I have during the past seven, it was largely thanks to her."[58] Lenchen and Engels had been trusted friends since 1845. Indeed, they were more than that; they were family. They were alike in every way, from their fastidious-ness to their love of drink and fun, and Lenchen knew exactly what Engels needed in order to work. By 1890, in her trademark linen cap and gold hoop earrings, she was directing a household of servants and acting as the matriarch of the Marx family. When Laura moved into a new home east of Paris, in the suburb Le Perreux, Lenchen went to help her.[59] When Tussy and Aveling were at the height of their war to defend Aveling's name, she waged as fierce a fight among party women as Engels did among the men.[60] It was she who graciously opened Engels's Regent's Park residence to assas-sins, revolutionaries, politicians, and journalists from every corner of the world. The talk was political, but if a guest felt inclined to sing, he was encouraged to do so, and the Bordeaux never stopped flowing.[61] Bernstein noted that the only requirement for Engels's guests was that they "be of some consequence intellectually."[62] Christmas under Lenchen's direction was legendary. The rooms were decorated with greens, the mistletoe stra-tegically hung so no one could pass without receiving a kiss, the table piled high with food. Lenchen's famous plum pudding, which she also sent to friends in Germany and France, ended the meal. Bernstein recalled Engels's delight in dramatically darkening the room and lighting the rum-drenched pudding to loud cheers.[63]

In 1890 Lenchen was seventy and, like Engels, slowing down. In October she became ill with a vague liver complaint.[64] Early in November, an alarmed Engels wrote Lafargue that she appeared to be having a recurrence of menstruation and was losing a lot of blood. The doctor did not know what the problem was, and apparently Lenchen would not allow him to conduct an examination. Engels brought in a second doctor, who suggested that she might have septicemia.[65] Two days later, on November 4, Lenchen died. At her bedside were Freddy, Engels, Tussy, Aveling, and two servants. Years later, in a letter to Johnny Longuet, Freddy wrote, "Nearly the last words which my mother spoke were, 'Explain to Freddy the name.' As she was saying that she was holding Tussy's hand in one hand and mine in another." Freddy was haunted by his mother's dying wish.[66]

Engels notified friends and family that the "good, dear, loyal Lenchen" was gone and, in a manner he had not done even when Lizzy Burns died, openly expressed his deep sense of loss.[67] "We had spent seven happy years together in this house," he told a friend in New York. "We were the only two left of the old guard of the days before 1848. Now here I am, once again on my own.... How I shall manage now I do not know."[68]

49

London, 1891

What fools these governments are! To think they can put such a
movement down by repression.

—Friedrich Engels[1]

LENCHEN WAS BURIED in Highgate Cemetery on November 7, in the same grave as Marx, Jenny, and their grandson Harry. Engels had tears in his eyes as he read a eulogy[2] describing her life while no doubt remembering the private sacrifices she had made for Marx and Jenny, from sharing their life of poverty to giving up her only child to protect Marx from his enemies and Jenny from the knowledge of her husband's betrayal. "We alone can measure what she was to Marx and his family, and even we cannot express it in words," Engels told those gathered to mourn her.[3] As for himself, "There has been sunlight in my house until now, and now there is darkness!"[4]

While she lived, Lenchen had protected those around her, and in death Engels showed her the same regard. In writing to Lenchen's closest living relative in Germany, her nephew, to explain her will, he fibbed about the man who was to inherit all her worldly goods. Lenchen's estate amounted to forty pounds, all of it left to Freddy. Engels told her nephew that "Frederick Lewis" was the "son of a deceased friend" whom Lenchen had adopted when he was small and whom she had brought up to be a "good and industrious mechanic." He explained that, out of gratitude and with Lenchen's permission, Freddy had taken the last name Demuth as his own.[5]

Freddy had been coming to Engels's home for years, and he continued

555

to do so after his mother's death, but Tussy noted that Engels was now irritable in his company. She blamed this on the fact that Engels was Freddy's father but had never declared himself as such. Tussy believed that for Engels, Freddy was a living reminder of a personal failing and a continual source of guilt. "We should none of us like to meet our pasts, I guess, in flesh and blood," she wrote Laura. Suggesting that she, too, felt tainted by what she believed to be Engels's abandonment of his son, Tussy added, "I know I always meet Freddy with a sense of guilt and of wrong done. The life of that man! To hear him tell of it all is a misery and a shame to me."[6]

Engels's younger socialist colleagues wanted to ensure that one of their own took Lenchen's place in his household to guard the Marx-Engels legacy.[7] Victor Adler, leader of the Austrian Social Democrats, wrote to Engels immediately, suggesting Kautsky's ex-wife Louise for the job.[8] Engels had admired Louise as a "nice little body"[9] in 1885 when she arrived from Vienna with her husband at the age of twenty-five. In nineteenth-century parlance the phrase "nice little body" meant "nice little somebody," but in Engels's case it probably also meant that he had noticed her fine figure. Louise and Karl Kautsky had lived in London and frequented the Engels home until 1888, when she'd returned to Vienna and her husband asked for a divorce. This soap opera had provided months of entertainment for socialists from Germany to France to London. Karl Kautsky had fallen in love with a young woman from the Salzburg Alps who after just five days jilted him in favor of his brother. Engels was astounded that Kautsky would want to leave Louise and equally astounded by Louise's "heroic" response to the affair—she accused Kautsky's friends of being unfair to him! After Kautsky's lover became engaged to his brother, he and Louise tried to work things out, but by 1890 their reconciliation had proved futile.[10]

The idea of this (to Engels's mind exceptional) woman joining him in London quickly took root. Five days after Lenchen's death he wrote Louise asking her to live with him.

> What I have been through these many days, how terribly bleak and desolate life has seemed and still seems to me, I need not tell you. And then came the question—what now? Whereupon, my dear Louise, an image, alive and comforting, appeared before my eyes, to remain there night and day, and that image was you. . . .
>
> If, as I fear, this day-dream of mine cannot be realized, or if you should think that the drawbacks and vexations would, so far as you are concerned, outweigh the advantages and pleasures, then let me know without beating

about the bush. I am far too fond of you to want you to make sacrifices for my sake.... You are young and have a splendid future in store. In three weeks' time I shall be seventy and have only a short while left to live.

Engels signed his letter "With undying love."[11]

Six days later thirty-year-old Louise Kautsky was on her way to London to become manager of Engels's household.[12] Aveling was supposed to send a check for ten pounds to Victor Adler, who would then give Louise the money to facilitate her trip. But Aveling's check bounced; it appeared that Engels had given Aveling the cash to cover the check but Aveling had pocketed it.[13] Engels sent Adler an apology and reimbursement for the check and expenses incurred. Of Aveling he wrote, "It's the slapdash literary Bohemian in Aveling that leads to this kind of thing." He promised to give him a "thorough dressing down."[14]

The business with Louise settled, Engels celebrated his seventieth birthday on November 28. The shadow of Lenchen's death hung over the festivities, though Engels admitted that with Louise's arrival "a little sunshine has returned." (He told a friend in New York, "She is a quite marvelous woman and Kautsky must have been out of his senses when he divorced her.")[15] Engels resisted the idea of making a fuss over his birthday, and as for the tributes that poured in from around the world, he told a friend in Paris, "Fate has decreed that, in my capacity as survivor, I should glean the honors due to the works of my deceased contemporaries, above all those of Marx. Believe me, I harbor no illusions whatever about that, or about the tiny portion of all this homage that falls to me by right." Yet even if Engels wasn't in the mood, friends had arrived from all over Europe expecting a party, so Engels obliged.[16] It lasted until 3:30 in the morning. Claret and sixteen bottles of champagne were drunk and twelve dozen oysters eaten. He told Laura, "I did my best to show that I was still alive and kicking."[17]

The Paris congress and the growing power of labor in the socialist movement spawned a plethora of meetings and conferences. One such was held in the fall of 1890 in Lille, France, a gathering of Lafargue's Workers' Party—the so-called Marxists—which Tussy and Aveling attended. Much to Tussy's surprise, a banner in the room declared "Under the Chairmanship of Eleanor Marx Aveling."[18] She had expected to be only a participant, but such was her new stature among workers in Europe that she was placed at the head of the event. From Lille, Tussy went with three Frenchmen to Halle, southwest of Berlin, to attend a meeting of the German party, where a struggle was under way between the old and new

557

guard. Tussy was again a star of the event, telling Aveling, who had stayed behind in France, "Of course everyone is asking me everywhere, especially the Berliners."[19] Both meetings endorsed a second May Day demonstration and another international workers' congress, this one to convene in Brussels in August 1891. Perhaps all too predictably, organizations immediately began jostling for position, each wanting to be *the* workers' party from their respective country.[20]

In early April 1891 Lafargue (whose Workers' Party was battling more moderate socialists with whom Longuet was aligned) and his comrade Guesde set out on a speaking tour of France's northern industrial region around Lille.[21] They visited three towns in three days—Wignehies, Fourmies, and Anor—and at each stop told a horrific tale of worker exploitation by industry and betrayal by the bourgeoisie. They were preaching to the choir; two men from Paris did not have to tell that crowd about suffering, and yet their words were reassuring to the neglected workers of the province, and their audiences grew.[22] Lafargue's rhetoric was far from mild: "Today the bourgeoisie is condemned in turn; it must disappear; its grave is dug; it remains only to push them into it."[23] A socialist newspaper described the tumult left in their wake: "In the workshops, in the cabarets, socialism is spoken of everywhere.... Employers are beginning to show anxiety over this agitation and are asking what they can do to check it."[24] Lafargue believed that May 1 would be the day these workers would show the world that they were united in strength with their fellows.

But when May 1 came, a peaceful protest by fifteen hundred striking textile workers in Fourmies turned violent. The group had gone to the town hall to present their demands, closely monitored by two infantry companies who stood guard alongside police. By evening, in the flickering light of torches held by the increasingly agitated crowd, some demonstrators had been arrested. Wives with children came to demand their release but were refused. Stones were thrown and troops, carrying a new gun called Le Lebel, rushed to protect the police. In the confused twilight a commander ordered his men to open fire. Some shot into the air, but not all: gunfire lasted for a full four minutes, and when it ended ten people were dead and up to sixty wounded. Among those killed were four teenagers or children.[25]

Lafargue wrote in *Le Socialiste* that the episode was a clear illustration that the French military worked for industry, not the people.[26] Strikes in the industrial north spread and more troops were sent in, the situation dangerously combustible. The government blamed the Workers' Party for the turmoil and accused Lafargue of conspiring with a local party leader named Hippolyte Culine to stir things up.[27] After an investigation, Lafargue was indicted in July for incitement to murder.[28] He was quoted as telling new military recruits, "If ever you are ordered to fire and in whatever circumstances, turn around and fire backwards." Lafargue denied ever uttering this statement, declaring himself too much a theoretician to advocate such violence.[29] Then again, anything he said in his defense was irrelevant; his trial was a farce. The four prosecution witnesses were all members of the Fourmies mill management, and all parroted almost the same words in their testimony. One read from notes hidden in his hat. The defense, meanwhile, presented 210 petitions from people who had attended the rally and vowed that another man, not Lafargue, had urged young soldiers to mutiny.[30] Nevertheless, the jury of employers, landowners, and businessmen needed only five minutes to reach a verdict. Lafargue was sentenced to a year in jail. He was to report to Sainte-Pélagie on July 30, 1891.[31]

In the intervening weeks Lafargue set out on a speaking tour, addressing huge audiences who knew he had been wronged. He wrote Engels, "The halls are packed. . . . I have never known such enthusiastic meetings; if elections were held at the present time we should certainly be elected in the North Department."[32] A martyr for the workers in the north, by the time Lafargue reported to prison in Paris he was a celebrity. He was in good spirits—he moved into Sainte-Pélagie with a trunk, manuscripts, and a bathtub[33]—and his mood only improved a month later, when a member of the Chamber of Deputies from Lille died suddenly. A special election was scheduled, and Paul put his name on the ballot. As an inmate he was allowed to run for office but he was not freed to campaign.[34] That decision, to keep Lafargue in jail, may have been the key to his success. He had a history of losing when he took to the stump, but Guesde, a master orator, campaigned in his stead, holding thirty-four rallies in thirty-eight days.[35] On election day, October 25, Lafargue won the most votes among the five first-round candidates, and he defeated his rival in the second round on November 8.[36] (Engels found out about his victory in London's *Daily News*, which reported it in a paragraph below a story about a wealthy widow found murdered.)[37]

Laura was now in the rare position of being proud of her husband. She told Engels a portrait of Paul published in the newspaper made him look "almost young and sheepish as when he came a-wooing Kakadou. . . . There's such a hubbub as you never saw in our press and political world. . . . Our own people are beside themselves in joy. They had not in the least expected so favorable an issue, having so long been used to fortune's cruelty."[38] On November 10 Lafargue was freed for the duration of his term in office.[39]

Seven days later Laura and Lafargue were being feted from one city to the next. The celebration began in Paris, where Workers' Party friends organized a dance in their honor that lasted until two in the morning.[40] The next day they traveled to Lille, Lafargue's new constituency, where electors literally carried him on their shoulders in triumph. Laura told Engels, "Me, a lot of women had seized upon, one on either side of me, taking hold of me and I don't know how many more following behind and very nearly lifting me off my feet." They arrived at the house that was listed as Lafargue's legal domicile in Lille but actually belonged to a friend, and were told several hundred men were waiting in a nearby hall, clamoring to hear Paul speak.

At eight o'clock we started for La Scala where the meeting was to take place. We managed to get in by a side door and once inside the hall I saw a sight such as I had never seen before. The body of the hall was crowded to suffocation, the gallery was stuffed and hundreds of men and women were making super human efforts to get in. The doors, which had been closed, were forced open and a second gallery (closed for repairs) was taken by storm and in a few seconds was as chock full as the other.

Laura said benches broke under the mass of bodies and a few windows were smashed. Finally Paul spoke, but the crowd, wanting more, would not leave the hall until he left. "The perspiration ran down Paul's face, he had an enormous bouquet on one arm and gave his other arm to his wife. I rather think he thought we should be crushed for he looked intensely unhappy as we moved on jammed and wedged in by his too enthusiastic electors." The madness continued outside in the street, where boys, women, and girls shouted *"Vive Lafargue!"* When the couple arrived "home," the crowd demanded another speech, which Lafargue duly gave. One woman told Laura, "If Lafargue is unseated there'll be a revolution in Lille."[41]

After years of missteps and disappointments, after watching her husband repeatedly try and fail at business, writing, even electoral office, this wild change of fortune for a woman as grounded in reality as Laura must have seemed too good to be true. It was. First there was an effort to disqualify Lafargue's victory because he had been born in Cuba and therefore was not French.[42] He argued vehemently for his French parentage and nationality, and in so doing sparked a major falling-out with Engels. In the course of a speech in which he tried to prove his "Frenchness," Lafargue was reported by Reuters to have said that he had not fought for France against the Prussians because he was doing his patriotic duty by channeling secret reports received from Prussians in the International, including those in the army, to their French opponents.[43] If true, Lafargue was admitting that Prussian members of the International had engaged in treason. Engels was terrified that that sort of statement would be used as grounds for another crackdown on socialists in Germany. He immediately wrote Laura to demand an explanation.[44]

Laura was crushed. Engels had allowed her to bask in Paul's rare victory for but a minute before he snatched it away with a harsh scolding and a serious accusation. She replied instantly,

> You must forgive me if I reply to the spirit rather than to the letter of it. And forgive me for saying that I consider the spirit of it most unjustifiable. It is on the strength of a Reuters' telegram that you fall foul of Paul in a way that I trust and believe to be wholly undeserved. I think Paul and I have done and suffered enough ever since we came over here to further and indeed invent the cause of internationalism — which primarily means the union of France and Germany — to be quit of charges of the kind. If Paul were not the soul of honor in all things public and political, I should not now be here and living with him, for he has faults enough and to spare of his own! Forgive me for saying that your letter has spoilt the short-lived pleasure I have had in Paul's election.[45]

Lafargue convinced Engels that he had not implicated the Prussian Internationalists in treasonous activities, and Engels accepted his explanation. The rift was repaired.[46] Paul's election was also approved, his having been deemed French enough to hold office. But there would be no more celebrations. Lafargue's debut speech at the Chamber of Deputies brought him fresh humiliation.

On December 8 all eyes in the chamber were on him when he urgently asked to speak. He tabled a motion for a complete amnesty for political prisoners and made a general and naive statement on the merits of socialism while calling for others in the chamber dominated by rich men to join him in defending the working class. He then caused an uproar among leftist members who might otherwise have supported him by appearing to embrace the conservative Catholic Church's "Christian socialism" and question the rectitude of the left's commitment to the separation of church and state.[47]

From the very start of Lafargue's speech, his august colleagues murmured. The murmurs grew to heckling as lawmakers across the political spectrum egged each other on in their abuse of this upstart. The chamber was in an uproar — Lafargue rambling on while trying to shout down the hecklers[48]—until the president, radical deputy Charles Floquet (who according to Lafargue fired remarks at him behind his back from the presidential chair), finally asked him to get to the point. Lafargue described the speech to Engels the next day as a "dynamite bomb" that had caused an "explosion."[49] It was that, but not in the way he implied. Even members of his own Workers' Party disavowed his address over the church issue.[50] Mortified, he avoided the chamber for months, and instead set out on a dizzying lecture tour that kept him away from Paris.

Laura did not accompany Paul because they did not have the money to pay for her travel. A miserably cold winter had descended on France, and she said that had she not used her father's old greatcoat as a blanket, she would have been frozen in her bed. In the midst of the electoral excitement Lafargue had failed to pay the rent and left Laura without any money to do so.[51] He wrote Engels that the landlady had already paid Laura several visits and asked if Engels could send her a check.[52] Engels was furious that Lafargue had let the situation reach a crisis point: "Why expose Laura to such humiliations when you know that one word from you—or from her—would be enough to prevent them?"[53]

Engels's nerves may have been raw because that fall he had spent weeks defending Aveling against a new series of attacks, in the process wasting valuable time writing letters to try to clear his name. One wonders whether he ever considered taking the two Marx daughters into his home and locking them out of the reach of their troublesome (and self-consumed) spouses. Both Lafargue and Aveling were well into middle age but neither seemed to have achieved anything close to the maturity required at that moment, personally or politically.

50

London, 1892

Do you realize now what a splendid weapon you in France have
had in your hands for forty years in universal suffrage; if only
people had known how to use it. It's slower and more boring
than the call to revolution, but it's ten times more sure.

—Friedrich Engels[1]

TUSSY'S PROFESSIONAL LIFE was entirely focused on the union movement, while Aveling continued to straddle the rag-and-bone world of socialist politics and the glittering world of the theater. Tussy described their lives to Laura as doing a "good deal of sweating for damned little pay." Aveling still had hopes his plays would be produced, but, she acknowledged, "the devil of it is that hopes won't pay bills." Toward that end she was doing "hack translations" for a magazine, as well as "type-writing" on a new and magical machine she had purchased. Overall, their lives consisted of unending labor: "Edward writes all sorts of things—good, bad and indifferent. We both have meetings and work of that sort in every spare hour. There's really no time to consider whether life is worth living or is an unmitigated nuisance."[2] Tussy's load had increased through 1891 in preparation for the International Socialist Workers' Congress in Brussels in August. More than 330 delegates from Europe and the United States, among them envoys from the American Federation of Labor, were to be on hand for the next bout in the struggle for control of the socialist movement.[3] The jealousies among the English surfaced almost immediately: Aveling's enemies used his many flaws to tarnish the "Marx clique."[4]

Despite the personal dramas, however, the Brussels meeting ended with what Engels called a Marxist mandate for the Second International: the ideas accepted by delegates were based on Marx's scientific socialism (with its emphasis on workers' needs), not the bourgeois socialism of rival factions in France and England. The congress put the Second International, he said, once again "at the precise spot where its predecessor left off."[5] There was a sense the socialist movement, trade unions, and the myriad parties representing workers in Europe had matured, that the gains they had made through decades of toil and resistance were solid and widespread, so much so that they could not be undone at the whim of a king or even bludgeoned out of existence by an army. The resolutions approved in Brussels emphasized the importance of unions and the need for workers to unite globally against capitalist forces, which had begun to align in federations to counter organized labor. The congress also called on workers to use the vote, if they had it, to force governments to address their needs. And, over objections by some delegates, a controversial resolution was adopted to the effect that war was the product of the capitalist system and socialists must be the party of peace.[6]

The year 1892 was proof of just how far workers' parties had come. In France, where Lafargue had been in flight from the Chamber of Deputies for more than four months, addressing rallies in forty-one cities,[7] his Workers' Party had won 635 seats on municipal councils and control of twenty-two local governments.[8] Engels said things were going swimmingly in Germany, too. But it was in England that year that history was made. The 1892 May Day demonstration in London was twice the size of the first rally. Six hundred thousand people crammed into Hyde Park. Surveying that crowd, Engels said, "The time is fast approaching when we shall be strong enough to let things come to a decisive battle."[9] The old soldier used the language of war, but the change he sought would come through elections.

In July three working-class men were elected members of the British Parliament: John Burns, who was the voice of the dockworkers' strike, won election from Battersea; J. Havelock Wilson, president of the National Amalgamated Sailors' and Firemen's Union of Great Britain and Ireland, won in Middlesbrough in Yorkshire; and Keir Hardie, a thirty-five-year-old Scotsman who had begun working in the mines when he was ten, won in South West Ham, in London's East End. They did not represent either the Liberals or the Tories; they were from a third, inchoate party, the Independent Labour Party. Their agenda was for and by the working class, and while socialism did not appear in the party's name, it was its theoretical foundation.[10]

There had been candidates in the past who claimed to represent workingmen, but they were envoys from the upper classes. Burns said they, and the early trade union leaders, wore good coats, long watch chains, and high silk hats; it was evident at a glance that they were not workers and would not understand the needs of a person who lived from day to day not knowing whether they would be able to feed their children or keep a roof over their heads. The new men who took to the stump representing the people *looked* like the people, like workers.[11] Many were self-educated, studying at night while working in mines or factories during the day. Marx and Engels's revolution was poignantly manifest when Keir Hardie entered the House of Commons not brandishing a red flag but wearing the cloth cap of a workingman.

Fresh from that triumph, 120 delegates met in January 1893 to formally launch the Independent Labour Party. To write a platform a fifteen-member committee was selected that included Aveling, Hardie, Tom Mann of the dockworkers' strike, and H. H. Champion, an English socialist and journalist who had been actively promoting just such a party.[12] At the end of four days the ILP's platform read as if Marx himself had written it: "collective owner- ship and control of the means of production, distribution and exchange"; an eight-hour day; the abolition of child labor; provision for the sick, aged, wid- ows, and orphans paid for by taxes on unearned income. Also included were free education through university, and arbitration and disarmament instead of war.[13] Hardie was made chairman of the party that would one day be a cornerstone of Britain's Labour Party.[14] Engels had watched the develop- ments with awe and admiration. He told Bebel in Berlin, "The workers have at last realized that they are capable of something if only they have the will."[15]

In 1893 the electoral gains continued, this time in Germany. Forty-four Social Democrats were elected to the Reichstag and more than 1.7 million votes were cast for the party.[16] The vote came in the months before the scheduled Third Congress of the Second International in Zurich. Engels would not attend the full congress, but as honorary chairman he was obliged to deliver a closing address. It would be the first International Congress he had attended in twenty-one years, since 1872, and he may have had a sense it would also be his last.

The man who entered the Zurich hall on the last day of the Second Inter- national Congress was no mere mortal; he was a legend, half of the brain trust that had created modern socialism. The faces in the crowd were largely unknown to him, but his was instantly recognizable to them. When he entered the room the General, whose beard was now white and whose shoulders stooped slightly, was greeted by thunderous applause from four hundred delegates representing eighteen countries who stood to salute him.[17] Behind him hung a portrait of Marx. He began his address pointing to his friend's picture and saying he could accept the congress's applause only as a "collaborator of the great man whose portrait hangs up there." Then he reflected on the distance traveled: "Just fifty years have passed since Marx and I entered the movement by publishing our first socialist articles. . . . Since then socialism has developed from small sects to a mighty party which makes the whole official world quail. Marx is dead, but were he still alive there would be not one man in Europe or America who could look back with such justified pride over his life's work."

He described the evolution of the International and declared it to be much stronger in 1893 than ever before. "In accordance with this we must continue to work on common ground. We must permit discussion in order not to become a sect, but the common standpoint must be retained. The loose association, the voluntary bond which is furthered by congresses, is sufficient to win us the victory which no power in the world can snatch from us again."[18] Engels declared the congress closed, and cheering delegates were once again on their feet. A voice in the crowd began singing the "Marseillaise," and soon the familiar rebel hymn filled the hall.

The socialist and workers' parties had made great advances indeed, but the Marx family players within them had not. Despite huge gains for socialist parties in France—thirty seats in the Chamber of Deputies and seven hundred thousand votes—Lafargue, his district redrawn to his disadvantage, lost his seat in elections in the fall of 1893.[19] (Engels had expected the result. He long before had told Lafargue that his constituents wanted to know that he was at work in the chamber for them, not roaming the country delivering speeches on behalf of the Workers' Party.[20] In response Lafargue had argued that he was a "traveling salesman of socialism.")[21]

Tussy's political life in London also suffered a setback, though—as always—it was not of her making. She had struggled day and night, from Ireland to Scotland, Germany to France, to organize laborers against cross-border strikebreaking. But even as her reputation grew because of her work, it was tarnished by association with Aveling's. He was increasingly isolated in the Independent Labour Party because he thought Hardie was trying to make himself the "king" of the workers. He further marginalized himself in a dispute with Tom Mann over items Aveling wanted the ILP to add to the party program (among them abolition of the monarchy).[22] In the spring of 1894 Aveling was expelled from the ILP. Ede Bernstein, without offering details, wrote in his memoirs the reasons were such that they "would have sufficed to land him in prison."[23]

Aveling had alienated Tussy's literary friends from the British Museum, the British socialists, and finally her union colleagues. But he had in his corner one man whose opinion carried enough weight to ensure doors remained open to him: Engels still had not been turned against him. This loyalty was all the more remarkable given the shock their relationship had suffered in 1892. Engels had agreed to allow Aveling to translate into English the German text of Engels's *Socialism: Utopian and Scientific.*[24] Clear and eloquent, it was an excellent introduction to Marx's ideas (it built on Engels's *Anti-Dühring* and would become one of the most important publications in Marxist literature). Engels was a perfectionist, but with this project in particular he wanted to make absolutely sure the translation was correct. Having declared Aveling's work on *Capital* substandard, he had reason for concern. Nevertheless he went ahead with the project.

The two men agreed that Engels would edit Aveling's translation and make every change he thought necessary; he would also contribute a preface. But to his dismay, the pages he received for review were not Aveling's manuscript but page proofs from the publisher: the book was one step away from publication and Engels had not even seen it. Any changes at that point would be costly. Aveling blamed the mix-up on the publisher, but Engels's cautious tone in his letters to Aveling suggest he believed the younger man had rushed the book—essentially a rough draft—to print against his wishes.[25] Such behavior was reckless in the extreme, given that Engels not only bankrolled many of Aveling's activities but that his approval was all that kept Aveling from ostracism by the few people who still agreed to associate with him. Once again Engels was forced to put aside his other work and concentrate on undoing the damage wrought by Aveling.

Aveling's theatrical star had also fallen. It had become apparent to all—even to himself—that he was not a talented playwright. In 1893 Tussy announced to Laura that one of his comedies, *The Frog,* had failed soon after opening: "A result I fully expected, because it was *not* a good play. He knew that too, but thought *that* might save it."[26] But even as his professional prospects dimmed, the theater became more important to him personally. His social life revolved around West End pubs and restaurants, and the theater reviews he continued to write gained him entrée, when he was lucky, in the company of a producer or on the arm of an obliging actress.

Tussy did not complain of isolation—she was too busy for that. But the strain of her life with Aveling (personal and financial) was evident in her increasing paranoia about her father's legacy and in her relations with Freddy Demuth.

Tussy saw Freddy often. Perhaps it was because she felt he had been wronged or out of love for Lenchen, whom she dearly missed, perhaps because he was an East End laborer, or perhaps because without knowing it she may have felt drawn to her older half brother. In 1890, at the time of

Lenchen's death, Freddy was thirty-nine and Tussy thirty-five. In 1892 Freddy's wife had left him and their son, Harry, and made off with all of Freddy's money as well as twenty-four pounds from a benefit fund placed in his care by fellow workers. In July of that year Tussy wrote frantically to Laura saying Freddy had to account for the money and had nowhere to go to make up the shortfall. Longuet did not respond to a letter from Freddy asking that Jennychen's loan be repaid, and Freddy refused to ask Engels for help. Tussy told Laura, seemingly sarcastically referring to Engels, whom she still believed to be Freddy's father, "It may be that I am very 'sentimental'—but I can't help feeling that Freddy has had a great injustice all through his life. Is it not wonderful, when you come to look things squarely in the face, how rarely we seem to practice all the fine things we preach—to others?" Laura sent Freddy fifty francs.[27]

As their relationship evolved, Tussy increasingly came to rely on Freddy. She had few other people to turn to. She felt alienated from Engels because of Louise Kautsky's presence, feared Engels had fallen completely under her sway and that rather than helping him protect the Marx literary legacy, Louise was intent on stealing it.[28] Tussy did not know that Bebel and Adler had discussed moving a party member into Engels's home to protect—or secure—the Marx-Engels material in the wake of Lenchen's death. She would have been horrified to know that such planning was taking place without either her or Laura being consulted. In her view all the Marx papers belonged to Marx's immediate heirs, of which there were two.

One of Lenchen's roles had been to help Engels sort through the thousands of pages of writing and correspondence Marx had gathered. Some of the letters were party business, but many others were personal. Tussy was alarmed when she learned Engels thought it perfectly reasonable that Louise should comb through them as Lenchen had. Her alarm grew when Louise suddenly married a Viennese doctor named Ludwig Freyberger and the two announced that they planned to live with Engels at his home.[29] The marriage sounded very much like a business arrangement, not a love match. (Louise herself told Tussy that until the day she agreed to marry Freyberger, they had been "the very best comrades but nothing more, with an unspoken intention on both sides to settle down in life together later on.")[30] Freyberger had arrived in London in 1892, but by 1893 Engels so trusted him that he witnessed Engels's will. Freyberger acted as a personal physician to Engels, and Tussy imagined all sorts of Svengali-like machinations by the pair to get Engels under their control. Tussy complained to Laura that she had not seen or talked to the General alone for months.[31]

*   *   *

For ten years Engels had been declaring—it was almost a mantra—that he must complete *Capital, Volume III*, and in May 1894 he did, sending the last sheaf of manuscript to the publisher.[32] He also immediately sent off copies of the entire unpublished work to Danielson in St. Petersburg for a Russian edition.[33] Engels described an incredible sense of relief not just for finishing, but for finishing just in time. That month he told a colleague in New York, "Not long ago I caught a cold, which left me in no doubt that I am now an old man at last. On this occasion, what I had previously been able to treat as a minor annoyance, pretty well laid me low for a week and kept me under draconian medical supervision for a whole fortnight after that." He described Freyberger's medical supervision as annoyingly thorough and Louise's vigilance as "doubled and tripled."[34]

But if Engels at seventy-four felt his body in decline, the third volume of *Capital* (and the fact that he still read newspapers in nine languages) was evidence his brain was not. He had inherited from Marx a disorderly pile of texts and notes, and out of that had produced an eight-hundred-page work that examined in brilliant detail monopoly capital and the creation of the world market. The book chronicled the development of the great "swindles" called the stock exchange[35] and described the "new variety of parasites" with "fabulous power" who run it.[36] *Volume III* examined the credit system and found that under it, the wage slave also became the creditor's slave, because he invariably consumed more than he could afford. Most significantly, the book chronicled the entire system's demise due to an inevitable fall in profit caused by capitalist overreach.[37]

With *Capital* out of the way, Engels planned at last to embark on his biography of Marx. After describing his many commitments and plans to Laura, he said, "That is my position: seventy-four years the which I am beginning to feel, and work enough for two men of forty. Yes, if I could divide myself into the F.E. [Friedrich Engels] of forty and the F.E. of thirty-four, which would just be seventy four, then we should soon be all right. But as it is, all I can do is to work on with what is before me and get through it as far and as well as I can."[38]

That summer the Avelings and the Freybergers went to Paris to stay with the Lafargues. One of Tussy's biographers has suggested that the visit resulted in a row over a rumor that Louise had had an affair with the married German party leader Bebel.[39] That certainly would have explained her speedy and rather strange union with Freyberger; Louise was pregnant when she married him.[40] In September, Louise accused Tussy of a "breach of confidence" for relating the story to Liebknecht, who then passed it on until it reached Bebel. In fact, Bernstein told Louise it was Bebel who had told another party member about their affair, but that was not the end of the rumors and counterrumors.[41]

In October the Freybergers accompanied Engels to the English coast at Eastbourne, where he suffered a slight stroke. He did not want anyone to know about this, but Tussy accused Louise of ghoulishly spreading the word among German socialists waiting to get their hands on the Marx-Engels legacy. The two women were still at loggerheads when Louise gave birth to a daughter on November 6. In the preceding weeks Engels and the Freybergers had moved into a new home, also on Regent's Park Road, because Engels's previous one was not big enough for a growing family.[42] These events alarmed Tussy to an unnatural and unhealthy degree. She felt utterly abandoned by Engels, who represented her most intimate connection to her father, both the man himself and his work.

Tussy was alone in London because Edward's doctors had told him to take a holiday. Apparently suffering from kidney trouble, he had gone to the Scilly Islands, off the coast of Cornwall, to recover. His articles for a London magazine about his sojourn sounded anything but afflicted. He wrote of beaches and cliff walks and a "fair-haired, blue-eyed girl" he met on the boat from Penzance: "I had seen her the day before in the Penzance Post Office, and invented a telegram that I might stick on a stamp her hands had touched. She was as easy and frank as she was beautiful."[43] In her delicate state his tactless stories would have pained Tussy if for no other reason than that they exposed the gulf between his life, however fanciful, and what she believed to be her dark reality.

In desperation Tussy wrote Laura that her presence in London was urgently needed: "It is impossible in a letter, a dozen letters to explain all the complications." Tussy claimed that Freyberger was spreading the word among socialists in London that she and Aveling had been "turned out by the General, and that *now* that things are in the hands of the Freybergers all will be different." She accused Louise of spreading the same report throughout Germany, along with personal calumnies against Tussy. "I don't think the poor old General even fully realizes what he is made to do, he has come to the condition where he is a mere child in the hands of this monstrous pair." Tussy said they bullied him and made him feel like an old man by constantly reminding him of what he was no longer capable of doing. She then expressed her terror at the possibility the Freybergers might be named sole literary executors of Marx's works, and she recalled Bebel saying the papers would fall into the right hands. "I should ask to know whose hands," Tussy told Laura. "If outsiders know we should, for when all is said and done this is *our* business and no one else's."[44]

Laura did not respond, which only made Tussy more frantic. In late November she wrote again, this time along with Aveling (who had goaded her on to new levels of paranoia). Tussy said if the Freybergers were not already in possession of Marx's papers they soon would be, and she used a notice in a German publication announcing that *Capital, Volume IV* would not be issued as evidence that Freyberger had persuaded Engels he was incapable of the task. She again begged Laura to come to London. Aveling added his own melodramatic note: "Come, *come*, COME. You have no idea of the immediate *importance* of it."[45]

If Tussy had bothered to ask Engels to see his will, her fears might have been allayed. It was explicit in directing that she should receive her father's works and letters.[46] But one wonders if even that would have calmed her—she seemed to have lost all reason. Indeed, this strong woman who boldly confronted the roughest strikebreakers, who mediated difficult political disputes, who stepped fearlessly into the hellholes of the East End, had lost her ability to communicate with a man she had known all her life and who had always had her best interests at heart. For his part, Engels was so utterly unaware of her fears that when he learned of them, his first response was to say to Laura that of course all Marx's manuscripts and correspondence belonged to her and Tussy. They could have no other destination.[47]

Aveling had broached the inheritance subject with Engels by showing him a letter Laura had written Tussy for that purpose. Tussy was not there when he produced it, but the Freybergers were, and Aveling reported that Freyberger took Engels aside to discuss the matter. Freyberger's remarks are unknown, but according to Aveling, after hearing what he had to say, Engels returned, veins standing out on his neck, shouting that the Marx daughters were involved in a conspiracy—though he failed to describe what it entailed. He was furious at the thought that Tussy and Laura mistrusted him. Aveling, of course, begged immunity, claiming he was only the messenger.[48]

Earlier, Engels had written a letter to "my dear girls" detailing his decisions about books that had belonged to Marx and him, and about provisions he would make to ensure that not only they but the Longuet children received part of his own estate. The letter was warmly generous, and showed that the man who had taken care of the Marx family all his life would continue to do so after his death.[49] Engels's anger over Tussy's fears may have reflected his sense that everyone around him was waiting for him to die. It was galling for a man of his pride, and doubly galling because he, too, was well aware of his mortality. He still had the work of two lifetimes—his own and Marx's—to complete, and he was realist enough to see that he would not live to finish even a fraction of it.

51

London, 1895

In this stern fighter and strict thinker beat a deeply loving heart.
—Vladimir Lenin[1]

THE WINTER OF 1895 was one of the coldest on record in London. Frost from January until March made the ground crackle underfoot while a bullwhip wind from the northeast lacerated the skin.[2] Water mains froze, and transportation in some areas came to a standstill. Engels told Kugelmann the city had been thrown back into the age of barbarism. This weather, however, suited Engels. It reminded him of Prussia and made him feel two decades younger than his seventy-four years.[3] Remaining indoors beside a huge fire, he kept up a vigorous correspondence with party members and planned his biography of Marx. Engels's attention was also on Russia. He corresponded frequently with allies in St. Petersburg and exiles in Switzerland, and had a steady stream of young Russians—mostly anarchists—arriving at his door. One of them, known simply as Stepniak, had fled Russia after assassinating an adjutant general in broad daylight in St. Petersburg in 1878.[4] Stepniak smiled easily, spoke gently, and was self-effacing, and yet for the average person he personified terror: he believed that if men and women were killed for political actions, their comrades must respond in kind.[5] Another frequent visitor was Georgy Plekhanov, whom Tussy considered a friend and who had founded the first Russian Marxist organization. Tussy translated Plekhanov's *Anarchism and Socialism*, his first English publication.[6]

But Engels's main correspondent on Russian affairs was Nikolai Danielson. In sometimes coded language, Danielson informed Engels about developments there, in particular the famine that had hit the countryside and the industrialization of the cities, which had significantly raised the temperature on simmering discontent. Marx's ideas were among those being absorbed by young people who wanted to end the czarist regime but did not know what the alternative might look like or how to achieve it. There had already been numerous assassination attempts on the czar, one of which, in 1887, led to the hanging of Alexander Ulianov, brother of Vladimir Illyich Ulianov, the future Vladimir Lenin.[7]

In 1894 the tyrannical Alexander III died and was replaced by his son Nicholas II. The new czar attempted to modernize the economy, but he did not end political repression.[8] Engels opined that "little Nicholas has done us the service of making revolution absolutely inevitable."[9] He wrote Danielson, "Capitalistic production works its own ruin, and you may be sure it will do so in Russia too.... At all events, I am sure the conservative people who have introduced capitalism into Russia, will be one day terribly astonished at the consequences of their doings."[10]

That year Vladimir Ulianov (he would not use the name Lenin until 1901) joined a Marxist circle in St. Petersburg. In 1895 he left Russia to visit Plekhanov and other colleagues in western Europe (he was one of the few young Russians who, somewhat surprisingly, did not appear at Engels's door).[11] In Paris he met Lafargue. The Frenchman was astonished that Russians not only read Marx, they understood him. He told Ulianov that in France, despite twenty years of propaganda, no one comprehended his father-in-law's work.[12]

In May, Engels confided to Laura that he had pains in his neck that drove him nearly mad. "The fact is this. Some time ago I got a swelling on the right side of the neck, which after some time resolved itself into a bunch of deep-seated glands infiltrated by some cause or other." He wanted to go to Eastbourne, perhaps hoping—though not truly believing—that the fabled sea air would ameliorate his condition. The Freybergers would accompany him, and he insisted that Laura and Lafargue, as well as Tussy and Aveling, join him, too.[13] Significantly, also in the party would be Sam Moore, the English translator of *Capital, Volume I* and Engels's lawyer. Moore was a British colonial official in Africa who was back in England on leave, and the General wanted him to amend his will to ease any concerns Tussy and Laura had about their father's writing.[14]

A physical man, Engels knew the signs of approaching death. He could barely speak, and he was so weak he did not have the strength to write: his normally multipage letters were reduced to a few sentences, then one sentence, and then sometimes just a word and his name. Still, on July 23, after Laura had returned to France, he summoned the strength to write four paragraphs. "To-morrow we return to London. There seems to be at last a crisis approaching in my potato field on my neck, so that the swellings may be opened and relief secured. At last!"[15] Elections had just been held in England, and the result was total defeat for the Independent Labour Party and the socialists. Even Keir Hardie lost because of an uproar he had caused in Parliament when he opposed congratulating the queen over the birth of a child to the Duchess of York. His reason was simple enough: Parliament would not send condolences to the families of 260 workers killed in a mine disaster.[16] In his letter Engels told Laura he was not surprised by the setback. He and Marx had seen socialist fortunes rise and fall as often as the capitalist cycle of financial crashes.[17]

Engels sounded optimistic about everything, his health included, but Moore confided to Tussy that his condition was grave. "There is so much work to be done which the General alone is capable of doing," Moore wrote, "his loss will be irreparable from a public point of view—to his friends it will be a calamity."[18]

It was also Moore who would tell Tussy that Freddy was her half brother, a revelation that would shatter her fragile world.

New tensions had arisen between Tussy and the Freybergers over who had the right not only to Marx's writings but to Engels's money. Tussy had long felt that Freddy suffered unduly for what she believed was Engels's and Lenchen's youthful indiscretion, and she may have raised the issue of Freddy being Engels's legal heir. Freyberger had witnessed Engels's will and knew that Engels had designated Louise as among those due to inherit a portion of the General's fortune. If Freddy were Engels's son, Louise's share would be at best diminished.

After Louise married Freyberger, Freddy said, his visits with Engels became less frequent, and he detected what he described as a "big change in the General." He cut short conversations with Freddy and seemed much colder toward him. Freddy implied that Engels had fallen under the Freybergers' influence and that they were trying to keep the two men apart, he believed for financial reasons. Tussy had again told Freddy that Engels was his father—a fact, Freddy said, that made Freyberger very angry, "because had Tussy been right you may imagine what it would have meant for them."[19] It is unknown whether Freddy had ever pressed his mother to reveal his father's identity, but it seems clear that even if he had, she did not tell him. At forty-four Freddy still had nothing more solid than rumors and family lore to explain his parentage. Recalling

Lenchen's mysterious deathbed statement about his name, he set out to discover the truth.

Tussy wanted not only answers but justice for Freddy. She went to Sam Moore and insisted that Engels was Freddy's father, perhaps in the hope that Moore might influence Engels to rewrite his will. But when Moore asked Engels, he vehemently denied it. According to Freddy, Engels told Moore he "could tell Tussy on his behalf that it was a damned lie and I will tell her myself when I see her the next time." (Freddy recalled that Moore later told him, "Knowing the General as well as I do I do not believe a single minute he would have denied it had he been your father.") But there was more: Engels apparently told Moore that *Marx* was Freddy's father, and Moore told Tussy.[20]

One can only imagine the horror Tussy felt at hearing those words. Not that she wouldn't be proud to claim Freddy as a brother, but that the father she idolized was capable of abandoning a child and betraying her mother and Lenchen. The pedestal she had erected in her heart and mind in his honor crumbled in an instant. In a lifetime of disappointments that, without doubt, would have been the worst. She accused Engels of lying.

On August 4, 1895, Tussy went to Engels's home to confront him. That he could not speak made his answer all the more devastating. On a slate Engels wrote the words Tussy did not want to see: Marx was Freddy's father. Tussy rushed out of the room and, forgetting her antipathy for Louise, threw herself into her arms, sobbing.[21] Louise, of course, already knew the story. She would later tell colleagues that Engels had given her the right to deny any rumors that he had disowned a son, not wanting such a blemish on his character to follow him to the grave. Louise explained that Engels had long ago claimed to be Freddy's father in order to spare the Marx family from disaster.[22]

The day after Tussy's meeting with Engels, he died of throat cancer.[23]

Engels's will lay in his desk drawer. True to his word, all Marx's manuscripts and letters were to be given to Tussy as his literary executor. Engels's furniture and household effects went to Louise.[24] To party members in Germany he left £1,000, all his books, and his own letters and manuscripts. His money he divided among Laura, Tussy, the Longuet children, and Louise.[25] Engels's estate was worth about £30,000[26] (about $4.8 million today), and after fees and bequests were paid, each Marx daughter received about £5,000.[27] To that point they had been used to living on about £150 a year.

Tussy now had more money than she knew what to do with, but she had lost everything else. More than the other Marx daughters, she had relied on Engels as a father, as a refuge, as a friend, and as a mentor. A rock in her turbulent life, he was much more dependable than either of her parents, second only to Lenchen in that regard. Now he was gone, and with him in one cruel blow also went all her illusions about her father. Freddy, too, was left adrift. He had been led to believe that Engels was his father only to have that belief repudiated on Engels's deathbed. He was then told that Marx was his father, but in his mind there was still uncertainty. He wrote Laura to say he and Tussy had reason to believe he was Marx's son. Freddy told Johnny Longuet years later, "Laura wrote neither denying or confirming what I said but noting that if my mother and the others did not speak about this during all these years, they without a doubt had serious reasons to do so."[28]

Engels's last wish was that his ashes be buried at sea, with no public funeral. Eastbourne, near Brighton, was his favorite spot on the coast, its chalky headland of nearly six hundred feet dropping precipitously into the crashing waters below. So it was to Eastbourne that Tussy and Aveling, accompanied by the old socialist Lessner and the new generation's Bernstein, went on August 27 to hire a boat for their farewell to the General. Despite rough seas the group rowed about six miles into the English Channel before they could finally bring themselves to stop and drop the urn containing the ashes of their unforgettable friend into the inky water below.[29]

Lenin would later say with much clarity, "The services rendered by Marx and Engels to the working class may be expressed in a few words thus: They taught the working class to know itself and be conscious of itself, and they substituted science for dreams."[30]

Tussy assumed the mantle Engels had taken on after Marx's death, determined to publish as many of her father's works as possible. She had always kept a frenetic schedule, but now she went into overdrive. She lectured incessantly, and when she was not lecturing, she wrote, and when she was not writing, she attended meetings. It was as if she did not want to stop moving for fear of what she would have to confront if she did. Her life unsettled in the extreme, she took a step that fall that offered a modicum of stability: she bought a home south of London in Sydenham, on a street called Jews Walk (which she proudly emphasized).[31] Sydenham was a suburb not unlike Maitland Park, but more remote and therefore within her budget. Tussy was aware, even if Aveling was not, how swiftly Engels's money could disappear, and once gone there would be nothing to replenish it. She was quick to tell Laura that while she had bought the house, Aveling had paid for the furniture, alluding to a property he owned that had increased in value.[32] It is hard to imagine that Aveling had owned property. In fact he may have told Tussy that story in order to explain a sudden influx of cash: his wife, Bell, had finally died, and as he had hoped and expected, her estate (though much diminished) went to him despite their decades apart.[33]

Tussy, too, now actually possessed something, and wrote a will shortly after Engels's death. Identifying herself as Eleanor Marx Aveling, wife of Edward Aveling, she bequeathed her estate and all the interest in her father's works to Aveling, with royalties going to the Longuet children. A year later, however, she amended the document to specify that royalties would go to Aveling during his life and to the Longuet children after his death.[34] Some have suggested Aveling pressured Tussy into making the change—Freddy said she was "mesmerized by that bastard."[35] It was indeed strange that she delayed benefit to the Longuet children; Tussy shared responsibility for them with Laura and considered herself a second mother to Johnny.

The Longuet children were certainly in need of help. Longuet was exceedingly loving toward them, but he simply could not raise them on his own.[36] He was in many ways like Marx himself: bohemian and political and struggling financially, but without the support of a wife or a Lenchen, not to mention an Engels to ease the way. Gradually, after his mother's death in 1891, he had begun to rely on Laura and Tussy. Laura frequently took in Jenny, known as Mémé, and Tussy watched over Johnny both during his visits to London and from a distance, when he was back with his father in France.[37] She worried that though gifted, Johnny might be lazy.[38] At seventeen he was conscious that he had disappointed his aunt by not yet having picked a career. She had suggested medicine, chemistry, or engineering, but he'd told Engels he wasn't interested in any of those and feared he might not be good at anything.[39] Two years later Johnny sent Tussy an article he had written, and while she said she was "very proud of my big little man," she was horrified at what might come of it. "I would not like to see you a journalist for anything in the world. . . . To write for a journal to live, that in the end is being forced to sell your pen, your conscience."[40]

Engels's death had proved the catalyst for a reconciliation between Laura and Tussy after twenty-three years of strained relations. Their letters were now free of the artificial warmth that had characterized them during that gap. Tussy joked that Laura had inherited their mother's beauty and gift of letter writing, while her own inheritance amounted to their father's nose.[41] Tussy had been conservative in her choice of residence purchased with Engels's money, but Laura and Lafargue had shown no such reserve. They bought a country estate about twenty miles south of Paris, at Draveil. It had thirty rooms, a pavilion, a billiards room, a studio and conservatory, as well as gardens, an orchard, one hundred fowl, and dozens of rabbits and sheep.[42] After years of living on the edge of financial ruin, Laura and Lafargue—fifty and fifty-three, respectively—relished their home and the security provided, as always, by Engels.

As bucolic as the Lafargues' life had become, Tussy's had grown complicated. In the spring of 1895 socialists held an evening of entertainment to raise money for the Fourth Congress of the Second International, to be held in London in the summer of 1896. Aveling organized the event and staged one of his plays, *In the Train*.[43] The one-act drama required the services of an actress named Lillian Richardson. Aveling played opposite her, and Will Thorne later remarked that Aveling became "very familiar" with Miss Richardson. (A note in the socialist press described her as the kind of traveling companion with whom anyone might fall in love.)[44] Suddenly Aveling seemed inclined to once again try to pitch his plays in the West End. And because he and Tussy now lived a train ride from the city, he was absent for long spells, sometimes all night.

Tussy may have hardly noticed. She was drowning in labor duties and her father's writings. She wanted to see *Capital, Volume IV* in print, and she busied herself publishing collections of Marx's other works, including a *Tribune* series she titled *Revolution and Counter Revolution in Germany in 1848*—an invaluable history of the period. (Years later it was determined that the bulk of the articles were by Engels, not Marx, but at the time Tussy was unaware of the mistake and soldiered on.) At forty-one she worked as feverishly as Engels had in his later years, when he consciously raced the clock of time.

Tussy's closest friends during this period were Laura, Freddy, Will Thorne and his wife, Ede Bernstein, Karl Kautsky, and faithful old Liebknecht, whom she had known from the time she was a child.[45] She may have clung to Liebknecht because of his connection to her youth, and he may have felt he had inherited a duty to protect her, now that Engels was no longer around. In the first two years after Tussy moved to Sydenham, Liebknecht traveled from Germany to visit her three times. Now seventy, he would not have found it an easy trip to make. In the spring of 1896 Tussy and Liebknecht strolled through the past. They went to Dean Street, which she was too young to remember, and Grafton Terrace, the scene of her youth. They stopped at the family's favorite pubs near Hampstead Heath, and Liebknecht told stories Tussy surely knew by heart but was eager to hear again,[46] these childhood fables now lifelines. But she was interested in the unvarnished version of the family's history, too. Since Engels's death, her father had become human for her, his frailties evident, even if he was still larger than life for party members. When Liebknecht published his reminiscences of Marx that year, Kautsky feared the details about his drinking, poverty, and personal habits would do infinite harm to his memory. But Tussy told Laura that while Liebknecht's story was muddled, she disagreed with Kautsky that humanizing Marx would undermine his teaching: "After all Marx the 'politician' and 'Thinker' can take his chance, while Marx the man (the man, the mere man as Karl Kautsky says), is less likely to fare well."[47] Indeed, she wrote Kautsky that Liebknecht's book could only help, because Marx "the *man* is least known, most misunderstood."[48] She even agreed to the publication of some of Marx's personal letters, though it was painful; she knew how much her father hated to have his "private life dragged into politics."[49] Having lived a lie her whole life, Tussy seemed eager that at least some of the truth should be known.

That eagerness was on full display a few months later. In July, Tussy threw a party at her home for delegates to the Second International Congress. German socialist Clara Zetkin, who had become her intimate friend, described the scene many years later to the director of the Marx-Engels Institute in Moscow. She said Tussy had promised her a big surprise, then pulled her away from the crowd to meet a youngish, slightly stooped man: "Here my dear Clara let me introduce you to my half brother, the son of Nimmy [Lenchen] and Mohr." Zetkin said the introduction impressed her deeply but seemed to make Freddy ill at ease, so they spoke about politics rather than anything personal. Later that night Tussy told Clara that though her father and Engels had lied, they had done the right thing, because despite her mother's great love for Marx, she could not have withstood the betrayal and scandal. But Tussy said she was angry that after their mother's death, Marx did not tell his daughters. She speculated that in his despair over the loss of his wife and Jennychen, he had not thought of it, though this theory felt weak to Tussy. It was hard to imagine that her father had been unconscious of his omission. Tussy said she regretted that she had not known Freddy was her half brother sooner, because she would have tried to be closer to him, although, she told Clara, she was making up for lost time.[50]

By the end of 1896 Tussy seemed to have reconciled herself to her family's hidden past. She bore regrets and deep scars, but like her mother she had learned to live with them. Out of necessity, Tussy had concluded a man could be great and flawed, and a man could be flawed and still worthy of love. It was true of her father, and she had come to believe it was also true of Aveling.

52

～๑

London, 1897

*I don't think you and I have been particularly bad people—and
yet, dear Freddy, it really seems as though we are being
punished.*

—Eleanor Marx[1]

IN JANUARY, AVELING produced one of his plays to raise money for a series
of science classes he wanted to offer. Acting opposite him was the twenty-
two-year-old daughter of a music teacher. Her name was Eva Frye, but
she was the same actress who had appeared with him a year earlier under
the name Lillian Richardson.[2] Aveling, now forty-seven, would have
been delighted to still have the wherewithal to charm and win a woman
half his age. His life with Tussy had become a working relationship, and
now that Engels was dead, a comfortable one at that. Besides, Tussy was
no longer the lively young girl once described by a Russian revolutionary
as slim and seductive. As she'd aged her body had spread; she appeared
shorter and wider. She also looked more like her father. If she were ever
described as beautiful, it would be because of an inner beauty. Tussy was
the opposite of a West End actress, and the latter, apparently, was what
Aveling was after.

Aveling held science classes near the theater district, which gave him a
reason to be in town late and also put him in close proximity to Eva. He
must have been absolutely smitten. For years he had been notorious for his
liaisons with women—he was, in fact, quite cavalier about them. But in
the case of Eva, Aveling wanted more than a fling. It might have been
because of his age; he may have feared she would soon tire of an older man
with no real prospects in the theater. Or it may have been stimulated by

his health; he had had an abscess on his side for more than two years, and he was not well.

Whatever the reason, Aveling married Eva on June 8 in Chelsea, where Eva resided. The marriage license identified him as Alec Nelson, a widower. There was no mention of his "wife" Eleanor, with whom he still lived.[3] In late June he went to St. Margaret's Bay, a trip he told Tussy he needed to take for medical reasons, though it was undoubtedly his honeymoon with Eva.[4] He was away for about two weeks, and when he returned to London, he moved back into Jews Walk with Tussy. But by August he was gone. He took everything he could sell and would not give Tussy his address, saying that if she needed to reach him, she could do so through a fellow actor.[5]

It is fair to assume that during the weeks between Aveling's marriage to Eva and the day he left Sydenham there had been quarrels at Jews Walk. It is also probable that during the months when Aveling's affair was building to a passionate pitch, relations between him and Tussy were at best strained. Still, it is unlikely that anything could have prepared Tussy for his abrupt and unconscionable departure. She did not know why, only that he was gone. Tussy turned to Freddy and in a rambling letter entreated him to go to a socialist meeting where she thought Aveling might turn up: "If he is there, then you could speak to him about it—he just couldn't run away in front of other people." She had written Aveling many letters through the designated actor but received no reply. She told Freddy she knew she was weak to write Aveling, "but one cannot wipe out fourteen years of one's life as though they had never been."[6]

It is not known if Freddy was successful in reaching Aveling, but the next day Tussy received a note from Edward saying, "I have come back. Shall be home early tomorrow morning." This was followed by a telegram reading, "Coming home one thirty definitely." She wrote Freddy after Aveling had returned, saying her "husband" seemed surprised she hadn't leaped into his arms. "He offered no word of excuse, and no explanation. I therefore said...that we must talk about business affairs and that I would never forget the treatment I had been subject to. He said nothing in reply." She asked Freddy to come to her house so Aveling could confront them together.[7] There was also mention of the lawyer Arthur Wilson Crosse, who had handled the distribution of Engels's property and had written Tussy's will.[8] Unfortunately much is left unsaid in those letters, and we have no response from Freddy at hand, so one can only guess what actually happened in Sydenham. If a confrontation with Aveling was to involve Tussy and Freddy, it must have concerned Freddy's paternity. If Crosse was involved, it could have been that Tussy wanted to amend her will in Freddy's favor, something Aveling would not have tolerated. (As it was, Aveling had already run through nearly half the money Tussy had inherited from Engels just two years before.) Now keeping two households, which he could ill afford, Aveling may have been trying to blackmail Tussy into giving him money by threatening to publicize the story of Freddy's birth. It was one thing for a few select party members to know the truth, but quite another to have the story widely broadcast.

On September 2 Tussy wrote Freddy, "Come if it is at all possible this evening. It is shameful to put this burden on you, but I am so lonely, and I am faced with a fearful situation — extreme ruin — everything to the last farthing — or utter disgrace before the whole world. It is terrible. Worse than I ever imagined. And I need someone to advise me. I know I must make a final decision.... So dear, dear Freddy come. I am broken. Your Tussy."[9]

Freddy despised Aveling, so it must have hurt him deeply when Aveling and Tussy came to some kind of agreement to remain together. In late September they traveled to Draveil to stay with Laura and Lafargue in their lavish new home. Laura did not detect any strain, and Tussy did not divulge the painful events of that summer. The only person who knew the full story was Freddy.

Back in London, Tussy went to work immediately on behalf of the Amalgamated Society of Engineers, who were striking for an eight-hour day. She called the strike nothing less than "civil war"[10] — her language was more radical than usual, perhaps reflecting her personal turmoil. William Collison, founder of the Free Labor Association, renewed his friendship with Tussy at this time.[11] They had known each other since 1890, when she was plotting the first May Day in London and teaching the "splendid figure of a man" Will Thorne to read and write. Collison described her as without religion but said her attitude in all aspects was Christian. And yet, sadly for her, she'd found a man who was a "moral wastrel.... The weaknesses she had excused on the ground of poverty only intensified when he entered into a kingdom of relative prosperity. He became unendurable, yet she endured him."[12]

Collison's association supplied nonunion labor and was often used by employers as a source of blacklegs to break up strikes, but out of regard for Tussy, he saw that his workers did not step in against the striking engineers.[13] During this period Collison recalled meeting Tussy on the street near Chancery Lane, where she stored some of her father's papers: "In very truth, I think she was dead then. Dead in heart and all womanly hope. I said little as we stood in the windy twilight . . . while I noticed the faded beauty of her face and hopeless eyes and the grief inscribed in deep drawn lines about her mouth. She seemed a little nervous also. She had fur or a boa, or a clinging scarf of lace around her neck and she played with it nervously."[14]

In January, despite receiving funds from abroad to support the strike, the engineers surrendered, having gained nothing.[15] That was Tussy's last professional fight; all the rest would be personal.

By now Tussy's main concern was for Aveling, who in addition to the abscess on his side had also developed congestion of the lungs and pneumonia. She told Laura that he was a skeleton and that his doctors said even a chill would be fatal. She wanted him to go to the seaside for warm air and sunshine, but she could not afford to go with him, his medical care in the weeks since their return from France having eaten dangerously into their depleted savings.[16] George Bernard Shaw described Aveling as back to his old trick of borrowing money with little or no intention of repaying. But too many people had been burned; he received shrugs instead of support.[17]

On January 13 Aveling went to the coast alone, and on that same day, Tussy wrote Freddy:

> Sometimes I have the same feeling as you, Freddy, that nothing will ever come right for us. I mean you and me. Naturally poor Jenny had her share of trouble and grief, and Laura has lost her children. But Jenny was glad to die, and it was so sad for the children, but sometimes I think it was all for the best. I would not have wished for Jenny that she should go through the life I have had to go through.[18]

When Aveling returned, his health had not greatly improved. He traveled often to London to see the doctor but would not allow Tussy to accompany him. (No doubt he also used his trips to see Eva.) Tussy was beside herself with worry—about his health and also about their finances. She told Natalie Liebknecht, "Sometimes I hardly know how I shall hold on!"[19]

Tussy had befriended a socialist named Edith Lancaster, whose family had sent her to a mental institution after she shamed them by conducting an extramarital affair.[20] (In the nineteenth century a woman was essentially the property of either her father or her husband, and in nearly all legal proceedings her word carried little weight against theirs.) In an 1898 letter to Lancaster, Tussy mused, "I often wonder why one goes on at all with all these fearful sufferings. Of course I'd not say so to my poor

Edward, but I often think it would be far easier to make an end of it. You see I have no little ones as you have."[21]

The situation became worse still in February. Aveling's doctors decided he needed surgery to remove the festering abscess that was making it impossible for his health to improve. There was no question about its importance, but Tussy despaired over the cost and had a vague feeling that more was amiss with Aveling than his health. She confided to Freddy that she was sure there were things Aveling was not telling her. "I know it is brutally selfish of me, but, dear Freddy, you are the only friend with whom I can be completely frank... you know what it is all about, and I am telling you what I would tell to no one else."[22] Tussy wanted Freddy to come to Jews Walk but he refused: he could not bear Aveling's presence. She understood his reluctance, but explained,

> There are people who lack a certain moral sense, just as many are deaf or short-sighted or in other ways afflicted. And I begin to realize that one is as little justified in blaming them for the one sort of disorder as the other. We must strive to cure them, and if no cure is possible, we must do our best. I have learned to understand this through long suffering... and so I am endeavoring to bear all these trials as well as I can.[23]

Two days later she added, "There is a French saying 'To understand is to forgive.' Much suffering has taught me to understand—and so I have no need to forgive. I can only love."[24]

Aveling entered University College Hospital on February 8 and underwent surgery the next day. Tussy took a room near the hospital so she could be on call day and night.[25] Nine days later doctors released him and suggested he go to Margate, on the coast, to recover. It was an expense Tussy could neither bear nor refuse. That time, she accompanied him.[26]

Based on her letters from this period, many of Tussy's correspondents would have thought she was the same vigorous woman she had always been, discussing party politics, the movement's history, her own work. But to intimate friends, especially Freddy and Natalie Liebknecht, she freely expressed her despair.[27] On March 1 she wrote her half brother,

> My dear, dear Freddy,
> Please don't regard my failure to write as negligence. The trouble is that I am exhausted, and often I have not the heart to write.... It is a bad time for me. I fear there is little hope left for me, and the pain and suffering are great.... I am ready to go and would do so joyfully. But so long as he needs help I am bound to remain. The only thing that has helped me is the friendship that has been

shown to me on every side. I cannot tell you how good different people have been to me. Why, I really do not know.[28]

Tussy and Aveling returned to London on March 27. Four days later Tussy killed herself. [29]

Tussy's surrender was the end result of a mighty cascade, a drowning. But the likely single reason for her suicide was a letter she'd received on the morning of March 31. A fellow socialist said the note threw "a very bad light" on a particular person—unquestionably Aveling—and it is likely that the letter informed Tussy of his marriage to Eva.[30] Aveling testified during a coroner's inquest that they had not argued that morning, and the maid did not mention a quarrel.[31] It may well have been that there was no need for tears or anger because Tussy knew immediately what course she would take. She had told Freddy the only thing that kept her alive was her obligation to care for Aveling. Whatever was in the letter relieved her of that duty.

At ten o'clock that morning Tussy sent her maid, Gertrude Gentry, to a local pharmacist with a note and one of Aveling's cards identifying him as Dr. Edward Aveling. The request was for chloroform and prussic acid (today commonly known as cyanide), which the note said were needed to kill a dog. Gentry returned with the chemicals and a book for Tussy to sign, because the substances were restricted. Tussy signed the register "EM Aveling."

Aveling was home when Tussy ordered the poison but left before Gentry returned with the packet. He announced that he was going to London, even though the day before he had been so weak he could not stand. Tussy asked him not to go but he ignored her, leaving her alone, waiting for a delivery of poison, fully aware of the terrible extent of his deceit. She went upstairs and wrote three letters, one to her lawyer, Crosse, in which she enclosed the letter she had received that morning.[32] Another was for Aveling: "Dear. It will soon be all over now. My last word to you is the same that I have said during all these long, sad years—love." Finally she wrote her nephew: "My dear, dear Johnny, My last word is addressed to you. Try to be worthy of your grandfather. Your Aunt Tussy."[33]

When Gentry returned from the pharmacist's she went to Tussy's room and found her lying in bed undressed. She was breathing but did not look well. Gentry asked if she was all right, and when Tussy didn't answer she summoned a neighbor. By the time she arrived, Tussy was dead.[34]

Aveling, meanwhile, had taken the train to London and went directly to the offices of the Social Democratic Federation. There he spoke to a member and made sure the fellow noted the exact time.[35] Ede Bernstein claimed that Aveling knew Tussy planned to kill herself, and her friends surmised that he wanted the time recorded to exculpate himself from her death.[36] Where he went after he left the SDF is a mystery, but he did not return to Sydenham until five in the evening. When he arrived, with Tussy's body still on the bed, he immediately searched for and found the letters she had written to him and Crosse. He tried to destroy them but was prevented from doing so by the coroner's official at the scene.[37]

Many years before, when Tussy had tried to kill herself by overdosing on opium, Havelock Ellis had said her friends were dismayed but not surprised. By 1898 her friends were even less so. Only two people were caught off guard by the tragedy: Liebknecht, who was released from prison in mid-March after serving a four-month term, could not comprehend it. He did not believe Tussy was suicidal, nor did he think Aveling responsible for driving her to it.[38] And then there was Laura. As warm as their relations had become, Tussy had not confided in her sister. Laura had no notion that life on Jews Walk was anything but felicitous. She was inconsolable when she heard that Tussy was dead.[39] Her reaction was no doubt shock and grief but also guilt that they had been estranged for so many years over Lissagaray, a man who ultimately played so little part in either of their lives.

On April 5 Tussy was cremated at the Necropolis Station at Waterloo. Wreaths had come in from socialist and workers' parties throughout Europe. The mourners who had gathered two years earlier at that same spot for Engels's rites had grieved for their loss but remembered a man who had had a full and rewarding life. Tussy's funeral was altogether different. The people who gathered to pay respects to her felt real heartache, not just over losing her in her prime, at the age of forty-three, but over her sufferings and their inability to ease them. Lafargue was there, as were Johnny Longuet, Hyndman, Bernstein, Will Thorne, and other party and labor friends. Those whose grief was too great for public airing, Freddy and Laura, were absent.[40]

Several people spoke, Aveling among them. He was described in a labor newspaper report as "dry eyed and theatrical in speech and manner." Said Bernstein, "If there were no party interests to take into consideration the people would have torn Aveling to pieces."[41] Bernstein spoke on behalf of the German socialists. He and his wife had become particularly close to Tussy after Engels's death, and he later wrote that he'd spent sleepless nights after her suicide blaming himself for not having wrested Tussy from Aveling's baleful influence. Finally Thorne spoke. One press report said that this giant of a workingman's words were barely audible because he was sobbing.[42]

★   ★   ★

After Tussy's suicide and before her cremation, the Sydenham coroner's office held an inquest into her death. The story generated considerable attention in the local paper, which ran a headline "Tragic Suicide at Sydenham." Aveling was called to testify, and, far from stricken, he came across as cocky. To the question "Was the deceased your wife," he cheekily responded, "Legally or not do you mean?" (He eventually settled on the latter.) Aveling claimed that he was not sure of Tussy's age and that she was in very good health, though she had several times threatened to kill herself. He said it was not unusual for her to say, "Let us end all these difficulties together." Next Gentry took the stand and explained the timeline of the morning of March 31. Finally the pharmacist, George Edgar Dale, was called. He was potentially in legal trouble because he had given poison to a person not authorized to receive it: "I thought Dr. Aveling was a qualified man. I thought it would be allowable to send it." He had understood Aveling to be a medical doctor and believed the note was in Aveling's handwriting.[43]

On April 4 the jury returned a verdict of suicide while in a state of temporary insanity. The coroner returned to Aveling the letters Tussy had written to him and her lawyer the morning of her death. Aveling destroyed them both.[44] Paul Lafargue and Charles Longuet had attended the inquest, and when it was over they and Aveling went to a nearby pub. It is not known whether they sympathized with Aveling over Tussy's death or loathed him for his supercilious performance before the coroner. The only thing that is known is that Longuet and Lafargue wanted Aveling to go with them to see Tussy's lawyer. Aveling refused.[45] The next day he went to a football match,[46] his problems, for the moment, over. At Tussy's death he had inherited nearly £2,000 in cash and £1,400 in property[47] and could now take up full-time residence with his lovely young wife, Eva.

As long as they had known him Tussy's friends had despised Aveling, but after her suicide their hatred knew no bounds. Bernstein had learned of his secret marriage and believed Aveling directly responsible for Tussy's death, if not complicit in it. He wanted him to stand trial.[48] To draw attention to the case he published Tussy's final letters to Freddy in Kautsky's socialist newspaper, Die Neue Zeit (The New Times), accompanied by a damning article on Aveling. The report was snapped up by the socialist press in London, but there were no grounds for prosecution, and by late summer Tussy's friends were forced to drop the matter. All they could do was shun Aveling (who was soon spotted in a fashionable London eatery accompanied by a young woman).[49]

According to Tussy's will, Aveling received all interest in and royalties from Marx's work, and he wasted no time in publishing yet another translation—Marx's *Value, Price and Profit*—which he and Tussy had been editing. In the introduction he said though he had done a good deal of the editing, the "most important part of the work has been done by her whose name appears on the title page"—Tussy. He then went on to extol his own efforts: "I am often asked what is the best succession of books for the student to acquire the fundamental principles of socialism...by way of suggestions one might say first Friedrich Engels's *Socialism: Scientific and Utopian*, then the present work, the first volume of *Capital* and the *Student's Marx*."[50] Aveling had had a hand in translating the first three, and he wrote the fourth.

But Aveling did not have long to live either. On August 2 he died in his reading chair in the Battersea apartment he shared with Eva.[51] His illness, which had so tormented Tussy earlier that year, finally killed him. Eva inherited the remainder of Engels's fortune, £852.[52]

Finally persuaded that Aveling was a fiend, Liebknecht declared that Tussy would now be referred to by her own name. She was gone, but once again, after too long, she would be known as Eleanor Marx.[53]

53

~⌒~

Draveil, France, 1910

Men fight and lose the battle and the thing they fought for comes
about in spite of their defeat, and when it comes turns out to be
not what they meant.

—William Morris[1]

ON A SUNDAY afternoon in the summer of 1910, two Russians bicycled up
to the Lafargues' house in Draveil. It was Vladimir Lenin and his wife,
Nadia Krupskaya. Lenin was in exile in Paris after leading the Bolshevik
faction of the Russian Social Democratic Labor Party in Russia's 1905
revolt.[2] In January of that year the rebellion Engels long foresaw had
erupted in St. Petersburg, when the military opened fire on a workers'
protest. The spark from that incident spread from city to city and throughout the countryside, where resentment had been growing for half a century over the end of serfdom's failure to improve the lives of those freed.
Not only were the czar and his government a target but also the industrialists who were trying to make the Russian economy mirror that of Western capitalist states. It was 1848 all over again, but the cataclysm was
confined to one country. By the time Lenin arrived in Paris, concessions
had been made. A legislative Duma was established and terms like "constitution," "political parties," and "trade unions" were being bandied
about. But, as had been the case in Western Europe at the start of the great
shift away from absolute monarchies, the Duma lacked real authority. The
reforms were more sop than substance, and the fuse remained lit.

Lenin was disgusted by the petty intrigues among the Russian émigrés
in Paris and retreated to study and writing. He had met Paul Lafargue in
1895, when the Frenchman had expressed surprise that Russians read and

589

understood Marx, and in 1910 he decided to pay that venerable party elder another visit. Lafargue was now sixty-eight and a hard-core Marxist. He rejected any conciliatory gestures toward nonsocialist government— socialists must either form the government or remain in the opposition (a position Marx, too, held in his earliest London days).[3] Easygoing and unflappable in his youth, Lafargue had become so hardened in his views by his late fifties that he had physically attacked a speaker at one socialist congress. Unyielding, he had to be forcibly removed from the platform.[4] He and Lenin were similarly intransigent, and the young Russian was pleasantly surprised to find in Lafargue such strong revolutionary views.[5]

Krupskaya described their visit: Lenin talked to Lafargue about his theoretical work while she toured the Lafargues' gardens with Laura. All the while, she said, she was marveling, "Here I am with Marx's daughter!" She examined Laura closely, but did not recognize any of Marx's physical traits in her.[6] Indeed, there was more Jenny von Westphalen than Karl Marx in Laura. In her later years Laura was truly lovely. She had aged gracefully, though friends remarked that she looked older than Lafargue, who was three years her senior.[7] Like her mother, she had long worked quietly, in the shadows, for the party. One incident, in 1893, had made that very clear. Laura had translated into French Engels's *The Origin of the Family* after another writer had made a hash of the job.[8] When the book was published, Engels had been surprised to see Laura's name left off the title page.[9] She told him, "I deleted the name myself, not thinking it necessary, for having once in a way been able to render you so slight a service, to proclaim it from the housetops as you were tolerably satisfied with my work, I was more than rewarded for it."[10]

Engels had had a deep appreciation for Laura's talents as a writer and translator[11](he stressed repeatedly that she was the best translator of her father's works in Paris), and he came to rely on her more in the busy years after Marx's death. Laura once told him, "I have in the first place to thank you for thinking of me. As I am in the habit of keeping in the background, I am very apt to be overlooked and forgotten. But you have at all times extended to his daughters the same noble friendship you had, and have, for Mohr!"[12] In the years after Engels's death and Tussy's suicide, Laura continued to work on the family's writing, tucked away and unnoticed at her estate at Draveil.

Lafargue, too, was largely out of political circulation.[13] He was the man who had introduced Marxism to France and Spain, and that would be his significant and enduring contribution to the movement. Recharged by the revolt in Russia, he made a brief return to electoral politics in 1905, but his campaign against the socialist powerhouse Etienne Millerand was doomed from the start. Lafargue did not even make it onto the first ballot.[14] He was as he appeared, a relic of radical politics past. His hair was as thick as it had been when he first courted Laura but was now pure white, as was his large mustache. His face was taut and sculpted, his bearing erect. He looked like a wealthy landowner—the very sort he had spent a lifetime ridiculing. In fact Lafargue was so convincing in that role that some fellow socialists denounced him as a "millionaire living in a chateau" who avoided his old friends because he did not want to give them money.[15] That criticism was not entirely fair. Lafargue and Laura were well known for their hospitality, inviting those toiling in Paris to parties and weekends in the country. Lafargue liked long meals and political talk that often descended into argument. Johnny's son, Robert-Jean Longuet, recalled being surprised by how vigorously Laura criticized Paul during political disputes: "As to him, he finished every reply in a deep voice with this formula... 'The women have long hair and short ideas,' which made Laura leap at him."[16]

Jennychen's children and grandchildren were often with the Lafargues, especially after Charles Longuet's death in 1903. But even while Longuet was alive, Laura had helped raise them. Despite a brief romance that had offended Tussy and Laura not long after his wife's death, Longuet never remarried. He worked on behalf of socialism as a writer and for a time served on the municipal council in Paris.[17] Johnny followed his father and grandfather into politics; he was a leading member of the French Socialist Party. Mémé consummated the stage dreams of the mother she never knew, becoming an opera singer. She did not marry.[18] Laura took great pride in her nephews and niece, but she had never lost that aura of sadness from her years in the Pyrenees when her own children had died. Dulling herself after a lifetime of pain and disappointment, she retreated into a haze. On many occasions neighbors remarked that Laura was drunk.[19]

On November 25, 1911, the Lafargues went to Paris to do some shopping, have dinner, and see a movie. Laura bought herself a new hat. The gardener, seeing them when they returned, noted how happy they seemed. They had had tea and cake after the cinema.[20] On the morning of November 26 the maid heard Lafargue open his window blinds, as he did every day, but after that there was silence. By ten she was disturbed that Laura had not called for breakfast, and sensing something was wrong summoned the gardener, Ernest Doucet, to check on Lafargue. Doucet knocked on his door but there was no response. He entered and found Lafargue dead in bed, dressed in the evening clothes he had worn the night before. Doucet next went to Laura's room. She too was dead, lying in her nightgown in the doorway to her dressing room.

Doucet sent his young son Roger off in the cold morning rain to find the mayor, who alerted the doctor. Police were stationed outside the Lafargue house while the investigation proceeded inside. The doctor who examined the couple said it seemed that Lafargue had injected Laura with a solution of potassium cyanide the night before and injected himself that morning. Lafargue had left Laura's body lying on the floor all night.[21] In those hours between his wife's death and his own, Lafargue methodically answered in writing the inevitable questions that would arise the next day and left several documents on his nightstand. He wrote out the text of a telegram to be sent to his nephew Edgar Longuet: "Monsieur and Madame Lafargue are dead, come quickly. Doucet, gardener." He left out a copy of his will and a letter to Doucet instructing him on distribution of the animals and fowl on the estate.[22] He also left a suicide note:

> Healthy in mind and spirit, I kill myself before pitiless old age, which would take from me one by one the pleasures and joys of existence and strip me of my physical and intellectual force, paralyzes my energy....For many years, I promised myself not to live past seventy years; I picked that year for my departure from this life and I prepared the mode of execution for my resolution: an injection of potassium cyanide. I die with the supreme joy of having the certitude that, in the very near future, the cause for which I have devoted some forty-five years will triumph. Long live Communism! Long Live International Socialism.
>
> Paul Lafargue.[23]

On his nightstand Lafargue also left a copy of *Plutarch's Lives*. The book was opened to the page describing the death of Cato the Younger, who stabbed himself with his sword and, to prevent a doctor from saving him, ripped out his bowels with his own dying hand.[24]

Lafargue had answered many questions except a very important one: did Laura submit willingly to his needle? Doucet's wife was sure they both wanted to die, that Lafargue would not have executed his plan if Laura had not agreed.[25] There was no murder-suicide investigation, but that issue remained and also the question why. Some said Lafargue was ill. He normally saw a doctor twice a year, but between July 1911 and the night of his death, he had seen a doctor once a week.[26] Others said the Lafargues had run through Engels's money as well as the funds Lafargue had inherited when his mother died in 1899, and could not bear to be poor again.[27]

Lafargue was sixty-nine when he died, two months shy of his seventieth birthday. Laura had just turned sixty-six.

★   ★   ★

Johnny Longuet—Jean to his associates—received tributes to the La-fargues from around the world. At thirty-five he was now the patriarch of the Marx family. Yet there was one older member who never did assume that mantle. Freddy Demuth rushed off a note to Jean, saying, "I have just learned the sad news of the end of Lafargue and my dear Laura and hasten to send you my condolence for such a grievous loss. All the papers here differ on their accounts of the sad end. And may I ask you if you will be so kind as to send me the details for it does not seem to me to be possible.... My dear Laura was so cheerful when I last heard from her."[28]

Now sixty, Freddy had not stopped wrestling with the question of his parentage. The year before, he had written Jean from the hospital, where he was due to have an operation he was not sure he would survive. He said, "Whatever I am it would be better for you to learn from me than from anybody else. Now I want to tell you the story of my father to the extent I am in a position to tell it." Freddy detailed events at the General's after Marx had died and Engels's deathbed disclosure to Tussy. "I have not given up hope to get to the truth and am still trying to do it as I am abso-lutely certain Marx was my father. Because of this operation, because my end is very near...I think it would be much better that I share what I know before this same information will come from other people."[29]

Freddy did not die. In fact, he lived until 1929, still searching for the truth.

A small funeral service was held for Lafargue and Laura on November 30, 1911, in Draveil, and then, on December 3, their coffins were conducted in a grand procession through Paris to Père-Lachaise cemetery.[30] The streets were awash in red flags, which seemed even brighter than usual because of the black mourning wear of the crowd. The procession, led by a band playing Chopin's "Funeral March," began at half past noon and took two hours to reach the cemetery. Despite a steady rain, the gathering that had begun with a few thousand people picked up more and more along the route.[31] Police estimated the crowd at 8,500; socialists put the number at 200,000.[32]

French, Poles, Germans, English, Italians, Spaniards, Belgians, Dutch, and Russians—many, many Russians—marched solemnly through the wet streets to the cemetery, which looked every bit a city of the dead. Laura and Lafargue were cremated there, and on the steps of the colum-barium, as the gray smoke from their bodies began to rise, the speeches commenced. It was as if the burial were not for two people but for an era, the era of Marx and Engels, the founding years. The new generation of leaders climbed the steps one by one to speak of the man and woman

593

being remembered that day and the movement they represented. Karl Kautsky was there for Germany, Keir Hardie for England, Jean Jaurès for France.[33] A police report noted that one of the speakers, "a Russian whose identity was not known," beseeched the crowd: "Fight. Fight always to arrive at that foreseen by the deceased—the victory of the proletariat."[34]

That speaker was Vladimir Lenin. He told the gathering that Lafargue symbolized two eras—that of the revolutionary French youth who marched side by side with workers to attack an empire, and another era, when the French proletariat under Marxist leadership waged war on the bourgeoisie in preparation for the ultimate triumph of socialism: "We can now see with particular clarity how rapidly we are nearing the triumph of the cause to which Lafargue devoted all his life." Those educated in the spirit of Marx, he said, were poised to establish a communist system.[35] They did, six years later in Russia, when Lenin and his Bolshevik colleagues seized power (though whether Marx would have recognized his ideas in their communist state is debatable). Freddy Demuth was the only one of Marx's children to live to see it.

He did the greatest literary feat a man can do. Marx changed the mind of the world.

— *George Bernard Shaw*

Acknowledgments

I could not have written the Marx family's story without access to their letters. I owe an enormous debt to two people in Moscow who made that possible: Andrei Shukshin, a former Reuters colleague, and Valerij Fomičev, a Marx expert and keeper of the archives at the Russian State Archive of Social and Political History. Andrei provided the key that unlocked many doors in Moscow, but the most important was at RGASPI, where he made contact with Dr. Fomičev. Dr. Fomičev subsequently and most generously agreed to provide me with access to hundreds of pages of Marx family letters and permission to use some in writing this book. He also gave me the rare treat of seeing Marx's original papers in their bomb-proof vault, deep under the archive. Both men devoted their valuable time to this project, and I fear may have set aside their own work to help me. In addition to the letters, they advised me over the course of several years, and Dr. Fomičev gave me his expert opinion as questions arose during my research. I cannot thank them enough for their kindness and patience. I would also like to thank Nora Mogilevskaya and the staff of the Social and Political State Library in Moscow for generously preparing materials so that when Andrei and I visited, we could get right to work. We found extremely important material at this library, which greatly advanced the project.

The other important cache of Marx family letters resides in Amsterdam, at the International Institute of Social History. The entire staff at that excellent facility deserves praise. During several visits they were consistently professional, knowledgeable, and pleasant. They made researching vast amounts of material relatively painless. I must mention one person in particular though, who sadly no longer works at the institute. Mieke Ijzermans not only provided a place to sleep during my stays in Amsterdam—as she has for countless other researchers—but she was a true friend. Mieke repeatedly acted on my behalf at the institute when I was back in London, arranging access to written material and photographs, and generally answering questions and sorting out problems in her lovely, calm way. She also gave me many tips during the course of my research without which I would have missed important elements in the story. I cannot thank her enough, and I am sure I am not alone in my gratitude for the warmth and assistance she provided researchers over the years.

Other institutions also provided invaluable help. Elisabeth Neu and the staff at the Friedrich-Ebert-Stiftung Study Center, Karl-Marx-Haus, in Trier, Germany, gave me access to files that helped me uncover some errors in previous Marx texts, most notably those involving photographs and dates. Elisabeth also patiently answered queries as they arose during the course of my research. Her information helped me avoid errors that had been picked up from one Marx biography to another. She also very kindly worked her network of Marx scholars to try to answer questions when I was otherwise stumped. I would like to thank the State Archives of the Free and Hanseatic City of Hamburg and the Principal National Archive of Saxony-Anhalt, Dessau, for giving me access to Westphalen family correspondence, which helped paint a clearer picture of the relations between Jenny and her brothers. My thanks to both institutions for their permission to use portions of the letters in this book.

In London, I cannot fail to mention the Marx Memorial Library, which is a clearinghouse of all things Marx, and the British Newspaper Library, which has an extremely good collection of international newspapers. Finally, my thanks to the British Library staff. Even though the facility is no longer located in the British Museum where Marx worked, it is still a researcher's dream. There was seemingly nothing it did not have or its staff could not find. In Kent, Michael Hunt at the Ramsgate Maritime Museum helped me better understand the workings of that resort town during the nineteenth century so I could place the Marx family at their favorite coastal spot.

Several individuals were also critical to this book. I had the privilege of discussing the Marx family with one of its descendants by phone from Paris, Frédérique Longuet-Marx, who along with her mother, Simone, and sister, Anne, answered questions about the family that only its members might know. I thank all three for their time and insight. Likewise, two scholars in England, whose works have long been the standard biographies on their subjects—David McLellan and Terrell Carver—generously answered questions that arose as I wrote. After having relied on their writings, it was a real comfort to be able to then turn by e-mail to Professor McLellan on Marx and Professor Carver on Engels for help on points that no doubt seemed minor to them but were major for me. David

King in London gave me access to his excellent Marx photo collection and patiently advised me on picture searches for some of the more difficult to find images. I am grateful that David has given me permission to use some of his images. Finally, there is one man in London who allowed me into Marx's world, literally. Sam Hart, the current owner of 28 Dean Street, graciously gave me a tour of the Marxes' former apartment, allowing me to feel what life in those cramped rooms must have been like for the family.

Juliane Matz was my long-distance assistant on this project. Not only did she handle the bulk of the German translations, but she discovered archival material in Germany of which I was unaware. She was talented, conscientious, and generous, never abandoning the project no matter the twists in her life, which took her during the course of our work from Britain to Germany to France to Ireland. She was a joy to work with. Thorsten Schülke helped translate some of the very difficult handwritten letters—not only was the nineteenth-century language a challenge, but some were barely legible. He was meticulous in his approach and an excellent translator. I also worked closely with Jan Vermeiren, who diligently translated dozens of handwritten letters as well as advised me on the nuances of German language, not to mention German and Austrian history. Also helping with translations were Ingrid Montbazet, Julia Riddiford, Charlotte Ryland, and Louise Miller. My thanks also to Nicolas Deakin for allowing me to use material from Havelock Ellis's papers in the British Library.

Finally, there would have been no book at all without the interest of three people: Jill Kneerim and Brettne Bloom at Kneerim & Williams, and Geoff Shandler at Little, Brown. The world was quite a different place when Jill took a chance on representing a book on Karl Marx's family. Marx had been declared dead—literally and theoretically—but she had the foresight to see that his family's story had merit. Brettne, who took on the project, not only helped me hone my ideas but she provided excellent advice in preparing a proposal and continued to give me sound guidance throughout the project. Her help went well beyond what was expected of an agent; it was invaluable. Geoff Shandler quite simply made this book come alive. Through his suggestions and questions, he helped me to see the family's story more clearly and better describe the turbulent times in which they lived. The book was a massive undertaking, but Geoff remained patient, gracious, and—perhaps most important for a writer—encouraging throughout. I was extremely fortunate to have had such a gifted editor to work with, and I thank him for helping me make the finished product the book I had hoped to write. My thanks also to Liese Mayer at Little, Brown for helping to make this project work at such a great distance, and Chris Jerome for her careful copyediting.

Personally I would like to thank my mother for putting up with eight years of neglect without complaint while I spent time with another family, and for allowing me to take over her kitchen table when I landed on her doorstep with computer in hand. Thanks to Lizzy, Mon, and Mark for their support and friendship. To John I say thank you for helping me write, edit, and research this book—for joining me in the Marx family's world. I could not have spent so much time in it without you.

Copyright Acknowledgments

Notes

In citing works here, short titles have been used, with full title and publishing details given in the Bibliography. Works or institutions frequently cited have been abbreviated as follows:

Dessau — Landeshauptarchiv Sachsen-Anhalt Abteilung Dessau
FE-PL — Friedrich Engels–Paul Lafargue and Laura Lafargue. *Correspondence, Volumes I–III.* Moscow: Foreign Languages Publishing House, 1959, 1960.
Hamburg — Freie und Hansestadt Hamburg Kulturbehörde Staatsarchiv
IISG — Internationaal Instituut voor Sociale Geschiedenis, Amsterdam
KMIR — McLellan, David (ed.), *Karl Marx, Interviews & Recollections.* London: Macmillan, 1981.
MECW — *Karl Marx and Frederick Engels. Collected Works, Volumes 1–50.* Moscow, London, New York: Progress Publishers, International Publishers, and Lawrence & Wishart, 1975–2004.
MEGA — Karl Marx and Friedrich Engels. *Historisch-kritische Gesamtausgabe. Werke, Schriften, Briefe.* Berlin: Akademie Verlag, 1927–ongoing.
Moscow — Rossiiskii gosudarstvennyi arkhiv sotsial'no-politicheskoi istorii, Moscow
REM — *Reminiscences of Marx and Engels.* Moscow: Foreign Language Publishing House, 1970.

Preface
1. Valerij Fomičev, "Helene Demuth Without Brethren," 970.

Prologue: London, 1851
1. MECW, Volume 16, 489.
2. Henry Mayhew, *London Labour and the London Poor,* 167.
3. MECW, Volume 38, 325; MEGA, III, Band 4, 85–86.

Part One: Marx and the Baron's Daughter

Chapter One: Trier, Germany, 1835
1. Honoré de Balzac, *Gambara,* 84.
2. Robert Payne, *Marx: A Biography,* 25.
3. H. F. Peters, *Red Jenny,* 5.
4. One historian, David Cargill, traced Jenny's family to Colin, Lord Campbell, first Earl of Argyll. Archibald Argyll was not, according to Cargill, a direct relation, but Jenny and her family believed him to be. Robert Payne, *Marx,* 26–27, 557.

5. Peter Stearns, *1848: The Revolutionary Tide in Europe*, 232–233.

6. Jürgen Reetz (ed.), *Vier Briefe von Jenny Marx aus den Jahren, 1856–1860*, Ferdinand von Westphalen to Ludwig and Carolyn von Westphalen, Apr. 10, 1831.

7. Peters, *Red Jenny*, 16; Louise von Westphalen to her parents, Dec. 15, 1831, Hamburg.

8. Louise von Westphalen to her parents, Dec. 20–22, 1831, Hamburg.

9. Louise von Westphalen to her parents, Jan. 4, 1832, Hamburg.

10. Peters, *Red Jenny*, 15, 18; Ferdinand von Westphalen to Wilhelm von Flourencourt, Nov. 26, 1830, Dessau.

11. Isaiah Berlin, *The Roots of Romanticism*, 8–9, 13.

12. E. H. Carr, *Michael Bakunin*, 14.

13. Berlin, *Roots of Romanticism*, 70–71.

14. Peters, *Red Jenny*, 15.

15. Steven Ozment, *A Mighty Fortress*, 157, 159.

16. Isaiah Berlin, *Karl Marx: His Life and Environment*, 29–32; Isaiah Berlin, *Political Ideas in the Romantic Age*, 80.

17. Eric Hobsbawm, *The Age of Revolution, 1789–1848*, 35.

18. Peters, *Red Jenny*, 1, 8; Robert Payne, *Marx*, 28.

19. R. J. W. Evans and Hartmut Pogge von Strandmann (eds.), *The Revolutions in Europe, 1848–49*, 14; Paul Lafargue, *The Right to Be Lazy*, 77–78; Hobsbawm, *Age of Revolution*, 139–140.

20. Alexis de Tocqueville, *The Recollections of Alexis de Tocqueville*, 66–67.

21. Hobsbawm, *Age of Revolution*, 140; Tocqueville, *Recollections*, 2–3.

22. Hobsbawm, *Age of Revolution*, 146.

23. Ozment, *Mighty Fortress*, 169; Carl Schurz, *The Reminiscences of Carl Schurz, Volume I, 1829–1852*, 104–105.

24. MECW, Volume 6, 21–22.

25. John Breuilly (ed.), *19th-Century Germany*, 113.

26. John Breuilly, *Austria, Prussia and Germany, 1806–1871*, 30.

27. Theodore S. Hamerow, *Restoration, Revolution, Reaction*, 34.

28. Jerrold Seigel, *Marx's Fate*, 40–41.

29. Peters, *Red Jenny*, 15.

30. Robert Payne, *Marx*, 23–24.

31. Wilhelm Liebknecht, *Karl Marx: Biographical Memoirs*, 65.

32. Oscar J. Hammen, *The Red 48ers*, 9.

33. Werner Blumenberg, *Karl Marx: An Illustrated History*, 6.

34. Ibid., 6–7; David McLellan, *Karl Marx: A Biography*, 2–3; Saul K. Padover, *Karl Marx: An Intimate Biography*, 2–3.

35. Blumenberg, *Illustrated*, 7; Jonathan Sperber (ed.), *Germany, 1800–1870*, 183.

36. Details about Heinrich Marx's legal training and the year he became a lawyer are unavailable. McLellan, *Karl Marx*, 4; Berlin, *Karl Marx*, 23; Padover, *Karl Marx*, 4.

37. Eleanor Marx to "Comrade," Oct. 1, 1893, Moscow; Liebknecht, *Karl Marx*, 163.

38. Boris Nicolaievsky and Otto Maenchen-Helfen, *Karl Marx: Man and Fighter*, 4.

39. McLellan, *Karl Marx*, 4; Blumenberg, *Illustrated*, 9; Berlin, *Karl Marx*, 17–20; Nicolaievsky and Maenchen-Helfen, *Karl Marx*, 4.

40. Padover, *Karl Marx*, 5–6.

41. McLellan, *Karl Marx*, 5; Blumenberg, *Illustrated*, 10; Padover, *Karl Marx*, 18.

42. Padover, *Karl Marx*, 17.

43. McLellan, *Karl Marx*, 1.

44. Berlin, *Karl Marx*, 23.

45. Ibid., 21; Padover, *Karl Marx*, 7; S. L. Gilman, "Karl Marx and the Secret Language of Jews," 31.

46. McLellan, *Karl Marx*, 4.

47. Blumenberg, *Illustrated*, 13.

48. Hammen, *Red 48ers*, 16.
49. Sperber (ed.), *Germany, 1800–1870*, 150.
50. Fritz J. Raddatz, *Karl Marx: A Political Biography*, 11; Nicolaievsky and Maenchen-Helfen, *Karl Marx*, 13.
51. McLellan, *Karl Marx*, 6; Blumenberg, *Illustrated*, 10; Nicolaievsky and Maenchen-Helfen, *Karl Marx*, 9; James M. Brophy, *Popular Culture and the Public Sphere in the Rhineland, 1800–1850*, 100–101.
52. Hal Draper and E. Haberkern, *Karl Marx's Theory of Revolution, Volume V: War & Revolution*, 20.
53. Nicolaievsky and Maenchen-Helfen, *Karl Marx*, 8.
54. Ernst Pawel, *The Poet Dying*, 8.
55. MECW, Volume 1, 4–9.

Chapter Two: Berlin, 1838
1. Friedrich von Schiller, *The Robbers*, 14.
2. McLellan, *Karl Marx*, 13–14; Padover, *Karl Marx*, 23, 28; Robert Payne, *Karl Marx*, 42, 44; MECW, Volume 1, 689.
3. MECW, Volume 1, 646.
4. Ibid., 651.
5. Ibid., 648.
6. Ibid., 653.
7. Robert Payne, *Karl Marx*, 45.
8. MECW, Volume 1, 657–658.
9. Françoise Giroud, *Jenny Marx ou la femme du diable*, 33.
10. MECW, Volume 1, 698.
11. Brophy, *Popular Culture and the Public Sphere*, 271.
12. Giroud, *Femme du diable*, 24; Hobsbawm, *Age of Revolution*, 283.
13. MECW, Volume 1, 689.
14. Padover, *Karl Marx*, 31.
15. McLellan, *Karl Marx*, 15, 19; Nicolaievsky and Maenchen-Helfen, *Karl Marx*, 29; Padover, *Karl Marx*, 32; Robert Payne, *Karl Marx*, 47.
16. Sperber (ed.), *Germany, 1800–1870*, 150.
17. MECW, Volume 1, 688.
18. Ibid., 11–21.
19. Robert Payne, *Karl Marx*, 49.
20. MECW, Volume 1, 18–19.
21. MECW, Volume 25, 24.
22. Eric Hobsbawm, *The Age of Capital, 1848–1875*, 48, 75 ; J. M. Roberts, *A History of Europe*, 327–328; Hobsbawm, *Age of Revolution*, 46, 61, 340.
23. Hobsbawm, *Age of Revolution*, 304; Hammen, *Red 48ers*, 18; Nicolaievsky and Maenchen-Helfen, *Karl Marx*, 33; McLellan, *Karl Marx*, 26.
24. MECW, Volume 1, 664–665.
25. Ibid., 517–528.
26. Ibid., 666–667.
27. Ibid., 670–671.
28. Franz Mehring, *Karl Marx: The Story of His Life*, 9.
29. Hammen, *Red 48ers*, 19–20; Robert Payne, *Karl Marx*, 79.
30. Ozment, *Mighty Fortress*, 187; Leszek Kolakowski, *Main Currents of Marxism, Volume I, The Founders*, 88; Seigel, *Marx's Fate*, 77.
31. KMIR, 3.
32. MECW, Volume 1, 674–675.
33. Ibid., 686–688.
34. Ibid., 691–692.

35. Jenny von Westphalen to Karl Marx, after May 10, 1838, Moscow.
36. Friedrich-Ebert-Stiftung Studienzentrum, Karl-Marx-Haus, Trier.
37. McLellan, *Karl Marx,* 27–28.

Chapter Three: Cologne, 1842

1. MECW, Volume 1, 707.
2. Ibid., 704.
3. Giroud, *Femme du diable,* 38; Peters, *Red Jenny,* 26; Robert Payne, *Karl Marx,* 89.
4. MECW, Volume 1, 696–697.
5. Ibid., 698.
6. Schurz, *Reminiscences,* 106–107; Hammen, *Red 48ers,* 23; Breuilly, *Austria, Prussia and Germany,* 29, 33.
7. Schurz, *Reminiscences,* 106–107.
8. Berlin, *Karl Marx,* 47.
9. Nicolaievsky and Maenchen-Helfen, *Karl Marx,* 41.
10. MECW, Volume 1, 379 ; McLellan, *Karl Marx,* 33; Francis Wheen, *Karl Marx: A Life,* 33.
11. MECW, Volume 1, 27–28.
12. Nicolaievsky and Maenchen-Helfen, *Karl Marx,* 41, 47; Mehring, *Karl Marx,* 32; Hammen, *Red 48ers,* 27; McLellan, *Karl Marx,* 42.
13. John Breuilly (ed.), *19th-Century Germany,* 99.
14. Lenore O'Boyle, "The Democratic Left in Germany, 1848," 379–380.
15. Ibid., 379.
16. McLellan, *Karl Marx,* 32; Luc Somerhausen, *L'Humanisme Agissant de Karl Marx,* 10.
17. Robert-Jean Longuet, *Karl Marx: Mon Arrière-Grand-Père,* 70.
18. Padover, *Karl Marx,* 19.
19. Brophy, *Popular Culture and the Public Sphere,* 125.
20. Karl Marx to Arnold Ruge, May 1843, MEGA, III, Band 1, 48–53.
21. Sperber (ed.), *Germany, 1800–1870,* 53.
22. McLellan, *Karl Marx,* 34.
23. MECW, Volume 1, 707.
24. Ibid., 709.
25. Ibid., 707.
26. Giroud, *Femme du diable,* 39–40.
27. Peters, *Red Jenny,* 28.
28. Jenny von Westphalen to Karl Marx, Sept. 13, 1841, MEGA, III, Band 1, 366–368.
29. Longuet, *Karl Marx,* 74; McLellan, *Karl Marx,* 35.
30. Padover, *Karl Marx,* 60–61; MECW, Volume 1, 109.
31. The law also gave censors the right to force publishers to fire editors deemed untrustworthy or to put up an unspecified security against violation of the rules by that person if they wished to retain him. MECW, Volume 1, 116, 119, 120, 123, 125, 131.
32. McLellan, *Karl Marx,* 35; Hammen, *Red 48ers,* 19–20; Sperber (ed.), *Germany, 1800–1870,* 193.
33. McLellan, *Karl Marx,* 61; Giroud, *Femme du diable,* 45; Peters, *Red Jenny,* 30; Padover, *Karl Marx,* 73; Robert Payne, *Karl Marx,* 89.
34. McLellan, *Karl Marx,* 37–38.
35. Ibid., 38; Berlin, *Karl Marx,* 54.
36. McLellan, *Karl Marx,* 38; Stearns, *1848,* 56; Nicolaievsky and Maenchen-Helfen, *Karl Marx,* 47–48, 50.
37. MECW, Volume 11, 8–9; Hamerow, *Restoration, Revolution, Reaction,* 7, 61–62.
38. Padover, *Karl Marx,* 65.
39. Brophy, *Popular Culture and the Public Sphere,* 49, 162.

40. MECW, Volume 1, 155, 162.
41. KMIR, 2.
42. McLellan, *Karl Marx,* 41.
43. MECW, Volume 1, 389.
44. McLellan, *Karl Marx,* 42–43.
45. MECW, Volume 1, 392.
46. Ibid., 220.
47. KMIR, 3.
48. Ibid., 5.
49. McLellan, *Karl Marx,* 44.
50. Hammen, *Red 48ers,* 28.
51. MECW, Volume 1, 394.
52. Ibid., 395.
53. Izumi Omura, Valerij Fomičev, Rolf Hecker, and Shun-ichi Kubo (eds.), *Familie Marx privat,* 416; Padover, *Karl Marx,* 72.
54. MECW, Volume 50, 497.
55. McLellan, *Karl Marx,* 46; Hobsbawm, *Age of Capital,* 51; Hamerow, *Restoration, Revolution, Reaction,* 17, 19, 47, 52.
56. MECW, Volume 1, 234, 254.
57. Ibid., 340, 342.
58. McLellan, *Karl Marx,* 48–50.
59. Peters, *Red Jenny,* 36.
60. MECW, Volume 1, 396–398; McLellan, *Karl Marx,* 47.
61. McLellan, *Karl Marx,* 50; Peters, *Red Jenny,* 38; Berlin, *Karl Marx,* 56; Wheen, *Karl Marx,* 12.
62. Padover, *Karl Marx,* 69; McLellan, *Karl Marx,* 50.
63. MECW, Volume 1, 397–398.

Chapter Four: Kreuznach, 1843
1. Pawel, *Poet Dying,* 271.
2. MECW, Volume 3, 572.
3. Ibid., 134; Longuet, *Karl Marx,* 82.
4. MECW, Volume 1, 728.
5. Longuet, *Karl Marx,* 85; Maenchen-Helfen and Nicolaievsky, *Karl und Jenny Marx: Ein Lebensweg.*
6. Arnold Ruge to Karl Marx, Aug. 10, 1843, MEGA, III, Band I, 409–410.
7. McLellan, *Karl Marx,* 61.
8. MECW, Volume 1, 399.
9. Ibid., 728.
10. Berlin, *Roots of Romanticism,* 94.
11. MECW, Volume 3, 573–574.
12. Giroud, *Femme du diable,* 52–53; Robert Payne, *Karl Marx,* 92.
13. MECW, Volume 1, 729.
14. REM, 279; Padover, *Karl Marx,* 76; McLellan, *Karl Marx,* 62.
15. Raddatz, *Karl Marx,* 77; Peters, *Red Jenny,* 41.
16. MECW, Volume 3, 175, 187; Padover, *Karl Marx,* 79; Seigel, *Marx's Fate,* 106–107.
17. Giroud, *Femme du diable,* 53–54.
18. Berlin, *Karl Marx,* 59.
19. Hammen, *Red 48ers,* 24; McLellan, *Karl Marx,* 63–64.
20. McLellan, *Karl Marx,* 64–65; Breuilly (ed.), *19th-Century Germany,* 46.
21. Padover, *Karl Marx,* 79.
22. Karl Marx to Arnold Ruge, Sept. 1843, MEGA, III, Band I, 54–57.

Part Two: The Fugitive Family

Chapter Five: Paris, 1843

1. Karl Marx to Arnold Ruge, Sept. 1843, MEGA, III, Band 1, 54–57.
2. François Fejtö (ed.), *The Opening of an Era: 1848*, 72–75; Somerhausen, *L'Humanisme*, 51–52, 54.
3. Edith Thomas, *The Women Incendiaries*, 3; Hammen, *Red 48ers*, 80.
4. Nicolaievsky and Maenchen-Helfen, *Karl Marx*, 66; Pavel Annenkov, *The Extraordinary Decade*, 63.
5. Fejtö (ed.), *Opening of an Era*, 75.
6. KMIR, 7; McLellan, *Karl Marx*, 73.
7. KMIR, 6–7.
8. REM, 82.
9. KMIR, 12.
10. Peters, *Red Jenny*, 44–45; Hammen, *Red 48ers*, 64.
11. Emma Herwegh's father has also been described as a Berlin banker. Carr, *Michael Bakunin*, 117; Peters, *Red Jenny*, 45.
12. Padover, *Karl Marx*, 88; Peters, *Red Jenny*, 45–46; Giroud, *Femme du diable*, 65–66.
13. Hobsbawm, *Age of Revolution*, 316–317; Hal Draper, *Karl Marx's Theory of Revolution, Volume 1, State and Bureaucracy*, 136–137.
14. Hobsbawm, *Age of Revolution*, 151, 324.
15. Eleanor Marx Aveling to Karl Kautsky, Sept. 7, 1895, Moscow; Nicolaievsky and Maenchen-Helfen, *Karl Marx*, 72.
16. Robert Payne, *The Unknown Karl Marx*, 97–100.
17. Pawel, *Poet Dying*, 5–7, 13, 68; Robert Payne, *Unknown Marx*, 97–100.
18. Eleanor Marx Aveling to Karl Kautsky, Sept. 7, 1895, Moscow.
19. Pawel, *Poet Dying*, 16, 190.
20. Hammen, *Red 48ers*, 70–71; McLellan, *Karl Marx*, 73.
21. McLellan, *Karl Marx*, 88–89; Nicolaievsky and Maenchen-Helfen, *Karl Marx*, 69; Padover, *Karl Marx*, 87.
22. Jenny's comments were from an unfinished memoir written in 1865 that remained as notes until it was finally published in 1965. KMIR, 19.
23. Hammen, *Red 48ers*, 79; McLellan, *Karl Marx*, 89; Somerhausen, *L'Humanisme*, 26; Nicolaievsky and Maenchen-Helfen, *Karl Marx*, 70; Mehring, *Karl Marx*, 62.
24. McLellan, *Karl Marx*, 88; Mehring, *Karl Marx*, 67.
25. McLellan, *Karl Marx*, 80.
26. MECW, Volume 3, 187.
27. McLellan, *Karl Marx*, 77; MECW, Volume 3, 147–148, 173–174.
28. Hammen, *Red 48ers*, 79; McLellan, *Karl Marx*, 90; Raddatz, *Karl Marx*, 47.
29. McLellan, *Karl Marx*, 89; Hammen, *Red 48ers*, 79; Padover, *Karl Marx*, 87; Nicolaievsky and Maenchen-Helfen, *Karl Marx*, 70.
30. McLellan, *Karl Marx*, 89; Padover, *Karl Marx*, 87.
31. Raddatz, *Karl Marx*, 47.
32. KMIR, 8–9.
33. MECW, Volume 11, 264–266.
34. All the Marx daughters were named Jenny after their mother—Jenny Julia Eleanor and Jenny Laura, for example—but only Jennychen used it as her first name. The other daughters were formally known as Eleanor and Laura. Omura, Fomičev, Hecker, and Kubo (eds.), *Familie Marx privat*, 447.
35. Eleanor Marx Aveling to Karl Kautsky, Sept. 7, 1895, Moscow.
36. MECW, Volume 1, 581–584 and Volume 3, 581.

Chapter Six: Paris, 1844

1. Carr, *Michael Bakunin*, 137.
2. Nicolaievsky and Maenchen-Helfen, *Karl Marx*, 82.
3. Attending the banquet: Mikhail Bakunin, Count Grigori Tolstoy, and the physician Sergei Botkin represented Russia. The French included socialist journalists Louis Blanc and Pierre Leroux, and future Bonapartist Felix Pyat. For the Germans, Ruge, Bernays, and Marx attended. Raddatz, *Karl Marx*, 53; Somerhausen, *L'Humanisme*, 26; Carr, *Michael Bakunin*, 126.
4. K. J. Kenafick, *Michael Bakunin and Karl Marx*. 15; Carr, *Michael Bakunin*, 3, 5, 18, 86, 90, 94.
5. Nicolaievsky and Maenchen-Helfen, *Karl Marx*, 54.
6. Carr, *Michael Bakunin*, 24, 110; Annenkov, *Extraordinary Decade*, 178.
7. Carr, *Michael Bakunin*, 167.
8. Ibid., 129.
9. KMIR, 11.
10. Stearns, *1848*, 27, 50, 60–61; Arnold Whitridge, *Men in Crisis*, 50–51.
11. Stearns, *1848*, 27, 50.
12. Hammen, *Red 48ers*, 90; Stearns, *1848*, 46–47; Roberts, *History of Europe*, 338–339; Evans and von Strandmann (eds.), *Revolutions in Europe, 1848–49*, 10.
13. Berlin, *Karl Marx*, 9–10.
14. McLellan, *Karl Marx*, 79–80; Padover, *Karl Marx*, 91; Nicolaievsky and Maenchen-Helfen, *Karl Marx*, 79.
15. Engels described the league as closely aligned to a secret French organization called the Society of the Seasons, led by veteran revolutionaries Auguste Blanqui and Armand Barbes. Karl Marx and Friedrich Engels, *The Cologne Communist Trial*, 39–40.
16. MECW, Volume 3, 313.
17. The economists Marx studied included David Ricardo, Adam Smith, and Jean Baptiste Say. The *1844 Manuscripts* became the basis of Marx's lifework and were completed in *Capital*. MECW, Volume 3, xvi–xvii, 270–273; McLellan, *Karl Marx*, 94–98.
18. MECW, Volume 3, 324.
19. Ibid., 273.
20. Hobsbawm, *Age of Revolution*, 212; Fejtö (ed.), *Opening of an Era*, 68–69.
21. Fejtö (ed.), *Opening of an Era*, 75.
22. McLellan, *Karl Marx*, 103–104.
23. Pawel, *Poet Dying*, 126.
24. MECW, Volume 3, 313.
25. Draper, *Karl Marx's Theory of Revolution*, 174–175, 177; Hamerow, *Restoration, Revolution, Reaction*, 35.
26. Longuet, *Karl Marx*, 107; Hammen, *Red 48ers*, 82; McLellan, *Karl Marx*, 103–104; Brophy, *Popular Culture and the Public Sphere*, 87.
27. MECW, Volume 38, 64; Raddatz, *Karl Marx*, 53; Carr, *Michael Bakunin*, 125.
28. MECW, Volume 20, 28; McLellan, *Karl Marx*, 103–104; Nicolaievsky and Maenchen-Helfen, *Karl Marx*, 81; Hammen, *Red 48ers*, 82; Whitridge, *Men in Crisis*, 196–197.
29. MECW, Volume 4, 24 and Volume 20, 28; McLellan, *Karl Marx*, 117.
30. Wheen, *Karl Marx*, 67.
31. Neighboring monarchs viewed Paris as frighteningly democratic (or as one writer said at the time, "unprincipled and revolutionary") and flooded the city with spies to ensure that the contagion did not spread. Annenkov, *The Extraordinary Decade*, 63; Robert Payne, *Karl Marx*, 106.
32. Nicolaievsky and Maenchen-Helfen, *Karl Marx*, 81–82.
33. MECW, Volume 3, 576–579.

34. Ibid., 580. (Others have said the would-be assassin's motive was frustration with the king for not listening to his complaints about corruption. The gunman, Heinrich Ludwig Tschech, was a former village mailman and ex–civil servant. He was executed. Brophy, *Popular Culture and the Public Sphere,* 85.)
35. MEGA, I, Band 2, 501.
36. Nicolaievsky and Maenchen-Helfen, *Karl Marx,* 82–83.
37. Somerhausen, *L'Humanisme,* 69.
38. MECW, Volume 3, 582–583.

Chapter Seven: Paris, 1845
1. Wheen, *Karl Marx,* 17.
2. McLellan, *Karl Marx,* 95, 115.
3. Ibid., 116; Seigel, *Marx's Fate,* 147.
4. KMIR, 5.
5. Marx and Engels, *Cologne Communist Trial,* 44.
6. Gustav Mayer, *Friedrich Engels: A Biography,* 3–4; Terrell Carver, *Engels: A Very Short Introduction,* 5; Carver, *Friedrich Engels: His Life and Thought,* 3.
7. MECW, Volume 2, 582.
8. Carver, *Engels, Short Introduction,* 3; Seigel, *Marx's Fate,* 148.
9. Mayer, *Friedrich Engels,* 9–10; Engels, *The Condition of the Working Class in England,* x; Hammen, *Red 48ers,* 30.
10. MECW, Volume 2, 511–512.
11. Ibid., 525.
12. Carver, *Friedrich Engels,* 31; Carver, *Engels, Short Introduction,* 3; Yelena Stepanova, *Frederick Engels,* 22.
13. MECW, Volume 2, 9.
14. Ibid., 10.
15. Carver, *Friedrich Engels,* 146.
16. MECW, Volume 2, 493.
17. Stepanova, *Frederick Engels,* 17.
18. Ibid., 19; Hammen, *Red 48ers,* 35–36; Mayer, *Friedrich Engels,* 19; Carver, *Friedrich Engels,* 64; Hammen, *Red 48ers,* 36.
19. Mayer, *Friedrich Engels,* 26; Hammen, *Red 48ers,* 39.
20. Mayer, *Friedrich Engels,* 4.
21. Ibid., 30; Carver, *Friedrich Engels,* 96–97.
22. John Smethurst, Edmund Frow, and Ruth Frow, "Frederick Engels and the English Working Class Movement in Manchester, 1842–1844," 340–341.
23. Ibid., 341.
24. Ibid., 342.
25. Edmund Frow and Ruth Frow, *Frederick Engels in Manchester,* 9, 11; Eleanor Marx Aveling to Karl Kautsky, Mar. 15, 1898, Moscow.
26. Engels, *Condition of the Working Class,* 61, 63, 65, 66.
27. Ibid., 91.
28. Ibid., 148.
29. Smethurst, Frow, and Frow, "Frederick Engels and the English Working Class Movement," 342.
30. Mayer, *Friedrich Engels,* 44; Mick Jenkins, *Frederick Engels in Manchester,* 16.
31. Smethurst, Frow, and Frow, "Frederick Engels and the English Working Class Movement," 343–344.
32. Carver, *Friedrich Engels,* 110–111; Hammen, *Red 48ers,* 77.
33. MECW, Volume 4, 8.
34. McLellan, *Karl Marx,* 118.

35. Giroud, *Femme du diable,* 62.
36. McLellan, *Karl Marx,* 116–117.
37. MECW, Volume 4, 55–76.
38. MECW, Volume 38, 9–10.
39. Ibid., 4, 17–18.
40. Nicolaievsky and Maenchen-Helfen, *Karl Marx,* 83–84.
41. REM, 222.
42. Nicolaievsky and Maenchen-Helfen, *Karl Marx,* 84.
43. Ibid., 84–85.
44. REM, 222.
45. MECW, Volume 38, 525–526.
46. REM, 222.

Chapter Eight: Brussels, Spring 1845

1. McLellan, *Karl Marx,* 143.
2. Fejtö (ed.), *Opening of an Era,* 161; Robert Payne, *Karl Marx,* 118.
3. MECW, Volume 4, 675.
4. Ibid., 676–677.
5. Somerhausen, *L'Humanisme,* 76.
6. Ibid., 75; Raddatz, *Karl Marx,* 284.
7. Longuet, *Karl Marx,* 114.
8. Ibid., 118.
9. McLellan, *Karl Marx,* 141; Nicolaievsky and Maenchen-Helfen, *Karl Marx,* 99–100.
10. Nicolaievsky and Maenchen-Helfen, *Karl Marx,* 100; Peters, *Red Jenny,* 62–63.
11. Nicolaievsky and Maenchen-Helfen, *Karl Marx,* 100.
12. McLellan, *Karl Marx,* 129; Fejtö (ed.), *Opening of an Era,* 57; KMIR, 20; Robert Payne, *Karl Marx,* 118–119.
13. MECW, Volume 38, 21–22; McLellan, *Karl Marx,* 130; Longuet, *Karl Marx,* 118.
14. KMIR, 20; McLellan, *Karl Marx,* 130; Longuet, *Karl Marx,* 118.
15. KMIR, 5–6.
16. Hess did not marry Sibylle until 1852, after his father died. Shlomo Avineri, *Moses Hess,* 16; Longuet, *Karl Marx,* 118.
17. KMIR, 20.
18. Peters, *Red Jenny,* 60; McLellan, *Karl Marx,* 129–130; Edna Healey, *Wives of Fame,* 78.
19. KMIR, 20; Peters, *Red Jenny,* 60.
20. KMIR, 60; Valerij Fomičev, "Helene Demuth Without Brethren," 970; Peters, *Red Jenny,* 61.
21. McLellan, *Karl Marx,* 130; Longuet, *Karl Marx,* 119; Mayer, *Friedrich Engels,* 66.
22. MECW, Volume 38, 9–10.
23. Ibid., 19–20.
24. Ibid., 10–11, 28–29.
25. Ibid., 572(n)
26. Mayer, *Friedrich Engels,* 65.
27. MECW, Volume 38, 13.
28. McLellan, *Karl Marx,* 130.
29. MECW, Volume 38, 19.
30. McLellan, *Karl Marx,* 143; Nicolaievsky and Maenchen-Helfen, *Karl Marx,* 133.
31. Longuet, *Karl Marx,* 120.
32. Whitridge, *Men in Crisis,* 293.
33. Stearns, *1848,* 31–32; Hobsbawm, *Age of Revolution,* 64; Roberts, *History of Europe,* 14.
34. Hamerow, *Restoration, Revolution, Reaction,* 81.
35. Stearns, *1848,* 28; Roberts, *History of Europe,* 221, 913.

36. Hobsbawm, *Age of Revolution*, 169; Fejtö (ed.), *Opening of an Era*, 24.
37. Evans and von Strandmann (eds.), *Revolutions in Europe, 1848–49*, 3; Derek Offord, *Nineteenth-Century Russia*, 20.
38. Annenkov, *Extraordinary Decade*, 62.
39. Offord, *Nineteenth-Century Russia*, 10; Hobsbawm, *Age of Revolution*, 160, 162.
40. Fejtö (ed.), *Opening of an Era*, 60.

Chapter Nine: London, 1845
1. Mayhew, *London Labour and the London Poor*, 296.
2. MECW, Volume 5, 3; McLellan, *Karl Marx*, 131–132.
3. MECW, Volume 5, 5.
4. McLellan, *Karl Marx*, 130.
5. MECW, Volume 3, 576, 578.
6. G. D. H. Cole and Raymond Postgate, *The British Common People 1746–1946*, 302, 305; Stearns, *1848*, 22.
7. McLellan, *Karl Marx*, 133; "On Your Marx," *The Guardian*, London, Feb. 4, 2006, 31; MECW, Volume 38, 574.
8. Mayhew, *London Labour and the London Poor*, 12–13, 15; Engels, *Condition of the Working Class*, 80, 84.
9. Engels, *Condition of the Working Class*, 61, 72–73.
10. Ibid., 78–80.
11. Ibid., 153; Stephen Halliday, *The Great Filth*, 43.
12. In describing Marx and Engels's 1845 Manchester trip, Marx biographers generally mention the time the two men spent in the library studying economics but not the impact that viewing Manchester life firsthand would have had on Marx. This is partly because the only real description of the trip comes from Engels years later, when he discusses days spent in the Chetham Library. There are no letters that describe the men's travels with Mary Burns, but it is inconceivable that they would not have employed her as a guide through Manchester's working districts for Marx's first trip to the heart of the industrial world. He had already read the economists; he had never actually witnessed the full social blight resulting from the system they championed, and it defies logic to think that he would have passed up the opportunity to do so. His impatience with theory and his hardened attitude toward fellow socialists when he returned to Brussels after his trip indicate a profounder experience in Manchester than one derived merely from books read in a cozy library alcove.
13. Engels, *Condition of the Working Class*, 36–37, 40.
14. Ibid., 58–59.
15. Mayhew, *London Labour and the London Poor*, 57–58.
16. Robert Winder, *Bloody Foreigners*, 196–197.
17. Engels, *Condition of the Working Class*, 40.
18. Mayhew, *London Labour and the London Poor*, 111, 118.
19. Ibid., 167, 476.
20. McLellan, *Karl Marx*, 133; Hammen, *Red 48ers*, 119.
21. Marx and Engels, *Cologne Communist Trial*, 40–41.
22. Ibid., 41.
23. MECW, Volume 26, 315–317; Marx and Engels, *Cologne Communist Trial*, 42–43.
24. E. P. Thompson, *The Making of the English Working Class*, 17–19.
25. Cole and Postgate, *British Common People*, 196.
26. Ibid., 202–203, 214.
27. Ibid., 249, 258; Francis Sheppard, *London 1808–1870*, 320–321.
28. Cole and Postgate, *British Common People*, 261–262.
29. Thompson, *English Working Class*, 194, 822.

30. A. N. Wilson, *The Victorians*, 43; Kenneth Morgan, *The Birth of Industrial Britain*, 84; Cole and Postgate, *British Common People*, 280.
31. Cole and Postgate, *British Common People*, 286; Sheppard, *London 1808–1870*, 327.
32. McLellan, *Karl Marx*, 133.
33. Marx and Engels, *Cologne Communist Trial*, 44; McLellan, *Karl Marx*, 133; Hammen, *Red 48ers*, 120.

Chapter Ten: Brussels, 1846
1. MECW, Volume 5, 41.
2. MECW, Volume 38, 527–528.
3. Ibid.
4. Ibid., 528.
5. REM, 223; Longuet, *Karl Marx*, 121.
6. MECW, Volume 38, 528–529.
7. McLellan, *Karl Marx*, 133–134.
8. MECW, Volume 5, xvi, 24; McLellan, *Karl Marx*, 135; Nicolaievsky and Maenchen-Helfen, *Karl Marx*, 103; Draper, *Karl Marx's Theory of Revolution*, 189.
9. MECW, Volume 5, 31.
10. MECW, Volume 26, 173 and Volume 5, 44; Carver, *Engels, Short Introduction*, 72.
11. MECW, Volume 5, 50.
12. Ibid., 52.
13. Ibid., 52, 74–75.
14. Ibid., 59.
15. MECW, Volume 47, 31.
16. *The German Ideology* was not published in full until 1932 in Moscow. McLellan, *Karl Marx*, 140–141.
17. MECW, Volume 4, 678–679, 721(n); Longuet, *Karl Marx*, 122–123; Nicolaievsky and Maenchen-Helfen, *Karl Marx*, 101.
18. McLellan, *Karl Marx*, 143; MECW, Volume 38, 39.
19. MECW, Volume 38, 573(n).
20. Longuet, *Karl Marx*, 124.
21. MECW, Volume 38, 533.
22. McLellan, *Karl Marx*, 143–144; Nicolaievsky and Maenchen-Helfen, *Karl Marx*, 108–109.
23. Marx and Engels, *Cologne Communist Trial*, 46.
24. Nicolaievsky and Maenchen-Helfen, *Karl Marx*, 109.
25. Marx and Engels, *Cologne Communist Trial*, 46.
26. McLellan, *Karl Marx*, 130.
27. Annenkov, *Extraordinary Decade*, 168–170; KMIR, 12–14; Nicolaievsky and Maenchen-Helfen, *Karl Marx*, 117–118.
28. McLellan, *Karl Marx*, 159.
29. MECW, Volume 6, 35–41; McLellan, *Karl Marx*, 146.
30. Annenkov, *Extraordinary Decade*, 171.
31. Fejtö (ed.), *Opening of an Era*, 362–365, 367.
32. MECW, Volume 38, 39; Nicolaievsky and Maenchen-Helfen, *Karl Marx*, 116–117.
33. McLellan, *Karl Marx*, 147.
34. MECW, Volume 38, 530–531; Carver, *Friedrich Engels*, 150–151.
35. Blumenberg, *Illustrated*, 65; Hammen, *Red 48ers*, 140–141.
36. MECW, Volume 38, 576(n).
37. Ibid., 532.
38. Ibid., 36–37.
39. Ibid., 42–43.

40. MECW, Volume 24, 131; McLellan, *Karl Marx*, 142; REM, 223.
41. KMIR, 20; McLellan, *Karl Marx*, 142.
42. Mayer, *Friedrich Engels*, 76.
43. MECW, Volume 38, 82, 89.
44. Ibid., 92.
45. Longuet, *Karl Marx*, 125–126; McLellan, *Karl Marx*, 142; Peters, *Red Jenny*, 69.
46. MECW, Volume 38, 51.
47. Ibid., 105.
48. MECW, Volume 38, 95–97; Annenkov, *Extraordinary Decade*, 171–172.
49. MECW, Volume 38, 101–102.
50. Hammen, *Red 48ers*, 145.
51. MECW, Volume 6, 176.
52. McLellan, *Karl Marx*, 148.
53. MECW, Volume 38, 591(n); McLellan, *Karl Marx*, 152.
54. McLellan, *Karl Marx*, 157; Robert Payne, *Karl Marx*, 131.

Chapter Eleven: Brussels, 1847
1. MECW, Volume 38, 149.
2. Marx and Engels, *Cologne Communist Trial*, 39–41; McLellan, *Karl Marx*, 154, 157.
3. Marx and Engels, *Cologne Communist Trial*, 40, 47; McLellan, *Karl Marx*, 156–157; Nicolaievsky and Maenchen-Helfen, *Karl Marx*, 111, 122–124.
4. Stearns, *1848*, 33.
5. MECW, Volume 10, 495.
6. Whitridge, *Men in Crisis*, 26; Stearns, *1848*, 34; Hamerow, *Restoration, Revolution, Reaction*, 76–77.
7. Hobsbawm, *Age of Capital*, 43–44.
8. Edgar Marx's birth date varies from Marx biography to biography. The Friedrich-Ebert-Stiftung Study Center in Trier has concluded that he was born on Feb. 3, 1847. The name on his birth certificate is Charles Louis Henri Edgar Marx, but he was known as Edgar or Musch. *Genealogy Marx*, Friedrich-Ebert-Stiftung Museum/Studienzentrum, Trier; Omura, Fomičev, Hecker, and Kubo, *Familie Marx privat*, 447.
9. Padover, *Karl Marx*, 128; MECW, Volume 38, 121.
10. MECW, Volume 38, 154.
11. Ibid., 158.
12. Ibid., 576(n).
13. Ibid., 108.
14. Ibid., 55, 90.
15. Ibid., 153.
16. Ibid., 154.
17. Ibid., 115, 587(n).
18. Ibid., 117.
19. Ibid., 120, 588(n).
20. Ibid., 117.
21. MECW, Volume 6, 585 and Volume 38, 587–588(n); Carr, *Michael Bakunin*, 139; McLellan, *Karl Marx*, 156–157.
22. MECW, Volume 6, 96–103, 341–357.
23. Ibid., 600.
24. Boris Nicolaievsky, "Toward a History of the Communist League, 1847–1852," 241.
25. Robert Payne, *Unknown Marx*, 18; Padover, *Karl Marx*, 115; Robert Payne, *Karl Marx*, 131; McLellan, *Karl Marx*, 142–143.
26. Nicolaievsky and Maenchen-Helfen, *Karl Marx*, 133.
27. MECW, Volume 38, 588(n).

28. Nicolaievsky and Maenchen-Helfen, *Karl Marx,* 128–129; Hammen, *Red 48ers,* 163; Longuet, *Karl Marx,* 127–128. (Today the Café au Cygne is known as the Maison du Cygne.)

29. Nicolaievsky and Maenchen-Helfen, *Karl Marx,* 131–132; MECW, Volume 38, 122–130.

30. Nicolaievsky and Maenchen-Helfen, *Karl Marx,* 129.

31. MECW, Volume 38, 141.

32. Longuet, *Karl Marx,* 128; Hammen, *Red 48ers,* 190.

33. MECW, Volume 38, 122, 143.

34. McLellan, *Karl Marx,* 163; Carr, *Michael Bakunin,* 123, 131.

35. Carr, *Michael Bakunin,* 146.

36. Kenafick, *Bakunin and Marx,* 41–42.

37. Carr, *Michael Bakunin,* 146.

38. MECW, Volume 38, 150–151.

39. McLellan, *Karl Marx,* 160–161.

40. MECW, Volume 6, 388–389.

41. REM, 153.

42. Marx was in fact twenty-nine years old during the league meeting that fall. KMIR, 14.

43. MECW, Volume 38, 592; McLellan, *Karl Marx,* 154–155; Nicolaievsky and Maenchen-Helfen, *Karl Marx,* 110–111.

44. MECW, Volume 6, 633–638.

45. Ibid., 585.

46. Ibid., 633.

47. MECW, Volume 38, 149.

Chapter Twelve: Brussels, 1848

1. Tocqueville, *Recollections,* 11–12.

2. Giroud, *Femme du diable,* 92–93; Peters, *Red Jenny,* 73.

3. Jenny Marx to Lina Schöler, Dec. 17, 1847, Moscow.

4. Jenny Marx to Lina Schöler, mid-Jan. 1848, Moscow.

5. Giroud, *Femme du diable,* 92–93.

6. MECW, Volume 6, 639.

7. Giroud, *Femme du diable,* 92–93.

8. Jenny Marx to Lina Schöler, mid-Jan. 1848, Moscow.

9. McLellan, *Karl Marx,* 163.

10. Peters, *Red Jenny,* 65.

11. MECW, Volume 38, 153; Carver, *Friedrich Engels,* 152.

12. McLellan, *Karl Marx,* 162; MECW, Volume 26, 523–524 and Volume 6, 695–696(n).

13. Roberts, *History of Europe,* 336.

14. MECW, Volume 6, 463, 465 and Volume 26, 523–524.

15. MECW, Volume 26, 523.

16. MECW, Volume 38, 152–154.

17. Nicolaievsky and Maenchen-Helfen, *Karl Marx,* 136; Raddatz, *Karl Marx,* 80.

18. MECW, Volume 6, 698.

19. Ibid., 698(n); Padover, *Karl Marx,* 129.

20. MECW, Volume 39, 60; Padover, *Karl Marx,* 129.

21. MECW, Volume 6, 481.

22. Ibid., 487–488.

23. Ibid., 489.

24. Ibid., 496.

25. Ibid., 500.

26. Ibid., 502.

27. Ibid., 506.
28. Ibid., 519.

Chapter Thirteen: Paris, 1848

1. Hamerow, *Restoration, Revolution, Reaction,* 87.
2. MECW, Volume 6, 559; Nicolaievsky and Maenchen-Helfen, *Karl Marx,* 141–142.
3. Wilson, *Victorians,* 127.
4. Hobsbawm, *Age of Capital,* 14.
5. Fejtö (ed.), *Opening of an Era,* 60–63, 65–66; Whitridge, *Men in Crisis,* 246–247.
6. Fejtö (ed.), *Opening of an Era,* 66.
7. Whitridge, *Men in Crisis,* 115–116; Stearns, *1848,* 123; Evans and von Strandmann (eds.), *Revolutions in Europe,* 55.
8. Stearns, *1848,* 53; Evans and von Strandmann (eds.), *Revolutions in Europe,* 56.
9. Fejtö (ed.), *Opening of an Era,* 116–118; Whitridge, *Men in Crisis,* 140–141, 146–147; Stearns, *1848,* 123, 125; Evans and von Strandmann (eds.), *Revolutions in Europe,* 57, 60.
10. Stearns, *1848,* 57, 124; Whitridge, *Men in Crisis,* 147.
11. Nicolaievsky and Maenchen-Helfen, *Karl Marx,* 141.
12. John J. Baughman, "The French Banquet Campaign of 1847–48," 1; MECW, Volume 6, 375; Stearns, *1848,* 6; Evans and von Strandmann (eds.), *Revolutions in Europe,* 32.
13. Pawel, *Poet Dying,* 17.
14. Stearns, *1848,* 71; Evans and von Strandmann (eds.), *Revolutions in Europe,* 32.
15. Baughman, "The French Banquet Campaign of 1847–48," 2–3, 6–9; MECW, Volume 6, 393.
16. MECW, Volume 6, 375.
17. Baughman, "The French Banquet Campaign of 1847–48," 32; Whitridge, *Men in Crisis,* 29.
18. Baughman, "The French Banquet Campaign of 1847–48," 14; Stearns, *1848,* 72.
19. Stearns, *1848,* 73; Whitridge, *Men in Crisis,* 27, 31, 32.
20. Stearns, *1848,* 73.
21. Ibid., 73–74; Hamerow, *Restoration, Revolution, Reaction,* 97; Whitridge, *Men in Crisis,* 36.
22. Tocqueville, *Recollections,* 11–12.
23. Evans and von Strandmann (eds.), *Revolutions in Europe,* 164.
24. A. J. P. Taylor, *The Struggle for Mastery of Europe, 1848–1918,* 6; Andrew Jackson Donelson, "The American Minister in Berlin on the Revolution of March, 1848," 357; Hamerow, *Restoration, Revolution, Reaction,* 98.
25. Longuet, *Karl Marx,* 131; Somerhausen, *L'Humanisme,* 236.
26. Hammen, *Red 48ers,* 193.
27. MECW, Volume 38, 82.
28. Hammen, *Red 48ers,* 193. (Eleanor Marx Aveling wrote Karl Kautsky on Mar. 15, 1898 [Moscow], that she had long been aware of an "unpleasant mystery" involving Engels's expulsion from Paris. The only thing she knew for certain was that there was a woman involved, and "from some words I heard a rather disreputable one at that.")
29. MECW, Volume 6, 643.
30. Nicolaievsky and Maenchen-Helfen, *Karl Marx,* 138–139.
31. Fejtö (ed.), *Opening of an Era,* 163.
32. Nicolaievsky and Maenchen-Helfen, *Karl Marx,* 143.
33. MECW, Volume 6, 567; Nicolaievsky and Maenchen-Helfen, *Karl Marx,* 143.
34. Hammen, *Red 48ers,* 196.
35. MECW, Volume 6, 559 and Volume 24, 136–137; Hammen, *Red 48ers,* 196–197.
36. Nicolaievsky and Maenchen-Helfen, *Karl Marx,* 143; MECW, Volume 24, 137.
37. MECW, Volume 6, 568, 581.
38. Ibid., 560 and Volume 24, 137.

39. MECW, Volume 6, 560.
40. KMIR, 20.
41. Nicolaievsky and Maenchen-Helfen, *Karl Marx,* 143; McLellan, *Karl Marx,* 177; Somerhausen, *L'Humanisme,* 217.
42. KMIR, 20.
43. Somerhausen, *L'Humanisme,* 237, 245.
44. Peters, *Red Jenny,* 74.
45. McLellan, *Karl Marx,* 177–178; Somerhausen, *L'Humanisme,* 245.
46. MECW, Volume 6, 651–652.
47. Ibid., 649.
48. Ibid., 650.
49. Hammen, *Red 48ers,* 198.
50. Marx and Engels, *Cologne Communist Trial,* 49; Nicolaievsky and Maenchen-Helfen, *Karl Marx,* 144.
51. Somerhausen, *L'Humanisme,* 239.
52. MECW, Volume 6, 561–562, 565; Somerhausen, *L'Humanisme,* 239–240; Nicolaievsky and Maenchen-Helfen, *Karl Marx,* 144.
53. Somerhausen, *L'Humanisme,* 240; KMIR, 20–21; MECW, Volume 6, 561, 565.
54. KMIR, 21; Somerhausen, *L'Humanisme,* 240–241.
55. KMIR, 21; Somerhausen, *L'Humanisme,* 241.
56. KMIR, 21.
57. MECW, Volume 6, 565; Somerhausen, *L'Humanisme,* 242.
58. KMIR, 21.
59. MECW, Volume 6, 565.
60. Ibid., 562.
61. Somerhausen, *L'Humanisme,* 242.
62. KMIR, 21.
63. Peters, *Red Jenny,* 76.
64. Nicolaievsky and Maenchen-Helfen, *Karl Marx,* 146.
65. KMIR, 21.

Chapter Fourteen: Paris, Spring 1848

1. MECW, Volume 4, 82.
2. KMIR, 21.
3. Peter Amann, "The Changing Outlines of 1848," 941; Nicolaievsky and Maenchen-Helfen, *Karl Marx,* 146; Padover, *Karl Marx,* 133.
4. Nicolaievsky and Maenchen-Helfen, *Karl Marx,* 147; Carr, *Michael Bakunin,* 149.
5. MECW, Volume 38, 169.
6. Raddatz, *Karl Marx,* 86.
7. Stearns, *1848,* 77.
8. MECW, Volume 7, 513.
9. Longuet, *Karl Marx,* 136.
10. Ibid., 135; McLellan, *Karl Marx,* 179.
11. Carr, *Michael Bakunin,* 149.
12. Hobsbawm, *Age of Capital,* 26.
13. Amann, "The Changing Outlines of 1848," 942.
14. Stearns, *1848,* 80.
15. Ibid., 179–180.
16. Thomas, *Women Incendiaries,* 21, 23.
17. Stearns, *1848,* 83.
18. Giroud, *Femme du diable,* 98.
19. MECW, Volume 21, 61.
20. Fejtö (ed.), *Opening of an Era,* 7; Hamerow, *Restoration, Revolution, Reaction,* 76–79, 84.

21. Sperber (ed.), *Germany, 1800–1870,* 54; MECW, Volume 11, 19–20.
22. Sperber (ed.), *Germany, 1800–1870,* 54, 57.
23. Schurz, *Reminiscences,* 108–109.
24. Stearns, *1848,* 64; Evans and von Strandmann (eds.), *Revolutions in Europe,* 29.
25. Priscilla Robertson, "Students on the Barricades: Germany and Austria, 1848," 375–376; Stearns, *1848,* 95–96.
26. Hamerow, *Restoration, Revolution, Reaction,* 99; Stearns, *1848,* 96; Evans and von Strandmann (eds.), *Revolutions in Europe,* 181.
27. Evans and von Strandmann (eds.), *Revolutions in Europe,* 186; Robertson, "Students on the Barricades," 376; Fejtö (eds.), *Opening of an Era,* 255.
28. Evans and von Strandmann (eds.), *Revolutions in Europe,* 62–63; Stearns, *1848,* 129–130.
29. Evans and von Strandmann (eds.), *Revolutions in Europe,* 106.
30. Schurz, *Reminiscences,* 119; Donelson, "The American Minister in Berlin," 358; Stearns, *1848,* 146; Whitridge, *Men in Crisis,* 218.
31. Schurz, *Reminiscences,* 119; Sperber (ed.), *Germany, 1800–1870,* 59.
32. Schurz, *Reminiscences,* 119.
33. Whitridge, *Men in Crisis,* 218.
34. Donelson, "The American Minister in Berlin," 358; Stearns, *1848,* 147.
35. Donelson, "The American Minister in Berlin," 360–361.
36. Ibid., 360.
37. Ibid., 360–361.
38. Ibid.
39. Schurz, *Reminiscences,* 120–121; Donelson, "The American Minister in Berlin," 363.
40. Schurz, *Reminiscences,* 121.
41. Donelson, "The American Minister in Berlin," 362.
42. Ibid., 370–371.
43. Offord, *Nineteenth-Century Russia,* 39–40.
44. Carr, *Michael Bakunin,* 150.
45. Liebknecht, *Karl Marx,* 63.
46. Marx and Engels, *Cologne Communist Trial,* 50; Amann, "Changing Outlines of 1848," 940.
47. Carr, *Michael Bakunin,* 151–152.
48. REM, 19; Nicolaievsky and Maenchen-Helfen, *Karl Marx,* 150–151; MECW, Volume 26, 324.
49. MECW, Volume 6, 657.
50. Karl Marx and Friedrich Engels, *Letters to Americans, 1848–1895,* 15.
51. Stearns, *1848,* 142; McLellan, *Karl Marx,* 180; Nicolaievsky and Maenchen-Helfen, *Karl Marx,* 152–153.
52. MECW, Volume 26, 324; Nicolaievsky and Maenchen-Helfen, *Karl Marx,* 152, 155; Hammen, *Red 48ers,* 214.
53. The Rhineland was the natural place for Marx to go. It still had the freest press laws and operated under Napoleonic law, which meant trial by jury if that became necessary. It was also home to businessmen who had financed him before and indicated they would do so again. And it had been the site of the first communist uprising in Germany. McLellan, *Karl Marx,* 181.
54. MECW, Volume 7, 3–7.
55. McLellan, *Karl Marx,* 181.
56. MECW, Volume 6, 558.

Chapter Fifteen: Cologne, 1848

1. Seigel, *Marx's Fate,* 173.
2. Nicolaievsky and Maenchen-Helfen, *Karl Marx,* 165; Sperber (ed.), *Germany, 1800–1870,* 60.
3. McLellan, *Karl Marx,* 182; Stearns, *1848,* 145; Donelson, "The American Minister in Berlin," 365.

4. Marx and Gottschalk's final falling-out was over funding the remnants of Herwegh's Legion, which Gottschalk favored but Marx did not. McLellan, *Karl Marx,* 182–183; Nicolaievsky and Maenchen-Helfen, *Karl Marx,* 164, 166–167; Hammen, *Red 48ers,* 222.

5. MECW, Volume 26, 122.

6. In his citizenship appeal Marx first wrote that he intended to edit a newspaper, but a final draft of his application eliminated that reference and stated simply, "After the events which took place recently, I returned to my country and now I intend to settle with my family in Cologne." A police report six days later said that Marx told authorities he was writing a book on economics and planned to live on the proceeds of his writings and the personal property of his wife. The police inspector called Marx "politically unreliable" but did not immediately act on his application. MECW, Volume 7, 537–538.

7. Peters, *Red Jenny,* 82-83; McLellan, *Karl Marx,* 181.

8. Hammen, *Red 48ers,* 222.

9. Luise Dornemann, *Jenny Marx: Der Lebensweg einer Sozialistin,* 103.

10. MECW, Volume 26, 127.

11. MECW, Volume 7, 69–70.

12. MECW, Volume 26, 127.

13. MECW, Volume 7, 15.

14. Whitridge, *Men in Crisis,* 47, 50; Stearns, *1848,* 76.

15. Whitridge, *Men in Crisis,* 50; Evans and von Strandmann (eds.), *Revolutions in Europe,* 35.

16. Evans and von Strandmann (eds.), *Revolutions in Europe,* 35; Whitridge, *Men in Crisis,* 51.

17. Whitridge, *Men in Crisis,* 52–53, 71; Evans and von Strandmann (eds.), *Revolutions in Europe,* 36.

18. Tocqueville, *Recollections,* 95, 102; Amann, "Changing Outlines of 1848," 946; Stearns, *1848,* 79; Whitridge, *Men in Crisis,* 66–67.

19. Whitridge, *Men in Crisis,* 66–67.

20. Evans and von Strandmann (eds.), *Revolutions in Europe,* 39; Stearns, *1848,* 85.

21. Tocqueville, *Recollections,* 107.

22. Ibid., 130–132; Taylor, *Struggle for Mastery in Europe,* 11; Amann, "A Journée in the Making: May 15, 1848," 44, 63–64; Stearns, *1848,* 86.

23. Whitridge, *Men in Crisis,* 66–67; Tocqueville, *Recollections,* 130.

24. Tocqueville, *Recollections,* 133–134.

25. Schurz, *Reminiscences,* 129.

26. Hamerow, *Restoration, Revolution, Reaction,* 102–104, 107; Stearns, *1848,* 41.

27. Hobsbawm, *Age of Capital,* 33.

28. Fejtö (ed.), *Opening of an Era,* 231.

29. Hamerow, *Restoration, Revolution, Reaction,* 114.

30. Ibid., 120–122; Breuilly, *Austria, Prussia and Germany,* 42–43.

31. Hamerow, *Restoration, Revolution, Reaction,* 123–124.

32. MECW, Volume 7, 72.

33. MECW, Volume 11, 41–42; Breuilly, *Austria, Prussia and Germany,* 42–43.

34. Hammen, *Red 48ers,* 223–224.

35. Nicolaievsky and Maenchen-Helfen, *Karl Marx,* 168.

36. MECW, Volume 26, 123.

37. Blumenberg, *Illustrated,* 86.

38. Schurz, *Reminiscences,* 139–140; KMIR, 15.

39. MECW, Volume 7, 45 and Volume 26, 126.

Chapter Sixteen: Paris, June 1848

1. Tocqueville, *Recollections,* 156.

2. Ibid., 146.

3. Stearns, *1848,* 88.

4. Fejtö (ed.), *Opening of an Era*, 90.
5. Whitridge, *Men in Crisis*, 99.
6. MECW, Volume 7, 124–127; Stearns, *1848*, 89; Whitridge, *Men in Crisis*, 99.
7. MECW, Volume 7, 128; Whitridge, *Men in Crisis*, 98.
8. Tocqueville, *Recollections*, 154, 175; MECW, Volume 7, 138.
9. Tocqueville, *Recollections*, 162; Whitridge, *Men in Crisis*, 100.
10. Tocqueville, *Recollections*, 150–151.
11. Stearns, *1848*, 92; Evans and von Strandmann (eds.), *Revolutions in Europe*, 41; Whitridge, *Men in Crisis*, 101–102.
12. Stearns, *1848*, 93; Evans and von Strandmann (eds.), *Revolutions in Europe*, 43; Pawel, *Poet Dying*, 53; Whitridge, *Men in Crisis*, 103.
13. Evans and von Strandmann (eds.), *Revolutions in Europe*, 43; Whitridge, *Men in Crisis*, 103.
14. MECW, Volume 7, 128.
15. Ibid., 130.
16. Ibid., 144.
17. Ibid., 146–147.
18. Ibid., 147 and Volume 10, 68.
19. MECW, Volume 7, 143.
20. Ibid., 478 and Volume 26, 126.
21. MECW, Volume 26, 126.
22. McLellan, *Karl Marx*, 183; Seigel, *Marx's Fate*, 199; REM, 156.
23. MECW, Volume 7, 74, 170, 194 and Volume 11, 36.
24. MECW, Volume 7, 176–179.
25. Ibid., 186.
26. Ibid., 554.
27. Ibid., 208.
28. Ibid., 383–384, 407–408, 581.
29. Ibid., 448, 452 and Volume 38, 182.
30. MECW, Volume 7, 653(n); Hammen, *Red 48ers*, 296; Nicolaievsky and Maenchen-Helfen, *Karl Marx*, 173.
31. Hammen, *Red 48ers*, 296.
32. Brophy, *Popular Culture and the Public Sphere*, 216–217, 224.
33. MECW, Volume 7, 582–583.
34. Hammen, *Red 48ers*, 297.
35. MECW, Volume 7, 574; Hammen, *Red 48ers*, 298.
36. Hammen, *Red 48ers*, 299–300.
37. MECW, Volume 7, 584.
38. Ibid., 442–443.
39. Hammen, *Red 48ers*, 287–289.
40. Ibid., 304.
41. Ibid., 304; Hamerow, *Restoration, Revolution, Reaction*, 181.
42. MECW, Volume 7, 444, 589.
43. Ibid., 452.
44. Ibid., 452–453.
45. Hammen, *Red 48ers*, 307.
46. MECW, Volume 7, 463; Hammen, *Red 48ers*, 307–309; Nicolaievsky and Maenchen-Helfen, *Karl Marx*, 175.
47. MECW, Volume 7, 455, 642(n); Hammen, *Red 48ers*, 310; Nicolaievsky and Maenchen-Helfen, *Karl Marx*, 175.
48. MECW, Volume 7, 455–456, 590.
49. Ibid., 593.
50. MECW, Volume 24, 140.
51. MECW, Volume 38, 540–541.

52. MECW, Volume 7, 459–460, 594.
53. Ibid., 513–514.
54. Ibid., 511.
55. Ibid., 526, 528–539.
56. Ibid., 515.
57. Ibid., 456.
58. Hammen, *Red 48ers,* 316.
59. Brophy, *Popular Culture and the Public Sphere,* 59.
60. MECW, Volume 38, 178.
61. Dornemann, *Jenny Marx,* 103–139.
62. KMIR, 16.
63. Biographers of Marx and Jenny have stressed the antagonisms between them and Ferdinand von Westphalen, which were real and many, both political and personal. But throughout her life, despite the difficulties, Jenny did not abandon her older brother or his wife, Louise: she wrote them regularly, exchanged family news, and frequently signed off with a "kiss from your loving sister." Her correspondence was full of the extraordinarily polite language used by her class when greeting fellow aristocrats, and it is therefore sometimes difficult to determine whether her words were more than social artifice. But I believe in many cases they were: these letters were expressions of affection for the life and family she had abandoned in marrying Marx—not that she would have exchanged him for them, but they may have given her a respite, however brief, from the struggle.
64. Ferdinand von Westphalen to Louise von Westphalen, June 10, 1847, Hamburg.
65. Ferdinand von Westphalen to Louise von Westphalen, Oct. 23, 1848, Hamburg.

Chapter Seventeen: Cologne, 1849

1. MECW, Volume 10, 70.
2. Stearns, *1848,* 119–121; Hammen, *Red 48ers,* 327–328, 330; MECW, Volume 11, 67; McLellan, *Karl Marx,* 193.
3. Stearns, *1848,* 121; Hammen, *Red 48ers,* 329, 331; Breuilly, *Austria, Prussia and Germany,* 49.
4. MECW, Volume 9, 453.
5. The Prussian Assembly's decision to take up the no-tax mantra so soon after Marx's article appeared may have been a coincidence, though it is possible that assemblymen read his piece and were inspired by his argument. MECW, Volume 7, 477.
6. MECW, Volume 11, 67; Hammen, *Red 48ers,* 340.
7. MECW, Volume 8, 36; Hammen, *Red 48ers,* 342, 345.
8. MECW, Volume 8, 36, 41.
9. Ibid., 46.
10. Hammen, *Red 48ers,* 347.
11. Marx was summoned to appear at the magistrate's offices in a case brought by former public prosecutor, now chief prosecutor, Hecker. At issue was a letter printed in the *Neue Rheinische Zeitung* attributed to a "Hecker," identified as a republican who had fled to New York. The piece was picked up in various Prussian newspapers and the prosecutor accused Marx of fabricating the letter and maliciously signing it "Hecker" to make it seem as if the prosecutor had republican leanings. When Marx appeared in court on November 14 for a hearing in the case, he firmly believed he would be arrested. A crowd of several hundred gathered to support him, and perhaps because of the threat of civil disorder, he was not jailed. MECW, Volume 7, 485–487; Volume 8, 495–496, 501, 503; Volume 38, 180; McLellan, *Karl Marx,* 195.
12. MECW, Volume 8, 504.
13. Ibid., 82.
14. MECW, Volume 38, 179.

15. MECW, Volume 8, 135, 588(n).
16. MECW, Volume 38, 190.
17. MECW, Volume 8, 312.
18. Ibid., 314.
19. Ibid., 316–317.
20. Ibid., 320, 322, 517–518.
21. Ibid., 323, 335, 338.
22. Ibid., 338–339.
23. Ibid., 520–521; McLellan, *Karl Marx,* 199; Nicolaievsky and Maenchen-Helfen, *Karl Marx,* 192; Stearns, *1848,* 183.
24. MECW, Volume 8, 527–528.
25. MECW, Volume 9, 487, 492–493, 496–497.
26. Ferdinand von Westphalen to Louise von Westphalen, Feb. 10, 1849, Hamburg.
27. Nicolaievsky and Maenchen-Helfen, *Karl Marx,* 191.
28. MECW, Volume 38, 192–193 and Volume 47, 613(n); McLellan, *Karl Marx,* 201–202; Nicolaievsky and Maenchen-Helfen, *Karl Marx,* 191.
29. MECW, Volume 38, 193.
30. MECW, Volume 11, 80, 83–85.
31. McLellan, *Karl Marx,* 203; Nicolaievsky and Maenchen-Helfen, *Karl Marx,* 195.
32. MECW, Volume 38, 196.
33. McLellan, *Karl Marx,* 202; Nicolaievsky and Maenchen-Helfen, *Karl Marx,* 181, 193–194.
34. Nicolaievsky and Maenchen-Helfen, *Karl Marx,* 194.
35. McLellan, *Karl Marx,* 203.
36. Hammen, *Red 48ers,* 386.
37. MECW, Volume 9, 451, 509; McLellan, *Karl Marx,* 203.
38. Carr, *Michael Bakunin,* 186, 190, 193; McLellan, *Karl Marx,* 203; Nicolaievsky and Maenchen-Helfen, *Karl Marx,* 195; Sperber (ed.), *Germany, 1800–1870,* 65.
39. Carr, *Michael Bakunin,* 166, 194.
40. MECW, Volume 9, 447; Hammen, *Red 48ers,* 391–392.
41. Mayer, *Friedrich Engels,* 13; Hammen, *Red 48ers,* 393. (A recent biography of Engels by Tristram Hunt disputes the story of Engels's encounter with his father, saying that it appeared too "pathos ridden" to be true. It was based on the account of one eyewitness and was held in the Wuppertal archives. Tristram Hunt, *The Frock-Coated Communist,* 175.)
42. MECW, Volume 9, 449, 508; Stearns, *1848,* 191; Carver, *Friedrich Engels,* 204; Hammen, *Red 48ers,* 392–393.
43. In an account of the events written many years later, Engels said that to his dismay many of the "gin-happy lumpenproletarians" sold their rifles that same evening to the bourgeoisie. MECW, Volume 9, 449 and Volume 10, 168, 602–603; Carver, *Friedrich Engels,* 204.
44. MECW, Volume 9, 514, 524 and Volume 10, 602–604.
45. MECW, Volume 9, 417.
46. MECW, Volume 11, 68.
47. Nicolaievsky and Maenchen-Helfen, *Karl Marx,* 197.
48. McLellan, *Karl Marx,* 203.
49. MECW, Volume 9, 418.
50. Ibid., 453–454, 467.
51. McLellan, *Karl Marx,* 204; Nicolaievsky and Maenchen-Helfen, *Karl Marx,* 197.
52. MECW, Volume 26, 128.
53. Nicolaievsky and Maenchen-Helfen, *Karl Marx,* 197.
54. Giroud, *Femme du diable,* 106.
55. MECW, Volume 9, 509; McLellan, *Karl Marx,* 204.

56. MECW, Volume, 24, 164.
57. MECW, Volume 9, 515; McLellan, *Karl Marx,* 204.
58. KMIR, 21.
59. McLellan, *Karl Marx,* 205.
60. KMIR, 21; McLellan, *Karl Marx,* 205; Carver, *Friedrich Engels,* 205.
61. MECW, Volume 11, 86.

Chapter Eighteen: Paris, 1849
1. MECW, Volume 11, 103.
2. Whitridge, *Men in Crisis,* 92.
3. W. H. C. Smith, *Second Empire and Commune,* 2.
4. Whitridge, *Men in Crisis,* 88.
5. W. H. C. Smith, *Second Empire,* 2, 7; Whitridge, *Men in Crisis,* 90.
6. Whitridge, *Men in Crisis,* 93; Stearns, *1848,* 216.
7. Whitridge, *Men in Crisis,* 91, 94.
8. Ibid., 84, 104, 106.
9. Ibid., 108.
10. MECW, Volume 9, 525 and Volume 38, 200; McLellan, *Karl Marx,* 205.
11. MECW, Volume 7, 150 and Volume 38, 209.
12. MECW, Volume 38, 199.
13. Stearns, *1848,* 217.
14. Whitridge, *Men in Crisis,* 179, 181–182.
15. Taylor, *Struggle for Mastery of Europe,* 30.
16. Stearns, *1848,* 217.
17. MECW, Volume 9, 478.
18. Tocqueville, *Recollections,* 245–246, 272–274.
19. Nicolaievsky and Maenchen-Helfen, *Karl Marx,* 203.
20. MECW, Volume 38, 546.
21. Ibid., 546–548; Pawel, *Poet Dying,* 46.
22. MECW, Volume 38, 202.
23. Ibid., 201.
24. Ibid., 200, 207.
25. KMIR, 22.
26. MECW, Volume 9, 480–481.
27. MECW, Volume 38, 211.
28. Ibid., 210–211, 605(n) and Volume 9, 526.
29. MECW, Volume 38, 208.
30. Ibid., 209–210.
31. Berlin, *Karl Marx,* 119.
32. MECW, Volume 38, 205.
33. Ibid., 209.
34. Ibid., 207–208.
35. McLellan, *Karl Marx,* 206.
36. MECW, Volume 38, 204–205.
37. Ibid., 212 and Volume 9, 527.
38. MECW, Volume 38, 212–213, 606.
39. Ibid., 212.
40. Ibid., 213.
41. Ibid., 606(n).
42. Ibid., 216.
43. Pawel, *Poet Dying,* 6–7, 71–72.
44. MECW, Volume 38, 216.
45. REM, 225.

Part Three: Exile in Victoria's England

Chapter Nineteen: London, 1849

1. Percy Bysshe Shelley, "Peter Bell the Third," *The Daemon of the World,* 39.
2. KMIR, 22; MECW, Volume 38, 607; Padover, *Karl Marx,* 151; Gustav Mayer, "Letters of Karl Marx to Karl Blind," 154–155.
3. Bernard Porter, *The Refugee Question in Mid-Victorian Politics,* 2–3.
4. Ibid., 22.
5. Daniel Pool, *What Jane Austen Ate and Charles Dickens Knew,* 30.
6. Ibid., 30; Halliday, *Great Filth,* 79.
7. Halliday, *Great Filth,* 133.
8. Ibid., 135, 204; Gilda O'Neill, *The Good Old Days,* 10.
9. Halliday, *Great Filth,* 77.
10. Porter, *Refugee Question,* 20, 25; Jenny Marx to Louise von Westphalen, Jan. 29, 1858, Moscow.
11. William C. Preston, *The Bitter Cry of Outcast London,* 8; Donald J. Olsen, *The Growth of Victorian London,* 12.
12. Mayhew, *London Labour and the London Poor,* 68–69, 104.
13. MECW, Volume 10, 280–282.
14. Ibid., 605–606.
15. MECW, Volume 38, 216.
16. Liebknecht, *Karl Marx,* 65, 68–69.
17. KMIR, 44–46; Liebknecht, *Karl Marx,* 69; McLellan, *Karl Marx,* 214.
18. Porter, *Refugee Question,* 28; Berlin, *Karl Marx,* 137.
19. Porter, *Refugee Question,* 25–26.
20. Liebknecht, *Karl Marx,* 82.
21. Berlin, *Karl Marx,* 13.
22. MECW, Volume 10, 596.
23. Ibid., 599 and Volume 38, 231; McLellan, *Karl Marx,* 214.
24. MECW, Volume 10, 623; McLellan, *Karl Marx,* 214.
25. MECW, Volume 38, 213; Hammen, *Red 48ers,* 403.
26. REM, 141.
27. MECW, Volume 38, 202–203.
28. REM, 142.
29. Ibid., 143–144; Carver, *Friedrich Engels,* 206; Hammen, *Red 48ers,* 403.
30. MECW, Volume 38, 217, 607(n); Tocqueville, *Recollections,* 272–273.
31. Winder, *Bloody Foreigners,* 179–181; KMIR, 22; Olsen, *The Growth of Victorian London,* 150.
32. KMIR, 22; Robert Payne, *Karl Marx,* 227–228; Wilson, *Victorians,* 141.
33. KMIR, 22.
34. MECW, Volume 38, 557–558.
35. Ibid., 549–550.
36. Ibid., 607(n).
37. MECW, Volume 10, 606.
38. *New York Daily Tribune,* December 1, 1852.
39. MECW, Volume 38, 219.
40. MECW, Volume 38, 224–225, 609(n).
41. Evans and von Strandmann (eds.), *Revolutions in Europe,* 166.
42. MECW, Volume 38, 226–227.
43. Ibid., 608(n).
44. MECW, Volume 10, 69, 127, 135.
45. Mehring, *Karl Marx,* 194.
46. MECW, Volume 38, 605(n); McLellan, *Karl Marx,* 219.

47. MECW, Volume 38, 605(n).
48. Ibid., 234.
49. Ibid., 555.
50. Ibid., 556–558.
51. KMIR, 23.
52. MECW, Volume 10, 281–285.
53. Ibid., 375.
54. MECW, Volume 38, 610(n).
55. MECW, Volume 10, 370, 681(n)
56. Robert Payne, *Unknown Marx,* 103, 107, 109.
57. MECW, Volume 38, 237.
58. MECW, Volume 10, 378–386.
59. Ibid., 381.
60. Porter, *Refugee Question,* 76, 81.
61. Berlin, *Karl Marx,* 134.
62. Liebknecht, *Karl Marx,* 81.
63. Berlin, *Karl Marx,* 143.
64. KMIR, 17–18.
65. MECW, Volume 38, 607(n); McLellan, *Karl Marx,* 213.
66. MECW, Volume 1, 674.
67. MECW, Volume 38, 557–558.

Chapter Twenty: Zaltbommel, Holland, August 1850

1. Jenny Marx to Karl Marx, Aug. 1850, Moscow.
2. Marjorie Caygill, *The British Museum Reading Room,* 29; Asa Briggs and John Callow, *Marx in London,* 50.
3. Caygill, 5–6.
4. MECW, Volume 38, 239–240.
5. Mayer, *Friedrich Engels,* 136; Raddatz, *Karl Marx,* 139.
6. Mayer, *Friedrich Engels,* 137.
7. Carver, *Friedrich Engels,* 139.
8. Mayer, *Friedrich Engels,* 138; Carver, *Friedrich Engels,* 139.
9. KMIR, xvii.
10. MECW, Volume 38, 274.
11. Jenny Marx to Karl Marx, Aug. 1850, Moscow; KMIR, 24.
12. KMIR, 59–60.
13. Ibid., 24.
14. McLellan, *Karl Marx,* 228.
15. Nicolaievsky and Maenchen-Helfen, *Karl Marx,* 156, 205.
16. KMIR, 22.
17. McLellan, *Karl Marx,* 228.
18. Marx and Engels, *Cologne Communist Trial,* 23.
19. Throughout his life and after his death, well into the twentieth century, Marx was accused of living a bourgeois existence while pretending to be the advocate of the workingman. The charge arose, as we see, early in his London life but more frequently after 1864, when journalists discovered that he lived in a large home seemingly surrounded by comfort. They did not know, however, that the facade of wealth was an illusion. The criticism was revived by Cold War–era biographers trying to discredit Marx by portraying him as a hypocrite. In fact, Marx's life was "bourgeois" in that he was an educated, middle-class Prussian and family man. Any material comfort on display came courtesy of Engels. Nicolaievsky and Maenchen-Helfen, *Karl Marx,* 217; McLellan, *Karl Marx,* 228.
20. MECW, Volume 10, 614–615.

21. REM, 292.
22. Liebknecht, *Karl Marx*, 106–107.
23. REM, 112; Liebknecht, *Karl Marx*, 104–105.
24. Liebknecht, *Karl Marx*, 104.
25. Ibid., 106–107.
26. McLellan, *Karl Marx*, 229.
27. Liebknecht, *Karl Marx*, 106–107; MECW, Volume 38, 618.
28. McLellan, *Karl Marx*, 229.
29. Liebknecht, *Karl Marx*, 106–107.
30. MECW, Volume 10, 625–626.
31. Ibid., 626–627.
32. Ibid., 628.
33. Ibid., 629.
34. Ibid., 483–484.
35. Ibid., 625, 633; Marx and Engels, *Cologne Communist Trial*, 62–63.
36. MECW, Volume 39, 60 and Volume 10, 627; Porter, *Refugee Question*, 41.
37. MECW, Volume 38, 240–241.
38. Ibid., 558–559.
39. Ibid., 241.
40. Ibid., 242.
41. Ibid., 250.

Chapter Twenty-one: London, Winter 1851

1. Marx and Engels, *Cologne Communist Trial*, 53.
2. Wilson, *Victorians*, 137–138, 144; Cole and Postgate, *British Common People*, 328, 366; Judith Flanders, *The Victorian House*, 290.
3. "Capitalism" as a word was coined by Proudhon and used in the 1840s by other socialist and communist writers, but it had not surfaced in the mainstream until the early 1850s. Marx himself did not use the word "capitalism" in the *Communist Manifesto*. Hobsbawm, *Age of Capital*, 13; Roberts, *History of Europe*, 376.
4. Hobsbawm, *Age of Capital*, 44–45; Sperber (ed.), *Germany, 1800–1870*, 73.
5. Sheppard, *London 1808–1870*, 98, 101.
6. Hobsbawm, *Age of Capital*, 13; Hammen, *The Red 48ers*, 90.
7. Hobsbawm, *Age of Capital*, 49–50; Sheppard, *London 1808–1870*, 71–72.
8. Hobsbawm, *Age of Capital*, 51.
9. Roberts, *History of Europe*, 329.
10. MECW, Volume 39, 21 and Volume 10, 500–502.
11. MECW, Volume 39, 96 and Volume 10, 502.
12. REM, 98; Liebknecht, *Karl Marx*, 57.
13. Berlin, *Karl Marx*, 13.
14. MECW, Volume 38, 270.
15. REM, 185; Flanders, *Victorian House*, 105–106; MECW, Volume 38, 251.
16. Mayer, *Friedrich Engels*, 143, 155, 157; Grenfell Morton, *Home Rule and the Irish Question*, 10; Wilson, *Victorians*, 76; MECW, Volume 41, 634(n); Carver, *Friedrich Engels*, 149.
17. MECW, Volume 38, 250.
18. Ibid., 252.
19. Ibid., 257.
20. Ibid., 297, 561.
21. MECW, Volume 10, 535.
22. MECW, Volume 38, 257.
23. The Marx apartment is often described by biographers as located on the second floor of the house, and that is where the Greater London Council affixed a blue historical

marker. The family inhabited the top story. There is also a dispute as to when the family moved into 28 Dean Street. Some biographers say the move occurred on December 2, 1850, but Marx wrote Engels a letter dated that day from 64 Dean Street. Also, on January 6, 1851, Marx told Engels he needed money for his landlady, who was "very poor." At 64 Dean Street the Marxes rented from a woman; at 28 Dean Street they rented from a man. Marx's first reference to his new address is in a letter to Engels dated January 27, 1851. Briggs and Callow, *Marx in London*, 43; Robert Payne, *Karl Marx*, 289; MECW, Volume 38, 251, 257, 269.

24. Liebknecht, *Karl Marx*, 94.
25. Briggs and Callow, *Marx in London*, 43.
26. Liebknecht, *Karl Marx*, 6.
27. MECW, Volume 38, 361.
28. Liebknecht, *Karl Marx*, 85.
29. Ibid., 54.
30. REM, 163–164.
31. Liebknecht, *Karl Marx*, 116.
32. Ibid., 117–118.
33. Gustav Mayer, "Neue Beitrage zur Biographie von Karl Marx," 54–66.
34. Paul Lafargue, *Karl Marx*, 26.
35. Liebknecht, *Karl Marx*, 115.
36. Some of them—the Italian Giuseppe Mazzini, France's Ledru-Rollin, Poland's Albert Darasz, and Marx's old nemesis Arnold Ruge—formed a group called the Central Committee of European Democracy. They declared that nationalism was dead and the opposition had to join hands across borders. MECW, Volume 38, 615(n) and Volume 39, 158.
37. Marx and Engels, *Cologne Communist Trial*, 168.
38. Liebknecht, *Karl Marx*, 94.
39. Marx and Engels, *Cologne Communist Trial*, 190.
40. MECW, Volume 38, 286.
41. Ibid., 287, 289–291.
42. Ibid., 323–324.
43. Ibid., 325; MEGA, III, Band 4, 85–86. (Eleanor Marx Aveling told Karl Kautsky in a letter dated March 15, 1898 [Moscow], that after Marx's death Engels had burned many letters among Marx's papers referring to himself. Engels also destroyed documents and letters in the spring of 1851 on the advice of Dr. Roland Daniels in Cologne, who said authorities in England were preparing to raid the homes of members of the Marx circle. If Marx had written Engels about Lenchen's pregnancy, the letter may have disappeared at that time.)
44. Marx and Engels, *Cologne Communist Trial*, 209; MECW, Volume 11, 304–305.
45. Porter, *Refugee Question*, 33.
46. Ibid., 86–87.
47. Ibid., 48, 57.
48. MECW, Volume 38, 355; Hamerow, *Restoration, Revolution, Reaction,* 206; Sperber (ed.), *Germany, 1800–1870,* 205; Marx and Engels, *Cologne Communist Trial,* 19.
49. MECW, Volume 38, 338.
50. Sperber (ed.), *Germany, 1800–1870,* 70.
51. Marx and Engels, *Cologne Communist Trial,* 20.
52. Ibid., 272.
53. Ibid., 19; MECW, Volume 38, 626–627(n).
54. Stieber was later the Prussian political police chief. It was not the first time Marx had run across a police agent operating under the alias Schmidt: in 1848, in a report in his newspaper, Marx had accused Stieber himself of pretending to be an artist named Schmidt while spying in Silesia. Schmidt, according to Marx and Engels, was the

name used by Prussian police spies. Peters, *Red Jenny*, 98; MECW, Volume 11, 410 and Volume 38, 183–184.

55. Peters, *Red Jenny*, 115.
56. KMIR, 24.
57. Jenny Marx (daughter) to Laura Lafargue, Dec. 24, 1868, Moscow.
58. Freddy's parentage is still a matter of debate for some Marx scholars. Some argue that Jenny would not have remained with Marx had she known Freddy was his son. But that is an argument from a twentieth-century perspective—a nineteenth-century woman would have had no good choice to make in this situation. Jenny's options would have been to return to Prussia and essentially become a humiliated ward of her family, her children's futures shadowed by scandal, or accept her husband's infidelity. Given Jenny's intense pride, the choice would have been clear. Others argue that an unidentified someone else in Marx's circle was the father, but if that was the case, why wouldn't he have married Lenchen? Why would Marx not have mentioned the situation to Engels? There would have been nothing to hide from his friend or from prying eyes. It is wholly consistent with Marx's personality that he would run from this responsibility—and wholly inconsistent that if Engels had been the father, he would have abandoned his son. Engels's decision to claim Freddy would have been the politically expedient thing to do. Personally, it was just one more instance in which Engels rescued Marx from disaster. In the early twentieth century, letters surfaced that contained evidence that Marx was Freddy's father. Stalin, alerted to their existence by the director of the Marx-Engels Institute, David Ryazanov, reportedly instructed him to bury what he called the "petty affair." Since the letters (Freddy Demuth to Jean Longuet, Sept. 10, 1910, Moscow; August Bebel to Ede Bernstein, Sept. 8, 1898, Moscow; Clara Zetkin to David Borisovich Ryazanov, Feb. 27, 1929, Moscow) have resurfaced, most recent scholarship has tended toward the belief that Freddy Demuth was Marx's son. Considering the personalities involved, contemporary accounts, logic, and the findings of Marx scholars in Russia, Germany, and Japan, I, too, have come to that conclusion. Valerij Fomičev, "Helene Demuth Without Brethren," 971–972; McLellan, *Karl Marx*, 249–250; MECW, Volume 38, 338.
59. KMIR, 24.
60. Marx and Engels, *Cologne Communist Trial*, 54–55, 59; MECW, Volume 38, 365 and Volume 11, 399.
61. MECW, Volume 38, 355, 359, 366.
62. Later, Marx and Engels said the imagined conspiracies of the exiles "provided governments the pretext they needed to arrest all sorts of people in Germany, to suppress indigenous movements and to use these wretched straw men in London as scarecrows with which to frighten the German middle classes." MECW, Volume 38, 366, 375; *Cologne Communist Trial*, 215.
63. MECW, Volume 38, 369.
64. Ibid., 623(n).
65. Fomičev, "Helene Demuth Without Brethren," 970; Wheen, *Karl Marx*, 170.
66. Raddatz, *Karl Marx*, 160.
67. MECW, Volume 38, 398.
68. McLellan, *Karl Marx*, 250; Robert Payne, *Karl Marx*, 267.
69. Peters, *Red Jenny*, 61, 104–105.
70. MECW, Volume 38, 402–403.
71. Fomičev, "Helene Demuth Without Brethren," 970.
72. MECW, Volume 40, 66.
73. MECW, Volume 38, 432, 629(n); Nicolaievsky and Maenchen-Helfen, *Karl Marx*, 225.
74. MECW, Volume 38, 431–432, 628–629(n).
75. Ibid., 629(n); Nicolaievsky and Maenchen-Helfen, *Karl Marx*, 225.
76. MECW, Volume 38, 409, 627(n); Berlin, *Karl Marx*, 145.

77. Nicolaievsky and Maenchen-Helfen, *Karl Marx,* 236.
78. MECW, Volume 38, 380; Berlin, *Karl Marx,* 146, 204; Nicolaievsky and Maenchen-Helfen, *Karl Marx,* 244.
79. MECW, Volume 38, 409.
80. Ibid., 425.

Chapter Twenty-two: London, 1852
 1. MECW, Volume 11, 103–104.
 2. MECW, Volume 38, 489.
 3. Ibid., 494.
 4. MECW, Volume 39, 569.
 5. MECW, Volume 38, 499–501.
 6. Schurz, *Reminiscences,* 384–386; Porter, *Refugee Question,* 108–109; Whitridge, *Men in Crisis,* 280.
 7. MECW, Volume 38, 488, 502, 508.
 8. Ibid., 635(n); Stearns, *1848,* 221.
 9. E. B. Washburne, *Recollections of a Minister to France, Part I,* 35.
10. MECW, Volume 38, 635–636(n).
11. Schurz, *Reminiscences,* 398–400.
12. MECW, Volume 38, 508.
13. Ibid., 519, 636(n).
14. Ibid., 635–636(n); Stearns, *1848,* 222.
15. Draper, *Karl Marx's Theory of Revolution,* 409.
16. MECW, Volume 38, 563.
17. KMIR, 24.
18. McLellan, *Karl Marx,* 233.
19. MECW, Volume 39, 3.
20. Ibid., 16.
21. Ibid., 6.
22. Ibid., 567.
23. Ibid., 20–21.
24. Ibid., 9.
25. Ibid., 570.
26. Ibid., 28.
27. Draper, *Karl Marx's Theory of Revolution,* 386.
28. REM, 250–251; KMIR, 24–25, 99–100.
29. Liebknecht, *Karl Marx,* 97, 151–152.
30. Flanders, *Victorian House,* 170–172; W. L. Burn, *The Age of Equipoise,* 17.
31. MECW, Volume 38, 637(n) and Volume 39, 71, 603(n).
32. MECW, Volume 39, 33.
33. MECW, Volume 11, 103–104, 106.
34. MECW, Volume 38, 475, 490–491.
35. MECW, Volume 39, 50.
36. Ibid., 59, 606(n).
37. Ibid., 59; Marx and Engels, *Cologne Communist Trial,* 86.
38. MECW, Volume 11, 426–427 and Volume 39, 59, 624–625(n).
39. MECW, Volume 39, 78–79, 81; KMIR, 25.
40. Halliday, *Great Filth,* 20.
41. KMIR, 25.
42. MECW, Volume 39, 85.
43. Ibid., 84–85.
44. Ibid., 85.
45. Ibid., 216.

46. Ibid., 93, 101, 611(n).
47. Ibid., 98.
48. Marx and Engels, *Cologne Communist Trial,* 276.
49. Laura Marx, writing for Edgar Marx, to Karl Marx, May 19, 1852, IISG.
50. This letter has been placed in the Marx story by other authors at various dramatic points in the family's history. But based on events, correspondence during other traumatic episodes, and Marx's response, I believe Jenny wrote it at this point. Jenny Marx to Karl Marx, undated, IISG.
51. MECW, Volume 39, 116–117.
52. Ibid., 124.
53. Ibid., 208.
54. Ibid., 148.
55. Ibid., 594(n), 610(n).
56. Ibid., 175.
57. Ibid., 182.
58. Ibid., 148–149.
59. MECW, Volume 39, 149 and Volume 38, 323 and Volume 11, 254.
60. MECW, Volume 39, 181–182.
61. Liebknecht, *Karl Marx,* 164; Raddatz, *Karl Marx,* 176; Mayhew, *London Labour and the London Poor,* 495.
62. MECW, Volume 39, 576–578.
63. Marx and Engels, *Cologne Communist Trial,* 60.
64. MECW, Volume 39, 144–145.
65. Ibid., 134.
66. Marx and Engels, *Cologne Communist Trial,* 26.
67. MECW, Volume 39, 142.
68. Marx and Engels, *Cologne Communist Trial,* 60, 114.
69. Ibid., 25, 66.
70. Ibid., 25.
71. MECW, Volume 38, 521 and Volume 39, 222–223, 226, 229–230, 240, 576–577, 624–625(n); Marx and Engels, *Cologne Communist Trial,* 87–88.
72. Marx and Engels, *Cologne Communist Trial,* 132.
73. Ibid., 105; MECW, Volume 39, 236.
74. MECW, Volume 39, 235, 247; Marx and Engels, *Cologne Communist Trial,* 106.
75. Marx and Engels, *Cologne Communist Trial,* 80–95, 265–266.
76. MECW, Volume 39, 215, 219.
77. Raddatz, *Karl Marx,* 114.
78. MECW, Volume 39, 241.
79. Ibid., 221.
80. Ibid., 216.
81. Marx and Engels, *Cologne Communist Trial,* 112.
82. Marx and Engels, *Cologne Communist Trial,* 29, 55, 112.
83. MECW, Volume 39, 577.
84. Ibid., 247.
85. Ibid., 232–233, 242, 255–256; Nicolaievsky and Maenchen-Helfen, *Karl Marx,* 222.
86. MECW, Volume 39, 386.
87. Ibid., 281.
88. Ibid., 264; Mehring, *Karl Marx,* 222.
89. MECW, Volume 39, 579.
90. Ibid., 259.
91. Ibid., 287, 580, 625(n).
92. Ibid., 288.
93. Mehring, *Karl Marx,* 223.

Chapter Twenty-three: London, 1853

1. Seigel, *Marx's Fate,* 274.
2. MECW, Volume 39, 386.
3. MECW, Volume 11, 621–625.
4. MECW, Volume 39, 272.
5. Ibid., 283.
6. Ibid., 273, 275.
7. KMIR, 25; REM, 230.
8. Mayhew, *London Labour and the London Poor,* 57, 195–196, 284.
9. Liebknecht, *Karl Marx,* 116–118.
10. Mayhew, *London Labour and the London Poor,* 478.
11. Derek Hudson, *Munby, Man of Two Worlds,* 22.
12. Liebknecht, *Karl Marx,* 131,139.
13. Jenny Marx to Wilhelm von Florencourt, Aug. 10, 1855, Moscow.
14. MECW, Volume 39, 581.
15. Preston, *The Bitter Cry of Outcast London,* 8.
16. Liebknecht, *Karl Marx,* 52.
17. Mayer, "Letters of Karl Marx to Karl Blind," 155.
18. REM, 251; Lafargue, *Karl Marx,* 26.
19. KMIR, 60–61; Liebknecht, *Karl Marx,* 126, 128–129.
20. KMIR, 61–62.
21. Ibid., 56-57.
22. REM, 251.
23. Francis Wheen, *Marx's Das Kapital,* 8.
24. Mayer, "Neue Beitrage zur Biographie von Karl Marx," 54-66; KMIR, 34–36.
25. MECW, Volume 39, 315.
26. Ibid., 293, 309.
27. Ibid., 308–309.
28. "Aleph," *London Scenes and London People,* 153–154.
29. KMIR, 101–102.
30. Jenny Marx (daughter) to Laura Lafargue, Dec. 24, 1868, Moscow.
31. KMIR, 25–26.
32. MECW, Volume 39, 406.
33. Ibid., 406, 453, 454, 458.
34. Ibid., 453.
35. Ibid., 589.
36. Ibid., 405, 646(n).
37. Ibid., 502, 506, 511.
38. Ibid., 481.
39. Halliday, *Great Filth,* 73, 143.
40. MECW, Volume 39, 483.
41. Halliday, *Great Filth,* 77–78.
42. MECW, Volume 39, 457, 462–463, 465.
43. Ibid., 464–465.
44. Ibid., 408, 423–426.
45. Ibid., 427–428.
46. Ibid., 434–436.
47. Ibid., 443.
48. Ibid., 436.
49. Ibid., 448–449.
50. Ibid., 421, 472, 477.
51. Ibid., 455.
52. Ibid., 485–486.

53. Ibid., 428.
54. Ibid., 421.
55. Edgar Marx to Karl Marx, Mar. 27, 1854, IISG.
56. MECW, Volume 39, 467, 469.
57. Ibid., 483–484.
58. Liebknecht, *Karl Marx,* 145.
59. KMIR, 63–65.
60. Laura Marx to Jenny Marx, Aug. 1854, IISG.
61. Jenny Marx (daughter) to Jenny Marx, July 10, 1854, Moscow; Olsen, *Growth of Victorian London,* 191.
62. Jenny Marx (daughter) to Jenny Marx, July 24, 1854, Moscow.

Chapter Twenty-four: London, 1855
1. MECW, Volume 39, 544.
2. Ibid., 509.
3. Ibid., 505, 658(n).
4. Schurz, *Reminiscences,* 393–395.
5. MECW, Volume 39, 296, 299; Porter, *Refugee Question,* 30.
6. Liebknecht, *Karl Marx,* 106–107.
7. MECW, Volume 39, 658; Liebknecht, *Karl Marx,* 109.
8. "Aleph," *London Scenes,* 271.
9. MECW, Volume 39, 505.
10. Ibid., 524.
11. Ibid., 522, 524–525.
12. Ibid., 526.
13. Ibid., 528.
14. Ibid.
15. Jenny Marx to Wilhelm von Florencourt, Aug. 10, 1855, Moscow.
16. Ibid.
17. MECW, Volume 39, 529.
18. Ibid., 530.
19. KMIR, 63.
20. Halliday, *Great Filth,* 86.
21. Jenny Marx to Wilhelm von Florencourt, Aug. 10, 1855, Moscow.
22. KMIR, 85.
23. Liebknecht, *Karl Marx,* 133–134, 179.
24. Ibid., 133–134.
25. MECW, Volume 39, 533.

Part Four: The End of *La Vie Bohème*

Chapter Twenty-five: London, Fall 1855
1. William Shakespeare, *Richard III,* 109.
2. MECW, Volume 39, 534, 613(n).
3. Ibid., 533, 534, 544.
4. Gosudarstvennaia Obshchestvenno-Politicheskaia Biblioteka, Moscow.
5. Jenny Marx to Ferdinand Lassalle, May 5, 1861, Moscow.
6. MECW, Volume 39, 536.
7. Ibid., 535.
8. Ibid., 526.
9. Ibid., 541.
10. Ibid., 543; Briggs and Callow, *Marx in London,* 46.
11. MECW, Volume 39, 550; Briggs and Callow, *Marx in London,* 46.

12. Jenny Marx to Wilhelm von Florencourt, Aug. 10, 1855, Moscow.
13. Jenny Marx to Louise von Westphalen, Jan. 29, 1858, Moscow.
14. MECW, Volume 39, 546.
15. MECW, Volume 41, 454.
16. MECW, Volume 39, 545.
17. Jenny Marx to Wilhelm von Florencourt, Sept. 22, 1855, Moscow.
18. Hobsbawm, *Age of Capital,* 99; Wilson, *Victorians,* 186, 199.
19. Wilson, *Victorians,* 178–179, 183.
20. Ibid., 173; Taylor, *Struggle for Mastery of Europe,* 49, 52.
21. Draper and Haberkern, *Karl Marx's Theory of Revolution, Volume V,* 82.
22. Offord, *Nineteenth-Century Russia,* 45.
23. In one post-1848 incident, the czar had forty-nine members of a literary club arrested. The organization, whose members included twenty-seven-year-old Feodor Dostoevsky, studied foreign authors, but it was also a cover for a socialist organization. Those arrested were sentenced to be executed in May 1849, and on the day scheduled they proceeded to the spot where they were to be shot. There Dostoevsky and his fellows waited, paralyzed by fear, until the surprise announcement that their sentence had been commuted and they would be sent to Siberia instead. Nicholas had cruelly taunted these intellectuals. Others he deported, lashed, or hanged. Fejtö (ed.), *Opening of an Era,* 397.
24. Ibid., 395.
25. MECW, Volume 39, 534.
26. Wilson, *Victorians,* 179–180, 193.
27. Ibid., 181, 183, 186.
28. August Ludwig von Rochau coined the term "realpolitik" in 1853. Sperber (ed.), *Germany, 1800–1870,* 22; MECW, Volume 39, 663–664; Porter, *Refugee Question,* 122, 165.
29. Taylor, *Struggle for Mastery of Europe,* 81.
30. MECW, Volume 39, 548–549.
31. Ibid., 550.
32. Ibid., 562.
33. Ibid., 557, 559–560.
34. KMIR, 26.
35. Wilson, *Victorians,* 411.
36. MECW, Volume 40, 8.
37. Ibid., 14.
38. Jenny Marx to Ernestine Liebknecht, mid-July 1856, Moscow.
39. MECW, Volume 40, 33.
40. Ibid., 41.
41. Ibid., 33.
42. MECW, Volume 40, 33, 44.
43. Ibid., 45.
44. Ibid., 46.
45. Ibid.
46. Ibid., 54.
47. Ibid., 49–50. (English men had been clean-shaved but began growing beards in tribute to fighters in the Crimea after the war.)
48. Ibid., 54–56.
49. Jenny Marx to Ernestine Liebknecht, mid-July 1856, Moscow.
50. The source of Eleanor Marx's nickname has been a topic of speculation by biographers. I discovered the answer in a letter written by Jennychen to her husband. Jenny Longuet to Charles Longuet, Mar. 31, 1876, Moscow.
51. Jenny Marx to Ernestine Liebknecht, mid-July 1856, Moscow.
52. MECW, Volume 40, 59, 63, 588(n).
53. Ibid., 63.

54. Ibid., 61.
55. Ibid., 66.
56. Ibid., 64.
57. Ibid., 67.
58. Ibid., 67, 71.
59. Olsen, *Growth of Victorian London,* 238.
60. MECW, Volume 40, 67, 71.
61. Briggs and Callow, *Marx in London,* 58, 60; Jenny Marx to Wilhelm von Florencourt, Oct. 4, 1856, Moscow.
62. Edgar von Westphalen to Ferdinand von Westphalen, Aug. 22, 1856, Dessau.
63. MECW, Volume 40, 68.
64. Jenny Marx (daughter) to Karl Marx, September 28, 1856, IISG.
65. MECW, Volume 40, 68.
66. Sheppard, *London 1808–1870,* 71–72; Hobsbawm, *Age of Capital,* 49.
67. Cole and Postgate, *British Common People,* 348; Hobsbawm, *Age of Capital,* 85.
68. MECW, Volume 40, 191.
69. Ibid., 74.
70. Ibid., 72.
71. Jenny Marx to Wilhelm von Florencourt, Oct. 4, 1856, Moscow.
72. Ibid.; KMIR, 26.
73. Jenny Marx to Wilhelm von Florencourt, Oct. 4, 1856, Moscow.
74. KMIR, 26.
75. Flanders, *Victorian House,* lii.
76. Jenny Marx to Wilhelm von Florencourt, Oct. 4, 1856, Moscow.
77. Briggs and Callow, *Marx in London,* 60.
78. Jenny Marx to Wilhelm von Florencourt, Oct. 4, 1856, Moscow.
79. Ibid.
80. Ibid.
81. KMIR, 26.
82. Raddatz, *Karl Marx,* 115.
83. MECW, Volume 40, 88.
84. Ibid., 68, 590(n).
85. MECW, Volume 40, 69; Pawel, *Poet Dying,* 181.
86. KMIR, 26.
87. MECW, Volume 40, 87.
88. Marx and Engels had tried to establish a *Tribune*-like relationship with the U.S. publication *Putnam's,* which paid handsomely. Marx had dinner in London in 1856 with Freiligrath, "Putnam's man" Frederick Law Olmsted, and another American. He found Olmsted a "quiet, genial soul" and came away with requests for articles. MECW, Volume 40, 68, 71, 88, 111.
89. Peters, *Red Jenny,* 118.

Chapter Twenty-six: London, 1857

1. MECW, Volume 41, 575.
2. MECW, Volume 40, 93–94.
3. MECW, Volume 41, 216.
4. Carver, *Friedrich Engels,* 140.
5. MECW, Volume 40, 96–97.
6. Ibid., 132, 563.
7. Ibid., 111.
8. Ibid., 564.
9. Ibid., 122, 125, 599–600(n). The encyclopedia was published in sixteen volumes in New York in 1858–1863. Authors of the entries were generally anonymous.

10. Ibid., 124–125.
11. Ibid., 565.
12. Caygill, *British Museum,* 12, 15, 29.
13. Jenny Marx to Louise von Westphalen, Jan. 19, 1858, Moscow; KMIR, 27.
14. MECW, Volume 40, 143, 146.
15. Ibid., 148.
16. Jenny Marx to Louise von Westphalen, Jan. 19, 1858, Moscow.
17. MECW, Volume 40, 191.
18. Ibid., 197.
19. Ibid.
20. Ibid., 199.
21. Ibid., 566.
22. Ibid., 224, 226, 249.
23. Ibid., 238.
24. Ibid., 202, 213.
25. Ibid., 203–204.
26. Ibid., 236.
27. Ibid., 215.
28. Ibid., 220.
29. Eventually the divorce was granted, but the dispute over finances continued until Lassalle acquired, through not entirely legal means, evidence of crimes committed by Count Edmund Hatzfeldt-Wildenburg. Lassalle threatened to go public with them unless the count gave his ex-wife part of his holdings. The count saw where his best interests lay and settled, making the countess and Lassalle rich for life. Raddatz, *Karl Marx,* 167, 171–172; Norman Davies, *Europe: A History,* 837; MECW, Volume 40, 23, 583–584(n).
30. MECW, Volume 40, 23.
31. Ibid., 270, 286.
32. Ibid., 255.
33. Ibid.
34. Ibid., 273.
35. Jenny Marx to Louise von Westphalen, Jan. 29, 1858, Moscow.
36. Wilson, *Victorians,* 260, 263.
37. Jenny Marx to Louise von Westphalen, Jan. 29, 1858, Moscow.
38. MECW, Volume 41, 571; Longuet, *Karl Marx,* 201, 204.
39. Jenny Marx (daughter), May 1, 1857, IISG.
40. Jenny Marx to Berthe Markheim, July 6, 1863, Moscow.
41. MECW, Volume 40, 295.
42. McLellan, *Karl Marx,* 293.
43. MECW, Volume 40, 286.
44. Ibid., 295.
45. Ibid., 295, 297.
46. Ibid., 304.
47. Ibid., 569.
48. Ibid., 374.
49. Ibid., 309–310, 312.
50. Ibid., 311.
51. Ibid., 312.
52. Ibid., 313.
53. Ibid., 315–316.
54. Ibid., 318.
55. O'Neill, *Good Old Days,* 10.
56. MECW, Volume 40, 328.

57. Ibid., 328–331.
58. Ibid., 332.
59. Ibid., 333–334, 347, 350.
60. Ibid., 335.
61. Pamela Horn, *Pleasures & Pastimes in Victorian Britain,* 125.
62. MECW, Volume 40, 339.
63. Yvonne Kapp, *Eleanor Marx, Volume I,* 32; MECW, Volume 40, 337.
64. MECW, Volume 40, 340.
65. Ibid., 341.
66. Ibid., 351.
67. Ibid., 353–354.
68. Ibid., 358.
69. Ibid., 364.
70. Ibid., 368.
71. Ibid., 369.
72. Ibid., 371.
73. Ibid., 369.

Chapter Twenty-seven: London, 1859

1. MECW, Volume 40, 397.
2. Ibid., 620(n).
3. Breuilly, *Austria, Prussia and Germany,* 63; MECW, Volume 40, 620(n).
4. Hamerow, *Restoration, Revolution, Reaction,* 240.
5. Taylor, *Struggle for the Mastery of Europe,* 58.
6. Breuilly, *Austria, Prussia and Germany,* 63; MECW, Volume 41, 617.
7. Jenny Marx to Louise von Westphalen, Feb. 10, 1859, Moscow.
8. MECW, Volume 40, 389–390.
9. Ibid., 400.
10. MECW, Volume 40, 547; KMIR, 27.
11. MECW, Volume 40, 402, 415.
12. Ibid., 406, 408.
13. Ibid., 404.
14. Ibid., 408.
15. Ibid., 416.
16. Ibid., 455.
17. Ibid., 435.
18. Ibid., 547.
19. Ibid., 446–447, 452.
20. Ibid., 454.
21. Ibid., 632–633(n).
22. Ibid., 520.
23. Ibid., 439.
24. Ibid.
25. Ibid., 462–463.
26. Padover, *Karl Marx,* 180; MECW, Volume 40, 635(n).
27. MECW, Volume 40, 457.
28. Ibid., 473.
29. McLellan, *Karl Marx,* 282, 286–288.
30. MECW, Volume 40, 471, 478.
31. McLellan, *Karl Marx,* 288.
32. MECW, Volume 40, 518.
33. Ibid., 473.
34. Ibid.

35. Ibid., 479.
36. Ibid., 572.
37. Ibid., 472.
38. Ibid., 484.
39. Ibid., 501.
40. Ibid., 489.
41. Ibid., 490.
42. Ibid., 491.
43. Ibid., 493.
44. Ibid., 575.
45. Ibid., 498–499.
46. Ibid., 511.
47. Ibid., 532–533.
48. Ibid., 496, 508, 548.
49. Ibid., 548.
50. Jenny Marx to Louise von Westphalen, Feb. 10, 1859, Moscow.
51. MECW, Volume 40, 569.
52. Ibid., 466.
53. Ibid., 572–573 and Volume 41, 571.
54. MECW, Volume 40, 573–576.
55. Ibid., 574.
56. Wilson, *Victorians,* 225–226.
57. MECW, Volume 40, 551.
58. MECW, Volume 41, 232, 246.
59. Liebknecht, *Karl Marx,* 91.
60. MECW, Volume 40, 631; McLellan, *Karl Marx,* 289.
61. MECW, Volume 40, 434.
62. McLellan, *Karl Marx,* 289.
63. Ibid., 290; MECW, Volume 40, 521.
64. McLellan, *Karl Marx,* 290.
65. MECW, Volume 40, 514, 637-638(n); MECW, Volume 17, 10–11.
66. MECW, Volume 40, 515.
67. McLellan, *Karl Marx,* 290.
68. Ibid., 291.
69. MECW, Volume 41, 80–83.
70. Ibid., 188, 576.
71. Ibid., 6.
72. Ibid., 43 and Volume 17, 28–29, 41–43, 46–48, 89; McLellan, *Karl Marx,* 290.
73. McLellan, *Karl Marx,* 290.
74. MECW, Volume 41, 6, 69, 261; Mehring, *Karl Marx,* 288.
75. MECW, Volume 41, 9.
76. Ibid., 13–14.
77. Ibid., 22–23.
78. Ibid., 24.
79. Ibid., 572.
80. Ibid., 114.
81. Ibid., 28.
82. MECW, Volume 17, 12–13.
83. MECW, Volume 41, 29.
84. MECW, Volume 17, 14–15.
85. MECW, Volume 41, 75.
86. MECW, Volume 17, 259, 279.
87. MECW, Volume 41, 33.

88. Ibid., 94.
89. Ibid., 56.
90. Ibid., 114.
91. Ibid., 34, 77.
92. Ibid., 567.
93. Ibid., 157; Offord, *Nineteenth-Century Russia,* 50; Hobsbawm, *Age of Revolution,* 200.
94. MECW, Volume 41, 567.
95. While Jenny's parents were alive, the Westphalens had given some money to another family as a safe investment. (Some of it was earned by Jenny for working as a secretary for her father.) But the family went bankrupt, and the Westphalens were not repaid until 1860, four years after the Marx family had moved to Grafton Terrace. Jenny received sixteen pounds. MECW, Volume 39, 526; Jenny Marx to Ferdinand and Louise von Westphalen, June 4, 1860, Moscow.
96. Jenny Marx to Ernestine Liebknecht, Oct. 13, 1863, Moscow.
97. Jenny Marx to Ferdinand and Louise von Westphalen, June 4, 1860, Moscow.
98. In her letter to Olive Schreiner (June 16, 1885), Tussy wrote that she remembered her father saying, "Jenny is most like me but Tussy is me." Havelock Ellis; "Havelock Ellis on Eleanor Marx," *Adelphi,* London, Sept.-Oct. 1935.
99. Nicolaievsky and Maenchen-Helfen. *Karl Marx,* 244.
100. MECW, Volume 41, 116.
101. Ibid., 120–121.
102. Ibid., 121.
103. Ibid., 129, 609(n).
104. Ibid., 167.
105. Ibid., 175–176.
106. Ibid., 177.
107. Ibid., 568.
108. Ibid., 179.
109. Ibid., 190.
110. Ibid., 191, 198–199.
111. Ibid., 193.
112. Ibid., 195.
113. Jenny Marx (daughter) to Karl Marx, Sept. 17, 1862, Moscow.
114. MECW, Volume 41, 197–198.
115. Ibid., 202.
116. Ibid., 198, 205.
117. Ibid., 212.
118. Ibid., 207.
119. Ibid., 208, 211.
120. Ibid., 214.
121. Ibid., 216–217, 573.
122. MECW, Volume 41, 216; Halliday, *Great Filth,* 8, 9, 14, 16.
123. MECW, Volume 41, 573.
124. Halliday, *Great Filth,* 8–9, 58.
125. MECW, Volume 41, 216.
126. Ibid., 573.
127. Ibid., 220–221, 224; Liebknecht, *Karl Marx,* 180.
128. MECW, Volume 41, 222, 231.
129. MECW, Volume 17, 26, 50, 69.
130. MECW, Volume 41, 227, 234, 239, 327; McLellan, *Karl Marx,* 292.
131. MECW, Volume 41, 327–328; McLellan, *Karl Marx,* 292.
132. MECW, Volume 17, 26.
133. REM, 20; MECW, Volume 44, 130.

Chapter Twenty-eight: London, 1861

1. MECW, Volume 41, 114.
2. Ibid., 573; Jenny Marx to Antoinette Philips, early May 1861, Moscow.
3. MECW, Volume 41, 574.
4. "Aleph," *London Scenes,* 156.
5. MECW, Volume 41, 574.
6. Ibid., 231, 262.
7. Ibid., 231.
8. Ibid., 230, 232.
9. Ibid., 243.
10. Ibid., 252, 257.
11. Ibid., 263.
12. Ibid., 247.
13. Ibid., 617(n).
14. Ibid., 252.
15. Ibid., 261.
16. Ibid., 264–265.
17. REM, 252–253; Chushichi Tsuzuki, *Eleanor Marx, 1855–1898,* 12.
18. Eleanor Marx Aveling to Karl Kautsky, Jan. 1, 1898, Moscow; Jenny Marx to Louise von Westphalen, Feb. 10, 1859, Moscow.
19. Eleanor Marx Aveling to Karl Kautsky, Jan. 1, 1898, Moscow.
20. Jenny Marx to Louise von Westphalen, Feb. 10, 1859, Moscow; MECW, Volume 41, 582.
21. REM, 252–253.
22. MECW, Volume 41, 572.
23. Ibid., 258, 261.
24. Ibid., 264; Padover, *Karl Marx,* 185.
25. MECW, Volume 41, 264.
26. Ibid., 266.
27. Ibid., 268.
28. Ibid., 268–269.
29. Padover, *Karl Marx,* 186.
30. MECW, Volume 41, 503.
31. Ibid., 576–578.
32. Ibid., 576.
33. Ibid., 577–578.
34. Ibid., 269–271.
35. Ozment, *Mighty Fortress,* 165.
36. MECW, Volume 41, 269–271.
37. Ibid., 273.
38. Ibid., 578–579.
39. Ibid., 278.
40. Ibid., 274–276.
41. Giroud, *Femme du diable,* 157.
42. Jenny Marx to Ferdinand Lassalle, first half of April 1861, Moscow.
43. Jenny Marx to Ferdinand Lassalle, May 5, 1861, Moscow.
44. MECW, Volume 41, 275.
45. Ibid., 289.
46. Ibid., 279.
47. Ibid., 283.
48. Ibid., 279.
49. Ibid., 277.
50. Jenny Marx to Ferdinand Lassalle, May 5, 1861, Moscow.

51. Ibid., MECW, Volume 41, 277.
52. MECW, Volume 41, 283.
53. Jenny Marx to Ferdinand Lassalle, May 5, 1861, Moscow; Giroud, *Femme du diable*, 164.
54. MECW, Volume 41, 337–338.

Chapter Twenty-nine: London, 1862
1. MECW, Volume 41, 411.
2. Wilson, *Victorians*, 243–244; "Aleph," *London Scenes*, 162; Hudson, *Munby*, 111.
3. "Aleph," *London Scenes*, 162.
4. Edward Royle, *Radical Politics, 1790–1900*, 67.
5. MECW, Volume 41, 335–336; Hudson, *Munby*, 111–113.
6. MECW, Volume 19, 109.
7. MECW, Volume 41, 291.
8. Ibid., 335–336.
9. MECW, Volume 19, 137–138; D. G. Wright, *Democracy and Reform, 1815–1885*, 64.
10. MECW, Volume 19, 137–138.
11. Hudson, *Munby*, 90, 113.
12. MECW, Volume 41, 376, 416.
13. Ibid., 4 and Volume 19, 10.
14. MECW, Volume 41, 414.
15. Ibid., 633(n).
16. Ibid., 344, 347.
17. Ibid., 402.
18. Ibid., 341; Kapp, *Eleanor Marx, Volume I*, 44.
19. MECW, Volume 41, 341.
20. Ibid., 340–341.
21. Ibid., 343–344.
22. Ibid., 344, 354.
23. Ibid., 344, 369, 376, 388.
24. Ibid., 354.
25. Ibid., 365.
26. Ibid., 379.
27. Jenny Marx to Ferdinand Lassalle, May 5, 1861, Moscow.
28. MECW, Volume 41, 380.
29. Ibid., 383.
30. Ibid., 389–390.
31. Robert Payne, *Karl Marx*, 334.
32. MECW, Volume 41, 389.
33. Ibid., 390; Eduard Bernstein, *My Years of Exile*, 158.
34. MECW, Volume 41, 389, 399.
35. Ibid., 389.
36. Ibid., 390.
37. Robert Payne, *Karl Marx*, 335.
38. MECW, Volume 41, 399, 403.
39. Ibid., 392.
40. Ibid., 401.
41. Ibid., 402.
42. Ibid., 401, 406.
43. Ibid., 405–406, 409.
44. Ibid., 411, 419.
45. Ibid., 411.
46. Ibid., 415–416.

47. Ibid., 417, 425.
48. Ibid., 414.
49. Ibid., 427.
50. Ibid., 582.
51. Ibid., 429.
52. MECW, Volume 19, 250.
53. MECW, Volume 41, 421.
54. Ibid., 436.
55. Ibid., 433; Jenny Marx to Ernestine Liebknecht, Jan. 16, 1863, Moscow.
56. Jenny Marx to Ernestine Liebknecht, Jan. 16, 1863, Moscow.
57. MECW, Volume 41, 433.
58. Jenny Marx to Ernestine Liebknecht, Jan. 16, 1863, Moscow.
59. MECW, Volume 41, 441.
60. Ibid., 442.
61. Ibid., 443.
62. Ibid., 444–445.
63. Ibid., 446–448, 455.
64. Ibid., 468.
65. Ibid., 474, 481.
66. Ibid., 488.
67. Ibid., 481.
68. Ibid., 482, 582.
69. Ibid., 488; Jenny Marx to Ernestine Liebknecht, Oct. 13, 1863, Moscow.
70. Jenny Marx to Karl Marx, early April 1862, Moscow.
71. MECW, Volume 41, 571.
72. Jenny Marx to Karl Marx, Aug. 1863, Moscow.
73. REM, 272; Longuet, *Karl Marx,* 204.
74. MECW, Volume 41, 571.
75. Jenny Marx to Karl Marx, early April 1862, Moscow.
76. MECW, Volume 41, 583; Jenny Marx to Karl Marx, Aug. 1863, Moscow.
77. MECW, Volume 41, 581.
78. Ibid., 584–585, 587.
79. Ibid., 585.
80. Ibid., 497, 587.
81. Ibid., 495.
82. Ibid., 500.
83. Ibid., 495.
84. Ibid., 499.
85. Ibid., 503.
86. Jenny Marx to Karl Marx, Jan. 1864, Moscow.
87. Ibid.
88. Jenny Marx to Ernestine Liebknecht, Dec. 10, 1864, Moscow.
89. Hudson, *Munby,* 173.
90. MECW, Volume 41, 507, 510.
91. Ibid., 508, 511.
92. McLellan, *Karl Marx,* 304; Padover, *Karl Marx,* 192.
93. Briggs and Callow, *Marx in London,* 62; Sheppard, *London 1808–1870,* 156. (The address was changed to 1 Maitland Park Road. Today apartment blocks occupy the site.)
94. Padover, *Karl Marx,* 193.
95. McLellan, *Karl Marx,* 325.
96. Kapp, *Eleanor Marx, Volume I,* 57; Briggs and Callow, *Marx in London,* 63.
97. MECW, Volume 41, 518, 520, 521, 522.
98. Ibid., 523.

99. Ibid., 524.
100. Ibid., 525.
101. Ibid., 170–171.

Part Five: From *Capital* to the Commune

Chapter Thirty: London, 1864
 1. MECW, Volume 20, 12.
 2. MECW, Volume 25, 266.
 3. Sheppard, *London 1808–1870,* 118.
 4. Slavery was not banned in the United States until 1865, with the ratification of the Thirteenth Amendment to the Constitution.
 5. Offord, *Nineteenth-Century Russia,* 57–59; Hobsbawm, *Age of Capital,* 223.
 6. Businesses and governments had opened the door a crack to labor organizations. Laws were changed to permit some unions and allow the possibility of strikes. But for many in the working class, this was far from enough. Sheppard, *London 1808–1870,* 118.
 7. MECW, Volume 41, 534.
 8. The violence included assassination attempts against Russian-appointed officials, and in such cases workers were blamed and executed. The Poles had hoped for help from the relatively liberal governments of France and England, but that assistance did not come. Davies, *Europe,* 828.
 9. McLellan, *Karl Marx,* 340.
10. MECW, Volume 41, 546–547.
11. Marx's dabbling in the stock market has been questioned by some scholars, who believe he may simply have wanted his uncle to believe he was engaged in "capital" transactions, not *Capital.* MECW, Volume 41, 543.
12. Jenny Marx to Ernestine Liebknecht, Dec. 10, 1864, Moscow.
13. MECW, Volume 41, 546.
14. Jenny Marx to Ernestine Liebknecht, July 16, 1864, Moscow.
15. Jenny Marx to Ferdinand von Westphalen, before May 29, 1865, Moscow.
16. Jenny Marx to Karl Marx and daughters, 1864, Moscow.
17. MECW, Volume 41, 552.
18. Ibid., 556.
19. Jenny Marx to Ernestine Liebknecht, Spring 1866, Moscow.
20. MECW, Volume 41, 553–554.
21. Jenkins, *Engels in Manchester,* 18.
22. MECW, Volume 41, 555, 558; McLellan, *Karl Marx,* 327.
23. MECW, Volume 43, 88.
24. In 1862 and 1863, Bismarck had, in his capacity as minister-president, tried to undermine liberal opponents by bribing or bullying journalists and trying to woo liberals into cooperation. Sperber (ed.), *Germany, 1800–1870,* 73; Breuilly (ed.), *19th-Century Germany,* 144, 151.
25. MECW, Volume 41, 556.
26. Ibid., 560.
27. MECW, Volume 42, 15–16.
28. Hobsbawm, *Age of Capital,* 49.
29. McLellan, *Karl Marx,* 341–342; Padover, *Karl Marx,* 223; Hobsbawm, *Age of Capital,* 136; Sheppard, *London 1808–1870,* 336–337.
30. Padover, *Karl Marx,* 223.
31. MECW, Volume 42, 3–4, 587–588(n).
32. Ibid., 3–4.
33. Ibid., 17–18.
34. MECW, Volume 20, 9–11.
35. MECW, Volume 42, 43–44.

36. Raddatz, *Karl Marx,* 123.
37. Carr, *Michael Bakunin,* 197, 201.
38. Ibid., 205, 207, 210.
39. Ibid., 220.
40. Ibid., 223.
41. Ibid., 227.
42. Ibid., 232–235.
43. Ibid., 242.
44. MECW, Volume 41, 492.
45. Carr, *Michael Bakunin,* 305.
46. Ibid., 308.
47. Ibid., 287, 295, 299, 301.
48. MECW, Volume 42, 18–19.
49. Nicolaievsky and Maenchen-Helfen, *Karl Marx,* 281.
50. Jenny Marx to Ernestine Liebknecht, Dec. 10, 1864, Moscow.
51. Pool, *What Jane Austin Ate,* 53, 78.
52. Giroud, *Femme du diable,* 177.
53. Jenny Marx to Ernestine Liebknecht, Dec. 10, 1864, Moscow.
54. MECW, Volume, 20, 19–20.
55. MECW, Volume 42, 86, 161.
56. *The Times,* London, Feb. 6, 1865.
57. MECW, Volume 41, 582.
58. Eleanor Marx to Laura Marx, Dec. 29, 1868, Moscow.
59. Ernestine Liebknecht to Jenny Marx (daughter), late Dec. 1865, IISG.
60. Leslie Derfler, *Paul Lafargue and the Founding of French Marxism,* 49.
61. Longuet, *Karl Marx,* 217–218.
62. Clemenceau became prime minister of France in 1906. Longuet, *Karl Marx,* 218.
63. Jacques Macé, *Paul et Laura Lafargue,* 25.
64. Derfler, *Paul Lafargue and the Flowering of French Socialism,* 2.
65. Lafargue said he was sent to London in 1865 with a message from the Paris IWMA. But his biographer, Leslie Derfler, has questioned whether he appeared in London in 1866 and also whether the IWMA would have entrusted a newcomer with a message of importance for the Central Committee in London. Derfler, *Founding of French Marxism,* 33; Lafargue, *Karl Marx,* 11; Macé, *Paul et Laura Lafargue,* 14–17.
66. Macé, *Paul et Laura Lafargue,* 16.
67. Lafargue, *Karl Marx,* 11.
68. MECW, Volume 42, 106.
69. Lafargue, *Karl Marx,* 11.
70. Ibid., 13–14.
71. Derfler, *Founding of French Marxism,* 34.
72. Eleanor Marx to Friedrich Engels, Feb. 13, 1865, Moscow.
73. Eleanor Marx to Friedrich Engels, Feb. 1865, Moscow.
74. MECW, Volume 42, 129–130.
75. The International's central committee was known as the Central Council until 1866, when it became the General Council. MECW, Volume 42, 140 and Volume 43, 545.
76. MECW, Volume 42, 144.
77. Ibid., 597(n).
78. Ibid., 227.
79. Ibid., 78.
80. MECW, Volume 20, 362.
81. Longuet, *Karl Marx,* 201.
82. MECW, Volume 42, 155.
83. *The Times,* London, Apr. 27, 1865.

84. MECW, Volume 42, 150.
85. MECW, Volume 20, 99–100.
86. MECW, Volume 42, 414.
87. Ibid., 150.
88. Ibid.
89. Jenny Marx to Ernestine Liebknecht, before May 27, 1865, Moscow.
90. Jenny Marx to Ferdinand von Westphalen, before May 29, 1865, Moscow; Jenny Marx to Ernestine Liebknecht, before May 27, 1865, Moscow.
91. Jenny Marx to Ferdinand von Westphalen, before May 29, 1865, Moscow; Edgar von Westphalen to Ferdinand von Westphalen, May 26, 1865, Dessau; Jenny Marx (daughter) to Ernestine Liebknecht, Nov. 10, 1865, Moscow.
92. Edgar von Westphalen to Ferdinand von Westphalen, May 26, 1865, Dessau.
93. Ferdinand von Westphalen to Edgar von Westphalen, Apr. 9, 1859, Dessau.
94. Jenny Marx to Ferdinand von Westphalen, before May 29, 1865, Moscow.
95. MECW, Volume 42, 160.
96. Ibid., 159.
97. Jenny Marx to Friedrich Engels, May 20, 1865, Moscow.
98. MECW, Volume 42, 172–174.
99. Ibid., 177
100. Ibid., 175.
101. Ibid., 178.
102. Ibid., 180.
103. Ibid., 183–184.
104. Ibid., 180, 184, 193, 196.
105. Ibid., 187–188.
106. Ibid., 213, 221.
107. Hudson, *Munby*, 216.
108. MECW, Volume 42, 228.
109. Ibid., 223–224, 228.
110. Ibid., 227.
111. Ibid., 249, 573–574,
112. Ibid., 225–226, 233.
113. Ibid., 233–234.
114. Ibid., 236, 250.
115. Ibid., 238.

Chapter Thirty-one: London, 1866

1. Germaine de Staël, *Delphine*, 371.
2. The three family friends were the Frenchman and '48er Eugene Dupont, the Swiss watchmaker Hermann Jung, and Konstanty Bobczynski, a forty-nine-year-old who arrived in London fresh from the 1863 Polish uprising. MECW, Volume 42, 250; Longuet, *Karl Marx*, 211.
3. Pawel, *Poet Dying*, 117–119.
4. Macé, *Paul et Laura Lafargue*, 21; Derfler, *Founding of French Marxism*, 25.
5. Derfler, *Founding of French Marxism*, 26.
6. Macé, *Paul et Laura Lafargue*, 25.
7. Ibid., 26; Derfler, *Founding of French Marxism*, 27.
8. Derfler, *Founding of French Marxism*, 29.
9. Macé, *Paul et Laura Lafargue*, 27–28; Derfler, *Founding of French Marxism*, 30–31.
10. Jenny Marx to Ernestine Liebknecht, Oct. 14, 1867, Moscow; Macé, *Paul et Laura Lafargue*, 28; Derfler, *Founding of French Marxism*, 32; Porter, *Refugee Question*, 35; Taylor, *Struggle for Mastery of Europe*, 101.
11. Derfler, *Founding of French Marxism*, 34.

12. Longuet, *Karl Marx,* 220.
13. MECW, Volume 20, 339.
14. MECW, Volume 42, 243.
15. Ibid., 243, 250.
16. Raddatz, *Karl Marx,* 66.
17. MECW, Volume 42, 250–251.
18. Ibid., 240; Olga Meier, Michèle Perrot, and Michel Trebitsch (eds.), *The Daughters of Karl Marx,* 5.
19. MECW, Volume 42, 241.
20. Ibid., 245–246.
21. Meier, Perrot, and Trebitsch (eds.), *Daughters,* 5.
22. MECW, Volume 42, 246.
23. Longuet, *Karl Marx,* 220.
24. REM, 82.
25. Macé, *Paul et Laura Lafargue,* 33.
26. MECW, Volume 42, 249.
27. Jenny Marx to Ernestine Liebknecht, Spring 1866, Moscow.
28. Jenny Marx to Ferdinand von Westphalen, Aug. 8, 1865, Moscow.
29. Meier, Perrot, and Trebitsch (eds.), *Daughters,* 6–7.
30. Ibid., 8.
31. MECW, Volume 42, 254.
32. Ibid., 262.
33. Ibid., 268; Jenny Marx to Ernestine Liebknecht, Spring 1866, Moscow.
34. D. G. Williamson, *Bismarck and Germany,* 10, 22–23; Breuilly, *Austria, Prussia and Germany,* 7; Sperber (ed.), *Germany, 1800–1870,* 85; MECW, Volume 42, 288.
35. Robert Payne, *Karl Marx,* 390; Mayer, "Letters of Karl Marx to Karl Blind," 155. (Some reports say Cohen hanged himself, others that he slashed his throat. In 1886 Bismarck told a session of the Reichstag that Cohen, whom he identified as Ferdinand Blind, was one of Marx's "pupils" and posthumously accused Marx of rearing assassins. Tussy wrote a protest letter to the German press in her and Laura's names.)
36. MECW, Volume 42, 272–273.
37. Ibid., 273–274.
38. Ibid., 274.
39. Ibid., 287.
40. MECW, Volume 20, 411.
41. MECW, Volume 42, 303–304.
42. Jenny Marx to Ernestine Liebknecht, Oct. 14, 1867, Moscow.
43. MECW, Volume 42, 306.
44. Ibid., 307–308.
45. Ibid., 308.
46. Ibid., 308–309.
47. Ibid., 309–310.
48. Ibid., 310.
49. Ibid., 313; Emile Bottigelli (ed.), *Lettres et documents de Karl Marx,* Karl Marx to Laura and Eleanor Marx, Aug. 28, 1866.
50. MECW, Volume 42, 313.
51. Jenny Marx (daughter) to Jenny Marx, Sept. 2, 1866, Moscow.
52. Jenny Marx (daughter) to Eleanor and Laura Marx, Sept. 6, 1866, Moscow; Eleanor Marx to Alice Liebknecht, Oct. 14, 1866, Moscow.
53. Meier, Perrot, and Trebitsch (eds.), *Daughters,* 9.
54. Jenny Marx to Ernestine Liebknecht, Oct. 14, 1867, Moscow.
55. MECW, Volume 42, 328.
56. Ibid., 321.

57. Ibid., 398.
58. Ibid., 331.
59. Ibid., 332.
60. Ibid.
61. Ibid., 576.
62. Ibid., 343–344.
63. Ibid., 383.
64. Ibid., 350–351.
65. Meier, Perrot, and Trebitsch (eds.), *Daughters,* 16; MECW, Volume 42, 352.
66. MECW, Volume 3, 248.

Chapter Thirty-two: London, 1867
1. Honoré de Balzac, *The Unknown Masterpiece,* 40.
2. MECW, Volume 42, 362–364.
3. Ibid., 357.
4. Ibid., 358.
5. Ibid., 366.
6. Ibid., 371.
7. Ibid., 369.
8. Ibid., 360–361.
9. Padover, *Karl Marx,* 203.
10. In this letter Marx addresses Jennychen as "Joe," which has been incorrectly described in several books as a reference to Louisa May Alcott's character Jo in *Little Women.* Alcott's book was not published until 1868, and Marx's letter was written in 1867. MECW, Volume 42, 369.
11. Ibid., 375.
12. Ibid.
13. Meier, Perrot, and Trebitsch (eds.), *Daughters,* 24–25.
14. In a note prepared for Tenge's visitor's book, Marx wrote of the "spell of feminine noble harmony" that tamed "life's wild frenzy." Meier, Perrot, and Trebitsch (eds.), *Daughters,* 27; Padover, *Karl Marx,* 204–205.
15. MECW, Volume 42, 371–372.
16. Ibid., 379–380.
17. Ibid., 361.
18. Ibid., 347–348.
19. Ibid., 381–382.
20. Ibid., 383, 394.
21. Meier, Perrot, and Trebitsch (eds.), *Daughters,* 17, 19.
22. Ibid., 16.
23. Jenny Marx (daughter), undated Maitland Park, IISG.
24. Jenny Marx (daughter) notebook, IISG; Meier, Perrot, and Trebitsch (eds.), *Daughters,* 16–17; MECW, Volume 42, 369, 649(n).
25. MECW, Volume 42, 396–397.
26. Jenny Marx to Ernestine Liebknecht, Oct. 14, 1867, Moscow.
27. Jenny Marx (daughter) to Jenny Marx, 1867, Moscow.
28. Ibid.
29. REM, 185.
30. MECW, Volume 42, 400.
31. Ibid., 402–405.
32. Ibid., 405.
33. REM, 26–27.
34. MECW, Volume 42, 405–406.
35. Ibid., 431; Padover, *Karl Marx,* 208.

36. MECW, Volume 42, 428.
37. Ibid., 451, 462; Carver, *Engels, Short Introduction,* 49–50.
38. MECW, Volume 42, 512.
39. Ibid., 444, 467.
40. Ibid., 443.
41. Ibid., 490.
42. McLellan, *Karl Marx,* 325.
43. MECW, Volume 42, 549.
44. Ibid., 453.
45. Ibid., 453–454.
46. Ibid., 458.
47. Ibid., 507.
48. Davies said Marx took his material history from Feuerbach, class struggle from Saint-Simon, dictatorship of the proletariat from Babeuf, labor theory from Adam Smith, surplus value from Bray and Thompson, and dialectic from Hegel. Davies, *Europe,* 837.
49. Berlin, *Karl Marx,* 15.
50. KMIR, 145.
51. MECW, Volume 35, 739.
52. Ibid, 748.
53. Ibid, 47–48.
54. Ibid., 181–182.
55. MECW, Volume 42, 514.
56. MECW, Volume 35, 195.
57. Ibid., 195.
58. Ibid., 510.
59. Marx differed with the economist Adam Smith, who said that capital commanded, or controlled, labor. Marx believed that capital commanded *unpaid* labor. MECW, Volume 35, 219, 534.
60. Ibid., 158–159.
61. Ibid., 162–164.
62. Ibid., 534.
63. Ibid., 570–571.
64. Ibid., 531.
65. Ibid., 202.
66. Ibid., 626.
67. Berlin, *Karl Marx,* 176.
68. MECW, Volume 35, 471, 87, 183.
69. Ibid., 241.
70. Ibid., 271.
71. Ibid., 336.
72. Ibid., 306–307.
73. Ibid., 750.
74. Ibid., 751.
75. MECW, Volume 42, 578–579.

Chapter Thirty-three: London, 1868

1. Lafargue, *Karl Marx,* 14.
2. MECW, Volume 42, 519.
3. Ibid., 535.
4. Ibid., 538.
5. Ibid., 517.
6. MECW, Volume 43, 25. (By way of comparison, Charles Dickens earned £33,000 in 1868 alone. Hobsbawm, *Age of Capital,* 332.)

7. MECW, Volume 42, 579.
8. Jenny Marx to Ernestine Liebknecht, Oct. 14, 1867, Moscow.
9. MECW, Volume 42, 529.
10. Padover, *Karl Marx,* 195.
11. Morton, *Home Rule,* 1, 3, 5; Wilson, *Victorians,* 77, 79, 80, 83; Hobsbawm, *Age of Revolution,* 201–202.
12. MECW, Volume 21, 190, 192 and Volume 42, 486.
13. Paul Rose, *The Manchester Martyrs,* 16.
14. Ibid., 13.
15. Ibid., 17–19.
16. Jenkins, *Engels in Manchester,* 18; REM, 88.
17. Rose, *Manchester Martyrs,* 28; Annie Besant, *An Autobiography,* 73–74.
18. Mayer, *Friedrich Engels,* 202; REM, 88; Rose, *Manchester Martyrs,* 75.
19. Rose, *Manchester Martyrs,* 38, 42; Besant, *Autobiography,* 75.
20. MECW, Volume 42, 501.
21. Ibid., 483.
22. Ibid., 431.
23. Ibid., 444.
24. Rose, *Manchester Martyrs,* 46; Besant, *Autobiography,* 75–76.
25. Rose, *Manchester Martyrs,* 67.
26. MECW, Volume 42, 460 and Volume 21, 121.
27. Rose, *Manchester Martyrs,* 70.
28. Ibid., 11; MECW, Volume 42, 484; Morton, *Home Rule,* 19.
29. Morton, *Home Rule,* 19.
30. MECW, Volume 42, 474.
31. O'Neill, *Good Old Days,* 225; Winder, *Bloody Foreigners,* 205.
32. MECW, Volume 42, 505–506.
33. Ibid., 479.
34. Meier, Perrot, and Trebitsch (eds.), *Daughters,* 42–43.
35. MECW, Volume 42, 483, 492, 666(n).
36. Ibid., 501–502.
37. Ibid., 503.
38. Ibid., 542, 553.
39. Flanders, *Victorian House,* 197; MECW, Volume 42, 72.
40. MECW, Volume 42, 538.
41. Ibid., 542, 548. (Eleanor Marx wrote in a letter to an unidentified "comrade" that after Lion Philips's death "the cousins became too respectable, too frightened" to continue their association with the Marxes. October 1, 1893, Moscow.)
42. MECW, Volume 42, 551.
43. Ibid., 554.
44. FE-PL, Volume I, 20.
45. Ibid., 22, 23.
46. MECW, Volume 42, 316.
47. Ibid., 547, 556, 557.
48. Padover, *Karl Marx,* 284.
49. Derfler, *Founding of French Marxism,* 58.
50. Meier, Perrot, and Trebitsch (eds.), *Daughters,* 32.
51. Jenny Marx (daughter) to Laura Lafargue, Apr. 7, 1868, Moscow.
52. MECW, Volume 43, 9–10.
53. Ibid., 25.
54. Ibid., 28.
55. Eleanor Marx, notebook, IISG.
56. Eleanor Marx to Lion Philips, undated (1863), Moscow.

57. MECW, Volume 42, 513, 525.
58. Lafargue, *Karl Marx,* 29.
59. O'Neill, *Good Old Days,* 225; Wilson, *Victorians,* 338.
60. Eleanor Marx to Lizzy Burns, Feb. 14, 1868, Moscow.
61. Jenny Marx (daughter) to Eleanor Marx, June 1868, Moscow.
62. MECW, Volume 43, 44.
63. Ibid., 50.
64. Ibid., 75.
65. Ibid., 72.
66. Jenny Marx (daughter) to Laura Lafargue, Dec. 24, 1868; MECW, Volume 43, 171. (Being a governess in nineteenth-century England was considered a respectable occupation for a middle-class woman in need of independent income, but she was treated by her employers as a servant. Pool, *What Jane Austen Ate,* 224.)
67. MECW, Volume 43, 171.
68. Ibid., 213.
69. Ibid., 199.
70. Jenny Marx (daughter) to Laura Lafargue, Jan. 7, 1869, Moscow.
71. Ibid.
72. MECW, Volume 43, 594(n).
73. Ibid., 130–131.
74. Ibid., 169–170.
75. Ibid., 214.
76. Olsen, *Growth of Victorian London,* 237; Cole and Postgate, *British Common People,* 354.
77. MECW, Volume 43, 171–172.

Chapter Thirty-four: London, 1869
1. Charles Prolès, *Gustave Flourens,* 92.
2. MECW, Volume 20, 478(n); Nicolaievsky and Maenchen-Helfen, *Karl Marx,* 283–284.
3. Nicolaievsky and Maenchen-Helfen, *Karl Marx,* 285.
4. Ibid., 286.
5. Mehring, *Karl Marx,* 394.
6. McLellan, *Karl Marx,* 360; MECW, Volume 44, 291.
7. MECW, Volume 43, 8.
8. Mehring, *Karl Marx,* 392.
9. MECW, Volume 42, 515, 520, 669(n); Mehring, *Karl Marx,* 393.
10. MECW, Volume 42, 520.
11. MECW, Volume 43, 173–174.
12. Derfler, *Founding of French Marxism,* 61.
13. MECW, Volume 43, 155.
14. Meier, Perrot, and Trebitsch (eds.), *Daughters,* 33–34.
15. Laura Lafargue to Karl Marx, Nov. 2, 1868, Moscow.
16. MECW, Volume 42, 178.
17. Derfler, *Founding of French Marxism,* 61.
18. Meier, Perrot, and Trebitsch (eds.), *Daughters,* 38.
19. MECW, Volume 43, 216.
20. Ibid., 243.
21. Ibid., 216.
22. Ibid., 225.
23. Ibid., 229.
24. Ibid., 214.
25. Meier, Perrot, and Trebitsch (eds.), *Daughters,* 37.
26. MECW, Volume 43, 217, 608(n).
27. Ibid., 287–288.

28. Ibid., 290.
29. Derfler, *Founding of French Marxism*, 66.
30. MECW, Volume 43, 243.
31. Ibid.
32. Thomas, *Women Incendiaries*, 34.
33. Meier, Perrot, and Trebitsch (eds.), *Daughters*, 63; Thomas, *Women Incendiaries*, 28.
34. Meier, Perrot, and Trebitsch (eds.), *Daughters*, 70.
35. Thomas, *Women Incendiaries*, 27.
36. Meier, Perrot, and Trebitsch (eds.), *Daughters*, 37.
37. Ibid., 46.
38. MECW, Volume 43, 262.
39. Meier, Perrot, and Trebitsch (eds.), *Daughters*, 38.
40. *Contemporary Review,* London, No. 6, June 1868, 317.
41. Karl Marx, Jenny Marx, and Friedrich Engels, *Lettres à Kugelmann*, 186–187.
42. MECW, Volume 43, 410, 528.
43. Meier, Perrot, and Trebitsch (eds.), *Daughters*, 40.
44. MECW, Volume 43, 270.
45. Ibid., 275.
46. Jenny Marx (daughter) to Jenny Marx, May 1869, Moscow; MECW, Volume 21, 48, 466(n).
47. MECW, Volume 43, 297; 618–619(n). (The upper ten thousand referred to the aristocracy and the literary and political classes. Wilson, *Victorians,* 274.)
48. MECW, Volume 43, 310, 623(n).
49. Ibid., 620(n).
50. Marx and Jennychen traveled to Germany together in September and returned before October 12. They stayed with the Kugelmanns in Hanover, and then Marx met with political associates. MECW, Volume 43, 353.
51. Meier, Perrot, and Trebitsch (eds.), *Daughters*, 49; Eleanor Marx Aveling to Karl Kautsky, Mar. 15, 1898, Moscow.
52. MECW, Volume 43, 295, 308.
53. Ibid., 303.
54. Jenkins, *Engels in Manchester*, 10; REM, 186.
55. MECW, Volume 43, 299.
56. Carver, *Friedrich Engels,* 141; Hunt, *Frock-Coated Communist,* 240.
57. MECW, Volume 43, 302–303.
58. MECW, Volume 43, 311; Mayer, *Friedrich Engels,* 253.
59. Meier, Perrot, and Trebitsch (eds.), *Daughters,* 51–52; Eleanor Marx to Jenny Marx (daughter), July 1969, Moscow.
60. MECW, Volume 43, 356–357.
61. Jeremiah O'Donovan Rossa, *My Years in English Jails,* 8–9, 30.
62. MECW, Volume 21, 101.
63. Bert Andreas (ed.), *Briefe und Dokumente de Familie Marx,* 131.
64. MECW, Volume 43, 546.
65. Ibid., 366.
66. Ibid., 365.
67. Morton, *Home Rule,* 13.
68. O'Donovan Rossa, *My Years,* 214.
69. MECW, Volume 43, 387.
70. Andreas, *Briefe und Dokumente,* 205.
71. MECW, Volume 43, 449.
72. Ibid., 640(n); Meier, Perrot, and Trebitsch (eds.), *Daughters,* 64(n).
73. Derfler, *Founding of French Marxism,* 65; David Wetzel, *A Duel of Giants,* 44.

74. Washburne, *Recollections,* 3.
75. Derfler, *Founding of French Marxism,* 75.
76. Washburne, *Recollections,* 7.
77. MECW, Volume 43, 419; Thomas, *Women Incendiaries,* 34.
78. Thomas, *Women Incendiaries,* 34.
79. Meier, Perrot, and Trebitsch (eds.), *Daughters,* 60–61.
80. MECW, Volume 43, 314–316.
81. Ibid., 644(n).
82. Ibid., 431.
83. Prolès, *Gustave Flourens,* 51.
84. Meier, Perrot, and Trebitsch (eds.), *Daughters,* 65–66.
85. MECW, Volume 43, 440.
86. Ibid., 646(n).
87. MECW, Volume 21, 101–102.
88. MECW, Volume 43, 444–445.
89. Charles Habeneck to Jenny Marx (daughter), 1870, Moscow.
90. Jennychen published eight articles in *La Marseillaise* from March 1 to April 24, 1870. MECW, Volume 21, 414–416 and Volume 43, 646(n).
91. O'Donovan Rossa, *My Years,* 98; MECW, Volume 21, 417–418.
92. MECW, Volume 43, 497; Marx, Marx, and Engels, *Lettres à Kugelmann,* 192.
93. O'Donovan Rossa, *My Years,* 198; MECW, Volume 21, 417–418.
94. MECW, Volume 43, 454–455.
95. MECW, Volume 21, 420.
96. MECW, Volume 43, 458.
97. Ibid., 461, 649(n); O'Donovan Rossa, *My Years,* 218.
98. MECW, Volume 43, 461.
99. Ibid., 458.
100. Ibid., 466.
101. Ibid., 423, 559.
102. Ibid., 559.
103. Because of the wording, a vote against extending Napoleon III's powers as emperor would also be a vote against democratic reforms supported by legislators, while a vote in favor of granting Napoleon new powers would be seen as a vindication of his rule and help shore up his flagging support. Washburne, *Recollections,* 26; MECW, Volume 43, 653(n), 656(n).
104. MECW, Volume 22, 3 and Volume 43, 522.
105. MECW, Volume 43, 656(n).
106. Ibid., 444.
107. Meier, Perrot, and Trebitsch (eds.), *Daughters,* 65.
108. MECW, Volume 43, 446.
109. Meier, Perrot, and Trebitsch (eds.), *Daughters,* 66.
110. MECW, Volume 43, 486.
111. Ibid., 556–557.
112. Derfler, *Founding of French Marxism,* 62.
113. MECW, Volume 43, 497.
114. Andreas, *Briefe und Dokumente,* 217.
115. MECW, Volume 43, 504–505.
116. Prolès, *Gustave Flourens,* 52.
117. MECW, Volume 44, 558.
118. MECW, Volume 43, 495.
119. Ibid., 442, 514.
120. Jenny Marx to Friedrich Engels, July 12, 1870, Moscow.

Chapter Thirty-five: Paris, Fall 1870

1. MECW, Volume 49, 35.
2. Washburne, *Recollections*, 26; Wetzel, *Duel of Giants*, 31, 37–38, 96, 110; Taylor, *Struggle for Mastery of Europe*, 203–204; Ozment, *Mighty Fortress*, 210.
3. Washburne, *Recollections*, 33–34.
4. Ibid., 55.
5. Andreas, *Briefe und Dokumente*, 224.
6. MECW, Volume 44, 591(n).
7. The Social Democratic Workers' Party was formed in August 1869 after breaking away from the General Union. Williamson, *Bismarck and Germany*, 48.
8. MECW, Volume 44, 3–4.
9. MECW, Volume 22, 4.
10. Ibid., 6.
11. Ibid., 3–7.
12. MECW, Volume 44, 40, 598 (n).
13. Ibid., 7, 35, 593(n).
14. Ibid., 32, 58.
15. Jennychen said she nicknamed Engels General Staff because of his military writing and because *Le Figaro* mistakenly spoke of the "general staff" as if the phrase described an individual. Andreas, *Briefe und Dokumente*, 229.
16. Washburne, *Recollections*, 54–55.
17. Ibid., 59–60.
18. MECW, Volume 44, 64–65, 71.
19. Prosper Lissagaray, *History of the Commune of 1871*, 1.
20. Washburne, *Recollections*, 65.
21. Meier, Perrot, and Trebitsch (eds.), *Daughters*, 69, 72, 74–75, 77.
22. MECW, Volume 44, 59.
23. Ibid., 65.
24. Washburne, *Recollections*, 100.
25. Ibid., 105–106; W. H. C. Smith, *Second Empire*, 56–57.
26. Washburne, *Recollections*, 108.
27. Ibid., 111.
28. Ibid., 126.
29. Ibid., 131.
30. Ibid., 109.
31. Ibid., 131.
32. Charles Longuet to Karl Marx, Sept. 5, 1870, Moscow.
33. MECW, Volume 44, 64–65.
34. Meier, Perrot, and Trebitsch (eds.), *Daughters*, 78–79.
35. Washburne, *Recollections*, 140–141.
36. Ibid., 133.
37. MECW, Volume 44, 560.
38. Robert Gildea, *The Third Republic*, 3.
39. Lissagaray, *History of the Commune*, 20; W. H. C. Smith, *Second Empire*, 57.
40. Lissagaray, *History of the Commune*, 21.
41. Washburne, *Recollections*, 208–209; Lissagaray, *History of the Commune*, 22.
42. Washburne, *Recollections*, 210; Lissagaray, *History of the Commune*, 23.
43. Washburne, *Recollections*, 212; Lissagaray, *History of the Commune*, 25.
44. Lissagaray, *History of the Commune*, 32.
45. Washburne, *Recollections*, 201.
46. REM, 186.
47. Among the young Russians arriving at Modena Villas was Herman Lopatin, the twenty-five-year-old son of an impoverished nobleman, who had fled to France and

then on to England after escaping prison in the Caucasus. He sought out Marx to convey a message of admiration from Russian youth. Next came nineteen-year-old Elizabeth Dmitrieff, who had left Russia for Switzerland. She became Elizabeth Tomanovskaya through marriage and was part of the IWMA in Geneva. Members sent her to London in the summer of 1870 to deliver a message to Marx. She was adopted by the family and became part of Marx's network of couriers to France. MECW, Volume 42, 530; Thomas, *Women Incendiaries*, 72–74; Carr, *Michael Bakunin*, 446.

48. Lafargue, *Karl Marx*, 17.
49. MECW, Volume 44, 105.
50. Marx, Marx, and Engels, *Lettres à Kugelmann*, 171; MECW, Volume 43, 548.
51. MECW, Volume 44, 81,102.
52. REM, 90; Lafargue, *Karl Marx*, 31.
53. Andreas, *Briefe und Dokumente*, 229.
54. Paul Lafargue to Karl Marx, late 1870, IISG.
55. Meier, Perrot, and Trebitsch (eds.), *Daughters*, 80–82.
56. Washburne, *Recollections*, 175, 267.
57. Meier, Perrot, and Trebitsch (eds.), *Daughters*, 82.
58. Washburne, *Recollections*, 235, 244, 271, 274.
59. Lissagaray, *History of the Commune*, 31.
60. Washburne, *Recollections*, 271.
61. MECW, Volume 44, 108.
62. MECW, Volume 22, 274 and Volume 44, 595(n), 606(n).
63. MECW, Volume 44, 97.
64. Ibid., 95–96.
65. O'Donovan Rossa, *My Years*, 227; Jenny Marx (daughter) to Kugelmann, Jan. 27, 1871, Moscow.
66. O'Donovan Rossa, *My Years*, 227.
67. Ibid., 237–238.
68. Washburne, *Recollections*, 290.
69. Alistair Horne, *The Terrible Year*, 53.
70. Lissagaray, *History of the Commune*, 33.
71. Part of Bismarck's aim in going to war with France was to prove Prussia's military superiority and by extension its natural dominance among the states of the German Confederation. His troops succeeded brilliantly. Their advanced weaponry and magnificent organization made quick work of the French army. The majority in the parliaments of the northern and southern German states agreed that the Prussian king should become the emperor of the Second Reich. As for Prussia's place in Europe, its defeat of France and Wilhelm's ascension as emperor shifted the balance of military and political power on the Continent from Paris to Berlin. Prussia could ask what it wanted of France. Williamson, *Bismarck and Germany*, 41, 65; Taylor, *Struggle for Mastery of Europe*, 210.
72. Horne, *Terrible Year*, 59; Lissagaray, *History of the Commune*, 34–35.
73. Horne, *Terrible Year*, 60; Washburne, *Recollections*, 320–321.
74. Lissagaray, *History of the Commune*, 26, 36.
75. Ibid., 36.
76. Washburne, *Recollections*, 323.
77. Horne, *Terrible Year*, 61; Washburne, *Recollections*, 324; Lissagaray, *History of the Commune*, 37.
78. Lissagaray, *History of the Commune*, 38–39.
79. Horne, *Terrible Year*, 61; Washburne, *Recollections*, 325.
80. Washburne, *Recollections*, 327–328; Lissagaray, *History of the Commune*, 41.
81. Thomas, *Women Incendiaries*, 50.
82. Horne, *Terrible Year*, 66; Lissagaray, *History of the Commune*, 56–57.

Chapter Thirty-six: Paris, 1871

1. Thomas, *Women Incendiaries*, 128.
2. Ibid., 51; Lissagaray, *History of the Commune*, 66.
3. Lissagaray, *History of the Commune*, 70, 77; Horne, *Terrible Year*, 72.
4. Lissagaray, *History of the Commune*, 207–209.
5. Ibid., 72.
6. Ibid., 72–73.
7. Ibid., 74.
8. Prolès, *Gustave Flourens*, 81.
9. Lissagaray, *History of the Commune*, 74.
10. Thomas, *Women Incendiaries*, 52; Lissagaray, *History of the Commune*, 78–79.
11. MECW, Volume 22, 323; Lissagaray, *History of the Commune*, 80.
12. Thomas, *Women Incendiaries*, 54.
13. Lissagaray, *History of the Commune*, 81.
14. Ibid., 84.
15. Ibid., 128–129.
16. W. H. C. Smith, *Second Empire*, 63.
17. MECW, Volume 22, 157, 288.
18. Ibid., 289.
19. MECW, Volume 44, 130–131.
20. Lissagaray, *History of the Commune*, 164.
21. Prolès, *Gustave Flourens*, 85–87; Lissagaray, *History of the Commune*, 166.
22. Prolès, *Gustave Flourens*, 87–90.
23. Ibid., 90; MECW, Volume 22, 326; Lissagaray, *History of the Commune*, 166.
24. Lissagaray, *History of the Commune*, 167–168; Horne, *Terrible Year*, 95.
25. Lissagaray, *History of the Commune*, 169.
26. Ibid., 185.
27. Ibid., 191.
28. Prolès, *Gustave Flourens*, 91.
29. *The Daily Telegraph*, London, April 5, 1871, 4.
30. Jenny Marx to Kugelmann, May 12, 1871, Moscow; MECW, Volume 22, 326.
31. Marx, Marx, and Engels, *Lettres à Kugelmann*, 192; Andreas, *Briefe und Dokumente*, xvii.
32. MECW, Volume 44, 129.
33. Meier, Perrot, and Trebitsch (eds.), *Daughters*, 91–92.
34. Ibid., 87.
35. Ibid., 99.
36. Ibid., 98–99.
37. Marx, Marx, and Engels, *Lettres à Kugelmann*, 192.
38. Jenny Marx (daughter) to Laura Lafargue, Apr. 18, 1871, Moscow; Marx, Marx, and Engels, *Lettres á Kugelmann*, 192.
39. Derfler, *Founding of French Marxism*, 99; Marx, Marx, and Engels, *Lettres à Kugelmann*, 192.
40. Lissagaray, *History of the Commune*, 273.
41. Derfler, *Founding of French Marxism*, 103–106; Macé, *Paul et Laura Lafargue*, 56–57.
42. Jenny Marx (daughter) to Karl and Jenny Marx, May 4, 1871, Moscow; Jenny Marx to Kugelmann, May 12, 1871, Moscow; Jenny Marx (daughter) to Friedrich Engels, May 9, 1871, Moscow.
43. Marx, Marx, and Engels, *Lettres à Kugelmann*, 173.
44. For all his praise, Marx saw from the start that the communards had blundered by delaying an assault on Versailles and failing to seize the treasury. MECW, Volume 44, 131–132.
45. Lissagaray, *History of the Commune*, 295.

46. Horne, *Terrible Year,* 114–115; Lissagaray, *History of the Commune,* 290–291; *The Times,* London, May 17, 1871, 5.
47. Lissagaray, *History of the Commune,* 306.
48. Horne, *Terrible Year,* 121; Thomas, *Women Incendiaries,* 151; Lissagaray, *History of the Commune,* 312, 314.
49. Horne, *Terrible Year,* 121.
50. Ibid., 112; Lissagaray, *History of the Commune,* 298, 314.
51. Lissagaray, *History of the Commune,* 300, 324; Thomas, *Women Incendiaries,* x.
52. After the Commune, the basilica of Sacré-Coeur was built on Montmartre as a symbol of "hope" and "repentance." Horne, *Terrible Year,* 139; Lissagaray, *History of the Commune,* 329.
53. Horne, *Terrible Year,* 133; *The Times,* London, May 31, 1871, 9.
54. *The Eastern Post,* London, Apr. 20, 1872, 20.
55. Horne, *Terrible Year,* 129, 131; *The Evening Standard,* London, May 25, 1871, 1; *The Evening Standard,* London, May 26, 1871, 1; *The Standard,* London, May 29, 1871, 5.
56. Thomas, *Women Incendiaries,* 166.
57. Lissagaray, *History of the Commune,* 366.
58. Ibid., 383.
59. MECW, Volume 44, 143.
60. Ibid., 151.
61. Horne, *Terrible Year,* 126.
62. MECW, Volume 44, 151.
63. Ibid., 153.
64. Jenny Marx to Karl Marx, undated (Spring 1871), Moscow.
65. Ibid.
66. Horne, *Terrible Year,* 137; Lissagaray, *History of the Commune,* 384–385, 489.
67. Lissagaray, *History of the Commune,* 484.
68. Ibid., 491.
69. *The Evening Standard,* London, May 31, 1871, 1.
70. Ibid.
71. Lissagaray, *History of the Commune,* 390–391.
72. *The Standard,* London, June 2, 1871, 5.
73. Horne, *Terrible Year,* 139; W. H. C. Smith, *Second Empire,* 65; Lissagaray, *History of the Commune,* 395.
74. Lissagaray, *History of the Commune,* 397.
75. Horne, *Terrible Year,* 139; Lissagaray, *History of the Commune,* 458–459.
76. MECW, Volume 44, 159; McLellan, *Karl Marx,* 368; Berlin, *Karl Marx,* 189.
77. MECW, Volume 22, 336.
78. Ibid., 355.
79. McLellan, *Karl Marx,* 372.
80. Nicolaievsky and Maenchen-Helfen, *Karl Marx,* 333.
81. *Pall Mall Gazette,* London, May 1871, 2065.
82. *The New York World,* June 3, 1871, 1.
83. *Chicago Tribune,* June 5, 1871, 1.
84. *The Evening Standard,* London, June 23, 1871, 5.
85. Lissagaray, *History of the Commune,* 465.
86. McLellan, *Karl Marx,* 366.
87. MECW, Volume 23, 223.
88. MECW, Volume 44, 158, 680(n).
89. Ibid., 564; Derfler, *Founding of French Marxism,* 108.
90. French police archives indicate that some of Lafargue's letters to Marx from Luchon were intercepted by French authorities and contained enough information to raise alarms and warrant his arrest. It is not clear which letters these were or whether they

still exist, so it is impossible to say what they may have contained. In any case, there may have been no need for an excuse to arrest Lafargue beyond his activities in Bordeaux. MECW, Volume 44, 153–154, 617(n); Derfler, *Founding of French Marxism,* 108.

91. Jenny Marx (daughter) to Friedrich Engels, July 5, 1871, IISG.
92. Jenny Marx (daughter) to "doctor" [Ludwig Kugelmann], Oct. 3, 1871, Moscow.
93. MECW, Volume 24, 460–461; Derfler, *Founding of French Marxism,* 109.
94. Georg Eckert (ed.), *Wilhelm Liebknecht Briefwechsel,* 478.
95. Derfler, *Founding of French Marxism,* 109.

Chapter Thirty-seven: Bagnères-de-Luchon, France, Summer 1871
1. MECW, Volume 22, 632.
2. Eckert (ed.), *Wilhelm Liebknecht Briefwechsel,* 478; MECW, Volume 22, 623.
3. Jenny Marx (daughter) to Friedrich Engels, July 5, 1871, IISG.
4. Eckert (ed.), *Wilhelm Liebknecht Briefwechsel,* 478; MECW, Volume 22, 623.
5. Ibid.
6. MECW, Volume 24, 460–461.
7. There is no indication to whom Tussy's letter was addressed. Also, in a letter to Kugelmann written after she described their ordeal in *Woodhull & Claflin's Weekly,* Jennychen said she was found at Fos to be carrying a letter to O'Donovan Rossa, not a newspaper. Eckert (ed.), *Wilhelm Liebknecht Briefwechsel,* 478–479, 484; MECW, Volume 22, 623–625 and Volume 44, 564.
8. Eckert (ed.), *Wilhelm Liebknecht Briefwechsel,* 414.
9. Ibid., 479–480; MECW, Volume 22, 625.
10. MECW, Volume 24, 460–461.
11. Eckert (ed.), *Wilhelm Liebknecht Briefwechsel,* 480–482; MECW, Volume 22, 625–627.
12. Eckert (ed.), *Wilhelm Liebknecht Briefwechsel,* 482–483; MECW, Volume 22, 628–629.
13. McLellan, *Karl Marx,* 373; Derfler, *Founding of French Marxism,* 113.
14. Eckert (ed.), *Wilhelm Liebknecht Briefwechsel,* 483; MECW, Volume 22, 630.
15. Paul Lafargue to Karl Marx, Apr. 16, 1871, IISG.
16. Derfler, *Founding of French Marxism,* 113.
17. W. H. C. Smith, *Second Empire,* 70; *The Standard,* London, June 3, 1871, 5.
18. MECW, Volume 44, 154.
19. Porter, *Refugee Question,* 217.

Part Six: The Red Terrorist Doctor

Chapter Thirty-eight: London, 1871
1. Vladimir Lenin, *Collected Works, Volume 17,* 143.
2. Lissagaray, *History of the Commune,* 413–414, 420–421; Horne, *Terrible Year,* 139.
3. Derfler, *Founding of French Marxism,* 157, 158; REM, 29.
4. On March 21 Longuet and a friend wrote: "The workingmen, those who produce everything and enjoy nothing, are they then forever to be exposed to outrage? The bourgeoisie, which has accomplished its emancipation, does it not understand that now the time for emancipation of the proletariat has come? Why, then, does it persist in refusing the proletariat its legitimate share?" Lissagaray, *History of the Commune,* 109.
5. Longuet's doctor friend Dourlen took him to the town of Saint Jean de Dieu, and from there, with the aid of a priest, Longuet made it into Belgium. Longuet, *Karl Marx,* 221.
6. REM, 162.
7. Ibid., 82.
8. KMIR, 106.
9. Jenny Marx (daughter) to Kugelmann, Oct. 6, 1871, Moscow.
10. KMIR, 107.

11. *New York Herald,* Aug. 30, 1871.
12. *Chicago Tribune,* Dec. 18, 1871.
13. MECW, Volume 22, 600.
14. KMIR, 111; MECW, Volume 44, 213.
15. MECW, Volume 22, 398.
16. *Public Opinion,* London, Aug. 19, 1871, 229 and Aug. 26, 1871, 262; MECW, Volume 22, 393.
17. MECW, Volume 44, 176–177.
18. Ibid., 206–207.
19. Ibid., 207.
20. Bakunin's group was called the International Alliance of Socialist Democracy. Carr, *Michael Bakunin,* 345, 352.
21. Ibid., 396, 404–407.
22. Ibid., 446.
23. Berlin, *Karl Marx,* 190.
24. REM, 290; KMIR, 103–105.
25. REM, 170–171.
26. MECW, Volume 22, 423–431.
27. Ibid., 426–427.
28. Jenny Marx (daughter) to "doctor" [Ludwig Kugelmann], Oct. 3, 1871, Moscow; Robert Payne, *Karl Marx,* 429.
29. MECW, Volume 44, 186.
30. MECW, Volume 22, 633–634; McLellan, *Karl Marx,* 377.
31. MECW, Volume 44, 220.
32. Ibid., 229.
33. Ibid., 216.
34. Ibid., 229.
35. Jenny Marx (daughter) to "doctor" [Ludwig Kugelmann], Oct. 3, 1871, Moscow.
36. MECW, Volume 44, 617(n).
37. Ibid., 228–229.
38. REM, 299.
39. Hobsbawm, *Age of Capital,* 308.
40. Jenny Marx (daughter) to the Kugelmanns, Dec. 21, 1871, Moscow.
41. MECW, Volume 44, 562.
42. MECW, Volume 23, 635.
43. In the midst of the family's work on behalf of refugees, Marx learned that his own status in England was in jeopardy. A contact in the British Home Ministry said the government was readying a bill to expel communists and International members. Marx's report of what he'd heard was reprinted in an English newspaper. Jennychen observed that if the family was expelled, its only option would be to move to the land of "Yankee Doodle Dandy." Jenny Marx (daughter) to the Kugelmanns, Dec. 21, 1871, Moscow.
44. FE-PL, Volume I, 32.
45. Jenny Marx (daughter) to Charles Longuet, Friday evening (Feb. 1872), Moscow.
46. Charles Longuet to Jenny Marx (daughter), before Feb. 15, 1872, Moscow.
47. Jenny Marx (daughter) to Charles Longuet, Feb. 17, 1872, Moscow.
48. Jenny Marx to Wilhelm Liebknecht, May 26, 1872, Moscow.
49. FE-PL, Volume III, 403–405; MECW, Volume 44, 283; Derfler, *Founding of French Marxism,* 114–115.
50. MECW, Volume 44, 574.
51. J. Roy to Charles Longuet, Jan. 19, 1872, Moscow.
52. FE-PL, Volume I, 46.
53. KMIR, 91.
54. Longuet, *Karl Marx,* 207.

55. Jenny Marx to Wilhelm Liebknecht, May 26, 1872, Moscow.
56. MECW, Volume 44, 32.
57. Jenny Marx (daughter) to the Kugelmanns, May 3, 1872, Moscow.
58. MECW, Volume 44, 575.
59. Eckert (ed.), *Wilhelm Liebknecht Briefwechsel*, 413–415.
60. REM, 250.
61. The Hungarian jeweler Leo Frankel, a former communard, showered her with attention, as did French lithographer Jules Johannard, another communard and member of the General Council. Both men were at least ten years her senior. Kapp, *Eleanor Marx, Volume I*, 145.
62. Ibid., 155–156.
63. Ibid., 160.
64. Jenny Marx (daughter) to the Kugelmanns, Dec. 21, 1871, Moscow.
65. FE-PL, Volume I, 46.
66. Jenny Marx (daughter) to Kugelmann, Jan. 22, 1872, IISG; Derfler, *Founding of French Marxism*, 119.
67. Macé, *Paul et Laura Lafargue*, 63.
68. MECW, Volume 44, 581.
69. Ibid., 327.
70. Ibid., 347.
71. Marx, Marx and Engels, *Lettres à Kugelmann*, 214–215.
72. Ibid., 216–217.
73. Derfler, *Founding of French Marxism*, 142.
74. FE-PL, Volume III, 463.
75. Derfler, *Founding of French Marxism*, 138.
76. FE-PL, Volume III, 428–429.
77. Lafargue did however leave a mark on Spain: in July he and a colleague established the New Madrid Federation, the first Marxist party in Spain and the direct parent of today's Spanish Socialist Party. Derfler, *Founding of French Marxism*, 138–141.
78. FE-PL, Volume III, 471.

Chapter Thirty-nine: The Hague, Fall 1872
1. MECW, Volume 23, 256.
2. MECW, Volume 44, 386, 387.
3. Ibid., 346–347.
4. Ibid., 387.
5. Ibid., 100, 283, 607(n).
6. Ibid., 385.
7. Ibid., 390.
8. Ibid., 396.
9. Offord, *Nineteenth-Century Russia*, 68; Carr, *Michael Bakunin*, 453.
10. Offord, *Nineteenth-Century Russia*, 76.
11. Hobsbawm, *Age of Revolution*, 197.
12. Ibid., 198.
13. MECW, Volume 44, 399.
14. McLellan, *Karl Marx*, 395.
15. MECW, Volume 44, 400.
16. Hobsbawm, *Age of Capital*, 308; MECW, Volume 44, 438.
17. McLellan, *Karl Marx*, 394.
18. MECW, Volume 44, 385.
19. Jenny Marx to Wilhelm Liebknecht, May 26, 1872, Moscow.
20. Carr, *Michael Bakunin*, 375–376; Offord, *Nineteenth-Century Russia*, 64.
21. Nicolaievsky and Maenchen-Helfen, *Karl Marx*, 347.

22. Ibid., 349; MECW, Volume 43, 595(n). Bakunin was apparently to have been involved in the translation of *Capital* undertaken by Nikolai Danielson, Nikolai Lyubavin, and Hermann Lopatin.

23. Nicolaievsky and Maenchen–Helfen. 350–351.

24. Fyodor Dostoevsky incorporated this crime into his novel *Demons*. Offord, *Nineteenth-Century Russia*, 64.

25. MECW, Volume 44, 398.

26. Nicolaievsky and Maenchen-Helfen, *Karl Marx*, 294.

27. REM, 163.

28. Nicolaievsky and Maenchen-Helfen, *Karl Marx*, 358.

29. MECW, Volume 44, 426.

30. Nicolaievsky and Maenchen-Helfen, *Karl Marx*, 359.

31. Nicolaievsky and Maenchen-Helfen, *Karl Marx*, 360; Padover, *Karl Marx*, 244; REM, 208.

32. MECW, Volume 44, 438–439.

33. KMIR, 90.

34. Ibid., 91.

35. Ibid., 113; FE-PL, Volume III, 473.

36. Nicolaievsky and Maenchen-Helfen, *Karl Marx*, 360–361.

37. Ibid 361; KMIR, 159.

38. MECW, Volume 44, 516.

39. REM, 210.

40. Bakunin's most notable International follower, James Guillaume, was also expelled. MECW, Volume 23, 249.

41. Padover, *Karl Marx*, 245.

42. Ibid., 246; REM, 212.

43. Marx's comments are based on three press reports, from *La Liberté, Der Volksstaat,* and *La Emancipation,* which the editors of MECW checked against one another for accuracy and consistency. MECW, Volume 23, 254–256.

44. Carr, *Michael Bakunin*, 430.

45. Ibid., 418.

46. Offord, *Nineteenth-Century Russia*, 65.

47. Carr, *Michael Bakunin*, 325, 353–354, 372.

48. Ibid., 456–457.

49. Ibid., 459, 461.

50. Ibid., 408.

51. Retirement had not suited Bakunin well. In 1874 he had gone to Bologna to take part in a (failed) bomb plot. Wearing dark glasses and dressed as a priest, he escaped. This would be the Russian giant's last revolt. Bakunin died in 1876. Carr, *Michael Bakunin*, 461, 478.

52. Jenny Marx–Charles Longuet Certificate of Marriage, Moscow.

53. Jenny Longuet to the Kugelmanns, Dec. 23, 1872, Moscow.

54. Jenny Longuet to Karl Marx, Oct. 30, 1872, Moscow.

55. Jenny Longuet to Karl Marx, undated (likely Fall 1872), Moscow.

56. MECW, Volume 44, 450.

57. Jenny Longuet to the Kugelmanns, Dec. 23, 1872, Moscow; Jenny Marx to Johann Philip Becker, Nov. 7, 1872, Moscow.

58. MECW, Volume 44, 455.

59. Meier, Perrot, and Trebitsch (eds.), *Daughters,* 113–114.

60. Jenny Longuet to Charles Longuet, Mar. 1873, Moscow.

61. Macé, *Paul et Laura Lafargue,* 68.

62. MECW, Volume 44, 457.

63. Ibid., 472, 517; Derfler, *Founding of French Marxism,* 153.

64. MECW, Volume 44, 527.

65. Ibid., 544, 676(n) and Volume 45, 456; Jenny Marx to Madame Longuet, Oct. 1874, Moscow; McLellan, *Karl Marx,* 389.
66. MECW, Volume 45, 468.
67. Derfler, *Founding of French Marxism,* 154.
68. Jenny Marx to Wilhelm Liebknecht, July 1873, Moscow.
69. Jenny Marx to Eleanor Marx, May 1873, Moscow; Marx, Marx, and Engels, *Lettres à Kugelmann,* 224–225.
70. Jenny Marx to Wilhelm Liebknecht, July 1873, Moscow.
71. MECW, Volume 45, 457(n), 460(n) and Volume 44, 607(n).
72. REM, 76; Berlin, *Karl Marx,* 213.
73. Jenny Longuet to Karl Marx, Apr. 24, 1874, Moscow.
74. REM, 76.
75. Jenny Marx to Eleanor Marx, May 1873, Moscow; Jenny Marx to Eleanor Marx, June 1873, Moscow.
76. Jenny Marx to Eleanor Marx, May 1873, Moscow.
77. Kapp, *Eleanor Marx, Volume I,* 146.
78. Eleanor Marx to Karl Marx, May 3, 1873, Moscow.
79. Jenny Marx to Wilhelm Liebknecht, July 1873, Moscow.
80. Kapp, *Eleanor Marx, Volume I,* 150.
81. MECW, Volume 44, 496. (One of the great tragedies of the Marx story is that after Marx's death Tussy and Laura burned letters they thought might offend a friend—Engels in particular—or which for their own reasons they did not want to become part of the Marx family record. Eleanor Marx to Laura Lafargue, Mar. 26, 1883, Moscow; B. Nicolaievsky, "Toward a History of the Communist League," 239.)
82. MECW, Volume 44, 506.
83. Jenny Marx to Eleanor Marx, June 1873, Moscow.
84. Kapp, *Eleanor Marx, Volume I,* 152.
85. Jenny Marx to Wilhelm Liebknecht, July 1873, Moscow.
86. Charles Longuet to Jenny Longuet, Friday morning, undated, Moscow.
87. Jenny Marx to Eleanor Marx, June 1873, Moscow.
88. Jenny Marx to Wilhelm Liebknecht, July 1873, Moscow.
89. MECW, Volume 44, 516.
90. Jenny Marx to Wilhelm Liebknecht, July 1873, Moscow.
91. MECW, Volume 44, 516.
92. Ibid., 538.
93. Ibid., 550.
94. MECW, Volume 45, 3.
95. Walt Contreras Sheasby, "Marx at Karlsbad," 91–97.
96. Taylor, *Struggle for Mastery of Europe,* 219; Hobsbawm, *Age of Capital,* 201.
97. In Germany, for example, Liebknecht and Bebel were sentenced to two years in prison in 1872 for their political activism and for belonging to the IWMA. MECW, Volume 45, 466(n).
98. Williamson, *Bismarck and Germany,* 48; Hobsbawm, *Age of Capital,* 62.
99. Offord, *Nineteenth-Century Russia,* 77; MECW, Volume 45, 461(n).
100. MECW, Volume 45, 33, 35.
101. MECW, Volume 24, 564.
102. Paul Lafargue to Karl Marx, July 26, 1874, IISG; Derfler, *Founding of French Marxism,* 155; FE-PL, Volume I, 48–49. (Between 1874 and 1878 Lafargue wrote at least twenty-eight letters to Engels asking for money.)
103. MECW, Volume 45, 21–22; Briggs and Callow, *Marx in London,* 71; A. E. Laurence and A. N. Insole, *Prometheus Bound,* 4.
104. REM, 254.
105. KMIR, 130.

106. MECW, Volume 45, 26, 29.
107. Ibid., 28.
108. Ibid., 27.
109. Ibid.
110. Jenny Longuet to Charles Longuet, Aug. 1874, Moscow.
111. MECW, Volume 45, 36.
112. Kapp, *Eleanor Marx, Volume I,* 153–154.
113. Jenny Marx to Madame Longuet, Oct. 1874, Moscow.
114. MECW, Volume 45, 34.
115. Ibid., 35.
116. Sheasby, "Marx at Karlsbad," 91–97.
117. Egon Erwin Kisch, *Karl Marx at Karlsbad,* 5–46.
118. MECW, Volume 45, 37.
119. KMIR, 93.
120. Meier, Perrot, and Trebitsch (eds.), *Daughters,* 118.
121. The report on the count may have confused him with Turgenev, who was also resident at Karlsbad. Turgenev was not the "chief of the nihilists" but is believed to have
   coined the phrase during his Berlin days, in the 1840s. MECW, Volume 45, 37.
122. REM, 284–285; KMIR, 91.
123. Eleanor Marx to Jenny Longuet, Sept. 5, 1874, Moscow; MECW, Volume 45, 46.
124. MECW, Volume 45, 52–53.
125. KMIR, 121.
126. Ibid., 165.

Chapter Forty: London, 1875
1. MECW, Volume 45, 31.
2. Jenny Longuet to Charles Longuet, mid-Aug. 1874, Moscow; Jenny Longuet to
   Charles Longuet, Aug. 8, 1874, Moscow; Jenny Longuet to Charles Longuet, Aug.
   28, 1874, Moscow.
3. Jenny Longuet to Charles Longuet, Aug. 1874, Moscow.
4. MECW, Volume 45, 38.
5. Jenny Longuet to Charles Longuet, Aug. 10, 1874, Moscow; Jenny Longuet to
   Charles Longuet, mid-Aug. 1874, Moscow.
6. Jenny Longuet to Charles Longuet, Aug. 28, 1874, Moscow.
7. Jenny Longuet to Charles Longuet, mid-Aug. 1874, Moscow.
8. Jenny Longuet to Charles Longuet, Sept. 1, 1874, Moscow.
9. Jenny Marx to Madame Longuet, Oct. 1874, Moscow.
10. KMIR, 130.
11. Jenny Marx to Wilhelm Liebknecht, May 26, 1872, Moscow.
12. MECW, Volume 45, 446.
13. Jenny Longuet to Madame Longuet, Dec. 25, 1874, Moscow.
14. Longuet, *Karl Marx,* 224.
15. Jenny Longuet to Madame Longuet, Dec. 25, 1874, Moscow.
16. Jenny Longuet to Madame Longuet, July 27 [1875], Moscow.
17. MECW, Volume 45, 75; Jenny Marx to Madame Longuet, June 1875, Moscow.
18. Jenny Marx to Madame Longuet, June 1875, Moscow; MECW, Volume 45, 66.
19. Eckert (ed.), *Wilhelm Liebknecht Briefwechsel,* 414.
20. Ibid., 421.
21. Ralph Miliband and John Saville (eds.), *The Socialist Register,* 183–184.
22. Gildea, *Third Republic,* 7–8.
23. MECW, Volume 45, 60–66.
24. Ibid., 63.
25. Ibid., 69.

26. Ibid., 467(n).
27. MECW, Volume 24, 89–90.
28. Ibid., 87.
29. Ibid., 94–95.
30. Ibid., 95.
31. Ibid., 99.
32. Padover, *Karl Marx,* 219.
33. "Though Marx has lived much in England and though he has written voluminously and forcibly in our language—though the illustrations and the main proofs of his chief work are drawn from English experience—he is here almost the shadow of a name. People may do him the honor of abusing him; read him they do not....He has a style of his own....A word will describe it: he abuses everybody, or at least everybody that is deemed by the world an authority; abuses in downright uncompromising fashion.... You encounter expressions oftener heard in a street corner discussion than in a philosophical debate." John Macdonnell, "Karl Marx and German Socialism," 384.
34. Jenny Marx to Eleanor Marx, Sept. 1875, Moscow.
35. Jenny Longuet to Eleanor Marx, Aug. 1875, Moscow.
36. MECW, Volume 45, 84–85.
37. Ibid., 82.
38. Kisch, *Karl Marx at Karlsbad,* 20.
39. KMIR, 124–125.
40. Blumenberg, *Illustrated,* 152.
41. MECW, Volume 45, 518.
42. REM, 298–299.
43. Jenny Marx to Natalie Liebknecht, Jan. 18, 1876, Moscow.
44. Jenny Longuet to Madame Longuet, Dec. 31, 1875, Moscow.
45. MECW, Volume 45, 96.
46. Ibid., 56.
47. REM, 217; Jenny Longuet to Eleanor Marx, Nov. 28, 1873, Moscow.
48. Jenny Longuet to Charles Longuet, Apr. 5, 1876, Moscow.
49. MECW, Volume 45, 120–121.
50. Jenny Marx to Madame Longuet, June 1875, Moscow.
51. Jenny Longuet to Madame Longuet, Dec. 31, 1875, Moscow.
52. Jenny Marx to Natalie Liebknecht, Jan. 18, 1876, Moscow.
53. MECW, Volume 45, 135–137.
54. He told Jennychen the question on everyone's lips was, " 'What do you think of Wagner?' It is highly typical of this latter-day Prusso-German imperial court musician that he, plus wife (the one who was divorced from Bülow), plus the cuckolded Bülow, plus their mutual father-in-law Liszt, should all four be living together harmoniously in Bayreuth, cuddling, kissing and adoring one another, and generally enjoying themselves." MECW, Volume 45, 143.
55. MECW, Volume 45, 149–150, 152.
56. Ibid., 444.
57. Tsuzuki, *Eleanor Marx,* 57; MECW, Volume 45, 191, 446; Hudson, *Munby,* 123.
58. MECW, Volume 45, 191.
59. Ibid., 446.
60. McLellan, *Karl Marx,* 407.
61. MECW, Volume 45, 122–123.
62. MECW, Volume 25, 27 and Volume 24, 195.
63. Draper and Haberkern, *Karl Marx's Theory of Revolution, Volume V,* 115.
64. MECW, Volume 25, 154.
65. MECW, Volume 45, 442.

Chapter Forty-one: London, 1880

1. Madame de Staël, *Delphine,* 304.
2. Just as Marx had been concerned for his own daughters, Engels had to prepare Pumps for something more than the proletarian life she was born to. In 1875 Engels and Lizzy had taken her to Germany, where she was entrusted to a chemist and his wife for a year and a half of "finishing" school. Jenny Longuet to Eleanor Marx, Sept. 1, 1874, Moscow; MECW, Volume 45, 104, 106.
3. MECW, Volume 45, 244.
4. Ibid., 274.
5. Ibid., 245.
6. Ibid., 267–268.
7. KMIR, 98.
8. Jenny Marx to Eleanor Marx, Nov. 20, 1877, Moscow.
9. MECW, Volume 45, 320.
10. Ibid., 447.
11. KMIR, 162.
12. Williamson, *Bismarck and Germany,* 55; Ozment, *Mighty Fortress,* 219.
13. Williamson, *Bismarck and Germany,* 58.
14. MECW, Volume 45, 312.
15. Jenny Longuet to Charles Longuet, Sept. 1878, Moscow; Jenny Marx to Eleanor Marx, Aug. 1878, Moscow.
16. Jenny Longuet to Charles Longuet, Sept. 14, 1878, Moscow.
17. MECW, Volume 45, 447.
18. Jenny Longuet to Charles Longuet, Sept. 14, 1878, Moscow.
19. MECW, Volume 45, 320; Hunt, *Frock-Coated Communist,* 271.
20. Jenny Longuet to Charles Longuet, mid-Sept. 1878, Moscow.
21. Jenny Longuet to Charles Longuet, Sept. 19, 1878, Moscow.
22. MECW, Volume 45, 361–362.
23. KMIR, 128.
24. MECW, Volume 45, 343.
25. Ibid., 354–356.
26. Ibid., 369.
27. Ibid., 371–372.
28. Ibid., 376.
29. Ibid., 373.
30. Ibid., 388.
31. MECW, Volume 24, 669(n); KMIR, 140.
32. MECW, Volume 24, 580–582; KMIR, 140–142.
33. Liebknecht, *Karl Marx,* 110; KMIR, 97.
34. Marx biographers generally say that Freddy's name did not appear in family correspondence until 1882, but a letter discovered in the Moscow archives mentions him two years earlier. The significance of the earlier date is that Jenny Marx was still alive and so aware of Freddy's presence in her daughters' lives. The reason Freddy repeatedly asked Longuet for repayment of money in later years has also been the source of much speculation. This letter explains the circumstances—Jennychen was in the habit of borrowing money from Lenchen and Freddy. Jenny Longuet to Charles Longuet, Oct. 24, 1880, Moscow; Jenny Longuet to Charles Longuet, Nov. 17, 1880, Moscow.
35. Ernest Belfort Bax, *Reminiscences and Reflections of a Mid and Late Victorian,* 70–71.
36. KMIR, 158–159
37. Ibid., 151.
38. Wilson, *Victorians,* 444.
39. KMIR, 144, 150.

40. MECW, Volume 46, 102–103.
41. Kapp, *Eleanor Marx, Volume I,* 211.
42. Jenny Marx to Eleanor Marx, Aug. 1878, Moscow.
43. Jenny Longuet to Charles Longuet, late Sept. 1880, Moscow.
44. FE-PL, Volume I, 63–64.
45. MECW, Volume 46, 32; Derfler, *Founding of French Marxism,* 154.
46. Longuet, *Karl Marx,* 228.
47. MECW, Volume 46, 95, 101.
48. MECW, Volume 45, 390.
49. Jenny Longuet to Charles Longuet, Aug. 1, 1880, Moscow.
50. MECW, Volume 46, 22–23 and Volume 24, 584–585.
51. Derfler, *Founding of French Marxism,* 177, 183.
52. MECW, Volume 24, 585.
53. Charles Longuet to Jenny Longuet, Aug. 24, 1880, Moscow.
54. Jenny Longuet to Charles Longuet, Sept. 29, 1880, Moscow.
55. Liebknecht, *Karl Marx,* 114; Jenny Longuet to Charles Longuet, Sept. 29, 1880, Moscow.
56. Bernstein, *My Years of Exile,* 150.
57. Bax, *Reminiscences,* 48.
58. Offord, *Nineteenth-Century Russia,* 81–82; MECW, Volume 46, 495(n).
59. Hartmann fell in love repeatedly, proposing marriage to Tussy and then to Pumps. Marx and Engels, meanwhile, kept him occupied with political work, and no doubt Engels gave him the money he needed to survive. KMIR, 150, 160; MECW, Volume 46, 95–96.
60. Bernstein, *My Years of Exile,* 152–153, 156–157.

Chapter Forty-two: London, 1881
1. Dornemann, *Jenny Marx,* 318–326.
2. Jenny Longuet to Charles Longuet, Nov. 22, 1880, Moscow.
3. Jenny Longuet to Charles Longuet, Nov. 10, 1880, Moscow.
4. Jenny Longuet to Charles Longuet, undated, Moscow; Jenny Longuet to Charles Longuet, Nov. 1880, Moscow.
5. Jenny Longuet to Charles Longuet, Nov. 1880, Moscow.
6. Jenny Longuet to Charles Longuet, undated, Moscow.
7. Charles Longuet to Jenny Longuet, Nov. 1880, Moscow.
8. Jenny Longuet to Charles Longuet, Sunday morning, Dec. 1880, Moscow.
9. Jenny Longuet to Charles Longuet, Nov. 10, 1880, Moscow.
10. MECW, Volume 46, 61.
11. Jenny Longuet to Charles Longuet, Jan. 1881, Moscow.
12. Jenny Longuet to Charles Longuet, Feb. 1881, Moscow.
13. Jenny Longuet to Charles Longuet, Jan. 13, 1881, Moscow.
14. The Longuets' house in Argenteuil was on the Boulevard Thiers, which was in later years renamed Boulevard Karl Marx. Longuet, *Karl Marx,* 230.
15. Jenny Longuet to Laura Lafargue, Apr. 1881, Moscow.
16. Jenny Longuet to Laura Lafargue, Apr. 22, 1881, Moscow.
17. MECW, Volume 46, 81.
18. Ibid., 81–82.
19. Kautsky's *Theories of Surplus Value* was based on his edit of Marx's material for *Capital, Volume IV.* Blumenberg, *Illustrated,* 159.
20. KMIR, 154–155.
21. Jenny Longuet to Charles Longuet, Nov. 10, 1880, Moscow; Bernstein, *My Years of Exile,* 158.
22. MECW, Volume 46, 82.
23. Ibid., 83.

24. Ibid., 89.
25. Ibid., 91.
26. Ibid., 96.
27. Ibid., 97.
28. Ibid., 106.
29. Ibid., 108.
30. Jenny Longuet to Jenny Marx, July 1881, Moscow.
31. MECW, Volume 46, 107.
32. Ibid., 109.
33. Ibid., 110.
34. Ibid., 116; Giroud, *Femme du diable*, 224.
35. MECW, Volume 46, 124.
36. Ibid., 124, 132.
37. Kapp, *Eleanor Marx, Volume I*, 187.
38. Morton, *Home Rule*, 23.
39. Eckert (ed.), *Wilhelm Liebknecht Briefwechsel*, 427–429; Morton, *Home Rule*, 25.
40. Bax, *Reminiscences*, 73–74; Joseph Clayton, *The Rise and Decline of Socialism in Great Britain*, 9.
41. Later, Shaw abandoned Marxism. James W. Hulse, *Revolutionists in London*, 111.
42. Bernstein, *My Years of Exile*, 159–160.
43. MECW, Volume 46, 104.
44. Meier, Perrot, and Trebitsch (eds.), *Daughters*, 134–135.
45. Ibid., 133.
46. MECW, Volume 46, 133, 134–135.
47. Ibid., 475.
48. MECW, Volume 46, 161; Liebknecht, *Karl Marx*, 43–44.
49. Meier, Perrot, and Trebitsch (eds.), *Daughters*, 138–139.
50. Ibid., 139.
51. Eleanor Marx to Jenny Longuet, Oct. 31, 1881, Moscow.
52. Liebknecht, *Karl Marx*, 158.
53. KMIR, 1.
54. Williamson, *Bismarck and Germany*, 58.
55. Eleanor Marx to Pytor Lavrov, Dec. 3, 1881, Moscow; Eleanor Marx to Jenny Longuet, Oct. 31, 1881, IISG; Jenny Longuet to Laura Lafargue, Dec. 2, 1881, Moscow.
56. MECW, Volume 46, 163; Bax, *Reminiscences*, 45.
57. Wheen, *Marx's Das Kapital*, 89.
58. MECW, Volume 46, 157, 165.
59. Ibid., 156.
60. MECW, Volume 24, 423–424; REM, 90.
61. MECW, Volume 46, 164.
62. Liebknecht, *Karl Marx*, 159.

Chapter Forty-three: London, 1882

1. William Shakespeare, *King Lear*, 30.
2. KMIR, 159.
3. Bernstein, *My Years of Exile*, 155.
4. MECW, Volume 46, 156.
5. Ibid., 157–158.
6. Ibid., 161.
7. Ibid., 158.
8. Ibid., 161.
9. Ibid., 184.
10. Flanders, *Victorian House*, 182.

11. Eleanor Marx to Jenny Longuet, Jan. 16, 1881, Moscow.
12. Jenny Longuet to Karl Marx, Dec. 3, 1881, Moscow.
13. MECW, Volume 46, 169.
14. Eleanor Marx to Jenny Longuet, Jan. 8, 1882, Moscow.
15. Jenny Longuet to Laura Lafargue, Dec. 1881, Moscow.
16. Jenny Longuet to Laura Lafargue, Dec. 2, 1881, Moscow.
17. Jenny Longuet to Laura Lafargue, Dec. 1881, Moscow.
18. MECW, Volume 46, 176–177.
19. Eleanor Marx to Jenny Longuet, Jan. 15, 1882, Moscow.
20. Jenny Longuet to Eleanor Marx, Jan. 23, 1882, Moscow.
21. Jenny Longuet to Eleanor Marx, Thursday, Apr. 1882, Moscow.
22. MECW, Volume 46, 184.
23. Ibid., 199.
24. Ibid., 213–215.
25. Ibid., 218.
26. Ibid., 227.
27. Ibid., 249.
28. Ibid., 253–254.
29. Ibid., 269.
30. Ibid., 262.
31. Ibid., 271–272.
32. Jenny Longuet to Karl Marx, Feb. 24, 1882, Moscow.
33. Jenny Longuet to Eleanor Marx, Mar. 23, 1882, Moscow.
34. Jenny Longuet to Eleanor Marx, Jan. 23, 1882, Moscow; Jenny Longuet to Eleanor Marx, June 10, 1882, Moscow; Jenny Longuet to Eleanor Marx, May 3, 1882, Moscow.
35. Jenny Longuet to Eleanor Marx, May 3, 1882, Moscow.
36. Jenny Longuet to Eleanor Marx, May 17, 1882, Moscow.
37. Jenny Longuet to Charles Longuet, undated, Moscow.
38. Jenny Longuet to Laura Lafargue, Mar. 1882, Moscow.
39. Jenny Longuet to Eleanor Marx, June 10, 1882, Moscow.
40. Jenny Longuet to Eleanor Marx, May 1882, Moscow.
41. MECW, Volume 46, 276; Longuet, *Karl Marx,* 234.
42. FE–PL, Volume I, 82–83.
43. MECW, Volume 46, 303.
44. Jenny Longuet to Laura Lafargue, July 1881, Moscow.
45. REM, 258.
46. MECW, Volume 46, 303.
47. Meier, Perrot, and Trebitsch (eds.), *Daughters,* 154–155.
48. Tsuzuki, *Eleanor Marx,* 66–67.
49. MECW, Volume 46, 303.
50. Ibid., 308.
51. Ibid., 356.
52. FE–PL, Volume I, 88–89.
53. MECW, Volume 46, 291.
54. FE–PL, Volume I, 101; Derfler, *Flowering of French Socialism,* 4.
55. FE–PL, Volume III, 479–480.
56. Jenny Longuet to Eleanor Marx, Sept. 5, 1882, Moscow.
57. Jenny Longuet to Eleanor Marx, Sept. 23, 1882, Moscow.
58. FE–PL, Volume I, 100–101.
59. MECW, Volume 46, 221; Derfler, *Founding of French Marxism,* 167.
60. Derfler, *Flowering of French Socialism,* 5.
61. MECW, Volume 46, 375.
62. Ibid., 394.

63. Ibid., 529(n).
64. Ibid., 399.
65. FE-PL, Volume I, 119.
66. Jenny Longuet to Eleanor Marx, Nov. 8, 1882, Moscow.
67. FE-PL, Volume I, 119.
68. Ibid., 117.
69. Jenny Longuet to Eleanor Marx, Sept. 5, 1882, Moscow.
70. Jenny Longuet to Eleanor Marx, Nov. 8, 1882, Moscow; Jenny Longuet to Eleanor Marx, Dec. 30, 1882, Moscow.
71. MECW, Volume 46, 419, 420.
72. Ibid., 425.
73. FE-PL, Volume III, 479–480.
74. MECW, Volume 46, 420–421.
75. Ibid., 421, 424.

Chapter Forty-four: London, 1883
1. Honoré de Balzac, *Lost Illusions,* 60.
2. Liebknecht, *Karl Marx,* 160.
3. MECW, Volume 24, 460–461.
4. MECW, Volume 46, 434.
5. Ibid., 440–441.
6. MECW, Volume 46, 456; REM, 346.
7. Friedrich Engels, *The Fourteenth of March 1883,* 21; FE-PL, Volume I, 121. (In nineteenth-century Britain, corpses remained in the home after death and the blinds were drawn to indicate mourning. They were not raised until after the funeral. Flanders, *Victorian House,* 32.)
8. MECW, Volume 24, 476.
9. MECW, Volume 46, 462–463.
10. Wheen, *Karl Marx,* 382; Robert Payne, *Karl Marx,* 500. (The headstone for the grave containing Marx, Jenny, and their grandson Harry was a simple flat stone. Engels and the family felt Marx's work was memorial enough, and no grander marker was needed. MECW, Volume 47, 17. The massive headstone in Highgate Cemetery today was installed by the Communist Party in 1956.)
11. REM, 256–257.
12. MECW, Volume 24, 463.
13. REM, 348.
14. MECW, Volume 24, 464.
15. Engels, *The Fourteenth of March 1883,* 11–13; REM, 348.
16. MECW, Volume 24, 469; REM, 350.
17. MECW, Volume 24, 469.
18. *The Coming Nation,* March 18, 1911, Greensburg, Indiana, 8; Raddatz, *Karl Marx,* 272.
19. Berlin, *Karl Marx,* 206.

Part Seven: After Marx

Chapter Forty-five: London, Spring 1883
1. MECW, Volume 46, 462.
2. Ibid., 465.
3. MECW, Volume 47, 3.
4. MECW, Volume 36, 5.
5. MECW, Volume 47, 13.
6. MECW, Volume 46, 466; 533(n).
7. MECW, Volume 47, 12.

8. FE-PL, Volume I, 124–125.

9. MECW, Volume 47, 3, 26, 561(n).

10. Tsuzuki, *Eleanor Marx,* 71.

11. Eleanor Marx to Laura Lafargue, Mar. 26, 1883, IISG. (Tussy said Engels also burned many letters referring to himself among Marx's papers. Eleanor Marx Aveling to Karl Kautsky, Mar. 15, 1898, Moscow.)

12. Warren Sylvester Smith, *The London Heretics,* 74; Tsuzuki, *Eleanor Marx,* 83.

13. Ellis quoted Shaw on Aveling. Ellis, "Havelock Ellis on Eleanor Marx," *Adelphi,* London, Sept./Oct. 1935.

14. KMIR, 120.

15. Warren Sylvester Smith, *London Heretics,* 74.

16. Tsuzuki, *Eleanor Marx,* 91–92.

17. Ibid., 91–92; Robert Payne, *Karl Marx,* 513. (This phrase was used in the eighteenth century by John Wilkes, lord mayor of London, who said: "I am the ugliest fellow in England yet give me half an hour in advance of the smartest beau in Great Britain, and I will undertake to gain the preference of the prettiest woman in the land." "Aleph," *London Scenes,* 31.)

18. Ellis, "Havelock Ellis on Eleanor Marx," *Adelphi,* London, Sept./Oct. 1935; Warren Sylvester Smith, *London Heretics,* 74.

19. Kapp, *Eleanor Marx, Volume II,* 204.

20. Less than a month after Marx's death, Engels wrote Zurich newspaper editor Eduard Bernstein on Aveling's behalf. MECW, Volume 47, 7.

21. Ibid., 26.

22. Aveling edited the newspapers *Progress* and *Freethinker.* Warren Sylvester Smith, *London Heretics,* 63–65; Besant, *Autobiography,* 288.

23. Beatrice Webb, *My Apprenticeship,* 301–302.

24. MECW, Volume 47, 28–29.

25. Derfler, *Flowering of French Socialism,* 6–7.

26. MECW, Volume 46, 375.

27. Derfler, *Flowering of French Socialism,* 8.

28. Ibid., 11.

29. Derfler, *Flowering of French Socialism,* 12; FE-PL, Volume I, 132.

30. FE-PL, Volume I, 138–139.

31. Ibid., 140.

32. Ibid., 139.

33. Ibid., 141–142.

34. MECW, Volume 47, 39–40.

35. Ellis, "Havelock Ellis on Eleanor Marx," *Adelphi,* London, Sept./Oct. 1935.

36. Bax, *Reminiscences,* 75.

37. O'Neill, *Good Old Days,* 226; MECW, Volume 47, 583(n).

38. Wright, *Democracy and Reform,* 98.

39. Hulse, *Revolutionists in London,* 79.

40. J. Bruce Glasier, *William Morris and the Early Days of the Socialist Movement,* 32.

41. Hulse, *Revolutionists in London,* 226.

42. May Morris, *William Morris: Artist, Writer, Socialist, Volume II,* xii.

43. MECW, Volume 47, 78.

44. Ibid., 60–61.

45. Gildea, *Third Republic,* 25.

46. FE-PL, Volume I, 162–163.

47. Gildea, *Third Republic,* 34.

48. Ibid., 35; FE-PL, Volume I, 148–150.

49. FE-PL, Volume I, 151.

50. Ibid.

51. Ibid., 155.
52. Meier, Perrot, and Trebitsch (eds.), *Daughters,* 175–176.
53. FE-PL, Volume I, 194–196.
54. MECW, Volume 47, 118, 122, 551(n).
55. FE-PL, Volume I, 217–219.
56. On her marriage Bell received £1,000, and she stood to eventually inherit part of her father's £25,000 estate. Kapp, *Eleanor Marx, Volume I,* 257–258.
57. Ibid., 257.
58. Eleanor Marx to Laura Lafargue, June 18, 1884, Moscow.
59. Bernstein, *My Years of Exile,* 161.
60. Eleanor Marx Aveling to Mrs. Bland, July 15, 1884, Moscow.
61. FE-PL, Volume I, 217–219.
62. MECW, Volume 47, 177.
63. Tsuzuki, *Eleanor Marx,* 99.
64. MECW, Volume 47, 167; Tsuzuki, *Eleanor Marx,* 107.
65. Michael Rive (ed.), *Olive Schreiner Letters, Volume I,* 48.
66. Ibid., 49.
67. Through Olive, Ellis got to know Tussy better, including her sexual history. Ellis mentioned one intriguing, though sadly vague, "sudden sexual initiation" Tussy experienced while lying on the sofa at her parents' home and at the hands of a "prominent foreign follower of her father's." Ellis wrote later that he forgot the fellow's name. Ellis, "Havelock Ellis on Eleanor Marx," *Adelphi,* London, Sept./Oct. 1935.
68. Ibid.
69. Yaffa Claire Draznin (ed.), *My Other Self,* 140; Ellis, "Havelock Ellis on Eleanor Marx," *Adelphi,* London, Sept./Oct. 1935.
70. Draznin, *My Other Self,* 141.
71. Tsuzuki, *Eleanor Marx,* 99.
72. Cole and Postgate, *British Common People,* 415–416, 421; Clayton, *Rise and Decline of Socialism,* 20–21; Bax, *Reminiscences,* 80.
73. Clayton, *Rise and Decline of Socialism,* 42.
74. Declaration to members of the Social Democratic Federation announcing the formation of the Socialist League, Jan. 10, 1885, signed by Edward Aveling, Eleanor Marx Aveling, Robert Banner, E. B. Bax, William Morris, John Mann, and others, IISG.
75. MECW, Volume 47, 248.

Chapter Forty-six: London, 1885

1. Eleanor Marx Aveling to George Bernard Shaw, June 2, 1885, Catalog of George Bernard Shaw Papers, British Library, London.
2. MECW, Volume 47, 244.
3. Ibid., 316.
4. Ibid., 244.
5. Ibid., 290.
6. Ibid., 244.
7. Ibid., 245, 249, 394.
8. Ibid., 394.
9. FE-PL, Volume I, 270–271.
10. MECW, Volume 36, 283.
11. Ibid., 235–236.
12. Ibid., 238–239.
13. MECW, Volume 47, 289, 296.
14. Engels corresponded with members of the Emancipation of Labor, including Vera Zasulich. She also belonged to the Narodnaya Volya, or People's Will, which had engaged in terrorist tactics against Alexander II and his ultrareactionary son Alexander

III—actions that brought more repression without a single gain for the workingman. Zasulich had fled Russia after shooting the governor of St. Petersburg and being acquitted—remarkably—by a jury. Offord, *Nineteenth-Century Russia*, 80, 88; Hulse, *Revolutionists in London*, 32–33.

15. Tsuzuki, *Eleanor Marx*, 121.
16. MECW, Volume 47, 405; Tsuzuki, *Eleanor Marx*, 122.
17. *The National Reformer*, London, May 4, 1884, 310.
18. Bax, *Reminiscences*, 109.
19. MECW, Volume 47, 274.
20. Eleanor Marx Aveling to Laura Lafargue, Apr. 12, 1885, Moscow.
21. Eleanor Marx Aveling to George Bernard Shaw, June 2, 1885, London, British Library, GBS Papers.
22. Tsuzuki, *Eleanor Marx*, 127.
23. Ellis, "Havelock Ellis on Eleanor Marx," *Adelphi*, London, Sept./Oct. 1935.
24. Ibid.
25. Ibid.
26. Miliband and Saville (eds.), *The Socialist Register*, 183–184, 187.
27. Vera Buchanan-Gould, *Not Without Honor: The Life and Writings of Olive Schreiner*, 221.
28. Tsuzuki, *Eleanor Marx*, 123–124.
29. Edward Aveling and Eleanor Marx Aveling, *The Woman Question*, 6, 8, 13, 16.
30. Eleanor Marx Aveling to George Bernard Shaw, June 2, 1885, London, British Library, GBS Papers; Tsuzuki, *Eleanor Marx*, 165.
31. Gustave Flaubert, *Madame Bovary*, trans. Eleanor Marx-Aveling, xx.
32. Williamson, *Bismarck and Germany*, 58–61.
33. Ibid., 46.
34. Clayton, *Rise and Decline of Socialism*, 26; MECW, Volume 47, 366.
35. O'Neill, *Good Old Days*, 156; Wilson, *Victorians*, 508.
36. Clayton, *Rise and Decline of Socialism*, 27.
37. MECW, Volume 47, 404, 408.
38. Clayton, *Rise and Decline of Socialism*, 27.
39. MECW, Volume 47, 413.
40. Derfler, *Flowering of French Socialism*, 48.
41. MECW, Volume 47, 413.
42. Ibid., 428.
43. Gildea, *Third Republic*, 35
44. MECW, Volume 47, 441, 452, 470.
45. Ibid., 436.
46. Meier, Perrot, and Trebitsch (eds.), *Daughters*, 193–194.
47. Ibid., 194.
48. Tsuzuki, *Eleanor Marx*, 135.
49. *Chicago Tribune*, Nov. 6, 1886, 9.
50. Meier, Perrot, and Trebitsch (eds.), *Daughters*, 194.
51. Tsuzuki, *Eleanor Marx*, 136.
52. Edward Aveling and Eleanor Marx Aveling, *The Working Class Movement in America*, 8.
53. *Chicago Tribune*, Nov. 6, 1886, 1.
54. Kapp, *Eleanor Marx, Volume II*, 158.
55. Ibid., 153.
56. MECW, Volume 47, 525.
57. Ibid., 530–532, 628(n); Tsuzuki, *Eleanor Marx*, 140.
58. MECW, Volume 47, 494 and Volume 48, 3.
59. *New York Herald*, Jan. 8, 1887, 5.
60. *Evening Standard*, London, Jan. 13, 1887, 4.

61. *New York Herald,* Jan. 14, 1887, 5.
62. *Evening Standard,* London, Jan. 13, 1887, 4.
63. Warren Sylvester Smith, *London Heretics,* 79.
64. Tsuzuki, *Eleanor Marx,* 117.
65. MECW, Volume 26, 617; *New York Herald,* Jan. 14, 1887, 5.
66. MECW, Volume 48, 16–17.
67. Bax, *Reminiscences,* 52, 55.
68. George Bernard Shaw, *The Doctor's Dilemma.*
69. Tsuzuki, *Eleanor Marx,* 165.

Chapter Forty-seven: London, 1887
1. Tsuzuki, *Eleanor Marx,* 168.
2. Derfler, *Flowering of French Socialism,* 69.
3. In the two decades starting in 1875, more than a quarter of the globe was seized by a half dozen European powers. Davies, *Europe, A History,* 848.
4. Hobsbawm, *Age of Capital,* 354–355.
5. Derfler, *Flowering of French Socialism,* 70.
6. MECW, Volume 47, 413.
7. Ibid., 5.
8. Macé, *Paul et Laura Lafargue,* 90.
9. FE-PL, Volume II, 19.
10. Fomičev, "Helene Demuth Without Brethren," 972.
11. In his will Freddy referred to Harry as "Mr. Harry Demuth my nephew known as my son." Kapp, *Eleanor Marx, Volume I,* 294.
12. Ibid., *Volume II,* 437.
13. FE-PL, Volume II, 40.
14. MECW, Volume 48, 542(n).
15. FE-PL, Volume II, 34–36.
16. Ibid., 28.
17. Tsuzuki, *Eleanor Marx,* 79, 115; Morris, *William Morris,* 226.
18. MECW, Volume 48, 73–74, 83, 105.
19. Bernstein, *My Years of Exile,* 202.
20. MECW, Volume 48, 91.
21. Ellis, "Havelock Ellis on Eleanor Marx," *Adelphi,* London, Sept./Oct. 1935.
22. Tsuzuki, *Eleanor Marx,* 168.
23. *To-Day,* London, June 1887, No. 43.
24. Ellis, "Havelock Ellis on Eleanor Marx," *Adelphi,* London, Sept./Oct. 1935.
25. Meier, Perrot, and Trebitsch (eds.), *Daughters,* 197–198.
26. Wilson, *Victorians,* 508.
27. MECW, Volume 48, 57.
28. Wilson, *Victorians,* 508.
29. MECW, Volume 48, 79, 536–537(n).
30. Wilson, *Victorians,* 509.
31. *Pall Mall Gazette,* London, Nov. 14, 1887, 1.
32. MECW, Volume 48, 113.
33. *Pall Mall Gazette,* London, Nov. 14, 1887, 5.
34. Morris, *William Morris,* 263.
35. Ibid., 252.
36. MECW, Volume 48, 113.
37. Wilson, *Victorians,* 510; Warren Sylvester Smith, *London Heretics,* 22.
38. Tsuzuki, *Eleanor Marx,* 155.
39. Meier, Perrot, and Trebitsch (eds.), *Daughters,* 202.
40. MECW, Volume 48, 119.

41. Tsuzuki, *Eleanor Marx,* 169–170.
42. Eleanor Marx Aveling to Laura Lafargue, Dec. 31, 1887, IISG.
43. Tsuzuki, *Eleanor Marx,* 173.
44. MECW, Volume 48, 198.
45. Ibid., 183.
46. Mayer, *Friedrich Engels,* 294.
47. Eleanor Marx Aveling to George Bernard Shaw, Dec. 16, 1887, GBS Papers. (Shaw said his fight with Aveling occurred in May 1887 over whether the new generation of socialists in England should be considered Marxist. Shaw said they should not, and Aveling attacked him in a series of letters, London, British Library, GBS Papers.)
48. MECW, Volume 48, 184, 192.
49. Ibid., 194.
50. Mayer, *Friedrich Engels,* 253.
51. MECW, Volume 48, 195, 202, 203.
52. Meier, Perrot, and Trebitsch (eds.), *Daughters,* 204–205.
53. Ibid., 207.
54. MECW, Volume 48, 208.
55. Ibid., 207.
56. Ibid., 211.
57. Olsen, *Growth of Victorian London,* 122; Wilson, *Victorians,* 521.
58. Will Thorne, *My Life's Battles,* 13.
59. Flanders, *Victorian House,* 370.
60. Winder, *Bloody Foreigners,* 215.
61. O'Neill, *Good Old Days,* 46; Anne Cowen and Roger Cowen, *Victorian Jews Through British Eyes,* xiv-xv.
62. Eleanor Marx Aveling to Laura Lafargue, June 24, 1888, IISG.
63. Paul Adelman, *The Rise of the Labour Party,* 12.
64. Kapp, *Eleanor Marx, Volume II,* 260.
65. Ibid., 510.
66. Eleanor Marx Aveling to Laura Lafargue, Dec. 31, 1888, IISG.

Chapter Forty-eight: London, 1889

1. William Stewart, *J. Keir Hardie: A Biography,* 38.
2. Adelman, *Rise of the Labour Party,* 10.
3. Clayton, *Rise and Decline of Socialism,* 56.
4. Thorne, *My Life's Battles,* 67.
5. Clayton, *Rise and Decline of Socialism,* 62.
6. MECW, Volume 48, 601(n); Adelman, *Rise of the Labour Party,* 12–13.
7. Thorne and Mann would become MPs; Burns would become an MP and a minister in a Liberal government. Cole and Postgate, *British Common People,* 427.
8. William Collison, *The Apostle of Free Labour,* 81.
9. Clayton, *Rise and Decline of Socialism,* 55.
10. Cole and Postgate, *British Common People,* 427–428.
11. Ibid., 427.
12. Thorne, *My Life's Battles,* 13.
13. Ibid., 80–81.
14. Ibid., 81.
15. MECW, Volume 48, 591(n); Cole and Postgate, *British Common People,* 428; Thorne, *My Life's Battles,* 80.
16. Thorne, *My Life's Battles,* 86.
17. MECW, Volume 48, 373, 379.
18. Tsuzuki, *Eleanor Marx,* 197.
19. Clayton, *Rise and Decline of Socialism,* 59.

20. Cole and Postgate, *British Common People,* 429.
21. MECW, Volume 48, 373.
22. Cole and Postgate, *British Common People,* 430.
23. Clayton, *Rise and Decline of Socialism,* 64.
24. MECW, Volume 26, 545.
25. MECW, Volume 48, 377, 487 and Volume 49, 479–480.
26. MECW, Volume 48, 312–313.
27. Ibid., 313.
28. Ibid., 286.
29. Ibid., 286, 287.
30. Ibid., 316; Meier, Perrot, and Trebitsch (eds.), *Daughters,* 210.
31. Derfler, *Flowering of French Socialism,* 75.
32. FE-PL, Volume II, 285; Derfler, *Flowering of French Socialism,* 75.
33. MECW, Volume 48, 348.
34. Ibid., 352; Derfler, *Flowering of French Socialism,* 74–75.
35. MECW, Volume 48, 353.
36. Derfler, *Flowering of French Socialism,* 76.
37. MECW, Volume 48, 352.
38. Ibid., 589(n); Derfler, *Flowering of French Socialism,* 77.
39. MECW, Volume 48, 392.
40. REM, 187.
41. MECW, Volume 48, 257–258.
42. FE-PL, Volume II, 363.
43. MECW, Volume 48, 605(n), 607(n).
44. Ozment, *Mighty Fortress,* 222; Williamson, *Bismarck and Germany,* 62.
45. Williamson, *Bismarck and Germany,* 62–63; Ozment, *Mighty Fortress,* 222.
46. Ozment, *Mighty Fortress,* 222–223.
47. Williamson, *Bismarck and Germany,* 64.
48. MECW, Volume 48, 481.
49. FE-PL, Volume II, 374.
50. MECW, Volume 48, 493.
51. *People's Press,* London, May 10, 1890, 5.
52. MECW, Volume 48, 493–494.
53. Ibid., 409.
54. *People's Press,* London, May 10, 1890, 7.
55. MECW, Volume 48, 494–495, 496.
56. MECW, Volume 49, 14.
57. MECW, Volume 48, 470.
58. MECW, Volume 49, 67.
59. MECW, Volume 48, 200.
60. Ibid., 84.
61. Bernstein, *My Years of Exile,* 169.
62. Ibid., 192, 196.
63. Ibid., 197.
64. MECW, Volume 49, 53.
65. Ibid., 65–66.
66. MECW, Volume 49, 67; Fomičev, "Helene Demuth Without Brethren," *Motherland,* 972.
67. MECW, Volume 49, 67.
68. Ibid., 67.

Chapter Forty-nine: London, 1891

1. MECW, Volume 49, 215.
2. Mayer, *Friedrich Engels,* 196.

3. REM, 191.
4. Mayer, *Friedrich Engels,* 196.
5. MECW, Volume 49, 69–71.
6. Eleanor Marx Aveling to Laura Lafargue, Dec. 19, 1890, Moscow.
7. Tsuzuki, *Eleanor Marx,* 247.
8. MECW, Volume 49, 88.
9. MECW, Volume 47, 265.
10. MECW, Volume 48, 224–225, 235.
11. MECW, Volume 49, 68–69.
12. Ibid., 72.
13. Ibid., 71.
14. Ibid., 87.
15. Ibid., 73.
16. Ibid., 82.
17. Ibid., 76.
18. Eleanor Marx Aveling to Friedrich Engels, Oct. 14, 1890, Moscow.
19. Eleanor Marx Aveling to Edward Aveling, Oct. 16, 1890, Moscow.
20. In Britain the intrasocialist fighting was vicious, and in France the two main socialist parties clawed at each other to expand their bases. The so-called Possibilists—more moderate socialists with whom Longuet was allied—concentrated their power in Paris. But Lafargue's Workers' Party had more followers in the normally conservative provinces, where industrialization was booming and workers were most needy. *Justice,* London, Feb. 21, 1891, 1; MECW, Volume 49, 127.
21. Derfler, *Flowering of French Socialism,* 85, 87–88.
22. FE-PL, Volume III, 88.
23. Derfler, *Flowering of French Socialism,* 88.
24. Ibid., 89.
25. Derfler, *Flowering of French Socialism,* 89–90; Macé, *Paul et Laura Lafargue,* 110–111.
26. Derfler, *Flowering of French Socialism,* 90.
27. Ibid., 91.
28. FE-PL, Volume III, 79(n).
29. Derfler, *Flowering of French Socialism,* 91–92.
30. Ibid., 93–94.
31. Macé, *Paul et Laura Lafargue,* 113; Derfler, *Flowering of French Socialism,* 94.
32. FE-PL, Volume III, 88.
33. Derfler, *Flowering of French Socialism,* 95.
34. FE-PL, Volume III, 106, 110–111.
35. Ibid., 112–113.
36. MECW, Volume 49, 269; Derfler, *Flowering of French Socialism,* 98.
37. Ibid., 288, 290.
38. FE-PL, Volume III, 127.
39. MECW, Volume 49, 293; FE-PL, Volume III, 131(n).
40. FE-PL, Volume III, 133.
41. Ibid., 134–135.
42. Ibid., 134(n).
43. FE-PL, Volume III, 137(n); MECW, Volume 49, 301–302.
44. MECW, Volume 49, 305.
45. FE-PL, Volume III, 137.
46. Ibid., 138, 144; MECW, Volume 49, 306–307.
47. FE-PL, Volume III, 146(n).
48. Derfler, *Flowering of French Socialism,* 104–106.
49. FE-PL, Volume III, 145–146, 148.
50. Derfler, *Flowering of French Socialism,* 105.

51. FE–PL, Volume III, 150–151.
52. Ibid., 112–113.
53. Ibid., 114.

Chapter Fifty: London, 1892
1. Derfler, *Flowering of French Socialism*, 110.
2. Eleanor Marx Aveling to Laura Lafargue, Dec. 19, 1895, Moscow.
3. MECW, Volume 49, 225, 584(n).
4. Clayton, *Rise and Decline of Socialism*, 37; MECW, Volume 49, 237, 238; Ferdinand Gilles, "Is He the Son-in-Law of Karl Marx?," London, Nov. 10, 1891.
5. MECW, Volume 49, 238.
6. Ibid., 584(n).
7. Derfler, *Flowering of French Socialism*, 108.
8. MECW, Volume 49, 621–622(n); Derfler, *Flowering of French Socialism*, 110.
9. MECW, Volume 49, 409.
10. Cole and Postgate, *British Common People*, 434; MECW, Volume 49, 468; Clayton, *Rise and Decline of Socialism*, 61; Stewart, *J. Keir Hardie*, 6–7, 68.
11. Adelman, *Rise of the Labour Party*, 17.
12. Ibid., 22.
13. Cole and Postgate, *British Common People*, 435; Clayton, *Rise and Decline of Socialism*, 75.
14. Clayton, *Rise and Decline of Socialism*, 72.
15. MECW, Volume 49, 479.
16. MECW, Volume 50, 154, 569(n).
17. Adelman, *Rise of the Labour Party*, 19–20; MECW, Volume 50, 574(n).
18. MECW, Volume 27, 404–405; Stepanova, *Frederick Engels*, 229.
19. Derfler, *Flowering of French Socialism*, 143; FE–PL, Volume III, 290; Gildea, *Third Republic*, 37.
20. MECW, Volume 50, 10, 113.
21. Derfler, *Flowering of French Socialism*, 140.
22. Tsuzuki, *Eleanor Marx*, 233, 237.
23. Ibid., 239.
24. MECW, Volume 49, 357–358, 359 and Volume 46, xvii.
25. MECW, Volume 49, 357–358.
26. Meier, Perrot, and Trebitsch (eds.), *Daughters*, 246.
27. Eleanor Marx Aveling to Laura Lafargue, July 26, 1892, Moscow.
28. Eleanor Marx Aveling to Laura Lafargue, Mar. 22, 1894, Moscow.
29. Meier, Perrot, and Trebitsch (eds.), *Daughters*, 247, 248, 250; Eleanor Marx Aveling to Laura Lafargue, Mar. 22, 1894, Moscow.
30. Kapp, *Eleanor Marx, Volume II*, 560.
31. Meier, Perrot, and Trebitsch (eds.), *Daughters*, 248.
32. MECW, Volume 50, 299.
33. Ibid., 308.
34. Ibid., 300.
35. MECW, Volume 37, 436.
36. Ibid., 541–542.
37. Ibid., 590.
38. MECW, Volume 50, 386–387.
39. Kapp, *Eleanor Marx, Volume II*, 566.
40. German socialist Clara Zetkin said later that the speculation among party members was that Victor Adler, Engels, or Bebel was the father of Louise's child, but that it was most likely Bebel. Terrell Carver, in his biography of Engels, said Engels had dealt with Pumps's out-of-wedlock pregnancy in a similar fashion, hurriedly arranging a

marriage with an accountant named Percy Rosler. Fomičev, "Helene Demuth Without Brethren," 971–972; Carver, *Friedrich Engels,* 161.

41. Kapp, *Eleanor Marx, Volume II,* 566–567.
42. Eleanor Marx to Laura Lafargue, Nov. 5, 1894, Moscow.
43. Tsuzuki, *Eleanor Marx,* 252–253.
44. Eleanor Marx Aveling to Laura Lafargue, Nov. 5, 1894, Moscow.
45. Meier, Perrot, and Trebitsch (eds.), *Daughters,* 258, 260.
46. MECW, Volume 50, 537.
47. Ibid., 395, 424–425.
48. Meier, Perrot, and Trebitsch (eds.), *Daughters,* 263; MECW, Volume 50, 425.
49. MECW, Volume 50, 364.

Chapter Fifty-one: London, 1895

1. REM, 65.
2. Halliday, *Great Filth,* 195; MECW, Volume 50, 441.
3. MECW, Volume 50, 477.
4. Stepniak's real name was Sergey Mikhaylovich Kravchinskiy. Bernstein, *My Years of Exile,* 214; Hulse, *Revolutionists in London,* 8.
5. Stepniak died in 1895 after being hit by a train in London. Hulse, *Revolutionists in London,* 28, 30–31.
6. Bernstein, *My Years of Exile,* 219; MECW, Volume 50, 611(n); Georgy Plekhanov, *Anarchism and Socialism.*
7. Offord, *Nineteenth-Century Russia,* 94.
8. Ibid., 97.
9. MECW, Volume 50, 455.
10. MECW, Volume 49, 538.
11. Offord, *Nineteenth-Century Russia,* 99.
12. Longuet, *Karl Marx,* 239.
13. MECW, Volume 50, 507.
14. Ibid., 395.
15. Ibid., 526.
16. Cole and Postgate, *British Common People,* 436–437; Adelman, *Rise of the Labour Party,* 23.
17. MECW, Volume 50, 526.
18. Ibid., 535.
19. Fomičev, "Helene Demuth Without Brethren," 972.
20. Fomičev, "Helene Demuth Without Brethren," 971.
21. Some scholars, who deny that Marx was Freddy's father, dispute the veracity of Engels's deathbed confession to Tussy, in part because they say the scene is too quintessentially "Victorian" to be true, and because details were based on an account given by Louise Kautsky years later. They also question whether Engels would have confided such important information to Louise. Separate from Louise Kautsky, Freddy Demuth recounted the same story. I believe it to be true in its most important details, that the episode is wholly consistent with the personalities involved, and that subsequent events indicate a revelation had occurred that changed Tussy's life. Fomičev, "Helene Demuth Without Brethren," 971; REM, 385; Blumenberg, *Illustrated,* 112.
22. Fomičev, "Helene Demuth Without Brethren," 971.
23. Liebknecht said that though Engels had throat cancer, he died of a stroke. REM, 148.
24. MECW, Volume 50, 612(n); Carver, *Friedrich Engels,* 253. (Ludwig Freyberger asked Tussy shortly after Engels's death to remove Marx's chair and bookcases. Ludwig Freyberger to Eleanor Marx, Oct. 4, 1895, IISG.)
25. MECW, Volume 50, 537–538, 541–542.
26. Carver, *Friedrich Engels,* 253.

27. Kapp, *Eleanor Marx, Volume II*, 611.
28. Fomičev, "Helene Demuth Without Brethren," 972.
29. Eleanor Marx Aveling to Karl Kautsky, Sept. 29, 1895, Moscow; Bernstein, *My Years of Exile*, 187, 191–192; Mayer, *Friedrich Engels*, 327; REM, 180. (Cremations began to be carried out in England only in 1885, and were still rare in the 1890s. Wilson, *Victorians*, 544.)
30. REM, 59.
31. *Justice*, London, July 30, 1898, 2.
32. Meier, Perrot, and Trebitsch (eds.), *Daughters*, 285.
33. Kapp, *Eleanor Marx, Volume I*, 258.
34. Eleanor Marx Aveling Last Will and Testament, Oct. 16, 1895, London, IISG; Codicil, Nov. 28, 1896, IISG.
35. Fomičev, "Helene Demuth Without Brethren," 972.
36. Frédérique Longuet-Marx, author interview; Kapp, *Eleanor Marx, Volume II*, 505(n).
37. FE-PL, Volume III, 26–27; MECW, Volume 49, 203.
38. Eckert (ed.), *Wilhelm Liebknecht Briefwechsel*, 453
39. Jean Longuet to Friedrich Engels, Dec. 31, 1893, IISG.
40. Eleanor Marx Aveling to Jean Longuet, July 14, 1895, Moscow.
41. Eleanor Marx Aveling to Karl Kautsky, Feb. 28, 1896, Moscow.
42. Eleanor Marx Aveling to Karl Kautsky, Sept. 28, 1897, Moscow.
43. Tsuzuki, *Eleanor Marx*, 278–279.
44. Thorne, *My Life's Battles*, 148.
45. Kapp, *Eleanor Marx, Volume II*, 632.
46. Ibid., 630.
47. Eleanor Marx Aveling to Laura Lafargue, Dec. 24, 1896, Moscow.
48. Kapp, *Eleanor Marx, Volume II*, 631.
49. Eleanor Marx Aveling to Karl Kautsky, July 19, 1897, Moscow.
50. Fomičev, "Helene Demuth Without Brethren," 971–972.

Chapter Fifty-two: London, 1897

1. *Justice*, London, July 30, 1898, 2.
2. Tsuzuki, *Eleanor Marx*, 296.
3. Ibid., 299.
4. Eckert (ed.), *Wilhelm Liebknecht Briefwechsel*, 455; Tsuzuki, *Eleanor Marx*, 300.
5. Freddy Demuth and Eduard Bernstein published Tussy's series of letters to Freddy written in the months leading up to her death. *Justice*, London, July 30, 1898, 2.
6. Eleanor Marx Aveling to Freddy Demuth, Aug. 30, 1897, *Justice*, London, July 30, 1898, 2.
7. Eleanor Marx Aveling to Freddy Demuth, Sept. 1, 1897, *Justice*, London, July 30, 1898, 2.
8. Eleanor Marx Aveling to Freddy Demuth, Aug. 30, 1897, *Justice*, London, July 30, 1898, 2.
9. Eleanor Marx Aveling to Freddy Demuth, Sept. 2, 1897, *Justice*, London, July 30, 1898, 2. (Some biographers have suggested that the secret Aveling was threatening to reveal was the fact that he and Tussy were not married. But that is highly unlikely, because she freely admitted her marital status to anyone who asked, as evidenced by her letters as soon as she began using the name Aveling.)
10. Tsuzuki, *Eleanor Marx*, 305.
11. Ibid., 306.
12. Collison, *Apostle of Free Labour*, 81–83.
13. Tsuzuki, *Eleanor Marx*, 306.
14. Collison, *Apostle of Free Labour*, 84; Tsuzuki, *Eleanor Marx*, 303.
15. Tsuzuki, *Eleanor Marx*, 307.

16. Meier, Perrot, and Trebitsch (eds.), *Daughters*, 299; Tsuzuki, *Eleanor Marx*, 310.
17. Tsuzuki, *Eleanor Marx*, 308–309.
18. Eleanor Marx Aveling to Freddy Demuth, Jan. 18, 1898, *Justice*, London, July 30, 1898, 2.
19. Eleanor Marx Aveling to Natalie Liebknecht, Feb. 1, 1898, Moscow.
20. Tsuzuki, *Eleanor Marx*, 297.
21. Eleanor Marx Aveling to Edith (no surname), [month illegible] 29, 1898, Moscow.
22. Eleanor Marx Aveling to Freddy Demuth, Feb. 3, 1898, *Justice*, London, July 30, 1898, 2.
23. Eleanor Marx Aveling to Freddy Demuth, Feb. 5, 1898, *Justice*, London, July 30, 1898, 2.
24. Eleanor Marx Aveling to Freddy Demuth, Feb. 7, 1898, *Justice*, London, July 30, 1898, 2.
25. Eleanor Marx Aveling to Jean Longuet, Feb. 9, 1898, Moscow.
26. Eckert (ed.), *Wilhelm Liebknecht Briefwechsel*, 463.
27. Eleanor Marx Aveling to Karl Kautsky, Mar. 15, 1898, Moscow.
28. Eleanor Marx Aveling to Freddy Demuth, Mar. 1, 1898, *Justice*, London, July 30, 1898, 3.
29. Tsuzuki, *Eleanor Marx*, 316.
30. Fellow socialist Robert Banner declared that he had seen the letter and that it depicted a "certain person," undoubtedly Aveling, badly. *Justice*, London, July 30, 1898, 3.
31. The local newspaper, the *Sydenham Examiner*, published a full transcript of the Coroner's Inquest into Tussy's death. *Sydenham Examiner*, London, Apr. 8, 1898, 5.
32. Tsuzuki, *Eleanor Marx*, 318–319.
33. Kapp, *Eleanor Marx, Volume II*, 697.
34. *Sydenham Examiner*, London, Apr. 8, 1898, 5.
35. Tsuzuki, *Eleanor Marx*, 319; *Justice*, London, July 30, 1898, 3.
36. *Justice*, London, July 30, 1898, 3.
37. Ibid.; Bernstein, *My Years of Exile*, 163; Tsuzuki, *Eleanor Marx*, 319.
38. Meier, Perrot, and Trebitsch (eds.), *Daughters*, 311.
39. Macé, *Paul et Laura Lafargue*, 149; *Justice*, London, Apr. 9, 1898, 2.
40. *Justice*, London, Apr. 9, 1898, 2. (Tussy's ashes were claimed by Aveling and kept at the headquarters of the Social Democratic Federation. They were then transferred to the Urn Park of Great Britain until 1921, when police raided the facility. Eventually they were turned over to the Marx Memorial Library in London. In 1957 Tussy's urn was added to the family grave at Highgate Cemetery. Tsuzuki, *Eleanor Marx*, 337.)
41. Tsuzuki, *Eleanor Marx*, 321.
42. *Justice*, London, Apr. 9, 1898, 2; Bernstein, *My Years of Exile*, 210.
43. *Sydenham Examiner*, London, Apr. 8, 1898, 5.
44. Bebel said it was obvious from Tussy's close relations with Freddy that she wanted to take care of him in her will and indicated as much in her instructions to Crosse, but that Aveling destroyed the letter. Fomičev, "Helene Demuth Without Brethren," 971.
45. Tsuzuki, *Eleanor Marx*, 323; *Justice*, London, July 30, 1898, 2.
46. *Justice*, London, July 30, 1898, 2.
47. Probate of Eleanor Marx Aveling's Last Will and Testament, Apr. 16, 1898, London, IISG; Tsuzuki, *Eleanor Marx*, 324.
48. *Justice*, London, July 30, 1898, 2; Meier, Perrot, and Trebitsch (eds.), *Daughters*, 311, 312.
49. *Justice*, London, July 30, 1898, 2.
50. Karl Marx (Eleanor Marx Aveling, ed.), *Value, Price and Profit*, introduction.
51. Tsuzuki, *Eleanor Marx*, 325.
52. Edward Aveling's Last Will and Testament, July 21, 1898, London, IISG; Probate of Aveling's will, August 17, 1898, IISG.
53. Tsuzuki, *Eleanor Marx*, 325.

Chapter Fifty-three: Draveil, France, 1910

1. Whitridge, *Men in Crisis*, 331.
2. Macé, *Paul et Laura Lafargue*, 172; Derfler, *Flowering of French Socialism*, 277.

3. Derfler, *Flowering of French Socialism*, 222.
4. Ibid., 225.
5. Ibid., 278.
6. Macé, *Paul et Laura Lafargue*, 172–173.
7. Ibid., 194.
8. MECW, Volume 50, 567(n).
9. Ibid., 216.
10. FE-PL, Volume III, 304–305.
11. MECW, Volume 47, 333.
12. FE-PL, Volume III, 304–305.
13. Derfler, *Flowering of French Socialism*, 158.
14. Ibid., 270–271.
15. Ibid., 158.
16. Longuet, *Karl Marx*, 243.
17. Clemenceau wrote a tribute to Longuet after his death in Paris on August 6, 1903. Longuet was sixty-four. *L'Action Régionaliste*, Paris, undated, 235–239.
18. Frédérique Longuet-Marx, author interview.
19. Macé, *Paul et Laura Lafargue*, 160.
20. Derfler, *Flowering of French Socialism*, 288; Macé, *Paul et Laura Lafargue*, 8, 179.
21. After the Lafargues' deaths the family changed the description of Laura's state upon discovery, saying that Doucet had found Laura seated at her dressing table, dead. But Macé said the first witness's testimony given after her body was discovered described her as lying on the floor. Macé, *Paul et Laura Lafargue*, 7–9.
22. Ibid., 9–10.
23. Ibid., 11–12.
24. Derfler, *Flowering of French Socialism*, 290; *Plutarch's Lives, Volume II*, 316.
25. Macé, *Paul et Laura Lafargue*, 9.
26. Ibid., 178.
27. Derfler, *Flowering of French Socialism*, 295.
28. Freddy Demuth to Jean Longuet, Nov. 29, 1911, Moscow.
29. Fomičev, "Helene Demuth Without Brethren," 972. (Marx biographers who dispute the assertion that Marx was Freddy's father contend that Freddy wrote this letter to Jean in an attempt to solicit money from him. This, however, is unlikely, because Freddy did not think he was going to survive the operation, so would have no need of money. Tussy's biographer Yvonne Kapp, however, points out that in his own will years later, Freddy bequeathed more than £1,971 to his "son." It could be that someone in the Marx-Longuet family made sure that Freddy received some of Karl Marx's royalty money, because it is nearly impossible that Freddy would have been able to save that amount from his salary. Kapp, *Eleanor Marx, Volume 1*, 294.)
30. Macé, *Paul et Laura Lafargue*, 183.
31. Ibid., 185; Louis Aragon, *The Bells of Basel*, 247.
32. Macé, *Paul et Laura Lafargue*, 184.
33. Derfler, *Flowering of French Socialism*, 300; Aragon, *Bells of Basel*, 248.
34. Macé, *Paul et Laura Lafargue*, 188.
35. Lenin, *Collected Works, Volume 17*, 304–305.

Bibliography

⌒⌒

Research Libraries
British Library, London. *George Bernard Shaw Papers, Havelock Ellis Papers.*
British Newspaper Library, London.
Freie und Hansestadt Hamburg Kulturbehörde Staatsarchiv (State Archives of the Free and Hanseatic City of Hamburg), Hamburg, Germany. *Hugo Friedrich Beneke Collection.*
Friedrich-Ebert-Stiftung Museum/Studienzentrum (Friedrich-Ebert-Stiftung Study Center), Karl-Marx-Haus, Trier, Germany.
Gosudarstvennaia Obshchestvenno-Politicheskaia Biblioteka (Socio-Political State Library), Moscow.
Internationaal Instituut voor Sociale Geschiedenis (International Institute of Social History), Amsterdam. *Marx/Engels Papers, Eleanor Marx Aveling Papers, Jenny Marx Papers, Laura Lafargue Papers, Paul Lafargue Papers, Jenny Longuet Papers, Charles Longuet Papers, and those of associates of the Marx family.*
Landeshauptarchiv Sachsen-Anhalt Abteilung Dessau (Principal National Archive of Saxony-Anhalt), Dessau, Germany.
Library of Congress, Washington, D.C.
Marx Memorial Library, London.
Rossiiskii gosudarstvennyi arkhiv sotsial'no-politicheskoi istorii (Russian State Archive of Social and Political History), Moscow. *Marx/Engels Papers, Jenny Marx Papers, Eleanor Marx Aveling Papers, Laura Marx Lafargue Papers, Paul Lafargue Papers, Charles Longuet Papers, Jenny Marx Longuet Papers, and those of associates of the Marx family.*

Collected Works
Marx, Karl, and Frederick Engels. *Collected Works, Volumes 1–50.* Moscow, London, New York: Progress Publishers, International Publishers Co. Inc., and Lawrence & Wishart. The English-language series began publication with Volume I in 1975 and ended with Volume 50 in 2004. It includes all Marx and Engels's published writings—among them the first three volumes of *Capital,* the *Communist Manifesto, The Eighteenth Brumaire of Louis Bonaparte, The Civil War in France, Socialism: Utopian and Scientific.* It also includes thirteen volumes of correspondence between the two men, their associates, and family.
Marx, Karl, and Friedrich Engels. *Historisch-kritische Gesamtausgabe. Werke, Schriften, Briefe* (known as MEGA). Frankfurt, Berlin, Moscow. Publication of this collection of Marx and Engels's writings began in 1927 in Moscow under the direction of the Marx-Engels Institute's founder, David Ryazanov. MEGA is an ongoing project involving

international scholars and is published by Akademie Verlag in Berlin. As of 2008, 55 volumes had been issued. When its projected 114 volumes are finished, MEGA will contain the entire body of Marx and Engels's work and correspondence.

Newspapers
The Chicago Tribune
The Coming Nation, Greensburg, Indiana
The Daily Chronicle, London
The Daily Telegraph, London
The Eastern Post, London
The Evening Standard, London
The Guardian, London
Justice, London
The National Reformer, London
The New York Daily Tribune
The New York Herald
The New York World
Pall Mall Gazette, London
People's Press, London
Public Opinion, London
The Standard, London
The Sydenham Examiner, London
The Times, London

Books and Journals
Ackroyd, Peter. *London: The Biography.* London: Vintage, 2001.
Adelman, Paul. *Gladstone, Disraeli and Later Victorian Politics.* Essex, UK: Longman Group, 1983.
———. *The Rise of the Labour Party, 1880–1945.* London and New York: Longman Group, 1986.
"Aleph" (pseudonym of William Harvey). *London Scenes and London People.* London: W. H. Collingridge, City Press, 1863.
Amann, Peter. "The Changing Outlines of 1848." *American Historical Review* 68, no. 4 (July 1963): 938–953.
———. "A Journée in the Making: May 15, 1848." *Journal of Modern History* 42, no. 1 (March 1970): 42–70.
Andreas, Bert, ed. *Briefe und Dokumente de Familie Marx aus der Jahren, 1862–1873.* Hannover: Archiv für Sozialgeschichte, 2 Band, 1962.
Annenkov, Pavel. *The Extraordinary Decade: Literary Memoirs.* Ann Arbor: University of Michigan Press, 1968.
Aragon, Louis. *The Bells of Basel.* New York: Harcourt, Brace, 1936.
Aveling, Edward. *The Student's Marx.* London: Swan Sonnenschein, 1892.
Aveling, Edward, and Eleanor Marx Aveling. *Shelley's Socialism.* London and West Nyack, NY: Journeyman Press, 1975.
———. *The Woman Question.* London: Swan Sonnenschein, Le Bas & Lowrey, 1886.
———. *The Working Class Movement in America.* London: Swan Sonnenschein, Lowrey, 1888.
Avineri, Shlomo. *Moses Hess: Prophet of Communism and Zionism.* New York and London: New York University Press, 1985.
Bakunin, Michael. *Marxism, Freedom & the State.* London: Freedom Press, 1998.
Balzac, Honoré de. *Lost Illusions.* London: Penguin, 1971.
———. *Old Goriot.* London: Penguin, 2006.
———. *The Unknown Masterpiece.* New York: New York Review Books, 2001.

Baughman, John J. "The French Banquet Campaign of 1847–48." *Journal of Modern History* 31, no. 1 (March 1959): 1–15.

Bax, Ernest Belfort. *Reminiscences and Reflections of a Mid and Late Victorian.* New York: Augustus M. Kelley, 1967.

Berlin, Isaiah. *Karl Marx: His Life and Environment.* New York and Oxford: Oxford University Press, 1996.

————. *Political Ideas in the Romantic Age.* Princeton, NJ, and Oxford: Princeton University Press, 2008.

————. *The Roots of Romanticism.* Princeton, NJ: Princeton University Press, 2001.

Bernstein, Eduard. *My Years of Exile: Reminiscences of a Socialist.* London: Leonard Parsons, 1921.

Besant, Annie. *Annie Besant: An Autobiography.* London: T. Fischer Unwin, ca. 1893.

Best, Geoffrey. *Mid-Victorian Britain 1851–75.* London: Fontana Press, HarperCollins, 1985.

Black, Clementina. *An Agitator.* New York: Harper & Brothers, 1895.

Blumenberg, Werner. *Karl Marx: An Illustrated History.* London and New York: Verso, 1998.

Bottigelli, Emile, ed. *Lettres et documents de Karl Marx.* Milan: Annali, Istituto Giangiacomo Feltrinelli, 1958.

Breuilly, John. *Austria, Prussia and Germany, 1806–1871.* London and New York: Longman, 2002.

————, ed. *19th-Century Germany: Politics, Culture and Society, 1780–1918.* London: Edward Arnold, 2001.

Briggs, Asa, and John Callow. *Marx in London.* London: Lawrence and Wishart, 2008.

Brophy, James M. *Popular Culture and the Public Sphere in the Rhineland, 1800–1850.* Cambridge: Cambridge University Press, 2007.

Buchanan-Gould, Vera. *Not Without Honor: The Life and Writings of Olive Schreiner.* London: Gould Hutchinson, 1949.

Burn, W. L. *The Age of Equipoise.* New York: Norton, 1965.

Carr, E. H. *Michael Bakunin.* London: Macmillan, 1937.

Carver, Terrell. *Engels: A Very Short Introduction.* Oxford: Oxford University Press, 1981.

————. *Friedrich Engels: His Life and Thought.* New York: St. Martin's, 1990.

Caygill, Marjorie. *The British Museum Reading Room.* London: Trustees of the British Museum, 2000.

Chancellor, E. Beresford. *The West End of Yesterday & Today.* London: Architectural Press, 1926.

Chernaik, Judith. *The Daughter: A Novel Based on the Life of Eleanor Marx.* New York: Harper & Row, 1979.

Clark, T. J. *The Absolute Bourgeois: Artists and Politics in France 1848–1851.* Berkeley and Los Angeles: University of California Press, 1973.

Clayton, Joseph. *The Rise and Decline of Socialism in Great Britain, 1884–1924.* London: Faber & Gwyer, 1926.

Clough, Arthur Hugh, ed. *Plutarch's Lives,* vol. 2. New York: Modern Library, 2001.

Cole, G. D. H., and Raymond Postgate. *The British Common People 1746–1946.* London: University Paperbacks, Methuen, 1961.

Collison, William. *The Apostle of Free Labour: The Life Story of William Collison.* London: Hurst and Blackett, Paternoster House, 1913.

Cowen, Anne, and Roger Cowen. *Victorian Jews Through British Eyes.* Oxford: The Littman Library, Oxford University Press, 1986.

Davies, Norman. *Europe: A History.* London: Pimlico, Random House, 1997.

Derfler, Leslie. *Paul Lafargue and the Flowering of French Socialism, 1882–1911.* Cambridge, MA, and London: Harvard University Press, 1998.

————. *Paul Lafargue and the Founding of French Marxism, 1842–1882.* Cambridge, MA, and London: Harvard University Press, 1991.

Donelson, Andrew Jackson. "The American Minister in Berlin on the Revolution of March, 1848." *American Historical Review* 23 (October 1917–July 1918): 355–371.

Dornemann, Luise. *Jenny Marx: Der Lebensweg einer Sozialistin.* Berlin: Dietz, 1971.

Draper, Hal. *Karl Marx's Theory of Revolution.* Vol. 1, *State and Bureaucracy.* New York and London: Monthly Review Press, 1977.

Draper, Hal, and E. Haberkern. *Karl Marx's Theory of Revolution.* Vol. 5, *War & Revolution.* Alameda, CA: Center for Socialist History, 2005.

Draznin, Yaffa Claire, ed. *My Other Self: The Letters of Olive Schreiner and Havelock Ellis, 1884–1920.* New York: Peter Lang, 1992.

Eckert, Georg, ed. *Wilhelm Liebknecht Briefwechsel mit Karl Marx und Friedrich Engels.* The Hague: Monitor, 1963.

Ellis, Havelock. "Havelock Ellis on Eleanor Marx." *Adelphi.* London: September/October 1935.

———. *My Life: Autobiography of Havelock Ellis.* Boston: Houghton Mifflin, 1939.

Engels, Friedrich. *The Condition of the Working Class in England.* Oxford: Oxford University Press, 1999.

———. *The Fourteenth of March 1883: Friedrich Engels on the Death of Karl Marx.* London: Martin Lawrence, 1933.

Engels, Friedrich, Paul Lafargue, and Laura Lafargue. *Correspondence.* 3 vols. Moscow: Foreign Languages Publishing House, 1959–1960.

Evans, R. J. W., and Hartmut Pogge von Strandmann, eds. *The Revolutions in Europe, 1848–49: From Reform to Reaction.* Oxford: Oxford University Press, 2002.

Fejtö, François, ed. *The Opening of an Era: 1848.* New York: University Library, Grosset & Dunlap, 1973.

Flanders, Judith. *The Victorian House.* London: HarperPerennial, 2003.

Flaubert, Gustave. *Madame Bovary: Provincial Manners,* Eleanor Marx Aveling, trans. London: Vizetelly, 1886.

Flourens, Gustave. *Ce qui est possible.* Paris: Garnier Frères, 1864.

Fomičev, Valerij. "Helene Demuth Without Brethren." *Motherland.* Moscow: August 9, 1992, 970–972.

Frow, Edmund, and Ruth Frow. *Frederick Engels in Manchester.* Manchester: Working Class Movement Library, 1995.

Gildea, Robert. *The Third Republic from 1870–1914.* London and New York: Longman Group, 1988.

Gilman, S. L. "Karl Marx and the Secret Language of Jews." Vol. 5, *Marx's Life and Theoretical Development.* London: Routledge, 1999.

Giroud, Françoise. *Jenny Marx, ou la femme du diable.* Paris: Robert Laffont, 1992.

Glasier, J. Bruce. *William Morris and the Early Days of the Socialist Movement.* London: Thoemmes Press, 1994.

Goethe, Johann Wolfgang von. *The Sorrows of Young Werther.* New York: Modern Library, 2005.

Halliday, Stephen. *The Great Filth: The War Against Disease in Victorian England.* Stroud, UK: Sutton, 2007.

Hamerow, Theodore S. *Restoration, Revolution, Reaction: Economics and Politics in Germany, 1815–1871.* Princeton, NJ: Princeton University Press, 1972.

Hammen, Oscar J. *The Red 48ers: Karl Marx and Friedrich Engels.* New York: Charles Scribner's Sons, 1969.

Healey, Edna. *Wives of Fame: Mary Livingstone, Jenny Marx, Emma Darwin.* London: Sidgwick & Jackson, 1986.

Hobsbawm, Eric. *The Age of Capital, 1848–1875.* London: Abacus, 2004.

———. *The Age of Revolution, 1789–1848.* London: Abacus, 2005.

———. *Revolutionaries.* London: Abacus, 2007.

Hoffmann, Leni, ed. *Mohr und General: Erinnerungen an Marx und Engels*. Berlin: Dietz, 1983.

Horn, Pamela. *Pleasures & Pastimes in Victorian Britain*. Stroud, UK: Sutton Publishing, 1999.

Horne, Alistair. *The Terrible Year: The Paris Commune, 1871*. London: Phoenix, 2004.

Hudson, Derek. *Munby, Man of Two Worlds: The Life and Diaries of Arthur J. Munby, 1828–1920*. Boston: Gambit, 1972.

Hulse, James, W. *Revolutionists in London: A Study of Five Unorthodox Socialists*. Oxford: Oxford University Press, 1970.

Hunt, Tristram. *The Frock-Coated Communist: The Revolutionary Life of Friedrich Engels*. London: Allen Lane, Penguin, 2009.

Jenkins, Mick. *Frederick Engels in Manchester*. Manchester: Lancashire and Cheshire Communist Party, 1951.

Jones, Peter. *The 1848 Revolutions*. London and New York: Longman Group, 1992.

Kapp, Yvonne. *Eleanor Marx*. Vol. I. New York: Pantheon, 1972.

————. *Eleanor Marx*. Vol. 2. New York: Pantheon, 1976.

Kenafick, K. J. *Michael Bakunin and Karl Marx*. Melbourne, Australia: A. Maller, Excelsior, 1948.

Kisch, Egon Erwin. *Karl Marx in Karlsbad*. Berlin: Aufbau, 1953.

Kolakowski, Leszek. *Main Currents of Marxism*. Vol. 1, *The Founders*. Oxford: Oxford University Press, 1978.

Krosigk, Lutz Graf Schwerin von. *Jenny Marx: Liebe und Leid im Schatten von Karl Marx*. Wuppertal: Verlag Fr. Staats, 1975.

Lafargue, Paul. *Karl Marx*. New York: Labor News, 1947.

————. *The Right to Be Lazy*. Chicago: Charles H. Kerr, 1989.

Lanjalley, Paul, and Paul Corriez. *Histoire de la Révolution du 18 Mars*. Boston: Adamant Media, 2006.

Laurence, A. E., and A. N. Insole. *Prometheus Bound: Karl Marx on the Isle of Wight*. Isle of Wight, UK: Crossprint, 1981.

Lea, F. A. *Shelley and the Romantic Revolution*. London: Routledge, 1945.

Lenin, Vladimir. *Collected Works*, vol. 17. Moscow: Progress Publishers, 1974.

Liebknecht, Wilhelm. *Karl Marx: Biographical Memoirs*. London: Journeyman Press, 1975.

Lissagaray, Prosper. *History of the Commune of 1871*, Eleanor Marx Aveling, trans. London: Reeves & Turner, 1886.

Longuet, Robert-Jean. *Karl Marx: Mon Arrière-Grand-Père*. Paris: Editions Stock, 1977.

Macdonnell, John. "Karl Marx and German Socialism." *Fortnightly Review*, London, March 1, 1875.

Macé, Jacques. *Paul et Laura Lafargue: Du droit à la paresse au droit de choisir sa mort*. Paris: L'Harmattan, 2001.

Maenchen-Helfen, J. Otto, and B. I. Nicolaievsky. *Karl und Jenny Marx: Ein Lebensweg*. Berlin: Verlag der Bücherkreis, 1933.

Marx, Karl. *Value, Price and Profit*, Eleanor Marx Aveling, ed. London: Swan Sonnenschein, 1898.

Marx, Karl, and Friedrich Engels. *The Cologne Communist Trial*. New York: International Publishers, Lawrence & Wishart, 1971.

————. *Letters to Americans, 1848–1895*. New York: International Publishers, 1953.

Marx, Karl, Jenny Marx, and Friedrich Engels. *Lettres à Kugelmann*. Paris: Editions Social, 1971.

Mayer, Gustav. *Friedrich Engels: A Biography*. New York: Alfred A. Knopf, 1936.

————. "Letters of Karl Marx to Karl Blind." *International Review for Social History* 4 (1939): 154–155.

————. "Neue Beitrage zur Biographie von Karl Marx." *Archiv für Geschichte des Sozialismus* 10 (1922): 54–66.

Mayhew, Henry. *London Labour and the London Poor*. London: Penguin, 1985.

McLellan, David. *Karl Marx: A Biography*. New York: Palgrave Macmillan, 2006.

———, ed. *Karl Marx: Interviews & Recollections*. London: Macmillan, 1981.

Mehring, Franz. *Karl Marx: The Story of His Life*. Ann Arbor: University of Michigan Press, 1962.

Meier, Olga, Michèle Perrot, and Michel Trebitsch, eds. *The Daughters of Karl Marx: Family Correspondence 1866–1898*. New York and London: Harcourt Brace Jovanovich, 1982.

Miliband, Ralph, and John Saville, eds. *The Socialist Register*. London: Merlin Press, 1976.

Morgan, Kenneth. *The Birth of Industrial Britain: Social Change 1750–1850*. Harlow, UK: Pearson Longman, 2004.

Morris, May. *William Morris: Artist, Writer, Socialist*. Vol. 2. Oxford, UK: Basil Blackwell, 1936.

Morton, Grenfell. *Home Rule and the Irish Question*. Essex, UK: Longman Group, 1980.

Murger, Henry. *Bohemians of the Latin Quarter*. Charleston, SC: BiblioBazaar, 2007.

Nicolaievsky, Boris. "Toward a History of the Communist League, 1847–1852." *International Review of Social History*, vol. 1, pt. 2, 1956.

Nicolaievsky, Boris, and Otto Maenchen-Helfen. *Karl Marx: Man and Fighter*. Philadelphia and London: J. B. Lippincott, 1936.

O'Boyle, Lenore. "The Democratic Left in Germany, 1848." *Journal of Modern History* 33, no. 4 (1961): 379–380.

———. "The Problem of an Excess of Educated Men in Western Europe, 1800–1850." *Journal of Modern History* 42, no. 4 (December 1970): 476–477.

O'Donovan Rossa, Jeremiah. *My Years in English Jails: The Brutal Facts*. Tralee, Ireland: Anvil Books, 1967.

Offord, Derek. *Nineteenth-Century Russia: Opposition to Autocracy*. Essex, UK: Longman, 1999.

Olsen, Donald J. *The Growth of Victorian London*. London: Peregrine Books, 1979.

Omura, Izumi, Valerij Fomičev, Rolf Hecker, and Shun-ichi Kubo, eds. *Familie Marx privat: Die Foto- und Fragebogen-Alben von Marx' Töchtern Laura und Jenny*. Berlin: Akademie, 2005.

O'Neill, Gilda. *The Good Old Days: Poverty, Crime and Terror in Victorian London*. London: Penguin, 2007.

Ozment, Steven. *A Mighty Fortress: A New History of the German People*. London: Granta, 2006.

Padover, Saul K. *Karl Marx: An Intimate Biography*. New York: New American Library, 1980.

Pawel, Ernst. *The Poet Dying: Heinrich Heine's Last Years in Paris*. New York: Farrar, Straus & Giroux, 1995.

Payne, Howard, and Henry Grosshans. "The Exiled Revolutionaries and the French Political Police in the 1850s." *American Historical Review* 68, no. 4 (July 1963): 945–973.

Payne, Robert. *Marx: A Biography*. New York: Simon & Schuster, 1968.

———, ed. *The Unknown Karl Marx*. New York: New York University Press, 1971.

Peters, H. F. *Red Jenny: A Life with Karl Marx*. New York: St. Martin's, 1986.

Pike, E. Royston. *"Hard Times": Human Documents of the Industrial Revolution*. New York and Washington: Frederick A. Praeger, 1966.

Plekhanov, Georgy. *Anarchism and Socialism*. London: Twentieth Century Press, 1906.

Pool, Daniel. *What Jane Austen Ate and Charles Dickens Knew: From Fox Hunting to Whist— The Facts of Daily Life in Nineteenth-Century England*. New York: Simon & Schuster, 1993.

Porter, Bernard. *The Refugee Question in Mid-Victorian Politics*. Cambridge, London, and New York: Cambridge University Press, 1979.

Preston, William C. *The Bitter Cry of Outcast London*. Bath, UK: Cedric Chivers, 1969.

Prolès, Charles. *Les hommes de la révolution de 1871: Gustave Flourens, Insurrection Crétois, 1867–1868, Siège de Paris 1870–71.* Paris: Chamuel, 1898.

Raddatz, Fritz J. *Karl Marx: A Political Biography.* Boston and Toronto: Little, Brown, 1978.

Reetz, Jürgen, ed. *Vier Briefe von Jenny Marx aus den Jahren, 1856–1860.* Trier, Germany: Karl-Marx-Haus, 1970.

Reminiscences of Marx and Engels. Moscow: Foreign Language Publishing House, 1970.

Rive, Michael, ed. *Olive Schreiner Letters.* Vol. 1, *1871–1899.* Oxford: Oxford University Press, 1988.

Roberts, J. M. *A History of Europe.* New York: Penguin, 1997.

Robertson, Priscilla. "Students on the Barricades: Germany and Austria, 1848." *Political Science Quarterly* 84, no. 2 (June 1969): 375–376.

Rose, Paul. *The Manchester Martyrs: The Story of a Fenian Tragedy.* London: Lawrence & Wishart, 1970.

Royle, Edward. *Radical Politics, 1790–1900: Religion and Unbelief.* London: Longman Group, 1971.

Salt, Henry S. *Company I Have Kept.* London: George Allen & Unwin, 1930.

Schiller, Friedrich von. *The Robbers.* London: Dodo Press, undated; first published 1781.

Schröder, Wolfgang, ed. *Sie können sich denken, wie mir oft zu Muthe war: Jenny Marx in Briefen an eine vertraute Freundin.* Leipzig: Verlag für die Frau, 1989.

Schurz, Carl. *The Reminiscences of Carl Schurz.* Vol. 1, *1829–1852.* Boston: Adamant Media, 2006.

Seigel, Jerrold. *Marx's Fate: The Shape of a Life.* University Park: Pennsylvania State University Press, 1993.

Shakespeare, William. *King Lear.* London: Penguin, 2005.

———. *Richard III.* London: Penguin, 2005.

Shaw, George Bernard. *The Doctor's Dilemma.* Teddington, UK: Echo Library, 2006.

Sheasby, Walt Contreras. "Marx at Karlsbad." *Capitalism Nature Socialism,* 12, no. 3 (September 2001).

Shelley, Percy Bysshe, *The Daemon of the World and Peter Bell the Third.* London: Dodo Press, undated.

———. *The Mask of Anarchy.* London: Reeves and Turner, 1887; New York: AMS Press, 1975.

———. *Prometheus Unbound.* Los Angeles: Black Box Press, 2007.

Sheppard, Francis. *London 1808–1870: The Infernal Wen.* Berkeley and Los Angeles: University of California Press, 1971.

Smethurst, John, Edmund Frow, and Ruth Frow. "Frederick Engels and the English Working Class Movement in Manchester, 1842–1844." *Marxism Today,* November 1970, 340–341.

Smith, Warren Sylvester. *The London Heretics, 1870–1914.* London: Constable, 1967.

Smith, W. H. C. *Second Empire and Commune: France 1848–1871.* London and New York: Longman Group, 1985.

Somerhausen, Luc. *L'Humanisme Agissant de Karl Marx.* Paris: Richard-Masse, 1946.

Sperber, Jonathan, ed. *Germany, 1800–1870.* Oxford: Oxford University Press, 2004.

Staël, Germaine de. *Delphine.* De Kalb: Northern Illinois University Press, 1995.

Stearns, Peter. *1848: The Revolutionary Tide in Europe.* New York: Norton, 1974.

Stepanova, Yelena. *Frederick Engels.* Moscow: Foreign Language Publishing House, 1958.

Stewart, William. *J. Keir Hardie: A Biography.* London: Independent Labour Party, 1921.

Taylor, A. J. P. *The Struggle for Mastery of Europe, 1848–1918.* Oxford: Oxford University Press, 1971.

Thomas, Edith. *The Women Incendiaries.* Chicago: Haymarket Books, 2007.

Thompson, E. P. *The Making of the English Working Class.* New York: Vintage, 1966.

Thomson, David. *Democracy in France Since 1870.* London, Oxford, and New York: Oxford University Press, 1969.

Thorne, Will. *My Life's Battles.* London: George Newnes, 1925.

Tocqueville, Alexis de. *The Recollections of Alexis de Tocqueville.* New York: Meridian Books, 1959.

Tsuzuki, Chushichi. *The Life of Eleanor Marx, 1855–1898: A Socialist Tragedy.* Oxford: Clarendon Press, 1967.

Washburne, E. B. *Recollections of a Minister to France, Part I.* New York: Charles Scribner's Sons, 1887.

Webb, Beatrice. *My Apprenticeship.* Cambridge: Cambridge University Press, 1979.

Weissweiler, Eva. *Tussy Marx: Das Drama der Vatertochter Eine Biographie.* Cologne: Kiepenheuer & Witsch, 2002.

Wetzel, David. *A Duel of Giants: Bismarck, Napoleon III and the Origins of the Franco-Prussian War.* Madison: University of Wisconsin Press, 2001.

Wheen, Francis. *Karl Marx: A Life.* New York and London: Norton, 1999.

———. *Marx's Das Kapital: A Biography.* London: Atlantic Books, 2006.

Whitridge, Arnold. *Men in Crisis: The Revolutions of 1848.* New York: Charles Scribner's Sons, 1949.

Williamson, D. G. *Bismarck and Germany, 1862–1890.* London and New York: Longman Group, 1986.

Wilson, A. N. *The Victorians.* London: Arrow Books, 2003.

Winder, Robert. *Bloody Foreigners: The Story of Immigration to Britain.* London: Abacus, 2005.

Wright, D. G. *Democracy and Reform, 1815–1885.* Essex, UK: Longman Group, 1970.

———. *Revolution and Terror in France, 1789–1795.* Essex, UK: Longman Group, 1974.

Zola, Emile. *Germinal.* London: Penguin, 2004.

Index

Note: The abbreviation KM in subheadings refers to Karl Marx.

About the Author

MARY GABRIEL was educated in the United States and France, and worked in Washington and London as a Reuters editor for nearly two decades. She is the author of two previous biographies: *Notorious Victoria: The Life of Victoria Woodhull, Uncensored,* and *The Art of Acquiring: A Portrait of Etta and Claribel Cone.* Mary Gabriel lives in Italy.